THE IMMIGRATION AND NATIONALITY ACT OF 1965

Along with the civil rights and voting rights acts, the Immigration and Nationality Act of 1965 is one of the most important bills of the civil rights era. The Act's political, legal, and demographic impact continues to be felt, yet its legacy is controversial. The 1965 Act was groundbreaking in eliminating of the white America immigration policy in place since 1790, ending Asian exclusion, and limiting discrimination against Eastern European Catholics and Jews. At the same time, the Act discriminated against gay men and lesbians, tied refugee status to Cold War political interests, and shattered traditional patterns of Mexican migration, setting the stage for current immigration politics.

Drawing from studies in law, political science, anthropology, and economics, this book will be an essential tool for any scholar or student interested in immigration law.

Gabriel J. Chin, a professor at the University of California, Davis School of Law, is a "paper grandson," descendant of an unauthorized migrant during Chinese Exclusion. Author of many articles on Asian American legal history, he is the coeditor with Carissa Hessick of *Strange Neighbors: The Role of States in Immigration Policy*, addressing recent state immigration restrictions. He has worked with students to lobby for the repeal of Jim Crow laws still on the books, including anti-Asian land laws in Kansas, New Mexico, and Wyoming, and for the posthumous admission to the California bar of Hong Yen Chang, excluded because of his race in 1890.

Rose Cuison Villazor is a professor at the University of California, Davis School of Law. She is the author of numerous articles on immigration and citizenship law, equal protection law, and critical race theory, and coeditor of two books: Loving v. Virginia *in a Post-Racial World* and *Asian Americans, Pacific Islanders, and the Law*. She has served as an Equal Justice Works Fellow in New York City representing immigrants in civil rights cases. In 2011, she received the Derrick A. Bell Award from the Association of American Law Schools Minority Section.

"Untitled." Copyright © Teresa Johnson. Used by permission of the artist.

President Lyndon B. Johnson signs the Immigration Act as Vice President Hubert Humphrey, Lady Bird Johnson, Muriel Humphrey, Sen. Edward (Ted) Kennedy, Sen. Robert F. Kennedy, and others look on. LBJ Library photo by Yoichi Okamoto.

The Immigration and Nationality Act of 1965

LEGISLATING A NEW AMERICA

Edited By

GABRIEL J. CHIN
University of California, Davis School of Law

ROSE CUISON VILLAZOR
University of California, Davis School of Law

CAMBRIDGE
UNIVERSITY PRESS

CAMBRIDGE
UNIVERSITY PRESS

32 Avenue of the Americas, New York, NY 10013-2473, USA

Cambridge University Press is part of the University of Cambridge.

It furthers the University's mission by disseminating knowledge in the pursuit of education, learning, and research at the highest international levels of excellence.

www.cambridge.org
Information on this title: www.cambridge.org/9781107084117

First published 2015

A catalog record for this publication is available from the British Library.

Library of Congress Cataloging in Publication Data
The Immigration and Nationality Act of 1965 : legislating a new America / edited by Gabriel J. Chin, Rose Cuison Villazor.
pages cm
Includes bibliographical references and index.
ISBN 978-1-107-08411-7 (hardback)
1. Emigration and immigration law – United States. 2. United States. Immigration and Nationality Act Amendments of 1965. 3. United States – Emigration and immigration – Government policy. 4. Refugees – Legal status, laws, etc. – United States. 5. Foreign workers – United States. I. Chin, Gabriel J. (Gabriel Jackson), 1964– editor. II. Villazor, Rose Cuison, editor.
KF4819.I4713 2015
342.7308′2–dc23 2015016875

ISBN 978-1-107-08411-7 Hardback

Contents

Notes on Contributors

Gabriel J. Chin is Professor of Law at the University of California, Davis School of Law, where he specializes in criminal law, immigration, and race. He earned a B.A. in History from Wesleyan and law degrees from Michigan and Yale. He is particularly interested in Asian American legal history. His paper, *The* Plessy *Myth: Justice Harlan and the Chinese Cases*, 82 IOWA L. REV. 151 (1996), won the Thurgood Marshall Award from the Midwest People of Color Legal Scholarship Conference, and *Segregation's Last Stronghold: Race Discrimination and the Constitutional Law of Immigration*, 46 UCLA L. REV. 1 (1996), won the Association of American Law Schools' Scholarly Paper Award. His article, *Effective Assistance of Counsel and the Consequences of Guilty Pleas*, coauthored with a student, was cited in the majority and concurrence in *Padilla v. Kentucky*, 130 S. Ct. 1473 (2010) and the majority and dissent in *Chaidez v. United States*, 133 S. Ct. 1103 (2013). He is regularly included on lists of the most-cited law professors. His law reform work with students has resulted in Ohio ratifying the Fourteenth Amendment and Kansas, New Mexico, and Wyoming repealing anti-Asian alien land laws that were still on the books. He and his students successfully petitioned for the posthumous admission of Hong Yen Chang, denied bar membership by the California Supreme Court in 1890 because of his race.

Valerie Francisco is an Assistant Professor in the department of sociology at the University of Portland. She works with a global perspective both in her scholarship and teaching. Dr. Francisco's research projects include a transnational study of Filipino migrant mothers in New York City and their families left behind in Manila, as well as participatory action research with Filipino immigrants working as caregivers in the United States. She has written about her findings in a dissertation entitled "Together But Apart: Dynamics of Filipino Transnational Families" and in journals including *Critical Sociology*, *The Philippine Sociological Review*, and *International Review of Qualitative Research*. Dr. Francisco also writes on the transnational activism that emerges from the social conditions of migration, separation, and migrant labor. Dr. Francisco's academic interests include global and transnational sociology, migration and immigration studies, diaspora with a special interest on the Philippine migration, gender and the family, racial and ethnic relations in the United States, labor, transnational social movements with regard to migrant workers, and international political economy. Dr. Francisco received her Ph.D. from the Department of Sociology at City University of New York, The Graduate Center.

Bill Ong Hing is Professor of Law at the University of San Francisco and Professor Emeritus at the University of California, Davis School of Law. He teaches immigration policy, rebellious lawyering, negotiation, and evidence. Throughout his career, he has pursued social justice by combining community work, litigation, and scholarship. He is the author of numerous academic and practice-oriented books and articles on immigration policy and community lawyering. His books include *Ethical Borders – NAFTA, Globalization and Mexican Migration* (Temple University Press, 2010); *Deporting Our Souls – Values, Morality, and Immigration Policy* (Cambridge University Press, 2006); *Defining America Through Immigration Policy* (Temple University Press, 2004); *Making and Remaking Asian America Through Immigration Policy* (Stanford University Press, 1993); *Handling Immigration Cases* (Aspen Publishers, 1995); and *Immigration and the Law – a Dictionary* (ABC-CLIO, 1999). His book *To Be an American: Cultural Pluralism and the Rhetoric of Assimilation* (NYU Press, 1997) received the award for Outstanding Academic Book in 1997 by the librarians' journal *Choice*. He was co-counsel in the precedent-setting Supreme Court asylum case, *INS v. Cardoza-Fonseca*, 480 U.S. 421 (1987). Professor Hing is the founder of, and continues to volunteer as General Counsel for, the Immigrant Legal Resource Center in San Francisco. He serves on the board of the Southeast Asian Refugee Center in Washington, DC, and also is a member of the Koshland Committee of the San Francisco Foundation.

Kevin R. Johnson is Dean, Mabie-Apallas Professor of Public Interest Law, and Professor of Chicana/o Studies at the University of California, Davis School of Law. He has published extensively on immigration law and policy and civil rights. *Opening the Floodgates: Why America Needs to Rethink Its Borders and Immigration Laws* (NYU Press, 2007), one of Johnson's recent books, has influenced the national debate over immigration reform. A magna cum laude graduate of Harvard Law School, he served as an editor of the *Harvard Law Review*. From 2006 to 2011, Johnson served on the board of directors of the Mexican American Legal Defense and Education Fund. He was named the National Association of Chicana and Chicano Studies 2008 Scholar of the Year. Johnson is an editor of the ImmigrationProf blog (http://lawprofessors.typepad.com/immigration/) and the regular immigration contributor to SCOTUSblog (http://www.scotusblog.com/). In 2003, Dean Johnson was elected to the American Law Institute.

Atticus Lee is a 2013 graduate of the University of California, Davis School of Law, and currently serves as law clerk to the Honorable Vanessa D. Gilmore, United States District Judge for the Southern District of Texas. While in law school, Atticus externed for the Honorable Samuel K. Feng of the San Francisco Superior Court and was a summer associate at Minami Tamaki LLP. Atticus also served as editor on the *UC Davis Law Review*, senior articles editor of *Environs: the UC Davis Environmental Law & Policy Journal*, clinic director of the Sacramento LGBT Community Pro Bono Legal Clinic, and as fundraising chair of the King Hall Intellectual Property Law Association. After graduating from law school, Atticus served as law clerk to the Honorable Kathleen N. A. Watanabe of the Fifth Circuit Court of Hawaii in Kaua'i, Hawai'i.

Jeannette Money is a faculty member in the Political Science Department at the University of California, Davis. Her research spans various dimensions of immigration policy: immigration control, immigrant integration, international cooperation on migration, and migration and development. Books include *Fences and Neighbors: The Political Geography of Immigration Control* (Cornell University Press, 1999), *Migration, Nation States, and International Cooperation* (Routledge, 2011), and *The Architecture of International Cooperation on Migration* (under review). Ongoing research focuses on the variation in nationality legislation and the incentives that politicians confront to make citizenship access easier or more difficult for immigrants. A second project explores the impact of emigration on the least-developed countries of the world.

Cerissa Salazar Parreñas is an alumna of the University of California, Davis School of Law, and works as a research associate at George Washington University. During her time as a research associate she has been instrumental in the study on "Decision-Making Practices of Urban Districts for Including and Accommodating English Language Learners in NAEP – School-Based Perspectives." The report presents findings from a study conducted by the George Washington University Center for Equity and Excellence in Education under the sponsorship of the National Center for Educational Statistics.

Rhacel Salazar Parreñas is Professor of Sociology and Gender Studies and Chair of the Department of Sociology at the University of Southern California. She was previously in the faculty at Brown University, University of California, Davis, and University of Wisconsin–Madison. She is known for her work on women's labor and migration in economic globalization. Her research has been featured in various news media outlets including NPR's *The World*, *Bloomberg News*, the *New York Times*, *Wall Street Journal*, *de Volkskrant*, and *American Prospect*. Her dissertation was made into a documentary, *The Chain of Love* (2000), by the public broadcasting station VPRO-TV in the Netherlands. Professor Parreñas has coedited three anthologies and has written four monographs as well as numerous peer-reviewed articles. Her latest book, *Illicit Flirtations: Labor, Migration and Sex Trafficking in Tokyo* (Stanford University Press, 2011), won the Distinguished Book Award in the Labor and Labor Movements Section of the American Sociological Association.

Giovanni Peri is Professor of Economics at the University of California, Davis, and Director of the Temporary Migration Cluster at UC Davis. He is also a Research Associate of the National Bureau of Economic Research in Cambridge, Massachusetts, a CESifo Research Professor, and IZA affiliate. He is editor of *Regional Science and Urban Economics* and member of the editorial board of five academic journals, including the *Journal of the European Economic Association*. He has published in several academic journals including the *American Economic Review*, the *Review of Economic Studies*, *The Review of Economics and Statistics*, the *Economic Journal*, and the *Journal of the European Economic Association*. He has done research on human capital, growth, and technological innovation. More recently he has focused on the impact of international migrations on labor markets, housing markets, productivity, and innovation of the receiving countries and on the determinants of international migrations. His research on immigration has been cited in several popular blogs and in media outlets including the *New York Times*, the *Wall Street Journal*, the *Washington Post*, and the *Economist Magazine*. He has received grants for the study of the impact of migrations from foundations and international organizations including the John D. and Catherine T. MacArthur Foundation, the World Bank, and the Volkswagen Foundation.

Robyn Magalit Rodriguez is an Associate Professor in the Department of Asian American Studies at the University of California, Davis. Her research is broadly concerned with understanding how processes of globalization, particularly international migration, impact the societies that migrants leave and the societies to which they move. Rodriguez's book, *Migrants for Export: How the Philippines Brokers Labor to the World* (University of Minnesota Press, 2010), won an Honorable Mention for Best Book in Social Science by the Association for Asian American Studies. Professor Rodriguez's book coauthored with Pawan Dhingra, *Asian America: Sociological and Interdisciplinary Approaches*, was recently published (Polity Press, 2014). Also recently published is an anthology, coedited with Ulla Berg, entitled *Transnational Citizenship across the Americas* (Routledge Press, 2014). Currently, Professor Rodriguez is finishing a book entitled *In Lady Liberty's Shadow: Race and Immigration in Post-9/11 New Jersey*, to be published by Rutgers

University Press. In addition to her books, Rodriguez has written more than thirty academic and nonacademic articles and book chapters.

Leticia M. Saucedo is Professor of Law at the University of California, Davis School of Law. She is an expert in employment, labor, and immigration law. She has developed courses in international and domestic service learning that explore the immigration consequences of crime and domestic violence in a post-conflict society. Professor Saucedo earned her A.B., cum laude, in 1984 from Bryn Mawr College and her J.D., cum laude, in 1996 from Harvard Law School, where she was managing editor of the *Harvard Latino Law Review*. After law school, she served as briefing attorney to Chief Justice Thomas Phillips of the Texas Supreme Court. She then became an associate at Fried, Frank, Harris, Shriver & Jacobson in New York City, where she was the recipient of the Fried Frank MALDEF Fellowship. From 1999 to 2003, she worked as a staff attorney for the Mexican American Legal Defense and Educational Fund in San Antonio, Texas, where she litigated employment and education cases. Saucedo's research interests lie at the intersections of employment, labor, and immigration law. Her law review articles have appeared in *Notre Dame Law Review*, the *Ohio State Law Journal*, the *Buffalo Law Review*, the *Richmond Law Review*, the *Harvard Journal of Law and Gender*, the *Harvard Latino Law Review*, the *University of Michigan Journal of Law Reform*, and the *Hispanic Journal of Behavioral Sciences*. She is a member of the American Law Institute.

Brian Soucek is Acting Professor and Martin Luther King Jr. Hall Research Scholar at the University of California, Davis School of Law, where he teaches and writes about antidiscrimination law, constitutional law, civil procedure, and immigration. Professor Soucek's previous articles on U.S. asylum and refugee law include "Social Group Asylum Claims: A Second Look at the New Visibility Requirement" (*Yale Law and Policy Review*, 2010) and "Copy-Paste Precedent" (*Journal of Appellate Practice and Procedure*, 2012). Soucek is a graduate of Yale Law School and Columbia University, where he received his Ph.D. in Philosophy in 2006. Professor Soucek clerked for U.S. District Judge Mark R. Kravitz and the Hon. Guido Calabresi of the U.S. Court of Appeals for the Second Circuit.

Kristina Victor is a doctoral candidate in the Political Science Department at the University of California, Davis, specializing in immigration studies, Latino politics, and political behavior. She is interested in how immigration to the United States influences politics, policy, and political behavior in the United States. Her work examines the political behavior of Latinos living in the United States, as well as the effect of immigration-related policies on Latinos living in the United States.

Rose Cuison Villazor is Professor of Law at the University of California, Davis School of Law. She teaches, researches, and writes in the areas of immigration and citizenship law, Asian Americans and the law, equal protection law, critical race theory, and property law. Her published law review articles include: "The Undocumented Closet" (*North Carolina Law Review*, 2013); "The Other *Loving*: Uncovering the Federal Regulation of Interracial Marriages" (*New York University Law Review*, 2011; "Rediscovering *Oyama v. California*: At the Intersection of Property, Race and Citizenship" (*Washington University Law Review*, 2010); and "Blood Quantum Land Laws: The Race versus Political Identity Dilemma" (*California Law Review*, 2008). She is coeditor, with Neil Gotanda and Robert Chang, of a forthcoming book, *Asian Americans and Pacific Islanders and the Law*, which will be published by New York University Press in 2016. Professor Villazor obtained an LL.M from Columbia Law School in 2006 and a J.D. from the American University Washington College of Law in 2000.

Foreword

As a son of parents who immigrated from Mexico in the 1920s, my interest in immigration comes naturally. And as an attorney who lived and practiced law by the Mexican border in Imperial County, I have witnessed the changes since 1965. My practice included clients who immigrated from Mexico. My appointment in 1979 by President Jimmy Carter to the Select Commission on Immigration and Refugee Policy provided me with a precursor to today's controversial issue of undocumented immigration.

The essays in this book underscore the historic changes the Immigration and Nationality Act of 1965 has brought. These changes were groundbreaking in abolishing racial and national origin discrimination in the admission of immigrants. Prior immigration laws had favored Western and Northern European countries, which contributed predominantly white, Protestant immigrants. After 1965, the majority of immigrants have been people of color, bringing ethnic and linguistic changes to the nation as a whole.

Not surprisingly, in the half-century since 1965, the United States has evolved into a very different country. Never before have I studied a collection of essays that so convincingly explain the effect of the 1965 Act and subsequent changes in the law. In my own state of California, the presence of Asians and Latinos, and particularly their children and grandchildren, have made minorities of color a majority of our residents. According to the 2010 Census, approximately 38.4 percent and 14.1 percent of the population in California are Latinos and Asians, respectively. Citizenship by birth and change of legal status has brought Asian Americans and Latinos into political prominence in state legislative and constitutional statewide offices, as well as in the U.S. Congress. National political observers credit their vote in the results of recent presidential races. And a majority of public school children are of color. Nor have the changes been limited to California; they are nationwide. I was recently invited to Knoxville, Tennessee, which is a community I have known for more than fifty years. Back then, there were no Latinos in Knoxville, or if they lived there, they were socially invisible. Today, there are tens of thousands of Latinos who have established at least three nonprofit organizations including a Latino Chamber of Commerce and a socially active organization that has recruited seventy-five volunteers to teach English, citizenship classes, computer skills courses, and similar practical courses. I was told that there are more than 80,000 Latinos in East Tennessee alone. Similar growth has been seen in many states that a few years ago had few Latinos. Nationwide, the number exceeds 10 million.

The changes the 1965 Immigration Act has caused were not always positive, however. In particular, the Act imposed restrictions on immigration from anywhere in the Western Hemisphere. The limitations might seem fair because the same restrictions are applied to other nations outside the Western Hemisphere. However, due to proximity, economics, and safety realities, immigration from Mexico and Central America has not subsided. They still come, but many without documents, to the point that we have millions who reside in the shadows. In 2014, Senate proposed a "comprehensive" immigration bill; unfortunately, the House of Representative has not acted. Thus, Congress has been unable to respond to the push/pull reality as represented by the Mexican and Central American immigrant situation. The political pressure to curtail the numbers has caused the federal government to deport hundreds of thousands of undocumented immigrants, often dividing families that include both citizen and noncitizen members.

The arrival of young children from Central America has brought forth some public protests seeking their immediate deportation. These are children who risked their lives by leaving their Central American neighborhoods, villages, and cities endangered by criminal gangs, poverty, war, and corruption. That some Americans have no heart to help those young children puzzles me.

The aim of family reunification and nondiscrimination (in the spirit of the Civil Rights Movement) in the 1965 Act is laudatory. But even that aim has been partially frustrated by per-country restrictions. Despite gains, gay couples and others similarly situated continue to experience discrimination. And potential immigrants from Africa, for example, have not profited from family reunification as have others.

On a personal basis, the work that has yet to be done takes me back to my youth and the Imperial Valley. I recall the calendars we had at home when I was a child during the Second World War. On display were the Mexican and American flags and photographs of President Roosevelt and President Camacho. There was a sense of brotherhood. In 1959, when I arrived in Imperial Valley, the border to Mexico seemed open. Workers from Mexicali crossed the border daily to work or shop. Residents of Imperial Valley, too, crossed daily to visit relatives, to shop, or to patronize an excellent Chinese restaurant. Others, like a fellow attorney and I, crossed to take lessons on how to write a more effective business letter in Spanish. There was a sense of community between the Imperial and Mexicali valleys.

How strange was my feeling when I recently visited Imperial Valley and came upon a high darkened fence separating the two countries, as the Berlin Wall had once divided that city. Unlike Berlin, commerce makes Mexico one of America's top three trading partners. But the wall is too tall for people. The Act of 1965 was a gigantic step forward, but since then our immigration policies have not kept up with today's reality. As the essays in this volume suggest, there is much work to be done.

Cruz Reynoso
Former California Supreme Court Justice and
University of California, Davis Professor of Law Emeritus

Introduction

Gabriel J. Chin and Rose Cuison Villazor

The Immigration and Nationality Act of 1965: Legislating a New America examines and explores the 1965 Immigration Act's origins and its legal, political, economic, and cultural effects. This book demonstrates the principal consequence of the law – ending formal discrimination in immigration law. At the same time, while the 1965 Immigration Act was in some sense a civil rights law, it was one of its era that perpetuated discrimination in certain ways.

On October 3, 1965, at a ceremony on Liberty Island in New York Harbor, President Lyndon B. Johnson signed into law the Immigration and Nationality Act Amendments of 1965, also referred to as the Hart-Celler Act.[1] A primary goal of the 1965 Immigration Act was to end the controversial National Origins Quota System that began in the 1920s.[2] In signing the 1965 Immigration Act, President Johnson famously stated, "This bill ... is not a revolutionary bill. It does not affect the lives of millions. It will not reshape the structure of our daily lives."[3] Fifty years later, it is clear that President Johnson was mistaken. The 1965 Immigration Act *did* precipitate a revolution – a demographic revolution. For nearly a century before 1965, the immigrant stream was overwhelmingly white. That resulted from nearly a century of federal laws designed to guarantee that immigrants to the United States were predominantly from the countries of Northern and Western Europe. Yet, since 1965, a supermajority of immigrants are people of color from Asia and Central and South America. This demographic paradigm shift – the electoral, cultural, and linguistic remaking of America – is a direct consequence of the 1965 Immigration Act's changes to U.S. immigration policy. In repealing the National

1 Pub. L. No. 89–236, 79 Stat. 911 (1965), so named after its sponsors, Senator Philip Hart of Michigan and Representative Emanuel Celler of New York.

2 Pub. L. No. 68-139, 43 Stat. 153 (1924).

3 *See* Ming Hsu Chen & Taeku Lee, *Reimagining Democratic Inclusion: Asian Americans and the Voting Rights Act*, 3 U.C.I. L. Rev. 359, 379 (2013) (discussing the legislative debates and President Johnson's statement about the 1965 Immigration Act).

Origins Quota System, the 1965 Immigration Act, like the Civil Rights Act of 1964 and the Voting Rights Act of 1965, adopted a norm of nondiscrimination. Section 2 of the Immigration Act provided that "no person shall ... be discriminated against in the issuance of an immigrant visa because of his race, sex, nationality, place of birth, or place of residence."[4] Today, California, Hawaii, New Mexico, Texas, and the District of Columbia are majority minority. Indeed, the United States is expected to become a majority minority nation as a whole by 2043.[5]

The 1965 Immigration Act did more than overturn the national origins quota. It also established the framework of our contemporary immigration law system – one that privileges select family members of U.S. citizens and lawful permanent residents as potential immigrants. Promoting a policy of family unification, the 1965 Immigration Act allocated unlimited visas to spouses, children, and parents of U.S. citizens and a limited number of visas to spouses and children of lawful permanent residents and siblings of U.S. citizens. Moreover, the 1965 Immigration Act provided that a limited number of visas would be conferred to skilled and unskilled workers and noncitizens seeking to escape countries because of persecution or fear of persecution on basis of race, religion, or political opinion. Upon arriving in the United States, all of these preferred immigrants – family members, workers, and refugees – acquire lawful permanent residency or "green cards." Noncitizens outside of these select categories for lawful permanent immigration may lawfully enter the United States, if at all, temporarily under various nonimmigrant visa categories.

This immigration system created half a century ago by the 1965 Immigration Act remains the bedrock of contemporary immigration law and policy. As policy makers consider what comprehensive immigration reform would look like, including addressing the existence of 11 million undocumented immigrants, it is essential to understand the system that we have today. We cannot do that without taking a close look at the 1965 Immigration Act.

IMMIGRATION BEFORE 1965: AMERICAN APARTHEID

The 1965 Immigration Act ended the controversial National Origins Quota System that began in the 1920s. The National Origins Quota System was explicitly structured to maintain the Caucasian racial makeup of the country. Under the system, Congress granted each country of the world at least 100 immigrant visas (what would now be called "green cards" granting "lawful permanent resident" [LPR] status) annually. Additional visas were allocated to some nations based on a formula that considered

4 8 U.S.C. § 1152(a)(1)(A).

5 *U.S. Census Bureau Projections Show a Slower Growing, Older, More Diverse Nation a Half Century from Now* (Dec. 12, 2012), www.census.gov/newsroom/releases/archives/population/cb12-243.html.

the number of Americans who traced their ancestry to that nation. Importantly, as intended, this system effectively privileged natives of some countries over others. People from England, Germany, and Ireland and other Western Europeans were particularly favored, while Southern and Eastern Europeans were disadvantaged.

The law's preference for white immigrants was also reflected by its treatment of people from Africa and Asia. Although in the 1920s as today many Americans traced their ancestry to Africa, quotas for African nations were the 100-visa minimum. The stated rationale was that it was impossible to determine from which country African Americans originated; the real reason was a racist desire to minimize African immigration.

The system also treated Asians differently. The anti-Asian immigration policy of the United States began in 1882 when Congress passed the Chinese Exclusion Act; other Asians were denied the right to immigrate over time, and they were almost entirely prohibited from immigrating under the quota system. In 1952, Congress finally allowed Asians from all nations to immigrate and naturalize. However, the restriction policy continued; large Asian countries such as China, India, and Japan received the minimum quota of 100, as did Asian countries with close connections to the United States such as South Korea and the Philippines. Notably, immigrants of Asian racial background, regardless of citizenship or place of birth, were charged to the quotas of their nation of racial ancestry. Under the so-called Asia Pacific Triangle provision, there was a worldwide, overall cap of 2,000 Asian immigrants per year.

Even among nominally favored groups, discrimination was embedded in the law. For example, under the quota system, natives of the Western Hemisphere could enter the United States free of the quota; based on a policy originating in the Monroe Doctrine, they were exempt from the numerical limits. This is shocking from a modern perspective given the concern in some quarters about immigration from Mexico; in principle, millions of Mexicans were welcome to immigrate. In practice, however, they could not. The law allowed federal immigration authorities to deny entry to would-be immigrants who were not literate or who were "likely to become a public charge." Therefore, for example, agricultural workers from Mexico normally had to enter the United States, if at all, as temporary workers, even though immigrant visas were available in theory.

THE 1965 IMMIGRATION ACT: THE END OF THE RACE LINE, IN PRINCIPLE AND PRACTICE

The 1965 Immigration Act ripped out the National Origins Quota System by its roots. It increased the number of visas available only marginally, but it eliminated race as a formal factor in immigration policy. Immigrants were to be judged as individuals, and admitted based on education, achievement, job skills, or family connections to U.S. citizens or LPRs. The refugee and asylum programs admitted people based on humanitarian concerns.

However, the number of visas available to any given country in the Eastern Hemisphere was capped at 20,000 (out of 170,000 total), and for the first time, Western Hemisphere immigration was limited, although by the region as a whole and without per-country limitations. (Per-country limitations were later added to the Western Hemisphere). The 1965 Immigration Act fundamentally altered the racial demography of the immigrant stream, directly leading to the United States heading toward a majority-minority population.

Crucially, the 1965 Immigration Act should be seen as part of a broader movement to protect civil rights and eliminate race as a factor in public policy. Indeed, the 1965 Immigration Act should be understood as a sibling of the other great civil rights laws of those years, the Civil Rights Act of 1964 and the Voting Rights Act of 1965. At the same time, the 1965 Immigration Act was a product of its era. If it ended formal racial discrimination, it also perpetuated discrimination based on sexual orientation and political opinion. It failed to account for the interests of Mexican migrant workers who had traveled to the United States for generations, but were restricted under the new law. It also had the effect of giving Africans few opportunities to come to the United States.

This book considers these various aspects of the 1965 Immigration Act to deepen our understanding of our contemporary immigration law system. It is divided into four parts that focus on various aspects of the law: its purported goal to eviscerate race discrimination and promote equality; the promotion of family unification; providing employment opportunities; and political and economic consequences.

PART I: NUANCED VIEWS OF THE INTENDED CONSEQUENCES OF 1965 IMMIGRATION ACT

Part I examines more closely the 1965 Immigration Act's purpose to remove discrimination in immigration law. The chapters in this part examine both the intended and unintended effects of the 1965 Immigration Act. Gabriel J. Chin makes the case that the 1965 Immigration Act should be regarded as an important piece of civil rights legislation. Several leading scholars have argued that the contemporary diversification of the United States was an unintended consequence of the 1965 Immigration Act. Chin challenges this conventional argument. Based on close reading of media records, the legislative history, as well as interviews with participants, Chin contends that when Congress passed the 1965 Immigration Act, it intended to end racism as an idea as well as a formal matter. Accordingly, it deserves to be considered a sibling of other celebrated (albeit imperfect) laws such as the Civil Rights Act of 1964 and the Voting Rights Act of 1965.

The next three chapters, by contrast, present more critical views on the 1965 Immigration Act. Contrary to the claim that the 1965 Immigration Act ushered in a new civil rights era, both Bill Ong Hing and Kevin Johnson argue that the 1965 Immigration Act did not remove all racial barriers to immigration. In particular, these two authors argue that the 1965 Immigration Act kept in place discriminatory barriers for African and Latino/a immigrants. Specifically, Hing maintains that when it comes to residents of African descent after the end of slavery, the 1965 Immigration Act played little role in facilitating the entry of African migrants to the United States. A close look at African migrants to the United States reveals that the vast majority entered as refugees or under the diversity visa lottery program that was established in 1990. The 1965 Immigration Act did nothing to make up for or correct decades of discrimination.

Johnson argues that the 1965 Immigration Act affirmatively discriminated against Latinos/as. In particular, Johnson points out that the Immigration Act of 1965 implemented for the first time numerical caps on immigration from Mexico, as well as all of Latin America. Mexican workers in particular had a special relationship with the United States based on migration and employment; abrupt restriction of their ability to immigrate deprived these people of color equal treatment under the law. Importantly, Johnson argues that this anti-Latina/o intent of the 1965 Immigration Act set in stone the modern American immigration enforcement state that has focused primarily on Latino/a immigrants.

Brian Soucek similarly presents a counternarrative to the view that the 1965 Immigration Act ended discrimination by focusing on the extent to which the law's refugee policy maintained restrictions based on nationality. Specifically, Soucek points out that to qualify for refugee status, those persecuted had to hail from a "Communist or Communist-dominated country," or "the general area of the Middle East" and thus maintained national origins restrictions. Refugee status was also provided for those "uprooted by catastrophic natural calamity as defined by the President." The 1965 Immigration Act, Soucek argues, turned refugee policy into another weapon of the Cold War, to be deployed largely as the president chose.

PART II: THE 1965 IMMIGRATION ACT AND IMPACT ON FAMILIES

Next, Part II conducts a closer look at the 1965 Immigration Act's stated policy of promoting family unification. In particular, the three chapters in this part examine which sorts of families benefited from the 1965 Immigration Act and the impact of the Act on other families. Rose Cuison Villazor underscores that the 1965 Immigration Act enabled millions of U.S. citizens and LPRs to bring their families to the United States and thus changed the racial and ethnic makeup of our country.

Yet, Villazor shows that family unification has not been meaningfully realized by millions of U.S. citizens and LPRs and their families. In particular, many families continue to be separated as a result of the visa backlog. Additionally, others are unable to unify because of the law's limited definition of who counts as family for purposes of immigration law.

Cerissa Salazar Parreñas and Rhacel Salazar Parreñas' chapter examines the role the 1965 Immigration Act plays in creating transnational families and households. It focuses on the extent to which limited visa programs for nonimmigrant workers and visa backlogs help form transnational families. As this chapter highlights, the physical distance and long separation in time under our contemporary immigration system have imposed significant emotional consequences and relational challenges to transnational households.

Atticus Lee's chapter contends that although the 1965 Immigration Act marked a new era of racial inclusivity, it also brought with it the sting of overt discrimination based on sexuality. Lee conducts a historical analysis of immigration law's exclusion of individuals based on sexual orientation – beginning with the 1965 Immigration act's definition of homosexuals as "aliens afflicted with … sexual deviation," prohibiting them from receiving visas and gaining admission into the United States, to the 2013 Supreme Court invalidation of the 1996 Defense of Marriage Act (DOMA). In so doing, Lee highlights the impact of immigration exclusion of gays on their right to establish families in the United States.

PART III: EMPLOYMENT-BASED IMMIGRATION AND THE 1965 IMMIGRATION ACT

Part III examines the ways in which the 1965 Immigration Act facilitates immigration based on employment. Leticia Saucedo's chapter conducts a historical analysis of the relationship between the 1965 Immigration Act and the termination of the Bracero Program with Mexico. As she explains, the debates surrounding the guest worker programs that led up to the 1965 Immigration Act centered on the work that citizens will do and what work immigrants will do and thus shaped the view of the types of immigrants that the United States desires. Further, she explains how 1965 Immigration Act failed to provide avenues for Bracero workers to participate in the Act's guest workers programs. Combined with the new Western Hemisphere quotas, the Act limited lawful entry of migrant workers who had a long tradition of working in the United States. Instead of considering the historical patterns of mobility influenced by the Bracero Program or the motivations and behaviors of immigrants themselves, the 1965 Immigration Act and ensuing laws focused on targeting the workplace and employer behavior. The combination of these factors helped entrench undocumented immigration and continues to shape contemporary discussions on comprehensive immigration reform.

Robyn Magalit Rodriguez and Valerie Francisco's chapter examines noncitizen and nonimmigrant workers, those who enter the United States on a temporary basis. Specifically, their chapter examines those workers who come on H-1 visas, which are reserved for noncitizens with Bachelor's degrees and able to work in a specialty occupation. H-1 visa holders are different from most other temporary workers because they have the skills that could enable them to adjust their status to LPR or green card holders. As this chapter highlights, a growing transnational migration industry have led H-1 visa holders to become vulnerable at different points of the labor migration. This includes becoming susceptible to abuse by employers who hold the power to help these workers gain green cards.

PART IV: THE 1965 IMMIGRATION ACT AND POLITICAL AND ECONOMIC IMPLICATIONS

Part IV turns to political and economic issues related to the 1965 Immigration Act and the future of U.S. immigration policy. Notably, both chapters provide a closer look at Mexican immigrants. Giovanni Peri's chapter focuses on the long-term economic impact of the 1965 Immigration Act. The immigration system established by the 1965 Immigration Act did not provide for a large inflow of immigrants as workers, particularly those without college educations. Peri's chapter analyzes how the 1965 Immigration Act's privileging of college-educated immigrants shaped economic outcomes for various groups. Peri compares Asian immigrants, who generally had higher education and entered based on employment-related visas, with Mexican immigrants, who generally had more limited educational backgrounds and entered as family-sponsored immigrants. The 1965 Immigration Act, Peri contends, led Mexicans to rely on their preexisting social networks to find work mainly in manual, unskilled occupations. By contrast, Asian immigrants, who were already a selected and highly educated group in 1965, had access to highly remunerated jobs. Overall, Peri argues, the large number of undocumented and the very low number of employer-sponsored immigration for Mexican immigrants suggests that the 1965 Act did not work very well for that group. Accordingly, Peri calls for a more labor-market-based immigration system, which he believes would work better for Mexican immigrants and would also be more beneficial to the United States.

Finally, Jeannette Money and Kristina Victor's chapter examines the demographic and political transformation of Mexicans and Mexican Americans, particularly in U.S. border communities. In particular, they document the demographic impact of the 1965 law in terms of increased permanence and increased illegality.

They contend that political empowerment was gradually enhanced through four channels: second-generation access to citizenship through birth on U.S. soil; legalization via the Immigration Reform and Control Act of 1986; increased naturalization when the Mexican government recognized a form of dual nationality in 1998; and finally, through geographic concentration. Additionally, they explore the political power of the Mexican and Mexican-American community to shape border security policy along the U.S.-Mexican border. Overall, their chapter illustrates the delayed but growing influence of the largest group of immigrants in the United States.

In sum, this book both celebrates and critiques the 1965 Immigration Act. In so doing, it aims to explain why our current immigration system operates the way that it does today, and seeks to offer guiding principles for what immigration law could look like in the future.

PART I

The Immigration and Nationality Act Amendments of 1965

Ushering in an Era of Racial Equality or Furthering Racial Discrimination?

1

Were the Immigration and Nationality Act Amendments of 1965 Antiracist?

Gabriel J. Chin

1.1 INTRODUCTION

In a remarkable fifteen-month span between July 1964 and October 1965, Congress passed and President Lyndon B. Johnson signed three landmark civil rights bills: the Civil Rights Act of 1964,[1] the Voting Rights Act of 1965,[2] and the Immigration and Nationality Act Amendments of 1965 (1965 Immigration Act).[3] These laws unquestionably marked a turning point in American history and dramatically changed American society.

Of the three, the last may be the least celebrated and the most consequential.[4] Half a century after the Civil Rights Act, African Americans and other people of color still experience dramatic disparities in wealth, income, education, employment, and access to health care compared to whites.[5] The Voting Rights Act revolutionized access to the ballot in many parts of the United States, but the Supreme Court has

1 Civil Rights Act of 1964, PUB. L. 88–352 (July 2, 1964).

2 Voting Rights Act of 1965, PUB. L. 89–110 (Aug. 6, 1965).

3 Immigration and Nationality Act Amendments of 1965, PUB. L. 89–236 (Oct. 3, 1965).

4 *Cf.* Nicholas Pedriana & Robin Stryker, *Rights and Their Translation into Practice: Toward a Synthetic Framework* (conference paper) (discussing relative successes of the Civil Rights Act of 1965, the Voting Rights Act of 1965, and the Fair Housing Act of 1968).

5 *See, e.g.*, ALGERNON AUSTIN, THE UNFINISHED MARCH: AN OVERVIEW (Economic Policy Institute, June 18, 2013); PEW RESEARCH CENTER, KING'S DREAM REMAINS AN ELUSIVE GOAL; MANY AMERICANS SEE RACIAL DISPARITIES (Aug. 22, 2013) (http://www.pewsocialtrends.org/files/2013/08/final_full_report_racial_disparities.pdf).

Professor of Law, University of California, Davis School of Law. This essay is a revised version of an earlier paper, Gabriel J. Chin, *The Civil Rights Revolution Comes to Immigration Law: A New Look at the Immigration and Nationality Act of 1965*, 75 N.C. L. REV. 273, 279 (1996). It also borrows, principally in the Introduction, from Gabriel J. Chin & Douglas M. Spencer, *Did Multicultural America Result from a Mistake? The 1965 Immigration Act and Evidence from Roll Call Votes*, 2015 ILLINOIS L. REV. 1239. Thanks to John Ormonde for excellent research assistance.

invalidated one critical provision[6] and indicated doubts about another.[7] The Act has also been outflanked in part by creative methods and techniques that have the effect of suppressing the vote of African Americans and other minorities without technically violating its terms.[8]

By contrast, the 1965 Immigration Act utterly succeeded in bringing race neutrality to the immigration stream. Before the 1965 Act, the vast majority of immigrants were Caucasians from Europe;[9] as a result, America's population in 1960 was 85 percent non-Hispanic white and 11 percent the descendants of enslaved Africans.[10] The almost total absence of immigrants of color was no accident; the United States had a Jim Crow immigration policy pursuant to which limiting immigration of non-preferred races was perhaps the single-most important goal.[11]

Under the National Origins Quota System, in effect until 1965, visas were allocated preferentially to Northern and Western European countries.[12] Because of their Jewish and Catholic populations, the countries of Southern and Eastern Europe were given fewer visas.[13] African immigration was restricted and discouraged.[14] Beginning with

[6] Christopher S. Elmendorf & Douglas M. Spencer, Administering Section 2 of the VRA after Shelby County, 115 COLUM. L. REV. (forthcoming 2015) *After Shelby County: Getting Section 2 of the VRA to Do the Work of Section 5* (discussing *Shelby County v. Holder*, 133 S. Ct. 2612 (2013), invalidating § 4 of the Voting Rights Act, which required some jurisdictions with histories of voting discrimination to preclear changes to election procedures).

[7] Christopher S. Elmendorf, *Making Sense of Section 2: Of Biased Votes, Unconstitutional Elections, and Common Law Statutes*, 160 U. PA. L. REV. 377 (2011) (discussing constitutional challenges to Section 2 of the Voting Rights Act); Luis E. Fuentes-Rohwer, *The Future of Section 2 of the Voting Rights Act in the Hands of a Conservative Court*, 5 DUKE J. CONST. L. & PUB. POL'Y 125 (2010).

[8] *See, e.g.*, SPENCER OVERTON, STEALING DEMOCRACY: THE NEW POLITICS OF VOTER SUPPRESSION 14 (2006); Gilda R. Daniels, *A Vote Delayed Is a Vote Denied: A Preemptive Approach to Eliminating Election Administration Legislation that Disenfranchises Unwanted Voters*, 47 U. LOUISVILLE L. REV. 57 (2008); Atiba R. Ellis, *The Cost of the Vote: Poll Taxes, Voter Identification Laws, and the Price of Democracy*, 86 DENV. U. L. REV. 1023 (2009); Janai S. Nelson, *The Causal Context of Disparate Vote Denial*, 54 B.C. L. REV. 579 (2013); Spencer Overton, *Voter Identification*, 105 MICH. L. REV. 631 (2007); Terry Smith, *Disappearing Districts: Minority Vote Dilution Doctrine as Politics*, 93 MINN. L. REV. 1680 (2009); Daniel P. Tokaji, *The New Vote Denial: Where Election Reform Meets the Voting Rights Act*, 57 S.C. L. REV. 689 (2006).

[9] *See* DEPARTMENT OF HOMELAND SECURITY, 2011 YEARBOOK OF IMMIGRATION STATISTICS, table 2.

[10] Paul Taylor & D'Vera Cohn, *A Milestone en route to a Majority Minority Nation* (Nov. 7, 2012) (http://www.pewsocialtrends.org/2012/11/07/a-milestone-en-route-to-a-majority-minority-nation/?src=rss_main).

[11] *See generally* ROGER DANIELS, GUARDING THE GOLDEN DOOR: AMERICAN IMMIGRATION POLICY AND IMMIGRANTS SINCE 1882 (2004); BILL ONG HING, DEFINING AMERICA THROUGH IMMIGRATION POLICY (2003); KEVIN R. JOHNSON, THE "HUDDLED MASSES" MYTH: IMMIGRATION AND CIVIL RIGHTS (2003).

[12] See Gabriel J. Chin, *The Civil Rights Revolution Comes to Immigration Law: A New Look at the Immigration and Nationality Act of 1965*, 75 N.C. L. REV. 273, 279 (1965).

[13] *Id.*

[14] *Id.* at 280 n. 21 (citing Bill Ong Hing, *Immigration Policies: Messages of Exclusion to African Americans*, 37 HOW. L.J. 237 (1994)).

the Chinese Exclusion Act, Asian immigration was almost entirely prohibited.[15] In addition, from 1790 to 1952, the privilege of naturalization was restricted by race.[16]

After 1965, the vast majority of immigrants have been from the Third World, particularly from Latin and South America and Asia.[17] As of 2012, only 63 percent of the U.S. population is non-Hispanic white.[18] The states of California, Hawaii, New Mexico, and Texas as well as the District of Columbia are majority minority as of 2012, and the United States as a whole is projected to become a majority minority nation by 2043.[19]

Scholars recognize that formally, the 1965 Act broke with the past.[20] However, many contend that the demographic shift was unwelcome and unanticipated. Eithne Luibheid contends that the "surge [of Asians and other nonwhites] was clearly an unintended consequence of the 1965 act and did not occur because lawmakers set out to right a wrong";[21] passage of the law was "a primarily cosmetic change, one that would not actually open the United States to significant Asian, Latin American, African or Caribbean migration"; thus, it was not "a complete rupture with the

[15] *Id.* at 280–82.

[16] IAN HANEY LÓPEZ, WHITE BY LAW: THE LEGAL CONSTRUCTION OF RACE (Rev. Ed., 2006).

[17] 2011 YEARBOOK, *supra* note 9.

[18] *U.S. Census Bureau Projections Show a Slower Growing, Older, More Diverse Nation a Half Century from Now* (Dec. 12, 2012) https://www.census.gov/newsroom/releases/archives/population/cb12-243.html.

[19] *Id.*

[20] *See, e.g.*, VERNON M. BRIGGS, JR., IMMIGRATION POLICY AND THE AMERICAN LABOR FORCE 62 (1984) ("Just as overt racism could no longer be tolerated in the way citizens treated their fellow citizens, neither could it be sanctioned in the laws that governed the way in which noncitizens were considered for immigrant status."); ROGER DANIELS, COMING TO AMERICA: A HISTORY OF IMMIGRATION AND ETHNICITY IN AMERICAN LIFE 338 (1990) (noting that the Civil Rights Act, Voting Rights Act, and Immigration Act "represent a kind of high-water mark in a national consensus of egalitarianism"); MALDWYN ALLEN JONES, AMERICAN IMMIGRATION 266 (2d ed., 1992). Jones wrote:

> By the early 1960s, however, anticommunist paranoia had waned, racial and ethnic stereotypes had lost some of their force, and Americans had become more tolerant of diversity. There was also growing awareness that the country was chronically short of skilled labor. Even so, it was not until Johnson's landslide victory in the 1964 presidential election had given Congress a more liberal complexion that reform at last reached its goal.

Id.; *see also* RONALD TAKAKI, A DIFFERENT MIRROR: A HISTORY OF MULTICULTURAL AMERICA 400–01 (1993) ("Moral consistency compelled lawmakers to remove the barriers to Asian immigration, and in 1965, Congress enacted a new immigration law.... By abolishing discrimination against Asian immigrants, this new law represented a sharp ideological departure from the traditional view of America as a homogeneous white society."); Nathan Glazer, *Introduction*, CLAMOR AT THE GATES: THE NEW AMERICAN IMMIGRATION 3, 7 (Nathan Glazer ed., 1985) (referring to the "liberal and open spirit of 1965" and the "moral satisfaction of passing a nondiscriminatory immigration act"); Charles B. Keely, *Immigration Policy and the New Immigration, 1965–76*, *in* SOURCEBOOK ON THE NEW IMMIGRATION: IMPLICATIONS FOR THE UNITED STATES AND THE INTERNATIONAL COMMUNITY 15, 24 (Roy S. Bryce Laporte ed., 1980)) (hereinafter SOURCEBOOK ON THE NEW IMMIGRATION).

[21] Eithne Luibheid, *The 1965 Immigration and Nationality Act: An "End" to Exclusion?*, 5 POSITIONS NO. 2, 501, 507 (1997).

long history of exercising racial and ethnic control through immigration."[22] Mae Ngai suggested that liberals in Congress believed that "opening Asiatic immigration in principle would not mean opening it in practice, at least not significantly."[23] Hugh Davis Graham explained that officials believed that "far from threatening to ethnically transform the nation, the immigration reform bill would, as a practical matter, produce a national origins system of immigration, but without the offensive quotas."[24]

Similarly, Erika Lee concluded: "The 1965 Act abolished the national origins quotas, but lawmakers still expressed a desire to facilitate immigration from Europe, and to limit – or at the very least, discourage – immigration from Asian, Latin America and Africa. Indeed, although a racial hierarchy was not explicitly written into the law as in 1924, it remained deeply embedded in the 1965 act's design and intent."[25] Bill Ong Hing explains that the 1965 law was "driven by [America's] desire to be seen as the egalitarian champion of the 'free world'," but that "Asian immigration after 1965 took the United States by surprise"[26] because "little attention was paid to what, if any, impact the reforms might have on Asian American communities."[27] Vernon Briggs writes that "it was anticipated that passage of the Immigration Act of 1965 would lead to a decline in Asian immigration."[28] Many other immigration scholars and historians agree.[29]

[22] *Id.* at 510.

[23] Mae M. Ngai, Impossible Subjects: Illegal Aliens and the Making of Modern America 246 (2004).

[24] Hugh Davis Graham, Collision Course: The Strange Convergence of Affirmative Action and Immigration Policy in America 61 (2002).

[25] Erika Lee, *A Nation of Immigrants and a Gatekeeping Nation: American Immigration Law and Policy*, in A Companion to American Immigration (Reed Ueda ed., 2006) *See also, e.g.*, George J. Borjas, Friends or Strangers: The Impact of Immigrants on the U.S. Economy 32 (1990) ("It is conceivable that some of the framers of the 1965 amendments saw the family-reunification provisions as a way of preserving the status quo in the national-origin mix of the U.S. population, without having to resort to explicit racial or national origin restrictions.").

[26] Hing, *supra* note 11, at 79.

[27] *Id.* at 39.

[28] Vernon M. Briggs, Jr. & Stephen Moore, Still an Open Door? U.S. Immigration Policy and the American Economy 19 (1994). Professor Briggs also stated that "some interest groups saw family reunification as a way to perpetuate the old national origins systems under a guise that was more politically acceptable." *Id.* at 17.

[29] *See* Irving Bernstein, Guns or Butter: The Presidency of Lyndon Johnson 259 (1996) ("No one anticipated the dramatic changes that would soon take place."); Briggs, *supra* note 20, at 79; Daniels, *supra* note 20, at 341, 344 ("Clearly, the 1965 law has not worked out as its proponents expected. The experts simply did not know what they were talking about . . ."); Jones, *supra* note 20, at 267 (claiming that the massive increase in Asian immigration "was entirely unexpected"); David M. Reimers, Still the Golden Door: The Third World Comes to America 73–76 (2d ed., 1992) (noting that many thought Asian immigration would not increase); Elizabeth Rolph, Immigration Policies: Legacy from the 1980s and Issues for the 1990s, at 10 (1992) (noting that Congressional interest in change in immigration law was spurred by "certain unanticipated consequences of the 1965 immigration reforms" including increase in Asian immigration);

The claim is not merely that the details of the operations of the Act were not anticipated; rather, it is that the preference for whites in practice was a condition of passage of the Act. David Reimers questions what "[Congress] would have done if this issue were clear in 1965,"[30] suggesting the possibility that the bill would not have passed, at least not without measures designed to minimize Asian and other nonwhite immigration.[31] Roger Daniels has no doubts: "[H]ad the Congress fully understood [the 1965 Act's] consequences, it almost certainly would not have passed."[32] Immigration restrictionists rely on the unanticipated consequences of the Act as a reason to repeal it.[33]

STEPHEN STEINBERG, THE ETHNIC MYTH 268 (1989) (noting that the dramatic increase in Asian immigration was "not fully anticipated at the time of its enactment"); RONALD TAKAKI, STRANGERS FROM A DIFFERENT SHORE 419 (1989); Robert Tucker, *Immigration and Foreign Policy: General Considerations, in* IMMIGRATION AND UNITED STATES FOREIGN POLICY 9 (Robert Tucker et al. eds., 1990) ("Asian immigration was expected to rise only very modestly as a result of the new legislation."); THEODORE H. WHITE, AMERICA IN SEARCH OF ITSELF: THE MAKING OF THE PRESIDENT, 1956–1980, at 363 (1982) ("new [A]ct … was noble, revolutionary-and probably the most thoughtless of the many acts of the Great Society."); PHILIP Q. YANG, POST-1965 IMMIGRATION TO THE UNITED STATES 18, 21 (1995) (noting that "both Congress and the Johnson Administration expected only a slight increase in Asian immigration" as a result of the 1965 Amendment); Franklin Abrams, *Immigration Law and its Enforcement: Reflections on American Immigration, in* SOURCEBOOK ON THE NEW IMMIGRATION, *supra* note 20, at 27 (stating that immigration of Asian professionals was unexpected); Edna Bonacich et al., *Korean Immigrant: Small Business in Los Angeles, in* SOURCEBOOK ON THE NEW IMMIGRATION 167, *supra* note 20, at 167 ("An unanticipated consequence of the new law has been a sharp rise in immigration from Asia."); Glazer, *supra* note 20, at 7; Nathan Glazer, *The Closing Door, in* ARGUING IMMIGRATION 37, 39 (Nicolaus Mills ed., 1994); Elizabeth Midgely, *Comings and Goings in U.S. Immigration Policy, in* THE UNAVOIDABLE ISSUE: U.S. IMMIGRATION POLICY IN THE 1980S, at 52 (Demetrios Papademetriou & Mark Miller eds., 1983) (stating that "not all of the effects of the new system in practice were anticipated" including the increase in Asian immigration); *The New Immigrants*, 5 CQ RESEARCHER 108, 108 (1995) (noting that one of the "effects of the new law [was] a largely unanticipated rise in immigration from … Asia"); David M. Reimers, *An Unintended Reform: The 1965 Immigration Act and Third World Immigration to the United States*, 3 J. AM. ETHNIC HIST. 9, 25 (1983); Peter Schuck, *The Emerging Political Consensus on Immigration Law*, 5 GEO. IMMIG. L.J. 1, 7 (1991) ("Kennedy administration officials predicted that only 5,000 Asians would migrate in the first year and virtually none thereafter …"); David Stewart, *Immigration Laws Are Education Laws Too*, 75 PHI DELTA KAPPAN 556, 556–57 (1994); Jan C. Ting, *"Other Than a Chinaman": How U.S. Immigration Law Resulted from and Still Reflects a Policy of Excluding and Restricting Asian Immigration*, 4 TEMP. POL. & CIV. RTS. L. REV. 301, 307 (1995).

30 REIMERS, *supra* note 29, at 76.

31 Professor Reimers concluded: "The bill might have passed anyway, in the civil rights and generally liberal climate of 1965, but perhaps not so easily or without other changes." *Id.*

32 DANIELS, *supra* note 20, at 338.

33 *See, e.g.*, LAWRENCE AUSTER, THE PATH TO NATIONAL SUICIDE: AN ESSAY ON IMMIGRATION AND MULTICULTURALISM 10–26 (1990) (arguing that consequences of the 1965 Act were unintended); S.L. Bachman, *As the Number of People Increases in Poor Nations, the Number of People at the Borders of Rich Countries Does, Too*, SAN JOSE MERCURY NEWS, Mar. 20, 1994, at 7C ("The Law of Unintended Consequences upsets planning."); Donald Devine, *Impending Debate on Immigration*, WASH. TIMES, May 1, 1995, at A16 ("Talk about your unintended consequences from government actions"); Otis Graham, Jr., *Tracing Liberal Woes To '65 Immigration Act*, CHRISTIAN SCI. MONITOR, Dec. 28, 1995, at 19.

It is important to understand the significance of the claim that the 1965 Immigration Act was a Cold War gesture not actually intended to eliminate racism root and branch. Immigration reform's centrality to the liberal project is exemplified by President John F. Kennedy's book *A Nation of Immigrants*, published posthumously in 1964 with an introduction written by Robert F. Kennedy.[34] Offering an understanding of race modern progressives might well embrace, it includes illustrations – and thus implicit comparisons – of KKK rallies, Nazi book burnings, and a nineteenth-century anti-Chinese riot in Denver. The president's book calls the Japanese American Internment "unreasoning discrimination" and notes that "[t]he same things are said today of Puerto Ricans and Mexicans that were once said of Irish, Italians, Germans, and Jews: 'They'll never adjust; they can't learn the language; they won't be absorbed.'"[35] Although not particularly academic, the book is remarkable, perhaps unique, because it was written by a sitting president who made and defended specific policy reforms that, as amended, became law.[36] The central idea was that U.S. law "should be modified" so that it admitted "those with the greatest ability to add to the national welfare, no matter where they are born."[37] Of course, this nice language is perfectly consistent with the argument that no change was intended. Perhaps legislative antiracism was situational. For example, Presidents Kennedy and Johnson, and Congress, might have understood immigration and domestic civil rights differently; conceivably, they recognized that it had to offer fair treatment to African Americans who were already in the United States, but that discriminating against Asians, Latinos, and Africans in foreign lands on the basis of their race was practically and morally different.

This chapter argues that the conventional view is not correct. Congress understood when it passed the 1965 Act that it was putting U.S. immigration policy on a race-neutral basis, and that the chips would fall where they might. It uses several pieces of evidence to support this conclusion. Contemporary recollections of participants, legislative history, and media reports all show that Congress and the administration understood that changing the law would change things on the ground. It concludes that the 1965 Act is justly considered to be part of the same movement that led to the other great civil rights statutes of the era.

1.2 IMMIGRATION LAW BEFORE 1965

Before 1965, U.S. immigration law was a branch of Jim Crow. Designed to maintain racial homogeneity, the national origins quota system based the number of visas

[34] John F. Kennedy, A Nation of Immigrants (rev. ed., 1964).

[35] *Id.* at 58.

[36] *Id. at* 113–21 (outlining proposal); *see also id.* at Appendix D (reprinting President Kennedy's July 23, 1963 address on immigration).

[37] *Id.* at 120.

awarded annually to natives of particular nations on the percentage of Americans who traced their ancestry to that country. The workings of the quota laws are described in detail elsewhere,[38] but the Immigration Act of 1924,[39] the first permanent quota law,[40] provided for about 150,000 immigrant visas annually. Visas were awarded to a country based on the number of American citizens who traced their ancestry to that nation based on the 1920 census. Each country received a minimum of 100 visas per year.[41]

In 1952, the formula was amended by the Immigration and Nationality Act of 1952, also known as the McCarran-Walter Act, so that nations were awarded quotas of one-sixth of 1 percent of the number of inhabitants of the United States who traced their ancestry to that country in 1920.[42] Because the proportion of eastern and southern Europeans in the population was smaller than that of northern and western Europeans, eastern and southern European nations received low quotas, some receiving only the token 100 visa minimum. Americans tracing their ancestry to southern and eastern European nations were instrumental in developing support for immigration reform in 1965.

Americans of African descent were not counted for purposes of awarding quotas to foreign nations.[43] The law also provided special restrictions on colonial immigration, which disproportionately affected persons of African descent.[44] As a result of these

38 *See, e.g.*, MARION T. BENNETT, AMERICAN IMMIGRATION POLICIES: A HISTORY 47–58 (1963) (describing the 1924 quota system); *id.* at 133–52 (describing the McCarran-Walter quota system); E.P. HUTCHINSON, LEGISLATIVE HISTORY OF AMERICAN IMMIGRATION POLICY, 1798–1965, at 468–74 (1981); *id.* at 187–96 (discussing 1924 quota law); *id.* at 303–11 (discussing the McCarran-Walter quota system); PRESIDENT'S COMM'N ON IMMIGRATION AND NATURALIZATION, WHOM WE SHALL WELCOME 83–109 (1953) [hereinafter PRESIDENT'S COMM'N]. *See generally* U.S. DEP'T OF JUSTICE, AN IMMIGRANT NATION: UNITED STATES REGULATION OF IMMIGRATION 1798–1991 (1991) (offering a historical overview of the immigration system).

39 Immigration Act of 1924, ch.190, 43 Stat.153 (amended 1952).

40 A temporary quota had been established in 1921. *See* Act of May 19, 1921, ch. 8, § 2, 42 Stat. 5, *amended by* Immigration Act of 1924, ch. 190, 43 Stat. 153 (repealed 1952).

41 *See* Immigration Act of 1924, ch.190, § ll(b), 43 Stat.153, 159 (amended 1952).

42 *See* Immigration and Nationality Act of 1952, ch. 477, § 201(a), 66 Stat. 163, 175 (amended 1965).

43 *See id.*; Immigration Act of 1924, ch. 190, § ll(d), 43 Stat. 153, 159 (amended 1952) (stating that "the term 'inhabitants in continental United States in 1920' does not include … the descendants of slave immigrants"). *See generally* Bill Ong Hing, *Immigration Policies: Messages of Exclusion to African Americans*, 37 How. L.J. 237 (1994) (discussing African immigration to the United States).

44 *See* Immigration and Nationality Act of 1952, ch. 477, § 202(c), 66 Stat. 163, 177–78 (amended 1965). Residents of colonies were denied the unlimited immigration privileges awarded to Western Hemisphere nations or full access to the quotas of their mother countries and instead received the minimum 100-per-year quotas, which effectively limited this form of immigration. The Act provided in pertinent part:

> Any immigrant born in a colony or other component or dependent area of a governing country for which no separate or specific quota has been established … shall be chargeable to the quota of the governing country, except that (1) not more than one hundred persons born in any one such colony or other component or dependent area overseas from the governing country shall be chargeable to the quota of its governing country in any one year.

Id.

factors and others, "[b]efore 1965, Africans represented less than one percent of the total immigrant population."[45] On paper at least, pre-1965 immigration policy particularly favored Canadians, Mexicans, Central and South Americans, and other residents of the Western Hemisphere.[46] While England, Germany, and Ireland had quotas so large that they were often unfilled, Western Hemisphere residents were subject to no numerical limitations.[47]

Control of the potentially massive numbers of would-be Asian immigrants was a special focus right up to the 1965 Act. American naturalization law discriminated against nonwhite immigrants from the first days of the Republic. America's first naturalization act in 1790 offered benefits only to whites;[48] persons of African descent were added in 1870.[49] When persons of "races indigenous to the Western Hemisphere" were added to the statute in 1940,[50] only members of Asian races remained ineligible to naturalize.

Asians were the only group whose immigration was restricted on the basis of race. A consistent feature of anti-Asian immigration laws was categorization by race and ancestry rather than by place of birth. For example, a person of Asian racial descent born and raised in Brazil was treated as Asian, not Brazilian.[51] By contrast, a Greek family could, theoretically, escape discrimination under the national origins quota system by bearing children in more favored countries. The Chinese Exclusion Act of 1882[52] was the first express racial restriction; as Japanese and Asian Indians began to immigrate, they too were excluded.[53] This process culminated in the Immigration

45 Hing, *supra* note 43, at 240.

46 *See* Leticia Saucedo, Chapter 9 in this volume, and Kevin R. Johnson, Chapter 3 in this volume.

47 *See id.;* Immigration and Nationality Act of 1952, ch. 477 § 101(a)(27)(C), 66 Stat. 163, 169 (amended 1965) (stating that the term "nonquota immigrant" includes "an immigrant who was born in Canada, the Republic of Mexico, the Republic of Cuba, the Republic of Haiti, the Dominican Republic, the Canal Zone, or an independent country of Central or South America"). For a discussion of Latino immigration and demographics, see Berta Esperanza Hernandez Truyol, *Building Bridges-Latinas and Latinos at the Crossroads: Realities, Rhetoric and Replacement*, 25 COLUM. HUM. RTS. L. REV. 369, 383–96 (1994).

48 *See* Act of Mar. 26, 1790, ch. 3, 1 Stat. 103, *repealed by* Act of Jan. 29, 1795, ch. 20, 1Stat. 414 (retaining restriction of naturalization to "free white person[s]").

49 *See* Act of July 14, 1870, ch. 254, § 7, 16 Stat. 254, 256.

50 Nationality Act of 1940, ch. 876, § 303, 54 Stat. 1137, 1140. Mexicans in territory ceded to the United States after the Mexican War were offered citizenship under the Treaty of Peace, Friendship, Limits, and Settlement with the Republic of Mexico, May 30, 1848, U.S.-Mex., art. IX, 9 Stat. 922, 930, and Indians were naturalized as a group by statute in 1924. *See* Act of June 2, 1924, ch. 233, 43 Stat.253.

51 *See* Hitai v. INS, 343 F.2d 466, 468 (2d Cir. 1965) (holding that a Brazilian of Japanese ancestry could not enter as a Brazilian, but only as a Japanese).

52 Act of May 6, 1882, ch. 126, 22 Stat.58, *repealed by* Act of Dec. 17, 1943, ch. 344, 57 Stat. 600.

53 *See* Act of Feb. 5, 1917, ch. 29, § 3, 39 Stat. 874, 876, *repealed by* Act of June 27, 1952, ch. 4, § 403(a) (13), 66 Stat. 163, 279. This legislation created the "Asiatic Barred Zone," prohibiting immigration of natives or descendants of natives of continental Asian countries. China was covered by the preexisting Chinese Exclusion Act, and Japanese immigrants were covered by the "Gentlemen's Agreement," a diplomatic understanding that Japan would not issue travel documents to laborers who wanted to

Act of 1924,[54] which tied immigration to the right to naturalization. "[A]lien[s] ineligible to citizenship" were excluded entirely under the 1924 law.[55]

This phrase was a euphemism for Asians because the Act defined an alien "ineligible to citizenship" as one covered by the Chinese Exclusion Act or otherwise racially ineligible.[56] Even though some United States citizens traced their ancestry to Asian countries, the quota allotment for Asia was zero.[57] After 1924, virtually no Asians could legally immigrate,[58] and any who were already here were prohibited from becoming naturalized citizens. Again, all of these laws operated on the basis of race, not nationality.

Reform was cautious and limited. In 1943, Congress repealed the Chinese Exclusion Act and allowed Chinese to naturalize, but only 100 racial Chinese worldwide were allowed to immigrate. In 1952, when all Asians were allowed to immigrate and the racial restriction on naturalization was lifted, the Asia Pacific Triangle provision limited worldwide Asian immigration to 2,000.

1.3 THE 1965 ACT AND ITS MOTIVATIONS

In 1965, American immigration law abruptly changed. The Immigration and Nationality Act Amendments of 1965[59] sometimes known as Hart-Celler, was

come to the United States. *See* BILL ONG HING, MAKING AND REMAKING ASIAN AMERICA THROUGH IMMIGRATION POLICY, 1850–1990, at 207–12 (1993) (reprinting portions of the Gentlemen's Agreement).

54 Immigration Act of 1924, ch. 190, 43 Stat. 153, *repealed by* Act of June 27, 1952, ch. 477, 66 Stat.163, 279. This law is also known as the Reed-Johnson Act or the National Origins Act.

55 *See id.* § 13(c), 43 Stat. at 162.

56 *See id.* § 28(c), 43 Stat.at 168.

57 *See id.* § ll(b), (c), (d), 43 Stat. at 159 (noting that "aliens ineligible to citizenship" were not counted as "inhabitants in the continental United States in 1920").

58 Asians were, however, allowed to enter if they were previously lawfully admitted and were returning from a trip abroad, were a minister of religion or a teacher, or were entering solely for purposes of study in an accredited school. *See id.* §§ 4, 13(c), 43 Stat. at 155,162. Filipinos, then nationals of the United States but not citizens, were permitted to travel to the United States but not to naturalize. *See* *Toyota v. United States*, 268 U.S. 402 (1925).

59 PUB. L. NO. 89–236, 79 Stat. 911 (codified as amended in scattered sections of 8 U.S.C.).

On July 23, 1963, President Kennedy sent his immigration reform proposal to Congress, where it was introduced as H.R. 7700 in the House and S. 1932 in the Senate. Congress held hearings on both bills. *See* HUTCHINSON, *supra* note 38, at 359–60. On January 13, 1965, President Johnson sent a similar immigration proposal to Congress which was introduced as H.R. 2580 in the House and S. 500 in the Senate. Hearings began in February of 1965 in the Senate and in March of 1965 in the House. *See id.* at 367–68. Less than one year passed between the last hearings on the Kennedy proposal and the first hearings on the Johnson proposal, and, as Senator Edward Kennedy explained, Johnson's "recommendations ... with very minor exceptions, paralleled those of President Kennedy." Edward M. Kennedy, *The Immigration Act of 1965*, 367 ANNALS AM. ACAD. POL. & SOC. SCI. 137, 142 (1966). Similarly, James J. Hines of the Office of the Legal Adviser, U.S. Department of State, did a section-by-section comparison of the administration's proposal and the bill that became law and found them substantially similar. *See* James J. Hines, *The Immigration Act of 1965*, 43 Interpreter Releases 59, 59–61 (1966). Accordingly, the hearings on H.R. 7700 and S. 1932 are relevant to the meaning of the final law.

structurally familiar in certain ways.[60] The new law provided for restricted immigration; a limit of 170,000 visas per year was imposed on the citizens of the countries in the Eastern Hemisphere.[61] Furthermore, no more than 20,000 visas per year could go to natives of any one nation.[62] The law's preference categories were based on employment skills or family connections to citizens or permanent resident aliens.[63] In addition, immediate relatives of citizens – spouses, parents, and unmarried children – could enter without numerical limitation, that is, regardless of whether one of the 170,000 Eastern Hemisphere (or 20,000 per country) visas were available, and without being charged against those limits.[64]

Western Hemisphere immigration was limited for the first time to 120,000, but without preferences or per-country limitations.[65] As in the Eastern Hemisphere, immediate relatives of citizens could enter without regard to the 120,000 annual limitation.[66] The law's revolutionary feature was its race neutrality: For the first time since the United States started regulating immigration, race was not a factor.

Congressional Statements about Racism

Congressional discussion of the 1965 Act supports the conclusion that its elimination of racial discrimination was sincere.[67] Many legislators contended that the laws should be changed because racial and national distinctions were bad in principle, not because of some particular exigency. Senator Edward M. Kennedy argued

60 For additional discussions of the Act's workings, see H.R. Rep. No. 89–745, at 8–23 (1965); S. Rep. No. 89–748, at 10–26 (1965), *reprinted in* 11 Oscar Trelles & James Bailey, Immigration and Nationality Acts: Legislative Histories and Related Documents, doc. 73 (1979), *and in* 1965 U.S.C.C.A.N. 3328, 3328–45 (1965).

61 *See* Immigration and Nationality Act Amendments of 1965, Pub. L. No. 89–236, § 1, 79 Stat. 911,911 (codified as amended in scattered sections of 8 U.S.C.).

62 *See id.* § 2, 79 Stat. at 911–12.

63 *See id.* § 3, 79 Stat. at 912–13 (establishing preference system).

64 *See id.* § 1, 79 Stat. at 911.

65 *See id.* § 8, 79 Stat. at 916 (defining "special immigrant" to mean native of an independent foreign country of the Western Hemisphere or Canal Zone, and the spouse and children of such person, as well as other certain other categories of person, such as permanent resident aliens returning from a temporary trip abroad, and certain active or retired employees of the U.S. government); *id.* § 21, 79 Stat. at 920–21 (providing that, effective July 1, 1968, immigration of "special immigrants" based on their Western Hemisphere nativity may not exceed 120,000 per year). Per-country limits were added in 1976.

66 *See id.* § 21(e), 79 Stat. at 921.

67 Of course, the "civil rights talk" could have been fluff. But perhaps the bill is entitled to a presumption of innocence through association; it had telling friends and enemies. Analysis of the roll-call votes of the Civil Rights Act of 1964, the Voting Rights Act of 1965, and the Immigration and Nationality Act Amendments of 1965 showed that the same basic coalition of senators and representatives supported and opposed the bills. *See* Gabriel J. Chin & Douglas M. Spencer, *Did Multicultural America Result From a Mistake? The 1965 Immigration Act and Evidence From Roll Call Votes*, 2015 Illinois L. Rev. 1239.

that the national origins quota system was "contrary to our basic principles as a nation."[68] Senator Joseph Clark insisted that "[t]he national origins quotas and the Asian-Pacific [sic] triangle provisions are irrational, arrogantly intolerant, and immoral."[69] Representative Paul Krebs argued that the national origins system was "repugnant to our national traditions," and that "[w]e must learn to judge each individual by his own worth and by the value he can bring to our Nation."[70] Representative Dominick Daniels argued that "[r]acism simply has no place in America in this day and age."[71] These kinds of arguments had been largely absent from earlier debates about immigration reform.[72]

This change in attitude extended to Asians. Representative Leonard Farbstein stated to his colleagues that he could not "believe that there is any Member of this House who would say a word in defense" of the Asia-Pacific Triangle provision.[73] Senator Kennedy announced that he was "especially gratified that we are wiping out the Asia-Pacific triangle … [A]fter almost 100 years, Asian peoples are no longer discriminated against in the immigration laws of our country."[74]

Others compared the bill to measures designed to eliminate domestic discrimination, such as the Civil Rights Act of 1964 and the Voting Rights Act of 1965. Reflecting the views of many, Representative Laurence Burton argued: "Just as we sought to eliminate discrimination in our land through the Civil Rights Act, today we seek by phasing out the national origins quota system to eliminate discrimination in immigration to this Nation composed of the descendants of immigrants."[75]

Officials recognized that racism in immigration was a civil rights issue because of its effect on Americans. Dean Rusk, for example, observed that immigration policy had significant domestic, as well as foreign, effects:

> [G]iven the fact that we are a country of many races and national origins, that those who built this country and developed it made decisions about opening our doors

68 111 CONG. REC. 24,225 (1965).

69 *Id.* at 24,501. It was unjust, Senator Clark continued, that "[a] brilliant Korean or Indian scientist is turned away, while the northern European is accepted almost without question." *Id.*

70 *Id.* at 21,778.

71 *Id.* at 21,787.

72 Surely some members of Congress held racially egalitarian views in those years, but they may have concluded that such an argument would be unpersuasive to the majority.

73 111 CONG. REC. 21,785 (1965); *see also id.* at 21,792 (remarks of Rep. Brademas) (noting that the bill "will repeal the Asia-Pacific triangle which has too long been an insult to those of oriental ancestry").

74 *Id.* at 24,227.

75 *Id.* at 21,783; *see also id.* at 21,765 (remarks of Rep. Sweeney) (making similar observation); *id.* at 21,768 (remarks of Rep. Giaimo); *id.* at 21,783 (remarks of Rep. Wolff); *id.* at 21,784 (remarks of Rep. Farbstein); *id.* at 21,796 (remarks of Rep. Gallagher) (mentioning Voting Rights Act); *id.* at 24,446 (remarks of Sen. Fong) ("Elimination of racial barriers against citizens of other lands is a logical extension of eliminating discrimination against American citizens."); *id.* at 24,563 (remarks of Sen. Edward Kennedy).

> to the rest of the world; that anything which makes it appear that we, ourselves, are discriminating in principle about particular national origins, suggests that we think… less well of our own citizens of those national origins, than of other citizens.[76]

In 1943 and 1952, Congress amended the law in favor of Asians. In 1965, as in earlier years, the fact that the United States was at war in Asia did not go unnoticed.[77] But the 1943 and 1952 liberalizations were quite different from what occurred in

[76] *See Immigration: Hearings Before Subcomm. No. 1 of the Comm. on the Judiciary, House of Representatives, on H.R. 7700 and 55 Identical Bills*, 88th Cong. 390 (1964), *reprinted in* 10A Trelles & Bailey, *supra* note 60, doc. 69A [hereinafter *Hearings on H.R. 7700*]; *see also id.* at 410 (remarks of Attorney General Robert Kennedy) (noting that the bill "would remove from our law a discriminatory system of selecting immigrants that is a standing affront to millions of our citizens"); *Immigration: Hearings on S. 500 Before the Subcomm. on Immigration and Naturalization of the Senate Comm. on the Judiciary*, 89th Cong. at 9 (1965), *reprinted in* 11 Trelles & Bailey, *supra* note 60, doc. 70 (remarks of Attorney General Katzenbach) ("I do not know how any American could fail to be offended by a system which presumes that some people are inferior to others solely because of their birthplace.… The harm it does to the United States and to its citizens is incalculable."); *Hearings Before the Subcomm. on Immigration and Naturalization of the Senate Comm. on the Judiciary on S. 1932 and other Legislation Relating to the Immigration Quota System*, 88th Cong. 31 (1964) (unpublished) [hereinafter *Hearings on S. 1932*] (remarks of Sen. Robert Keating). Keating stated:

> Moreover, by eliminating from the law the pernicious implications of racial inferiority contained in the Asia-Pacific Triangle provisions, the United States would no longer be in the position of having on its books a legal slap in the face of our … own citizens of Asian background who can be justly proud of their record of attainments as Americans.

Id. Even opponents of reform, such as W.B. Hicks, Jr., Executive Director of the Liberty Lobby, understood this point. Hicks acknowledged the insult to Americans when the law discriminated against those of similar ethnic or national backgrounds:

> I would like to say that the people I have seen, the witnesses, coming before this committee to object to the quota system have made a very deep impression on me. Apparently the quota system is not an insult to foreigners so much as it is to Americans of foreign parentage of identifiable racial strains such as the Italian-Americans and Chinese-Americans, who feel that the quotas make them less valuable or that Congress feels they are less valuable as American citizens than others, and I can well understand their feelings. I think the people who subscribe to Liberty Lobby would agree with me on this, that we do not like the idea of discrimination based on race resulting in a feeling of being insulted on the part of our American citizens.

Hearings on H.R. 7700, *supra* note 76, at 852.

[77] *See, e.g.*, TAKAKI, *supra* note 29, at 418 ("Seeking to promote anti-Communism abroad and to present itself as a democracy to peoples engaged in anticolonialist struggles in Latin America, Africa, and Asia, the United States felt compelled to abandon the national-origins quota."); *id.* (noting the important role of the Civil Rights Movement in awakening "the moral conscience of America"); Abba P. Schwartz, *Foreign and Domestic Implications of U.S. Immigration Laws*, 50 DEP'T ST. BULL. 675 *passim* (1964) (discussing foreign policy difficulties caused by McCarran-Walter). Desegregation of the immigrant stream, like the public schools, was clearly, in part, a cold war imperative, and to some extent served the interests of caucasians. See Derrick A. Bell, Jr., Brown v. Board of Education *and the Interest-Convergence Dilemma*, 93 HARV. L. REV. 518, 524 (1980); Mary L. Dudziak, *Desegregation as Cold War Imperative*, 41 STAN. L. REV. 61 (1988); John Hayakawa Torok, *"Interest Convergence" and the Liberalization of Discriminatory Immigration and Naturalization Laws Affecting Asians*, 1943–65 in CHINESE AMERICA: HISTORY AND PERSPECTIVES 1995, at 1, 8 (Chinese Historical Society of America ed., 1995).

1965. The 1943 and 1952 reforms compromised war aims in order to ensure effective racial restriction. In addition, there were fail-safe mechanisms to ensure only a tiny number of Asians could immigrate.

In 1943, in legislation sometimes called the "Chinese Repealer," Congress granted a worldwide quota of 105 to racial Chinese.[78] Notions of racial equality were not an important motivating force.[79] Indeed, several members of Congress pointed out that other allies, such as India and Philippines,[80] did not benefit from the proposed bill,[81] and that the miniscule quota actually insulted Chinese people because it did not offer equality with Europeans.[82] Importantly, these critics argued neither for extending token recognition to other allies nor for full equality for Chinese; instead, the opposed reform entirely. Maintaining restriction of Asians was more important than helping win World War II.

In 1952, the McCarran-Walter Act eliminated the remaining bars against Asian naturalization and awarded all Asian countries immigration quotas, most of which were the hundred-per-year minimum.[83] This, too, was a war and Cold War measure.[84] Just as in 1943, the 1952 law provided strict controls on the admission of

78 *See, e.g.*, 89 CONG. REC. 8582 (1943) (remarks of Rep. Fred Busbey). Representative Judd assured his colleagues that "[t]here are no loopholes whereby persons of the Chinese race who were born in Hong Kong, for example, and therefore are British citizens, could come in under the British quota." *Id.* at 8588.

79 While there was an occasional reference to racial equality – *see, e.g., id.* at 8593 (remarks of Rep. Judd) – the circumstances, in addition to the avowed military purposes of the bill, belie any such purpose. Indeed, during the hearings on the bill, when a witness admitted that he supported "social equality among all the races," Representative Leo Allen replied: "I thank you for giving your views. You have done your cause more harm than anybody else." *Hearings on Repeal of the Chinese Exclusion Acts, H.R. 1882 & H.R. 2309, Before the House Comm. on Immigration and Naturalization*, 78th Cong. 40–41 (1943).

80 *Id.* at 8584. Representative Jenkins shared this view. *See id.* at 8598. *See also id.* at 8593. Senator Hiram Johnson argued:

> China is not our only Ally subject to our exclusion laws. What about our brave Allies the Filipinos, and what about all the potential Allies in the Orient, the natives of India, Burma, Malaya, the Dutch East Indies, and others? Is not this proposed legislation a deliberate slap in the face for all Asiatic peoples, except only the Chinese?

ld. at 9999 (statement of Sen. Hiram Johnson).

81 *See* H.R. REP. NO. 78–732, pt. 2, at 1–2 (1943). India and the Philippines would later be awarded minimum quotas.

82 89 CONG. REC. 8584 (1943) (remarks of Rep. Bennett). Representative Thomas Jenkins, likewise, stated that "I do not rate the Chinese as being so ignorant and so easy as not to notice how they are being fooled and discriminated against." *Id.* at 8599.

83 *See* Immigration and Nationality Act of 1952, ch. 477, § 201(a), 66 Stat. 163, 175 ("[T]he minimum quota for any quota area shall be one hundred.").

84 *See, e.g.*, DANIELS, *supra* note 20, at 329 (stating that the 1952 liberalization "should be seen as a fruit of the Cold War"); ROBERT A. DIVINE, AMERICAN IMMIGRATION POLICY, 1924–1952, at 173–74 (1957); HING, *supra* note 11, at 37–38 ("The ideological Cold War between capitalism and communism made the United States acutely conscious of how its domestic policies, including immigration, were perceived abroad.").

Asians. While the near-absolute prohibition on Asian immigration was eliminated, Congress replaced it with the Asia-Pacific triangle, a geographic area subject to special restrictions. Congress awarded each triangle country a minimum quota of one hundred,[85] but the total immigration from the triangle was limited to two thousand.[86] Thus, if more than twenty countries came into being within the triangle, all triangle countries would have their individual quotas reduced.

In addition, following the 1943 Chinese Repealer model, the McCarran-Walter Act retained a racial test solely for persons tracing more than half of their ancestry to countries in the Asia-Pacific triangle. Such persons were charged against the quota of their racial homeland rather than their country of birth.[87] As one commentator acknowledged, the triangle provision was "an obvious device to prevent such persons, because of their race, from immigrating to the United States under the possibly large quotas of their country of birth, or in the case of Western Hemisphere countries, from coming into the United States on a non-quota basis."[88]

Asian peoples could not have missed the import of these provisions, which presumably gave them little reason to align with the United States rather than the Soviet bloc. The self-defeating effect of the law appears not only in hindsight, but was emphasized by congressional critics who favored greater liberalization. However, the reasoning of this group was not that the bill was insufficiently egalitarian, but that its remaining discriminations against Asians were unwise in light of the Korean War and the global struggle with communism.[89] Senator William Benton suggested

[85] *See* Immigration and Nationality Act of 1952, ch. 477, § 201(a), 66 Stat. 163, 175. China and Japan received marginally larger quotas. *See* PRESIDENT'S COMM'N, *supra* note 38, at 99–101 tbl.S (noting that China received a quota of 105 and Japan a quota of 185).

[86] *See* Immigration and Nationality Act of 1952, ch. 477, § 202(e), 66 Stat. at 178 (stating that "any increase in the number of minimum quota areas above twenty within the Asia-Pacific triangle shall result in a proportionate decrease in each minimum quota of such area in order that the sum total of all minimum quotas within the Asia-Pacific triangle shall not exceed two thousand"). This feature of the law was removed in 1961. *See* Act Amending the Immigration and Nationality Act and For Other Purposes, PUB. L. NO. 87–301, § 9, 75 Stat. 650, 654 (1961); H.R. REP. NO. 87–1086, at 45 (1961), *reprinted in* 1961 U.S.C.C.A.N. 2950, 2979. Thus, after 1961, new countries in the triangle could be recognized without diminishing the quotas of preexisting nations.

[87] *See* Immigration and Nationality Act of 1952, § 202(b), 66 Stat. at 177, *repealed by* Immigration and Nationality Act Amendments of 1965, Pub. L. No. 89–236, § 2, 79 Stat. 911, 911–12.

[88] ABBA P. SCHWARTZ, THE OPEN SOCIETY 109 (1968).

[89] This point was noted by the administration as well. *See* Memorandum by the Director of the Bureau of the Budget to the President, May 9, 1952 (noting that Walter bill contained a racial attribution feature, which because it "would apply only in Asia and nowhere else in the world, would call into question the meaning and sincerity of the gestures made by the bill.... The Kremlin is always quick to seize upon any half measure as proof of democratic duplicity."), *reprinted in* I U.S. DEP'T OF STATE, FOREIGN RELATIONS OF THE UNITED STATES, 1952–1954, GENERAL ECONOMIC AND POLITICAL MATTERS 1591 (1983); *see also id.* at 1595 ("These restrictions would announce to the peoples of Asia 'the United States still considers you undesirable. We're going to have one set of rules for everyone else in the world and a special set of rules for you. We want to make sure that too many of you won't come over.'").

that the bill was "potentially more costly, more damaging to the national interest, than any major bill which has come to the floor with so little understanding about it on the part of the Senate as a whole."[90] Benton explained:

> What folly it is for us, Mr. President, to spend hundreds of billions of dollars on defense and to incur more than 100,000 casualties in Korea, and then to undercut this great investment of our boys' blood and their parents' money by passing a bill which turns the world against us …
>
> [W]e can totally destroy that investment, and can ruthlessly and stupidly destroy faith and respect in our great principles, by enacting laws that, in effect, say to the peoples of the world:
>
> "We love you, but we love you from afar. We want you but, for God's sake, stay where you are."[91]

Benton went so far as to suggest that the earlier Asian Exclusion laws contributed directly to Japan's attack on Pearl Harbor.[92]

Senator McCarran was unmoved. He explained:

> [T]he cold, hard truth is that in the United States today there are hard-core, indigestible blocs who have not became [sic] integrated into the American way of life, but who, on the contrary, are its deadly enemy. The cold, hard truth, Mr. President, is that today, as never before, untold millions are storming our gates for admission; and those gates are cracking under the strain. The cold, hard fact is, too, Mr. President, that this Nation is the last hope of western civilization; and if this

90 98 Cong. Rec. 5149 (1952). Benton was in an excellent position to evaluate the effects of propaganda on foreign policy; he had been both an assistant secretary of state involved in the founding of the United Nations, and the founder of a major Madison Avenue advertising agency, Benton & Bowles. For a discussion of his activities, see generally Sidney Hyman, The Lives of William Benton (1969).

91 98 Cong. Rec. 5150 (1952).

92 Senator Benton reported that he:

> happened to be in Japan in 1937 on the anniversary of the day when the United States enacted its Oriental Exclusion Act. [sic] To my astonishment, I saw black flags break out all over Tokyo, even draped on buildings. It was a national day of mourning in Japan, a day of humiliation. No man knows the extent to which the Oriental Exclusion Act, by which we insulted the proud peoples of Asia, was responsible for the temper of the Japanese people which lead to the attack upon the United States at Pearl Harbor.

Id. at 5157; *see also id.* at 5616 (making similar comment). A 1943 memorandum by a State Department official offers some support for this view:

> The burning hostility of such men as the late Admiral Yamamoto toward the United States, and the desire and intention and plans and efforts of such men to make war upon and defeat the United States were animated in no small part by their view of and emotions regarding this matter of discrimination on our part against the race of which they were and are members.

Memorandum by the Advisor on Political Relations, June 9, 1943, *reprinted in* U.S. Dep't of State, Foreign Relations of the United States, 1943, China 777 (1957).

> oasis of the world shall be overrun, perverted, contaminated, or destroyed, then the last flickering light of humanity will be extinguished. A solution of the problems of Europe and Asia, Mr. President, will not come as we transplant these problems en masse to the United States of America.[93]

The 1965 law, then, differed from the 1943 and 1952 reforms in two important ways. First, supporters of the 1965 Act advanced antiracist as well as practical arguments. Second, the 1965 Act contained no fail-safe, no insurance policy – that is, numerical or racial restrictions ensuring that only a limited number of nonwhite people could take advantage of the available immigration slots.

Contemporary Recollections of Participants

In 1995 and 1996, a number of participants shared their recollections – some faded – of the drafting and adoption of the 1965 legislation. When trying to determine what people meant to accomplish through particular actions, what they say has some bearing.[94] The responses were remarkably uniform. President Gerald R. Ford, for example, was the House minority leader in 1965, and a supporter of the bill. He remembered that Asian immigration was expected to increase substantially. "As I recall, it was anticipated that the 1965 Amendments would substantially increase the number of Asian immigrants. As the Republican Leader in the House of Representatives at the time, I favored that result."[95]

The bill came out of the Democratic-controlled House Judiciary Committee, and its Subcommittee Number One, which was responsible for immigration.[96] Peter Rodino, Jr., later chairman of the House Judiciary Committee itself, recognized that there was enormous unsatisfied immigration demand in Asia.[97] Representative

93 98 CONG. REC. 5330 (1952).

94 I do not mean to weigh in on the controversy over using legislative history to construe statutes. *See* Kevin R. Johnson, *Responding to the "Litigation Explosion": The Plain Meaning of Executive Branch Primacy Over Immigration*, 71 N.C. L. REV. 413, 425–31 (1993) (discussing debate and collecting authorities). First, no one questions that the 1965 Act eliminated the national origins quota system and formal consideration of race from the immigration laws. Moreover, this chapter examines what Congress and the administration thought they were doing when they changed the law. In answering this question, legislative history and other evidence is surely relevant. At the same time, the "'plain meaning'" rule – that the best evidence of congressional purpose is the "plain meaning of the text" – renders doubtful the claim that the racial diversification of the immigration stream was accidental. *See id.* at 426. It is implausible that Congress did not know that ending discrimination would create opportunities for previously excluded groups.

95 Letter from President Gerald R. Ford to Gabriel J. Chin 1 (Jan. 29, 1996) (on file with author).

96 *See* CONGRESSIONAL STAFF DIRECTORY 1966, at 217 (Charles Brownson ed., 1966) (noting that Subcommittee No. 1 had "[s]pecial jurisdiction over immigration and nationality").

97 *See* Telephone Interview with Peter Rodino, Jr., Retired Member of Congress (Mar. 8, 1996) (transcript on file with author).

Rodino recognized at the time that the increase in Asian immigration "could be substantial."[98] Judiciary Committee member Robert Kastenmeier also expected that "many more Asians would be coming to the United States."[99] Subcommittee member Don Edwards recalled that he knew "there would be more" Asian immigrants.[100] Jack Brooks,[101] Charles Mathias,[102] and Arch Moore,[103] all members of the Immigration Subcommittee, also anticipated increased Asian immigration, although not at the level that actually occurred.

According to Dale DeHaan, then advisor to Senator Edward Kennedy, supporters of the bill in the Senate recognized that more Asians would be coming.[104] Aware of some scholarly opinions to the contrary, DeHaan disagrees with them.[105]

Kennedy and Johnson administration officials who worked on the bill had no doubt about its effects. Washington attorney Myer Feldman was Deputy White House Counsel to President Kennedy and White House Counsel to President Johnson.[106] Feldman states that both Kennedy and Johnson believed that "[w]hether the immigrant was from Asia, Africa, Italy or eastern Europe, or whether the immigrant was from England, France or Belgium, was not an acceptable basis for discrimination between them."[107] Speaking of Asian immigration, Feldman writes: "[W]e did expect there would be an increase and we welcomed it."[108]

98 *Id.* at 9.

99 Telephone Interview with Robert Kastenmeier, Retired Member of Congress (Jan. 12, 1996) (transcript on file with author).

100 Telephone Interview with Don Edwards, Retired Member of Congress (Jan. 16, 1996) (transcript on file with author).

101 *See* Letter from Jack Brooks, Retired Member of Congress, to Gabriel J. Chin 1 (Jan. 17, 1996) (on file with author) ("As I recall the thought was that a few more Asians would enter and that it would modify the national origin system which had limited the number of Asian immigrants for a few years.").

102 *See* Telephone Interview with Charles Mathias, Retired United States Senator (Feb. 9, 1996) (transcript on file with author).

103 *See* Telephone Interview with Arch Moore, Jr., Retired Governor of West Virginia and Member of Congress (Jan.18, 1996) (transcript on file with author).

104 *See* Letter from Gabriel J. Chin to Dale DeHaan, Former Staff Member for Senator Edward M. Kennedy 1(Dec. 16, 1995) (on file with author) (containing transcribed notes of interview). After leaving Senate service, Mr. DeHaan remained active in refugee and immigration matters. He was director of immigration and refugee services for the National Council of Churches and the Church World Service, and later U.N. Deputy High Commissioner for Refugees. In 1990, he was named to the U.S. Commission for the Study of International Migration and Cooperative Economic Development. *See* Robert Pear, *Centralized Immigration Control Urged*, N.Y. TIMES, June 3, 1990, at A22 (announcing Commissioner DeHaan's appointment).

105 *See* Letter from Gabriel J. Chin to Dale DeHaan, *id.* at 1.

106 *See* WHO'S WHO IN AMERICA 1274 (50th ed. 1996).

107 Letter from Myer Feldman, Former White House Counsel, to Gabriel J. Chin 1–2 (Feb. 2, 1996) (on file with author).

108 *Id.* at 2.

Nicholas deBelleville Katzenbach was Deputy Attorney General under Kennedy before becoming Attorney General under Johnson.[109] Katzenbach said in 1996 that he was "surprised [but] not astounded" at the percentage of nonwhite immigration under the 1965 Act, but that he would not have been surprised at the time the bill was passed if 50 percent turned out to be nonwhite.[110] Although the details, such as Southeast Asian immigration following the Vietnam War, could not have been anticipated, "the general phenomenon" of increased Asian immigration "should have been predictable, [and he] think[s] was" predicted when the bill passed.[111] W. Willard Wirtz, then Secretary of Labor, generally shared Attorney General Katzenbach's views.[112] Norbert A. Schlei,[113] Assistant Attorney General in the Justice Department's Office of Legal Counsel under Robert Kennedy, worked on the original draft of the bill with Adam Walinsky.[114] Both recalled that Asian immigration was expected to increase; Walinsky points out that "you'd have to be a real dope not to know that the number would go up." He added: "How could anybody think when we were repealing the Asia-Pacific Triangle that you wouldn't get a significant increase in immigration from China? That just doesn't make any sense. It's just stupid."[115] Thomas Ehrlich, President Emeritus of Indiana University and now a Stanford professor, worked on the original draft of the bill when he was on the legal staff of the State Department.[116] He says that he and

[109] During his remarks on the floor of the Senate, Robert Kennedy thanked ten people for their work on the bill, including Adam Walinsky; the first two were Attorney General Katzenbach and Assistant Attorney General Schlei. *See* 111 CONG. REC. 24,498 (1965).

[110] *See* Telephone Interview with Nicholas deBelleville Katzenbach, former Attorney General (May 20, 1996) (transcript on file with author).

[111] *Id.*

[112] *See* Telephone Interview with W. Willard Wirtz, former Secretary of Labor (Aug. 7, 1996) (transcript on file with author).

[113] Schlei's background is remarkable; editor-in-chief of the Yale Law Journal and first in his graduating class, he clerked for Justice Harlan on the Supreme Court and coauthored a prize-winning book with Yale Professor Myers McDougall. *See* 2 WHO'S WHO IN AMERICA, *supra* note 106, at 3705. Six years out of law school, he was an Assistant Attorney General under Robert Kennedy, where he advised the White House on such matters as the Cuban Missile Crisis and integration of the University of Mississippi. *See id.*

[114] Since leaving the Justice Department, in addition to practicing law in New York, Walinsky has been one of the most provocative and interesting critics of the criminal justice system. *See* Adam Walinsky, *The Crisis of Public Order*, ATLANTIC MONTHLY, July 1995, at 39, 39; 140 CONG. REC. S124965-01 (daily ed. Aug. 25, 1994) (noting Walinsky's ultimately successful efforts to establish a Police Corps, which occurred in 1994 by virtue of PUB. L. NO. 103–322, tit. XX, § 200104, 108 Stat. 2049, 2050 (1994) (codified at 42 U.S.C. § 14093 (1993))).

[115] Telephone Interview with Adam Walinsky, former Attorney, Office of Legal Counsel, U.S. Dep't of Justice (May 31, 1995) (transcript on file with author); telephone Interview with Norbert Schlei, former Assistant Attorney General (Dec. 18, 1995) (transcript on file with author).

[116] *See* WHO'S WHO IN AMERICA, *supra* note 106, at 1173.

Assistant Secretary of State Abba Schwartz intended to "open up the gates, and . . . it happened just [that] way."[117]

Legislative History: Asian Immigration Will Increase

In 1964 and 1965, there seems to have been no serious question that the racial demographics of the immigration stream would change. In an early use of the term "the new immigration" in the context of the 1965 Act, Senator Edward Kennedy explained that Americans need not fear the people who would be brought in under the bill: "[T]he people who comprise the new immigration – the type which this bill would give preference to – are relatively well educated and well to do. They are familiar with American ways."[118] Kennedy argued only that the change would not be traumatic, not that there would be no change.

If only southern and eastern European immigration would be increased, then the following exchange about security measures between Representative Michael Feighan and State Department official Abba Schwartz makes little sense:

MR. FEIGHAN. The reason I ask [about changes in security procedures] is that the existing patterns of immigration to the United States have been in force for some time, thus permitting the development of security techniques and procedures which fit those patterns. *The administration proposal could very well change those patterns to such an extent that you would be required to operate in new and uncharted waters. Is that a realistic possibility?*

MR. SCHWARTZ. We certainly believe you are correct, Mr. Chairman. *There may be people coming in greater numbers from different areas of the world.* That certainly would be taken into account. I can imagine that if numbers were to increase of persons coming from areas where we do not have extensive personnel, or experienced people, that certainly would have an effect and we would have to take care of that.[119]

117 Telephone Interview with Thomas Ehrlich, President Emeritus, Indiana University and Former Attorney, State Department (Feb. 9, 1996) (transcript on file with author).

118 111 CONG. REC. 24,228 (1965).

119 *Hearings on H.R. 7700*, *supra* note 76, at 511–12 (emphasis added). The administration's draft of the bill gave the president discretion to award Ireland, Germany, and England extra visas over and above the ordinary per-country limitation. Dean Rusk explained:

> This is partly because we do not wish to interrupt *too precipitately* longstanding patterns of movement of peoples from those countries who have long sent us substantial numbers of emigrants [sic]. I think it would work a hardship if we were to apply this 10-percent rule right away to some of the countries who have been sending us large numbers every year.

Id. at 403 (emphasis added). President Johnson's message to Congress proposed a five-year phase-in of the new law, so that the "possibility of *abrupt* changes in the pattern of immigration from any nation [could be] eliminated." H.R. EXEC. DOC. 89-52, at 2 (1965), *reprinted in* 10 TRELLES & BAILEY, *supra* note 60, doc. 68 (emphasis added). In fact, Congress adopted a three-year phase-in period. *See infra*

Senator Paul Douglas made no bones about the effect of the bill: "I would say the fundamental question is simply this. Should we not admit more of the hundreds of thousands of people in eastern Europe, southern Europe, southeastern Europe and Asia who want to come here[?]"[120]

Many witnesses predicated an increase in Asian immigration. If few subscribed to witness Rosalind Frame's prediction that after forty years of immigration under the new law, there could be more than 114 million Chinese living in the United States,[121] groups such as The Citizens for a Sensible, Security-Minded Immigration Law[122] and The Daughters of the American Revolution,[123] among several others,[124] agreed that the bill would offer advantages to "immigrants from the overpopulated, socially, and economically deprived countries, such as China, India, and Africa [sic]."[125]

Many witnesses and legislators also recognized that existing law was unfair to would-be Asian immigrants;[126] and that there was unsatisfied immigration demand

note 207 (discussing this provision). The Senate Judiciary Committee report explained that "*[d]uring the interim*, this procedure will not affect the flow of immigration from large quota countries." S. REP. NO. 89–748, at 14 (1965), *reprinted in* 11 TRELLES & BAILEY, *supra* note 60, doc. 73 (emphasis added).

120 *Hearings on S. 500*, *supra* note 76, at 167.

121 *See id.* at 821.

122 *See Hearings on H.R. 7700*, *supra* note 76, at 1012 ("Asia and Africa ... [will] receive the largest quotas.").

123 *See id.* at 736 ("[S]uch a change in our existing laws would appear to be an outright accommodation to the heaviest population explosions throughout the world-India, Asia, and Africa. Certainly these countries could naturally be expected to take full advantage of such an increased quota opportunity.").

124 Mrs. Myra C. Hacker testified that the Hart Bill "would realine [sic] quotas to countries and be based on the relation of their populations to world population." *Id.* at 764. Representatives of the Greenwich Women's Republican Club explained that immigrants "will begin to come more and more from Asia where the pressures of the population explosion are felt most heavily." *Id.* at 819. Another commentator explained:

> In the preamble to the Constitution, the founders of this great Republic made it abundantly clear that they were leaving the fruits of their struggle as a legacy to us, their "posterity." We, their posterity, are either emigrants, or descendants of emigrants, from the white nations of northern Europe in the majority ... We are neither Asiatic nor African.

Id. at 1017 (statement of Matthew McKeon); *see also id.* at 1014 (statement of Fla. State Rep. George B. Stallings, Jr.) ("The enemies of [McCarran-Walter] do not like America as it is, its institutions and its culture. They want to make America over in the image of Asia, Africa, or eastern and southern Europe."); *Immigration: Hearings on H.R. 2580 Before Subcomm. No. 1 of the House Comm. on the Judiciary*, 89th Cong. 443–44 (1965) (same), *reprinted in* 10 TRELLES & BAILEY, *supra* note 60, doc. 69 [hereinafter *Hearings on H.R. 2580*]. *Hearings* (comments of Tyre Taylor of the Southern States Industrial Council) (noting that immigrants are typically the poorest people from "overpopulated, hunger-racked" nations).

125 *Hearings on H.R.7700*, *supra* note 76, at 664.

126 Senator Edward Kennedy said that elimination of the Asia-Pacific triangle concept was "one of the most laudable aspects of the entire bill." 111 CONG. REC. 24,776 (1965). Senator Hart stated that "[d]iscriminatory provisions against immigrants from eastern and southern Europe, token quotas

in Asia.[127] Many officials recognized that Asian immigration would increase. Edward Kennedy[128] and Attorney General Katzenbach[129] predicted that would-be Asian immigrants would benefit from the reforms.

for Asian and African countries, and implications of race superiority in the Asia-Pacific triangle concept, have no place in the public policy of the United States." *Id.* at 24, 238. Senator William Proxmire stated that the bill "would break the pattern of inconsistency that has discriminated against immigration from southern and eastern Europe and Asia." *Hearings on S. 500*, *supra* note 76, at 857–58. Representative William Ryan was one of many who recognized unfairness in the fact that "[t]he quota for Ireland is larger than that for all of Asia." *Hearings on H.R. 2580*, *supra* note 124, at 165; *see also id.* at 194 (remarks of Rep. Paul Fino) (making similar observation); *Hearings on H.R. 7700*, *supra* note 76, at 234 (remarks of Rep. Edward Patten) ("[T]he countries of India, China, Israel, Australia, New Zealand, and many others are allowed only 100 people per year."); *id.* at 240 (remarks of Rep. Seymour Halpern) (mentioning discrimination against Asia, among other areas); *id.* at 278 (remarks of Rep. Harold Donohue); *id.* at 317 (remarks of Rep. John J. Rooney); 111 CONG. REC. 21,769 (1965) (remarks of Rep. John Lindsay); *id.* at 24,781 (remarks of Sen. Abraham Ribicoff) (mentioning discrimination against southern and eastern Europe and Asia).

Oregon's Senator Neuberger quarreled on this point with Senator Ervin, who was hesitant about reform. Ervin asked whether, given that one in four people in the world was Chinese, Neuberger advocated admitting 65 million Chinese to the United States so they would have the same representation here. Without quite agreeing, Neuberger did insist that there had been unfairness: "I am even more concerned if there [sic] are one out of four that they are not truly represented in our society. It shows we have been excluding them for one reason alone and that is their ancestry." *Hearings on S. 500*, *supra* note 76, at 551.

127 Mrs. Ray Erb mentioned the long waiting lists in some Asian countries, *see Hearings on S. 500*, *supra* note 76, at 703–04, as did Senator Fong, *see* 111 CONG. REC. 24,447, 24,448 (1965), and Representatives Ryan, *see id.* at 21,781, and Yates, *see id.* at 21,793 (discussing "heavily mortgaged Eastern quotas"). David Carliner, testifying in support of the bill on behalf of the ACLU, pointed out that in addition to unsatisfied immigration demand in Italy and Greece, there was also unsatisfied demand:

> [T]o some extent from Eastern Europe and from Asia. I think that under this bill we redress the balance by letting those people come in, and in a historical sense, to give the Chinese a preference today would perhaps be a discrimination in their favor. But if someone has been getting a discrimination for 100 years, he cannot complain if somebody else gets a discrimination for the next 100 years.

Hearings on S. 500, *supra* note 76, at 448. According to Carliner, "[t]he critical problem is that the people in Greece, in China, to some extent in India, are seeking to come here in large numbers." *Id.* at 455. Senator Leverett Saltonstall, after mentioning discriminatory effects against southern and eastern Europe and Asia, explained: "Today there are many quota numbers available in some countries where there is little pressure for immigration, while in other areas, where there are many persons who wish to immigrate to the United States, few quota numbers are available and the quotas are heavily oversubscribed." 111 Cong. Rec. 24,441 (1965). He mentioned five countries: China, Italy, Greece, Poland, and Portugal. *See id.*

128 According to Senator Kennedy, "[t]he principal beneficiaries of the new system are those countries which have large backlogs of applicants for immigration, but have relatively small quotas." *Hearings on S. 500*, *supra* note 76, at 2. Kennedy named China and Japan, and seven other countries. *See id.*

129 Katzenbach said southern and eastern Europe would benefit and "the Asian countries would get some benefit." *Hearings on H.R. 2580*, *supra* note 124, at 23.

Senator Ervin, ambivalent but ultimately a supporter of the bill, seemed to assume that China[130] and India[131] would take the maximum quota, and noted that the bill "would provide for at least possible, substantial increases in immigration from" a list of countries with small quotas, including Bhutan, Burma, Cambodia, China, Mongolia, India, Indonesia, Korea, Laos, Pakistan, Thailand, Western Samoa, and Vietnam.[132] Representative George Miller of California, after speaking of a U.S. Air Force Academy graduate of Japanese American ancestry, said: "I feel that we can accept more people here or we can perhaps better arrange the quotas to take in people from places and areas that are now given an insufficient quota."[133]

Representative Arch Moore, in explaining what the status of Japan, China, and the Philippines would be after the bill was passed, told Congress precisely how the system would work: 20,000 per year would be the upper limit for them just as for every other country.[134] As a result, the United States could "look forward to an increased number of each of the groups … referred to."[135] Similarly, Senator Fong stated that there was no need to fear that an increase of Asian immigration would "upset the historical and cultural pattern of American life. An objective examination of the facts dispels this fear as groundless"[136] because of historical patterns of Asian assimilation.

Opponents of reform also recognized that Asia would benefit. Representative O.C. Fisher, an opponent, stated that "[t]here is simply no way of estimating the number of refugees, Asiatics, Africans, and others, who would be admissible.… The big increase under the Celler proposal would come primarily from Africa, Asia, and some from southern Europe."[137] Even Representative Frank Chelf, a subcommittee member who supported the national origins quota system, said that the bill should be rejected, but Asian immigration should increase:

> As I recall … in 1952 we … recognized the Japanese, Koreans, Chinese, and the others. In other words, the Asian countries and this so-called affront of exclusion was removed. While I agree … that this is only a token recognition – and I also agree … that there ought to be an additional recognition – how much, at this

[130] *See Hearings on S. 500*, *supra* note 76, at 64, 359, 571.
[131] *See id.* at 66, 196, 280, 530.
[132] *Id.* at 210–11.
[133] *Hearings on H.R. 7700*, *supra* note 76, at 189.
[134] *See* 111 CONG. REC. 21,590 (1965).
[135] *Id.* at 21,591. Representative Pelly stated that "[i]t is not that I register fear that they might come in because they make wonderful citizens." *Id.* Moore added that "[p]eople who attack what we are doing here today say that it will let millions of orientals come into the United States," and found that result unlikely. *Id.*
[136] *Id.* at 24,467.
[137] *Hearings on H.R. 2580*, *supra* note 124, at 157–58.

> juncture, I am unable to say, but in all good conscience and sincerity, I do agree … we should eventually recognize them by a larger number.[138]

Senators Spessard Holland,[139] John McClellan,[140] and Robert Byrd[141] also recognized that Asian immigration would increase.

In April 1966, before the full effects of the new law could be known, an Immigration and Naturalization Service employee writing about the law was certain that Asian immigration would increase.[142] After discussing the elimination of the Asia-Pacific triangle provisions, he wrote:

> This amendment will have the effect of making immigrant visas available to aliens who were previously chargeable to quotas so greatly oversubscribed that visas could not be issued to them for many years to come. *The amendment will lead to an increase in the number of visa petitions filed with the Service.* The fact that even the preference portions of some quotas were heavily oversubscribed had discouraged many relatives and prospective employers from filing petitions to accord aliens a preference classification.[143]

138 *Hearings on H.R. 7700*, *supra* note 76, at 393; *see also id.* at 847 (statement by Rep. Chelf) (stating to Chinese-American witness: "I favor an increased quota for your people.").

139 Senator Spessard Holland of Florida, a supporter of McCarran-Walter, noted:

> [T]he bill, as it is now disclosed on the floor, assumes to open the door to immigration to this country equally wide to people from all the countries of the world, making no distinction between them … [T]he Oriental, the African, the Malayan, and various other people from all parts of the earth are to be equally accepted for immigration into this country and for admission to citizenship.
>
> All I am calling attention to is that many people in my State of Florida do not agree with that principle, and they have objected to it.
>
> ….
>
> I merely state that when we open our doors wide to all the oriental nations of this earth, with some 700 to 800 million in 1 country alone, and with countless other millions in other nations, and when we offer to admit them on terms of exact equality with people from our own forefather nations, we are making a radical departure of which I cannot, and do not approve.

111 CONG. REC. 24,778–79 (1965). Senator Robert Kennedy did not deny Holland's claim: "The Senator talks about opening the doors wide. The doors are open only to those who can make a contribution." *Id.* at 24,779.

140 Senator McClellan asked, "Will the addition of still more minority groups from all parts of the world lessen or contribute to the increasing racial tensions and violence we are currently witnessing on the streets of our major cities?" *Id.* at 24,556. "Remember that under this bill, immigration will shift from those European countries that contributed most to the formation of this Nation to the countries of Asia and Africa." *Id.* at 24,557.

141 *See id.* at 23,794 ("[R]evising our immigration laws by removing the Asia-Pacific triangle provisions will add to the many social problems that now confront us across the Nation."). A West Virginia newspaper placed in the record claimed that Senator Robert Byrd was concerned that elimination of the quota system "would swell the flow of immigrants from Asia and the newly emerging countries." *Id.* at 24, 542.

142 *See* Robert Lindsey, *The Act of October 3 1965*, 14 I & N. REP. 103, 103 (1966).

143 *Id.* at 104 (emphasis added).

He also recognized that the overall pattern of immigration would change in favor of relatives and skilled immigrants, and nonpreference immigration would be virtually unavailable.[144]

Media Reports

People thinking about immigration, years before the results of the 1965 Act were known, predicted that ending discrimination against Asians would result in more of them coming over. For example, in his 1963 book *American Immigration Policies*, former U.S. Representative Marion T. Bennett criticized Senator Philip Hart's 1962 proposal to end quota preferences for Northern European nations. Bennett wrote:

> *China and India ... would ... ultimately be the European-successor to our immigration largesse.* The 1961 Indian census reported 438 million people in that country. The 1953 Chinese census reported 583 million Chinese and in 1962 President Kennedy said there were 650 million in Communist China alone. *The possibility that they might not take advantage of relaxed immigration restrictions is remote.*
>
> Their quotas have been oversubscribed for years. One of the arguments advanced for greater Chinese immigration is that the Chinese quota is only 205 annually. It is pertinent to note, however ... that nonquota Chinese immigration is much greater than the world average of two and one-half times quota immigration.[145]

What is obvious in retrospect was also observed at the time: liberalization would mean benefits for countries with large populations and high immigration demand.

The news media did not overlook the likely effects of the 1965 law on Asian immigration. *U.S. News & World Report* was unambiguous: "Under rules just approved by Congress, officials forecast these changes in the flow of immigrants to [the] U.S... FROM ASIA: Many more immigrants expected, since racial restrictions on Indians and Orientals are wiped out."[146] "Nobody has estimated the number of Chinese who

[144] He explained:

> There was no need for an alien who was a native of England, Ireland or Germany, for example, to seek a preference classification, when non-preference visas were readily available. However, on and after July 1, 1968, such aliens will be competing for immigrant visas on equal terms with natives of countries which heretofore have had heavily oversubscribed quotas, such as Greece, Italy and, China. It is highly probable that af(t)er July 1, 1968, the pattern of recent years will be greatly changed, with all or nearly all of the immigrant visas subject to the numerical limitation ... being issued to preference immigrants.

Id. at 111–12.

[145] BENNETT, *supra* note 38, at 274 (emphasis added) (footnote omitted). Hart later introduced the bill that became the 1965 Act. *See also Editorial, New Quota for Old*, BOSTON REC. AM., Jan. 16, 1965 (noting irony that "those nations with large numbers of people who would like to emigrate to the U.S. are generally allotted the smallest quota").

[146] *A New Mix for America's Melting Pot*, U.S. NEWS & WORLD REP., Oct. 11, 1965, at 55.

will apply to enter the U.S.," the magazine reported, but "[t]he potential is large."[147] Days after President Johnson signed the bill, the *Christian Science Monitor* reported that it would contribute to a "multinational and multiracial United States."[148] The *Los Angeles Times* explained: "What is ahead is an even more diverse mix of populations, favoring the Italian, Spanish and Greek, becoming to the Latin-American, inviting the Oriental and African. When we add to this the rapid rise of the native Negro population, we see at once that we will have much more of what President Kennedy called the pluralistic society."[149] In November 1965, *Scientific American*, reporting on the new law, noted that Asians, as well as Southern Europeans, would have increased opportunities to immigrate.[150] Major newspapers reported that the demographics of the immigration stream would change or that the bill was intended to benefit Asians, including the *Boston Herald*,[151] *Chicago Tribune*,[152] *Los Angeles Times*,[153] *The New York*

[147] *Id.* at 57.

[148] Saville Davis, *Immigration Change, Papal Visit Mesh*, CHRISTIAN SCI. MONITOR, Oct. 5, 1965, at 1.

[149] Richard Wilson, *New Soup in the Melting Pot*, L.A. TIMES, Sept. 23, 1965, at A5.

[150] *See Equitable Immigration*, SCI. AM., Nov. 1965, at 48.

[151] *See, e.g.*, *Immigration Law May Be Revised*, BOSTON SUN. HERALD, Jan. 3, 1965, § 1, at 80 (noting that "[i]t is more difficult for [Southern and Eastern Europeans, Africans and Asians] to immigrate to the U.S. Most attempts at revising the law would alter this balance."); Cabell Phillips, *Congress Seen Approving New Immigration Law*, BOSTON HERALD, May 23, 1965, § 1, at 25 ("Critics have long argued that [the National Origins Quota System] tended to favor the Western European countries at the expense of other regions, particularly the Far East."); Irene Saint, *How Immigration Bill Would Affect Boston Area*, BOSTON HERALD, Jan. 17, 1965, § 4, at 1 (noting that Asian countries, among others, would benefit from reform).

[152] Willard Edwards, *Alien Bill Called Democratic Bid for Votes*, CHI. TRIB., Sept. 22, 1965, § 1A, at 4 (noting that bill will have the effect of "increasing the flow from southern Europe and other areas whose flow is restricted under the present system"); William Moore, *Senators Cite Heritage, Plea for Alien Bill*, CHI. TRIB., Sept. 21, 1965, § 1B, at 8 ("Supporters of repeal say that African and Asian countries need more immigration permits."); Aldo Beckman, *House Approves Immigration Measure*, CHI. TRIB., Aug. 26, 1965, N1 (reporting that Rep. O.C. Fisher "said the new law will shift the main stream of immigrants from western and central Europe to Africa and Asia."); *Alien Bill Warning Issued*, CHI. TRIB., July 30, 1965 at A12 ("A Senate judiciary committee, nearing the end of hearings to wipe out the national origins quotas in the immigration system, today heard the proposal attacked as one that could result in 220,000 Chinese coming into the United States annually"); *Drive Started for New Law on Immigrants*, CHI. TRIB., Feb. 11, 1965 at C16 (noting that Attorney General Katzenbach "asserted that the system 'discriminates heavily against immigration from southern and eastern Europe and Asiatic countries.").

[153] John H. Averill, *Senate Starts Debate on Immigration Reform*, L.A. TIMES, Sept. 18, 1965, at 11 ("A nearly empty Senate opened debate on the administration's immigration reform bill that would make it easier for southern Europeans and Asians to enter the United States."); Robert Barkdoll, *Immigration Reform Bill OKd by House Unit*, L.A. TIMES, July 23, 1965, at 1 ("Mr. Johnson recommended such legislation last January on grounds that the quota system which favors northern Europeans and all but excludes Asians, is 'incompatible with our basic American tradition.'"); *Immigration Innovations Spelled Out*, L.A. TIMES, May 26, 1965 at A2 ("Principal beneficiaries of the Immigration Law Reform Bill are the people of Eastern Europe and Asia, [State Department official Abba] Schwartz told a press conference."); Editorial, *Liberals and the Immigration Law*, L.A. TIMES, Mar. 1, 1965 at A4 (current system "favors immigrants from northwestern Europe whole tending to exclude people from Eastern

Times,[154] and the *Washington Post*.[155] Indeed, the argument that an increase in Asian immigration is surprising is the revisionist view. A 1966 article in *American Legion Magazine* insisted that the multiplicity of newspaper reports predicting an increase in Asian immigration were foolish.[156]

Sources of the New Immigration: Families and Professionals

The few estimates that were offered support the idea that an increase in Asian immigration was expected. Major news outlets reported that overall immigration would increase, including the *Los Angeles Times*,[157] the *Chicago Tribune*,[158] and

Europe and Asia."); John H. Averill, *Wirtz Sees Jobless Cut in Immigration Changes*, L.A. TIMES, Feb. 26, 1965 10 ("Eliminating the quota system would increase immigration from southern Europe and Asia."); Davis Kraslow, *Defections Raise Doubts on Immigration Reform*, L.A. TIMES, Feb. 21, 1965 at C16 ("The proposed reform measure would democratize the quota system, permitting a greater influx from Greece, Italy, Poland, Portugal, Spain and non-Communist Asia."); AP, *Johnson Urges Reforms in Immigration*, L.A. Times, Jan. 14, 1964 at 3 ("("Sen. Philip A. Hart (D-Mich.), the first witness, said that 'discriminatory provisions against immigrants from Eastern and Southern Europe, town quotas for Asian and African countries, and implications of race superiority … have no place in the public policy of the United States."); Editorial, *Revising the Immigration Law*, L.A. TIMES, Jan. 15, 1964, at A4 (under quota system, "Asians were excluded completely, although the law was amended in 1952 to allow a minimum quota of 100 from every country. Thus, Andorra, which has a population of 6,500, has a quota of 100; Japan, with 94 million, has a quota of 185.")

154 Cabell Phillips, *Immigration Law Comes Into Effect*, N.Y. TIMES, Dec. 2, 1965, at 10 (the law's "principal beneficiaries will be close relatives – living in such low-quota countries as Italy, Greece and Nationalist China – of persons who have already become citizens or resident aliens of the United States … There will be no country by country quotas, and the national of an Asian or African country will receive the same consideration as a citizen of France or Germany."); *id.* (noting that old law discriminated against southern and eastern Europe and "most other regions of the world. Most nations of Asia and Africa, for example, had had token annual quotas of only 100 under this system."); Cabell Phillips, *Johnson Pushing for Aliens Law*, N.Y. TIMES, May 23, 1965 at 20 ("Critics have long argued that the system tended to favor the Western European countries at the expense of other regions, particularly the Far East."); C.P. Trussell, *Rusk Says U.S. Immigration Laws Delight Foes*, N.Y. TIMES, Aug. 1, 1965 at 2 (noting that one problem with existing law was "the differential treatment to which persons of Asian ancestry are subjected.").

155 Editorial, *Choosing Immigrants*, WASH. POST, June 30, 1965 at A24 (current law "has conditioned admittance to this country on ethnic grounds, discriminating flagrantly against Eastern and Southern Europeans and against Orientals."); *LBJ Attacks Quota Immigration System*, WASH. POST, Jan. 6, 1965 ("Asians and people born in Asia or of Asian ancestry are limited to 100 immigrants per country per year");

156 *See* Deane Heller & David Heller, *Our New Immigration Law*, AM. LEGION MAG., Feb. 1966, at 6, 9. This and other misinterpretations of the law, according to the authors, were "a bit of faking" on the part of the press. *Id.* at 41.

157 William F. Buckley Jr., *Immigration Bill Opens the Door to More Folks than We Can Handle*, L.A. TIMES, Aug. 30, 1965 at A6 ("[T]he looseness of the bill's provisions (and that looseness is sometimes commendable, as when special provisions are made to admit political refugees), could well result in substantially increasing the annual flow, up towards a half million persons per year."); AP, *Immigration Policy Hit as Unjust, Outdated*, L.A. TIMES, Aug. 25, 1965, at 18 ("The proposed new system is expected to result in an annual increase in immigration of about 50,000").

158 *Alien Bill Warning is Issued*, CHI. TRIB., July 30, 1965 at A12 ("Proponents of the revision have estimated that if the quota system is junked, about 330,000 immigrants a year will be admitted, or about 50,000 more than the average for the last 10 years.")

the *Washington Post*.[159] Administration officials predicted that Asian immigrants would account for 94,972 of the 820,910 immigrants expected during the five-year phase-out of the quota system that was proposed by President Kennedy;[160] this was an increase over the 15,000 or so who came in each year during the 1950s, but, because of increasing numbers in the late 1950s and 1961–5, about the same proportion as had come in under McCarran-Walter.[161]

Senator Fong predicted that about 20 percent of quota spots would go to the Asia-Pacific triangle once the new law was in full effect[162] – more than a 300 percent increase over their share in the 1950s, and over 1,300 percent more than their official quota of 2,000 (1.53 percent of all visas) under McCarran-Walter. Concretely, 20 percent of the 170,000 per year Eastern Hemisphere quota under the new law would be 34,000 for Asia (not counting non-quota immigration).

If hard estimates are scarce, impressionistic information is more plentiful. The 1965 law offered preferences to skilled immigrants and to family members of U.S. citizens or permanent resident aliens. The legislative record indicates that Congress understood that Asians would take advantage of both aspects of the new law.

Asian Family Reunification

Congress perceived clearly the problem of divided families Americans separated from family members eligible to immigrate except for their race. Many immigrants, Massachusetts Senator Saltonstall explained, "have spouses, children, parents, brothers or sisters still abroad whom they wish to bring to this country to join them."[163] Legislators recognized that this problem applied with special force to Asians. The experience of passing many private bills,[164] necessary to reunite families or alleviate other severe hardships, was not forgotten in the debate on the 1965 law. Robert Kennedy, for example, testified as Attorney General about the problems Americans

159 Editorial, *Immigration Changes*, WASH. POST, Mar. 11, 1965 at A24 ("there would be an actual increase of approximately 60,000 immigrants over the number now admitted each year.")

160 *See Hearings on H.R. 7700*, *supra* note 76, at 589.

161 *See* INS, U.S. DEPARTMENT OF JUSTICE, STATISTICAL YEARBOOK OF THE INS, 1991 29 (1992). Although Asian countries had no quotas or small quotas during this period, many Asians immigrated nevertheless, through special bills for refugees, relatives, scientists, and the like. *See infra* notes 288–96 and accompanying text.

162 *See Hearings on S. 500*, *supra* note 76, at 118, 147.

163 111 CONG. REC. 24,441 (1965). Although there were family reunification preferences under McCarran-Walter for low-quota countries, they were rapidly exhausted.

164 A look though the private bills section of a volume of *Statutes at Large* suggests the magnitude of the private bill solution. *See, e.g.*, An Act for the Relief of Thelma Margaret Hwang, PRIV. L. NO. 85-94,71 Stat. A39 (1957); An Act for the Relief of Kuo York Chynn, PRIV. L. NO. 85–96, 71 Stat. A39 (1957); An Act for the Relief of Yun Wha Yoon Holsman, PRIV. L. NO. 85–97, 71 Stat. A39 (1957); An Act for the Relief of Chong You How, PRIV. L. NO. 85–102, 71 Stat. A41 (1957).

had bringing in an immediate relative who was "Italian or Australian, Spanish or Portuguese, Japanese or Korean, Indian or Filipino."[165] Senator Neuberger explained that

> we on the west coast have a large number of citizens who are second, third, and fourth generation Americans, but whose ancestors were born in China, Japan, Korea, other Asiatic countries-the Philippines – in order to reunite some of these families requires my putting in a number of private bills every year.[166]

Congress recognized that the volume of Asian family reunification immigration would be significant. For example, Representative John Lindsay noted that in 1964, "[t]he great majority of the immigrants who entered the country over and above their national quotas were admitted because they were the wives, husbands, or children of U.S. citizens. Persons in any one of these three categories last year alone accounted for … almost 8,000 from Asia."[167] As a result, non-quota family reunification immigration from Asia was nearly four times quota immigration.[168] That these facts were before Congress when it passed the bill suggests that when they continued to be true, it was no surprise.

Asian Professionals

The record also shows that Congress was well aware that significant numbers of Asian professionals would immigrate once they had a chance. One after another, legislators regaled each other with stories about real or hypothetical Asian professionals who could not be admitted because of their racial ancestry.[169] These

[165] *Hearings on S. 500*, *supra* note 76, at 216. He repeated this comment as New York's junior senator. *See* 111 CONG. REC. 24,482 (1965).

[166] *Hearings on S. 500*, *supra* note 76, at 548.

[167] *Hearings on H.R. 2580*, *supra* note 124, at 413. Many other members of Congress made the same point. Representative James Roosevelt wrote that an American citizen of Indian ancestry would have difficulty bringing in a brother or sister, while a British neighbor would find it easy. *See Hearings on H.R. 7700*, *supra* note 76, at 320. Representative Thomas Gill of Hawaii, stated: "Reuniting families, particularly when you deal with the various Chinese quotas and the Asian [sic] Pacific triangle quota, is very important to Hawaii." *Id.* at 179; *see also id.* at 305 (statement of Rep. Joseph Minish) (noting that a Chinese constituent was unable to bring in her sister from Hong Kong); *cf. id.* at 697 (statement by a member of a social welfare agency that the wife and child of an American physician could not enter).

[168] Representative Byron Rogers also spoke about family immigration pulling in large groups, *see Hearings on H.R. 7700*, *supra* note 76, at 78, and he later mentioned Indian or Italian family members. *See id.* at 83.

[169] Senator Allott spoke of a Chinese nurse who faced deportation. *See* 111 CONG. REC. 24,473 (1965). Senator Clark noted that a "brilliant Korean or Indian scientist is turned away, while the northern European is accepted almost without question.… While Plato and Dante would have a hard time getting into the United States … Confucius or Lao-tze could not get in at all." *Id.* at 24,501. Senator Robert Kennedy mentioned three professionals who could not get in because of the quota system: a Greek

stories were only anecdotes, but it was clear that the number of Asian professionals who would immigrate was thought to be significant. Indeed, Representative Arch Moore, a supporter of the bill, was concerned about the brain drain from Asia:

> In the Asia-Pacific triangle countries, there isn't a very wholesome attitude about us from the standpoint of our immigration policies; and yet, here we become a scavenger for brain power in the same part of the world. It just seems to me that while we may in a very logical way, by removing the national origins system, remove the stigma of placing a greater value on one citizen over another, we jump right back into the fire in another respect when we set up these magnets to pull out their choicest citizens.[170]

chemist, a Korean radiation specialist, and a Japanese microbiologist. *See id.* at 24,482. Representative Thomas Gill spoke of a doctor of Chinese descent, who, he thought, was a native to the Philippines, who could not get into Hawaii. *See Hearings on H.R. 7700*, *supra* note 76, at 180. Senator Paul Douglas explained that a Chinese engineer in Evanston, Illinois, was unable to obtain permanent residency for his Chinese wife, a nurse, who had entered on a student visa. *See Hearings on S. 500*, *supra* note 76, at 153. According to Senator Neuberger, a cancer expert sought by a medical school was kept out because of the Asia-Pacific triangle rule. *See id.* at 550–51. A representative of the ACLU stated that a hypothetical "brilliant physicist living in Hong Kong who is Chinese," *id.* at 450, would not be able to come in. Attorney General Katzenbach testified that there were "innumerable" cases in which the quota system damaged the United States by keeping out professionals, including a "brilliant" Indian cardiac surgeon. *See id.* at 10. He also observed that an Indian brain surgeon would likely be excluded or subjected to a very long wait, but a common laborer from Ireland could easily enter. *See Hearings on H.R. 2580*, *supra* note 124, at 17. Attorney General Robert Kennedy said skilled workers from the United States would go to "Italy, Germany, England, and Japan," just as we took their skilled workers. *Hearings on H.R. 7700*, *supra* note 76, at 427. Similarly, after Senator Kennedy noted that the Asia-Pacific triangle restrictions would be eliminated by the bill, Maryland Senator Tydings noted that his family doctor was Chinese, that his son had a close Korean friend, and exclaimed with apparent passion:

> Why if a man can make a great contribution – a doctor, a writer, a scientist, or a scholar – the fact ... that he should be kept out, when we arbitrarily bring anybody in from northern Europe whether they can make a contribution or not, merely because the quota of northern Europe is not filled, just does not make sense.

Hearings on S. 500, *supra* note 76, at 657. John Lindsay explained: "A high proportion of those who most want to come to America and who would be of most benefit to us are ineligible. A very few countries are given high quotas which they don't use. Other countries with vastly larger populations ... are given tiny quotas." *Hearings on H.R. 7700*, *supra* note 76, at 115. Senator Fong also advised the Senate Judiciary Committee of Nobel prize–winning scientists who had managed to make it in, including a number of Asians. *See Hearings on S. 1932*, *supra* note 76, at 98 (listing immigrants from Europe and Asia who have won Nobel prizes).

170 *Hearings on H.R. 2580*, *supra* note 124, at 223. A critic writing in *The New Republic* argued that the law would "suck in the doctors and engineers that underdeveloped countries need at home." T.R.B. from Washington, *Who Should Enter?*, THE NEW REPUBLIC, Feb. 20, 1965, at 4, 4. Clearly, this was a reference to underdeveloped third-world nations, not Germany or England. *See also Hearings on H.R. 2580*, *supra* note 124, at 374 (statement of W.B. Hicks, of the Liberty Lobby) ("Should we deprive the underdeveloped nations of the world of the cream of their limited supply of doctors, engineers, and teachers by making these skills the No. 1 preference in our immigration law, and at the same time, spend millions on programs designed to develop such skills in those nations?"); 111 CONG. REC. 21,775(1965) (remarks of Rep. Durward Hall).

Similarly, Labor Secretary Wirtz suggested that the quality of skilled immigration would increase because Asian immigration would open up. After discussing the small quotas available to the Asia-Pacific triangle countries, Wirtz said, "under the new bill there will be situations in which a more skilled person will come in where under the old bill a less skilled person from a country whose quota was not filled would have come in."[171]

There was also evidence that once opportunities to immigrate were made available, Asians would take full advantage of them. In September 1966, before the law was fully implemented,[172] and therefore before its consequences could be fully known, British economist Brinley Thomas predicted that Asian immigration would increase.[173] His argument was based not only on logic but on the results of 1962 legislation,[174] making it easier for professionals to enter the United States.

The 1962 statute allowed "large numbers of alien scientists and engineers to achieve immigrant status within a relatively short period of time."[175] As a result, immigration of European scientists and engineers increased by 23 percent, but "that of Asians increased by no less than 182 per cent. This indicates that skilled Asian immigration has a remarkably high elasticity with respect to a moderate liberalizing of the restrictions."[176] The author concluded:

> If the relatively minor supplement to the law in October 1962 led to an almost threefold increase in the influx of highly qualified Asians, one wonders what the basic alteration in the principles of selection enacted in 1965 is likely to do. One can only surmise that the process of creaming off skills from the poorest areas of the world will be intensified.[177]

Members of Congress working on the 1965 bill were aware of the 1962 law and its effects.[178] In short, rather than concluding that immigration of Asian professionals *should have been* no surprise, it seems more probable that it *was* no surprise to any member of Congress who listened to the testimony and debates on the bill.

[171] *Hearings on S. 500*, *supra* note 76, at 114.

[172] Under the law, the national origins quota system was not fully abolished until 1968. *See* Immigration and Nationality Act Amendments of 1965, PUB. L. NO. 89–236, § 1, 79 Stat. 911, 911 (providing that each country would have at least the same quota as it had under McCarran-Walter until June 30, 1968, but unused quota slots would be used for oversubscribed countries).

[173] *See* Brinley Thomas, *From the Other Side: A European View*, 367 ANNALS AM. ACAD. POL. & SOC. SCI. 63, 68 (1966).

[174] Act of Oct. 24, 1962, Pub. L. No. 87–885, 76 Stat. 1247. Technically, the bill allowed entry over and above the quota of certain immigrants who, by virtue of their skills, were entitled to first preference entry under McCarran-Walter, but whose countries' quotas were exhausted. *See* S. REP. NO. 87–2276, *reprinted in* 1962 U.S.C.C.A.N. 4204 (reporting favorably on S. 336, describing in particular its effect on worthy Chinese who wished to immigrate).

[175] Thomas, *supra* note 173, at 67.

[176] *Id.* at 67–68.

[177] *Id.* at 68 (emphasis added).

[178] *See, e.g.*, *Hearings on S. 1932*, *supra* note 76, at 13 (testimony of Senator Philip Hart) (noting the immigration "has not, in fact, flowed in the national origins channels set forth in the 1952 Act"); 111

The Evidence Supporting a Prediction of No Asian Influx

There is some evidence that members of Congress and other informed sources doubted that Asian immigration would increase as a result of the bill. Some of it is ambiguous.[179] Even the most compelling, however, does not outweigh the evidence to the contrary.

Attorney General Robert Kennedy's Prediction

The 1964 prediction by then Attorney General Robert Kennedy, is the centerpiece of the widespread belief that no one expected an Asian influx as a result of immigration reform. According to *Fortune*, for example, "Attorney General Robert Kennedy told the Senate that 5,000 Asian immigrants might come the first year, 'after which immigration from that source would virtually disappear.'"[180] The interpretation that Robert Kennedy's words constituted a projection that Asian immigration would quickly become a thing of the past has been cited in the halls of Congress;[181] by academics including Bill Ong Hing,[182] David Reimers,[183] Roger Daniels,[184] Peter Schuck,[185] Nathan Glazer,[186] Vernon Briggs,[187] Nicolaus Mills,[188] and Michael Teitelbaum;[189] published in respected

CONG. REC. 24,226 (1965) (chart including all admissions under special legislation, including this act, described as the "act of Oct. 24, 1962").

179 *See, e.g.*, *Hearings on S. 500*, *supra* note 76, at 563 (testimony of Sen. Claiborne Pell) ("Maybe there will be a huge surge from India or a huge surge from Africa, but I would tend to doubt it."). Senator Strom Thurmond, who voted against the bill, stated that he did not "believe that the immigration formula in the proposal now before the Senate, if properly administered, will result in drastic or undesirable changes in the patterns of immigration into the United States." 111 CONG. REC. 24,237 (1965).

180 Scott McConnell, *The New Battle Over Immigration*, FORTUNE, May 9, 1988, at 89, 94.

181 *See, e.g.*, *Legal Immigration Reform Proposals: Hearing Before the Subcomm. on Immigration and Claims of the House Judiciary* Comm., 104TH CONG. 134 (1995), *available in* 1995 WL 306792 (testimony of Mark Krikorian, of the Center for Immigration Studies) (citing Robert Kennedy's testimony); 132 CONG. REC. 27,397 (1986) (statement of Rep. Donnelley, quoting Robert Kennedy's prediction).

182 *See* HING, *supra* note 11, at 39–40.

183 *See* DAVID M. REIMERS, STILL THE GOLDEN DOOR 77 (1st ed. 1985); Reimers, *supra* note 29, at 9, 16. *But see infra* note 209 and accompanying text (discussing Professor Reimers's current view about the meaning of Robert Kennedy's comment).

184 *See* DANIELS, *supra* note 20, at 341 ("Members of [Johnson's] administration, almost certainly in good faith, had testified before Congress that few Asians would come in under the new Jaw . . .").

185 *See* Schuck, *supra* note 29, at 7.

186 *See* Glazer, *supra* note 20, at 7.

187 *See* Briggs & Moore, *supra* note 28, at 19 ("[I]t was anticipated that passage of the Immigration Act of 1965 would lead to a decline in Asian immigration." (citing Attorney General Robert Kennedy's testimony)).

188 *See* Nicolaus Mills, *Introduction: The Era of the* Golden Venture, *in* ARGUING IMMIGRATION 1, 17 (Nicolaus Mills ed., 1994).

189 *See* Michael S. Teitelbaum, *Skeptical Noises About the Immigration Multiplier*, 23 INT'L MIGRATION REV. 893, 895 (1989).

news outlets like the *Economist*,[190] the *San Francisco Chronicle*,[191] the *Los Angeles Times*,[192] the *Christian Science Monitor*,[193] the *Baltimore Evening Sun*,[194] and *Financial World*;[195] and used as ammunition by anti-immigration activists like Lawrence Auster,[196] Leon Bouvier,[197] Peter Brimelow,[198] and Otis Graham.[199] The perceived meaning is completely wrong, making it possibly the most pervasive legend in immigration history.

Even under McCarran-Walter, Asian immigration in 1964 was 21,279,[200] and had averaged 15,000 per year in the 1950s.[201] Is it possible that Robert Kennedy thought that Asian immigration would "virtually disappear" after 1966; that he believed *eliminating* restrictions would *diminish* immigration?[202] This interpretation makes

[190] *See Yes, They'll Fit in Too*, THE ECONOMIST, May 11, 1991, at 17 (The 1965 reform "has had large, and largely unintended, consequences. Robert Kennedy, the then attorney-general, was wildly wrong when he told a congressional committee that 5,000 immigrants might come from Asia in the first year 'but we do not expect that there would be any great influx after that.'").

[191] *See* Ramon G. McLeod, *A Call for an Immigration Policy*, S.F. CHRON., July 4, 1991, at Al, A6:

> In 1964, the late Robert Kennedy told a congressional hearing that an immigration law ending quota systems would result in at most about 5,000 people immigrating from Asia. Almost 4 million Asians immigrated after the law went into effect in 1965. Such unanticipated results … have been the hallmark of recent immigration debate.

Id.; *see* Ramon G. McLeod, *1965 Immigration Reform Law Opened Door for Asians*, S.F. CHRON., July 4, 1988, at A5 (describing the contrast between the prediction and the large increase in immigration in the Bay Area).

[192] *See* Douglas Massey, *Immigration Adjustments Ignore the Chain Effect of Family Eligibility*, L.A. TIMES, Apr. 6, 1988, pt. 2, at 7 (Op-Ed column by a sociology professor at the University of Chicago) (citing Kennedy quote as example of unpredictability of immigration law changes).

[193] *See* John Dillin, *Asian Americans: Soaring Minority*, CHRISTIAN SCI. MONITOR, Oct. 10, 1985, at 3 ("Seldom has any public official been so wrong.").

[194] *See* Linda Seebach, *Let's Vote on a U.S. Immigration Policy*, BALTIMORE EVENING SUN, May 8, 1995, at 9A. (editorial commentary by a California newspaper editor).

[195] *See* Kermit Lansner, *Who Will Be an American?*, FINANCIAL WORLD, Apr. 17, 1990, at 100.

[196] *See* Auster, *supra* note 33, at 20–23 (describing Kennedy's approach as "divorce[d] from reality").

[197] *See* LEON F. BOUVIER & LINDSEY GRANT, HOW MANY AMERICANS? 79 (1994) (dealing with the environmental impact of immigration). Bouvier is also concerned about the racial makeup of the nation. See LEON F. BOUVIER & CAREY B. DAVIS, IMMIGRATION AND THE FUTURE RACIAL COMPOSITION OF THE UNITED STATES 7–19 (1982). For a critique of the environmental argument against immigration, see Peter L. Reich, *Environmental Metaphor in the Alien Benefits Debate*, 42 UCLA L. REV. 1577 *passim* (1995).

[198] *See, e.g.*, PETER BRIMELOW, ALIEN NATION: COMMON SENSE ABOUT AMERICA'S IMMIGRATION DISASTER 78 (1995) (quoting and mocking Kennedy's purported prediction).

[199] *See* Graham, *supra* note 33, at 19 ("Attorney General Robert Kennedy predicted 5,000 immigrants from the entire Asia-Pacific Triangle, 'after which immigration from that source would virtually disappear.'").

[200] *See* BUREAU OF THE CENSUS, U.S. DEP'T OF COMMERCE, HISTORICAL STATISTICS OF THE UNITED STATES, COLONIAL TIMES TO 1970, at 106 (1976)

[201] *See* 1991 STATISTICAL YEARBOOK, supra note 161, at 49.

[202] Question: What bizarre phenomenon would make 5,000 Asians want to immigrate in 1965, but none thereafter?

no sense. Close examination of the hearing record where the statement was made shows why his testimony was misunderstood.

Attorney General Kennedy was testifying about the administration's version of the bill, which continued the historical practice of imposing no numerical limitation on Western Hemisphere immigration. Asians could not take advantage of that, however, because of McCarran-Walter's Asia-Pacific Triangle limitation, restricting worldwide immigration of racial Asians to 2,000. The proposed bill, however, would, for the first time, extend the privilege of unlimited Western Hemisphere immigration to persons of Asian ancestry who were native to the region.[203] The question was:

> Mr. FEIGHAN. Mr. Attorney General, what influx or increase in nonquota immigrants would you consider likely by the abolition of the Asia-Pacific triangle and the relationship of the same upon the nonquota immigration from the Western Hemisphere?
>
> Attorney General KENNEDY. I would say for the Asia Pacific triangle it would be approximately 5,000, Mr. Chairman, after which immigration from that source would virtually disappear; 5,000 immigrants could come in the first year, but we do not expect that there would be any great influx after that.[204]

Kennedy was asked to comment on the increase in Asian immigration from the Western Hemisphere, which would result from granting them non-quota immigration privileges. Kennedy replied that 5,000 Asians would immigrate from the Western Hemisphere as a result of the change, not that 5,000 Asians would immigrate from all the countries of the world. To the contrary, during the same hearing,[205] Robert Kennedy filed written projections estimating that 94,972 Asians – not 5,000 – would immigrate in the first five years of the proposed law.[206] Testimony by Secretary of State Dean Rusk[207] and Justice Department officials makes clear that Kennedy was predicting that 5,000 Asians living in the Western Hemisphere would immigrate when they were eligible to do so, not that 5,000 Asians worldwide would come to the United States.[208] A few people got it right, including David Reimers in

[203] Recall that under McCarran-Walter, in effect when Kennedy was testifying, persons of Asian descent, wherever born, were relegated to the tiny quotas of their countries of racial ancestry.

[204] *Hearings on H.R. 7700*, *supra* note 76, at 418.

[205] *See id.* at 431 (statement of Rep. Poff) (referring to "[t]he document which the Attorney General presented for inclusion in the record").

[206] *See id.* at 589.

[207] *See id.* at 406 (testimony of Dean Rusk) ("The elimination of the Asia-Pacific triangle would result in an estimated 5,000 or 6,000 persons annually entering the United States *from nonquota areas*, who are now chargeable to highly oversubscribed quota areas within the Asia-Pacific triangle." (emphasis added)).

[208] Assistant Attorney General Schlei, for example, was asked about the repeal of the Asia-Pacific triangle quota and its effects on non-quota immigration. He replied:

> I understand it is estimated, about 5,000 people who would like to come to the United States and are in either nonquota areas [i.e., the Western Hemisphere], or in areas where there are no waiting lists, such as England, Ireland, and Germany, but are now unable to come because they

his more recent work,[209] but the myth persists. The best evidence that the framers of the 1965 Act believed it would not increase Asian immigration turns out to be a misunderstanding.

Focus on Southern and Eastern Europe and Backlogs on Wait Lists

When it considered the law, Congress may well have been focusing on remedying injustices to southern and eastern Europeans.[210] Several commentators have relied on this point as partial support for the idea that the increase in Asian immigration was unforeseen.[211] Perhaps the possibility of significant Asian immigration was just overlooked, but this is implausible. Leaving aside the many affirmative statements that Asian immigration would increase, remarks by members of Congress noting the injustices to would-be Asian immigrants seem to suggest that Asians were not ignored by the people who were considering the law.[212]

Under McCarran-Walter, when a visa was not available, an alien could be placed on a waiting list and thus become part of a country's "backlog." Some have pointed to the fact that the largest waiting lists for visas were in Italy and Greece at the time the bill was passed.[213] The relatively smaller backlogs in China, say, might have indicated a lower demand for immigration, and hence supported the conclusion that not many Asians would want to immigrate after the reforms. But this analysis ignores the issue of relative quotas; a backlog of 50,000 is not daunting if a nation's quota is 25,000 per year; a backlog of 5,000 might be insuperable for a would-be immigrant from a nation with a quota of 100. The real question is not the backlog in absolute terms, but the length of the wait for a visa. This point did not escape members of Congress; among many others, Senator Saltonstall pointed out that more than 40,000 people were on the waiting list for visas under the Chinese quota,[214] which made for the wait of more than 380 years for a visa, given China's annual quota of

> had Asiatic ancestors. *We would, therefore, get 5,000 immigrants within the first year from that source, but from then on it would disappear.*

Id. at 482 (emphasis added); *see also id.* (testimony of Office of Legal Counsel attorney Adam Walinsky) (noting that 5,000 Asians would come as a result of the change).

[209] *See* REIMERS, *supra* note 29, at 74–76.

[210] *See Hearings on H.R. 7700*, *supra* note 76, at 215 (remarks of Rep. John Murphy) (focusing on Italian, Greek and Polish immigrants); *id.* at 219 (remarks of Rep. William Ryan); *id.* at 274 (remarks of Rep. James J. Delaney); *id.* at 300 (remarks of Rep. Roland Libonati).

[211] *See* DANIELS, *supra* note 20, at 341; HING, *supra* note 53, at 39–40; YANG, *supra* note 29, at 21.

[212] *See, e.g.*, *Hearings on S. 1932*, *supra* note 76, at 10–11 (testimony of Sen. Philip Hart) ("Let us restore equality and fair play in our selecting immigrants. Discriminatory provisions against immigrants from eastern and southern Europe, token quotas for Asian and African countries, and implications of race superiority in the Asia-Pacific Triangle concept have no place in the public policy of the United States.").

[213] *See, e.g.*, REIMERS, *supra* note 29, at 76, 92–93; Reimers, *supra* note 29, at 16.

[214] *See* 111 CONG. REC. 24,441 (1965).

105. That Chinese would put their names on a list, even though, as Senator Fong noted, the quota was "for all practical purposes exhausted in perpetuity,"[215] indicates a desire to immigrate to the United States of almost religious intensity.

Structural Protections against Asian Immigration

Arguably, supporters of the bill might have expected little increase in Asian immigration because, as in 1943 and 1952, protections against unlimited immigration were built into the statute.[216] To the extent that this argument suggests that there would be some upper limit on immigration, it is, of course, correct. If it suggests that the limits would ensure low proportions of Asian immigration, it is implausible because the structure of the 1965 law was so different from previous statutes that there was no reasonable basis for predicting that it would prevent "overrepresentation" from any particular region of the world.

One important restriction in the 1965 law was the 20,000 per country annual limitation, which was designed to avoid "opening up the gates to a vast flood from some particular country."[217] There are hints in the legislative history that the "particular countries" Congress was concerned with were Asian. Representative Feighan, for example, Chairman of the House Judiciary Committee's subcommittee with jurisdiction over immigration, stated that repeal of the Asia-Pacific triangle concept "has met with strong reactions from our allies and friends in Asia who have come to regard it as the same kind of personal affront as the old Chinese Exclusion Act."[218] In the next breath, he added that "the proposed selective system of immigrant admissions included in the bill guarantees that no country can receive a disproportionate number of the total visas authorized."[219] The fact that he thought of the per-country limitation might be read to suggest some connection between disproportionate immigration on the one hand and Asians on the other. Similarly, Representative Giaimo noted that the bill would repeal the Asia-Pacific triangle provisions, but immediately stated that "[i]t is important to note that this new law will not open the floodgates of immigration as charged by opponents of the bill."[220]

There is countervailing evidence suggesting that the 20,000 cap was not created with Asians in mind.[221] However, even if the 20,000 per country annual limitation was intended to restrict Asian immigration, compared to prior restrictive laws – limiting

[215] *Id.* at 24,447.

[216] *See, e.g.* REIMERS, *supra* note 29, at 74–75.

[217] 111 CONG. REC. 24,763 (1965) (remarks of Sen. Dirksen).

[218] *Id.* at 21,585.

[219] *Id.*

[220] *Id.* at 21,767.

[221] *See* Telephone Interview with Norbert Schlei, *supra* note 115 (explaining that the per-country limit was imposed because of southern and eastern European nations).

Chinese immigration to 105, as the 1943 act had done, or all Asian immigration to 2,000 – a maximum of 20,000 per country could more reasonably be called an open-door policy than a restriction. Representative Moore, explaining that Asians would be treated the same as persons from other parts of the world, showed the arithmetic:

> It does not mean that that number, 20,000, of Chinese, Japanese, or Filipinos are immediately going to come into this country, but the upper limitation [of the number] to which they would be entitled would be that number.... People who attack what we are doing here today say that it will let millions of orientals come into the United States. I wanted to place in the RECORD the observation that there is no one in this House who need fear such an event occurring.[222]

Moore was right; millions of Asians would not enter each year. But Moore recognized the possibility that just three Asian countries could send 60,000 per year, thirty times as many as all Asians worldwide had been officially allowed under McCarran-Walter. This was a revolutionary increase compared to past treatment of Asian immigration.

Another potential safeguard was a Western Hemisphere quota limitation.[223] Representative Fisher, echoing arguments from the 1943 and 1952 debates, argued that "there are about half a million Chinese living in the Western Hemisphere, many of whom would like to come into this country if they could, but who are prohibited now from doing so because of the triangle provision."[224] The law protected against this eventuality by imposing, for the first time, a 120,000 annual limit on Western Hemisphere immigration. But this restriction also was insignificant compared to those that were eliminated.

Celler, Masaoka, Rusk

The best evidence that members of the administration or Congress thought there would be little Asian immigration are the public statements of three knowledgeable

[222] 111 CONG. REC. 21,590–91 (1965). Representative Thomas Pelly, who asked the question which engendered that response, stated that

> I would like to say to the gentleman that I would not fear that amount of those persons coming in. I have a great amount of Japanese, Chinese, and Filipinos in my district. It is not that I register fear that they might come in because they make wonderful citizens. I want to make that clear.

Id. at 21,591.

[223] The restriction was not in the House bill reported by the Judiciary Committee and was, in fact, narrowly rejected as a floor amendment. However, it was in the version approved by the Senate, and was accepted by the Conference, thus becoming part of the law. Immigration and Nationality Act Amendments of 1965, PUB. L. NO. 89–236, §§ *B(a)*, 21(e), 79 Stat. 911, 916, 921 (defining Western Hemisphere natives as "special immigrants" and limiting their numbers to 120,000 per year).

[224] 111 CONG. REC. 21,774 (1965).

participants, House Judiciary Committee Chairman Emanuel Celler, Japanese American Citizens League officer Mike Masaoka, and Secretary of State Dean Rusk.[225] Celler's oft-cited remarks suggest that he believed non-white immigration would be limited:

> Mr. Chairman, claim has been made that the bill would bring in hordes of Africans and Asians. This is the answer to that false charge: Persons from African and Asian countries would continue to come in as heretofore, but would be treated like everyone else. *With the end of discrimination due to place of birth, there will be shifts to countries other than those of northern and western Europe.* Immigrants from Asia and Africa will have to compete and qualify in order to get in, quantitatively and qualitatively, which, itself, will hold the numbers down. *There will not be, comparatively, many Asians or Africans entering this country.*
>
> ....
>
> Mr. Chairman, since the peoples of Africa and Asia have very few relatives here, comparatively few could immigrate from those countries, because they have no family ties in the United States ... *There is no danger whatsoever of an influx from the countries of Asia and Africa.*[226]

Although Celler acknowledged that there would be shifts in the immigration stream, he also seemed to say that there would not be "comparatively" many Asian or African immigrants; that is, that there would be no huge influxes.

Mike Masaoka, longtime JACL officer and advocate of immigration reform, insisted that fears of a "'flood' of immigration from the Orient" were "groundless."[227] Because 74 percent of the visas were designated for family reunification, the small numbers of Asians here would not be able to take advantage of them, with the result that "the general pattern of immigration which exists today will continue for many years yet to come."[228] Dean Rusk, likewise, commented that "[a]ny increase in the volume of immigration resulting from the proposed amendments would be rather limited against the actual volume of Asian immigration into the United States between 1953 and 1963."[229]

[225] A number of commentators rely on Representative Celler's statements. *See, e.g.*, BRIGGS & MOORE, *supra* note 28, at 17; TAKAKI, *supra* note 29, at 419; Reimers, *supra* note 29, at 16. Professors Briggs and Reimers also rely on Mike Masaoka's statements, as does Professor Daniels. *See* DANIELS, supra note 20, at 341; Reimers, *supra* note 29, at 16. Lawrence Auster and Professor Reimers also rely on Dean Rusk's testimony. *See* Auster, *supra* note 33, at 21; REIMERS, *supra* note 29, at 75–76.

[226] 111 CONG. REC. 21,757–58 (1965) (emphasis added).

[227] *Id.* at 24,503.

[228] *Id.*

[229] *Hearings on S. 500*, *supra* note 76, at 4849; *accord Hearings on H.R. 2580*, *supra* note 124, at 90; *Hearings on H.R. 7700*, *supra* note 76, at 389. Similarly, although he believed that Asians would account for approximately 20% of Western Hemisphere immigration, Senator Fong suggested the possibility that the Asian American population might never exceed one percent of the total. *See Hearings on S. 500*, *supra* note 76 at 119.

One possible explanation for the remarks is that people were simply stretching the truth to get a bill passed;[230] given the unpopularity of immigration reform in general and Asian immigration in particular, this would hardly be surprising.[231] If so, it does not necessarily mean that others shared a concern that a truthful prediction about an increase would be fatal to the bill. Celler and Masaoka had been defeated in 1952; McCarran-Walter had been passed despite racial restrictions they deeply opposed. Indeed, forty-one years later, when the long-serving Celler's views finally prevailed, he reminded his colleagues that he "inveighed against this national origins theory a way back in 1924,"[232] when Congress passed the first permanent quota law. Even if the traditional fear of Asian immigration had diminished in the minds of other legislators by 1965, it would be understandable if Celler and Masaoka were still concerned with the "kiss of death" that Senator McCarran predicted in 1952 would destroy any bill eliminating special restrictions on Asian immigration.[233] When Masaoka observed that "the slant of my eyes ... ha[s] nothing to do with the slant of my heart,"[234] he might have suspected that others would not agree.[235]

[230] As Adam Walinsky observed in this context, "people in debate say all kinds of things." *See* Telephone Interview with Adam Walinsky, *supra* note 115.

[231] Louis Harris, *The Harris Survey: U.S. Public is Strongly Opposed to Easing of Immigration Laws*, WASH. POST, May 31, 1965, at A2 (reporting that public opposed immigration reform by a 2-1 margin, and that Asians were tied for last place with Russians in the "most preferred" category, and second to Russians on the "least preferred" category).

[232] 111 CONG. REC. 21,579 (1965).

[233] *See* 98 CONG. REC. 5329 (1952); *id.* at 5624. Former Assistant Attorney General Schlei believes this may be the explanation for Celler's comments:

> [T]he standard lore was that it was utterly impossible to change the national origins quota system because there was such an entrenched feeling in Congress and in the country that everyone wanted the same racial, national make-up of the immigrant stream, but when I began to promote that Bill and to talk to people about it in the Congress, I found that it was not anywhere near as totally accepted a proposition as everybody had thought.... [A]lmost everybody felt bad about our immigration laws and felt that something needed to be done about it.... But Celler was a fellow who had struggled with immigration for a generation, and he I think, feared that if the word was around that this was going to totally change the stream of immigration, the Bill might lose, so I think he tried to develop arguments (and we probably helped him) to reassure those people that if there was a change it certainly wouldn't be sudden ... I think Celler was trying to think of every argument he could to reassure the conservative people that what we were doing was not going to blow everything up like a bomb; it was going to be a gradual change and not all that great.

Telephone Interview with Norbert Schlei, *supra* note 115.

[234] *Hearings on S. 500*, *supra* note 76, at 626.

[235] Perhaps it was no coincidence that Masaoka's comment came from a Japanese American, rather than an American of other Asian descent, because by 1965, the major Japanese immigration to the United States was over. Compared to other Asian groups, the influx of Japanese immigrants was small. *See* J. Wareing, *The Changing Pattern of Immigration into "the United States, 1956–75*, 63 GEOGRAPHY 220, 221 (1978) ("In Asia, despite the spectacular rise in numbers, the trend was not universal and immigration from Japan actually declined after 1965 because of the continuing buoyancy of the Japanese economy and the competition for visas."). By the end of the 1970s, the first

Equally plausible is that these comments, taken in the context of the entire history of the bill, were sincere, *and have proved to be accurate.* What would constitute an "influx" or a "flood"? When attempting to alleviate fears of Asian immigration from the Western Hemisphere, Mike Masaoka argued that "[e]ven if all the million [persons of Asian descent] from Latin America … came in at one time … they still would not equal the number of Asiatics in this country. And the total number of Asiatics in this country is less than one-half of one percent."[236] A million in one day from one region of the world would not be a huge influx. Similarly, Robert Kennedy argued that an increase of 2 percent in the Italian-American proportion of the total U.S. population over a course of years would not constitute an alteration of the ethnic makeup of the country.[237] What seem to be very large shifts in absolute terms, we are told, are *de minimis;* what to one person might seem like a flood, to another is merely diversity.

Edward Kennedy explained that the bill "will not inundate America with immigrants from any one country or area, or the most populated and economically deprived nations of Africa and Asia…. *[N]o country can be given more than 10 percent of the total annual quota.*"[238] The protection was that no country could have more than ten percent, but that did not preclude, say, Mexico, India, the Philippines, El Salvador, China, Viet Nam, El Salvador, Korea, Cuba, and the Dominican Republic from having 100 percent. Thus, when he advised that "[t]he principal beneficiaries of the new system are those countries which have large backlogs of applicants for immigration, but have relatively small quotas," that is, countries with high immigration demand, he named China and Japan as two of the nine countries that had the most to gain.[239] The result was not that there would be no change in the immigration stream, but that "the ethnic pattern of immigration under the proposed measure is not expected to change *as sharply as the critics seem to think.*"[240] Indeed,

full decade of the law's operation, Japanese-Americans fell from being the largest Asian subgroup to the third largest, behind Chinese-Americans and Filipino-Americans. *See* ROGER DANIELS, ASIAN AMERICA: CHINESE AND JAPANESE IN THE UNITED STATES SINCE 1850, at 321–22 (1988); *see also* HING, *supra* note 11, at 106 ("A variety of factors have combined to limit the impact of the 1965 Amendments on Japanese America."). This phenomenon was predicted before the 1965 bill became law. *See Hearings on H.R. 7700*, *supra* note 76, at 725 (statement of James Carey, President of the International Brotherhood of Electrical Workers) (noting the economic boom in Japan and predicting that "very few Japanese would become emigrants [sic] to the United States today even if all bars were down"). *But cf. Hearings on S. 500*, *supra* note 76, at 727 (testimony of Chinese-American leader Jack Wong Sing) (stating, much more ambiguously, "[l]et it not be said that Chinese immigration would be opened"); *see also Hearings on H.R. 7700*, *supra* note 76, at 846 (asserting that any increase would be limited).

236 *Hearings on S. 500*, *supra* note 76, at 627; *accord Hearings on H.R. 7700*, *supra* note 76, at 890–91.

237 *See Hearings on S. 500*, *supra* note 76, at 217.

238 *Id.* at 2 (emphasis added).

239 *Id.*

240 *Id.* (emphasis added).

the bill provided for a phasing out of the National Origins Quota System, designed to make sure that the traditional sources of immigration were protected *for three years*.[241] The clear implication of this provision is that after 1968, sources of immigration could change more rapidly.

In these terms – a million in a day is not a huge influx, a 2 percent increase over a period of decades is not a huge influx, acceptance of a sharp (if not too sharp) change in the immigrant stream – there still has not been an influx of Asian immigrants. Compared to the population of Asia as a proportion of the world population, the percentage of Asians in the immigrant stream does not represent a huge influx. Compared to the population of the United States, the percentage of Asians in the immigrant stream does not represent a huge influx. In absolute terms, the United States is a long way from becoming a distinctly Asian country.

In addition, Celler, Masaoka, and Rusk knew what is sometimes obscured today: by 1965, McCarran-Walter had failed to maintain an immigrant stream that reflected America's racial makeup as of 1952 or 1924; in particular, it had failed to limit the number of Asian immigrants. A series of special laws admitted refugees,[242] relatives,[243] and others,[244] in response to particular political and economic exigencies, even though no quota numbers were available for them.[245] As Richard Poff, a member of the House Judiciary Committee Subcommittee Number One in 1964, explained:

> [McCarran-Walter's] purpose has been called worthy and unworthy. Whether the concept is sound or unsound, the purpose worthy or unworthy, debate is no longer relevant. The question is moot. The purpose has not been achieved. The national origins system has not maintained the ethnic ratios of the American population which prevailed in 1920.... For the last 3 years, for every immigrant entering under the quota system, there were two entering by other means, entirely within the law as amended by Congress from time to time.[246]

[241] *See* Immigration and Nationality Act Amendments of 1965, Pub. L. No. 89–236, § 1, 79 Stat. 911, 911; *see also supra* note 207 (discussing this provision).

[242] *See, e.g.*, Refugee Relief Act of 1953, ch. 336, 67 Stat. 400 (codified at 50 U.S.C. app. § 1971 (a)-(q)) (omitted in current 50 U.S.C. app. due to provision that statute would lapse on Dec. 31, 1956).

[243] *See, e.g.*, Act of Sept. 22, 1959, Pub. L. No. 86–363, §4, 73 Stat. 644, 644 (providing for relief of backlog by admitting, as non-quota immigrants, certain relatives on waiting lists) (current version at 8 U.S.C. § 1153 (1994)).

[244] *See* Act of Oct. 24, 1962, Pub. L. No. 87–885, § 2, 76 Stat. 1247, 1247 (admitting certain skilled immigrants from waiting lists as non-quota immigrants).

[245] *See generally* Helen F. Eckerson, *Immigration and National Origins*, 367 Annals Am. Acad. Pol. & Soc. Sci. 4, 10–14 (1966) (discussing laws providing for admissions outside the quota system established by McCarran-Walter).

[246] 111 Cong. Rec. 21,772 (1965); *see also* H.R. Rep. No. 89–745, at 11 (1965) (making similar observation). As one member of Congress put it, "[t]he basic inequities in the existing quota system have impelled Congress to enact numerous laws during the past dozen years to meet emergency conditions." 111 Cong. Rec. 23,677 (1965) (remarks of Rep. Cunningham).

Thus, under McCarran-Walter – that is, from 1953 to 1965 – there were roughly 28,000 quota numbers allotted to Asia,[247] but 238,507 Asian immigrants.[248] Representative Moore noted that between 1953 and 1963, 119,677 immigrants came to the United States from China, Japan, and the Philippines, and 109,000 were non-quota immigrants.[249]

Senator Hart informed the Senate Judiciary Committee that while China had a quota of 1,000 for the 1953–62 period, actual entrants were 3,600 more; in spite of Japan's annual quota of 185, 48,169 immigrants arrived.[250] A "limited" increase over a quota of 2,000 is one thing; a "limited" increase from a situation where Asians are already coming in at a rate geometrically in excess of their quota, the situation Celler, Masaoka, and Rusk were discussing, is another.

Was the Issue Left Vague because Congressional Antiracism Was Sincere?

Perhaps the best evidence of the attitude of Congress in 1965 is what they did *not* say or do. In the committees and on the floor of Congress, some people said Asian immigration would increase a little or a lot, and others suggested those concerns were overblown. The only formal estimates covered the transition period, not the much more important time during which the law would be in full effect. If ethnic changes in the immigrant stream were an important consideration to the members of Congress who were neither extreme antiracists nor racists,[251] why did they not insist on hard projections, or structural protections in the law against that eventuality?[252]

247 *See Hearings on S. 500*, *supra* note 76, at 308–25 (listing quotas for all nations).

248 *See* BUREAU OF THE CENSUS, *supra* note 6, at 108 (giving annual admissions statistics).

249 *See* 111 CONG. REC. 21,590 (1965). In 1931–40, 3.1% of the 528,000 immigrants were from Asia; 3.5% of the approximately 1,000,000 immigrants admitted between 1941–50 were from Asia; in 1951–60, of 2,515,000 immigrants, 6% were from Asia. *See* 1991 STATISTICAL YEARBOOK, *supra* note 161, at 29. Thus, in absolute and proportionate terms, Asian immigration had been increasing substantially for decades.

250 *See Hearings on S. 1932*, *supra* note 76, at 13.

251 Sitting in the first session of the 89th Congress were many who had opposed the Civil Rights Act of 1964 because of its fundamental principle, and signed the Southern Manifesto. For example, Senators James O. Eastland, Allen Ellender, Sam Ervin, Spessard Holland, John McClellan, and Strom Thurmond voted against both the Civil Rights Act of 1964, *see* 110 CONG. REC. 14,511 (1964), and the Voting Rights Act of 1965, *see* 111 CONG. REC. 11,751–52 (1965); only Ervin switched sides and voted for the Immigration and Nationality Act Amendments of 1965. *See id.* at 24,783. Each of these men and ninety or so other members of Congress signed a statement entitled "Deviations from the Fundamentals of the Constitution," subsequently known as the Southern Manifesto, the 1956 pledge of resistance to *Brown v. Board of Education* endorsed by almost every member of the Southern contingent in both houses of Congress. *See* 102 CONG. REC. 4515–16 (1956). Of the Southern senators, only Lyndon Johnson, Estes Kefauver, and Albert Gore declined to sign. *See* RICHARD KLUGER, SIMPLE JUSTICE 752 (1976).

252 Senator Eastland argued that "it would be a grave mistake if we proceeded with haste to adopt new concepts unsupported by detailed factual surveys and studies," 11 CONG. REC. 24,545 (1965), but his view did not prevail. Many commentators observe that increasing racial toleration domestically was a

It may be that race really was not a major issue to a majority in Congress. McCarran-Walter's supporters could not make political hay out of it, moderates were unconcerned about the race of new immigrants, and liberals thought it was fair for previously excluded groups to have a chance to enter in greater numbers. That is, perhaps Congress as a whole truly meant to eliminate the race factor from immigration policy.

Statements of David Burke, then Senator Edward Kennedy's Chief of Staff, suggests that this motive might have existed: "If you can ever find some nobility in public policy, elimination of the Triangle was one of [those] instances, I think, because it certainly wasn't going to bring any acclamation to Ted Kennedy or his brother Bobby."[253] "Scare" argumentation invoking a renewed threat of the yellow peril would have been ineffective: "[I]n those days … if the guys from Alabama, or Mississippi, or Georgia, if that was the best they could come up with, it was not a concern. The Asian immigration was not a concern. It was not a threat."[254] According to Congressman Peter Rodino, Jr., given the tenor of the times, no legislator who wanted to avoid being tagged a racist would have insisted on racial estimates.[255]

Senator Charles Mathias, who was in the House in 1965, said it was fair to assume that the bill would have passed even had its effects been known at the time. "After all, the bill was fairly dramatic in abandoning the original quota system, and it was opening the gates wider than they had been opened."[256] In Robert Kastenmeier's view, the bill would have passed even if its effects had been known at the time: "I don't know that somebody around here would quibble about whether it is one-half or one-third, or one-quarter, but I guess most of us who supported the bill would have said, 'well, that's not an unreasonable figure.'"[257] Immigration Subcommittee member Don Edwards also believes the bill would have passed even if its effects had been known at the time.[258] Arch Moore, Jr., also a member of the House Judiciary Committee subcommittee responsible for immigration, believes that awareness of the full consequences of the bill with regard to Asian immigration "probably would have caused some difficulty with the bill. Whether or not it would have been sufficient to have defeated the bill, which had widespread administration support,

factor in passing the bill. *See, e.g.*, *supra* note 112 (listing sources discussing increased racial toleration). But why was this important if the 1965 Act was McCarran-Walter with a fresh coat of paint? A change in racial attitudes signaled that a substantive, not merely formal, change in immigration policy was possible.

253 Telephone Interview with David Burke, Former Chief of Staff to Senator Edward.

254 *Id.*

255 *See* Telephone Interview with Peter Rodino, Jr., *supra* note 139.

256 Telephone Interview with Charles Mathias, *supra* note 144. Senator Mathias did note that he was speculating. *See id.*

257 Telephone Interview with Robert Kastenmeier, *supra* note 141.

258 *See* Telephone Interview with Don Edwards, *supra* note 142.

I doubt it."[259] Similarly, James Corman, then a member of the House Judiciary Committee, "would have supported the bill" even if its effects in increasing Asian immigration had been known.[260]

President Ford's opinion that "[t]he existing laws were clearly out of date with unrealistic quotas and racial bars" is also consistent with an intent to create real change.[261] Dale DeHaan explained that the race of new immigrants was simply not a serious issue for most supporters of the legislation, especially given the context of other civil rights legislation that was being passed at the time.[262]

Participants from the administration echo these views. President Johnson's counsel Myer Feldman agrees that arguments about changes in the immigrant stream would have been unavailing: "Certainly, the argument against 'more blacks,' 'more Asians,' or 'more Poles' was unpersuasive."[263] "I have no reason to believe," Feldman says now, "that the commitment to ending discrimination would have been less if its effects in increasing the percentage of Asians had been perceived at the time of passage."[264] Katzenbach also believes the bill would have passed even if its effects were known at the time,[265] as do Schlei[266] and Walinsky.[267] While Thomas Ehrlich does not know how others would have reacted to advance knowledge of the bill's effects, it would not have made a difference to him or, he believes, to State Department official Abba Schwartz.[268] If these views are representative, and if indeed some did not forecast a significant increase in nonwhite immigration in 1965, perhaps the reason was that the question was not decisive.

This is not to say that full disclosure of the racial consequences would not have caused a ripple in Congress or the administration. Some officials said that if the full consequences had been known, that would have given some supporters pause.[269] However, not being entirely free of anxiety is not inconsistent with real change. It would not be surprising, for example, if even a sincere supporter of civil rights legislation felt a twinge when confronting the concrete effects of ending favoritism

[259] Telephone Interview with Arch Moore, Jr., *supra* note 145; *see also id.* (making similar comment).

[260] Telephone Interview with James Corman, Former Member of Congress (Jan. 18, 1996) (transcript on file with author).

[261] Letter from President Gerald R. Ford to Gabriel J. Chin, *supra* note 137, at 1.

[262] *See* Letter from Gabriel J. Chin to Dale DeHaan, *supra* note 146, at 1.

[263] Letter from Myer Feldman to Gabriel J. Chin, *supra* note 107, at 2.

[264] *Id.* Referring to the absolute numbers of immigrants admitted, he explains that "we did not anticipate the high level of immigration that followed the enactment of the law. However, I doubt that if we had ... that [it] would have changed our policy." *Id.*

[265] *See* Telephone Interview with Nicholas deBelleville Katzenbach, *supra* note 110.

[266] *See* Telephone Interview with Norbert Schlei, *supra* note 115.

[267] *See* Telephone Interview with Adam Walinsky, *supra* note 115.

[268] *See* Telephone Interview with Thomas Ehrlich, *supra* note 117.

[269] *See, e.g.*, Telephone Interview with Peter Rodino, Jr., *supra* note 97; Telephone Interview with David Burke, *supra* note 299; Telephone Interview with Thomas Ehrlich, *supra* note 117.

for whites. The reality that a white member of Congress could lose his seat might make him look at the Voting Rights Act from a different perspective.

The Assimilation Assumption

Members of Congress may have felt comfortable admitting a greater proportion of nonwhites because they assumed immigrants would assimilate. Representative John Tunney, for example, assured his colleagues that "[t]here is no bidden nefarious motive behind the bill to undermine our American way of life."[270] Congress assumed that immigrants wanted to come to the United States to share this way of life.[271] Representative Paul Findley explained: "[T]he Statue of Liberty … still stands as an inspiration and a hope to those millions beyond our borders who long for an opportunity to share in the American heritage. To them, America is a promised land, a place of refuge, a place where people can live in dignity and without fear."[272]

Congress agreed with Presidents Kennedy[273] and Johnson[274] that foreigners were allowed to immigrate to the extent that it was perceived to be a benefit to America. Thus, Representative Feighan insisted that "the interests of the United States were at all times first and foremost" when Congress drafted and passed the bill.[275]

[270] 111 CONG. REC. 21,791 (1965).

[271] *See, e.g., id.* at 21,597 (remarks of Rep. Donald Irwin) ("[T]here is still room for those in need of shelter and those in search of freedom."); *id.* at 21,787 (remarks of Rep. Jeffery Cohelan) ("[T]oday we find countless thousands who look to this great melting pot as a land of freedom and opportunity …").

[272] *Id.* at 21,783.

[273] In a letter to Congress, President Kennedy argued that his reforms would "provide a sound basis upon which we can build in developing an immigration law that serves the national interest and reflects in every detail the principles of equality and human dignity to which our nation subscribes… [The national origins quota system] should be modified so that those with the greatest ability to add to the national welfare, no matter where they were born, are granted the highest priority. The next priority should go to those who seek to be reunited with their relatives."

[274] *See Remarks at the Signing of the Immigration Bill, Liberty Island, New York, in* 2 PUB. PAPERS OF THE PRESIDENTS OF THE UNITED STATES: LYNDON B. JOHNSON 1965, at 1037, 1038 (Oct. 3, 1965) (stating that "[t]hose who can contribute most to this country – to its growth, to its strength, to its spirit-will be the first that are admitted to this land"); *Remarks to Representatives of Organizations Interested in Immigration and the Problems of Refugees,* in 1 PUB. PAPERS OF THE PRESIDENTS OF THE UNITED STATES: LYNDON B. JOHNSON 1963–64, at 123, 123 (Jan. 13, 1964) ("What is the training and qualification of the immigrant who seeks admission? What kind of citizen would he make, if he were admitted?"); *see also Annual Message to the Congress on the State of the Union,* in 1 PUB. PAPERS OF THE PRESIDENTS OF THE UNITED STATES: LYNDON B. JOHNSON 1963–64, at 112, 116 (Jan. 8, 1964) ("[A] nation that was built by immigrants of all lands can ask those who now seek admission: 'What can you do for our country?' But we should not be asking: 'In what country were you born?'").

[275] 111 CONG. REC. 21,585 (1965) (remarks of Rep. Feighan). Senator Pastore also noted:

> John Kennedy's immortal test – Ask not what America can do for you – ask only what you can do for America – would still be his test.… [I]t makes no difference what the race is, it makes no difference what the nationality is, it makes no difference what the place of birth is. What counts is the contribution that a person can make to this great America of ours.

Id. at 24,562–63.

Accordingly, the law "carefully establishes conditions which guarantee against any influx of refugees who might be openly or covertly hostile to American principles."[276]

If America was looking out for itself, not the huddled masses, why could it so blithely eliminate racial and national tests? The answer was that individuals were nothing less than individuals, and factors like race, religion, color, or place of birth were irrelevant because they said nothing about a particular person.[277] This focus on individuality was not just an acknowledgment of the idea that all people are morally equivalent despite deep differences; it was also a claim that they actually bear fundamental similarities.[278] Representative Silvio Conte noted the achievements of Italian Americans but then suggested that this kind of background was irrelevant: "The single overriding point is that aliens should and must be evaluated as individuals not as incorrigible vassals of a racial, ethnic, or national strain. They must be evaluated as future Americans, not as former Italians, or

[276] *Id.* at 21,770 (remarks of Rep. Jacob Gilbert).

[277] President Johnson made this point in his signing message, saying that the national origins quota system "violated the basic principle of American democracy – the principle that values and rewards each man on the basis of his merit as a man." *Remarks at the Signing of the Immigration Bill, Liberty Island, New York*, *in* 2 PUB. PAPERS, *supra* note 274, at 1038; *see also* 111 CONG. REC. 21,594 (1965) (remarks of Rep. Peter Rodino) ("This long overdue change recognizes the dignity of the individual and is predicated on the principle that one person is no less desirable than any other person regardless of his race or place of birth."); *id.* at 21,759 (remarks of Rep. Clark MacGregor) (noting that the "fundamental American attitude [is] to ask not where a person comes from, or to prejudge a person on the basis of his place of birth, but to evaluate his personal qualities"). Representative Bernard Grabowski stated that immigration should be

> based on the worth and integrity of each individual without regard to his country or religion.... [Admission] will be based on what skills a person has to offer and whether he already has close relatives in this country.... It is time that we start to consider what an individual has to contribute, not whether those of his same nationality are preponderate in this country.

Id. at 21,764; *see also id.* at 21,771 (remarks of Rep. Jacob Gilbert) ("It is our birthright that we are a nation of men, women and children, each an individual, and not a pawn of society or the State. This measure is testimony of America's regard for the worth of the individual."); *id.* at 21,778 (remarks of Rep. Paul Krebs) ("We must learn to judge each individual by his own worth and by the value he can bring to our Nation."); *id.* (remarks of Rep. Seymour Halpern) ("Americans are concerned with a man's merit and personal integrity, and not with his ethnic background or racial stock."); *id.* at 21,784 (remarks of Rep. Frank Annunzio) ("We have always measured a man's worth by his capacity to contribute and not by his religious beliefs or nation of origin."); *id.* at 21,786 (remarks of Rep. Henry Helstocki) ("[W]e are seeking an immigration policy which will reflect America's ideal of equality of all men without regard to race, color, creed, or national origin ...").

[278] *See id.* at 21,784 (remarks of Rep. Leonard Farbstein) ("Embodied in this bill is a realization and a recognition which has become widespread in this Nation rather belatedly. Indeed, even now it is not yet accepted in all quarters. I am speaking of the recognition of the basic equality of all men."); *id.* at 21,787 (remarks of Rep. Dominick Daniels) ("The very basic contention that 'all men are created equal' is negated by our immigration policy. A policy which flies in the face of our national ideals by holding that some races and some ethnic groups make better Americans than others."); *id.* at 21,807 (remarks of Rep. Paul Fino) (noting "fundamental truth that all men, regardless of race, color or religion, are created equal").

Greeks, or Congolese, or Ethiopians, or anything else."[279] "We have learned," said Edward Kennedy, "that there is no difference between people who participate in the life of our Nation."[280] Furthermore, Robert Kennedy explained that evaluating individuals on "their merit … is the whole philosophy of the immigration bill, and that that was the whole philosophy of the civil rights bills of 1963 and 1964 and the voting rights bill of 1965."[281]

On the other hand, even if "in the United States we judge a man by what he is and not by where his ancestors came from, what his religion is or what color his skin is,"[282] we still judge him. As Edward Kennedy put it, "[f]avoritism based on nationality will disappear. Favoritism based on individual worth and qualifications will take its place."[283]

One component of individual worth and qualification was that the new immigrant assimilate and become a good citizen.[284] Representative Moore explained:

> In addition to the existing numerical quota limitations, intending immigrants must satisfy strict moral, mental, health, economic, and national security requirements. The law is long and detailed on the specific criteria to be applied in testing the qualifications of applicants. The objective of these tests is obvious: To insure that those aliens admitted are of good character, healthy, will not be a burden on our economy, and will not endanger our form of government and way of life.[285]

[279] *Id.* at 21,818.

[280] *Id.* at 24,777.

[281] *Id.* at 24,778.

[282] *Id.* at 21,787 (remarks of Rep. Dominick Daniels); *see also Special Message to Congress on Immigration, in* 1 PUB. PAPERS OF THE PRESIDENTS OF THE UNITED STATES: LYNDON B. JOHNSON 1965, at 37, 39 (Jan. 13, 1965) ("No move could more effectively reaffirm our fundamental belief that a man is to be judged – and judged exclusively on his worth as a human being.").

[283] 111 CONG. REC. 24,226 (1965); *see also id.* at 24,238 (remarks of Sen. Philip Hart) (making similar point); *id.* at 24,564 (remarks of Sen. Thomas Dodd) (describing the provisions of the bill).

[284] *See id.* at 21,765 (remarks of Rep. Brock Adams). He stated:

> I am very proud of the people who live in [my] District who have been patient for many years in the face of America's inadequate immigration policies. They number among our finest citizens, and a look at the people this bill will help the most shows they are among the best people of our community. This is shown by the warm affection they enjoy in the community and by such statistical factors as the low school dropout rate, low crime rate, low incidence of welfare, and a high degree of participation in all civic endeavors.

Id.; *see also id.* at 21,796 (remarks of Rep. Roman Pucinski) ("We need good citizens, good Americans from all the four comers of the world."); *id.* at 21,799 (remarks of Rep. Edward Roybal) ("[W]e have always been an outward-looking people, coming as we do from many ethnic and cultural backgrounds – a true melting pot of the strength and diversity that has made America great.").

[285] *Id.* at 21,780.

The United States could welcome new immigrants without fear of damaging its special history and tradition, because the new immigration would assimilate to the United States just as had the old.[286]

But the form of assimilation suggested by the legislative history was cosmopolitan and fluid; it did not demand that immigrants' history would be wiped clean as they arrived at LaGuardia Airport, or that the United States would be denied the cultural contributions of people from foreign lands. The words of Senator Saltonstall capture both the respect for immigrant contributions to a dynamic and evolving culture and the assumption of assimilation that the bill embodied: "The homogeneity of American life has been enhanced by the efforts of many groups of heterogeneous people."[287]

President Johnson[288] and members of Congress asserted that new immigrants would weave themselves into the fabric of a unitary America without eradicating cultural distinctiveness. Representative Rodino, for example, stated:

> Surely one of the greatest sources of the strength of America is to be found in the diversity of the groups making up our Nation. Each group has brought its traditions, its culture, its individual genius, and these in turn have become part of the American heritage. Diversity marks the various contributions to this heritage; unity has been the outgrowth of a shared experience, of shared values. The American Nation today stands as eloquent proof that there is no inherent contradiction between unity and diversity.[289]

Senator Edward Kennedy also made clear that new immigrants would assimilate:

> Another fear is that immigrants from nations other than those in northern Europe will not assimilate into our society. The difficulty with this argument is that it comes 40 years too late. Hundreds of thousands of such immigrants have come here in recent years, and their adjustment has been notable.... The fact is, Mr. President, that the people who comprise the new immigration – the type which this bill would

[286] *See, e.g., id.* at 21,769 (remarks of Rep. John Lindsay) ("The law, obviously, must be geared to this country's absorptive capacity."); *id.* at 21,779 (remarks of Rep. Seymour Halpern) ("We are not a stagnant people, nor a nation stuck in its ways. Ours is a dynamic and ever-progressing society, always receptive to fresh insights and new ideas, while at the same time, preserving those principles which have made our Nation great."); *id.* at 21,783 (remarks of Rep. Lester Wolff) (arguing that the claim that many immigrants would be "hard to assimilate ... [has] no foundation and crumble[s] when exposed to the facts of immigration reform").

[287] *Id.* at 24,441; *see also id.* at 24,501(remarks of Sen. Joseph Tydings, citing an INS official) ("Their gradual fusion with the multinational immigrants who came to this land before and after them has helped to produce an amalgamated society which has no parellel [sic] in the world.").

[288] *See Remarks at the Signing of the Immigration Bill, Liberty Island, New York, supra* note 274, at 1039 ("From a hundred different places or more they have poured forth into an empty land, joining and blending in one mighty and irresistible tide.").

[289] 111 CONG. REC. 21,594 (1965).

> give preference to – are relatively well educated and well to do.... They share our ideals. Our merchandise, our styles, our patterns of living are an integral part of their own countries. Many of them learn English as a second language in their schools. In an age of global television and the universality of American culture, their assimilation, in a real sense, begins before they come here.[290]

Emanuel Celler more than once told a story that palpably communicates its message of pluralistic harmony:

> If you go to my district [in Brooklyn, New York] you will find people of all nationalities. And to give you an idea of the pluralistic character of my district, which is symptomatic [sic] of many, many districts in the Nation, I would like to tell you a story.
>
> A man goes into a Chinese restaurant, and there, to his amazement, he sees a Negro waiter – a Negro waiter in a Chinese restaurant. And he says to the waiter, "What is the specialty of the house?" And the Negro waiter says, "Pizza pie."
>
> "Pizza pie in a Chinese restaurant?"
>
> And he said, "Yes, this is the Yiddish neighborhood."
>
> That gives you some idea of what is happening in this country and what is happening is good for the land because all those races are amalgamated and they are here for a good, common purpose, the weal and the welfare of our Nation, to which all these diverse races make contribution.[291]

[290] *Id.* at 24,228. Senator Kennedy continued:

> Let us erase forever today the stereotype of the immigrant in our history. The cities of America no longer have the foreign neighborhoods, the cultural islands, separate, unassimilated, a drag on the Nation. They are gone and policies based on them should be gone... The people who will be admitted under [the bill] will continue to adjust to our country with the speed and dispatch of past immigrants.

Id. at 24,777.

[291] *Id.* at 21,757. Representative Durward Hall, likewise, explained:

> Mr. Chairman, from the "melting pot" which certainly we were, and had to be, has come an American culture, a culture no less unique than that of any other established nation in the world.... Persons from many nations and many nationalities and many ethnic groups all contribute to this culture. But it is also important to recognize that as they have changed America, so has America changed them. The result is a nation which in combining the best of each ethnic group has, in effect, like a great, fine hybrid, surpassed each predecessor, and has provided a standard of living that surpasses that of any country from which all our forebears once immigrated. *Id.* at 21,775; *see also id.* at 24,467 (remarks of Sen. Hiram Fong) ("As a nation of immigrants, we have developed a racially heterogeneous society in which citizens of many cultures and ethnic origins live and work side by side to make the American dream a reality."); *id.* at 24,781 (remarks of Sen. Joseph Tydings) ("In his book, 'A Nation of Immigrants,' President Kennedy reminded us that the three ships that discovered America flew the Spanish flag, sailed under an Italian captain, and included as members of their crew an Irishman, a Negro, an Englishman, and a Jew.").

In short, the law would not assume that a person could not be a good American because of race, color, or place of birth, but it did assume that people would come here because they wanted to assimilate into this society. Even a legislator who recognized that it might not be easy for white Americans to get used to unfamiliar languages and colors could insist that anyone, in time, could become a part of "the adventure and opportunity that America means,"[292] and share in the "dream of America."[293]

1.4 CONCLUSION

The 1965 Act is widely misunderstood. In conjunction with other landmark civil rights bills of the time, it intended to take race out of America's immigration policy. Although there is sometimes good reason to question the true motives behind particular laws, the Congress of Camelot and the Great Society was perhaps the most racially progressive America has ever seen. If these legislators were racial hypocrites, the Voting Rights Act of 1965 and the Civil Rights Act of 1964 become very problematic – were they spurious, also?

Fortunately, the evidence in support of the argument that Congress passed the 1965 Act only because it believed there would be little change in the racial demographics of the immigrant stream is limited. The evidence, in fact, actually shows the opposite. This change is revolutionary, given how recently American interests in winning World War II, the Korean War, and the Cold War were subordinated to the more important policy of racial restrictions on immigration. Knowing that nonwhites would be likely to take advantage of the equalized opportunities, Congress passed the law anyway. When Robert Kennedy announced that "[i]t will not matter whether they come from Italy or Germany or whether they come from some countries in the Far East,"[294] he seems to have been telling the truth.

[292] *Id.* at 24,562 (remarks of Sen. Pastore).
[293] *Id.* at 21,783 (remarks of Rep. Philip Burton).
[294] *Hearings on H.R. 7700, supra* note 76, at 421.

2

African Migration to the United States

Assigned to the Back of the Bus

Bill Ong Hing

2.1 INTRODUCTION

This book project, timed for the fiftieth anniversary of the 1965 immigration amendments, recognizes many significant effects the amendments have had on the United States. In many ways – particularly with respect to dramatic demographic changes in Latino and Asian Pacific American communities – the amendments might be regarded as integral to the perpetuation of the United States as a land of immigrants. Yet, when it comes to residents of African descent after the end of slavery,[1] the 1965 changes have had relatively little to do with facilitating the entry of African migrants to our shores.

Under current immigration laws – largely framed by the 1965 Act with some revisions in 1990 – the primary means of immigration is through family reunification or employment categories. The family categories require a prospective immigrant to have a U.S. citizen or lawful permanent resident spouse or parent; U.S. citizens also can petition for siblings. Most employment visas are set aside for professionals, corporate executives, outstanding scientists, educators, athletes, other skilled persons, and investors. A diversity visa lottery program was established subsequent to the 1965 Act as well.

Notwithstanding an increase in employment visas in 1990, the unlimited number of immediate relatives (spouses, parents, and children) of adult U.S. citizens and the large number of visas available for other relatives make clear that family reunification remains the primary policy goal of U.S. immigration laws. Africans, however, have not been able to take advantage of this policy to the same extent as many Asians and Latinos have. Certainly, some gradual change over the past twenty years has occurred. However, while African countries each had 20,000 visas available to them under the numerically restricted family and occupational categories after 1965, and

[1] Rhonda V. Magee, *Slavery as Immigration?*, 44 U.S.F. L. REV. 273 (2009).

about 27,000 visas after 1990, no African country has come close to reaching its ceiling.

Newcomers of African descent can be found in the United States, of course. In the first two decades of the nineteenth century, Africans from the small island of Cape Verde began to settle in the northeast in places like New Bedford, Massachusetts. They worked in seafaring occupations and as agricultural laborers in the cranberry industry. Members of the immigrant community dissociated themselves from African Americans and maintained an ethnicity as Portuguese colonists.[2] By 1850, there were 551 African immigrants in the United States and 2,539 in 1900. Between 1900 and 1950, 31,000 Africans entered the country. Many came as students sponsored by missionaries, and returned to Africa to spread their faith to their former townspeople and tribesmen.[3] Significant increases did not occur until the 1960s. In 1960, there were 35,355 African migrants, but by 1990, the number was 363,819. By 2000, the figure reached 881,300, but the number represented only 3 percent of the total immigrant population in the United States.[4] However, the African migrant population almost doubled within ten years, and the 2010 census counted a total of almost 1.7 million.[5] The largest subgroups of African descent are illustrated in Table 2.1.

This boom is surprising on many levels; given the segregation and open racial antipathy that existed in the United States up until the civil rights movement, many Africans who emigrated in the last century chose to migrate to European countries.[6] The 1994 implementation of the 1990 Immigration Act, which established the Diversity Visa Program,[7] was arguably meant to allow skilled Africans, among other immigrants, a means to enter the country. This program, pushed for by business leaders looking to employ skilled laborers, established a lottery for prospective immigrants to the United States. Under the law, individuals who have a high school diploma (or its equivalent), as well as two years of work experience in an occupation that requires a minimum of two years of training or experience, may

2 John W. Frazier, Joe T. Darden, & Norah F. Henry, The African Diaspora in the U.S. and Canada at the Dawn of the 21st Century 97 (2010).

3 *Id.*

4 Olanipekun Laosebikan, From Student to Immigrant: Diasporization of the African Student in the United States 6 (2012) (Ph.D. dissertation, University of Illinois at Urbana-Champaign) (on file with author); Shimantini Shome, Assimilation of Somali Refugees and Immigrants in the Kansas City Area 12 (2011) (Ph.D. dissertation, University of Kansas) (on file with author).

5 Immigration Policy Center, African Immigrants in America: A Demographic Overview (June 2012), *available at* http://www.immigrationpolicy.org/just-facts/african-immigrants-america-demographic-overview

6 Bill Ong Hing, *Immigration Policies: Messages of Exclusion to African Americans*, 37 Howard L. J. 237 (1994).

7 Immigration Act of 1990, PL 101–649, Nov. 29, 1990, 104 Stat. 4978.

TABLE 2.1. *Largest African migrant communities in the United States, 2012*

Nigerians	228,166
Ethiopians	177,909
Egyptians	153,735
Ghanaians	127,802
Kenyans	99,115
Somalis	85,700

Source: 2012 American Community Survey, table B05006: "Place of Birth for the Foreign-Born Population in the United States." The Somali figure is a 2010 estimate.

enter a visa lottery for one of 50,000 immigrant visas to enter the United States.[8] This requirement threatened to shut out African immigrants who could otherwise benefit from the program; according to 2013 statistics from the UNESCO organization, 38 percent of African adults are illiterate.[9] Two-thirds of these adults are women. Applicants are also required to apply electronically, and data reveals that an average of only 15 percent of Africans have Internet access.[10]

Despite these barriers, the African immigrant population has flourished in many pockets of the United States. From the Cape Verdean community in Boston, to the large Nigerian population in Houston, to "Little Ethiopia" in Washington, DC, and Somalis in the Twin Cities of Minnesota, African enclaves have been able to take root in America. African immigrants are concentrated in a limited number of states. As of 2010, the largest African foreign-born populations were in California (158,953), New York (158,878), Texas (136,112), Maryland (125,470), and Virginia (89,290).[11] The states of Georgia, Virginia, North Carolina, Maryland, Ohio, and Pennsylvania also have relatively large numbers of African immigrants.[12] This distribution generally reflects the pattern for black Americans, with some notable exceptions. Few African immigrants live in the five comparatively rural southeastern states (Louisiana, Mississippi, Alabama, Mississippi, Tennessee, and South Carolina) that have larger black American populations. And unlike the black American population,

8 8 U.S.C. § 1153(c).

9 United Nations Educational, Scientific and Cultural Organization, Literacy and non-formal education, *available at* http://www.unesco.org/new/en/dakar/education/literacy/

10 The World Bank: Internet Users per 100 people, *available at* http://data.worldbank.org/indicator/IT.NET.USER.P2/countries?display=map

11 Kristin McCabe, Migration Policy Institute: African Immigrants in the United States (July 21, 2011), *available at* http://www.migrationpolicy.org/article/african-immigrants-united-states/

12 *Id.*

large African immigrant enclaves have developed in Minnesota and the state of Washington.[13]

Their presence is indicated in many ways. Senegalese organize celebrations and traditional wrestling matches at local parks and invite friends; Ethiopians, Eritreans, Somalis, and Sudanese broadcast poetry about their experience in the United States; Ghanaians of the Ashanti ethnic group appoint local leaders with the ceremony and regalia of the Akan tradition in Ghana. Nigerians establish houses of worship that are branches of religious denominations in their home country. In parts of the country, these communities have grown in size and visibility. For example, Ethiopians are prominent in the taxi business in Washington, DC, and Nigerians can be found in a range of businesses and professions, including nursing, medical doctors, social workers, cooks, and industrial workers.[14]

African immigrants to the United States have had their origins in West Africa and in Anglophone countries. In 2009, the Anglophone countries of Nigeria, Ghana, Kenya, Liberia, Cameroon, and Sierra Leone together accounted for 46 percent of all black African immigrants.[15] In 2010, more than one-fifth (21.8 percent) of African immigrants spoke only English, while nearly half (49.1 percent) reported speaking it "very well."[16] More than one-third of African immigrants work in professional jobs, and 40 percent hold a Bachelor's degree or higher education,[17] compared to 28.5 percent of adult U.S.-born citizens with a Bachelor's degree or higher.[18]

A close look at African migrants to the United States reveals that the vast majority entered as refugees or under diversity visa lottery program that was established in 1990. Thus, the 1965 Act played little role in facilitating their entry. However, the framework of the Act has provided the basis for some African migration and, if continued, will serve as the foundation for future African immigrants to the United States much as it did for the remaking of Asian America.[19]

In this chapter, I discuss the immigration categories under which African migrants have arrived in the United States and explain how the 1965 framework can facilitate future entry. The review of how African migrants arrived also provides an opportunity to take a closer look at some of their communities across the country.

13 *Id.*

14 Evans Eze, Africans in the Diaspora: Contrasting International Immigration: A Study of West African Immigrants in the Baltimore/Washington Area 4–5 (2002) (Ph.D. dissertation, American University) (on file with author).

15 McCabe, *supra* note 11.

16 *Id.*

17 *Id.*

18 U.S. Census Bureau: American Community Survey 2012, *available at* http://quickfacts.census.gov/qfd/states/00000.html

19 Bill Ong Hing, Making and Remaking Asian America through Immigration Policy, 1850–1990 (1993).

The examples include Ethiopian, Somali, and West African communities. In the process, their refugee and immigrant experiences in the United States provide us with an overview of the challenges that such migrants face in America.

2.2 IMMIGRATION DATA

Throughout the history of immigration to the United States, Africans have been underrepresented as a voluntary immigrant group. While voluntary black African migration to the United States has existed since the abolition of slavery in 1865, such immigration was intermittent.[20] Before 1965, Africans represented less than 1 percent of the total immigrant population; twenty years ago, Africans constituted only 2.3 percent of all immigrants, but today, they are about 10 percent. Before the latter half of the twentieth century, the low numbers may have been attributable to the fact that most of the African continent was controlled by Europe; immigration simply was not an option for more than a handful of elite Africans. But even after most African countries attained independence in the 1950s and 1960s, African immigration to the United States remained low. In the mid- to late 1900s, those African immigrants who did migrate first looked to Europe as the destination, in part because of prior relationships.[21] Those who wanted to come to the United States did not find easy routes because of the close family restrictions and narrow employment categories of the 1965 Amendments.

In real numbers, this means that in the 1920s, for example, of 4.1 million immigrants, 6,286 were from Africa; in the 1950s, of 2.5 million immigrants, 14,092 were African. In the 1970s, Africans numbered 80,779 of the total 4.5 million, and in a typical year such as 1987, there were 15,730 Africans of the total 601,516 immigrants. Today, more than a million immigrants enter the United States annually, and approximately 100,000 are from Africa.

Immigration data make clear that the 1965 Act did not facilitate drastic changes in the number of Africans who became immigrants in the United States. In the decade from 1960 to 1969 (before the full effect of 1965 Act could be felt), 3.2 million immigrants became lawful permanent residents of the United States.[22] Of that figure, more than a third (1.13 million) was from Europe. Some 358,000 were from Asia, and more than 440,000 were from Mexico alone. Less than 1 percent of the total (23,780) was from Africa, most of whom were from Egypt (5,581), South Africa (4,360), and Morocco (2,880).

20 Sadie Pendaz, Collective Identity and African American Views of Africa, African Immigrants, and Immigrant Entitlements 50 (2010) (Ph.D. dissertation, University of Minnesota) (on file with author).

21 Bill Ong Hing, *Immigration Policies, supra* note 6.

22 Department of Homeland Security, Office of Immigration Statistics, 2012 *Yearbook of Immigration Statistics*, table 2.

Four decades later, from 2000 to 2009, the numbers appear to be relatively better for Africans attaining lawful permanent resident status. Of a total of 10.3 million immigrants during that period, 759,734 (7.3 percent) were African, compared to 1.3 million Europeans, 3.5 million Asians, and 1.7 million Mexicans. However, as we will see, of the 759,734 Africans who became lawful permanent residents, many were actually admitted initially as refugees under the 1980 Refugee Act or the 1990 diversity visa program rather than through the 1965 Act provisions. Most of the growth in the African migrant community has occurred since 1990. Before 1990, the main source countries were Nigeria, Ethiopia, and Egypt, but since 1990, the flow is much more diverse. Civil wars, social upheaval, and historical connections have promoted more migration of Somalis, Sudanese, and Liberians as well as Nigerians, Ethiopians, and Egyptians.[23]

Consider the data comparing African with Asian and Mexican migrants from four sample years after 1990: 1997, 2001, 2006, and 2012 (Tables 2.2–2.5).

The data disclose that while African migration to the United States grew from about 47,000 and 44,000 in 1997 and 2000, respectively, by 2012, the figure was well over 100,000. However, the growing number is attributable primarily to figures such as almost 49,000 refugees who became immigrants in 2006, and the constant flow of Africans entering under the diversity lottery program – for example, more than 16,000 as early as 1997, and more than 18,000 in 2012.

Although the number of African refugee admissions appeared to be tapering off by 2012, the refugee figures for many African countries remain steady, as illustrated in Table 2.6.

Of the 121,000 refugee visas set aside for 1994, 7,000 were designated for Africa, up from 3,000 for 1993. This compares with 45,000 for East Asia, 55,000 for Eastern Europe and the former Soviet Union, 4,000 for Latin America and the Caribbean, and 6,000 for the Near East and South Asia. For 2013, of the 70,000 refugee visas set aside, 12,000 were for Africa, compared to 30,000 for the Near East/South Asia and 15,000 for East Asia.[24]

2.3 AFRICAN STUDENTS: RELEVANT TO AFRICAN MIGRATION HISTORY

The history of African foreign students to the United States, many of whom remained permanently, represents a record of early African immigration to the United States. Oddly enough, this record also serves as evidence of the historical

[23] Shome, *supra* note 4, at 12.

[24] Department of Homeland Security, Office of Immigration Statistics, 2012 *Yearbook of Immigration Statistics*, table 14.

TABLE 2.2. *Immigrants in 1997*

Region or country	Total	Immediate relatives of US citizens[a]	Family preference categories	Employment preference categories	Refugees and asylees	Diversity program
All countries	798,378	321,008	213,331	90,607	112,158	49,374
Africa	47,791	16,293	3,610	3,665	7,651	16,224
>Ethiopia	5,904	1,647	171	99	1,056	2,881
>Ghana	5,105	1,807	621	234	80	2,605
>Nigeria	7,038	3,339	352	611	67	2,357
>Somalia	4,005	172	29	10	3,607	181
Asia[b]	265,812	103,058	73,197	47,945	30,835	8,254
>India	38,071	13,926	14,229	9,204	462	115
>Philippines	49,117	25,506	16,196	7,075	68	18
Mexico	146,865	71,293	68,996	3,081	60	9

[a] The immediate relative category includes the spouses and unmarried minor children of U.S. citizens, as well as the parents of adult U.S. citizens. The family preference categories include the adult, unmarried sons and daughters of U.S. citizens, married sons and daughters of U.S. citizens, siblings of adult U.S. citizens, and the spouses and unmarried sons and daughters of lawful permanent resident aliens.

[b] Many Asian countries such as China, Korean, India, and the Philippines do not qualify for diversity visas because they do not have historically low rates of immigration to the United States.

Source: U.S. Department of Justice, Immigration and Naturalization Service, 1997 *Statistical Yearbook of the Immigration and Naturalization Service*, table 8. Numbers such as for IRCA legalization and suspension of deportation relief are not included.

TABLE 2.3. *Immigrants in 2000*

Region or country	Total	Immediate relatives of US citizens	Family preference categories	Employment preference categories	Refugees and asylees	Diversity program
All countries	849,807	347,870	235,280	107,024	65,941	50,945
Africa	44,731	16,720	4,206	4,351	3,365	15,810
>Ethiopia	4,061	1,537	355	107	270	1,778
>Ghana	4,344	1,741	587	223	46	1,737
>Nigeria	7,853	3,593	477	805	78	2,822
>Somalia	2,465	142	31	10	1,817	461
Asia	265,400	101,748	81,238	59,365	13,342	7,244
>India	42,046	11,543	14,267	15,557	466	101
>Philippines	42,474	17,830	14,207	10,167	22	12
Mexico	173,919	88,997	77,857	3,950	51	4

Source: U.S. Department of Justice, Immigration and Naturalization Service, 2000 *Statistical Yearbook of the Immigration and Naturalization Service*, table 8. Numbers such as for IRCA legalization and suspension of deportation relief are not included.

TABLE 2.4. *Immigrants in 2006*

Region or country	Total	Immediate relatives of US citizens	Family preference categories	Employment preference categories	Refugees and asylees	Diversity program
All countries	1,266,264	580,483	222,229	159,081	216,454	44,471
Africa	117,430	42,079	5,642	6,437	44,808	18,032
>Ethiopia	16,157	4,500	551	143	7,595	3,357
>Ghana	9,367	6,759	738	370	342	1,129
>Nigeria	13,459	7,379	1,217	1,123	740	2,942
>Somalia	9,462	355	15	11	9,045	36
Asia	422,333	180,339	83,972	80,635	67,011	8,314
>India	61,369	22,608	14,525	17,169	6,841	30
>Philippines	74,607	34,354	16,020	23,733	272	10
Mexico	173,753	94,663	62,998	8,864	491	16

Source: Department of Homeland Security, Office of Immigration Statistics, 2006 *Yearbook of Immigration Statistics*, table 10. Numbers such as for cancelation of removal relief are not included.

TABLE 2.5. *Immigrants in 2012*

Region or country	Total	Immediate relatives of US citizens	Family preference categories	Employment preference categories	Refugees and asylees	Diversity program
All countries	1,031,631	478,780	202,019	143,998	150,614	40,320
Africa	107,241	49,730	7,804	4,763	26,312	18,187
>Ethiopia	14,544	6,768	1,193	178	4,669	1,718
>Ghana	10,592	7,159	808	291	95	2,220
>Nigeria	13,575	8,718	1,544	768	153	2,352
>Somalia	5,204	894	100	15	4,154	38
Asia	429,599	150,254	86,742	91,591	82,680	13,336
>India	66,434	20,497	11,433	33,408	895	27
>Philippines	57,327	30,229	17,735	9,250	31	10
Mexico	146,406	92,053	41,724	7,858	508	7

Source: Department of Homeland Security, Office of Immigration Statistics, 2012 *Yearbook of Immigration Statistics*, table 10. Numbers such as for cancelation of removal relief are not included.

TABLE 2.6. *Refugee admissions*

Region or Country	1994	1997	2000	2003	2006	2009	2012
Africa	5,861	6,069	17,624	10,719	18,129	9,678	10,629
>Eritrea	6	7	94	23	538	1,571	1,346
>Ethiopia	328	197	1,347	1,702	1,271	321	620
>Liberia	610	231	2,620	2,957	2,346	385	69
>Somalia	3,555	4,974	6,026	1,994	10,357	4,189	4,911
>Sudan	1,220	277	3,833	2,139	1,848	683	1,077

Source: U.S. Department of Justice, Immigration and Naturalization Service, 2000 *Statistical Yearbook of the Immigration and Naturalization Service*, table 24; Department of Homeland Security, Office of Immigration Statistics, 2012 *Yearbook of Immigration Statistics*, table 14.

barriers Africans have faced in their immigration to the United States. Even before 1965, higher education was a major conduit by which Africans established contact with the United States, first as nonimmigrants on student visas. In some respects, African students who came in the 1970s provided the nucleus for African immigrant communities in the United States today.[25]

In 1870, Congress extended the right to citizenship through naturalization beyond "free white persons" to those of African descent.[26] In spite of the 1870 expansion, the 1917 enactment of a literacy test for immigration became a major barrier to African immigration. Similarly, once the 1924 quota system was enacted, limiting the annual number of immigrants who could be admitted from any country to 2 percent of the number of people from that country who were living in the United States in 1890, the quota for Africans was tiny. Significantly, the 1924 act also designated students as nonimmigrants rather than immigrants – helping permanently establish in immigration law the notion of foreign students as temporary sojourners. This had important consequences for the immigration of African students and any possible aspirations they might have toward naturalization.[27]

The U.S. government has a history of using education as a feature of foreign policy, and that philosophy was displayed during the early entry of African students. Initially, the U.S. government mostly relied on religious and philanthropic organizations to take the lead in educational exchange. In 1949, 888 African students were studying in the United States; two-thirds received full or partial scholarships from Liberia and Ethiopia.[28] But then, from 1959 to 1961, hundreds of East African students traveled to the United States for education as part of airlifts from East Africa. In September 1959, eighty-one students were airlifted from Nairobi, Kenya, to New York. This

25 Laosebikan, *supra* note 4, at 5; Pendaz, *supra* note 20, at 50.

26 Bill Ong Hing, Defining America through Immigration Policy 36 (2004).

27 Laosebikan, *supra* note 4, at 67–68.

28 *Id.* at 109.

was the first of three flights, the other two occurring in 1960 and 1961. The efforts were supported on the American front by notable icons like Martin Luther King, Jr., Harry Belafonte, Sidney Poitier, and Jackie Robinson. A charismatic young Kenyan senator, Thomas Mboya, was able to solicit scholarships for the students once they arrived. Eventually, President John F. Kennedy gave the efforts full support.[29] President Barack Obama's father was one of the early students from Kenya.

By 1963, the number of African students had more than doubled. Close to 5,000 students were here, most dependent on sponsorships from their own governments, private organizations, the United States, or some combination. The majority were male; only 619 were female; and most were from Egypt (1,136), Nigeria (813), and Kenya (697).[30]

About a decade later (1974), the African student number grew to 18,400, then doubled again by 1983, fueled by rising fortunes of countries like Nigeria, reaping the benefits of the discovery of oil in the late 1950s and able to afford to send masses of high-school-educated youth to foreign countries in search of development degrees. By 1993, there were 42,690 African nationals studying in the United States.[31]

Their desire to pursue education in the United States began many years prior to arrival in the United States. Prospective foreign students were encouraged while in their native lands to seek a U.S. education by a wide range of influences. The presence of American missionaries in Africa, American-sponsored "exchange programs," and family members or friends who had previously studied abroad in the United States all contributed to the ubiquity of the American image.[32]

The students – even the early ones – experienced racial challenges. A 1949 report highlighted increasing encounters of African students with racism and prejudice. A 1950 editorial by Aliyu Olumide Fafunwa, a Nigerian student who later became minister of education back home, recounted several incidents with racism that baffled him given the image of democracy the United States had worked so hard to cultivate. By 1965, challenging conditions (including financial) faced by African students had become so widespread that Congress held a special committee hearing on the issue. The African students were identified as a vulnerable, at-risk population.[33]

Depending on the era and the program, many African students wanted to remain in the United States. In one 1970 survey of students from Cameroon, Kenya, Nigeria, Rhodesia, Tanzania, Uganda, and Zambia who had graduated, 64 percent returned home, 16 percent stayed for practical training, and about 15 percent stayed for further study or for another reason.[34] However, in a subsequent 1973 survey of a different set of graduates, only 20 percent returned home; most who stayed did so

29 *Id.* at 94–95, 97.
30 *Id.* at 98–99.
31 *Id.* at 99–100.
32 *Id.* at 165.
33 *Id.* at 109–12.
34 *Id.* 116–18.

to pursue graduate degrees. Others were able to adjust status based on employment categories of the 1965 Act.[35] Some commentators have classified this latter group as part of a "brain drain" phenomenon attached to the skilled preference categories of the 1965 Act.[36]

A curious side effect of African students and migrants relates to diversity in higher education. African immigrants and their offspring are disproportionately represented in Ivy League schools in comparison to native-born blacks (described as those who have four native-born grandparents). Ivy League colleges in particular have trumpeted the presence of these students as evidence of their efforts toward increasing racial diversity. Some believe that this takes place at the expense of native-born blacks.[37]

2.4 WEST AFRICANS – PRIMARILY NOT REFUGEES

Most of the migrants of African descent who have not entered as refugees are from West Africa, from countries such as Nigeria, Liberia, Ghana, Togo, Guinea, and Sierra Leone. While many may have entered as students in the past, the presence of West Africans has increased significantly since the early 1990s, fueled by the institution of the Diversity Visa Program.[38] The communities are diverse, with a range of experiences and backgrounds.

Ghanaians

Ghanaians choose settlement destinations in the United States based on who invited them or whom they knew prior to coming. Knowing others helps minimize

[35] *Id.* at 119–20.

[36] *Id.* 120–21.

[37] *Id.* at 173. The report of a first-generation Ghanian-American student accepted by all eight Ivy league schools stirred up the tension between black Americans and recent African immigrants. A 2007 study covered by the *Washington Post* found that one-quarter of black students admitted to elite colleges were African immigrants, even though they only represented 13 percent of America's college-age black population. The study's authors offer several theories on why black immigrants do better, including "to white observers black immigrants seem more polite, less hostile, more solicitous and 'easier to get along with.' Native blacks are perceived in precisely the opposite fashion." Lani Guinier, a Harvard professor, argued instead that schools were attempting to "resolve historic wrongs against native black Americans by enrolling immigrants who look like them" but had different experiences. "In part, it has to do with coming from a country . . . where blacks were in the majority and did not experience the stigma that black children did in the United States," Guinier said. Either explanation creates a divide – as if Africans can only succeed at the expense of black Americans. Arit John, *Why the All-Ivy League Story Stirs Up Tensions between African Immigrants and Black Americans*, The Wire, Apr. 1, 2014, at http://www.thewire.com/politics/2014/04/why-the-all-ivy-league-story-stirs-up-tensions-between-african-immigrants-and-black-americans/359978/

[38] Eze, *supra* note 14, at 3.

loneliness and isolation as well as homesickness. In Chicago, for example, numerous outlets for Ghanaian and Nigerian populations – churches, organizations, social events, and festivals – are helpful. Chicago also boasts many African grocery stores and restaurants.[39]

Ghanaians living in Chicago generally work in labor-intensive jobs. Some are very poor, while others have good-paying jobs. All speak English, largely because English remains the official language in Ghana.[40] Most Ghanaians desire to bring family members to the United States, but the expense is prohibitive to most. The cost of visas and plane tickets can be thousands of dollars per person. Also, the backlogs in some family visa categories such as second and fourth preferences can take years. The fact that the invited family member may be totally financially dependent on the petitioner also can be discouraging financially.[41]

Many Ghanaians have relocated from their first place of residence in the United States. For example, most Ghanaians who live in Cincinnati first lived in other urban areas (mainly on the eastern seaboard) of the United States before moving.[42] The sense that Cincinnati is a prosperous place to live, as well as a running joke among Ghanaians who believe Ohio translates to "*Eho ye*" or "good place economically" in Twi (an Akan language that is the principal native language of Akan lands in Ghana, spoken over much of the southern half of that country), helped convince some Ghanaians to resettle in the city.[43]

The Ghanaian population in Cincinnati grew from about 100 people in the early 1990s to about 1,500 as of 2008. As Tables 2.2 through 2.5 illustrate, the diversity visa lottery program facilitated the entry of many of these Ghanaian immigrants. Most come because they have friends and relatives who sponsored them, and they presume that getting a job in the midwest is easier than on the immigrant-saturated eastern seaboard.[44] In fact, new arrivals have found jobs relatively easily in manufacturing and in nursing homes.[45]

The first group of Ghanaians to settle in Cincinnati were professionals and their families in the early 1990s. These immigrants found homes in the city, assisted others in job and housing searches, and in some cases physically helped transport people from other cities to Cincinnati. In the city, most Ghanaian grocery shops are located in the areas of Forest Park and Fairfield; however, unlike Washington, DC's

39 Tara M. Boadu, Experiences of Recent African Immigrants Living in United States 13 (2003) (Ph.D. dissertation, The Chicago School of Professional Psychology) (on file with author).

40 *Id.* at 7.

41 *Id.* at 13.

42 Ian E.A. Yeboah, Black African Neo-Diaspora: Ghanaian Immigrant Experiences in the Greater Cincinnati, Ohio, Area 31 (2008).

43 *Id.* at 33.

44 *Id.* at 33.

45 *Id.* at 33.

"Little Ethiopia," no Ghanaian ethnoscapes truly exist in the city. The majority of Ghanaians live mostly in the suburbs rather than in the inner city, and even within the suburbs, immigrants are dispersed throughout the neighborhoods.[46]

The greatest expectations that Ghanaians have is to provide financial help to family and friends here and back home and to assist family and friends back home to immigrate to the United States. Their biggest problems relate to financial and social challenges and support (including racism and discrimination), as well as working below their skill and education levels. In spite of their English-language abilities, they still have communication problems, and are homesick and worry about family problems back in the home country.[47]

Ghanaians' own families have high expectations – sometimes unrealistic – for the immigrants here. The immigrants can feel tremendous pressure to live up to these expectations, even if they are not attainable. Some are made to feel as though they are the family bank. Some relatives in Ghana go bankrupt because they have borrowed large sums of money in anticipation of receiving a windfall from the immigrant. For those who cannot help their families, the impact can be great. They isolate themselves out of shame because they could not do what was expected for their loved ones. Some never return to their country because of the shame and guilt of not being able to achieve these financial goals.[48] Many are undocumented, having overstayed their visas. Of course this makes it difficult to find work and can be exploited; they fear being caught and for that reason avoid unnecessary contact with people. They are concerned with being trapped, arrested, and deported.[49]

In spite of these challenges, most Ghanaians display remarkable resilience. In the face of many problems, they are tenacious and driven to succeed, not letting problems get them down. They stay focused on their goals, which helps distract them from their problems. In spite of their challenges (including being undocumented), they are positive about their future. They live by a principle of Ghanaian culture, under which it is taboo to verbalize negativity about oneself.[50]

West Africans Generally

As a highly educated African group from oppressive, nondemocratic, nonindustrial nations that have relatively weak relations with the United States, West Africans are considerably different from many other contemporary immigrant groups. Some West Africans have described their presence in the United States as temporary.

46 *Id.* at 36.
47 Boadu, *supra* note 39, at 68–69.
48 *Id.* at 129–30.
49 *Id.* at 149.
50 *Id.* at 135.

Some come with the hope of acquiring training that would improve their economic chances in their countries of origin. Even after living in the United States for decades, significant numbers avoid describing themselves as either American or African American, rejecting the adaptation pattern followed by other immigrant groups. They generally associate with other African immigrant groups, particularly those of the same ethnic origin, and frequently speak of plans to return home. Even those who settled in the 1960s continue to call themselves African.[51]

West Africans in most cases come to escape economic and political instability in their home countries or to earn money to send back to the home country. Once here, they struggle both to provide for themselves and to support a usually large family back home. The desire to return home is restrained by the fact that the economic and political troubles one escaped by emigrating have yet to abate. So the problem becomes less one of returning home than one of ensuring continued residence in the United States.[52]

Sub-ethnicity plays an important organizing role among West African immigrants in the Baltimore/Washington, DC area. West Africans tend to cluster along the lines of ethnic, tribal, and national origins. One example are Yorubas, an ethnic group from southwestern Nigeria, referred to by others as Nigerians while they identify themselves as Yorubas. In Nigeria, Yoruba ethnic identity is constructed in a social context that emphasizes Yoruba ethnicity. In the United States, however, the terms "Ibos" (another ethnic group) and "Yoruba" are no longer a sufficient differentiation because of the presence of different African immigrant subgroups. Instead, national origin – Nigerian, Ghanaian, Liberian, Senegalese, and the like – is used by West African immigrant community members to define subgroups. Most non–West Africans are largely unaware of these internal distinctions. However, major differences exist among these populations.[53]

West Africans are migrating from a relatively economically depressed region of the world, and their numbers probably contain many individuals with a propensity to stay on in the United States. This is true even though West African countries have very little social, economic, cultural, and political links to the United States.[54] Given the colonial experiences of the West African immigrant, English and French are the major language of the colonial masters, which were imposed on the colonized population. A significant percentage of the West African immigrant population is bilingual: the colonizers' language and a mother tongue.[55]

51 Eze, *supra* note 14, at 9.
52 *Id.* at 10.
53 *Id.* at 15.
54 *Id.* at 20.
55 *Id.* at 17.

Some research has been done on the claim that West African immigrants are ambivalent about being in the United States and their desire to return home. In a 1991 study, 30 percent of African immigrants planned to return and resettle back home within five years. Another 59 percent planned to go back within ten years and nearly 10 percent planned never to return to Africa.[56] About ten years later, a separate study of West Africans found that 91 percent planned to return to Africa in the future, while 8.6 percent planned never to return.[57]

Despite expressions of nostalgia for West Africa, many migrants continue to make their lives in the United States. On average, they reported to have three European Americans and three African Americans as their closest friends; 96.3 percent claimed to have friends and members of their own ethnic group in the area. More than 87 percent claimed their best friends to be fellow West Africans. Given that they lived in the United States at least three to five years and knew English, these results point at low interaction with native-born Americans.[58] A contradictory image emerges, that of being resourceful, hardworking, and economically disadvantaged, but marginally alienated. A self-description of alienation is evident among highly successful professionals and entrepreneurs as well.[59] West Africans are black, well educated, and often possess occupational and cultural skills that are incompatible with many nations. In the United States, they often lack adequate access to networks that can provide a broad variety of resources ranging from jobs to child care, housing, and social life, which could also be attributable to racism and discrimination. A great portion are young – 65.8 percent of those in the Baltimore/Washington, DC, area are between the ages of seventeen and forty. It is possible they may simply lack techniques for coping with life in the American settings.[60]

West Africans may want to remain in the United States for various reasons. For example, a Nigerian student's initial short-term plan to come for education may evolve into a permanent stay. Curiously, continued ties to Nigeria can actually extend the stay here. In a period of economic downturn in Nigeria, friends back home may urge the student to stay in the United States because nothing is happening back home.[61] Like other immigrant groups, the presence of relatives already living in the United States also can influence migrants to stay. These migrants may be prime to consider a more permanent transition because they have left home as a result of disillusionment, weariness with war, frustration with ethnic and tribal discrimination, or a general attitude of not being able to fit into the particular social and economic order.[62]

[56] *Id.* at 64.
[57] *Id.* at 64.
[58] *Id.* at 64.
[59] *Id.* at 64.
[60] *Id.* at 71.
[61] *Id.* at 65–66.
[62] *Id.* at 66.

West African immigrants' social structure was modified as a result of migration and continues to undergo further transformation as reflected in such concrete facts as occupational pursuits, educational attainments, and religious and social patterns. The transformation involves relationships between personality, culture, and social structure.[63] Those in the Baltimore/Washington, DC area are a marginally successful immigrant group in terms of economic and professional status. They are relatively well educated: 46.3 percent of West Africans have college degrees; an additional 41.5 percent have graduate degrees; 8.5 percent only completed high school; and 3.7 percent are not high school graduates, but have engaged in occupational training, such as welding.[64]

A majority in Baltimore/Washington, DC are employed in nonprofessional areas such as taxi drivers, cooks, and other service industries. A few are managers, administrators, professionals, or technical specialists. Rates of self-employment are low compared with other ethnic groups such as Korean and Israeli immigrants. Those who are employed earned about $25,000 per year in 2000.[65]

Transnationalism

As West Africans decide and are able to remain in the United States more permanently, they maintain transnational existence and identity. Transnationalism views immigration as a multidimensional process, which includes demographic, political, economic, cultural, and familial factors. It involves various links between two or more settings, rather than a discrete event constituted by a permanent move from one nation to another. As a perspective on human immigration, transnationalism addresses the major concerns of both micro and macro perspectives. Like the micro tradition, transnationalism emphasizes the importance of networks, contexts, and local values. Yet, like macro approaches to immigration, transnationalism also considers the large-scale economic, political, and legal structures within which immigrants develop their communities and lives. This is useful for understanding immigrants' motives. The concept emphasizes immigration as an ongoing process through which ideas, resources, and people change locations and develop meanings in multiple settings. The idea is that by retaining social, cultural, and economic links, immigrants can surmount the impediments traditionally associated with long distances and international borders.[66]

To assist with adjustment, a variety of African-oriented activities such as schools, day care centers, churches, leisure clubs, publications, restaurants, shops, and

63 *Id.* at 51.
64 *Id.* at 63.
65 *Id.* at 63.
66 *Id.* at 8.

nightspots have been created in the Baltimore/Washington, DC area so that a semblance of the African life can be experienced in the United States. West Africans maintain links to the country of origin and interact with co-nationals and ethnic group members; they learn of methods through which issues of national and ethnic affiliation are interpreted.[67]

Despite the many mechanisms that permit them to maintain a transnational existence, many West Africans remain troubled by their mixed loyalties. Even the most economically successful often contrast America's favorable economic and occupational environment to its communal and cultural liabilities. Most universally regard their home country as a better place for their children. Home is regarded as safer, with fewer violent social problems – other than the few warring countries, such as Sierra Leone and Liberia – and does not impose the manifold generational conflicts West Africans confront when raising children in the United States.[68]

The experience of transnationalism is trying. While West Africans build communities and networks to deal with the social and cultural dimensions of ties to two places and enjoy economic benefits from immigration, most are not quite comfortable with this status. Transnationals still confront many of the social, economic, and identity-related problems associated with traditional categories of immigration and may encounter new difficulties as well in the future.[69]

Family

Family issues can be a central source of unhappiness about being in the United States. Upon entering an urban environment in an industrial society, the family necessarily undergoes some reorganization. For West African families back home, ten to fourteen children is not uncommon, as children are seen as a form of wealth and are crucial part of the agricultural work in the fields. Having many children means cultivating large portions of agricultural farmland, which in the long run transforms into wealth from surplus harvest. However, the trend among West African immigrants is toward a smaller family size; the West African immigrant family has, on average, 2.7 children. Their siblings back home have 6.3 children per family. Having many children in the Baltimore/Washington, DC area would be a hindrance, putting strain on earnings.[70]

In the authoritarian, patriarchal family structure in West Africa, the husband makes the decisions and the wife abides by them. Among Baltimore/Washington, DC migrants, most of the married respondents reported that wives were consulted

[67] *Id.* at 72.
[68] *Id.* at 72–73.
[69] *Id.* at 73.
[70] *Id.* at 75–76.

before important family decisions were made. A more egalitarian status arrangement in the West African immigrant family was apparent compared with the authoritarian, patriarchal pattern of family arrangements in West African countries.[71] The democratization of a formally authoritarian or patriarchal family is evident. Most spouses are more frequently employed.[72]

Family, ethnic membership, and ties to other relatives remain strong in West African immigrant communities.[73] Migrants continue to consult with members of the same ethnic group for advice and guidance on important issues. Most recognize the importance of living close to relatives and consulting with members of their families before making important decisions. Many feel that contacts with friends and ethnic group members are important for finding a job or starting and developing a business.[74]

Minority Status

As Africans, West African immigrants are conscious of their minority status and of the status of African Americans in the United States. However, they are much more concerned about the threat of assimilation into American culture, a culture that discriminates against them yet provides them with better economic status than back home. The effect of their perception of discrimination and prejudice influences their ability to integrate into the American mainstream.

They have strong informal ethnic ties with ethnic group members.[75] Connections to their various ethnic groups provide West African immigrants with resources, including access to jobs and means to normalize their status in the Baltimore/ Washington, DC metropolitan community.[76] They are proficient in English and their African language. Use of their mother tongue holds steady among West African immigrants here. Their African language is spoken more often at home; English is used at work and to conduct their daily business. They have maintained traditional food habits and modified menus to include American food. They have both European-American and African-American friends, prefer African music, but also like reggae and hip-hop.[77] Their social structure has been modified, yet they tenaciously hold on to their African identities.[78]

71 *Id.* at 77.
72 *Id.* at 108–09.
73 *Id.* at 108–09.
74 *Id.* at 66, 91–92.
75 *Id.* at 109.
76 *Id.* at 106.
77 *Id.* at 124–25.
78 *Id.* at 129.

The extreme negative stereotyping of Africa in the media significantly devalues African culture in the eye of many Westerners. The nature of these stereotypes is a very "short step to racism."[79] Even the undignified portrayal of hunger in Africa by relief organizations serves to undermine the valuation of African people in America. As such, an important question is raised as to whether this portrayal of Africa as an impoverished and backward continent in academic, political, media, and other circles manifests itself in a different receptivity toward Africans, relative to other blacks in America.[80]

The immigration of West Africans is often considered in light of the West African status as black Africans and, accordingly, is seen as a metaphor for the relationship between white America and African Americans in the United States.[81] West Africans are victims of discrimination due to being black and African immigrants. They experience racial and ethnic name calling or insulting comments based on African stereotypes. This happens anywhere: at work, in school, and even in public.[82]

The problems that West Africans face in the areas of race and identity are associated with being black immigrants, but also with how they relate to African Americans, and what they believe Americans think of them as Africans. Of course, it would be a mistake to think they have never thought about their skin color, even in racially homogeneous countries like Ghana. For example, lighter-skinned Ghanaians sometimes are regarded as more beautiful and intelligent than the average person with darker skin.[83]

Yes, Africans are subjected to racism and discrimination in their home country, but the problem is conceptualized differently than in the United States. In Ghana, for example, discrimination is primarily based on the ethnic group with which one identifies. Ashantis are the predominant group and are considered to be the top of the social hierarchy. Ethnic groups in the less developed and more poverty-stricken northern regions are relegated toward the bottom of the social hierarchy.[84]

A different aspect of these difficult issues relate to West Africans' views of African Americans. Negative sentiment about African Americans is not uncommon among West Africans, including references to stereotypes they may hold about African Americans (e.g., "they are too lazy to work").[85] Nigerians may use the term "akata" to refer to black Americans, which translates as "wild animal." Some Nigerians

[79] *Id.* at 43.
[80] *Id.* at 43–44.
[81] *Id.* 45.
[82] Boadu, *supra* note 39, at 77.
[83] *Id.* at 107–09.
[84] *Id.* at 109.
[85] *Id.* at 112.

use akata to mean "ghetto" as well, as in "dressed like an akata girl," for wearing sweatpants in public.[86]

Some comments and attitudes stem from lack of understanding. West Africans may know little about African American history or culture. They believe African Americans are not in touch with their roots. Some expressed concern about being associated with or mistaken for an African American. They do not like the idea that Americans are going to stereotype them as African Americans.[87]

Economic Mobility

Some distinctions are clear between those West Africans who came before 1990 and those who came after. Those who settled in the 1960s, 1970s, and 1980s have made moderate progress up the socioeconomic ladder. Those who settled in the 1990s (primarily diversity lottery winners) are more upwardly mobile economically, work harder in two or three jobs, and have a higher average income, as well as a greater quantity and better quality of material possessions than do those who came in prior decades. Education has largely made occupational improvement possible for them. But the absence of a large middle class is apparent.

Those in higher income brackets are mostly married, with working spouses, or educated. Many who have succeeded in entering the middle class usually have done so by virtue of employment made possible by college education, except for those who settled in the 1990s. Most 1990s settlers drifted away from formal college education, instead participating in job training that provides them faster job opportunities. Unlike earlier immigrants who came for educational purposes, with the hope of returning back once they completed school, those of the 1990s are mostly economic immigrants, who escaped economic hardship in the various countries and come to settle, with little or no hope of returning back; they escaped economic destitution in their home country resulting from economic plunder and mismanagement by the leadership and rulers of their countries.[88] West African immigrants of the 1990s are economic migrants who settled with little or no hope of returning back, choosing instead to position themselves economically and call America their home.[89]

The line dividing these two groups is clear. Those who entered before 1990 focused on education; those after focused on economic opportunity. Within the short period of immigration, the 1990s group surpassed the earlier group in terms of

[86] Arit John, *Why the All-Ivy League Story Stirs Up Tensions Between African Immigrants and Black Americans*, The Wire, Apr. 1, 2014, at http://www.thewire.com/politics/2014/04/why-the-all-ivy-league-story-stirs-up-tensions-between-african-immigrants-and-black-americans/359978/

[87] Boadu, *supra* note 39, at 112–13.

[88] Eze, *supra* note 14, at 108, 122.

[89] *Id.* at 112.

socioeconomic status and homeownership. By the early 2000s, 11.7 percent reported annual incomes higher than $51,000, and 25 percent already own homes.[90]

2.5 REFUGEE ADMISSIONS

The population and migration levels illustrated in Tables 2.1 through 2.6 make clear the role refugee admissions have played thus far in the creation of African migrant communities in the United States. For example, the correlation between refugee admissions and the Ethiopian and Somali population figures is evident. Given the steady flow of refugees from Ethiopia and Somali and their adjustment to lawful immigrant status, the Ethiopian and Somali migrant populations of 202,715 and 120,102, respectively, by 2012 is not surprising.

The Refugee Act of 1980 empowers the president, in consultation with Congress, to establish annual refugee quotas and designate different geographic areas of the world for refugee admissions.[91] Between 1980 and 1988, the majority (69.2%) of the admissions ceiling was reserved for those from Asia, primarily Vietnam. For the next five years, refugees from the former Soviet Union commanded the highest proportion of the ceiling (41.8 percent). On the other hand, between 1980 and 1994, the ceilings for African refugees comprised a mere 3.1 percent of the total pool, in spite of the fact that Africa accounted for the highest number of refugees worldwide at the time. The ceiling for African refugees was 1,500 (0.6 percent) in 1980, when only 955 actually were admitted, which increased to 7,000 (5.7 percent) in 1994, when only 5,856 were actually admitted.[92]

Historically, refugees from African countries that were under the sway of a specific European country during the colonial era tended to seek asylum in that country. In addition, the proximity of Africa to Europe may also explain why more Africans sought asylum in various European countries than in the United States. On the other hand, in some cases, such as with Ethiopians, distance did not seem to be a factor even through the mid-1990s; more Ethiopian refugees resettled in the United States during an early crisis than in any other country, including Italy, with whom Ethiopia has had close historical ties.[93] From 1982 to 1992, Ethiopians were the dominant African refugee group admitted.[94] However, as Table 2.6 illustrates, by 1994, thousands of Somali and Sudanese refugees were admitted, surpassing

[90] *Id.* at 122.

[91] Bill Ong Hing, Making and Remaking Asian America, *supra* note 19, at 127.

[92] Madeleine Wong, Emerging Patterns of African Refugee Resettlement in the United States 81–84 (1995) (M.A. thesis, Florida Atlantic University) (on file with author); *see also* Table of African refugee quotas from 1980 to 1994, and actual admissions, at 82, 86.

[93] *Id.* at 87–88.

[94] *Id.* at 92.

Ethiopians at the time. And although the number of African refugees reached a high of more than 18,000 in 2006, new admissions remain in the 10,000 range for the time being.[95]

African refugees have fled their homes for different, overlapping reasons: civil conflict, danger to their lives, closed opportunities, or being targeted because of ethnicity or tribal affiliation. They left their homes under hurried, chaotic, and dangerous circumstances. When civil war began in their home countries, they were "scattered" or "ran into the bush," separated from family members – some still to this day.[96] They did not know when, if ever, they would be able to return to their home countries. This made leaving friends and family behind particularly painful. Many do not even know the whereabouts of some of their children or siblings.[97]

Often African refugees have been victims or witnesses to violence, rape, torture, and murder. They have been forced to leave homes under the most heinous circumstances. Some saw family members getting murdered while themselves hiding.[98] Every single refugee had a family member or friend killed, raped, or tortured in conflict back home. Quite a few themselves had been imprisoned, tortured, or raped. Their resilience is exceptional, but at times the past makes day-to-day living difficult, as they suffer with posttraumatic stress.[99] As illustrated in the specific discussions of Ethiopian, Somali, and Sudanese refugees that follow, refugee adjustment in the United States is a challenge.

2.6 REFUGEE RESETTLEMENT

Refugee resettlement in the United States was not given much consideration prior to 1960. Once admitted, refugees relied on their own resources or on private aid to adjust to their new home. Federal responsibility for resettlement strategies began to change with the arrival of Cuban refugees in 1959. In 1975, a special interagency task force coordinated the evacuation and resettlement of Southeast Asian refugees.[100] The Refugee Act of 1980 was implemented in light of the ever growing numbers of refugees entering the United States, aimed to narrow the focus on the issue of admissions to a more comprehensive approach that included the problems of resettlement.[101]

95 Table 2.6.

96 Tamar E. Mott, Pathways and Destinations: African Refugees in the US 132 (2006) (unpublished Ph.D. dissertation, The Ohio State University) (on file with author).

97 *Id.* at 132.

98 *Id.* at 132.

99 *Id.* at 210–11.

100 Wong, *supra* note 92, at 56; BILL ONG HING, MAKING AND REMAKING ASIAN AMERICA, *supra* note 19, at 128–29.

101 *Id.* at 126–31.

During the height of refugee resettlement in the late 1970s and 1980s, the government pursued a strategy of settling refugees where it was convenient for the host society, not necessarily where the best support group of family, friends, and fellow nationals existed. At one point, the strategy was to isolate refugees in order to speed their Americanization. At the same time, the Office of Refugee Resettlement (ORR) encouraged resettled populations to organize so that they could represent themselves for resources and services. In so doing, it required them to incorporate under state government rules and regulations, which were foreign to the traditional types of organizations with which the refugees were familiar.[102]

After unfavorable reviews of resettlement efforts with Southeast Asian refugees through the mid-1980s, the ORR attempted better planning of the distribution of refugees across the country. Widespread dispersal remained the goal, but more care was used in selecting sites. ORR set about resettling refugees by considering job opportunities, housing availability, viable voluntary organizations, service providers, and the existence of refugee populations, hoping to minimize negative economic effects the refugees might cause.[103]

Under this revised approach, African refugees have been distributed throughout the country. From 1983 to 2004, as Table 2.7 illustrates, the states that received the most African refugee arrivals were Florida, California, and Minnesota. However, focusing more closely on the later years of the data (2000–2004), Table 2.8 shows that Minnesota, Texas, and New York led the states with the most distribution.[104] Then, even more recently, from 2010 to 2012, Table 2.9 shows that Texas, California, New York, Arizona, and Ohio have become the leading destinations for African refugees.

The location of different African refugee groups in the United States varies by country of origin. Refugees from Ethiopia and Somalia have been resettled to similar locations, with large clusters in California, Texas, Minnesota, and Georgia. However, significant secondary migration – the phenomenon of refugees relocating within the United States – affects the ultimate locations of these populations. For example, significant numbers of secondary migrants have relocated to Ohio and Minnesota; the second-largest Somali community in United States is actually located in Columbus, Ohio, which cannot be determined by simple assessment of the state data from ORR. Flows out of California, Texas, and Georgia also are significant.[105]

[102] Kathryn Myers Moran, Community, Cohesion, and Conflict: Ethiopian Refugees in Los Angeles 304 (1996) (Ph.D. dissertation, University of California, Los Angeles) (on file with author).

[103] Bill Ong Hing, Making and Remaking Asian America, *supra* note 19, at 131–32.

[104] Mott, *supra* note 96, at 64.

[105] *Id.* at 66.

TABLE 2.7. *African refugee arrival distributions, 1983–2004*

Florida	21,369
California	20,888
Minnesota	18,124
Texas	14,815
New York	12,371
Georgia	10,095
Virginia	8,414
Washington	7,366
Pennsylvania	6,684
Arizona	6,054

Source: DHS Yearbook of Immigration Statistics, 2004.

TABLE 2.8. *African refugee arrival distributions, 2000–2004*

Minnesota	10,230
Texas	6,572
New York	5,792
Georgia	4,696
California	3,876
Pennsylvania	3,740
Arizona	3,560
Virginia	3,507
Maryland	2,695
Ohio	2,679

Source: DHS Yearbook of Immigration Statistics, 2004.

The patterns of Liberian and Sudanese secondary migration differ from their East African counterparts. Sudanese have been placed and largely remain in the south and southwest – Texas, Arizona, Tennessee, Georgia – as well as New York. In contrast, the largest number of Liberians resettled along the east coast – New York, Pennsylvania, New Jersey, Rhode Island, Maryland – as well as Minnesota.[106] The same states that received the largest number of initial refugee arrivals between 2000

[106] *Id.* at 66.

TABLE 2.9. *African refugee arrival distributions, 2010–2012*

Texas	9,243
California	8,975
New York	6,192
Arizona	4,962
Ohio	4,697
Washington	4,445
Minnesota	3,722
Georgia	3,616
Colorado	3,264
Connecticut	1,735
Missouri	1,241

Source: DHS Yearbook of Immigration Statistics, 2012.

and 2004 – Minnesota and Ohio – also received the largest number of secondary migrants between 2000 and 2005.[107] About 13 percent of Minnesota's foreign-born in 2000 were from Africa – a higher percentage than any other state in the country. Most come as refugees from Liberia, Somalia, and Sudan.[108]

The concentration of African refugees in specific geographic regions reveals the importance of family, economic, social, educational, and, in some cases, climatic factors in determining the initial and secondary patterns of settlement. States with generous assistance programs also attract both secondary and primary refugee migrants due to the presence of potential sponsors. The presence of a large cohort of a particular ethnic community tends to be a significant factor in the decision of where refugees settle.[109]

2.7 ETHIOPIANS

Given the significant numbers of refugees that have entered from Ethiopia and Somalia since 1990, a more in-depth look at those communities in the United States is informative. The experience of the smaller Sudanese refugee community also provides opportunities for interesting observations.

[107] *Id.* at 69.

[108] Stephanie L. Mitchell, Assimilation and Acculturation: The Effects of Family, Religion, and Culture on the Public Education of Somali Females in Rural Southwest Minnesota 17 (2012) (Ph.D. dissertation, Capella University) (on file with author).

[109] Wong, *supra* note 92, at 115.

First-Wave Royalists

Ethiopians who entered from 1920 to 1974 are often referred to as the first wave, royalists, or exiles.[110] The first Ethiopians who came to the United States were cousins of Emperor Haile Selassie or children of nobility who came as students. After Ethiopian patriots chased out the Italians with the assistance of the British army and Royal Air Force in 1941, reforms included instituting English language as the second official language and medium of instruction. That further encouraged interest in studying in the United States.[111]

Many of the first wave were beneficiaries of scholarships offered by the United States Agency for International Development (USAID) in addition to financial support from the emperor. Selassie saw the possibility for students educated abroad to become agents of modernization.[112] Thousands of Ethiopians studied in American universities, as well as in France and the United Kingdom, and many returned to serve in various professional capacities that strengthened the emperor's governance. After the 1950s, the United States had replaced France as the main destination for Ethiopian students because of strong U.S.-Ethiopia diplomatic ties.

Scores of students stayed in the United States, especially after Selassie was overthrown in 1974 by the army and a group of junior officers proceeded to impose a military dictatorship.[113] Ethiopian students in the United States were politically active, with left-wing tendencies.[114] Many in the first wave came from Addis Ababa, the capitol, or other urban areas that developed in the late nineteenth and early twentieth centuries. In contrast, their parents or grandparents came from the countryside as rural-urban migrants; some of them may have resettled in the capital as part of the emperor's retinue.[115]

Almost all of the first generation of Ethiopians who came to the United States were members of the ruling elite; they were blue-blooded aristocrats. The group found it hard to assimilate. The royalist generation distanced themselves from African Americans as long as they could when they first arrived.[116] Still, Ethiopians in the United States in the 1960s participated in the fight against racial segregation

[110] Mohammed Hamid Mohammed, Imagining and Performing Habasha Identity: The Ethiopian Diaspora in the Areas of Washington, D.C. 38 (2006) (Ph.D. dissertation, Northwestern University) (on file with author); Moran, *supra* note 102, at 90; Kassahun Haile Kebede, Double Engagements: The Transnational Experiences of Ethiopian immigrants in the Washington, D.C., Metropolitan Area 52 (2012) (Ph.D. dissertation, Syracuse University) (on file with author).

[111] Mohammed, *supra* note 110, at 38–40.

[112] Kebede, *supra* note 110, at 71–72.

[113] For further Ethiopian history, *see id.* at 67–69.

[114] Mohammed, *supra* note 110, at 41.

[115] Moran, *supra* note 102, at 39.

[116] Kebede, supra note 110, at 108.

and in the civil rights movement. Some embraced the "transformative effects of the Black Power Movement" and many came to regard themselves as both African American and Ethiopian American.[117]

Many of those who settled in the United States represented a middle class with a high educational and professional backgrounds. The royalists were small in number but high on the social profile, living scattered across the United States. Over time, their work led to solid careers, reaching executive positions or starting their own businesses.[118] Eventually, many of these "exiles" who arrived in the United States before the revolution were able to find some legal status, through marriage or work, in order to remain permanently.[119] Some were granted political asylum.[120] Others who were unable to obtain lawful permanent resident status were given extended voluntary departure status; some simply became undocumented by overstaying their visas.[121]

The royalist members of the first wave left Ethiopia in the 1970s. Many attended the same schools together in Ethiopia and in the United States. Their families worked for the government and most led privileged lives. They became dissatisfied with the imperial administration's resistance to change and unwillingness to introduce political reform.[122] For many royalists, coming to the United States was almost like a homecoming; even those who had never been to the United States were influenced by three decades of the U.S. presence in Ethiopia.[123] After the military government was overthrown in 1991, many royalists went home, only to realize that the home they imagined existed only in their minds.[124]

Second-Wave Revolutionaries

The second wave, referred to as revolutionaries by some,[125] entered from 1974 to 1991. This was a larger group, traumatized by civil war, that was largely responsible for the creation of Little Ethiopia in Washington, DC – today the U.S. city with the highest concentration of Ethiopians.[126]

117 *Id.* at 109–10.
118 Mohammed, *supra* note 110, at 42; Moran, *supra* note 102, at 116.
119 Moran, *supra* note 102. at 90.
120 For example, when the revolutionary war in Ethiopia commenced and Selassie was deposed in 1974, a number of students intending to earn university degrees were stuck in Seattle, Washington; many became asylum seekers and remained in the state. JOSEPH W. SCOTT & SOLOMON A. GETAHUN, LITTLE ETHIOPIA OF THE PACIFIC NORTHWEST 52 (2013).
121 Moran, *supra* note 102. at 90.
122 Kebede, *supra* note 110, at 71–72.
123 *Id.* at 75.
124 *Id.* at 77–78.
125 *Id.* at 52.
126 Mohammed, *supra* note 110, at 42–43.

The 1974 deposing of the monarchy (the Ethiopian Revolution) revamped the social, economic, political, and ideological landscape of Ethiopia. One of the first political targets was breaking any links with the United States while moving more toward the Soviet camp. American- and European-educated leftists along with students in higher institutions of learning in Ethiopia fought for change. The military took full advantage of this fertile climate, bringing in a junta to fill the power vacuum following the discrediting of the octogenarian monarch. The last triggering factor was the first major famine in the early 1970s that students and scholars accused the emperor of hiding.[127]

The United States responded politically with its power to accept refugees. As part of its strategic containment of communism and its anti-Soviet stand, the United States allowed Ethiopian refugees to resettle in the United States; this occurred in tandem with the expanded definition of refugees in the 1980 Refugee Act.[128] During the 1980s, the United States airlifted thousands of Ethiopian refugees suffering in Sudan and Kenya. More than 33,000 were resettled, and Ethiopians constituted 93 percent of all African refugees admitted to the United States during the decade.

Thousands more refugees were resettled in the 1990s, including some who had been students sent to socialist countries but then defected to Western Europe when the Soviet Union crumbled. This radicalized generation came of age in the 1960s and 1970s and was often associated with Ethiopian student movement. They were organized and vocal, and, ironically, condemned Western imperialism. They embraced Marxism and idolized Ho Chi Minh and Che Guevara.[129]

The second wave came with complicated cultural and political baggage. Many tried to continue their political agenda, raising money and resources for their comrades in Sudan and Ethiopia. After their arrival with extended family members, Ethiopian restaurants, businesses, churches, and media organizations sprang up in the District of Columbia. A large number took low-level jobs as cab drivers and parking lot attendants, despite their relatively high educational profile; many refugees were young people who held high school degrees or less, yet aspired to higher-level employment opportunities.[130] Some who accepted these jobs were professionals with graduate degrees and extensive higher-level experience. This group absorbed the first wave in terms of influence, asserting their own ethnic "Habasha" or east African character.[131]

[127] *Id.* at 44.
[128] *Id.* at 46.
[129] Kebede, *supra* note 100, at 81–82.
[130] Mohammed, *supra* note 110, at 47; Moran, *supra* note 102, at 116.
[131] Mohammed, *supra* note 110, at 47.

Third-Wave Diversity Visa Winners

The third wave began entering in 1991 and continues today. Many have entered on the diversity visa lottery program. After the collapse of the Soviet Union, the reestablishment of improved relationships between Ethiopia and the United States resulted in a decreasing number of Ethiopian refugees. These changes coincided with the introduction of the diversity visa lottery in the immigration reforms of 1990. By 2006, Ethiopia reached its annual cap of 3,500. Over a ten-year period, more than 50,000 Ethiopian lottery winners and their family members would enter. Hundreds of thousands apply every year, and the U.S. embassy in Addis Ababa is the busiest consular office among the foreign diplomatic missions in the city.[132]

By the 1990s, when the diversity visa lottery was in full swing, the Ethiopian economy hit rock bottom. The Ethiopian government had spent billions to flush out ethnic insurgents. Support from the Soviet Union dried up in 1989 as it focused on the problems that led to its eventual collapse. In 1991, a coalition of rebels ousted the socialist military regime and adopted neoliberal economic policies. Under a structural adjustment program of the World Bank, Ethiopia privatized most, if not all, of government-owned properties and laid off thousands of employees. The plan was to funnel resources toward producing goods for export, but the strategy did not work, and no meaningful recovery followed.[133]

The migration of diversity visa lottery winners was facilitated by several factors beyond the dire economy. The new Ethiopian government lifted a ban on outmigration, and exit passports became obtainable. Members of previous generations of emigrants were allowed to visit. Those visitors whetted the appetite of prospective migrants, and they also used the family visa categories for qualified relatives. The implementation of the diversity visa was timely for Africans, even though the program was intended to bring more Europeans to America and was aimed at mitigating the effect of the immigration laws, which favored those with relatives in the United States. In Africa, Ethiopia, Ghana, and Nigeria especially benefited from the diversity visa program. From 2005 to 2009, a total of 14,958 Ethiopians settled in the United States using diversity visas. The diversity visa group constitutes about a quarter of Ethiopians who arrive each year.[134] Most Ethiopian diversity visa recipients come from modest or poor backgrounds. They are not executives, aristocrats, or political activists.[135]

Of course, not all diversity visa winners are of lower economic status and not all who win make it to the United States. Before a visa can be granted, diversity

[132] *Id.* at 49.
[133] Kebede, *supra* note 110, at 91–92.
[134] *Id.* at 92.
[135] *Id.* at 93.

winners have to have an affidavit of support or a job waiting for them in the United States. Each winner has to pay nonrefundable immigrant visa processing and surcharge fees of $819. The average Ethiopian cannot afford this amount. Richer families search for lucky winners to arrange sham marriages for members of their family that could make them eligible for immigration. In return, they cover all the expenses for both their own family member and the lottery winner. A 2007 report from the Government Accountability Office showed an increase in "fraudulent DV marriages" from many parts of the world, including Addis Ababa. The report stated that in Addis Ababa, "fraudulent DV couples go to great lengths to try to prove their relationship is legitimate, including backdated marriage certificates and staged wedding photographs, and some even incur pregnancies for the sake of the visa."[136]

Unlike previous generations, the diversity visa generation benefited from access to existing Ethiopian migrant networks in the United States for information about jobs and housing. They have followed in the footsteps of the revolutionaries by starting their own businesses, most of which serve multiethnic communities.[137] The main difference of the diversity visa generation from the previous clusters is that they hail from different regions of Ethiopia, a product of the lottery's randomness. They have lowered the educational profile of Ethiopian immigrants. But diversity visa members call themselves the "true face" of Ethiopia and regard themselves as an accurate reflection of the existing situation in Ethiopia.[138]

The number of third-wave immigrants, along with good relations between the United States and Ethiopia, has strongly impacted the cultural, social, and business networks within the Ethiopian community. Since the 1990s, the number of churches, restaurants, and community organizations has increased many times, strengthening the ethos established by the earlier group.[139]

First Waves to Los Angeles

Although Washington, DC has become the site of "Little Ethiopia," the experience of Ethiopian migrants in other parts of the United States also is important. For example, the earliest Ethiopian settlers to Los Angeles were among the college-educated members of the highest pre-revolutionary classes. The refugee group that followed was from lower socioeconomic backgrounds, with less education.[140]

In Los Angeles, the first two waves of Ethiopians lived in specific residential neighborhoods and buildings. Most of the clusters were in areas containing high

[136] *Id.* at 93 (citing GAO at 4).
[137] *Id.* at 93–94.
[138] *Id.* at 95–96.
[139] Mohammed, *supra* note 110, at 50.
[140] Moran, *supra* note 102, at 138–39.

percentages of other minority communities, like African Americans and Latinos, where rent was low.[141] Early Ethiopian restaurants and businesses were distributed throughout Los Angeles.[142] By the mid-1990s, an Ethiopian business district had been established, where several restaurants and an import shop were located within the same block.[143]

The young Ethiopian refugees who arrived in Los Angeles had extremely high expectations and ambitions. They sought higher levels of education to obtain good jobs, such as professional or managerial positions, or wanted to establish their own businesses.[144] Most – exiles and refugees – spoke of returning home someday. They recalled good times back home rather nostalgically.[145]

For the first two waves of Ethiopians to Los Angeles, the Ethiopian Orthodox Church and a self-help group served important roles in Ethiopian cohesion for many parts of the community.[146] The church was attractive to the traditionally oriented individuals. On the other hand, the self-help group was more important for those who identified with the Ethiopian national label, in contrast with those who identified themselves as Eritrean even prior to Eritrea's independence in the early 1990s.[147] Ethiopians came together through the church or other groups for spiritual, self-help, and recreational purposes, and to support famine relief in the homeland.[148]

Ethiopian Migrant Identity

Ethiopian migrants who have come to the United States in the past half-century are products of Ethiopia's ideological seesaw and of major developments in the United States. Transformations in Ethiopia from semifeudal state to semi-capitalist economy through the mid-1970s, to the Soviet takeover in the 1980s, to reincorporation into global capitalism and the neoliberal agenda since 1991 mean that Ethiopians who have departed for the United States did so from different situations and for various reasons. These situations defined why people immigrated and shaped the frames through which each group interpreted the behavior of other groups and their own identity in the United States.[149]

Given economic and social globalization, the construction and perpetuation of identity today likely is the outcome of strong transnational networks. Many Ethiopian

[141] *Id.* at 139.
[142] *Id.* at 140.
[143] *Id.* at 309.
[144] *Id.* at 181.
[145] *Id.* at 183.
[146] *Id.* at 215–22.
[147] *Id.* at 261.
[148] *Id.* at 233.
[149] Kebede, *supra* note 110, at 70.

immigrants enter a strong transnational community, where they come into contact with co-nationals. The networks and institutions they encounter cultivate and perpetuate a sense of group racial consciousness and cultural identity.[150]

Regardless of whether the construction of Habasha identity is a stunt or a visual truth, Ethiopian migrants have made repeated efforts to reimagine themselves as a significant collective group. Intense debate has been swirling around black identity, which once was monolithic and taken for granted. Ethiopian migrants are engaging the host society on their own terms.[151]

Like racial identities, cultural identities also are on the line when people immigrate. Immigrants construct social fields and practice bicultural identities that connect the sending and receiving countries. This involves integrating with the culture of the receiving country to a certain degree while simultaneously maintaining ties to the culture of the sending country. The dynamics at work are the accommodation to American mainstream society combined with the continuation of traditional Ethiopian cultural practices, producing not a split identity but a transnational construction.[152]

As in the West African migrant context,[153] the transnational localities Ethiopian migrants create are hot spots for their communities. They provide a milieu where immigrants can enjoy being transmigrants. Transnationalism is not about being constantly on the move for them; their networks remain strongly grounded in particular places.[154]

Ethiopians are clearly involved in transnational politics. The topic pervades almost everything and remains a staple of conversation, even in restaurants. Ethiopian cab drivers lecture passengers about latest political developments in Ethiopia; parking lot attendants are adept at spreading word about when a demonstration will be held, and mobilizing the community.[155]

However, the political views of Ethiopian migrants certainly are not uniform. Ethiopians who came to the United States at the end of the first wave in the mid-1970s were clearly anticommunist; they were monarchists who still dreamed of restoring the monarchy.[156] By the time the larger waves were admitted during the 1980s and 1990s, they too were disillusioned with socialism, and the United States accepted them with open arms.[157] Today, activists may organize public rallies and prolonged formal meetings on Ethiopian issues, but community leaders disagree

[150] *Id.* at 116.
[151] *Id.* at 122.
[152] *Id.* at 122–23.
[153] *See* notes 39–65, *supra*, and accompanying text.
[154] Kebede, *supra* note 110, at 134.
[155] *Id.* at 144.
[156] *Id.* at 164.
[157] *Id.* at 163.

about strategies for shaping homeland politics. Some migrants advocate armed struggle as the only viable alternative for bringing about political change; others reject the call for any kind of violence, hoping and expecting that the government will once again open up.[158]

In the face of these divergent views, remittances to the homeland remain steady and strong. Some migrants send money to their families back home from time to time as a "compensation for" absence.[159] However, the vast majority send remittances to families, close relatives, and friends because the latter need money. The transfers are a lifeline, far more significant than any token for absence.[160]

The Ethiopian government has seized on this opportunity, officially urging immigrants to invest. Embassy officials in the District of Columbia go door to door in Ethiopian neighborhoods urging patriotic entrepreneurs to make investments in Ethiopia. A radio program paid for by the Ethiopian government advertises investment opportunities.[161] Given such a consistent and large flow of cash (from Ethiopians all over the world), in 2008, Ethiopia was the first African country to set up diaspora bonds, which are issued by the state-run power company. The plan is to use bonds to build the largest hydroelectric dam on the continent.[162]

Integration into U.S. Society

Most Ethiopian migrants are economically driven. Jobs are scarce in Ethiopia's urban areas, and unemployment remains high. Yet a cultural barrier – *yilunnta* – complicates the issue. *Yilunnta* is when someone experiences intense shame because of what others think and say about one's family based on the kind of work family members do. *Yilunnta* robs people of the willingness to take any kind of work available. For example, it would be unthinkable for a college graduate to work at a local gas station in Ethiopia, as they do here in the United States. In addition, it is culturally acceptable for working-age adults in Ethiopia to continue to live with their parents, especially while they are attending school.[163]

When Ethiopians come to the United States, *yilunnta* sometimes has its day. Finding jobs for Ethiopian immigrants was one of the greatest challenges for sponsoring agencies and families during the 1980s. Most immigrants either turned down job offers or walked off jobs. The major complaints were that the jobs they were offered were too menial; migrants felt that they were not appreciated for the

[158] *Id.* at 198.
[159] *Id.* at 236.
[160] *Id.* at 236–37.
[161] *Id.* at 216.
[162] *Id.* at 238.
[163] *Id.* at 124.

skills they had. Sponsors who had gone to great lengths to find employment were frustrated, not understanding the cultural background.[164] Over time, attitudes among the migrants were forced to change.[165] But even then, to the dismay of some sponsors, some immigrants of this generation wanted to go to school full time while the sponsoring families were helping out.[166]

Race has become an important factor in Ethiopian integration in the United States. Ethiopians in the District of Columbia are ambivalent about being classified as African or black, and often resent such classifications. Interestingly, some of the earlier Ethiopian immigrants to the United States "socialized with and had a better understanding of African Americans than the Ethiopians who came later."[167] Just like most other immigrants, Ethiopians arrive with their own racial ideologies and categories that can be very different from those in the United States. In Ethiopia, the racial categories are based on a combination of color, hair type, facial features, and sometimes socioeconomic status. Because they emphasize phenotypic features, at least two racial categories – black (*Shankilla* or *tiqur*) and reddish-brown (*qey*) – are present. "Black" is a term reserved for low-status groups, especially people who live in peripheral areas. The ruling groups – the Amhara and Tigre, which most Ethiopian immigrants belong to – consider themselves to be racially different and "superior" to the *Shankilla*.[168] The struggle for the creation of transnational identities must be seen and understood at different levels. It may involve struggle against preexisting racial categories that may eclipse and even deny other ethnic identities. Some individuals may want to be viewed as "ethnic American" or even as American, period.[169]

The diverse backgrounds of Ethiopian migrants influenced the identities of their children. Many of the royalist generation who migrated in the early 1970s were college-educated, English-speaking professionals and belonged to the elite class. In the United States, they built solid careers that afforded them a better standard of living, and they rank high on the economic and social profile, for example, as World Bank experts or university professors. They were more concerned with their children's performance in school and with integration in American culture than with whether or not their children were bicultural or held onto some aspect of Ethiopian identity.[170] The royalist generation did not have the benefit of tightly knit

164 *Id.* at 124–25.
165 *Id.* at 125–26.
166 *Id.* at 125.
167 Mohammed, *supra* note 110, at 42; Kebede, *supra* note 110, at 102–03.
168 Kebede, *supra* note 110, at 107–08.
169 *Id.* at 269.
170 *Id.* at 271.

Ethiopian immigrant communities. As a result, they may not have been able to socialize their children in strong Ethiopian traditions.[171]

Today, almost all second-generation Ethiopians used the label Ethiopian American. Some even add another identity to the ethnic label: Ethiopian African American. They are mostly well educated and do not see themselves as having fixed identities. During their teen years, they experienced degrees of uncertainty, ambivalence, and even confusion about who they were. They needed to see beyond borders and national groups.[172]

Ethiopian Americans who moved to or were born in the suburbs had a variety of experiences. Children of the royalists of the early 1970s were there because their parents had a better economic standing. They were often rejected by African Americans, but were treated as African Americans by whites; they were extremely ambivalent about where exactly they fit in. In adulthood, they continued to search for identity. A shift in identity sometimes happened because of a trip to Ethiopia, because of a college course, or through informal conversations with a schoolteacher. Their continued exclusion by African Americans is a major reason why some of the second generation desire to construct an Ethiopian-American identity.[173] They are black but they are "different blacks" than African Americans.[174] Some may emphasize intra-racial differences, while others dwell on historical and cultural differences that set them apart from native blacks.[175] In fact, the most important factor behind transnationalism for those in the second generation is discrimination that they experience.[176]

African migrants sometimes feel that American blacks, whom they thought would welcome them as brothers, are giving them the cold shoulder. Part of the problem appears to be linguistic. Some migrants in the South found it difficult to understand the blacks' accent at times, and blacks found it hard to understand African migrants. The reluctance of some Africans to initiate conversations, coupled with their clipped, unfamiliar accent, can also lead American blacks to conclude that the Africans are distant and haughty.[177]

The second generation regard themselves as Americans, regardless of what others think. They are emotionally attached to America, but not without being critical. Being independent and free are cherished qualities about being American.[178] Some

[171] *Id.* at 272.
[172] *Id.* at 282–83.
[173] *Id.* at 290.
[174] *Id.* at 292.
[175] *Id.* at 292.
[176] *Id.* at 319.
[177] Mesghina Ghebremedhin, The Adaptation of Eritrean Migrants in the Los Angeles City Area 101 (1997) (Ph.D. dissertation, Biola University) (on file with author).
[178] Kebede, *supra* note 110, at 302–03.

feel that they have not suffered from racism or discrimination. They know African Americans are the most discriminated group in U.S. society and that they are treated better because they make other people know that they are Ethiopian. Others see racism as something normal and natural in America but refuse to be trapped by it or excessively concerned. Still others definitely feel victimized by racism.[179]

Having grown up where cultures intersect and overlap, the second generation sees themselves well equipped with resources that enable them to blend and juggle identities. They cannot be pigeonholed into one culture. Their identities, their lives, and their thinking make sense to themselves in terms of both Ethiopian and American identities. They have components of both identities, a duality that is desirable in a globalized world.[180] Being connected to their homelands is an integral part of their identities.[181]

Many of the second generation traveled to Ethiopia because they wanted to know what the country and the people looked like – a phenomenon often referred to as "roots tourism."[182] They were interested in learning the culture and language, but also in doing business and being part of development activities. Going to Ethiopia gave them answers about how and why Ethiopians are culturally different from members of other African ethnic groups.[183] The journeys helped them appreciate the culture, become attached, develop friends, and understand their parents better, while participating in helping the needy.[184]

The second generation agrees with their parents on the fundamental values of Ethiopian transnational politics, among which the democratization of Ethiopia is central. They too closely monitor what transpires in Ethiopian politics.[185] Many are involved in charitable activities (mainly sponsoring children), fund-raisers for nongovernmental organizations operating in Ethiopia, or working themselves in Ethiopia. Child sponsorship is their most common involvement in transnational activity, helping orphans, collecting monthly contributions, and paying living expenses.[186]

The second generation challenges and resists the established, normative, and even determinative categorization of them as African Americans, although most have nothing against that group. They do not feel fully accepted by mainstream groups, whether that group is Ethiopians, African Americans, or Americans. The

[179] *Id.* at 305–06.
[180] *Id.* at 314.
[181] *Id.* at 315.
[182] *Id.* at 331.
[183] *Id.* at 331–32.
[184] *Id.* at 333.
[185] *Id.* at 344.
[186] *Id.* at 359–62.

labels "American" or "Ethiopian" do not sufficiently describe their belonging and identities. They feel up to the task of interacting, working, and living with different identity groups; they have cultural competencies to blend and juggle identities. Many of them feel that being transnational means being American.[187]

While second generation regard themselves as Ethiopians and Ethiopian Americans, "Ethiopian" and "Habasha" are conspicuously and interchangeably used as self-identifiers. Being Ethiopian runs through their blood. They have experienced frustration as they try to bridge contradictions and chasms related to negotiating Ethiopian identity.[188] An internal controversy about being or not being Ethiopian is related to language. Some of the second generation speak at least one Ethiopian language but prefer English as their primary language. Many parents sought to prevent the loss of language, so some of the second generation are fairly proficient in an Ethiopian language.[189]

The second generation stands at the forefront of having constant and frequent interaction with American society. They have become the face of Ethiopia in America. They are aware of media portrayals that continue to advance the image of a poverty-stricken and violence-ridden African continent that is falling off the cliff of progress.[190] In response, many of the second generation engage in "educating" Americans or "fighting the Discovery Channel" by citing and invoking Ethiopian cultural and historical achievements.[191] This is an extension of their childhood experiences when they were "the only black" or "the only Habasha" in their classrooms, forced to speak on behalf of the entire continent.[192]

2.8 SOMALI REFUGEES

When Barkhad Abdi and three other amateur Somali actors from Minnesota learned they had won major roles in the new Tom Hanks movie, "Captain Phillips," they tore off their clothes and jumped into the Pacific Ocean. Abdi and his fellow actors from Minneapolis portray Somali pirates who hijacked an American cargo ship off the Horn of Africa in 2009 and took its captain, played by Hanks, hostage. Abdi and the other three Somali actors – Faysal Ahmed, Barkhad Abdirahman, and Mahat M. Ali – all answered an open casting call at the Brian Coyle Community Center, a hub of Minneapolis's large Somali population, in November 2011. Generic fliers sought actors for what was described only as a new Tom Hanks movie. More than

[187] *Id.* at 387.
[188] *Id.* at 294.
[189] *Id.* at 296.
[190] *Id.* at 334.
[191] *Id.* at 338.
[192] *Id.* at 338.

700 aspiring actors showed up, filling the center. Casting director Debbie DeLisi said she chose Minneapolis because the city has the largest population of Somalis in the United States. Another casting call was held in Columbus, Ohio, also home to a growing Somali population.[193]

Abdi was working as a limousine driver in Minnesota when he attended an open casting call. Born in Mogadishu in 1985, he described the Somalia of his early childhood as "a very peaceful place. Everyone loved each other, everyone was a neighbor, there was a community." The country's crippling civil war broke out in 1991, when he was six. "It turned overnight to chaos, killing and guns," he said. "It was a very scary time for me and my family." His family fled for Yemen the following year, and emigrated to the United States when Abdi was fourteen, finally settling near Minneapolis.[194]

The casting director was right to hold auditions in Minneapolis. The U.S. Census says roughly 25,000 Somalis live in Minnesota, while local advocates peg the number as high as 100,000.[195] In 2010, the American Community Survey estimated the total Somali-born population in the United States to be about 85,700. The Minnesota Historical Society estimates it at more than 100,000.[196] Whatever the actual population, given the tragedy and history of Somalian displacement, the fact of Abdi's resettlement to Minneapolis is no surprise.

An independent nation since only the 1960s, the east coast African nation of Somalia is home to 7 million Sunni Muslims. The country, about the size of Texas, is populated by nomads and herdsmen who must compete with war, poverty, and drought as they try to find grazing land for their animals. As a result of drought, famine, and the corrupt regime of warlord Mohamed Farrah Aidid, the Somali capital of Mogadishu fell in 1988, and for three years war raged until the U.S. military intervened. Somalia and the United States were allies during the Cold War, and from 1983 to 1990, Somalia received almost $500 million worth of military resources including physical military presence. Between 1983 and 1990, 500,000 people died before the violence and hostility was contained; 300,000 were victims of starvation.[197]

[193] *How Tom Hanks recreated cargo ship skipper's Somali hostage ordeal in true-story movie, Captain Phillips*, THE DAILY TELEGRAPH, Oct. 11, 2013, at http://www.dailytelegraph.com.au/news/how-tom-hanks-recreated-cargo-ship-skipper8217s-somali-hostage-ordeal-in-truestory-movie-captain-phillips/story-fniocx4q-1226738483698

[194] Tim Walker, *Captain Phillips actor Barkhad Abdi struggles financially despite Oscar nomination*, THE INDEPENDENT, Mar. 5, 2014, at http://www.independent.co.uk/arts-entertainment/films/news/captain-phillips-actor-barkhad-abdi-struggles-despite-oscar-nomination-9171593.html

[195] Jeff Baenen, *'Captain Phillips' features Minn. Somali actors*, ASSOCIATED PRESS, Oct. 12, 2013, at http://www.dailyherald.com/article/20131012/entlife/710129957/

[196] Minnesota Historical Society, Becoming Minnesotan: Stories of Recent Immigrants and Refugees, at http://education.mnhs.org/immigration/communities/somali

[197] Mitchell, *supra* note 108, at 1.

Twenty years after the United States formally ended its mission to Somalia,[198] the country is still torn by the effects of civil war, the collapse of the Somali government, and a series of natural disasters including one of the worst droughts in history. Two million Somalis were displaced to other African countries. Some are still living in refugee camps today. Another 800,000 people left Somalia and are living elsewhere in the world, including, Canada, Great Britain, Australia, and the United States.[199] The total number displaced out of a total population of about 9 million makes the Somali diaspora one of the largest globally, proportionate to population size.[200]

Somali migrants who came to the United States as refugees are attempting to begin their lives anew, determined to overcome the tragedy of forcible displacement. Like most refugees, they have suffered the trauma of losing loved ones and all their belongings, having been uprooted from their homes.[201] They were forced to leave behind everything they know – their language, their culture, their personal property, and their loved ones. Most are focused on issues of survival and resettlement – finding adequate housing, coping with cultural adjustment, overcoming loss and isolation, and learning English. There may also be a danger that the hostilities of the civil war, which was mainly along clan frontiers, may still be prevalent in the new refugee communities, thus complicating resettlement efforts.[202]

The Twin Cities metropolitan area is estimated to have more than half of the arrivals from Somalia. The foreign-born population in Minnesota more than doubled during the 1990s from 110,000 to 240,000. They tend to settle in metropolitan areas, especially in St. Paul-Minneapolis.[203] Four of every five Somalis in the state live in Minneapolis, with 80 percent living in South Minneapolis. The Twin Cities area has become the de facto "capital" of the Somali community in North America, although some Somalis have started settling in smaller towns around southern Minnesota and western Wisconsin.[204] Nearly a third of Minnesota public school students speak Somali at home. Aside from being home to the largest Somali community in the United States, the Twin Cities also are among the top American receiving areas for other eastern African migrants.[205]

[198] The United States formally ended the mission to Somalia in 1994, which cost $1.7 billion and left 43 U.S. soldiers dead and another 153 wounded. Annabel Lee Hogg, *Timeline: Somalia, 1991–2008*, The Atlantic, Dec. 22, 2008, at http://www.theatlantic.com/magazine/archive/2008/12/timeline-somalia-1991–2008/307190/

[199] Mitchell, *supra* note 108, at 1; Thadeus Joseph Shio, Housing Experiences of Somali immigrants in the Twin Cities, Minnesota – A Housing Careers Perspective 23 (2006) (Ph.D. dissertation, University of Minnesota) (on file with author).

[200] Shome, *supra* note 4, at 141–42.

[201] Shio, *supra* note 200, at 4.

[202] *Id.* at 12.

[203] *Id.* at 14–15.

[204] *Id.* at 26.

[205] Pendaz, *supra* note 20, at 51–52.

Most Somalis who live in Minnesota came directly to the United States as refugees. One-third came directly from refugee camps; many experienced torture. Others settled first in another state and then relocated to the state, largely because of the established Somali community and the availability of unskilled jobs. The initial wave was attracted to Minnesota by the presence of food-processing jobs, while others were sent directly from refugee camps or were attracted to other states by job opportunities. Some also were drawn to small Minnesota cities by meat-processing plants and industries that do not require English proficiency.[206]

Thus, the adults primarily fill jobs that do not require strong English skills, or in stores that provide businesses and services to other Somali migrants.[207] They work in multiple fields, including the hospitality industry, janitorial services, food and beverage, parking lot attending, taxi driving, and assembly line work. On the other hand, some skilled workers were hired as teachers, accountants, interpreters, and entrepreneurs.[208]

Challenges to Adjustment

Somali refugees face many challenges to adjustment in the United States. Because of limited English proficiency, they often encounter problems learning how to cope with different legal, social service, employment, and housing systems in the United States.[209] Most are extremely disadvantaged, having experienced severe psychological trauma. The English language is unfamiliar to them, as are U.S. societal norms and customs.[210] More than a quarter of Somali households are headed by females with no husband present, and about 70 percent of those households live in poverty.[211]

In spite of overall receptivity in places like the Twin Cities, the reaction to Somalis is not always positive. Some areas witnessed protests and calls to limit their numbers. In Lewiston, Maine, the mayor openly criticized an influx of Somali migrants, a position that was echoed by a white supremacist group.[212] Somali students, especially boys, are vulnerable to pressures of drugs, gangs, and belligerence. Elders attribute this to the fact that there is often a lack of male influence in the family where a patriarch is crucial to maintaining cultural norms; many fathers, uncles, and older brothers were killed in clan warfare in Somalia, making single motherhood an unnatural reality for Somali mothers. The role of patriarch often goes to an adolescent boy who has neither the maturity nor the desire to keep a family together.

[206] Mitchell, *supra* note 108, at 17; Shio, *supra* note 200, at 4, 26.
[207] Shio, *supra* note 200, at 26.
[208] Ahmed Ismail Yusuf, People of Minnesota: Somalis in Minnesota 534 (2012).
[209] Shio, *supra* note 200, at 28.
[210] Shome, *supra* note 4, at 14.
[211] Shio, *supra* note 200, at 28–29.
[212] But in the same town, 4,000 supporters showed up at a rally. *Id.* at 24.

He may look for an outlet, such as other young men in the same situation, becoming involved in criminal behavior.[213] If convicted, these young men face deportation to Somalia despite an absence of a functioning government back home.[214]

Most Somali refugees have, however, successfully come together to adapt to their new life in America. For example, in Kansas City, Missouri, where 5,000 refugees settled by 2011,[215] Somali refugees stay connected and flourish as a community through activities that bring them to places that have visible elements of Somali material culture and also to places that might not have a visible Somali-ness. Over time, these places have become centralized sites of congregation, where community members meet and discuss their lives and problems, while ruminating about life back home. The Somali Foundation, a community-based organization, serves as such a connector for the community. Also, areas in the city have evolved with concentrations of Somali ethnic businesses that not only provide the community with Somali goods and services but also serve as meeting places.[216]

While the Somalis who live in the Twin Cities area are there because of refugee resettlement efforts and secondary migration due to employment and social attractions, the Somalis in Kansas City came because of the efforts of Jewish Vocational Service, a contracted refugee service agency based in Kansas City. The city provides affordable housing and educational opportunities apart from ample job opportunities to people with limited language skills.[217] Most of the refugees live in the low-income, northeastern part of the city – historically an immigrant destination in the city. Other than Somalis, the area is populated by Mexican immigrants and African Americans.[218]

The refugees think of themselves as members of a distinctive ethnic community, and they are extremely proud of their Somali identity. They wish to preserve their cultural heritage, even as they interact and absorb elements of the host society. They are aided by both formal and informal community organizations that provide them infrastructure to form networks;[219] to keep their values intact, Somalis have formed

[213] Mitchell, *supra* note 108, at 31.

[214] Eric Jeffrey Ong Hing, *Deportation into Chaos: The Questionable Removal of Somali Refugees*, 38 U.C. Davis L. Rev. 309 (2004). Successive transitional governments have remained on the verge of collapse. A militant Islamic insurgency has left the country ravaged and in a perpetual state of insecurity despite, or perhaps because of, an intervention by the Ethiopian military from December 2006 to January 2009. The Somali situation has now become one of the world's worst humanitarian and security crises, with the Ethiopian military intervention, combined with the U.S. bombings of suspected militant hideouts, setting in motion a chain of catastrophic events. Officials estimate that 20,000 civilians were killed between December 2006 and 2010. Shome, *supra* note 4, at 35–40.

[215] Shome, *supra* note 4, at 12.

[216] *Id.* at 158–59, 162–64.

[217] *Id.* at 19.

[218] *Id.* at 158.

[219] *Id.* at 159.

their own mosques, cultural organizations, and community programs.[220] Most Somalis follow Islamic law and traditions, with women wearing long dresses with scarves or veils. Sharia law strictly prohibits premarital sex, alcohol, and drugs. In keeping with Islamic law, many men refuse to shake hands with the opposite gender or touch women in any manner.[221]

Jewish Vocational Services contracts with the U.S. Committee for Refugees and Immigrants for resettling Somalis and other refugees in Kansas City. Its services include case management, citizenship classes, transitional cash assistance, pre-drivers education, clothing-housewares-furniture distribution, health care, transportation assistance, employment services, and relationship enhancement classes (e.g., personal communication). Counseling services include assisting refugees and immigrants in changing or adjusting immigration status and a variety of paralegal services to those trying to navigate the sometimes intimidating and complicated procedures necessary to become U.S. citizens.[222]

The Somali Foundation assists the rapidly growing population of Somali refugees and immigrants with the goal of adjusting socially in the United States and to live in economic security and good health. The community-based organization provides services, education, and advocacy while striving to honor Somali culture. The organization was founded in 1999 by Somali refugees who sensed the community's dire need for understanding English, overcoming culture shock, and fighting poverty.[223] Tutoring, English as a Second Language (ESL) classes for adults, citizenship classes, a women's program on financial management, nutrition advice, and health and safety programs are featured. Summer employment opportunities for low-income migrants also are available.[224] The Foundation provides a comprehensive youth program that includes group work on issues such as substance abuse prevention, domestic violence, and black history. The youth program also organizes recreational activities such as soccer and basketball.[225]

Most Somali children coming to the United States have never attended school. Those lucky enough to attend school (mostly boys) prior to entry did so for no more than a few years. Many Somalis are illiterate in their own language. The absence of an established heritage of literacy makes learning in English doubly difficult. This contributes to making the initial educational experience in the United States frightening and uncertain.[226]

[220] Chris Thomlinson, *Somalis Find Home, Hope in Minnesota; Lifestyle: Three of every five immigrants from impoverished nation live here, far from clan warfare*, Los Angeles Times, Nov. 30, 1997.

[221] *Id.*

[222] Shome, *supra* note 4, at 73–77.

[223] *Id.* at 79–80.

[224] *Id.* at 80–81.

[225] *Id.* at 81.

[226] Mitchell, supra note 108, at 1–2.

Different age groups face different integration challenges. For those who come at an early age, integration issues become intertwined with the challenges of adolescence. The need to be accepted by peers and not standing out are acute in the younger Somalis. Some have Somali friends with whom they spend time on weekends, but they are alone at school or at work. Most want to wear American clothes and get rid of any accent in order to fit in with American classmates and coworkers.[227] Interestingly, the younger refugees in Kansas City did not embrace American culture fully. In the future, they want their own children to speak Somali and to be aware of their cultural and religious heritage. Those with younger siblings look out for them, making sure that they go to the *madrassa* – religious classes – and do not spend time with the "wrong crowd."[228]

Arguably, older refugees face more difficulties, grappling with a multitude of issues. They take longer to learn English, to learn to drive, or to learn even the smallest everyday tasks. Memories of their lives in their native country, loss of that life and relatives, the wait and insecurity in the refugee camps, and resettlement in a totally alien society are a lot to absorb.[229] In Somalia, where everyone is Muslim, they were at war because of clan rivalries; people fought because of their clans or sub-clans. The refugees came here and were beginning to have a more secure life until 9/11. At that point, they sensed hatred from other communities because of their religion. Somali refugees found themselves under fire and were made to feel defensive about their faith. They were confronted by coworkers who wanted them to "choose sides."[230] Many refugees were frustrated with some encounters and members of the broader community who did not know where Somalia was and thought it was part of Saudi Arabia. These older Somalis found it hard to concentrate on work because of heightened feelings of "otherness" in the United States. This forced many to recoil further into their own community, far from the host society.[231]

Somalis are known to have a distinct mentality that has contributed to some material success for a number of refugees within the short period that they have been in the United States. Part of the "Somali way" meant trying their absolute best to not apply for public assistance for cash (some received Medicaid or food stamps), or if they had to apply, only relying on it for a short time. Although they may qualify for an initial eight-month refugee assistance package during the resettlement period, many got off the system early to pursue entrepreneurial opportunities like driving cabs or trucks, or opening restaurants, grocery stores, halal meat shops, money

[227] Shome, *supra* note 4, at 103.
[228] *Id.* at 104.
[229] *Id.* at 104.
[230] *Id.* at 108.
[231] *Id.* at 109.

transfer centers, or clothes shops.[232] Fewer than 4 percent of Somalis in Minnesota receive public assistance.[233]

Employment is viewed as both an economic and social imperative. Although their jobs helped pay bills and they were grateful to have them, Somali refugees were not particularly proud of doing many of these jobs or being among the unemployed. Regardless of educational background or area of expertise, Somali refugees would accept work in the lowest-paying sectors.[234] Those without work were greatly frustrated at the inability to find any work. Finding employment was a challenge due to low English language proficiency and being unqualified.[235]

Gender roles are affected by the refugee experience as well. Somalis come from a patriarchal society, where all children are a blessing of God, but greater symbolic value is placed on a male than a female child. Traditionally, a strict division of labor makes women responsible for dealing with domestic tasks, from finding and preparing food, to child-rearing and water and firewood collection. In Somalia, the women were left with little time for involvement in community decisions or education. Women always played a significant role in the economy, but they were generally at home. The civil war affected gender roles beginning in 1988, even for those who eventually came to the United States as refugees. The conflict separated families, and many women were required to take responsibility for their families. They shed traditional roles as caregivers and, both in Dadaab (the Kenyan UNHCR refugee camp) and in the United States, these women have had to fend for themselves and their children.[236]

Somali women in Kansas City work shoulder to shoulder with men, and sometimes they are the sole breadwinners in their families. Some got the very first jobs of their lives in Kansas City. They have to leave their children with relatives, mostly parents/in-laws/grandparents, during the day. But they still carry out all the household chores as usual and do not really have a say in major decisions of the family; those are still made by their husbands. Things are different for some younger Somali women, who are getting married here in the United States. They make decisions for their family whenever necessary, and their husbands are fine with that. Others prefer to stay home with children and perhaps work only part time; some go out and get jobs because their husband's income is insufficient to cover all household expenses.[237]

[232] *Id.* at 167–68.

[233] Chris Thomlinson, *Somalis Find Home, Hope in Minnesota; Lifestyle: Three of every five immigrants from impoverished nation live here, far from clan warfare*, Los Angeles Times, Nov. 30, 1997.

[234] Shome, *supra* note 4, at 172.

[235] *Id.* at 170.

[236] *Id.* at 105–06.

[237] *Id.* at 106.

Somali men in Kansas City are mostly not supportive of women who work or who plan on pursuing a career. Some young, educated men sneer at Somali girls planning to go to graduate school. According to them, women should marry and have children because that is what Somalis do. Many men feel disconcerted when their wives work. Some women think men voice objections to send a message that they are still "in charge." Younger Somali women do not put up with domestic violence and have obtained divorces in order to have a chance at happiness.[238]

In Columbus, Ohio, where another small Somali community has been established, most Somali refugees befriend only those of the same background and ethnicity. Some want it that way and do not even know other non-Somalis in the same apartment building. They do not think the other neighbors are bad, but the refugees often are only acquainted with those of the same tribe or subgroup.[239] There are, however, some Somalis in Columbus who are more integrated and do not live near other Somalis.[240]

On the other hand, some tensions can be found between different Somali ethnic groups even in Columbus, for example, between "Somali Somalis" and the "Somali Bantu." The friction stems from their histories in Somalia. The Bantu were treated terribly in Somalia. So even in the United States, a lack of trust between groups is often noticeable.[241]

Conflict between Somalis and African Americans in Columbus also has emerged. Some Somalis would rather live in white neighborhoods than with African Americans. They perceive African Americans as more aggressive than whites. At times, resettlement agencies and city officials have been brought in to mediate tension between the groups.[242]

Most Somali refugees are interested in becoming U.S. citizens. The primary reasons are practical. They want to relinquish their refugee status for U.S. citizenship because that allows them to get better jobs and enables their college-age children to qualify for in-state tuition and possible scholarships. U.S. citizenship also allows them to travel more freely – including back to Kenya (where refugee relatives can still be found) and perhaps even to parts of Somalia like Puntland (a self-governing and self-proclaimed autonomous region of northern Somalia) or Somaliland. They also know that U.S. citizenship provides them with an opportunity to sponsor the immigration of family members left behind in Dadaab and Somalia to the United States under family preference categories.[243] Beyond the practicalities, many Somali

[238] *Id.* at 107.
[239] Mott, *supra* note 96, at 217.
[240] *Id.* at 217.
[241] *Id.* at 220.
[242] *Id.* at 222.
[243] Shome, *supra* note 4, at 118.

migrants who have become citizens wear U.S. flag pendants and brooches because they view citizenship as a kind of lucky charm; citizenship is viewed as guaranteeing their legal status and entitling them to full membership in American society.[244]

Remittances

Sending money to their families back in Somalia or in Kenya refugee camps when possible is a moral obligation for Somalis in the diaspora. Remittances are their way of showing their relatives and extended family back in the Dadaap camps, elsewhere in Kenya, or in Somalia that they have not been forgotten. The United Nations estimates that $1.6 billion in remittances is sent back annually by Somali migrants living in North America and Europe,[245] which exceeds the official international aid to the country of Somalia. Migrants feel tremendous pressure to send money, especially to the remaining relatives in the camps. Somalis often have to make great sacrifices in their new lives just to be able to send money back to the family. Tension arises within families when migrants here are not able to send money to all the remaining relatives in Dadaab. Those in the United States often have to forego many requirements of daily life to send money; those left behind find it difficult to comprehend why those who left cannot send money back.[246]

2.9 SUDANESE REFUGEES

Due to violence and war in Sudan, many Sudanese are searching for safety. Sudanese refugees started arriving in the United States in the early 1990s, when the UNHCR determined that their lives were at high risk in the receiving countries of Kenya, Uganda, Ethiopia, and Egypt. Since then, Sudanese refugees continue to be admitted into the United States under yearly quotas allocated to African countries.[247] As Table 2.6 illustrates, almost 4,000 Sudanese refugees were admitted in 2000, and close to 2,000 in 2006.

In 2000, several families and individuals from southern Sudan were granted refugee status and sponsored by churches around the United States. Maryville, Tennessee, was one such site where about seventy refugees were placed.[248] Maryville,

[244] *Id.* at 121.

[245] *Somali diaspora's remittances cast a lifeline*, AFRICARENEWAL, May 2013, at http://www.un.org/africarenewal/magazine/may-2013/somali-diaspora%E2%80%99s-remittances-cast-lifeline

[246] Shome, *supra* note 4, at 146–47.

[247] Dominic A. Itto, Self-Sufficiency and Adjustment Among Sudanese Refugees in Tennessee 32 (2008) (Ph.D. dissertation, Walden University) (on file with author).

[248] Caitlin T.S. Teaster, The Acculturation Sudanese Refugees in Maryville, Tennessee: Has Self-Sufficiency Been Achieved? 8 (2010) (M.A. thesis, East Tennessee State University) (on file with author).

30 minutes from Knoxville, is predominantly white (91.2 percent). Minorities make up 8.2 percent, with only 3.2 percent black or African American.[249] In fact, Sudanese refugees have become the second-largest African refugee group in Tennessee, after Somalis.[250] Tennessee had about 1,500 Sudanese households by 2008.[251]

The Lost Boys

During the Second Sudanese Civil War from 1983 to 2005 between the central Sudanese government and the Sudan People's Liberation Army,[252] thousands of young boys were away from their villages grazing cattle when their homes were pillaged. More than 20,000 boys and a few girls escaped and walked for three months to Ethiopia. Once there, they made a home in camps in Ethiopia along the Sudanese border; many were younger than four. Four years later, war broke out in Ethiopia and refugees were given 48 hours to leave. They were met by gunfire, and some jumped into the Gilo River, only to be swept away by turbulent currents; others were eaten by crocodiles or attacked by hippos. The survivors spent 1.5 years living in the Sudanese bush on their way to a Kenyan refugee camp. By then, they had walked more than a thousand miles. About 3,400 were offered refugee status in the United States and placed across the country in Texas, Kansas, California, Massachusetts, and other states. They came to be known as the "lost boys" of Sudan.[253]

Some of the lost boys were among the seventy Sudanese refugees that were placed in Maryville, resettled by Bridge Refugee and Sponsoring Services in concert with local churches. Others who came to Maryvale migrated as individuals or in family units.[254]

Adjustment Challenges

Life is hard for the Sudanese refugees in America. Most who arrived could not read or write English fluently. Traumatized by war and living in refugee camps, they were unable to complete basic tasks. Those who came to the United States as adults without an education find it challenging to become self-sufficient.[255] Those with children say, "My hope is for my children. That is why I came here." They

[249] *Id.* at 36.
[250] Itto, *supra* note 248, at 9.
[251] *Id.* at 41.
[252] Teaster, *supra* note 249, at 11–21. About 2.5 million Sudanese were killed and millions were displaced during the war. *Id.*
[253] *Id.* at 22–23.
[254] *Id.* at 38.
[255] *Id.* at 62–63.

believe that their children will have a bright future.[256] Although English is widely spoken and taught in Sudanese schools (especially south Sudan, where English is the official language), many Sudanese refugees arrive with poor English skills. Sudanese Islamic government policy during the early 1980s imposed the Arabic language as a medium of instruction in the predominantly Christian south. Those who went to school during this period had little opportunity to learn English.[257]

The lost boys received tremendous support from foster parents and other groups upon arrival in the United States. Other Sudanese refugees received help from voluntary agencies for about six months and were left to struggle on their own after that, regardless of their economic situation.[258] The lost boys tended to be more successful than those who migrated as a family unit. In fact, the lost boys were provided educational services in English at the UNHCR's Kakuma Refugee Camp in Kenya while they awaited sponsors.[259] Other Sudanese were unable to receive an education because of war and violence. For forty years, Sudan had little infrastructure to support educational services. Those who came here with children were unable to focus on education. Those who grew up outside of Sudan actually had an easier time of adjusting to life in the United States.[260]

The lost boys, who are now in their thirties and having done the best among the Sudanese refugees, desire to return to Sudan with their education, knowledge, and influence. Other children who arrived as primary students and those born in the United States have bright futures. They have been socialized in American culture and understand cultural norms. They have learned English. They do not desire to return to Sudan.[261]

Unfortunately, many who came as high school students are gravitating to the subculture of the streets. Sudan was never their home because of war; upon arriving here, America was not their home because they did not have the opportunity to learn English. They have found it hard to find jobs. Drugs, specifically marijuana, have become a new means of income for this group, and more importantly an identity. They are torn between two nations, neither of which is home. They were not "lost boys," but they are lost now. In contrast, their younger siblings have not seemed to follow this path.[262]

Employment and family income are related to self-sufficiency. Most working Sudanese refugees (86.7 percent) in other parts of Tennessee, like Nashville, were

[256] *Id.* at 72–73.
[257] Itto, *supra* note 248, at 30.
[258] *Id.* at 6.
[259] *Id.* at 31.
[260] Teaster, *supra* note 249, at 64–65.
[261] *Id.* at 62–63.
[262] *Id.* at 63.

employed as laborers or production workers. Those mostly low-paying jobs do not create the means or incentive for most Sudanese refugees to escape poverty. Almost 28 percent had a college education before coming to the United States, but only 13.3 percent found white-collar jobs here. One contributing factor is lack of information about the labor market. Many Sudanese refugees rely heavily on temporary employment agencies for job seeking and placement. These agencies operate as middlemen between business owners and job seekers by hiring them as cheap laborers and assigning them to work at production companies or warehouses under contracts. This practice often amounts to exploitation of refugees and immigrants because some of their wages are appropriated by the agencies as commissions.[263]

Unlike economic immigrants, many political refugees from Sudan dream of returning to their homeland. Thus, they may resist adopting values and behaviors they perceive as foreign by protecting their cultural heritage, part of which is the language. Many Sudanese refugee families rarely speak English at home; as a result, improvement in English language is often slow, especially among the older members of the refugee community.[264]

Thus, many still consider themselves temporary migrants in the United States, hoping to return to their homeland once the security situation there improves. For them, long-term plans for permanent settlement are deferred. They often express a desire to return or at least pay a visit to Sudan in the near future. One reason for this attitude is obvious: economic hardship and difficulty adjusting to Western culture have led some Sudanese refugees to view life in the United States negatively. However, conditions in their homeland may not have improved, or may have further deteriorated since they left, and beginning a new life in one's own homeland might prove even more difficult than staying in one's new country.[265]

Sudanese refugee women have different challenges. They have much less education than do their male counterparts. Hardly any have higher than a middle school education.[266] Families can have difficulty merging traditional Sudanese norms with the norms of American culture. Often there is a backlash against traditional roles for Sudanese women in the United States. Women's empowerment came to these women literally overnight. Among the married couples that moved to the United States together or who married soon after arrival, there is still a level of patriarchy. Men assume ultimate power. Sudanese men in communities such as the one in Maryville, who are in their thirties but not in school, are desperately

[263] Itto, *supra* note 248, at 79–81.
[264] *Id.* at 83.
[265] *Id.* at 87–88.
[266] Teaster, *supra* note 249, at 52.

searching for a wife to harness respect and authority. In contrast, the younger men attending college are not in a hurry to marry, and say that when they decide to look for a wife, they will be looking for a wife who will be an equal.[267]

2.10 CLOSING

The 1965 Act has had relatively little to do with the establishment of African migrant communities in the United States. As Tables 2.2 through 2.5 illustrate, compared to immigrants from Mexico and Asian countries, the numbers of African immigrants to the United States in the family and employment categories established in 1965 is small. In 1997, twenty years after the legislation, fewer than 24,000 Africans can be counted as immigrants if the refugees and diversity lottery winners are subtracted from the Table 2.2 total immigrant figure. In contrast, the adjusted Asian immigrant figure is almost ten times greater (226,000), and Mexican immigrants alone totaled nearly 147,000 immigrants that year. The relative figures have gradually improved for African immigrants over the years, but even as recently as 2012 (Table 2.5), the adjusted African immigrant number is 62,742 compared with 333,583 Asian and 145,891 Mexican immigrants.

An analysis of the 1965 Act family provisions over time does show a gradual increase of African immigrants in those categories. From Tables 2.2 through 2.5, we can calculate that in 1997, 2000, 2006, and 2012, the number of African family category immigrants grew from 19,963 to 20,926, 47,721, and 57,534, respectively. Note, however, that even with the expansion of the employment categories in 1990, the African employment visa figures for those years are not particularly strong, at, respectively, 3,665, 4,351, 6,437, and 4,763.

Thus, the trends illustrate that over time, the family immigration categories of the 1965 Act are beginning to be more useful for prospective African immigrants. As African immigrants arrive in whatever category – be it through employment, as refugees, or as diversity lottery winners – they are beginning to make more use of the family reunification categories. As I have noted previously in the quintessential example of the Asian American experience,[268] the 1965 Act family categories may not have been intended to facilitate the growth of African migrant communities, but over time they can. Prospective African migrants may have been euphemistically assigned to the back of the bus under the 1965 Act, but they are not confined there.

An important sign that African migrants will be using the family categories more is their interest in naturalization. As the prior discussion notes, many African migrants know that a benefit of citizenship through naturalization is the ability to petition for

[267] *Id.* at 66–68.

[268] *See* BILL ONG HING, MAKING AND REMAKING ASIAN AMERICA, *supra* note 19.

a wider range of family members.[269] Table 2.10 illustrates the growing naturalization figures for African migrants from just over 10,000 in 1991 to almost 75,000 by 2012; the naturalization figures for Nigerians, Ethiopians, and Somalis are particularly noteworthy. Nearly half of all African migrants are naturalized U.S. citizens; 46.1 percent of African immigrants were naturalized U.S. citizens in 2010, compared to 43.7 percent of the foreign-born population in the country as a whole.[270]

Considering African migrant communities in the context of the 1965 Act also provides a good opportunity to be reminded of the diversity of this segment of the foreign-born U.S. population. This chapter provides only a limited review of a handful of examples: Ghanaians, Ethiopians, Somalis, and Sudanese. A more complete review would continue with good descriptions of such communities as Eritreans in the Los Angeles area,[271] Liberians in places like Johnson City, Tennessee,[272] or Providence, Rhode Island,[273] Tanzanians in Wichita, Kansas,[274] and of course Nigerians, the largest African migrant group in the United States with heavy concentrations in Texas, California, New York, Maryland, Illinois, New Jersey, and Georgia.[275]

In spite of the diversity, the review of communities discussed in this chapter does highlight many commonalities. Most have experienced racism or discrimination, yet have a challenging relationship with African Americans. Their search for identity has become anchored in transnational experiences while relying on the formation of community organizations and churches here in America. Women's equality in the United States and the migration experience has very much affected gender roles – not without tension. The second generation is Americanized, but also has evolved with a transnational identity. And in spite of the fact that many in the older generation still dream of going back home, remittances to friends and relatives are high in the face of growing naturalization rates to obtain U.S. citizenship.

The review of refugee admissions in the context of African migration also serves as a reminder that the United States continues to be generous on the one hand, but also needs to work to better resettlement efforts on the other. High incidents

[269] *See* note 244, *supra*, and accompanying text.

[270] Immigration Policy Center, African Immigrants in America: A Demographic Overview (June 2012), *available at* http://www.immigrationpolicy.org/just-facts/african-immigrants-america-demographic-overview.

[271] *See* Ghebremedhin, *supra* note 178.

[272] *See* Zon Gangbayee Quewea, Community Involvement Liberians in Johnson City, Tennessee: An Exploratory Pilot Study (2008) (Ph.D. dissertation, East Tennessee State University) (on file with author).

[273] *See* Mott, *supra* note 96.

[274] Mohamed A. M. Dosi, Leonce Rushubirwa, & Garth A. Myers, *Tanzanians in the Land of Oz: Diaspora and Transnationality in Wichita, Kansas*, SOCIAL & CULTURAL GEOGRAPHY 8.5 (2007): 657–71.

[275] Kwasi Sarkodie-Mensah, Nigerian Americans, 2007, available at: http://www.everyculture.com/multi/Le-Pa/Nigerian-Americans.html.

TABLE 2.10. *Naturalization of African migrants for specific years*

Region or country	1991	1994	1997	2000	2003	2006	2009	2012
Africa	10,468	16,073	15,996[a]	25,850	28,529	50,397	60,383	74,775
>Ethiopia	1,476	2,375	1,994	2,774	3,820	5,397	8,698	8,803
>Ghana	680	1,145	1,588	2,035	2,831	4,760	4,819	5,344
>Nigeria	1,804	3,464	3,537	4,135	5,691	8,652	9,298	9,322
>Somalia	107	154	171	1,247	2,235	4,242	3,818	9,286
Asia	168,296	193,842	193,591	331,136	196,972	263,516	276,375	257,035
>India	13,286	20,940	21,206	42,198	29,761	47,542	52,889	42,928
>Philippines	34,450	40,777	30,898	46,563	29,043	40,500	38,934	44,958
Mexico	22,878	46,169	142,569	189,705	55,946	83,979	111,630	102,181

[a] The decline in naturalization among African migrants in 1997 to 15,996 was preceded by higher figures in 1995 (18,495) and 1996 (26,970). The African naturalization figure continued to drop in 1998 (12,467), then dramatically increased in 1999 (20,401).

Source: U.S. Department of Justice, Immigration and Naturalization Service, 2000 *Statistical Yearbook of the Immigration and Naturalization Service*, table 49; Department of Homeland Security, Office of Immigration Statistics, 2012 *Yearbook of Immigration Statistics*, table 21.

of racial and ethnic conflict, high levels of unemployment, and high numbers of refugees living in homeless shelters point to weaknesses in the resettlement process. Refugees are sometimes located in cities that are not a good match, with high costs of living, high crime and unemployment rates, lack of support networks, and agencies without experience with certain populations.[276] Refugees are often attracted to places where relatives or friends already live and where public assistance is accessible. But geographical movement itself increases instability and makes certain kinds of adjustment more difficult.[277]

Cultural orientation sessions in refugee camps – for example, for Somalis in Kenya – lacked content, depth, and specificity. Many refugees were totally neglected. Somalis who escaped the horrors in Somalia are resilient and self-sufficient; these qualities should have been tapped into, to provide other refugees who attended the sessions with tools that might have been used in the United States. If the refugee cultural orientation sessions had been used as a learning environment to encourage the refugees to share and learn the strategies that some of them had used in negotiating a new environment and culture in Dadaab, it would have equipped the Somalis better to deal with the resettlement process in the United States.[278]

While most refugees agree on the importance of mastering English on arrival and the necessity of knowing English for long-term economic and social services, many point out that teaching English to newcomers is not a priority of the refugee resettlement program in the United States. The objective of the U.S. resettlement program is for refugees to attain self-sufficiency within sixty days of arrival. So the focus is much more on helping refugees get a job right away. Learning English is mostly neglected in the interest of working right away. People working in the resettlement agencies generally expect the refugees to learn English on their own, through communication with English speakers in the workplace or English classes taken during nonworking hours.[279]

To facilitate assimilation, policy makers should ensure refugee representation in the planning, implementation, and evaluation of resettlement services. Cities can play a big role. Cities are responsible for organizing and regulating many activities of daily urban life that may seem mundane, but are critical to social and economic inclusion of its residents.[280] Similarly, the role of community-based organizations to aid in the assimilation of refugees needs to be strengthened and expanded.[281]

[276] Mott, *supra* note 96, at 262.
[277] Itto, *supra* note 248, at 89.
[278] Shome, *supra* note 4, at 63–64.
[279] *Id.* at 99.
[280] *Id.* at 175.
[281] *Id.* at 177.

Refugees typically arrive with only a few personal belongings, and starting a new life in a foreign land is a huge challenge. In their initial moments here, the task is to help them face reality and work toward building a new life. However, that can only happen with the continuing support of the host community; short-term community assistance is not enough to help refugees get on their feet. Continuous commitment over a longer period is necessary to ensure a smooth transition into self-reliance.[282] Refugee resettlement needs to be understood and approached as a process over time, not a static one-time experience.[283] This is a wake-up call for intervention by human services department and refugee resettlement agencies to improve support systems that will help non-self-sufficient refugees realize their potential by seeking out employment opportunities, participating in community affairs, and making the move from dependence to public assistance to economic self-sufficiency. The idea is to help refugees achieve a better life than the one they fled, and many feel that their dreams can only become true when they are given a chance to reshape their family life outside public welfare programs.[284]

In closing, the importance of refugee admissions and the diversity visa lottery program to the establishment of African migrant communities in the United States must be underscored. The 1980 Refugee Act and the creation of the diversity visa program in the early 1990s are fundamentally responsible for the communities as we now know them. However, given the growing trend in using the family reunification categories of the 1965 Act, at long last we can finally say that the Act will serve as a positive vehicle for further expansion of African migrant communities in the United States. Sadly, we have to wonder if that trend and possibility is short-lived, given perennial attacks on the family reunification categories by some members of Congress[285] and, most recently, a serious proposal to eliminate the diversity visa lottery program.[286] If those proposals actually become law, then prospective African migrants would, once again, be relegated to the back of the bus.

[282] Itto, *supra* note 248, at 23.

[283] Ghebremedhin, *supra* note 178, at 163–69.

[284] Itto, *supra* note 248, at 91.

[285] *See* Bill Ong Hing, Deporting Our Souls – Values, Morality and Immigration Policy 118–39 (2006).

[286] S.744 passed by the U.S. Senate in the spring of 2013 would eliminate the diversity visa program as well as several family categories such as siblings and older married sons and daughters of U.S. citizens. *See* Immigration Policy Center, A Guide to S.744: Understanding the 2013 Senate Immigration Bill, available at: http://www.immigrationpolicy.org/special-reports/guide-s744-understanding-2013-senate-immigration-bill.

3

The Beginning of the End

The Immigration Act of 1965 and the Emergence of the Modern U.S.-Mexico Border State

Kevin R. Johnson

3.1 INTRODUCTION

In the celebratory wake of passage of the Civil Rights Act of 1964,[1] Congress enacted the Immigration Act of 1965.[2] Consistent with the growing popularity of the extension of civil rights to racial minorities in the United States, the 1965 Act eliminated the discriminatory national origins quotas system from the U.S. immigration laws as well as the last vestiges of the infamous Chinese exclusion laws.[3] At a special signing

[1] Pub. L. No. 88–352, 78 Stat. 241 (codified as amended in scattered sections of 28 and 42 U.S.C.).

[2] Immigration Act of 1965, Pub. L. No. 89–236, 79 Stat. 911 (codified as amended in scattered sections of 8 U.S.C.).

[3] *See id.* § 1, 79 Stat. at 911 (codified as amended at Immigration and Nationality Act (INA) § 201, 8 U.S.C. § 1151). The 1965 Act did considerably more than simply remove the discriminatory quotas from the immigration laws. Congress firmly admonished that "[n]o person shall receive any preference or priority or be discriminated against in the issuance of an immigrant visa *because of his race, sex, nationality, place of birth, or place of residence* …" Pub L. No. 89–236, § 2(a), 79 Stat. at 911–12 (codified as amended in the INA § 202, 8 U.S.C. § 1152) (2006) (emphasis added).

Congress originally adopted the quotas system in 1924, a time when xenophobic sentiment was at one of its periodic zeniths in American history. *See generally* JOHN HIGHAM, STRANGERS IN THE LAND: PATTERNS OF AMERICAN NATIVISM, 1860–1925 (2002 ed.) (analyzing the political movement culminating in congressional enactment of the national origins quotas system). For analysis of how

A version of this chapter originally appeared at 34 IMMIGRATION AND NATIONALITY LAW REVIEW 3 (2013), and is reprinted by permission of William S. Hein & Co. Inc. Thanks to Gabriel "Jack" Chin and Rose Cuison Villazor for organizing this book project and editing the book. Leticia Saucedo, Elizabeth Keyes, and Deep Gulasekaram provided comments on a draft of this chapter. Conversations with Cruz Reynoso over a number of years helped inform the analysis in this chapter. Raquel Aldana and other participants in a workshop on the chapters to the book in February 2014 at UC Davis School of Law also provided thoughtful comments. I also benefited from comments on this paper at presentations at Suffolk and the University of Cincinnati law schools and at the Critical Race Theory Conference at Yale Law School (by video) in the spring of 2014. Thanks also to UC Davis law student Jake Leraul for research assistance and editorial support in the preparation of this chapter. Stephanie Padilla also provided editorial assistance in finalizing this chapter.

ceremony steps away from the Statue of Liberty, President Lyndon B. Johnson proudly proclaimed that the new immigration law was "one of the most important acts of this Congress and of this administration."[4] This is nothing less than an extraordinary statement coming in an era in which Congress enacted a series of momentous civil rights laws.

Characterizing the Immigration Act of 1965 as a welcome by-product of the civil rights movement, most observers have praised the legislation in unqualified terms. For example, in an important book analyzing the impact of the U.S. immigration laws on shaping the development of the Asian American community in the United States, Bill Hing characterized the 1965 Act as reforming the American immigration laws in the spirit of the "new global egalitarianism."[5] In considering the legislation's role in opening the door to immigration from Asia to the United States, Jack Chin proclaimed that the legislation brought "[t]he civil rights revolution ... to immigration law."[6]

The praise for the Immigration Act of 1965 reflects the law's civil rights inspiration, hopes, and dreams. However, it fails to capture fully and accurately the entirety of this pivotal piece of immigration legislation. This chapter explores long-ignored, and substantial, negative civil rights consequences of the 1965 Act with which the nation continues to grapple to this day.

As is well known, the nation's racial sensibilities slowly but surely changed over the course of the twentieth century, with the dismantling of Jim Crow and the end of de jure segregation of whites and African Americans in U.S. social life. In light of the dramatic changes in the nation's racial sensibilities, the United States found it increasingly difficult to defend the racially discriminatory quotas system that served as the foundation of the U.S. immigration laws. Criticism, including

democratic nations consistently produce racially discriminatory immigration laws, see DAVID SCOTT FITZGERALD & DAVID COOK-MARTIN, CULLING THE MASSES: THE DEMOCRATIC ORIGINS OF RACIST IMMIGRATION POLICY IN THE AMERICAS (2014); *see also* DANIEL J. TICHENOR, DIVIDING LINES: THE POLITICS OF IMMIGRATION CONTROL IN AMERICA (2002) (analyzing history of political compromises in American immigration legislation).

4 *President Lyndon B. Johnson's Remarks at the Signing of the Immigration Bill, Liberty Island, New York Oct. 3, 1965*, PUBLIC PAPERS OF THE PRESIDENTS OF THE UNITED STATES: LYNDON JOHNSON, 1965, at 1037, 1037 (1966).

5 BILL ONG HING, MAKING AND REMAKING ASIAN AMERICA THROUGH IMMIGRATION POLICY 1850–1990, at 18 (1993); *see also id.* at 185 (noting that "the egalitarian 1965 amendments ... abandoned the racial national-origin quotas system"). Professor Hing also recognized shortcomings in the legislation. *See, e.g., id.* at 40–41.

6 Gabriel J. Chin, *The Civil Rights Revolution Comes to Immigration Law: A New Look at the Immigration and Nationality Act of 1965*, 75 N.C. L. REV. 273 (1996). One member of Congress later lamented what he characterized as the excessive influence of the civil rights movement on the passage of the 1965 Act. *See* Rep. Lamar Smith & Edward R. Grant, *Immigration Reform: Seeking the Right Reasons*, 28 ST. MARY'S L.J. 833, 888 (1997) ("Unfortunately, just as the immigration debate in the 1920s had been unduly affected by the rise of nativism, *the debate in 1965 was unduly influenced by a very different movement, that to secure civil rights of all Americans.*") (emphasis added).

from President Harry Truman[7] and Senator (later President) John F. Kennedy,[8] grew as the inconsistency between the discriminatory quotas system and the emerging antidiscrimination norms in post–World War II America became increasingly evident. The blatant discrimination in the immigration laws, as well as racial discrimination generally in American social life, became nothing less than a foreign policy embarrassment for the U.S. government – and one that seriously handicapped the nation's Cold War efforts to persuade hearts and minds around the world of the righteousness of the American cause.[9] The foreign policy impetus for elimination of the national origins quotas system resembled that which contributed to the pressures for the desegregation of American society.[10]

Rooting the Immigration Act of 1965 in a mass movement that galvanized the nation, the administration of President Lyndon B. Johnson rallied civil rights support for immigration reform. The end of the discriminatory national origins quotas system benefited large numbers of prospective immigrants from Asia, who since the late nineteenth century had been largely denied lawful admission into the United States.[11]

However, despite eliminating blatant racial discrimination in immigrant admissions, the Immigration Act of 1965 also made less well-known changes to the

7 *See* PUBLIC PAPERS OF THE PRESIDENTS OF THE UNITED STATES: HARRY S. TRUMAN 441 (1952–53) (explaining that he vetoed the Immigration & Nationality Act of 1952 because it perpetuated the discriminatory national origins quotas system and emphasizing that "immigration policy is … important to the conduct of our foreign relations and to our responsibilities of moral leadership in the struggle for world peace"). President Truman justified the veto, which Congress overrode, on the grounds that the quotas system was premised on the discriminatory view "that Americans with English or Irish names were better people and better citizens than Americans with Italian or Greek or Polish names. It was thought that people of West European origin made better citizens than Rumanians or Yugoslavs or Ukrainians or Hungarians or Balts or Austrians. Such a concept … violates the great political doctrine of the Declaration of Independence that 'all men are created equal.'" *Id.* at 443.

8 *See* JOHN F. KENNEDY, A NATION OF IMMIGRANTS (rev. ed. 1964).

9 *See* Chin, *supra* note 6, at 282–86 (exploring foreign policy motivations for the congressional repeal of the bar on immigration from Asia); J. Donald Kingsley, *Immigration and Our Foreign Policy Objectives*, 21 LAW & CONTEMP. PROBS. 299, 303–06 (1956) (examining negative U.S. foreign policy consequences resulting from the exclusion of Asian immigrants under the U.S. immigration laws); *see also* Allegra M. McLeod, *The U.S. Criminal-Immigration Convergence and Its Possible Undoing*, 49 AM. CRIM. L. REV. 105, 162 (2012) ("In the mid-twentieth century, when it became increasingly embarrassing for the United States to prohibit the naturalization of Chinese immigrants as China was a valued ally in the war effort, foreign policy concerns rather than humanitarian ones began to bring about the dismantling of facially exclusionary immigration provisions.") (footnote omitted).

10 *See generally* MARY L DUDZIAK, RACE AND THE IMAGE OF AMERICAN DEMOCRACY (2002) (analyzing the foreign policy impetus to end racial segregation in the United States); Derrick Bell, Brown v. Board of Education *and the Interest Convergence Dilemma*, 93 HARV. L. REV. 518 (1980) (to the same effect).

11 *See, e.g.*, Chae Chan Ping v. United States (*The Chinese Exclusion Case*), 130 U.S. 581 (1889) (upholding one of many Chinese exclusion laws that restricted immigration from China to the United States).

law that unquestionably did not further the cause of civil rights. Those changes restricted the migration of noncitizens from Latin America to the United States. Many of the changes represented significant amendments to the original bill, which proponents added to attract the necessary votes for its enactment. As discussed later in this chapter, the compromise provisions deserve outright condemnation by the same civil rights advocates who championed the law and lavished praise upon it with the Act's passage.

Intentionally and unmistakably designed to restrict immigration from Latin America, some major features of the Immigration Act of 1965 in fact are wholly inconsistent with the nation's efforts to extend civil rights to racial minorities in the United States. Nor are they in line with the antidiscriminatory spirit behind the abolition of the national origins quotas system. In fact, by placing a ceiling on immigration from Latin America, important features of the 1965 Act operated to deny equal treatment under the law to a discrete group of noncitizens of color – Latina/os.

The Immigration Act of 1965 added to U.S. immigration law a new and effective form of racial discrimination that is considerably more sophisticated than the crude national origins quotas system. It imposed an annual ceiling of 120,000 immigrants from the Western Hemisphere, the very first express numerical limitation in U.S. history on immigration from the region, which of course includes Mexico. Readily admitting its goals, Congress backed the ceiling as part of a necessary effort to thwart a feared mass migration of Latina/o immigrants to the United States likely to result from a feared dramatic increase in population in Latin America.

The legislative history of the Immigration Act of 1965 unequivocally reveals the palpable fear that, absent bold new restrictive steps, Latina/o immigrants – with Latin America experiencing what was popularly referred to as a "population explosion" – might well overrun American society.[12] As we shall see in Section 3.3, concerns with a mass migration from Latin America came to dominate U.S. immigration law and enforcement over the next fifty years and continues to concern many Americans today.

[12] *See* Kevin R. Johnson, *Race, the Immigration Laws, and Domestic Race Relations: A "Magic Mirror" into the Heart of Darkness*, 73 IND. L.J. 1111, 1131–33 (1998). For expression of such sentiments by an influential scholar, see SAMUEL P. HUNTINGTON, WHO ARE WE?: THE CHALLENGES TO AMERICA'S NATIONAL IDENTITY (2004). Ediberto Roman, *The Alien Invasion?*, 45 HOUS. L. REV. 841 (2008) provides a sustained response to claims that the United States is being overrun by immigrants. *See also* Kevin R. Johnson & Bill Ong Hing, *Who Are We? National Identity in a Multicultural Nation: The Challenge of Immigration Law and Immigrants*, 103 MICH. L. REV. 1347 (2005) (criticizing Huntington's analysis).

For analysis of the evolution of U.S. immigration law and policy in the period after World War II, see Philip Eric Wolgin, Beyond National Origins: The Development of Modern Immigration Policymaking, 1948–1968, Ph.D. Dissertation, Department of History, UC Berkeley (2011).

Seeking to fill a gap in the scholarly literature,[13] this chapter examines what may be described as the anti-Latina/o underside of the Immigration Act of 1965. It seeks to challenge the myth that the 1965 Act represents an unqualified civil rights success that brought racial neutrality, objectivity, and equality to American immigrant admissions.

The bottom line is that, despite its much-revered place in American immigration history, the 1965 Act's pro–civil rights reputation is not wholly deserved. The legislation in fact unmistakably intended to cap immigration from Latin America to the United States.[14] In so doing, Congress redirected the admission of immigrants away from the Western Hemisphere. Moreover, the law established a sturdy foundation from which the modern American immigration enforcement state has evolved, with disparate racial impacts on Latina/os achieved through facially neutral and ostensibly fair means.[15]

Despite its birth at the height of the national civil rights movement, the Immigration Act of 1965 set the stage for the creation and implementation of a myriad of restrictive immigration laws and enforcement measures directed primarily at Latina/os. Most importantly, the new law transformed millions of legal immigrants from Mexico into undocumented ones subject to deportation and particularly vulnerable to exploitation and discrimination by employers and others in the United States. With broad public support, those measures have been expanded dramatically in the new millennium. The results represent nothing less than a staggering revolution in immigration enforcement, with rapidly escalating numbers of removals of immigrants from the United States – approximately 400,000 a year, an astronomical increase of more than tenfold in the last twenty years. Not coincidentally, the disparate focus of the American removal machinery has yielded disproportionate number of removals of Latina/os from the country. In response to

[13] One of the few pieces of scholarship devoted to the exclusionary aspects of the 1963 Act is Eithne Luibheid, *The 1965 Immigration and Nationality Act: An "End" to Exclusion?*, 5 Positions 501 (1997).

[14] *See* Leticia M. Saucedo, *Mexicans, Immigrants, Cultural Narratives, and National Origin*, 44 Ariz. St. L.J. 305, 329–30 (2013). *See generally* Natalia Molina, How Race is Made in America: Immigration, Citizenship, and the Histories of Racial Scripts (2014) (providing a historical analysis of how persons of Mexican ancestry, including immigrants, were racialized in the United States from 1924 to 1965).

[15] *See generally* Kevin R. Johnson, *A Case Study of Color-Blindness: The Racially Disparate Impacts of Arizona's S.B. 1070 and the Failure of Comprehensive Immigration Reform*, 2 UC Irvine L. Rev. 313 (2012) (analyzing how modern U.S. immigration laws and their enforcement, as well as the failure of Congress to pass comprehensive immigration reform, have racially disparate results on Latina/o immigrants and U.S. citizens). As one prominent federal court of appeals judge observed, "ever-increasingly, seemingly ethnically-neutral laws are enacted that disproportionately burden the rights of Latino immigrants, and disproportionately of Mexican immigrants." Kim McLane Wardlaw, *The Latino Immigration Experience*, 31 Chicana/o-Latina/o L. Rev. 13, 44 (2012).

the much-publicized number of removals, a nascent political movement emerged to put an end to the escalating deportations.[16]

In the five decades since passage of the Immigration Act of 1965, U.S. immigration law and its enforcement have built on the anti-Latina/o roots of the legislation. As a result, immigration enforcement has focused on restricting immigration from Mexico and deporting Mexican immigrants from the United States. The transformation of border enforcement has been so complete that many American political leaders in 2015 firmly believe that curbing Mexican immigration is what U.S. immigration law and border enforcement should almost exclusively focus on – a mindset that has resulted in increasingly stringent enforcement efforts at the U.S./Mexico border supported by ever-growing appropriations of resources. Some contemporary immigration reform proposals even call for an additional "border surge" to greater control, if not seal, the border.[17]

This chapter critically examines how the 1965 Act fueled the development of a series of interlocking laws and enforcement programs designed to restrict immigration from Latin America to the United States. By the dawn of the new millennium, enforcement measures that impact Latina/os unquestionably dominate modern American immigration law and enforcement. Indeed, one might claim that, over the last fifty years, the United States replaced the *Chinese* exclusion laws of the nineteenth and twentieth centuries with legislation akin to the *Mexican* exclusion laws of the new millennium.

In essence, the Immigration Act of 1965 reallocated opportunities for lawful immigration from Latin America to Asia. On the one hand, the Act contributed to the growth in legal immigration from Asia.[18] On the other hand, the law placed an artificial ceiling on legal migration from Mexico wholly disconnected from its high, and increasingly unsatisfied, demand for immigration fueled by labor demand to the United States. Through these means, the 1965 Act dramatically transformed the relative distribution of legal Asian and Latina/o immigrants coming to the United States legally.

Liberalization of migration from Asia, while simultaneously restricting immigration from Latin America, contributed to significant changes in the racial demographics of immigration – and the entire United States – after 1965. By imposing a rigid ceiling on Latina/o immigration, the Immigration Act of 1965 spurred the growth of a large – and steadily expanding – population of unauthorized Mexican immigrants. This increased the proportion of Mexican immigrants subject

16 *See* #Not1More Deportation, available at http://www.notonemoredeportation.com/, last visited Aug. 8, 2014.

17 *See* Lawrence Downes, *Nogales Is Not Falluja*, N.Y. Times Taking Note (June 20, 2013), available at http://takingnote.blogs.nytimes.com/2013/06/20/nogales-is-not-falluja/), last visited Aug. 29, 2014.

18 *See* Chin, *supra* note 6, at 303–21. Considerable evidence suggests that Congress at some level anticipated that the law would result in an increase in immigration from Asia. *See id.*

to removal from the United States. Transforming lawful migrants into unlawful ones, the operation of the law contributed to the public's increasingly negative view of Latina/o immigration and the perceived need for ever-greater enforcement. Ultimately, the unpopularity of the new undocumented population transformed the domestic politics of immigration and progressively changed the overall direction of U.S. immigration law and its enforcement.

The changing racial composition of the overall immigrant population – legal and unauthorized – has contributed to the public's sporadic outbursts of animus directed at immigrants (often with anti-Mexican and anti-Latina/o undertones), frequent calls for immigration reform, and the frenzied advocacy for heightened enforcement of existing immigration laws. The racial demographics of modern immigration also fueled demands for a variety of reforms to the immigration laws that would change the racial demographics of the flow of legal immigrants to the United States.[19] In the end, the combination of legal maneuvers greatly limited legal immigration from Mexico to the United States and, by so doing, created significant incentives for undocumented immigration as a way to satisfy Mexican demand for immigration. Although the immigration laws endeavored to suppress powerful economic and demographic forces, it could not eliminate them, with the ultimate result being that Latina/os become the largest minority group in the United States.

Section 3.2 of this chapter analyzes the compromises in the Immigration Act of 1965 and the 1976 amendments, as well as their anti-Latina/o impacts. Section 3.3 summarizes how the 1965 legislation served as a linchpin to the dramatic changes in the nature and focus of American immigration enforcement – with distinctly anti-Mexican, anti-Latina/o effects – and have created the current immigration dilemma that the nation finds itself in today.

3.2 THE BEGINNING: WESTERN HEMISPHERE LIMITS, PER-COUNTRY CEILINGS, AND MORE RESTRICTIONS

Mainstream U.S. immigration histories praise the Immigration Act of 1965 as a monumental civil rights achievement. It is frequently offered as one of many proud examples of the transformation of American social life that came in the wake of the Supreme Court's groundbreaking decision in *Brown v. Board of Education*.[20]

19 A well-known example of the efforts to increase the number of white immigrants to the United States is the "diversity" visa program, which Congress added to the immigration laws in 1990; diversity visas were designed to facilitate greater migration to the United States from Europe. *See* Stephen H. Legomsky & Cristina Rodríguez, Immigration and Refugee Law and Policy 350–54 (5th ed. 2009) (explaining genesis and operation of the diversity visa program).

20 347 U.S. 483 (1954). As with *Brown*'s promise of full desegregation, *see generally* Derrick Bell, Silent Covenants: Brown v. Board of Education and the Unfulfilled Hopes for Racial

The Immigration Act of 1965 deserves praise for abolition of the discriminatory national origins quotas system. Unfortunately, the amendments had largely ignored but nonetheless devastating long-term impacts on Latina/o immigration to the United States. Specifically, the Act's Western Hemisphere annual ceiling of 120,000 immigrants proved to be a critically important first step in what became a generation of increasingly anti-Latina/o immigration measures. Moreover, the law cleared the way for the subsequent trajectory of U.S. immigration policy and enforcement unmistakably directed at Latinas/os, a keen if not myopic focus that shows no sign of change as the law celebrates its fiftieth anniversary.

Little critical attention has been paid to the long-term impacts of the Immigration Act of 1965 on immigration from Mexico, as well as from all of Latin America, to the United States. Few scholars, even those generally critical of the modern racial effects of the nation's immigration laws, have linked the Act to the distinctly anti-Mexican slant of modern American immigration enforcement. Commencing that task, this chapter contends that, although the 1965 Act markedly improved the prospects for lawful immigration from Asia to the United States, it began a process of firmly restricting legal immigration from Latin America, and specifically Mexico. That process fundamentally transformed U.S. immigration law and its enforcement to what it is today, with a primary focus on increasingly stringent enforcement of the U.S./Mexico border with little regard for the humanity of the people most directly affected.

It was almost as if Congress viewed migration to the United States as a zero-sum game, with restrictions on immigration from Latin America constituting a necessary concession for any liberalization of other restrictions on legal migration. Politically speaking, the 1965 Act reflected a compromise between advocates of the elimination of the national origins quotas system – and easing of the restrictions on migration from Asia – and proponents of restrictions to prevent future mass immigration from Latin America. As we shall see, the ultimate results of the compromise are striking. By redirecting legal immigrants from Latin America to Asia to the United States, "the Immigration Act of 1965 is perhaps the *most important nation shaping statute ever enacted – at least in the modern era*."[21]

As explained in detail later in this chapter, the restrictions placed on legal migration from Mexico contributed greatly to the steady growth of the undocumented Mexican population that today numbers in the millions. Specifically, the 1965 Act marked the beginning of a series of escalating restrictions on Mexican migration

REFORM (2004) (analyzing how the Supreme Court's decision in *Brown v. Board of Education* remains to be fully realized), the civil rights promise of the 1965 Act also remains to be fully realized.

21 Peter H. Schuck, *Immigration Policy: Myths, Realities, and Reforms*, 51 WASHBURN L.J. 189, 189 (2012) (emphasis added) (footnote omitted).

and greatly bolstered immigration enforcement, both of which contributed to the emergence of public concern about the number of Mexican immigrants – legal and unauthorized – in the United States.

The disparate racial impacts of the 1965 Act do not end with formal restrictions on immigration from Mexico. The reforms figured prominently in facilitating the creation over time of the contemporary, palpably negative public image of the undocumented immigrant, popularly known as the "illegal alien," from Mexico. With news reports focusing attention on undocumented immigration for many years, the public increasingly came to equate the ordinary undocumented immigrant – who study after study shows generally comes to this country for nothing more than to work and rejoin family – with criminal elements that necessitate a tough law enforcement response.[22] In so doing, the law and its enforcement built on, and reinforced, anti-Mexican sentiment prevalent in the United States.

Make no mistake about it: the Immigration Act of 1965 unquestionably represents an improvement over the discriminatory national origins quotas system that had locked the stream of immigrants into the racial demographic composition of the U.S. population as of 1920.[23] It eliminated that much-criticized system, removed discriminatory barriers to immigrate to the United States from Asia, and provided a brand new veneer of neutrality, objectivity, and fairness to the American immigration system. Nonetheless, a closer look reveals that the 1965 Act commenced an intentional, sustained, and systematic process by the U.S. government to limit legal migration to the United States from Mexico as well as from the rest of the Western Hemisphere.

Softening the immediate blow to prospective Mexican and other Latin American immigrants to the United States, Congress pursued an incremental approach, which served to obscure the ultimate anti-Latina/o purposes and impacts of the sequential reforms to the immigration laws. With the passage of the 1965 Act, Congress took the initial step in restricting Latina/o immigration by imposing an annual numerical ceiling on immigration from the entire Western Hemisphere.[24]

The hemispheric ceiling at first glance appeared objective, neutral, and fair, at least in part, because it ensured that all nations in the world had some type of immigration ceiling. Its application, as a practical matter, however, placed the heaviest burden on prospective migrants from Mexico, the nation with the greatest demand of any country

[22] *See generally* LEO R. CHAVEZ, THE LATINO THREAT: CONSTRUCTING IMMIGRANTS, CITIZENS, AND THE NATION (2008) (analyzing the American media's construction of Latina/o immigrants as a threat to American society).

[23] *See* Johnson, *supra* note 12, at 1127–31.

[24] *See* Immigration Act of 1965, Pub. L. No. 89–236, § 2, 79 Stat. 911, 911–12 (1965) (codified as amended at INA § 202(a), 8 U.S.C. § 1152(a)).

in the hemisphere – as well as on Earth – for immigration to the United States. The ceiling directly harmed potential Latina/o immigrants. At a most fundamental level, the artificially low ceiling failed to account for the huge demand in Mexico, as well as most of Latin America, for migration to the United States.

A little more than a decade after passage of the 1965 Act, Congress took an important second step toward significantly restricting Latina/o immigration to the United States. Repealing the Western Hemisphere ceiling, it extended the per-country ceilings to all nations in the hemisphere in the Immigration and Nationality Amendments of 1976. In so doing, Congress moved forward in its effort to formally cap Latina/o immigration, with the per-country ceiling having a dramatic and immediate adverse effect on immigration from Mexico – indeed, the cap immediately reduced legal immigration from that nation to the United States by approximately one-half. Completing the task initiated in 1965, the 1976 amendments directly placed a cap on legal immigration from Mexico, as well as from every other nation in Latin America.

As discussed in Section 3.3, subsequent decades saw the U.S. government systematically build on the basic purpose of the Western Hemisphere and per-country ceilings and pursue a series of greatly enhanced and increasingly aggressive measures with the unmistakable intention of limiting migration from Mexico. Restricting migration from Mexico ultimately emerged as the dominant goal of U.S. immigration policy.

The transformation of the law has been so complete that today, limiting Mexican immigration is considered by much of the public and many policy-makers to be the primary – and entirely necessary and proper – goal of U.S. immigration law and its enforcement. Fueled by anti-Mexican animus and related fears that a "population explosion" in Latin America would result in a tidal wave of Latina/o immigration, that goal is popular among segments of the American public. The objective of restricting immigration from Latin America has helped justify nothing less than punitive measures directed at immigrants, dramatic increases in appropriations for border enforcement, and record numbers of detentions and removals of noncitizens.

Over the last fifty years, one of the legacies of the Immigration Act of 1965 is greatly enhanced enforcement of the U.S.-Mexico border. In contemporary times, the government of Mexico and many persons of Mexican ancestry in the United States (citizens and immigrants), as well as significant numbers of other Americans, frequently contend that the U.S. immigration laws and their enforcement are nothing less than racist. Although restrictionists often deeply discount, if not simply ignore, the claims of racial discrimination, the critics, as this chapter demonstrates, have identified something worthy of scrutiny.

The 1965 Act: Restricting Immigration from Latin America

The Immigration Act of 1965 imposed an annual ceiling of 120,000 immigrants to the United States from nations in the Western Hemisphere.[25] The new ceiling had significant consequences in no small part because travel and migration within North America is relatively easy. Migration is facilitated by the fact that the United States shares a land border of thousands of miles with its two contiguous neighbors. Consequently, the United States historically has had close economic, social, and political ties with both Mexico and Canada. Part of that relationship includes the fact that both nations for many generations have sent significant numbers of immigrants to the United States.

Focus for a moment on the nature of the complex political, economic, and social relationship between the United States and Mexico. Most of the territory that is popularly known as the American Southwest, including much of Arizona, California, Colorado, New Mexico, Texas, and Utah, at one time was part of Mexico. As provided under the Treaty of Guadalupe Hidalgo ending the U.S.-Mexican War in 1848[26] – a war that mainstream histories characterize as little more than an acquisition of territory accomplished through American military aggression – many Mexican citizens in the annexed territories became legal U.S. citizens.

Due to geographic proximity, the large and growing population of Mexican ancestry in this country, and the economic disparities between the nations, it is no surprise that much of the modern demand for migration to the United States would come from citizens of Mexico. From the mid-1800s to 1965, migrants from Mexico flowed each year to the United States, particularly to the American Southwest.[27] After 1965, greater numbers of migrants from Mexico began settling outside the border region, including in the Midwest and South. As discussed later in this chapter, a number of states and localities that experienced an increase in their Latina/o immigrant population in the early years of the twenty-first century responded with the passage of immigration enforcement laws. Often enacted in racially hostile environments, these laws were designed to discourage undocumented immigrants from living in the jurisdictions covered by the laws by making their lives difficult.

The regular flow of migrants from Mexico to the United States over the nineteenth and twentieth centuries contributed to the emergence of durable cross-border employment and family networks. Those networks remain intact and, in fact, continue to grow, contributing to the regular and relatively constant flows of

[25] *Id.* § 21(e), 79 Stat. at 921 (repealed 1976).

[26] *See* Treaty of Peace, Friendship, Limits, and Settlement, Feb. 2, 1848, United States-Mexico, 9 Stat. 922, Treaty Series No. 207, 9 Bevans 791.

[27] *See* Gerald P. López, *Undocumented Mexican Migration: In Search of a Just Immigration Law and Policy*, 28 UCLA L. Rev. 615, 641–72 (1981).

migrants from Mexico to the United States, most of whom are attracted by wages in the North that are significantly higher on the average than those generally available in the South. Historically, family members and social networks in the United States also have influenced the migration flows.

As a result, demand for immigration from Mexico consistently has been greater than that of any other nation in North America.[28] Demand for migration from Mexico has been fueled, in no small part, by the great demand of employers in the United States for relatively inexpensive labor.

Even though the employment of undocumented immigrants in the United States generally is prohibited by law, jobs have been readily available for undocumented immigrants who enter the United States. Access to economic opportunity thus remains the most powerful magnet attracting Mexican immigrants to the United States.

Students of immigration fully appreciate that readily available employment opportunities create a powerful economic incentive for Mexican citizens to migrate to the United States. Without the availability of jobs, immigration, lawful and unauthorized, from Mexico would be dramatically reduced.

Pre-1965 Mexican Immigration and U.S.-Mexico Border Enforcement

Before Congress passed the Immigration Act of 1965, the U.S. immigration laws had never previously imposed quotas, ceilings, or fixed limits on immigration to the United States from any nation in the Western Hemisphere. Before 1965, the U.S. government flexibly enforced the U.S. immigration laws with respect to Latin America. Without a ceiling applicable to Mexican nationals, those laws lent themselves to flexible enforcement. Through variable, as opposed to fixed, admission numbers and adjustable rather than rigid enforcement policies, the law in operation accommodated much of the demand for immigration from Mexico to the United States. The law, as enforced, had the distinct advantage of allowing for adaptation of legal migration flows to the nation's labor needs.

Given that legal migration to the United States could generally accommodate many, if not most, of the prospective Mexican migrants before 1965, the pressures for undocumented immigration were more or less manageable through relatively modest border enforcement measures. The border was much less militarized and fortified than it would become. For obvious reasons, especially the risks of detection and the potentially lethal harms that may result from irregular crossings through remote, inclement locales, unauthorized immigration is generally much less preferable for prospective migrants than lawful migration is. The U.S. immigration

[28] See Table 3.1 (presenting data reflecting that a large percentage of legal immigration to the United States comes from Mexico).

laws in place before 1965 tended to limit incentives for immigration outside of the legal channels, with fewer numbers of undocumented immigrants making the existing restrictions easier to enforce.

The lack of express legal restrictions on immigration from the Western Hemisphere before 1965 should not be understood to mean that the U.S. immigration authorities allowed uncontrolled immigration from the hemisphere. Although the U.S.-Mexico border was much more permeable than it would ultimately become, immigration controls were firmly in place. In fact, U.S. immigration officials for the most part effectively and efficiently managed Mexican migration during the first half of the twentieth century. They did so, however, utilizing much less rigid, even though occasionally vigorous, means than hemispheric and per country ceilings, and did not find it necessary to regularly employ the kinds of aggressive and extremely costly law enforcement measures that prevail along the contemporary U.S.-Mexico border today.

The enforcement of the various provisions of the U.S. immigration laws that exclude certain categories of noncitizens from the country significantly limited Mexican migration, as well as migration from other developing nations populated by people of color. For example, U.S. immigration officers aggressively enforced the bar on the admission of noncitizens into the United States deemed "likely at any time to become a public charge,"[29] known as the "public charge exclusion," in a manner so as to restrict the migration of poor and working people from Mexico.[30] In addition, to limit the overall size of the Mexican immigrant population in this country, the U.S. government regularly deported immigrants. As discussed later in the chapter, however, the numbers of noncitizens deported each year was significantly smaller than they have been in the early years of the twenty-first century.

At various times before 1965, the U.S. government engaged in what amounted to ad hoc deportation campaigns, in no small part triggered by periodic yet regular outbursts of public concern with immigration from Mexico. The most well-known mass enforcement campaign of this variety is the 1954 military operation in the American Southwest that was officially dubbed "Operation Wetback"; it resulted in the deportation of tens of thousands of Mexican immigrants from the United States.[31] Similarly, an unfortunate episode that has been the subject of considerable

[29] *See* Immigration & Nationality Act (INA) § 212(a)(4), 8 U.S.C. § 1182(a)(4).

[30] *See* Kevin R. Johnson, *Public Benefits and Immigration: The Intersection of Immigration Status, Ethnicity, Gender and Class*, 42 UCLA L. REV. 1509, 1519–28. (1995) (analyzing critically the history of the public charge exclusion in the U.S. immigration laws).

[31] *See generally* JUAN RAMÓN GARCÍA, OPERATION WETBACK: THE MASS DEPORTATION OF MEXICAN UNDOCUMENTED WORKERS IN 1954 (1980) (analyzing the military-style mass removal campaign directed at Mexican immigrants known as "Operation Wetback" implemented by General Joseph Swing, then Commissioner of the Immigration and Naturalization Service).

scholarly criticism and legislative hearings in recent years,[32] state and local governments, with the support of the U.S. government, during the Great Depression engaged in a concerted effort resulting in the removal of approximately one million persons of Mexican ancestry, including U.S. citizens, from the United States. Immigrants from Mexico unquestionably were the focal point of both of these deportation campaigns.

In sum, through exclusions and removals done largely at the discretion of immigration enforcement authorities, the U.S. government for the most part effectively and efficiently managed labor migration from Mexico for the first sixty-five years of the twentieth century. The management of enforceable laws served to limit the overall size of the undocumented Mexican immigrant population in the United States. By so doing, the U.S. government at the same time was able to ensure that American employers had access to a ready pool of Mexican labor, with the number of workers expanding in boom times and contracting during economic downturns. Even though racial discrimination at times was a problem, there was room for flexible enforcement of the immigration laws due to the lack of a rigid fixed ceiling on Western Hemisphere immigrants and Mexican immigrants in particular.

The Western Hemisphere Ceiling

One might wonder why, in a time of the steady expansion of the civil rights of racial minorities in the United States, Congress in 1965 decided on a new limit of 120,000 immigrants from the Western Hemisphere per year, with predictable and intentionally detrimental impacts on Latina/o immigration.[33] The answer to this question is an elementary matter of politics. As is ordinarily the case with major pieces of legislation, the Immigration Act of 1965 represented compromises between competing political forces with dramatically different goals, agendas, and constituencies.[34] A majority of Congress ultimately concluded that the bargains included in the final version of the

32 *See generally* Francisco E. Balderrama & Raymond Rodríguez, Decade of Betrayal: Mexican Repatriation in the 1930s (rev. ed. 2006) (documenting the history of the repatriation of persons of Mexican ancestry during the 1930s).

33 The Immigration and Nationality Act of 1965 created the Select Commission on Western Hemisphere Immigration, which in 1968 released the Report of the Select Commission on Western Hemisphere, available at http://babel.hathitrust.org/cgi/pt?id=uc1.32106001216958;view=1up;seq=5, last visited Aug. 29, 2014. The report proposed the implementation of a ceiling on Western Hemisphere immigration, with an exception for those fleeing Fidel Castro's Cuba. The commission, however, could not reach consensus on the specific number at which the Western Hemisphere ceiling should be set. *See* Brian Soucek, The Last Preference: Refugees and the 1965 Immigration Act (Chapter 4 in this volume). As a result of congressional inaction, the Western Hemisphere ceiling of 120,000 provided by the 1965 Act was put into effect in 1968.

34 Senator Edward Kennedy describes the various compromises in the legislative process culminating in the final version of the Immigration Act of 1965 in Edward M. Kennedy, *The Immigration Act of 1965*, 367 Annals 137 (1966).

Act were necessary in order to pass immigration reform legislation – and eliminate the national origins quotas system.[35]

On the one hand, pro-immigrant advocates with the fervor of the civil rights movement behind them stridently demanded removal of the discriminatory national origins quotas system from the U.S. immigration laws.[36] The burgeoning antidiscrimination principle in large part animated the civil rights agenda and the forceful political push for reform, making it nothing less than a moral imperative. The 1965 Act's pro–civil rights aspects, ardently pursued by the Johnson administration and civil rights and immigrant rights groups, was the publicly trumpeted centerpiece of the reform effort.

On the other hand, restrictionists, many of whom were not particularly concerned with the expansion of civil rights to racial minorities, and with very different immigration goals in mind, demanded concessions. In exchange for the elimination of the national origins quotas system, some legislators and advocacy groups sought meaningful limits on immigration from Latin America. Expressing alarm about the projections of dramatic growth in the population of the Western Hemisphere, restrictionists deeply feared a literal tidal wave of uncontrolled immigration. Many supporters of new controls on immigration no doubt believed that Mexico was the primary immigration threat that necessitated aggressive restrictions. As a price to be paid for abolition of the national origins quotas system, the restrictionists strongly supported a ceiling on immigration from the Western Hemisphere, as well as a more rigorous certification process in order to obtain certain employment visas.[37]

35 *See* Hiroshi Motomura, *Whose Alien Nation?: Two Models of Constitutional Immigration Law*, 94 MICH. L. REV. 1927, 1934 (1996).

36 In response, some prominent members of Congress, including one particularly well-known opponent of the civil rights laws, spoke out in defense of the national origins quotas system. *See, e.g.*, S. Rep. No. 89–748, at 56, *reprinted in* 1965 U.S.C.C.A.N. 3328, 3350 (Additional Views of Sen. Ervin) (defending national origins quotas system against allegations of invidious discrimination and declaring that such allegations constitute "mischievous nonsense and sanctimonious propaganda"); 111 CONG. REC. 24237 (Sept. 17, 1965) (comments of Sen. J. Strom Thurmond) ("There is no merit in the contention that the quota system is racist or morally wrong.... No apology is necessary for an immigration law based on the national origins quota system and I make none."); *see also* U.S. Senate, Comm. on Judiciary, Subcomm. on Immigration and Naturalization, July 21, 1965, in 11 OSCAR M. TRELLES & JAMES F. BAILEY, IMMIGRATION AND NATIONALITY ACTS: LEGISLATIVE HISTORIES AND RELATED 1950–1978, at 801 (1979) (Statement of Sam Baccala, Americanism Chairman of the Baltimore District, American Legion) ("[T]here is a lot of talk about the [Immigration and Nationality] Act being discriminatory. I do not know what is discriminatory about it ... and I do not know what is wrong with being discriminatory.... The proposed changes ... will discriminate against gangsters, idiots, prostitutes, and some other undesirables. So the proposed changes are discriminatory, and there is nothing wrong with them.").

37 *See* E.P. HUTCHISON, LEGISLATIVE HISTORY OF AMERICAN IMMIGRATION POLICY 1798–1965, at 375–79 (1981) (explaining how the Western Hemisphere ceiling and the more rigorous labor certification process for employment visas were added to the original bill as part of a compromise

Both sides compromised in order to achieve passage of the Immigration Act of 1965. The precise nature of the legislative bargain turned out to be incredibly costly to future generations of prospective Latina/o immigrants. That cost was often overshadowed by the overwhelmingly positive contemporaneous public statements about the new law. Those statements focused more on the civil rights inspiration for the legislation than on the ultimate package of reforms in the bill passed by Congress.[38]

The House Report to 1976 amendments to the immigration laws aptly summarized the compromise in the 1965 legislation as follows:

> *To a considerable extent, passage of the provision for a ceiling on Western Hemisphere immigration came about because a sufficient number of those opposed to it agreed to accept it as the price that had to be paid in order to insure passage of legislation abolishing the national origins quotas system which dated back to the 1920's.* This latter goal was the primary purpose of the 1965 legislation since its inception, and this emphasis accounts in large part for the very limited consideration given to the actual implementation of the Western Hemisphere ceiling during the 1965 debate.[39]

Several members of Congress frankly acknowledged that the law placed a ceiling on immigration from the Western Hemisphere because of fears of a mass migration from Latin America:

> The most compelling reason for placing a numerical ceiling on immigration from the Western Hemisphere relates to *the worldwide population explosion and the possibility of a sharp increase in immigration from Western Hemisphere countries. Testimony before the Judiciary Committee identified Latin America as the area of greatest future population growth.*[40]

The Senate Report mentioned the need to put a halt to "*unrestricted* immigration" from the Western Hemisphere countries under preexisting law.[41] The report further mentioned the perceived unfairness of not subjecting nations in the West to limitations when immigration from nations in the Eastern Hemisphere in fact was limited.[42]

allowing for the congressional enactment of the legislative package abolishing the national origins quotas system).

38 *See* text accompanying notes 2–6.

39 H.R. Rep. 94–1553, 94th Cong., 2d Sess. 2 (1976) (emphasis added), *reprinted in* 1976 U.S.C.C.A.N. 6073, 6075.

40 H.R. Rep. No. 89–745, at 46, 48 (Additional views of Representatives MacGregor, McCulloch, Poff, Cramer, King, Hutchinson, and McClory) (emphasis added).

41 S. Rep. No. 89–748, at 18 (emphasis added), *reprinted in* 1965 U.S.C.C.A.N. at 3336.

42 *See id.* at 17–18.

The Western Hemisphere ceiling did not go unchallenged. The Senate Report to the 1965 Act includes the "Separate Views of Mr. Kennedy of Massachusetts, Mr. Hart, and Mr. Javits," which criticized the new Western Hemisphere ceiling:

> [A]t no other time in the history of our immigration policy have we disturbed or altered the unique relationship that exists among the nations of the New World.... *Now, despite the absence of any real immigration problem, and the presence of more stringent qualitative controls on entry to this country, it is proposed that we take this historic step backward in our otherwise progressive Western Hemisphere policies.... The majority of the hemisphere immigrants come to us from our closest neighbors – Canada and Mexico. We have long welcomed especially the contributions of these nations to our culture and society.*[43]

Consistent with the celebratory mood surrounding the passage of the legislation, the House and Senate reports on the 1965 Act highlighted how the reforms repealed the discriminatory national origins quotas system. At the same time, this legislative history, although properly acknowledging that the legislation imposed new restrictions on immigration from the Western Hemisphere, tended to minimize the significance of the new hemispheric ceiling and conveniently ignored the intended impacts of the legislation on prospective Latina/o immigrants.[44]

From a pragmatic political perspective, the decision to downplay the anti-Latina/o impacts of the new Western Hemisphere ceiling was entirely understandable. In an era marked by the growing dominance of the antidiscrimination principle in American public life, there was little political upside to publicizing the restrictive anti-Mexican, anti-Latina/o aspects of the 1965 Act. The new Western Hemisphere ceiling and its stated purpose were fundamentally antithetical to the increasingly popular civil rights values that served as the impetus to the immigration reform movement and the demand for abolition of the discriminatory national origins quotas system.

In fairness, the Immigration Act of 1965's elimination of the national origins quotas system was properly characterized as being a positive change to the U.S. immigration laws. The abolition of that system ended decades of discriminatory exclusion of Asian and other disfavored groups, once deemed under the law to be unworthy of admission into the United States. It also signaled the end of immigration laws that on their face discriminated on the basis of race.

The elimination of that discriminatory system in the Immigration Act of 1965, however, is far from the whole story. In an influential book analyzing the emergence of "illegal aliens" in modern American law and social life, Mae Ngai insightfully

[43] *Id.* at 59 (emphasis added).

[44] *See* H.R. Rep. No. 89–745, at 46; S. Rep. No. 89–748, at 17–18, *reprinted in* 1965 U.S.C.C.A.N. 3328, 3336.

summarizes the anti-Latina/o underpinnings of the 1965 Act.[45] She accurately observes that "[t]he abolition of the national origins quotas system garnered the most attention and *defined the law as a progressive measure*."[46] However, far from a "progressive measure," the 1965 Act, due to logrolling in a time when Latina/os had limited political clout, had potent restrictionist support and clearly discriminatory intents and purposes.

Indeed, the 1965 Act's Western Hemisphere ceiling attracted the strong endorsement of "one of the most restrictionist organizations" of the era, the powerful American Legion.[47] The fact that a group seeking to restrict immigration from Latin America supported passage of the legislation unquestionably signals that the legislation should not necessarily be classified as an unqualified civil rights achievement.

Even though knowledgeable observers could see that Mexico would be the nation most directly affected by the new Western Hemisphere ceiling, the House and Senate reports failed to identify by name the specific nation whose citizens would be *most* affected. The explanation for that omission is painfully obvious. Highlighting the specific detrimental impact of the Immigration Act of 1965 on migration from Mexico would effectively admit that the new ceiling would have discriminatory, country-specific impacts. Although such restrictive impacts were entirely consistent with the legislation, a candid admission of those impacts might have damaged U.S. foreign relations with Mexico, a neighbor and extremely important regional ally of the United States. Officials in the State Department expressed concerns that a Western Hemisphere ceiling alone might adversely affect diplomatic relations with all of the nations of Latin America.[48]

The blue ribbon Select Commission on Immigration and Refugee Policy in 1981 matter-of-factly explained the discriminatory purposes underlying the bargain struck by Congress in the Immigration Act of 1965:

> The United States was … far from free of prejudice … and one part of the 1965 law reflected change in policy that was in part due to antiforeign sentiments. Prejudice against dark-skinned people … remained strong. *In the years after World War II, as the proportion of Spanish-speaking residents increased, much of the*

45 *See* Mae M. Ngai, Impossible Subjects: Illegal Aliens and the Making of America 258–64 (2004); *see also* Gerald P. López, *Don't We Like Them Illegal?*, 45 UC Davis L. Rev. 1711 (2012) (analyzing critically how the operation of the U.S. immigration laws have facilitated the creation of the undocumented immigrant population in the United States).

46 Ngai, *supra* note 45, at 255 (emphasis added).

47 *Id.* at 260; *see* David M. Reimers, Still the Golden Door: The Third World Comes to America 69–72 (2d ed. 1992) (summarizing the position of the American Legion in advocating for the passage of the Immigration Act of 1965).

48 *See, e.g.*, 111 Cong. Rec. 21,809–10 (1965) (Letter of U.S. Department of State, Undersecretary of State and various comments).

> *lingering nativism in the United States was directed against those from Mexico and Central and South America.... Giving in to ... pressures as a price to be paid for abolishing the national origins system, Congress put into the 1965 amendments a ceiling [on Western Hemisphere immigration] to close the last remaining open door of U.S. policy.*[49]

Unfortunately, anti-Latina/o animus has a deep, if not proud, tradition in the United States. Racism has adversely affected the civil rights of persons of Mexican ancestry living in this country for decades.[50] Such sentiment has historically had a pronounced influence on U.S. immigration law and its enforcement.[51] John F. Kennedy himself acknowledged that migrants from Mexico and Puerto Rico "often receive the same discriminatory treatment and opprobrium that were faced by other waves of immigrants."[52] Sadly enough, racial animosity, which has been inflamed in modern times by the lengthy, deeply divisive national debate over immigration reform, has flared in episodic outbursts of hate violence directed at

[49] U.S. SELECT COMM'N ON IMMIGRATION AND REFUGEE POLICY, STAFF REPORT: U.S. IMMIGRATION POLICY AND THE NATIONAL INTEREST 208 (1981) (emphasis added) (footnote omitted). Not long after passage of the 1965 Act, one commentator observed that the Western Hemisphere ceiling

> applies to countries that never before were subject to any numerical limitation scheme. But it is only the latest expression of a continuing refrain in immigration legislation, which began with the passage of the Chinese Exclusion Act some 85 years ago. *It is the fear of being overwhelmed by great numbers of economically oppressed people who cannot readily be assimilated. In the debates prior to the passage of the new law some senators expressed fears of population explosions. It can be conjectured that in large part these fears were a reaction to the continuing unrest in Latin America coupled with our apparent inability to resolve the problems adequately.*

Thomas J. Scully, *Is the Door Open Again? – A Survey of Our New Immigration Law*, 13 UCLA L. REV. 227, 230 (1966) (emphasis added) (footnote omitted); *see* Kevin R. Johnson, *"Melting Pot" or "Ring of Fire"?: Assimilation and the Mexican-American Experience*, 85 CAL. L. REV. 1259, 1279–86 (1997) (analyzing popular concerns with assimilation of persons of Mexican ancestry into U.S. society).

Another important factor likely contributed to the admittedly anti-Latina/o bent of the 1965 Act. For a variety of reasons, the civil rights concerns of Latina/os, including those surrounding immigration law and enforcement, have not historically been thought of as core civil rights concerns. *See* Juan F. Perea, *The Black/White Binary Paradigm of Race: The "Normal Science" of American Racial Thought*, 85 CAL. L. REV. 1213 (1997); Richard Delgado, *Rodrigo's Fifteenth Chronicle: Racial Mixture, Latino-Critical Scholarship, and the Black-White Binary*, 75 TEX. L. REV. 1181 (1997). Thus, the impacts of the Western Hemisphere ceilings on potential Latina/o immigrants were not necessarily viewed as discriminatory in the same way that the Jim Crow laws, or the Chinese exclusion laws, were generally viewed.

[50] *See, e.g.*, Hernandez v. Texas, 347 U.S. 475 (1954) (holding that the exclusion of U.S. citizens of Mexican ancestry from juries in a Texas county violated the Fourteenth Amendment). *See generally* Rodolfo F. Acuña, Occupied America: A History of Chicanos (7th ed. 2010) (chronicling the long history of institutional racism against Chicana/os in the United States).

[51] *See generally* ALFREDO MIRANDÉ, GRINGO JUSTICE (1990) (analyzing the historical influence of anti-Mexican animus on U.S. border enforcement).

[52] KENNEDY, *supra* note 8, at 63.

Latina/o immigrants, as well as state and local immigration enforcement measures discussed later in this chapter.[53]

Racial anxieties provided the necessary political traction for the Western Hemisphere ceiling, which responded to the perceived threat of a mass migration from Mexico and Latin America. As we shall see in Section 3.3, such sentiment continues to influence modern U.S. immigration law and its enforcement.

Given the legislative history of the 1965 Act, it is difficult to deny that the admitted desire of Congress to limit Latina/o migration – and the general animosity held by segments of the public toward Latina/o immigrants – contributed to significant support for the legislative package and helped ensure its passage. Congress's primary immigration fear at the time of the passage of the 1965 Act was the mass migration of Latina/os from Latin America to the United States.

In sum, it should not be surprising that anti-Latina/o sentiment, which is particularly strong in certain regions of the United States (and has grown significantly in other areas in the last fifty years), influenced a critical compromise in a major piece of immigration reform legislation. Nor should it be a surprise, given the political forces at work, that the Immigration Act of 1965, which ultimately contributed greatly to the growth of the undocumented Mexican immigrant population, commenced an extended process of escalating restrictions on migration from Mexico, as well as the rest of Latin America, to the United States. The Act, in effect, established restrictions on immigration from Mexico as a legitimate policy goal, a goal that over time grew to dominate American immigration law and its enforcement.

To fully appreciate the political dynamics resulting in passage of the Immigration Act of 1965, one must keep in mind that Latina/os were in a far different place in terms of raw political power in 1965 than in 2015. Congress passed the 1965 Act decades before Latina/os wielded formidable political power in the United States. In the America of the 1960s, Latina/os exerted limited political clout, especially on the national political scene. Unlike today, the Democratic and Republican Parties in 1965 did not aggressively compete for Latina/o voters as a much-cherished constituency, with the well-known ability to influence the outcome of national, state, and local elections. Latina/o civil rights organizations concerned with immigration were not politically powerful. Not many Latina/o civil rights groups such as the Mexican American Legal Defense and Educational Fund, National Council of La Raza, and

[53] *See* Kevin R. Johnson & Joanna Cuevas Ingram, *Anatomy of a Modern Day Lynching: The Relationship Between Hate Crimes Against Latina/os and the Debate Over Immigration Reform*, 91 N.C. L. Rev. 1613 (2013) (analyzing how the contemporary failure of Congress to enact comprehensive immigration reform and the continued heated public ferment over immigration have contributed to hate crimes directed at Latina/o immigrants); *see also* Richard Delgado, *The Law of the Noose: A History of Latino Lynching*, 44 Harv. C.R.-C.L. L. Rev. 297 (2009) (studying the largely unknown history of lynching of Latina/os in the United States).

Latino Justice existed. Consequently, in a political milieu in which Latina/os were viewed as, at best, marginal players, an anti-Latina/o immigration reform measure was much more likely to be passed in Congress then than it would be today.

It goes without saying that the growth of Latina/o political power is attributable to the fact that, despite growing restrictions in the immigration laws as well as heightened enforcement, the Latina/o population has grown dramatically in the last half-century.[54] Latina/o voters in modern times can greatly influence, if not ultimately determine, the outcome of elections. As a result, Latina/o civil rights and immigrant rights activists, and Latina/os today generally, exercise considerable political power; political candidates of both major political parties aggressively pursue Latina/o votes. Moreover, Latina/os in contemporary politics enjoy the vigilant and aggressive protection of advocacy groups that carefully scrutinize immigration legislation. To fully understand the anti-Latina/o aspects of the Immigration Act of 1965, one must consider Latina/o political power at that particular historical moment, not think of such power as it exists today.

Labor Certification with Teeth

Public concern with the perceived labor market impacts of immigration has flared regularly in U.S. immigration history. State and federal legislatures, for example, passed laws in the 1800s to respond to "coolie labor" from China, which was alleged to unfairly compete with domestic workers.[55] Consistent with that history, certain members of the 1965 Congress worried about the downward pressures on the wage scale caused by a potential mass migration of immigrants from Latin America to the United States.

In the compromises culminating in the enactment of the Immigration Act of 1965, Congress responded to the demand of organized labor to increase the rigor of the labor certification process necessary to secure certain employment visas. By so doing, Congress made it more difficult to obtain the relatively limited number of employment visas and further restricted the limited opportunities for legal immigration to the United States by low- and medium-skilled workers. Of course, Mexico is the home of many of those would-be migrants. Concern with Mexican

[54] While Latina/o political power has grown over the last fifty years, it remains constrained by the fact that a significant portion of Latina/os in the United States are not citizens and cannot vote. *See* Kevin R. Johnson, *A Handicapped, Not "Sleeping," Giant: The Devastating Impact of the Initiative Process on Latina/o and Immigrant Communities*, 96 CAL. L. REV. 1259 (2008).

[55] *See, e.g.*, 1862 Cal. State 462, Ch. 339 (An Act to Protect Free White Labor Against Competition with Chinese Coolie Labor). *See generally* RONALD TAKAKI, STRANGERS FROM A DIFFERENT SHORE: A HISTORY OF ASIAN AMERICANS (1989) (analyzing history of discrimination in the United States against persons from Asia, including widespread discrimination against Chinese immigrants in the United States in the 1800s).

labor, as well as capping Latin American migration, influenced the push to place a ceiling on immigration from the Western Hemisphere.[56]

Both the labor certification amendments and the Western Hemisphere ceiling were added to the bill in the legislative process as part of a package of compromises to secure the votes necessary for passage of the 1965 legislation. Although not part of its original bill, the Johnson administration supported the amendments to the legislation that toughened labor certification and understood that the increased vigors of the process would place a de facto cap on immigration from the Western Hemisphere.

A member of Congress at the time, Peter Rodino later observed that the dual purpose of the labor certification provision – the protection of American labor and the numerical restriction of Western Hemisphere immigration – is apparent from the House report explaining the provisions of the Immigration Act of 1965:

> The amended section 212(a)(14) represents a substantial departure from existing law. Presently, the provisions of section 212(a)(14) operate only when the Secretary of Labor invokes them by certification which has the effect of excluding any intending immigrant, within the scope of certification, who would likely displace a qualified American worker, or whose employment in the United States would adversely affect the wages and working conditions of workers similarly employed in the United States. This procedure is reversed under the amendment. Responsibility is placed upon the intending immigrant to obtain the Secretary of Labor's clearance prior to issuance of a visa. *The committee is aware of what appears to be an increasing desire of natives of the countries of the Western Hemisphere to immigrate to the United States.*[57]

As amended by the 1965 Act, the invigorated labor certification process requires a noncitizen applicant for certain categories of employment-based immigrant visas to secure U.S. Department of Labor approval. Specifically, the Department must affirmatively certify that American workers are not available to perform the desired work at the prevailing wage and that the employment of immigrant workers will not negatively affect the wages and conditions of domestic workers.[58] Congress

[56] *See* Enid Trucios-Haynes, *Temporary Workers and Future Immigration Policy Conflicts: Protecting U.S. Workers and Satisfying the Demand for Global Human Capital*, 40 BRANDEIS L.J. 967, 975 (2002) (summarizing the history of efforts in the U.S. immigration laws to protect domestic labor, including the labor certification amendments in the Immigration Act of 1965 that serve "as a functional numerical control on Western Hemisphere immigration").

[57] Peter W. Rodino, *The Impact of Immigration on the American Labor Market*, 27 RUTGERS L. REV. 245, 255 (1974) (quoting H.R. Rep. No. 745, 89th Cong., 1st Sess. 14 (1965)) (emphasis added).

[58] *See* INA § 212(a)(5)(A), 8 U.S.C. § 1182(a)(5)(A); 8 C.F.R. § 656.2 (2013). As amended, that section provides that

> [a]ny alien who seeks to enter the United States for the purpose of performing skilled or unskilled labor is inadmissible, unless the Secretary of Labor has determined and certified to the Secretary

tightened the requirements for labor certification in the hopes of protecting American workers from what had been characterized as unfair competition by noncitizen labor.[59]

The labor certification requirement buttresses a plethora of other restrictions on labor migration in U.S. immigration law that all are ostensibly designed to protect domestic workers. Most importantly, current law generally restricts the vast majority of the limited number of employment-based immigrant visas to high-skilled workers, for whom labor certification is not generally required. Those restrictions on lawful labor migration, combined with labor certification and the Western Hemisphere ceiling, serve as a brake on the immigration of labor and contribute to the pressures for undocumented migration from Mexico and other developing nations. Many would-be immigrant workers are left without viable avenues for lawful admission into the United States and, as a consequence, resort to migration outside legally approved channels.[60]

The End of the Bracero Program

An important change to U.S. immigration law occurred, almost contemporaneously with the passage of the 1965 Act, which significantly limited lawful labor migration – particularly of low-wage agricultural workers – from Mexico to the United States. The year 1964 marked the end of the "Bracero Program," which since World War II had allowed tens of thousands of "guest" workers, referred to in Spanish as "braceros" (with "brazos" meaning arms), from Mexico to temporarily come lawfully to the United States to work the fields.[61] Open exclusively to Mexican citizens, this guest worker program, which permitted the regular legal migration of agricultural workers, had been created and implemented pursuant to bilateral agreements between the U.S. and Mexican governments.

> of State and the Attorney General that (I) there are not sufficient workers who are able, willing, qualified . . . and available at the time of application for a visa . . . and (II) the employment of such alien will not adversely affect the wages and working conditions of workers in the United States similarly employed.

[59] *See* Legomsky & Rodríguez, *supra* note 19, at 307–32 (explaining the operation of the labor certification process necessary to secure certain types of employment visas).

[60] *See* Kevin R. Johnson, *The Intersection of Race and Class in U.S. Immigration Law and Enforcement*, 72 Law & Contemp. Probs. 1, 13–15 (2009).

[61] *See* John A. Scanlan, *Immigration Law and the Illusion of Numerical Control*, 36 U. Miami L. Rev. 819, 829–30 (1982) (noting that, in an attempt to restrict immigration, the Immigration Act of 1965 "subjected Western Hemisphere immigration for the first time to an annual numerical limitation" and came at roughly the same time as the dismantling of the Bracero Program) (footnote omitted). *See generally* Kitty Calavita, Inside the State: The Bracero Program, Immigration, and the I.N.S. (1992) (analyzing critically the creation and operation of the Bracero Program).

Migration under the auspices of the Bracero Program helped build on the previously discussed well-established employment and family networks that historically have fueled migration from Mexico to the United States. Its demise reduced opportunities for lawful labor migration from Mexico.

Supported by growers in the United States seeking access to a low-wage labor force, the Bracero Program constituted a major avenue for the legal migration of agricultural workers from Mexico. Along with the new Western Hemisphere ceiling imposed by the Immigration Act of 1965 and the tightening of labor certification for certain employment visas, the dismantling of this major guest worker program contributed significantly to pressures for increased undocumented migration by Mexican citizens seeking employment, especially in agriculture, in the United States.[62]

In large part due to the demise of the Bracero Program, undocumented Mexican workers today dominate the ranks of farm laborers in the United States. While migrants from Mexico long have filled farm labor jobs – and still do today – what changed was their immigration status. The transformation of the immigration status of the agricultural labor force was due to the end of lawful admission of Mexican workers through the Bracero Program. Because of the change in the law, growers in the post-1965 period in effect replaced *legal* Mexican workers with *undocumented* Mexican labor.

The reduction in the number of lawful immigrants from Mexico admitted to the United States did not diminish the robust demand by Mexican workers to come work in the United States. Nor did these measures in any way reduce the demand by American employers, particularly in the agricultural, construction, and service industries, for relatively inexpensive labor. With the expansion of the U.S. economy, especially in the 1990s, demand for such labor grew substantially.

In short, the series of new restrictive immigration measures simply ignored the powerful economic incentives for labor migration from Latin America. U.S. immigration law to this day fails to consider the demand for immigration by foreign citizens seeking to pursue economic opportunity in the United States and the demand by profit-maximizing American employers for relatively inexpensive labor, as well as the differential demand for migration between nations. The Immigration Act of 1965 simply did not address the need for immigrant labor in agriculture that increased as a result of the end of the flow of temporary workers from Mexico under the Bracero Program. Consequently, undocumented Mexican

62 For analysis of the failure of Congress in the Immigration Act of 1965 to address the increased demand for workers resulting from the demise of the Bracero Program, see Leticia M. Saucedo, The Impact of 1965 Immigration and Nationality Act on the Evolution of Temporary Guest Worker Programs, or How the 1965 Act Punted on Creating a Rightful Place for Mexican Worker Migration (Chapter 9 in this volume).

workers replaced temporary workers from Mexico who previously had come to the United States legally.

The Restrictive Impacts

Congress added the new Western Hemisphere ceiling and tighter labor certification requirements as a compromise to ensure passage of the Immigration Act of 1965. Along with the elimination of the Bracero Program, the features of the new law resulted in an increase in the unmet demand in Mexico for legal labor migration to the United States. Demand for relatively inexpensive labor by American employers continued. Unmet immigration demand ultimately helped fuel the emergence of the large, and growing, undocumented Mexican immigrant underclass that lives and works in the United States.[63]

As immigrants were denied lawful entry into the country year after year, the number of undocumented immigrants in the United States grew slowly but surely over time. That population today comprises approximately 11–12 million people, with a majority of this population originating in Mexico. Given the unrealistic efforts to artificially restrain immigration demand in Mexico, many would-be immigrants from that country have circumvented the law and came without proper authorization to live and work in the United States.

The 1976 Amendments: The Extension of the Per Country Ceilings to the Western Hemisphere

A little more than a decade after passage of the Immigration Act of 1965, Congress took another major step toward restricting Mexican immigration to the United States. In 1976, Congress passed the Immigration and Nationality Act Amendments of 1976, which built on the 1965 legislation to even more directly restrict immigration from Mexico and all of Latin America. This legislation, among other things, did so by extending the per-country ceilings from nations in the Eastern Hemisphere to those in the Western Hemisphere and further tightening the labor certification requirements for employment visas.[64]

The 1976 amendments represented a major change to the Immigration Act of 1965. At a most fundamental level, Congress for the very first time in American history formally and directly placed a fixed, legally enforceable ceiling on annual migration from Mexico. This as a practical matter means that, *despite the fact that*

[63] *See* NGAI, *supra* note 45, at 261.

[64] Immigration and Nationality Act Amendments of 1976, Pub. L. No. 94–571, § 2, 90 Stat. 2703, 2703 (codified as amended at, inter alia, INA § 201(a), 8 U.S.C. § 1151(a)). For a brief summary of the impacts of the 1976 amendments on labor certification and the negative impacts on potential immigrants from the Western Hemisphere, see Afterword, *The Immigration and Nationality Act Amendments of 1976*, 14 SAN DIEGO L. REV. 326, 329–30 (1976).

Mexico has the greatest demand in the world for immigration to the United States, it has the exact same annual ceiling as every other nation.[65]

In signing the Immigration and Nationality Act Amendments of 1976 into law, President Gerald Ford expressed reservations about the negative impact of extending the per country ceilings on legal immigration from Mexico to the United States:

> I am concerned ... about one aspect of the legislation which has the effect of reducing the legal immigration into this country from Mexico. *Currently about 40,000 natives of Mexico legally immigrate to the United States each year. This legislation [through imposition of the per country ceiling on Mexico] would cut that number in half.*
>
> The United States has a very special and historic relationship with our neighbor to the south. In view of this special status we have with the Mexican Government and the Mexican people, I will submit legislation to the Congress in January to increase the immigration quotas for Mexicans desiring to come to the United States.[66]

President Carter later endorsed legislation that would have increased the number of immigrant visas to 50,000 annually for Canada and Mexico, a proposal that Congress rejected in 1976.[67]

The House Report also acknowledged the impacts of the imposition of a per county ceiling on immigration from Mexico:

> Based on a review of existing data, a uniform ceiling for each country ... would be preferable. This would permit an equitable distribution of immigration from throughout the hemisphere and from throughout the world. Problems with illegal immigration will exist whether immigration from Mexico is limited to 20,000 or 35,000 per year or not at all. While permitting 35,000 immigrants a year from Mexico would ease their demand slightly, this would only increase the waiting lists and the demand throughout the rest of the hemisphere....
>
> The decision by this Committee to limit all countries to 20,000 has been based primarily on the desire that this legislation mark the final end of an immigration quota system based on nationality, whether the rationale behind it be the alleged national origins of our citizenry, as it was in the past, or geographical proximity – the argument previously advanced for preferential treatment of Canada and Mexico. *The proposed legislation rejects the concept of a "special relationship" between this*

65 There are certain exceptions to the per-country ceilings, including for noncitizens who marry U.S. citizens. *See* LEGOMSKY & RODRÍGUEZ, *supra* note 19, at 251–52 (describing generally the exceptions).

66 Gerald R. Ford, President of the United States, *Statement by the President on Signing H.R. 14535 into Law* (Oct. 25, 1976), *in* 12 WEEKLY COMPILATION OF PRES. DOCUMENTS 1548 (emphasis added).

67 *See* Message from the President of the United States, *Undocumented Aliens*, H. Doc. No. 95–202, 95th Cong., 1st Sess., Aug. 4, 1977, at 6.

> *country and certain other countries as a basis for our immigration law, in favor of a uniform treatment for all countries.*[68]

Nothing appears to have come of President Ford's promise in the signing statement to the 1976 amendments to propose legislation to increase the immigration ceiling for Mexico and thus to bring it closer to pre-1965 levels. Congress never passed such a law. Nor has Congress taken any meaningful steps in the intervening thirty-five-plus years to meaningfully ameliorate the impacts of the 1976 reduction on legal Mexican migration.[69]

The greater Mexican-American community in the United States immediately recognized the impacts of the 1976 amendments. At the time of the signing of the bill, an article in the *New York Times* reported that:

> Mexican-Americans are strongly opposed to the new law … *Legal Mexican immigration to this country has been averaging 40,000 people a year in recent years. Under the new law, that number would be cut in half.*
>
> *A spokesman for the Immigration Service said that the pressures caused by the reduced quota for Mexico would probably produce an increase in the number of Mexicans seeking to enter the United States illegally.*
>
> Al Perez, associate counsel of the Mexican-American Legal Defense and Educational Fund, said that Chicanos were "very opposed" to the new law because its impact on Mexicans, he said, is discriminatory.[70]

In the 1976 amendments, Congress reformed the immigration laws while ignoring the great demand in Mexico for immigration to the United States just as it did in the Immigration Act of 1965. Without consideration by the U.S. immigration laws for the demand of migration by the citizens of any specific nation, Congress imposed the same annual ceiling on all nations around the world.

As mentioned in the House Report, Congress rejected proposals that would have allowed larger numbers of immigrants from Canada and Mexico based on the historic relationship, including more than a century of immigration, between the United States and those nations.[71] The hearings on the legislation made it readily apparent that the per-country quotas would reduce Mexican

68 H.R. Rep. 94–1553, 94th Cong., 2d Sess. 9 (1976), *reprinted in* 1976 U.S.C.C.A.N. 6073, 6081 (emphasis added).

69 For contemporary legislative proposals focused on easing restrictions on immigration from Mexico, see, for example, Samuel W. Bettwy, *A Proposed Legislative Scheme to Solve the Mexican Immigration Problem*, 2 San Diego Int'l L.J. 93 (2001).

70 Philip Shabecoff, *Ford Signs Immigration Bill Aiding Residents of Western Hemisphere*, N.Y. Times, Oct. 24, 1976, at 26 (emphasis added).

71 *See* James Francis Bailey, Immigration and Nationality Legislative Histories and Related Documents, 1977–1986, at 64–65 (1987).

immigration.[72] Although expressing concern with the increase in "illegal aliens" from Mexico, Congress moved forward with the uniform per-country ceilings that ultimately added further pressures for undocumented immigration from Mexico.[73]

To this day, the per-country ceilings remain a cornerstone of the U.S. immigration laws. They continue to have a pronounced impact on the flow of legal immigration from countries such as Mexico and other developing nations, populated predominantly by people of color. "[B]y extending the system of formal equality in admission to all countries, *the ... law [as amended] ... creat[ed] greater opportunities for migration from Asia and Africa but severely restricted it from Mexico, the Caribbean, and Latin America*."[74]

Put simply, the 1965 Act, as extended by the 1976 amendments, was a double-edged sword for prospective immigrants to the United States from the developing world. Immigrants from Asia benefited substantially from the elimination of discriminatory quotas and other exclusionary provisions. At the same time, prospective Latina/o immigrants lost out on lawful immigration opportunities through the imposition of new, unprecedented numerical ceilings established without considering the demand for immigration to the United States in Mexico and the rest of Latin America.

How the Per-Country Ceilings Suppress Legal Latina/o Immigration

Depending on nothing other than their country of origin, the per-country ceilings mean that similarly situated noncitizens may face dramatically longer waiting periods to lawfully immigrate to the United States. The longer the delay, the greater the incentive for immigration to this country outside avenues authorized by law. As the U.S. immigration laws currently operate, long lines of many years ultimately are determined by the prospective immigrants' national origin.

Because of the per-country ceilings, many would-be Mexican immigrants today experience significant impediments to lawful admission into the United States. The per-country ceilings create lengthy delays for immigrants from developing nations populated by people of color with high demand for immigration to the United States, such as Mexico, the Philippines, and India, and significantly shorter waiting

72 *See id.*

73 *See, e.g.*, Hearings Before the Subcomm. on Immigration, Citizenship, and International Law of the Comm. on Judiciary, House of Representatives, *Illegal Aliens*, 94th Cong., 1st Sess. (1975); *see also Illegal Aliens: Analysis and Background*, U.S. H. Rep., Comm. on Judiciary, 95th Cong., 1st Sess. (1977) (examining impacts of undocumented immigration on the United States).

After applying the per-country ceilings to the Western Hemisphere nations in 1976, Congress in 1978 established one worldwide ceiling of 290,000 covering both hemispheres. *See* Pub. L. No. 95–412, 92 Stat. 907 (1978).

74 Ngai, *supra* note 45, at 263 (emphasis added) (footnote omitted); *see* Elizabeth Keyes, *Race and Immigration, Then and Now: How the Shift to "Worthiness" Undermines the 1965 Immigration Law's Civil Rights Goals*, 57 How. L.J. 899 (2014).

periods for people from almost all other nations, including most of Europe and the developed world.[75] The ceilings have the greatest impacts on citizens of countries with the highest demand for immigration to the United States, primarily nations in the developing world populated by people of color, which have an annual demand for immigration far in excess of the annual ceiling.

Consider the contemporary impacts of the per-country ceilings on immigration from Mexico. In July 2013, the U.S. government processed visa applications filed by unmarried sons and daughters of U.S. citizens[76] from most nations submitted in *June 2006*; at the same time, it was processing the applications of Mexican citizens submitted in *August 1993*, almost thirteen years earlier, for a total waiting period of more than twenty years.[77] In that month, the U.S. government processed visa applications for unmarried sons and daughters of lawful permanent residents who applied in *November 2001*, compared to *November 1993* for applicants from Mexico, with a total wait of nearly two decades. The significant delay for issuance of both types of family immigrant visas, which Congress created in order to promote the reunification of families, results from nothing other than the national origin of the visa applicants, the high demand for migration to the United States from Mexico, and the ordinary operation of the per-country ceiling.[78]

Delays of twenty or more years for lawful immigration to the United States are simply not realistic for noncitizens seeking to rejoin their parents and other close family members in the United States.[79] Family members may die before the U.S. government issues immigrant visas to noncitizens waiting in decades-long lines. Prolonged delays to rejoin immediate family members understandably create virtually irresistible incentives for noncitizens to migrate outside the avenues available under the law.

Given the formidable barriers to legal migration that ignore the great demand for migration from Mexico, it is not mere coincidence that the largest

[75] *See* Kevin R. Johnson & Bernard Trujillo, Immigration Law and the US-Mexico Border 125–27 (2011); *see also* Bernard Trujillo, *Immigrant Visa Distribution: The Case of Mexico*, 2000 Wis. L. Rev. 713 (analyzing critically the negative impacts of the per country ceilings on legal immigration from Mexico).

[76] *See* U.S. Dep't of State, Bureau of Consular Affairs, Visa Bulletin 2 (July 2013), available at http://www.travel.state.gov/visa/bulletin/bulletin_5993.html.

[77] *See id.*

[78] *See* INA § 203(a)(2), 8 U.S.C. § 1153(a)(2).

[79] In one case in which the California Supreme Court authorized an undocumented immigrant from Mexico to be licensed as an attorney, the noncitizen in question initially had applied for a lawful permanent resident visa in 1994 based on his parent's lawful immigration status in the United States but had not been issued one by the time that the court issued its opinion in 2014. *See In re* Garcia, 58 Cal. 4th 440, 447–48, 165 Cal. Rptr. 3d 855, 860–61, 315 P.3d 117, 121–22 (2014).

Moreover, children of visa applicants who "age out" (*i.e.*, turn twenty-one) before their visa is issued must move to the back of the line for an immigrant visa. *See* Scialabba v. Cuellar de Osorio, 134 S. Ct. 2191 (2014).

component – approximately 60 percent – of the undocumented immigrant population in the United States originates in Mexico. This large component of the undocumented population directly results from the long lines for immigrant visas for Mexican applicants, which are generally among the longest of all nations, as well as the highest demand in the world for migrating here.

The popular conception of undocumented Mexican immigrants as "law breakers" fails to acknowledge their unequal treatment under modern U.S. immigration laws. Besides the delays imposed on persons eligible for lawful immigration and the imposition of an unrealistic ceiling on immigration from Mexico, many Mexican citizens who desire to migrate to the United States simply are not eligible for any kind of family or employment visa. Put differently, despite claims that undocumented immigrants should have waited in "line" like any other noncitizen seeking admission, there is no line for many of them to wait in to immigrate to the United States lawfully.

The immigration reforms in 1965 and 1976 helped transform what were legal immigrants before 1965 into the undocumented Mexican "shadow" population in the United States, which now numbers in the millions. The bottom line is that "[t]he number of migrants entering the United States from Mexico did not change very much after 1965. What changed was their legal status."[80]

In summary, the new per-country ceilings have resulted in years-long waits for lawful admission to come to the United States for many visa applicants from Mexico. Many other would-be immigrants today lack any legal avenue for coming to the United States. As a direct consequence, the undocumented immigrant population, with a majority of this population being from Mexico, increased significantly after implementation of the Western Hemisphere ceiling by the 1965 Act and the extension of the per-country ceilings to Latin America under the 1976 amendments.

The Per-Country Ceilings and Differential Demand for Immigration

There are a number of determinants that influence the overall demand of a nation's citizens to migrate to the United States, including relative employment opportunities between nations, geographic proximity to this country, historical migration patterns, existing employment and family networks, differences (or lack thereof) of culture and language, and a myriad of other political, social, and economic factors. As previously discussed, those factors in combination help explain why citizens of Mexico generally seek to migrate to the United States in far greater numbers than do citizens of Canada.

80 Douglas S. Massey, *Response to Joseph Carens' The Case for Amnesty*, *in* JOSEPH H. CARENS, IMMIGRANTS AND THE RIGHT TO STAY 75 (Joseph H. Carens ed., 2010).

The per-country ceilings applied to the nations of the Western Hemisphere in 1976 literally impose a proverbial "one size fits all" approach to migration from nations across the globe. The fixed ceiling fails to account for historical, economic, political, and social factors that shape immigration demand from any particular nation. In fact, the relative demand of a nation's citizens to immigrate to the United States is wholly ignored by, and completely irrelevant to, the ceilings and the available avenues for legal immigration under the U.S. immigration laws.

As the "one size fits all" moniker suggests, the approach of the modern U.S. immigration law does not fit all nations well or equally. That is exemplified by the fact that the lines for certain immigrant visas are extremely long for citizens of the nations with highest immigrant demand, such as Mexico, compared to the lines of citizens of other nations for immigration to the United States.

An alternative immigration admissions scheme that is more flexible, like that which existed in the United States with respect to Mexico and the rest of Latin America before 1965, would be a more realistic approach to effectively managing modern migration to the United States. Such a system would permit the reasonable accommodation of a nation's demand for migration. The system could be based on demand for migration in light of the comparative economic opportunity between nations, national ties as well as family and employment networks, and historical migration patterns, all of which directly affect a nation's demand for immigration to this country.

The simple fact of the matter is that if the modern U.S. immigration laws more closely approximated the demand for immigration to this country, the incentives for unauthorized immigration would be significantly reduced. Consequently, the population of undocumented immigrants in the United States would likely be much smaller than it is today. Moreover, if better-calibrated laws were able to more closely approximate immigration demand, the U.S. government would find it significantly easier to enforce the law. Unrealistic restrictions make effective and efficient enforcement difficult, if not impossible. With more realistic restrictions, extraordinary efforts and expenditures would not be necessary to enforce the immigration laws.

In contrast, the current immigration regime in the United States cannot reasonably be characterized as flexible and adaptable, or effectively and efficiently enforced. Unrealistic, rigid limits on immigration, with little relationship to immigration supply and demand, have proven extremely difficult for U.S. immigration authorities to enforce. That difficulty has resulted in the creation and maintenance of a large undocumented population in this country. The existence of that population, in turn, has helped spawn widespread public dissatisfaction with the contemporary American immigration system. All of these factors militate in favor of fundamental reform of the U.S. immigration laws, a task that has eluded Congress for more than a decade.

The Disparate Impacts of Uniform Limits

One might point out that the Western Hemisphere ceiling in the Immigration Act of 1965 and the per-country ceilings added to nations in the hemisphere in 1976 apply to Canada as well as Mexico. At least superficially, that fact tends to undermine any claim that the law was in some way anti-Mexican. But a failure to consider the relative demand for labor migration between nations in this analysis is mistaken. The magnitude of demand of Canadian nationals in 1965 to immigrate to the United States was quantitatively much less than the robust demand in Mexico for access to the U.S. labor market – demand that has persisted in modern times in which the U.S. economy continues to recover from a deep economic recession.

Canada's demand for labor migration to the United States for the most part has been satisfied by available legal channels since 1965, just as it was before Congress passed the 1965 Act. Skilled labor plentiful in Canada ordinarily can migrate lawfully to the United States, while low-skilled workers abundant in Mexico generally cannot. Undocumented immigration simply is not a necessary option for the vast majority of Canadians seeking to migrate to the United States.

The relative difference between Canada and Mexico in demand for immigration can be explained in large part by the fact that Canada's economy has historically been, and continues to be, stronger than Mexico's, providing more jobs with higher average wages and more generous benefits to its workers. This is true despite the fact that Mexico's developing economy has grown over the last five decades and the Mexican population for the most part is far from impoverished. Canada's economy has long provided for employment with wages and benefits closely resembling those available in the U.S. labor market. Even though it has grown in recent years, Mexico's economy, however, historically has not provided comparable employment opportunities and does not do so today.

As a consequence of the differential economies of the neighboring nations of North America, the Western Hemisphere and per-country ceilings do not have much of an impact on Canadian migration, and certainly nowhere near the extent that they have on migration from Mexico. Undocumented immigration of Canadians exists but is much smaller in magnitude than immigration from Mexico.

It is not readily apparent why U.S. immigration laws should not favor immigration from the nation's neighbors, Canada and Mexico, over other nations around the world. This is what the flexible laws in place as a practical matter did before passage of the Immigration Act of 1965 and implementation of the Western Hemisphere ceiling.

Besides sharing lengthy borders with its two neighbors, the United States has long and special relationships with both of its North American neighbors that differ in quantity and quality from virtually all other nations in the world. The relationships have deepened significantly with the emerging economic integration of North America achieved through the 1994 implementation of the North American Free Trade Agreement (NAFTA).[81]

Unlike trade between the North American nations, U.S. immigration law fails to treat its neighbors differently with respect to labor migration than it treats nations all over the world. Indeed, the per-country ceilings treat Canada and Mexico the same way they treat any other nation, such as Iceland, New Zealand, Denmark, or Zimbabwe. The ceilings completely fail to recognize the deep, enduring, and growing relationships between the United States and its North American neighbors, as well as the existing migration demands of citizens of those nations to migrate to the United States.

When it comes to labor migration in the Western Hemisphere, the U.S. government has insisted that its immigration laws not reflect the nation's long-standing political, economic, and social ties with Canada and Mexico. The U.S. government, for example, steadfastly rejected the discussion of possible free labor migration in North America during the negotiations culminating in NAFTA. One might reasonably surmise that the U.S. government refused to discuss possible labor migration because of a possible public fear of a possible mass migration from Mexico to the United States. Opposition to the ratification of NAFTA might have grown if the trade accord, which was already controversial without addressing immigration, would have liberalized labor migration to better meet immigration demand in North America.[82]

Public concern with a possible mass migration from Mexico and Latin America has grown significantly in the United States since 1965.[83] Still, the concern was strong enough to convince Congress in 1965 to include the Western Hemisphere ceiling in the Immigration Act of 1965. In that vein, many of the post-1965 immigration

[81] *See* North American Free Trade Agreement Dec. 17, 1992, Can.-Mex.-U.S., 32 I.L.M. 605 (entered into force Jan 1, 1994). *See generally* Bill Ong Hing, Ethical Borders: NAFTA, Globalization, and Mexican Migration (2010) (analyzing critically the impacts of the globalization of the world economy, including the implementation of the North American Free Trade Agreement in 1994, on migration from Mexico to the United States).

[82] *See* Kevin R. Johnson, *Free Trade and Closed Borders: NAFTA and Mexican Immigration to the United States*, 27 UC Davis L. Rev. 937, 965–71 (1994). There may be nations other than Mexico with close historic and other ties with the United States that might deserve consideration in deciding on the propriety of the per-country ceiling on migration.

[83] Such concerns can be seen with the much-published increase in 2014 of unauthorized immigration from Central America. *See* Frances Robles, *Fleeing Gangs, Children Head to U.S. Border*, N.Y. Times, July 9, 2014.

enforcement measures focus directly on reducing undocumented migration from Mexico. Public concern in the United States for Canadian immigration generally has been almost nonexistent compared to public concern for Mexican immigration.

Moreover, worries about possible mass migration from Mexico unquestionably continue to influence, if not dominate, modern U.S. immigration law and policy as well as public opinion. The fact that many of the immigrants from Mexico are racially and culturally different from the Anglo-American norm contributes to some of the concerns with immigration among the general public. The widespread nature of such fears in American society, combined with the perpetual concern of a mass migration from Mexico to the United States, make it unlikely in the short term that we will see much of a loosening of the restrictions on labor migration between the nations of North America.

The New "Illegal Alien" – the Undocumented Mexican Worker

The few avenues for lawful admission into the country for low- and medium-skilled workers, combined with other restrictions on migration in the Immigration Act of 1965 and 1976 amendments, the elimination of the Bracero Program, and the failure of U.S. law to account for the demand for labor migration (as well as the encouragement by employers and, at times, the U.S. government for foreign citizens to come work in the United States), all contributed to a growth of the undocumented immigrant population in the United States. This much-publicized growth exacerbated what much of the American public popularly believed to be the "illegal alien problem."[84]

The law's many restrictions on legal migration from Mexico facilitated the consistent increase in the post-1965 period of the size of the undocumented Mexican population. Negative publicity accompanying this growth helped create the increasingly popular public impression that the immigration of "illegal aliens" from Mexico is nothing less than out of control, a drumbeat that grabbed national headlines and the attention of political leaders. As Attorney General William French Smith put it in 1983, "we have lost control of our borders."[85]

Rather than place blame on the restrictiveness of the immigration laws and the virtual impossibility of their effective and efficient enforcement through ordinary means, political leaders blamed the federal government for an alleged failure

[84] *See* Kevin R. Johnson, *The New Nativism: Something Old, Something New, Something Borrowed, Something Blue*, in IMMIGRANTS OUT!: THE NEW NATIVISM AND THE ANTI-IMMIGRANT IMPULSE IN THE UNITED STATES 165, 171–81 (Juan F. Perea ed., 1997) (analyzing the resurgence in nativist sentiment, much of it directed at Mexican immigrants, in the United States in the period from 1960 to the 1990s).

[85] *Immigration Reform and Control Act of 1983: Hearings on H.R. 1510 Before the Subcomm. on Immigration, Refugees, and International Law of the House Comm. of the Judiciary*, 98th Cong., 1st Sess. 1 (1983) (testimony of Attorney General William French Smith).

to enforce the immigration laws. Undocumented Mexicans, often disparaged as "illegal aliens," emerged in the public debate as foreign, shadowy enemies of the American people. The general public often views the group as dominated by nonwhite criminals and public benefit abusers deserving of – and indeed requiring – aggressive border enforcement measures and removal efforts.

The distinctly negative view of undocumented immigrants helps rationalize the widespread belief that undocumented immigrants possess no legal right to live and work in the United States and can be treated in harsh fashion. Such treatment is popular even though millions of undocumented immigrants as a matter of fact live and work in this country, constitute integral parts of our economy and communities, and American employers eagerly demand their labor.

The negative social construction of the "illegal alien"[86] that characterizes, and reinforces, undocumented immigrants as a dangerous social evil has concrete legal and policy consequences at the federal, state, and local levels. It is relied on by many policy makers to legitimize the use of increasingly aggressive – arguably punitive – measures directed at undocumented Mexican immigrants, such as mass removals, detention, and the dramatically increased imposition of criminal penalties for immigration violations. The specter of the nation being overrun by "illegal aliens" contributes to resilient public support for committing unprecedented, and consistently increasing, resources directed toward combating undocumented immigration from Mexico.

A number of corollaries flow from the negative characterization of undocumented Mexican immigrants in American social life. First, the U.S. government should engage in the Herculean task – whatever the costs, financial, moral, and otherwise – of sealing the U.S.-Mexico border with the goal of halting the continued flow of "illegal aliens" into the country. Second, the government should deport as many undocumented Mexican immigrants as possible from the United States.[87] As discussed in Section 3.3, both corollaries have profoundly influenced U.S. immigration enforcement policies in the modern era.

Public concerns with immigration from Mexico ultimately led the U.S. government to declare what would become the moral equivalent of war on "illegal aliens." Heavily armed border enforcement and large military-style operations can be found

86 *See generally* Kevin R. Johnson, *"Aliens" and the U.S. Immigration Laws: The Social and Legal Construction of Nonpersons*, 28 U. Miami Inter-Am. L. Rev. 263 (1996–97) (examining critically the use of the dehumanizing and racially-charged term "alien" to refer to noncitizens); D. Carolina Nuñez, *War of the Words: Aliens, Immigrants, Citizens, and the Language of Exclusion*, 2013 BYU L. Rev. 1517 (analyzing terminological issues in immigration law).

87 *See* Bill Ong Hing, *Institutional Racism, ICE Raids, and Immigration Reform*, 44 USF L. Rev. 307, 325–33 (2009) (summarizing the history of restrictions in the U.S. immigration laws on migration from Mexico to the United States).

in the U.S.-Mexico border region.[88] Indeed, reminiscent of science fiction movies of a generation past, unmanned drones now patrol the southern border with Mexico. Consequently, the U.S.-Mexico border region has in fact been radically transformed over the last twenty years.

The Limited Effectiveness of Amnesty Programs

Amnesty programs were a core component of the omnibus immigration legislation known as the Immigration Reform and Control Act of 1986 (IRCA).[89] The programs regularized the immigration status of hundreds of thousands of undocumented immigrants living in the United States, including many originally from Mexico. Since 1986, Congress has occasionally provided for the regularization of the immigration status of various groups of unauthorized noncitizens, including certain migrants from Central America and Haiti.[90]

Although resulting in the legalization of hundreds of thousands of migrants, the amnesty programs unquestionably did not, and could not prevent the subsequent growth of undocumented immigrant population in the United States. That failure is rather obvious today given that the undocumented immigrant population is in the neighborhood of 11–12 million people, much larger than it was twenty years ago.

Despite several amnesty programs, the undocumented population has not declined over the last fifty years. Rather, it grew substantially in the years following the implementation of the amnesties granted to undocumented immigrants by the 1986 and subsequent acts of Congress. This growth demonstrates the limited effectiveness of the dramatic escalation of enforcement measures, such as the sanctions imposed on the employers of undocumented immigrants and the militarization of the U.S.-Mexico border.[91] Because such measures have failed to halt unauthorized labor immigration, a new undocumented population emerged to replace previous undocumented immigrants who were able to regularize their immigration status.

Larger social, political, and economic forces above and beyond allegedly poor enforcement help explain the subsequent growth of the undocumented immigrant population in the United States. In the 1986 and subsequent reforms,

[88] *See generally* JOSEPH NEVINS, OPERATION GATEKEEPER AND BEYOND: THE WAR ON "ILLEGALS" AND THE REMAKING OF THE U.S.-MEXICO BOUNDARY (2d ed. 2010) (documenting the increasing militarization of the U.S.-Mexico border and specifically the implementation of "Operation Gatekeeper" near San Diego, California in the 1990s).

[89] Immigration Reform and Control Act of 1986, Pub. L. No. 99–603, 100 Stat. 3359 (1986); *See* LEGOMSKY & RODRÍGUEZ, *supra* note 19, at 1178–79 (discussing the operation of the various legalization programs under the Immigration Reform and Control Act of 1986).

[90] *See* Nicaraguan Adjustment and Central American Relief Act, Pub. L. No. 105–100, 11 Stat. 2160 (1997); Haitian Refugee Immigration Fairness Act, Pub. L. 105–277, 112 Stat. 2681–5389 (1998).

[91] *See* INA § 274A, 8 U.S.C. § 1324(a).

Congress failed to meaningfully expand the avenues for legal immigration in an effort to rationally manage the demand for immigration from Mexico, as well as other nations, which was artificially suppressed by the Immigration Act of 1965 and the 1976 amendments. In turn, limited opportunities for legal immigration contributed to escalating pressures for immigration outside legally sanctioned avenues, pressures that increased with the substantial expansion of the U.S. economy in the 1990s and the concomitant expansion in the demand for labor. Employer sanctions and other enforcement measures implemented were simply incapable of meaningfully limiting undocumented immigration in light of the strong economic forces at work.

Although programs provided relief to certain undocumented immigrants in the country, Congress has failed to amend the immigration laws to provide meaningful relief from removal (and a path to legalization) for subsequent undocumented immigrants. Registry, for example, is a form of relief from deportation that allows noncitizens who have been in the United States since 1972 to regularize their immigration status.[92] Congress has not moved forward the year of eligibility for registry since 1986. Consequently, perpetually fixed in time to noncitizens present in the United States since 1972, each year fewer undocumented noncitizens are eligible to utilize registry to regularize their immigration status. The mere passage of time thus renders the registry provision increasingly obsolete. There has been no suggestion that Congress will intervene to remedy this obsolescence.

Moreover, Congress has restricted and eliminated forms of relief from removal, which allowed for the regularization of the immigration status of undocumented immigrants. In the 1996 immigration reforms, for example, Congress replaced previously available, relatively generous forms of relief from removal with forms of relief, such as cancellation of removal, with more restrictive eligibility requirements.[93] Those forms of relief, for example, are unavailable to noncitizens convicted of an ever-expanding number of crimes.

In sum, Congress has provided paths to legal status for undocumented immigrants in the form of amnesties in the 1986 and later acts. However, through inaction and affirmative restrictions on available and relatively general forms of relief, Congress also effectively narrowed the channels for undocumented immigrants to regularize their immigration status. Congress failed to meaningfully expand the opportunities for lawful migration by Mexican workers, which in turn increased the incentives for undocumented immigration.[94] Ultimately, ever-tougher border enforcement has

[92] *See* INA § 249, 8 U.S.C. § 1259.

[93] *See* Kevin R. Johnson et al., Understanding Immigration Law 321–23 (2009) (describing generally modern forms of relief from removal).

[94] *See* Legomsky & Rodríguez, *supra* note 19, at 625–26.

been unable to ensure obedience to unrealistic restrictions on immigration under the U.S. immigration laws.

The Limits of Border Enforcement

Throughout the post-1965 period, U.S. border enforcement officers, even with greatly increased resources and enforcement tools at their disposal, have been unable to enforce the existing legal restrictions on immigration, which fail to account for the high demand for immigration to the United States. This is strong evidence that the restrictions in the current immigration laws are unrealistic and simply unenforceable in the face of existing economic realities.

Consider that *before* the unprecedented border enforcement buildup by the U.S. government over the last twenty-plus years, the undocumented population in the United States in the early 1990s was about 3.5 million.[95] By 2011, the undocumented population had not declined but, in fact, had more than tripled to an estimated 11 million people, with approximately 60 percent of the total from Mexico.[96] The undocumented population in the United States levelled off – and, at least briefly, decreased in size – primarily due to the combination of a global recession beginning in 2008 and the accompanying decline in the labor demand in the United States. Generally speaking, undocumented immigration continues in the face of increasing enforcement and despite the fact that unauthorized migration can be extremely dangerous, with migrants regularly dying on the treacherous journey through remote and intemperate deserts and mountains from Mexico to the United States.

By some accounts, the U.S. government today fails to effectively manage Mexican immigration. Not coincidentally, public concern with immigration, especially with the racial, cultural, and other perceived differences about the majority of the new, both legal and undocumented, immigrants to the United States, increased as the Latina/o-dominated undocumented population did.[97]

95 *See* Robert Warren & John Robert Warren, *Unauthorized Immigration to the United States: Annual Estimates and Components of Change, by State, 1990 to 2010*, 47 INT'L MIGRATION REV. 296, 315 (2013) (Table 3) (providing estimates).

96 *See* Jeffrey Passel & D'Vera Cohn, *Unauthorized Immigrants: 11.1 Million in 2011* (Pew Research, 2012), *available at* http://www.pewhispanic.org/2012/12/06/unauthorized-immigrants-11-1-million-in-2011; *see also* Rose Cuison Villazor, *The Undocumented Closet*, 92 N.C. L. REV. 1 (2013) (analyzing critically the "closet" in which the millions of undocumented immigrants live in the United States).

97 *See, e.g.*, PETER BRIMELOW, ALIEN NATION 11 (1995) (expressing alarm with increased immigration of racial minorities, particularly Latina/os, to the United States because "[r]ace and ethnicity are destiny in American politics"); VICTOR DAVIS HANSON, MEXIFORNIA: A STATE OF BECOMING (2003) (lamenting alleged changes to California brought by what the author perceives to be a prolonged, and uncontrolled, mass immigration to the United States from Mexico); HUNTINGTON, *supra* note 12, at 59–80 (expressing concerns with the "Hispanicization" of immigration to the United States); GOV. RICHARD D. LAMM & GARY IMHOFF, THE IMMIGRATION TIME BOMB: THE FRAGMENTING OF AMERICA 76–98 (1985) (opining on the adverse impacts on mass immigration to the United States of non-Anglo-Saxon immigrants who allegedly fail to assimilate into American society).

With demand for labor migration unsatisfied by the normal operation of the U.S. immigration laws, undocumented migration from Mexico predictably increased over time. That growth, in turn, resulted in heightened public concern with undocumented Mexican immigrants and the U.S. government's adoption of a variety of aggressive immigration enforcement responses. A vicious cycle emerged that ensured increasing public concern with immigration followed by heightened enforcement measures due to a growing undocumented immigrant population. Unfortunately, Congress failed to make significant changes to the laws for legal labor migration to the United States, which would have helped reduce the incentives for undocumented immigration, shrank the undocumented population, and made public concern with immigration less pressing.

The Impacts of the 1965 and 1976 Acts on Mexican Migration

The impacts of the 1965 and 1976 amendments to the immigration laws can be seen in the relatively constant percentage of total legal immigrants coming from Mexico to the United States from 1960 to 1980 (Table 3.1).

The statistical data in the table reflects the impacts of the Immigration Act of 1965 and the 1976 amendments. After passage of each piece of legislation, legal immigration from Mexico immediately dropped as a percentage of overall immigration. Although those drops show that the changes in the law had quick impacts, demand for immigration from Mexico to the United States persisted. Throughout this period, Mexico contributed roughly one-third of the nation's legal immigrants annually. One could observe that the 1965 and 1976 amendments to the immigration laws appear to have effectively capped legal immigration from Mexico at one-third of all immigrants to the United States.

Despite growth in overall legal immigration and the demand for immigration in light of economic growth in the United States, legal Mexican immigration was kept relatively constant as a percentage of overall immigration throughout the 1960–80 period. The Western Hemisphere ceiling and other measures thus had the impact desired by Congress of placing a ceiling on legal migration from Mexico. Immigration levels from Mexico presumably would have been greater without the limitations added by Congress in 1965 and 1976.

One can reasonably conclude that through the Western Hemisphere and per-country ceilings Congress has achieved its intended result – effectively placing an upper limit on immigration from Mexico and avoiding a mass influx of immigrants from that country. The demand for migration from Mexico grew, however, and resulted in a steady stream of legal and unauthorized immigrants, which ensured that Mexico remained the number-one nation sending immigrants to the United States.

TABLE 3.1. *Legal immigration from Mexico to the United States, 1960–1980*

Fiscal year	Immigrants from Mexico	Total legal immigrants	% Mexican of total
1960	32,708	103,031	31.7
1961	41,143	120,485	34.1
1962	55,291	133,321	41.5
1963	55,253	142,207	38.9
1964	32,967	123,753	26.6
1965	37,969	137,262	27.7
1966	45,163	134,438	33.6
1967	42,371	151,673	27.9
1968	43,563	238,745	18.2
1969	44,623	138,503	32.2
1970	44,499	138,033	32.3
1971	50,105	149,002	33.6
1972	64,040	151,601	42.2
1973	70,141	157,181	44.6
1974	71,586	154,882	46.2
1975	62,205	150,549	41.3
1976	57,863	154,625	37.4
1977	44,079	189,503	23.2
1978	92,367	224,390	32.3
1979	52,096	161,408	32.2
1980	56,680	164,566	34.4

Note: Average for the 1960–1980 period is 30.1%.
Source: *See* Historical Statistics of the United States, Millennial Edition On-Line, edited by Susan B. Carter, Scott Sigmund Gartner, Michael R. Haines, Alan L. Olmstead, Richard Sutch, & Gavin Wright, Cambridge University Press 2006. For an analysis of additional data on migration from Mexico in the post-1965 period reaching similar conclusions as those presented here, see Douglas S. Massey, *Immigration Statistics for the Twenty-First Century*, 631 ANNALS 124, 138–39 (2010).

3.3 THE END: U.S.-MEXICO BORDER ENFORCEMENT POST-1965

This section outlines modern border enforcement measures that have disparate impacts on immigrants from Mexico. It contends that these measures are rooted in the restrictive designs of the Immigration Act of 1965 and the 1976 amendments.

Those two pieces of legislation had a dramatic impact on American immigration law and enforcement, redirecting the law toward an escalating Mexican-oriented focus.

In the years following passage of the 1965 Act, the legislative and executive branches took a series of increasingly aggressive steps designed to curb undocumented immigration to the United States from Mexico and to reduce the undocumented population created in no small part due to the implementation of the Immigration Act of 1965. Proponents of the greatly enhanced enforcement measures often emphasize that, unlike those pursued during past dark chapters of American immigration history, the modern immigration laws are neutral, objective, and not facially discriminatory. Based on the superficial appearance of objectivity added to the U.S. immigration laws by the 1965 Act and subsequent amendments, restrictionists frequently press for the laws to be stringently enforced.

Defenders of tough enforcement of the modern U.S. immigration laws frequently seek to legitimize the law because of its facial neutrality, as epitomized by both the Western Hemisphere and the per-country ceilings. They can colorably, if not convincingly, claim that the laws and their enforcement are not discriminatory and therefore should be enforced in the name of adherence to the powerful moral imperative of the "rule of law."

As is the case in other areas of American law,[98] dispelling the claims of color-blindness in the modern U.S. immigration laws is a formidable task. Unlike the days of old, the laws no longer expressly discriminate on the basis of race. Blatantly discriminatory monikers such as the "Chinese exclusion laws" and "Operation Wetback" fortunately are something of this nation's past. As we have seen, however, the per-country ceilings, in combination with other aspects of the immigration laws and their enforcement, clearly have disparate national origin and racial impacts. As intended by Congress, the impacts fall most heavily on prospective immigrants from Mexico, but also disparately affect noncitizens of color from other developing nations with consistently high demand for immigration to the United States, such as India and the Philippines.

The restrictive impacts should not be surprising in the least. Beginning with the Immigration Act of 1965, Congress took a series of affirmative steps to restrict immigration from the Western Hemisphere. However, the disparate impacts are obscured by, and can be defended by resort to, the seemingly objective and facially neutral nature of the modern U.S. immigration laws.

Similar racially disparate impacts follow inexorably from most of the heightened border enforcement measures – measures taken in the effort to combat the inability of the immigration laws to meet migration demand – implemented by the U.S. government in the post-1965 period. Many of those enforcement measures

[98] *See* Neil Gotanda, *A Critique of "Our Constitution is Color-Blind,"* 44 STAN. L. REV. 1 (1991).

admittedly had the intent of reducing undocumented immigration from Mexico. It goes without saying that, as demonstrated in this section, persons of Mexican ancestry, and Latinas/os generally, often quite reasonably consider themselves to be the primary targets of the modern U.S. immigration enforcement bureaucracy. They represent the overwhelming number of noncitizens removed from the country nowadays.

An important independent development of relatively recent origin complicates the analysis. National security fears that emerged after the events of September 11, 2001 resulted in a plethora of measures initially directed at more strictly regulating the migration of Muslims, Arabs, and others perceived as more likely than other noncitizens to be involved in terrorist activity, broadly defined. However, such fears quickly translated into growing popularity among members of Congress, as well as among the general public, for the increased militarization of the U.S.-Mexico border and for directing many aggressive enforcement measures at undocumented Mexican immigrants (and immigrants generally), often in the name of protecting national security.[99] Even though there is little evidence that the southern border with Mexico has ever been breached by any person seeking to engage in what reasonably can be characterized as terrorist activity, political leaders after 2001 regularly invoked public safety to justify increased immigration enforcement efforts along the U.S.-Mexico border.

The Expanded Use of the Criminal Justice System in Immigration Enforcement

Over the last several decades, Congress has passed a series of tough immigration enforcement laws that have built on the restrictions in the Immigration Act of 1965. These laws greatly expanded the grounds for removal – and effectively made removal mandatory – for many criminal activities, narrowed the available forms of relief from removal, dramatically increased the use of detention and criminal law as immigration enforcement tools, and significantly restricted judicial review of removal and related decisions by the Executive Branch.[100] During roughly the same time period, Congress, with the support of the president, has appropriated record funding for border enforcement, which has allowed for the progressively greater militarization of the U.S.-Mexico border with enhanced technology, extension of

[99] *See* Kevin R. Johnson & Bernard Trujillo, *Immigration Reform, National Security After September 11, and the Future of North American Integration*, 91 MINN. L. REV. 1369, 1386–87, 1396–1404 (2007).

[100] *See, e.g.*, REAL ID Act, Pub. L. 109–13, 119 Stat. 231, 302–311 (2005); Uniting and Strengthening America by Providing Appropriate Tools Required to Intercept and Obstruct Terrorism (USA PATRIOT) Act, Pub. L. No. 107–56, 115 Stat. 272, 342–362 (2001); Illegal Immigration Reform and Immigrant Responsibility Act, Pub. L. No. 104–208, 110 Stat. 3009–546 (1996).

the border fence, and ever-increasing numbers of enforcement personnel on the ground. As these developments suggest,

> [t]he deportation of "criminal aliens" is now the driving force in American immigration enforcement. In recent years, the Congress, the Department of Justice, the Department of Homeland Security, and the White House have all placed criminals front and center in establishing immigration enforcement priorities.... *In effect, federal immigration enforcement has become a criminal removal system.*[101]

For the past decade, Congress has periodically considered comprehensive immigration reform proposals that would expand in certain modest respects the avenues for legal immigration, including the possible creation of a new guest worker program that would expand legal labor migration. Many of the proposals also would create a path to legalization and possible eligibility for U.S. citizenship for undocumented immigrants. In addition, border enforcement is an integral part of virtually all reform proposals.

Although proposals have resurfaced time and again, Congress has found itself for well over a decade unable to cobble together the sufficient bipartisan support necessary to enact a major piece of immigration reform legislation.[102] Latina/o advocacy groups have expressed deep frustration with the failure of Congress to pass a reform bill. As this book goes to press, Congress appears to be at its most recent stalemate in the efforts to pass immigration reform.

As part of a concerted political push to demonstrate its commitment to enforcement and to hopefully convince Congress to enact comprehensive immigration reform, the executive branch, beginning in the 1990s, has pursued aggressive enforcement measures that have resulted in a series of records for the number of noncitizens removed from the United States. Significantly heightened and inflexible enforcement of the immigration laws by the administrations of both Democratic and Republican presidents, rather than any equally large recent surge in undocumented immigration, has resulted in the record numbers of removals. Political priorities have changed dramatically as public concern with immigration – especially from Mexico – progressively increased in the fifty years since Congress passed the Immigration Act of 1965. In essence, removals in 2015 are a high political priority for the executive branch in a way that they unquestionably were not in 1965, 1976, or, for that matter, 1990.

Building on the increasingly tough enforcement measures passed by Congress, the signature immigration enforcement program of the Obama administration

[101] Ingrid V. Eagly, *Criminal Justice for Noncitizens: An Analysis of Variation in Local Enforcement*, 88 NYU L. Rev. 1126, 1128 (2013) (emphasis added) (footnotes omitted).

[102] *See* Mary Fan, *The Case for Crimmigration Reform*, 92 N.C. L. Rev. 75, 77–80 (2013).

(until dismantled in 2014), called Secure Communities, contributed significantly to the consistently high numbers of removals.[103] The program required state and local law enforcement agencies to share information with federal immigration enforcement authorities about immigrants who are arrested and to detain noncitizens possibly subject to removal until federal immigration authorities can take them into custody. Officials at the highest level of the Obama administration, including the president himself, regularly proclaimed that Secure Communities targeted dangerous "criminal aliens" and contended that the program was a necessary and essential measure to protect public safety.

After the initial implementation of Secure Communities, the Obama administration generated considerable controversy when it announced that state and local participation in the program was mandatory, not voluntary. State and local law enforcement agencies therefore were told that they could not refuse to cooperate with U.S. immigration authorities in sharing information about noncitizens who are arrested and must place "immigration holds" – that is, detain noncitizens for the U.S. government for possible immigration violations – on them.

Secure Communities deviated from the historically rigid separation of state and local criminal law enforcement from federal immigration enforcement. That separation had been justified on the entirely reasonable policy consideration, which continues to be embraced by a number of law enforcement professionals, that immigrant communities are significantly less likely to cooperate with state and local police agencies in ordinary criminal law enforcement activities if those agencies are perceived by noncitizens to be part and parcel of the nation's immigration enforcement apparatus. Full cooperation with local law enforcement authorities would not appear likely, for example, if legal and undocumented immigrants fear that reporting a crime to local police might result in their deportation from the United States because local police work closely with federal authorities in immigration enforcement.[104] Because of perceived

[103] For commentary critical of the Secure Communities program, see Aarti Kohli, Peter K. Markowitz, & Lisa Chavez, Chief Justice Earl Warren Institute of Law and Social Policy, *Secure Communities by the Numbers: An Analysis of Demographics and Due Process* (Oct. 2011); Katarina Ramos, *Criminalizing Race in the Name of Secure Communities*, 48 CAL. W.L. REV. 317 (2012); Rachel R. Ray, *Insecure Communities: Examining Local Government Participation in U.S. Immigration and Customs Enforcement's "Secure Communities" Program*, 10 SEATTLE J. SOC. JUST. 367, 337–38 (2011). *See generally* Hiroshi Motomura, *The Discretion that Matters: Federal Immigration Enforcement, State and Local Arrests, and the Civil-Criminal Line*, 58 UCLA L. REV. 1819 (2011) (analyzing state and local government involvement in federal immigration enforcement).

[104] *See, e.g.*, McLeod, *supra* note 9 (criticizing the growing reliance on the criminal law as a means of enforcing the U.S. immigration laws); Jennifer M. Chacón, *Overcriminalizing Immigration*, 102 J. CRIM. & CRIMINOLOGY 613 (2012) (to the same effect); Juliet P. Stumpf, *The Crimmigration Crisis: Immigrants, Crime, and Sovereign Power*, 56 AM. U.L. REV. 367 (2006) (analyzing the increased confluence of immigration law and criminal law and coining the phrase "crimmigration law").

excesses in the breadth of Secure Communities, some states and localities, including California, passed laws attempting to restrict the extent of local police cooperation with U.S. immigration authorities with respect to minor, nonviolent criminal offenders.[105]

Despite the administration's public safety justification for its immigration enforcement measures, many noncitizens charged with but not necessarily convicted of relatively minor criminal offenses – and thus who cannot reasonably be said to pose a serious risk to public safety – were removed from the country under the auspices of Secure Communities. "Immigration and Customs Enforcement records show that a vast majority, 79 percent, of people deported under Secure Communities had *no criminal records or had been picked up for low-level offenses, like traffic violations and juvenile mischief*."[106]

For example, one undocumented Mexican immigrant who was dubbed the "tamale lady" faced possible removal from the United States based on her arrest for trespassing by local police in Sacramento, California; she had been arrested while selling home-made tamales in front of a Wal-Mart store.[107] As required by Secure Communities, local police detained the noncitizen and turned her over to U.S. immigration authorities, which threatened her with deportation. It strains credulity to believe that an undocumented immigrant trying to scratch out a living for herself and her U.S. citizen children by selling tamales truly represents a serious risk to the public safety and, based on that transgression alone, warrants removal from the country. A public outcry convinced the U.S. government to halt its efforts to deport the tamale lady.

Cases like those are more common than one might imagine due to mandatory reporting, including for such relatively minor criminal offenses as driving an

[105] *See, e.g.*, A.B. 4, 2013–14 Cal. Legis. (signed by the governor, Oct. 5, 2013) (California "Trust Act").

[106] Editorial, *Immigration Bait and Switch*, N.Y. TIMES, Aug. 17, 2010, at A22 (emphasis added); *see* Ginger Thomson & Sarah Cohen, *More Deportations Follow Minor Crime, Data Shows*, N.Y. TIMES, Apr. 7, 2014, at A1 (stating that the U.S. "government records shows that since President Obama took office, two-thirds of the nearly two million deportation cases involve people who had committed minor infractions, including traffic violations, or had no criminal record at all. Twenty percent – or about 394,000 – of the cases involved people convicted of serious crimes, including drug-related offenses . . . ."); Kavitha Rajagopalan, *Deportation Program Casts Too Wide a Net*, NEWSDAY (New York), June 24, 2011, at A34 ("Secure Communities purports to search for repeat illegal immigrant offenders or those charged with major crimes. *In practice, most people deported under the program have had no criminal record at all and were picked up on minor offenses, like speeding.*") (emphasis added); *see also* Adam B. Cox & Thomas J. Miles, *Policing Immigration*, 80 U. CHI. L. REV. 87 (2013) (finding in an empirical study that the Secure Communities program does not focus on high-crime areas but instead targets communities with large Hispanic populations, thereby undermining the claims of the U.S. government that the program is designed to protect public safety).

[107] *See* Ruben Navarrette Jr., *Don't Deport the "Tamale Lady,"* CNN, Aug. 2, 2012 available at http://www.cnn.com/2012/08/01/opinion/navarrette-deportation-sacramento, last visited Aug. 29, 2014.

automobile without a valid driver's license (or trespassing), required by Secure Communities. Their persistence demonstrates that if public safety was in fact the true purpose of the program, the program cast an overbroad, over-inclusive net. One might reasonably conclude that the true regulatory goal above all others in the Obama administration's immigration enforcement agenda has been to maximize removal numbers and trumpet the results as demonstrating the president's commitment to immigration enforcement. The administration frequently argues that the hundreds of thousands of removals demonstrate that the border has been secured and that Congress now should move forward with the enactment of comprehensive immigration reform.

Further suggesting that the U.S. government is hyperaggressive in its immigration enforcement efforts, the Supreme Court, known for its conservatism, has regularly rejected the government's overzealous attempts to remove from the United States long-term lawful permanent residents with deep ties to the community for what can be reasonably characterized as minor criminal offenses.[108] In 2013, for example, the Court rejected the removal order of a long-term lawful permanent resident with U.S. citizen children based on a single criminal conviction hinging on possession of what amounted to two or three marijuana cigarettes,[109] a transgression that would currently be legal in several states. Such an offense would not seem to pose a serious risk to public safety, especially when combined with the fact that the offender was an established U.S. resident with no other criminal record. The Obama administration nonetheless pushed for removal all the way to the Supreme Court. This case is not an outlier. Put simply, the executive branch regularly takes zealous litigation positions to defend its aggressive removal efforts, only to have a conservative Court, which one might expect to be sympathetic, frequently reject them.

To add to the concerns with the impacts of the Secure Communities program, its operation unquestionably had racially disparate impacts. These impacts directly resulted from the fact that the operation of the criminal justice system in the United States itself historically has disproportionate impacts on minority communities. Local police departments are frequently accused of profiling Latina/os and other racial minorities in law enforcement activities, including run-of-the-mill traffic stops. Profiling of Latina/os has long been a persistent problem in ordinary criminal law enforcement, just as it is in immigration enforcement. Stops for "driving while black" and "driving while brown" are well-known phenomena in minority communities across the country.

[108] *See, e.g.*, Vartelas v. Holder, 132 S. Ct. 1479 (2012) (rejecting the removal order based on a criminal conviction for a relatively minor role in small-time counterfeiting scheme); Carachuri-Rosendo v. Holder, 560 U.S. 563 (2010) (declining to affirm the removal order based on a criminal conviction for possession of one tablet of a prescription drug).

[109] *See* Moncrieffe v. Holder, 133 S. Ct. 1678 (2013).

When the federal removal machinery relies on state and local arrests to take immigration enforcement action as Secure Communities did, one can reasonably expect immigrants of color – with the largest number of this group being from Mexico – to be adversely affected because of the racially disparate effects of state and local policing. Racially disparate rates of arrests inexorably result in racially disparate removals of noncitizens handed over by state and local law enforcement authorities to U.S. immigration authorities. Consequently, through the operation of Secure Communities, many immigrants of color arrested by local police were ultimately placed by federal immigration authorities in removal proceedings. As we shall see, the result is that hundreds of thousands of Latina/o immigrants have been removed in recent years from the United States.

Racial Profiling in Immigration Enforcement

Even when exclusively in the hands of the U.S. government, immigration enforcement in the United States long has been challenged as discriminating against persons of Mexican ancestry. Public concerns, especially among Latina/os, with the discriminatory enforcement of immigration laws contribute to the ferocity of the public debate over immigration reform and the perception among Latina/os and others that immigration has become a pressing civil rights concern.

For a variety of reasons, fears of discriminatory immigration enforcement are at their zenith when state and local law enforcement agencies work with the U.S. government in regulating immigration and pursuing aggressive enforcement of the immigration laws. Generally speaking, besides being under local political pressures that are more enforcement oriented – at times even tinged with anti-immigrant and racial animus – than those existing at the national level, state and local police cannot reasonably be expected to be as familiar as their federal counterparts are with the well-known complexities of the U.S. immigration laws. That limited familiarity makes fair, effective, and racially neutral enforcement difficult.

Federal

Admittedly, U.S. immigration enforcement at the ground level historically has targeted persons of apparent Mexican ancestry. The U.S. government today pursues aggressive race-based enforcement of this type in the interior of the United States as well as in the U.S.-Mexico border region.

The fact that Mexican immigrants are the single highest priority of U.S. immigration authorities is symbolized in modern times by the erection and ever-popular extension of the fence along the United States' southern border with

Mexico.[110] Construction of the border fence has been extremely expensive and, at the same time, of uncertain utility in reducing the nation's undocumented immigrant population.

Despite its great costs and at best uncertain enforcement benefits, the fortification and extension of the border fence has unquestionably contributed to the circumstances resulting in thousands of migrant deaths. Mexican nationals comprise the overwhelming majority of those dying in the desert and mountains along the U.S.-Mexico border.[111] In contrast to the highly popular focus on the southern border with Mexico, fortifying the United States' northern border with Canada has never been a particularly high priority of American policy makers and the general public.

Importantly, the immigration enforcement focus of the American immigration bureaucracy on persons of Mexican ancestry goes much further than the symbolism of the southern border fence. Federal border enforcement officers routinely rely on "Mexican" or "Hispanic appearance" in deciding to pursue ordinary immigration enforcement actions; despite the vagueness, ambiguousness, and breadth of these descriptors, the Supreme Court has sanctioned their consideration.[112] This form of racial profiling has contributed to consistently high removal rates of Latina/o immigrants in the early years of the new millennium.

State and Local

As the analysis of the Secure Communities program demonstrates, the beginning of the twenty-first century has seen dramatically greater involvement of state and

[110] *See* Secure Fence Act, Pub L. No. 109–367, 120 Stat. 2638 (2006); *see also* Pratheepan Gulasekaram, *Why a Wall?*, 2 UC IRVINE L. REV. 147 (2012) (analyzing the political and symbolic significance of the "border wall" between the United States and Mexico).

[111] *See* Bill Ong Hing, *The Dark Side of Operation Gatekeeper*, 7 UC DAVIS J. INT'L. L. & POL'Y 121 (2001) (considering the many deaths directly resulting from the border enforcement operation known as Operation Gatekeeper along the U.S.-Mexico border in southern California).

[112] *See, e.g.*, United States v. Martinez-Fuerte, 428 U.S. 543, 562–63 (1976) (refusing to find a Fourth Amendment violation based on an immigration officer's decision to send a vehicle to secondary inspection at an immigration checkpoint miles away from the border based on apparent Mexican ancestry of the occupants of the vehicle); United States v. Brignoni-Ponce, 422 U.S. 873, 885–86 (1975) (holding that, consistent with the Fourth Amendment, "Mexican appearance" could be one factor among many that justifies an immigration stop of a vehicle by the Border Patrol in the U.S.-Mexico border region). *See generally* Kevin R. Johnson, *How Racial Profiling in America Became the Law of the Land: United States v. Brignoni-Ponce and Whren v. United States and the Need for Truly Rebellious Lawyering*, 98 GEO. L.J. 1005 (2010) (analyzing how the Supreme Court in *Brignoni-Ponce* sanctioned racial profiling in immigration enforcement). *But see* United States v. Montero-Camargo, 208 F.3d 1122, 1135 (9th Cir. 2000) (en banc) (distinguishing *Martinez-Fuerte* and *Brignoni-Ponce* and holding that "Hispanic appearance" could not be a factor in an immigration stop in the U.S.-Mexico border region in large part because large numbers of persons in the general population of that region, including U.S. citizens and lawful immigrants, fall into that broad category).

local governments in immigration enforcement.[113] Passed overwhelmingly by California voters in 1994, the initiative known as Proposition 187 was a well-known precursor to the many immigration enforcement laws of this variety passed by state legislatures in the first decade of the new millennium. Like many of the contemporary state and local immigration measures, the initiative would have required local police to assist with immigration enforcement and went so far as ban undocumented children from public schools, contrary to a Supreme Court ruling.[114]

Besides increasingly cooperating with federal authorities through programs like Secure Communities, many states, including Alabama, Arizona, Georgia, and South Carolina, and localities, such as Hazleton, Pennsylvania, Farmer's Branch, Texas, and Fremont, Nebraska, enacted record numbers of laws ostensibly designed to facilitate immigration enforcement. At the same time, those laws have struck fear in the hearts of immigrants, lawful and not, and Latina/os generally. Anti-Latina/o animus, which grew perceptibly as the Latina/o population increased in these locales and local political leaders exploited rising tensions, has often marred the vocal political movements pressing for the passage of state and local immigration enforcement laws.

The Supreme Court has repeatedly emphasized that the "'[p]ower to regulate immigration is *unquestionably … a federal power.*'"[115] Despite this seemingly clear directive, state and local governments have enthusiastically moved in recent years into the realm of immigration enforcement. Political motivations have fueled the movement for passage of the laws. Given the emphatic statement by the Supreme Court confirming the unquestioned federal authority over immigration, it is not surprising that courts have held that many of the state and local immigration

113 *See generally* STRANGE NEIGHBORS: STATE AND LOCAL REGULATION OF IMMIGRATION POLICY (Carissa Byrne Hessick & Gabriel J. Chin eds., 2014).

114 *See* Kevin R. Johnson, *An Essay on Immigration Politics, Popular Democracy, and California's Proposition 187: The Political Relevance and Legal Irrelevance of Race*, 70 WASH. L. REV. 629 (1995); Johnson, *supra* note 31; Plyler v. Doe, 457 U.S. 202 (1982) (invalidating a Texas law that in effect barred undocumented immigrants from public schools).

115 Chamber of Commerce v. Whiting, 131 S. Ct. 1968, 1974 (2011) (citation omitted) (emphasis added); *See* Arizona v. United States, 132 U.S. Ct. 2492, 2498–99 (2012). For an analysis of recent developments in federal preemption of state and local immigration enforcement laws, see Kit Johnson & Peter J. Spiro, *Debates, Immigration Preemption after* United States v. Arizona, 101 U. Pa. L. Rev. Online (Dec. 28, 2012), available at http://www.pennlawreview.com/debates/index.php?id=47, last visited Aug. 29, 2014; Kerry Abrams, *Plenary Power Preemption*, 99 VA. L. REV. 601 (2013); Pratheepan Gulasekaram & S. Karthick Ramakrishnan, *Immigration Federalism: A Reappraisal*, 88 N.Y.U. L. REV. 2074 (2013); Stella Burch Elias, *The New Immigration Federalism*, 74 OHIO ST. L.J. 703 (2013); Lucas Guttentag, *The Forgotten Equality Norm in Immigration Preemption: Discrimination, Harassment, and the Civil Rights Act of 1870*, 8 DUKE J. CONST. LAW & PUB. POL'Y 1 (2013); Karla Mari McKanders, *Federal Preemption and Immigrants' Rights*, 3 WAKE FOREST J.L. & POL'Y 333, 334 (2013).

enforcement measures, in whole or in part, impermissibly intrude on the federal power to regulate immigration.[116]

State and local political leaders seek to justify state and local immigration enforcement laws on the ground that the federal government has failed to enforce U.S. immigration laws effectively. These leaders frequently make the exaggerated assertion that the federal government had failed to enforce the laws despite the dramatic increases in removals and annual removal records discussed later in the chapter. Whatever its veracity, the persistence of the claim of the lack of federal immigration enforcement reveals a generalized frustration at the state and local levels with the perceived ineffectiveness of federal enforcement of the immigration laws. This frustration is exacerbated by the oft-publicized fact that millions of undocumented immigrants live in the United States.

State leaders, notably Arizona Governor Jan Brewer, have vociferously criticized the alleged failure of the U.S. government to enforce the immigration laws and argued that this failure justifies increased state enforcement efforts. Those leaders also regularly point to the fact that, despite many attempts, Congress has failed to intervene and pass comprehensive immigration reform.

In the name of enhancing immigration enforcement, a growing number of state immigration enforcement laws require state and local law enforcement officers to assist the federal government in its enforcement efforts. Section 2(B) of Arizona's SB 1070, popularly known as the "show your papers" law, is the most well-known example of a state law of this type. It requires state and local police to verify the immigration status of persons whom they reasonably suspect are in the United States in violation of the federal immigration laws, leaving considerable discretion to the officers.[117] Although invalidating core provisions of SB 1070 as conflicting with the federal power to regulate immigration, the Supreme Court declined to strike down Section 2(B); in so doing, however, the Court left the door open to future challenges of the section as applied by state and local law enforcement agencies to individual cases.[118] Commentators expressed concern that the implementation of Section 2(B) would result in increased racial profiling of Latina/os.[119]

[116] *See* Arizona v. United States, 132 S. Ct. 2492, 2498–99 (2012); City of Hazleton v. Lozano, 724 F.3d 297 (3d Cir. 2013), *cert. denied*, 134 S. Ct. 1491 (2014); Villas at Parkside Partners v. Farmers Branch, 726 F.3d 524 (5th Cir. 2013) (en banc), *cert denied*, 134 S. Ct. 1491 (2014). *But see* Keller v. City of Fremont, 719 F.3d 931 (8th Cir. 2013) (rejecting in large part a constitutional challenge to local immigration enforcement ordinance), *cert. denied*, 134 S. Ct. 2140 (2014).

[117] *See* Ariz. S.B. 1070, 49th Leg., 2d Sess. § 2(B) (2010).

[118] *See* Arizona v. United States, 132 S. Ct. 2492, 2507–10 (2012).

[119] *See, e.g.*, Kristina M. Campbell, *(Un)Reasonable Suspicion: Racial Profiling in Immigration Enforcement After Arizona v. United States*, 3 WAKE FOREST J.L. & POL'Y 367 (2013); Marjorie Cohn, *Racial Profiling Legalized in Arizona*, 1 COLUM. J. RACE & L. 168 (2012); Andrea Christina Nill, *Latinos and S.B. 1070: Demonization, Dehumanization, and Disenfranchisement*, 14 HARV. LATINO

A high-profile piece of civil rights litigation offers an illustration of the concerns with the racially discriminatory enforcement of the federal immigration laws by state and local police agencies. In 2013, a district court ruled that the Maricopa County (Arizona) Sheriff's Office (MCSO), headed by controversial Sheriff Joe Arpaio, popularly known as "America's Toughest Sheriff," had engaged in a pattern and practice of unconstitutional treatment of Latina/os, including U.S. citizens, in its law enforcement efforts.[120] In essence, the court found that the MCSO's aggressive immigration enforcement activities violated the constitutional rights of Latina/os, including lawful immigrants and U.S. citizens.

Knowledgeable observers could not be surprised by the judicial finding of MCSO's unlawful pattern of racial discrimination. Arizona has long been at the forefront of states seeking to bolster immigration enforcement, with critics regularly claiming that the state's conduct in fact discriminates against persons of Mexican ancestry, including U.S. citizens and lawful immigrants. Federal authorities had investigated the Sheriff's Office for civil rights violations for years. In addition, Sheriff Arpaio regularly makes insensitive statements about undocumented immigrants and has consistently championed tough measures that amounted to little more than the rounding up of Latina/os as a form of immigration enforcement.[121]

Hundreds of Thousands of (Latina/o) Removals

The Obama administration's immigration enforcement measures contributed to an incredible increase in the number of noncitizens – lawful permanent residents as well as undocumented immigrants – removed from the United States. Today, the U.S. government regularly deports in the neighborhood of 400,000 immigrants a year. In fiscal year 2012, for example, Immigration and Customs Enforcement removed more than 409,000 noncitizens from the United States.[122] By way of

L. REV. 35 (2011); David A. Selden et. al., *Placing S.B. 1070 and Racial Profiling into Context, and What S.B. 1070 Reveals About the Legislative Process in Arizona*, 43 ARIZ. ST. L.J. 523 (2011); *see also* McKanders, *supra* note 116, at 334 (observing that whether *Arizona v. United States* will result in greater racial profiling in violation of Constitution "has been widely debated").

120 *See* Melendres v. Arpaio, 784 F.3d 1254 (9th Cir. 2015).

121 *See* Mary Romero, *Are Your Papers in Order?: Racial Profiling, Vigilantes, and "America's Toughest Sheriff"*, 14 HARV. LATINO L. REV. 337, 345–52 (2011); *see also* Kevin R. Johnson, *Immigration and Civil Rights: State and Local Efforts to Regulate Immigration*, 46 GA. L. REV. 609 (2012) (analyzing the adverse civil rights impacts on Latina/os of state and local efforts to regulate immigration through increased local law enforcement involvement in immigration enforcement).

122 *See* Immigration & Customs Enforcement, FY 2012: ICE Announces Year-End Removal Numbers, Highlights Focus on Key Priorities and Issues New National Detainer Guidance to Further Focus Resources (Dec. 21, 2012), available at http://www.ice.gov/news/releases/1212/121221washingtondc2.htm, last visited Aug. 29, 2014. In fiscal year 2013, removals dropped somewhat to 368,644. *See* U.S. Immigration & Customs Enforcement, *FY 2013: ICE Announces Year-End Removal Numbers* (Dec. 19, 2013), available at http://www.ice.gov/news/releases/1312/131219washingtondc.htm, last visited Aug. 29, 2014.

comparison, removals by the U.S. government were at slightly more than 30,000 in 1990.[123]

At bottom, *the nation has experienced a greater than tenfold increase in annual removals in a little more than twenty years*. Due to enforcement, detention, and removal machinery expanded over time with strong public support, the number of removals have grown at a fast pace since the turn of the century.

Widely publicizing its high numbers of removals, the Obama administration has emphatically made enforcement and removals through programs like Secure Communities its highest immigration enforcement priority. Indeed, it is little known that this administration arguably has deported more noncitizens than any presidential administration in American history.[124] That jarring fact may surprise some observers given that President Obama has consistently voiced support for comprehensive immigration reform and received strong political support from Latina/o voters.

The available data plainly reveals that Mexicans and Central Americans today are disproportionally represented among the noncitizens removed from the United States.[125] In fiscal year 2013, for example, Mexico accounted for nearly 68 percent of all removals; *removals from Mexico, Guatemala, Honduras, and El Salvador account for more than 94 percent of all removals*.[126] Thus, Latina/os constitute the vast majority of removals under modern U.S. immigration enforcement. Consequently, as the nation removes hundreds of thousands of noncitizens year in and year out, it deports record numbers of Mexican and Central American noncitizens annually as well. These undisputed racial and national origin consequences are often ignored, or minimized, by proponents of ever-greater immigration enforcement.

Disparate removal outcomes can be directly traced back to the congressional enactment of the Immigration Act of 1965 and the 1976 amendments, with their new and inflexible restrictions on legal immigration from Mexico and Latin America through the Western Hemisphere ceiling and per country caps. As discussed previously, these changes in the law effectively transformed thousands of lawful Mexican and Latin American immigrants into undocumented ones subject

[123] *See* U.S. Dep't of Homeland Security, Yearbook of Immigration Statistics: 2011 (Table 39), available at http://www.dhs.gov/yearbook-immigration-statistics-2011–3, last visited Aug 29. 2014. The administration also has set records for numbers of immigrant detentions as a means of immigration enforcement. *See* César Cuauhtémoc García Hernández, *Immigration Detention as Punishment*, 61 UCLA L. REV. 1346, 1348 (2014).

[124] The removal statistics released by the Obama administration have been questioned. *See* Brian Bennett, *Figures Skew Number Obama Deports*, L.A. TIMES, Apr. 1, 2014, at A1. It is unquestionable, however, that the administration has annually removed hundreds of thousands of noncitizens from the United States.

[125] *See* U.S. Dep't of Homeland Security, *supra* note 123 (Table 40).

[126] *See* U.S. Immigration & Customs Enforcement, *FY 2013*, *supra* note 122.

to removal from the United States. Moreover, with considerable public support, the laws triggered a series of events (and programs such as Secure Communities) resulting in a prolonged and concerted effort by the U.S. government to significantly reduce immigration from Mexico and Latin America and deport undocumented immigrants.

The disparate impacts of hundreds of thousands of removals annually have not been lost on persons of Mexican ancestry, and Latina/os generally, living in the United States. Many Latina/os view the current U.S. immigration laws and the enforcement machinery as nothing less than racially discriminatory. Immigrant and civil rights groups vigorously contest the disparate impacts of the various enforcement and removal measures. Each year, removals result in the separation of hundreds of thousands of families, including those with family members who are U.S. citizens and lawful immigrants, and disrupt and frighten noncitizens across the United States.[127]

Along these lines, advocacy groups seek to protect the civil rights of immigrants and U.S. citizens against the government's increasingly aggressive efforts to remove immigrants, including lawful permanent residents who, as previously discussed, have had brushes with the law. In turn, deeply held concerns that the operation and enforcement of the U.S. immigration laws is discriminatory contribute to the contentious nature of the national debate over immigration reform.

3.4 CONCLUSION

In good ways and bad, the Immigration Act of 1965 dramatically changed the racial dynamics of modern U.S. immigration law and its enforcement. Like many pieces of immigration legislation, the legislation included a series of compromises, some that could be viewed as pro–civil rights and worthy of celebration, but others with negative civil rights impacts that deserve to be criticized.

On the positive side of the civil rights ledger, the 1965 Act eliminated racial restrictions on immigration and abolished the discriminatory national origins quotas system, the bedrock of the U.S. immigration law for more than four decades. By so doing, Congress opened the doors to significantly increased lawful immigration from Asia, which had been severely restricted through express racial restrictions

[127] Commentators have criticized the large number of removals of immigrants for separating families, including families with U.S. citizen children. *See* Shani M. King, *U.S. Immigration Law and the Traditional Nuclear Conception of Family: Toward a Functional Definition of Family that Protects Children's Fundamental Human Rights*, 41 COLUM. HUM. RTS. L. REV. 509 (2010); David B. Thronson, *You Can't Get Here from Here: Toward a More Child-Centered Immigration Law*, 14 VA. J. SOC. POL'Y & L. 58 (2006); Marie Weisenberger, *Broken Families: A Call for Consideration of the Family of Illegal Immigrants in U.S. Immigration Enforcement Efforts*, 39 CAP. U.L. REV. 495 (2011).

on immigration in place for generations. These aspects of the reforms are entirely consistent with the powerful antidiscrimination principle that energized the civil rights movement.

On the negative side of the civil rights ledger, the Immigration Act of 1965 triggered a series of objective, color-blind moves that nonetheless have had severe disparate impacts on immigration from Mexico, and Latin America generally, and have resulted in a dramatic increase in the deportation of Latina/os from the United States. The anti-Latina/o aspects of the law directly responded to a growing fear among many Americans that the nation faced the potential of an uncontrolled influx of immigrants from Latin America to the United States. Congress expressly voiced concern with the "population explosion" in the region and relied on it as a justification for the annual ceiling on immigration from the Western Hemisphere.

More onerous limitations were placed on Latina/o immigration with the extension of the per-country ceilings to Mexico and all other nations in 1976. The application of the per-country ceiling to Mexico has had dramatic impacts on legal immigration from the country. By creating long backlogs of immigrant visas for prospective Mexican immigrants, the ceilings resulted in long delays for legal immigration by noncitizens from nations that annually send large numbers of immigrants to the United States. By so doing, the 1976 amendments created strong incentives for undocumented immigration.

In the end, Congress in 1965 and 1976 transformed thousands of previously legal Mexican migrants into disfavored and increasingly unpopular "illegal aliens" subject to possible removal from the United States. Moreover, because of the uncertain immigration status of undocumented workers, this component of the labor market is subject to exploitation by employers and others.

Increased public awareness of the growing undocumented Mexican population contributed to enactment of increasingly tougher immigration laws and heightened immigration enforcement. Political leaders and candidates seized on undocumented immigration as a popular, and deeply divisive, political issue. Over the last decade, state and local governments also enthusiastically sought to join the efforts in immigration enforcement. The escalating enforcement fervor built on, and reinforced, long-existing anti-Mexican, anti-Latina/o animus in American social life.

Today, both federal and state immigration enforcement unquestionably targets immigrants from Mexico. The contemporary public debate about immigration and immigration reform often centers almost exclusively on "illegal aliens" from Mexico. This anti-Mexican emphasis of the public debate, which at times might aptly be described as something akin to hysteria, is readily apparent to persons of Mexican ancestry and Latina/os generally. Consequently, race is front and center of the modern public ferment over immigration, immigration enforcement, and immigration reform.

In essence, the Immigration Act of 1965 created the necessary foundation for a series of anti-Mexican immigration enforcement measures pursued by the U.S. government over the next 50 years. This chapter has focused on a number, but far from all, of the significant legal and regulatory restrictions on Mexican immigration since 1965 and the enhanced enforcement of the U.S./Mexico border. The Mexican-oriented escalation in immigration enforcement is exemplified by the Secure Communities program and racial profiling in federal and state immigration enforcement, which have resulted in record numbers of removals of Mexican immigrants from the United States during the Obama administration. These measures effectively doubled down on the anti-Latina/o underside of the 1965 Act and helped make immigration enforcement one of the most pressing Latina/o civil rights concerns of the new millennium.[128]

The costly compromises made by civil rights advocates to abolish the discriminatory quotas system in the Immigration Act of 1965 serve as a cautionary tale for proponents of contemporary immigration reform: compromises must be made with great caution in seeking to secure passage of a comprehensive immigration reform package that includes a much-cherished path to legalization for undocumented immigrants. Although ensuring the elimination of the discriminatory national origins quotas systems that benefited immigrants from Asia, the concessions to restrictionists necessary to ensure passage of the Immigration Act of 1965 have been nothing less than devastating to Latina/o immigrants. Learning from the past, the nation must be vigilant to ensure that contemporary compromises to restrictionists in contemporary immigration reform measures are not unduly costly in similar ways to, and effectively sacrifice, while claiming to vindicate, immigrants' rights.[129]

[128] *See* Cristina M. Rodríguez, *Immigration, Civil Rights & the Evolution of the People*, 142 DAEDALUS 228 (2013) (exploring the meaning of immigration as a civil rights issue).

[129] *See generally* ALFONSO GONZALES, REFORM WITHOUT JUSTICE: LATINO MIGRANT POLITICS AND THE HOMELAND SECURITY STATE (2014) (contending that segments of the contemporary immigrant rights movement has been willing to make excessive concessions to immigration enforcement in advocating for comprehensive immigration reform).

4

The Last Preference

Refugees and the 1965 Immigration Act

Brian Soucek

On October 3, 1965, President Lyndon Johnson traveled to the Statue of Liberty to sign Public Law 89–236, the 1965 amendments to the Immigration and Nationality Act. After joking with congressmen from New York and New Jersey about whose state they were in, the president delivered a stirring description of "one of the most important acts of this Congress and of this administration": ending "the harsh injustice of the national origins quota system."[1] Henceforth, Johnson said, immigrants to the United States would "come because of what they are, and not because of the land from which they sprung."[2]

Having hailed the end of the national origins quotas, President Johnson then turned to his second topic: the announcement of a new immigration initiative *based entirely on national origins*.[3] The speech heralded the launch of the Cuban airlift.

The contradiction at the heart of President Johnson's signing statement reflected tensions in the 1965 Act itself – specifically, tensions stemming from its treatment of refugees.[4] Where the primary purpose of the Act was to do away with discriminatory

[1] Signing of the Immigration Bill, The President's Remarks at the Ceremony on Liberty Island, with His Offer of Asylum for Cuban Refugees. October 3, 1965, 1 Weekly Comp. Pres. Docs. 364, 364–65 (Oct. 11, 1965).

[2] *Id.* at 366.

[3] *Id.*

[4] This tension was not lost on the Johnson administration. Asked during House Immigration Subcommittee hearings in March 1965 about whether "the administration proposal for immigration reform removes all discrimination from the law," Attorney General Katzenbach replied: "Yes … Of course, you could get into the situation of refugees, and I suppose there the political situation in the country of their birth – not the country of their birth – affects those that you would admit." *Immigration: Hearings on H.R. 2580 Before Subcommittee No. 1 of the House Committee on the Judiciary*, 89th Cong. 41 (1965).

Acting Professor, UC Davis School of Law. I am grateful for the enthusiastic and skillful research assistance provided by UC Davis law students John Ormonde and Joseph Uzarski. Thanks also to Professor Sarah Song and other participants at the UC Davis School of Law's Roundtable on the 1965 Immigration Act for their comments on an earlier draft of this chapter.

national origin quotas, the refugee preference was explicitly tied to communist and Middle Eastern countries. Where the rest of the Act aimed to bring immigration priorities in line with contemporary economic and social needs, its provisions for refugees failed to address even the most obvious demands of the time – most notably, the tens of thousands of Cubans then looking to flee the Castro regime. And where the 1965 Act can otherwise be seen as an assertion of Congressional control over the numbers and types of immigrants the United States would admit, the protection of refugees was largely left to the discretion – not always wanted – of the executive branch.

This chapter tells how the ad hoc nature of postwar U.S. refugee policy provided a crucial impetus for the broader immigration reforms of 1965. But refugee policy itself largely escaped such reform, and the formalizing of admissions based on family ties and employment skills – the hallmarks of the 1965 Act – only made ad hocery all the more prevalent when humanitarian crises and political opportunity required admissions outside these bases. The desire to "deal with" refugee admissions once and for all ran up against a recognition of the vast and ever-changing needs of displaced persons, and choices between settled rules and adaptive discretion had to be made – not for the last time.

4.1 REFUGEE POLICY BEFORE THE 1965 ACT

The national origins quota system the 1965 Immigration Act replaced was not just a moral failure[5] but a practical one as well. In fact, given its moral failings, perhaps the best thing that can be said about the quota system is that it didn't work. Several of the nations favored under the quota system failed to come anywhere close to using their yearly allotments,[6] and stop-gap measures to relieve growing backlogs in other countries accounted for a growing proportion of yearly admissions. So too did a series of temporary, sometimes emergency measures designed to address refugee crises throughout the world. By 1965, only one in three immigrants being admitted to the United States was entering under the quota system.[7] Special exceptions had swallowed the rule.

5 The deep-seated racism of the national origins quota system is well described in other chapters in this book, especially Chapters 1 and 2.

6 Between 1953 and 1962, for example, Great Britain and Ireland used only 38% or fewer of their allotted visas under the quota system. *See* H. COMM. ON THE JUDICIARY, SUBCOMM. NO. 1, 88TH CONG., STUDY OF POPULATION AND IMMIGRATION PROBLEMS: ADMINISTRATIVE PRESENTATIONS (I) 25 Chart 2 (1963).

7 H.R. REP. NO. 89–745, at 11 (1965); *see* STAFF OF S. COMM. ON THE JUDICIARY, 96TH CONG., U.S. IMMIGRATION LAW AND POLICY: 1952–1979, 52 (Comm. Print 1979) (prepared at the request of Senator Edward M. Kennedy) [hereinafter "USILP"].

Exceptions to the quota system started being made for refugees not long after passage of the Immigration and Nationality Act in June 1952. In July 1953, Congress enacted the "first non-quota refugee legislation"[8]: a resolution allowing for the admission of 500 orphans adopted abroad by American servicemen and other federal workers.[9] More significant was the Refugee Relief Act of 1953, which authorized 214,000 non-quota visas, 205,000 of which were meant for refugees, "escapees," and "expellees."[10] Its provision of 2,000 visas for Chinese refugees – at a time when the official quota for China was set at 105 immigrants per year[11] – suggests the extent to which the 1953 Act subverted the racial (and racist) balance struck only one year previous, when the INA was passed.[12] The Refugee Relief Act was only meant to last until the end of 1956, although ultimately, 18,656 unused visas were doled out in legislation passed in September 1957.[13]

Events occurring during the two and a half years the Refugee Relief Act was in effect showed how hard it was for even short-term legislation to keep pace with national and international demands. In the fall of 1956, the thwarted uprising in Hungary produced a flood of refugees, only 6,000 or so of whom could be brought to the United States under the Refugee Relief Act's provisions.[14] The remaining 32,000 Hungarian refugees who eventually resettled in the United States all came through a more discretionary route: the Attorney General's "parole" authority.

[8] USILP, *supra* note 7, at 17.

[9] Act of July 29, 1953, Pub. L No. 83–162, 67 Stat. 229 (1953).

[10] USILP, *supra* note 7, at 17; Refugee Relief Act of 1953, Pub. L. No. 83–203, § 2, 67 Stat. 400 (expired Dec. 31, 1956). Refugees were defined as those, outside of communist countries, who had fled persecution; escapees were refugees who had fled communist countries due to racial, religious, or political persecution; and expellees were refugees of German origin who had been forced out of Eastern Europe. *Id.*

[11] Gabriel J. Chin, *The Civil Rights Revolution, Comes to Immigration Law: A New Look at The Immigration and Nationality Act of 1965*, 75 N.C. L. Rev. 273, 291 nn.68–69 (1996).

[12] Rep. Walter Judd, a Republican from Minnesota, added the Asian refugee provisions as a last-minute floor amendment. Ignoring Asian refugees from communist countries would, he argued, not only undermine the Refugee Relief Act's professed anticommunist agenda; it would also constitute "the worst act of racial discrimination ... in our immigration laws since the disastrous 1924 so-called Exclusion Act, which also ignored one-half of the people in the world." Philip Eric Wolgin, Beyond National Origins: The Development of Modern Immigration Policymaking, 1948–1968, Ph.D. dissertation, Department of History, UC Berkeley (2011), at 148, *available at* http://escholarship.org/uc/item/1vr7k843.

[13] USILP, *supra* note 7, at 17; The Refugee-Escape Act of 1957, Pub. L. No. 85–316, 71 Stat. 639 (1957). The 1957 law expanded the definition of the term "refugee-escapee" to encompass those fleeing not just communist countries but also countries "within the general area of the Middle East," due to persecution "on account of race, religion, or political opinion." *Id.* § 15(c)(1). This was the language eventually incorporated in the refugee provision of the 1965 Act. *See* Act of October 3, 1965, Pub. L. No. 89–236, § 2(d)(7), 79 Stat. 911, 913 (1965).

[14] USILP, *supra* note 7, at 18.

Section 212(d)(5) of the Immigration and Nationality Act allowed the Attorney General to parole aliens into the country "for emergent reasons or for reasons deemed strictly in the public interest."[15] Then as now, those brought to the United States under the parole provision are not officially "admitted"; the law requires their return to the country from which they came once "the purposes of such parole shall, in the opinion of the Attorney General, have been served."[16] But unlike the current provision, which requires that parole be granted temporarily, on a case-by-case basis, and only when the need is an "urgent humanitarian" one,[17] the parole authority in place pre-1965 offered no such constraints.

Nor were many limitations observed in practice. Rather than proceeding case by case, the parole authority was increasingly invoked group by group, or crisis by crisis. The temporary parole of Hungarian refugees in 1956 and 1957 was followed by legislation in 1958 that allowed those refugees to make their status permanent after two years in the United States.[18] Then, in a twelve-month period in 1961 and 1962, more than 58,000 Cubans were paroled into the United States;[19] around the same time, the Attorney General paroled 15,000 Chinese refugees from Hong Kong, again drastically subverting the limits placed on Asian immigration under the national quota system.[20] In addition to these discretionary *executive* ventures beyond the quota system, Congress too passed legislation during this period authorizing non-quota immigration by refugees from the Azores and Indonesia.[21]

The fascinating interaction between the executive and legislative branches on the question of refugees – at times a tug-of-war, at other times a game of hot potato – can best be seen in two laws passed in the early 1960s: the Fair Share Refugee Act of 1960[22] and the Migration and Refugee Assistance Act of 1962.[23]

The year leading up to the Fair Share Act's passage had been dubbed the "World Refugee Year" by President Eisenhower.[24] The Act itself, introduced by Representative Francis Walter, one of the architects of the 1952 INA (also known as the McCarran-Walter Act), explicitly authorized the Attorney General to use his

[15] 8 U.S.C. § 1182(d)(5)(A) (1952).
[16] *Id.*
[17] 8 U.S.C. § 1182(d)(5)(A) (2012). If the parolee qualifies as a refugee, *see* 8 U.S.C. § 1101(a)(42) (2012), the current parole provision requires the Attorney General to "determine[] that compelling reasons in the public interest with respect to that particular alien require that the alien be paroled into the United States." 8 U.S.C. § 1182(d)(5)(B) (2012).
[18] Hungarian Refugees Act, Pub. L. No. 85–559, 72 Stat. 419 (1958).
[19] USILP, *supra* note 7, at 46.
[20] *Id.*
[21] USILP, *supra* note 7, at 21. The Azorean Refugee Act marked the first time the United States specifically provided for refugees fleeing a natural disaster. *See* Wolgin, *supra* note 12, at 157.
[22] Pub. L. No. 86–648, 74 Stat. 504 (1960).
[23] Pub. L. No. 87–510, 76 Stat. 121 (1962).
[24] USILP, *supra* note 7, at 22.

parole powers for two years (July 1960 to July 1962) on behalf of refugee-escapees[25] who fell under the mandate of the U.N. High Commissioner for Refugees[26] ("UNHCR") – generally, refugees remaining in Western European camps. The number of paroled refugees was not to exceed one-fourth the number of refugees resettled in other countries, and the legislation was set to expire in 1962. Congress did provide, however, for the refugees to be admitted as regular immigrants after two years' residence.[27]

The Fair Share Refugee Act thus reflected a somewhat awkward blend of congressional and executive power: Congress was explicitly authorizing an exercise of discretion that the Attorney General, at least arguably, already possessed, even as Congress was purporting to limit the duration and scope of the exercise. Meanwhile, by relying on the parole power, Congress was avoiding any conflict with the INA's admissions quotas for regular immigrants, while at the same time going beyond parole by preapproving parolees' future admission as regular immigrants – subject, of course, to the Attorney General's discretionary choice not to terminate their parole in the interim.

The Migration and Refugee Assistance Act of 1962 canceled the Fair Share Act's expiration date. As a result, between 1960 and 1965, nearly 20,000 refugees were paroled into the country under the Fair Share Act's largesse.[28] The Migration and Refugee Assistance Act law did still more: it appropriated funds and authorized the president to assist refugees under the UNHCR's mandate, as well as those whose assistance served the security and foreign policy interests of the United States.[29] Under the terms of the 1962 law, "refugees" were not limited to those fleeing communist countries (although an additional provision allowing the president to help refugees in the United States who had fled a Western Hemisphere nation because of racial, religious, or political persecution was clearly directed at Cuba).[30] Still, despite its breadth, the Act's refugee definition was still not as broad as that of the United Nations – whose 1951 Refugee Convention, which the United States had not yet ratified, protected those with a well-founded fear of persecution on account of race, religion, national origin, membership in a particular social group, or political opinion.[31] Without going quite that far with its protections in the 1962 Act, Congress had once again expanded the executive

25 *See supra* note 13 for the definition of "refugee-escapee."
26 Fair Share Refugee Act, Pub. L. No. 86–648, § 1, 74 Stat. 504 (1960).
27 *Id.* § 3.
28 USILP, *supra* note 7, at 47.
29 Migration and Refugee Assistance Act, Pub. L. No. 87–510, § 2(b), 76 Stat. 121 (1962).
30 Abba P. Schwartz, The Open Society 142 (1968).
31 Convention Relating to the Status of Refugees, July 28, 1951, 189 U.N.T.S. 150, Art. I, A(2), *available at* http://www.unhcr.org/3b66c2aa10.html.

branch's discretionary power to assist refugees, unhampered by the increasingly irrelevant constraints of the 1952 INA.

4.2 REFUGEE POLICY IN THE 1965 ACT

The ad hoc refugee legislation of the 1950s and 1960s, along with the increased use of the executive's discretionary parole authority – discretion sometimes prodded by Congress – together produced a kind of safety valve that lessened the pressures of, and on, the INA's quota system. The INA's proponents, especially Representative Walter, may actually have promoted use of the executive's parole authority precisely in order to sidestep the claim – made by Presidents Truman, Eisenhower, Kennedy, and Johnson, among others – that the outmoded national origin restrictions were failing to meet the country's contemporary domestic and foreign policy needs.[32]

At the same time, however, growing use of the parole authority and special non-quota legislation undermined any arguments that the INA's defenders might have made about the continued necessity of the quotas. Given that, by 1965, the quotas had come to account for only a third of U.S. immigration,[33] it was hard to argue that the racial balancing at which those quotas aimed still remained essential to the United States' national interests. The growth of non-quota immigration in the years leading up to the 1965 Act thus proved the quotas unnecessary, even as it might also have reduced the urgency of getting rid of them.

If the ad hocery of mid-century U.S. immigration policy was prompted at least in part by the limitations of the national origin quotas, doing away with the latter presumably offered the opportunity to rein in the former. And yet the genealogy of the refugee provisions in the 1965 Act reveals divisions not just *between* Congress and the executive, but *within* Congress, about whether ad hoc legislation and executive discretion were really all that bad. Ultimately, the 1965 Act reflects deep ambivalence about just how flexible immigration policy needs to be – and the extent to which such flexibility is compatible with Congressional control over immigration.

Attempts to undo the INA's quotas date back at least to President Truman, who vetoed the McCarran-Walter Act when it was passed in 1952. Representative Walter's death in May 1963 presented reformers an opportunity – or would have, had Walter's replacement as chair of the House Immigration Subcommittee, Representative Michael Feighan, proven more amenable to reform. It was only after Feighan, a Democrat who had represented Ohio for twenty-two years, won the 1964 primary in his immigrant-heavy

[32] Wolgin, *supra* note 12, at 153, n.77 (citing Stephen Thomas Wagner, The Lingering Death of the National Origins Quota System: A Political History of United States Immigration Policy, 1952–1965, Ph.D. Dissertation, Harvard University (1986), at 305–06).

[33] *See* 111 Cong. Rec. 24225, 24225–26 (Sept. 17, 1965) (statement of Senator Kennedy).

district by a slim plurality that he stopped holding up the immigration bill that the Kennedy administration had earlier proposed; for the first time, public hearings were scheduled, though they did not lead anywhere during the 88th Congress.[34]

Before a similar bill was reintroduced in the 89th Congress the following year, President Johnson deployed his fabled powers of persuasion, taking Feighan on Air Force One, reminding him that immigration reform was part of the Democratic platform, and – taking no chances – stacking the House Immigration Subcommittee, which grew from five to nine members.[35] At least partially swayed by the president's efforts, Representative Feighan held hearings on the administration's proposal between March and June 1965.[36] Parallel hearings in the Senate, run by Senator Edward Kennedy, extended from February to August.[37]

Representative Celler, the chair of the House Judiciary Committee and a bitter foe of Feighan's,[38] complimented the administration's proposal for "allow[ing] broad authority to the President, because of the need of flexibility in an immigration fabric."[39] According to Celler, flexibility was especially necessary in regard to refugees, who "almost by definition, are uprooted suddenly."[40]

The administration bills of 1964 and 1965 – mostly identical in their particulars – gave the president increased flexibility to deal with refugees in two specific ways. First, they allowed the president to allot a certain percentage (20 percent in 1964, reduced to 10 percent in 1965) of annual quota visas to refugees who were

> oppressed or persecuted, or threatened with oppression or persecution, because of their race, color, religion, national origin, adherence to democratic beliefs, or their opposition to totalitarianism or dictatorship, and to persons uprooted by natural calamity or military operations who are unable to return to their usual place of abode.[41]

Second, the administration bills broadened the terms of the Fair Share Act, removing its previous limitation to refugees who fell under the mandate of the

34 Dan Cordtz, *Immigration Reform: Bill's Smooth Passage Reflects New Complexion in Congress*, WALL ST. J., Oct. 4, 1965, at 16; *see also* Edward M. Kennedy, *The Immigration Act of 1965*, 367 ANNALS AM. ACAD. POL. & SOC. SCI. 137, 141 (1966) ("The Senate and House hearings during 1964 were the first significant Congressional inquiries into the merits of the national-origins quota system since the enactment of the Immigration and Naturalization Act of 1952. No additional action was taken, however ...").

35 Cordtz, *supra* note 34, at 16.

36 USILP, *supra* note 7, at 55.

37 *Id.*; *see also* Kennedy, *supra* note 34, at 142.

38 *See* Cabell Phillips, *Old Feud Erupts on House's Floor*, N.Y. TIMES, July 10, 1965, at 26.

39 *Immigration: Hearings on H.R. 7700 Before Subcommittee No. 1 of the House Committee on the Judiciary*, 88th Cong., 2d Sess., 8 (1964).

40 *Id.*

41 H.R. 7700, 88th Cong. § 2 (1964); H.R. 2580, 89th Cong. § 3 (1965).

UNHRC.[42] Where the UNHCR mandate failed to extend much beyond Europe, the administration bills allowed for the parole of any "refugee-escapee" who, because of race, religion, or political opinion, had fled from a communist country or the Middle East.[43] In addition to these two new, or newly expanded, powers, the Attorney General's parole authority under INA § 212(d)(5) was to remain untouched.

The flexibility given the executive branch thus stemmed partly from the bill's redundancies. Faced, say, with a political refugee from a communist country, executive branch officials would be able to respond in any of three ways: (1) offer admission using one of the approximately 16,000 quota visas (10 percent of the total allotment) that the president could reserve for those fleeing persecution or disaster; (2) parole the refugee into the United States under the terms of the expanded Fair Share Act, which was capped at one-quarter of the number of refugees accepted by other countries, and under which parolees could gain official admission after two years residence; or (3) parole the refugee into the country under § 212(d)(5), which had no numerical cap, but under which parolees could not be officially admitted unless further legislative action was taken, as it was for the Hungarian parolees of the 1950s.

Constraints on executive discretion were, therefore, largely illusory: taken together, the disjunctive provisions nearly always would have left room for the president to admit, or at least parole, anyone or any group he chose. Little practical significance, then, rode on the specific definitions enshrined in the proposed legislation. Yet Congress jealously guarded its power to set them: one reason the bills untethered the Fair Share Act's refugee definition from that of the UNHCR was because of Congressional concern about the United States delegating "to any international organization the authority to determine who is and who is not a refugee."[44]

The bills proposed by the administration only nominally survived to become law. H.R. 2580, the administration bill introduced by Representative Celler in 1965, eventually passed the House, but not before being fundamentally transformed. Once again, it was Representative Feighan who got in the way of the administration's plans. On June 1, 1965, Feighan introduced a bill of his own: H.R. 8662, which he touted as "a very large step in the direction of regaining and maintaining [Congress's] authority for regulating immigration into the United States."[45] In regard to refugees, this meant not just reducing the types of discretion given to the executive branch

[42] H.R. 2580, 89th Cong. § 13 (1965).

[43] *Id.* For these purposes, the "Middle East" meant the area from Morocco to Pakistan west to east, and from Turkey to Saudi Arabia and Ethiopia north to south.

[44] *Immigration: Hearings on H.R. 7700 Before Subcommittee No. 1 of the House Committee on the Judiciary*, 88th Cong., 2d Sess., 488 (1964) (question by Rep. Feighan for the Hon. Norbert A. Schlei, Assistant Attorney General).

[45] 111 Cong. Rec. 12087, 12089 (June 1, 1965) (statement of Rep. Feighan).

to admit or parole refugees but also limiting who would count as a refugee in the first place.

The Feighan bill proposed a cap of 225,000 immigrant admissions per year, with no more than 20,000 coming from any single country.[46] This ceiling was somewhat misleading, however, as it applied only to Eastern Hemisphere admissions. Feighan himself thought the traditional distinction between quota-limited Eastern Hemisphere admissions and unlimited Western Hemisphere admissions was just the sort of national origin discrimination that Congress was trying to end, and yet he deferred to "Government spokesmen that repeal of the special nonquota status for . . . the Western Hemisphere [was] unacceptable at [that] time."[47] Feighan did, however, propose to eliminate another way around the numerical cap: the executive's parole authority.

Aside from Western Hemisphere admissions, what Feighan envisioned was a totalizing quota system, without ad hoc legislative or discretionary executive exceptions, in which immigrants would be admitted according to seven ordered preferences. After six family- and employment-based categories, the seventh preference would allow up to 10 percent of yearly admissions (minus those used for the first preference, given to spouses, parents, and unmarried children of U.S. citizens) for refugees who fled a communist country "because of persecution or fear of persecution on account of race, religion, or political opinion."[48] A further provision in Feighan's bill allowed the president, in consultation with the Secretary of State, to dedicate up to half of the visas left over after the seven preferences had been applied to refugees "uprooted by natural calamity or military operations."[49]

Feighan's two quota-capped refugee provisions – the preference allotment for refugees from communist countries and the non-preference allotment for disaster and war refugees – were together meant to render unnecessary the Fair Share Act and similar large-scale uses of the parole authority. Feighan's bill explicitly repealed the former and, in the analysis section, expressed the hope that, going forward, the parole power of § 212(d)(5) would be limited to the "purposes originally intended – the temporary receptions of persons arriving in the United States without documentation and under emergent circumstances, e.g. shipwrecked crewmen, and so forth."[50] Restricting parole to individual emergencies was meant not only to curb executive discretion but also to ensure that refugees were admitted under a

[46] *Id.* at 12088.

[47] *Id.* For more on the debates over Eastern versus Western Hemisphere admissions, see Chapter 3 in this volume.

[48] 111 CONG. REC. at 12090. Half of the seventh preference quota could instead be used to admit aliens who had been physically present in the United States for two years. *Id.*

[49] *Id.* at 12091.

[50] *Id.* at 12093.

single system, free of UN control, in which, significantly, no one would be forced to "carry the *stigma of parole* as a condition of their entry."[51]

Compared to the administration bills, Feighan's proposed legislation was clearly an attempt to tie U.S. immigration policy to the proverbial mast, constraining future choices not only of the executive but also of Congress, whose crisis-specific legislation (like the bills concerning Hungary, the Azores, and Hong Kong) and private immigration bills[52] would no longer be needed. What Feighan hoped for was a more deliberate immigration policy – something better planned than the country's previous series of improvisational responses to successive world crises. (Of course, the United States had never actually responded to each and every crisis – a fact that only added to the discriminatory nature of the country's immigration scheme.) Further, Feighan justifiably sought to avoid provisional solutions such as parole, in which refugees were allowed into the country but not officially admitted. This was the stigmatizing limbo Feighan had decried. At the same time, while Feighan thought that his bill would make ad hoc, crisis-driven legislation unnecessary, it did nothing to bar it. Nor did Feighan's bill eliminate the Attorney General's statutory parole authority, even if Feighan did express a view about how Congress intended parole to be used.

Importantly, the refugee definitions in Feighan's bill were decidedly more political than those in the administration bills. Quota refugee visas in the administration bills were allotted to those fleeing natural disasters, military operations, or persecution due to race, color, religion, national origin, and political opinion.[53] The administration bill's second refugee provision, its extension of the Fair Share Act, only applied to those fleeing communist countries or the Middle East, but its reaffirmation of the Attorney General's parole authority had no such limitation. By contrast, Feighan's bill would have limited quota visas to refugees fleeing communism. And while Feighan's bill did make a potential allowance for victims of natural disasters or war, Feighan's stated interpretation of parole would not have allowed it to serve as a stop-gap protection for groups persecuted by anyone other than communists. In sum, Feighan's bill shared the humanitarian protections of the administration bills, but unlike their broad understanding of persecution,[54] Feighan's bill viewed persecution in purely Cold War terms.

51 *Id.* at 12089 (emphasis added).

52 *Id.* at 12089.

53 *See supra* note 41 and accompanying text. The political opinion protected in Rep. Feighan's bill was limited to that which favored democracy or opposed totalitarianism.

54 The administration bill came closest to adopting the refugee definition found in the 1951 U.N. Convention. The only category omitted was "membership in a particular social group." That said, the administration's bills (and Feighan's) swept beyond the UN's definition by offering refuge to victims of natural calamities in addition to victims of intentional persecution.

The proposals before Congress in the middle of 1965 thus differed fairly starkly in the amount of discretion they granted, in the number of potential refugees they allowed, in the permanence or provisionality of the refugee policies they envisioned, and finally in their willingness to distinguish among certain refugees based on their national origin. In time, a deeply amended version of H.R. 2580 emerged from Representative Feighan's subcommittee, passed the House of Representatives on August 25, 1965, and then – with one additional change to the refugee provisions at each stage – received approval from the Senate on September 22 and cleared the Conference Committee on September 29. The final product was partly a compromise between the alternatives on offer, partly a decision favoring one or the other, and partly just a dodge.

Like the Feighan bill, the 1965 Act in its final form replaced the national origin quota system with seven preference categories, the last of which was dedicated to refugees. Less generous than previous iterations, the Act that passed set aside 10,200 immigrant visas – 6 percent of the overall yearly total – for aliens in noncommunist countries who *either*: (1) fled a communist country or the Middle East and were unable or unwilling to return "because of persecution or fear of persecution on account of race, religion, or political opinion"; or – thanks to an addition made in the Senate – (2) were "uprooted by catastrophic natural calamity as defined by the President."[55] Following the example of the Fair Share Act, which the 1965 Act officially repealed, refugees entering under the seventh preference were not granted admission, but they could adjust their status after two years' residence. In a departure from the Fair Share Act, refugees' initial status was not called "parole," but "conditional entry." This, according to the Senate Judiciary Committee report, was to avoid any "connotation unfavorable to the alien" conveyed by the term "parole." Representative Feighan's worry about the stigma caused by parole's second-tier immigration status was thus reduced to, and addressed as, a worry about terminology.

The persecution provision in the 1965 Act went beyond the Feighan bill by including refugees from the Middle East alongside those who fled communist countries. Yet while it adopted the refugee-escapee protection of the administration bills – which had borrowed from the Fair Share Act while leaving out its link to the UNHCR mandate – the 1965 Act did *not* give the president one of the broader powers offered by the administration bills: the authority to grant 10 percent of the annual quota visas to refugees *anywhere*, so long as they faced persecution on account of race, color, religion, national origin, or political belief. Protections based on color and, most significantly, national origin did not make it into the final version

[55] Act of October 3, 1965, Pub. L. No. 89–236, § 3(a)(7), 79 Stat. 911 (1965). The Act allowed the president to use half of the conditional entry visas allowed under the refugee allotment for the adjustment of status of parolees who had lived in the United States for two years. *Id.*

of the 1965 Act at all. In fact, given the geographic restrictions that *did* make it in, the omission of discrimination based on nationality was doubly felt. The 1965 Act did not just fail to protect refugees fleeing national origin discrimination; it actually enacted such discrimination itself.[56]

Like its predecessor bills, the Act left intact the Attorney General's parole authority under INA § 212(d)(5). But the House and Senate Committee reports both noted their

> express intent … that the parole provisions of the [INA], which remain unchanged by this bill, be administered in accordance with the original intention of the drafters of that legislation. The parole provisions were designed to authorize the Attorney General to act only in emergent, individual, and isolated situations, such as the case of an alien who requires immediate medical attention, and not for the immigration of classes or groups outside the limit of the law.[57]

The "express intent" asserted by lawmakers in both the House and Senate did not go unchallenged. Senator Philip Hart, who had introduced the administration's bill in the Senate and assisted Senator Kennedy as its floor manager there, argued that although certain legislative reports "might seem to attempt to exclude [the parole provision's] application to large groups of refugees[,] … [w]e cannot predict accurately what the future holds." Therefore, Hart said, the parole provision should "continue to let our Nation respond quickly in dire emergency situations where freedom and lives of individuals are at stake."[58]

Making clear that he had the large-scale parole of refugee groups in mind, Senator Hart immediately went on to speak of the 250,000 Cubans who had fled to the United States since 1959.[59] As he observed, the version of H.R. 2580 that emerged from the Senate Judiciary Committee and eventually passed in the Senate included a provision, "geared specifically to exiles from Cuba,"[60] which would allow parolees from the Western Hemisphere who had fled persecution based on race, religion, or political opinion to become permanent residents after two years in the United

56 The explicit national origin discrimination in the 1965 Act – limited as it was to refugees fleeing communist countries and the Middle East – was exacerbated by the practical reality that the Immigration and Naturalization Service only "conducted conditional entry examinations in Frankfurt, Hong Kong, Rome, Vienna and Athens." Charlotte J. Moore, Cong. Research Serv., 96th Cong., Review of U.S. Refugee Resettlement Programs and Policies 12 (Comm. Print 1980).

57 H.R. Rep. No. 89–745, at 15–16 (1965); S. Rep. No. 89–748 (1965), *reprinted in* 1965 U.S.C.C.A.N. 3328, 3335.

58 111 Cong. Rec. 24225, 24239.

59 *Id.*

60 *See* Kennedy, *supra* note 34, at 146.

States. The point of the provision was to provide a regular status to the hundreds of thousands of Cubans who were then living in the United States as parolees.

The adjustment provision was removed, however, by the conference committee when it reconciled the House and Senate bills, and the provision never made it into the 1965 Act. Instead of providing Cuban parolees a route to permanent status, the 1965 Act, in its final version, punted: it referred the question of what should be done about Cuban refugees to a Select Commission on Western Hemisphere Immigration.[61] For Cubans already living in the United States, the "stigma of parole" would have to be removed through future legislation.

4.3 AFTER 1965: DISCRETION AND CONTROL

Despite the fact that it provided the country's "first permanent statutory basis for the admission of refugees,"[62] the 1965 Act's refugee scheme embraced so many tensions that its permanence was bound to be temporary.

For one thing, the Act provided no protection for refugees fearing persecution in countries that were not communist or Middle Eastern. The national original discrimination inherent in this limitation was in such tension with the spirit of the Act as a whole that the section containing the refugee and other preference categories had to be exempted from the Act's general nondiscrimination provision.[63] Even so, the protection the Act offered those fleeing communist countries in the Eastern Hemisphere did nothing for the thousands of refugees arriving in the United States each month from communist Cuba in the Western Hemisphere; the Act made no provision for them at all.

The Cuban problem also underscored another tension in the Act: the seventh preference was intended to regularize refugee admissions, providing a Congressionally set quota within the overall yearly immigration flow. And yet the quota that Congress set was clearly inadequate to meet even contemporary needs. Continued use of the executive's parole power – for groups, not just for individuals, as Congress (or at

[61] Act of Oct. 3, 1965, Pub. L. No. 89–237, § 21(b)(4), 79 Stat. 911, 919 (1965). The Select Commission was a fifteen-member body charged with determining whether a cap should be placed on the number of immigrants coming from within the Americas. The version of H.R. 2580 that passed the House had not placed a quota on Western Hemisphere immigration. An amendment in the Senate, however, proposed a limit of 120,000, which would go into effect in 1968 unless Congress, after receiving the Select Commission's recommendations, decided otherwise. *See id.* at § 21(e); *see also* Kennedy, *supra* note 34, at 147.

[62] Deborah E. Anker & Michael H. Posner, *The Forty Year Crisis: A Legislative History of the Refugee Act of 1980*, 19 SAN DIEGO L. REV. 9, 17 (1981).

[63] *See* Act of Oct. 3, 1965, Pub. L. No. 89–237, § 2(a), 79 Stat. 911, 911 ("No person shall receive any preference or priority or be discriminated against in the issuance of an immigrant visa because of his race, sex, nationality, place of birth, or place of residence, *except as specifically provided in … section 203*." (emphasis added)).

least the House and Senate Committee reports) insisted it intended – was therefore inevitable. President Johnson made this immediately clear when he included as part of his signing statement for the 1965 Act an announcement of the Cuban airlift, with its "open-ended invitation for thousands of Cuban refugees to enter the United States" as parolees.[64]

Given the obvious, continued need for the flexibility that the parole power offered, and given the fact that the 1965 Act did nothing to change the statutory basis for the parole power, Congress's stated intention to limit the use of parole is hard to credit. Congress claimed to be reasserting its constitutional authority over immigration in the 1965 Act; it purported to be establishing rules that would govern refugee admissions for the foreseeable future. But by failing to address obvious contemporary needs, and by choosing not to restrict the discretionary power the executive had used to meet such needs in the recent past, Congress seemed to have recognized, at least implicitly, that a more flexible approach was necessary. Congress may well have wanted to *appear* to be setting firm limits on immigration even as it expected that the executive branch would exceed those limits whenever humanitarian need or national interests so required.

This, in any event, is what happened in the fifteen years following passage of the 1965 Act. Nearly 350,000 Cubans were paroled into the United States between 1965 and March 1980; the Cuban airlift that began soon after President Johnson's Statue of Liberty speech lasted for more than seven of those years.[65] From 1975 to 1979, more than 200,000 Indochinese refugees also received parole. Unlike the Cuban refugees, those fleeing Vietnam and Cambodia satisfied the national origin requirements of the 1965 Act. So too did the 35,000 or so refugees from the Soviet Union who were paroled during the same period.[66] For those groups, the challenge was quantitative rather than qualitative: parole was needed because the seventh preference was simply too small. By the end of 1978, 126,000 refugees had been granted conditional entry under the 1965 Act's official refugee quota – only 12 percent of those who had benefited from the INA's parole provision.[67]

As in the years leading up to the 1965 Act, the quotas chosen by Congress were again made largely irrelevant in the decade and a half after the Act's passage by the repeated use of executive discretion. Yet, as before, it is not entirely clear how much Congress actually minded.[68]

64 Anker & Posner, *supra* note 62, at 19.

65 Larry Nackerud, Alyson Springer, Christopher Larrison, & Alicia Issac, *The End of the Cuban Contradiction in U.S. Refugee Policy*, 33 INT'L MIGRATION REV. 176, 188 tbl. 1 (1999).

66 *See* Moore, *supra* note 56, at 13–15.

67 *Compare id.* at 12, *with id.* at 15.

68 *See, e.g.*, *Refugee Act of 1979: Hearings Before the H. Subcomm. on Immigration, Refugees, and Int'l Law*, 96th Cong. 40 (1979) (statement of Dick Clark, Ambassador at Large and U.S. Coordinator for

In 1966, Congress allowed Cuban parolees to become permanent residents after two years in the United States,[69] just as Hungarian parolees had been allowed to do in the 1950s; those who adjusted their status were not counted against the immigration quotas then in place. Laws passed in 1977[70] and 1978[71] extended the same opportunity to refugees from Vietnam, Laos, and Cambodia. In passing such laws, Congress effectively ratified the Attorney General's circumvention of both Congressionally established quotas and the exclusion provisions of ordinary immigration law.

Further, Congress repeatedly voted to fund the resettlement of refugees who had been paroled into the country at the Attorney General's discretion. Between fiscal years 1966 and 1979, more than $1.1 billion was devoted to the Cuban refugee program alone.[72] The Indochina Migration and Refugee Assistance Act of 1975[73] extended $155 million to Vietnamese and Cambodian refugees. Additional appropriations approved in 1978 lacked the country-specific focus of earlier bills, although given the expectation that most of the money would serve refugees from the Soviet Union, it became known as the "Soviet and other" program.[74]

Of course, these adjustment and funding decisions do not show that Congress fully endorsed the executive branch's parole decisions. The Attorney General's decision to invoke the parole authority might just have forced Congress's hand. The alternative, after all, was to brand increasing numbers of refugees with the continued "stigma of parole" and to force states, local communities, or private charities to shoulder the costs of those parolees' resettlement.

In fact, many in Congress did voice displeasure with the expansive way the parole authority was being used.[75] A 1979 Congressional Research Service report specifically noted that "Members of Congress have been concerned with the virtually unlimited discretion open to the Attorney General in authorizing parole."[76] But there are reasons to believe that reports of these concerns might have been somewhat exaggerated.

Refugee Affairs) ("The parole authority was originally intended to admit individual hardship cases, but with an unrealistically low ceiling of 17,400 regular refugee admissions per year, we have increasingly had to stretch its purpose – *with Congressional concurrence* – to admit large groups of refugees such as the Hungarians, Cubans, and Indochinese." (emphasis added)).

69 *See* Act of November 2, 1966, Pub. L. No. 89–732, 80 Stat. 1161.

70 Act of October 29, 1977, Pub. L. No. 95–145, 91 Stat. 1223.

71 Act of October 5, 1978, Pub. L. No. 95–412, 92 Stat. 907.

72 Moore, *supra* note 56, at 27.

73 Pub. L. No. 94-23, 89 Stat. 87. Funding was eventually extended through fiscal year 1981. *See* Moore, *supra* note 56, at 29.

74 Moore, *supra* note 56, at 33.

75 *See, e.g.*, Edward M. Kennedy, *Refugee Act of 1980*, 15 Int'l Migration Rev. 141, 144 (1981) (describing "what many Members of Congress" – though not Kennedy himself – "saw as the misuse of the Attorney General's parole authority in admitting large groups of refugees").

76 USILP, *supra* note 7, at 77.

For one thing, "virtually unlimited discretion" is hardly what the Attorney General had been exercising. The 1979 CRS report itself went on to observe that "traditionally, the Attorney General authorizes parole only upon a recommendation of the Secretary of State and after consultation with the Congress ..."[77] A 1977 House hearing concerning the parole of 15,000 Indochinese refugees provides an instructive example of the process.[78] In that case, the Secretary of State had, with the president's permission, made a request to Attorney General Griffin Bell that he use his parole authority on behalf of the 15,000 refugees.[79] Attorney General Bell responded that because INA § 212(d)(5) "expressly requires that the exercise of discretion be based on facts showing the emergent or public interest reasons for parole,"[80] the State Department would need to furnish facts sufficient to justify parole. Bell then "immediately met with" the ranking members of the relevant committees in the House and Senate;[81] the chair of the House Immigration Subcommittee subsequently called a hearing so that members of his subcommittee could consider their collective position on the parole request and the public might become better informed about the refugee crisis at hand.[82] Especially interesting was a discussion that arose during the hearings about whether the Attorney General would exercise his parole authority even if a majority of those he consulted in Congress were against his doing so. The previous Attorney General, Edward Levi, had "made it very clear to the Members that he consulted" that he would not grant parole if they advised against it;[83] less committally, Attorney General Bell testified only that he would try to avoid that situation, not wanting to "get into an open warfare with the House Judiciary Committee about a matter."[84]

The point of this example is that the Attorney General's parole authority was, in practice, anything but unfettered. Parole was used only after a sufficient factual case had been developed elsewhere in the executive branch and consultation – both informal and, sometimes, as here, formal – had produced some level of consensus between the administration and interested members of Congress.

Moreover, to the extent that this consultative process may still have left too much discretion with the Attorney General, one of the people most concerned about this seems to have been the Attorney General himself! Asked his view of the parole

77 *Id.* The report went on to caution, however, that consultation with Congress was not, at the time, statutorily required. *Id.*

78 *Admission of Refugees into the United States Part II: Hearings Before the H. Subcomm. on Immigration, Citizenship, and Int'l Law*, 95th Cong. (1977).

79 *Id.* at 4–8.

80 *Id.* at 5.

81 *Id.* at 13–14.

82 *Id.* at 24.

83 *Id.* at 21.

84 *Id.* at 22.

power at the 1977 hearing, Attorney General Bell explained that the text of the parole provision speaks of "alien, singular," and thus, "it would appear it was not intended to be used for large groups."[85] Although he acknowledged that the statute had been interpreted more broadly since the Eisenhower administration's parole of the Hungarians, Bell testified that "vagueness in the law" pushed him to "consult with the appropriate committees of the Congress" rather than purporting to exercise "sole discretion."[86]

I stress this point because it complicates the view, sometimes offered, that "immigration policy has been formulated through a competitive dialogue between the political branches."[87] The dialogue is clear; whether it has generally been competitive is another matter. Just as I questioned earlier whether Congress really meant to cabin executive discretion in 1965 – given that the statute it passed did nothing to amend § 212(d)(5) and failed to address the most pressing refugee problem of the time – so too can we question just how grasping the executive was in trying to solidify or expand its control over refugee admissions in the years after the 1965 Act. Congressional limit-setting, inflexible and quickly outdated, and executive discretion, always potentially arbitrary, may have needed each other.

Returning to the question of how strongly Congress objected to executive discretion: perhaps the strongest evidence that Congressional concerns on this score may have been overstated is the fact that when Congress finally did overhaul U.S. refugee policy in the Refugee Act of 1980,[88] executive discretion over refugee admissions was not much changed.

Once again, rhetoric at the time suggested otherwise. According to Senator Edward Kennedy, one of the things the Refugee Act accomplished was to "replace[] the use of the 'parole authority' with new statutory language *asserting Congressional control over the entire process of admitting refugees*."[89] This is clear hyperbole. The 1980 Act, unlike the 1965 Act, *did* amend the parole provision, preventing the Attorney General from paroling "an alien who is a refugee" unless he determines that "compelling reasons in the public interest with respect to that particular alien require that the alien be paroled into the United States rather than" being admitted under the newly established

85 *Id.* at 13.

86 *Id.* at 14. Testifying before Congress in 1979, Leo Cherne, chairman of the Citizens Commission on Indochinese Refugees, observed: "We have had, through the parole system, the at times ironic situation of the Attorney General who about 1 year ago, was far from persuaded that he had the right to use the parole mechanism for more than handfuls of people." *Refugee Act of 1979 Hearings*, *supra* note 68, at 93; *see also* USILP, *supra* note 7, at 77 ("Attorney General Griffin Bell has indicated on numerous occasions that he is personally uncomfortable with the use of the parole provision for the mass admission of refugees, a purpose for which it was not originally intended.").

87 Adam B. Cox & Cristina M. Rodríguez, *The President and Immigration Law*, 119 YALE L.J. 458, 509 (2009).

88 Refugee Act of 1980, Pub. L. No. 96–212, 94 Stat. 102.

89 Kennedy, *supra* note 75 (emphasis added).

refugee process.[90] At the same time, the new system gave *the president* the power to set the number of refugees allowed entry each year.[91] "[A]ppropriate consultation" with Congress was required, but this only formalized the voluntary process that had taken place before;[92] the law did "not set forth what action [was] required to conclude the consultation process"[93] – which is to say, it did not say what would happen if the president and Congress disagreed about refugee levels.[94]

The upshot of the 1980 Act, then, was that the Attorney General needed individualized reasons for paroling refugees outside the ordinary process,[95] but the president was given the discretion to determine how many refugees could enter through that ordinary process. The net change on executive branch discretion was hardly negative.

The years immediately after passage of the 1980 Refugee Act bear this out. Concerned about the number of refugees that would be admitted,[96] Congress initially set the refugee quotas for 1980, 1981, and 1982 at 50,000 per year.[97] But just as the president was allowed to set the refugee cap in the years after 1982, so too could he go beyond the 50,000 in the first few years if he consulted with Congress and determined that a larger number was "justified by humanitarian concerns or … otherwise in the national interest."[98] This is what indeed happened: in 1981, the first full year in which the Refugee Act governed, the number of refugee admissions requested by the president was 271,000,[99] a far cry from the 50,000 envisioned in a law passed only months earlier.

90 Refugee Act of 1980, Pub. L. No. 96–212, 94 Stat. 102, 108.

91 Stephen H. Legomsky, *The Making of United States Refugee Policy: Separation of Powers in the Post-Cold War Era*, 70 WASH. L. REV. 675, 676 (1995) ("In the Refugee Act of 1980 Congress virtually wrote the President a blank check to decide how many overseas refugees to admit and which ones.").

92 *See* Kennedy, *supra* note 75, at 146 ("The goal of the Act was to … writ[e] into law what we were doing by custom and practice."); Anker & Posner, *supra* note 62, at 84 ("The Refugee Act deliberately institutionalizes what was previously an informal, *ad hoc* process of consultation.").

93 H. Rep. No. 96–608, 96th Cong., at 15 (1979).

94 Attorney General Bell had described the consultation requirement as a "report-and-wait provision": the executive branch would report to Congress and then allow Congress (an unspecified period of) time to act. *Id.* A proposed one-house legislative veto provision did not survive in the final version of the bill – to the apparent dismay of many in Congress. One account attributes the close vote (207-192) in the House to a desire for stronger Congressional control. *See* Anker & Posner, *supra* note 62, at 63.

95 The old parole provision was still in place as well, but it was now limited only to non-refugees.

96 Kennedy, *supra* note 75, at 146 ("A major concern was … the fear that the new legislation would somehow open the 'flood gates' to millions of refugees around the world.").

97 Refugee Act of 1980, Pub. L. No. 96–212, 94 Stat. 102, 103. Although this raised the worldwide limitation on overall immigration from 290,000 to 320,000, it was thought that the restrictions on parole would mean that actual immigration would not really change. *See* S. Rep. 96–256, 96th Cong., at 5 (1979).

98 Refugee Act of 1980, Pub. L. No. 96–212, 94 Stat. 102, 103.

99 *See* 126 CONG. REC. 31611, 31612 (Dec. 2, 1980). The vast majority of these – 168,000 – were intended for Indochinese refugees.

Even this extraordinary divergence from the adjustable cap set by the 1980 Act does not fully capture the extent to which executive discretion continued to control refugee admissions after the 1980 reforms. As Senator Kennedy later wrote, "the ink was hardly dry" on the 1980 Refugee Act when the Mariel Boatlift put the Act's limits, and its procedures for exceeding those limits, to the test.[100] The Carter administration first sought to admit 12,000 Cuban refugees under the Act's "unforeseen emergency" provision,[101] but then the number leaving Mariel Harbor for Florida quickly swelled to 125,000,[102] and the administration changed course. Even as Senator Kennedy urged the administration to expand reliance on the unforeseen emergency provision, the administration claimed that "Congress never intended the Act to accommodate large numbers of refugees arriving directly on our shores."[103] Not wanting to set a precedent by labeling the Cubans "refugees" under the Act, the administration instead resorted to parole.[104]

Eventually, President Carter successfully requested – as his predecessors had since Eisenhower – that Congress fund the parolees' resettlement. Another ad hoc path toward permanent residence was eventually established for the class of parolees who had come to be legally known as the Cuban-Haitian Entrants.[105]

4.4 AFTER 1965: NATIONAL ORIGIN DISCRIMINATION

The pairing of Cubans and Haitians was a response to widespread complaints about differences in the ways those groups had long been treated. Cubans had benefited not only by the unprecedented use of the parole authority already described but also from the generous route from parole to permanent residency established by Congress in 1966.[106] Not so the nearly 8,000 Haitians who fled by boat in the 1970s and, in particular, the 25,000 Haitians who arrived in South Florida at the same

[100] Kennedy, *supra* note 75, at 141. The mass emigration from Muriel Harbor in Cuba began in April, 1980, the month that the Refugee Act of 1980 went into effect.

[101] Refugee Act of 1980, Pub. L. No. 96–212, 94 Stat. 102, 103.

[102] Nackerud et al., *supra* note 65, at 188; *see also* JOHN A. SCANLAN, *Immigration Law and the Illusion of Numerical Control*, 36 U. MIAMI L. REV. 819, 859 (1982) ("Approximately 130,000 Cubans arrived in South Florida in five months; 88,000 arrived in May of 1980 alone.").

[103] Kennedy, *supra* note 75, at 154.

[104] *Id.* at 142; *see also* Scanlan, *supra* note 102, at 858 ("The Mariel influx shattered the illusion that the United States can, under all circumstances, select its own refugees. It revealed, as no other event has, our proximity to a politically unstable part of the world capable of producing hundreds of thousands of refugees and displaced persons.").

[105] This path was not set until the Immigration Reform and Control Act of 1986 Pub. L. No. 99–603 § 202, 100 Stat. 3359, 3404.

[106] Act of Nov. 2, 1966, Pub. L. No. 89–732, 80 Stat. 1161.

time as the Cuban exodus from Mariel[107] – most of whom were branded economic migrants rather than political refugees.[108]

The difference in treatment reflected the kind of national origin discrimination explicitly endorsed in the 1965 Act, with its preference for refugees fleeing communist countries. More troubling, if less explicitly, it also reflected the racial discrimination the 1965 Act was supposed to have ended.[109] Cuban refugees were mainly white; Haitians mostly black.[110]

The government's eventual solution – conflating the groups under the Cuban-Haitian Entrant category – was itself discriminatory in its own ways. Not only was the category limited to those who had entered before October 10, 1980 – the end of the Mariel boatlift, but not the end of widespread Haitian migration[111] – but the hybrid category, yet another ad hoc exception to established refugee law, discriminated against those whose national origin was other than Cuban or Haitian.

This all-too-familiar problem recalls the second main tension in the 1965 Act: the lingering specter of national origin discrimination. We have already seen how, in regard to the first tension left unresolved in 1965, the 1980 Refugee Act purported to cabin the executive *discretion* which the earlier law had failed to contain. The 1980 Refugee Act similarly sought to end the *discrimination* that the 1965 Act – for all its heralded progress in regard to the national origins quotas – had instituted in regard to refugee admissions.

According to Senator Kennedy, the 1980 Act's first objective was to "repeal[] the previous law's discriminatory treatment of refugees by providing a new definition of refugee" – one that conformed to the UN Protocol Relating to the Status of Refugees, which the United States had ratified in 1968.[112] Eliminating what a House Report referred to as "discrimination on the basis of outmoded geographical and ideological considerations,"[113] the 1980 Act defined refugees as those with a "well-founded fear of persecution on account of race, religion, nationality, membership in a particular social group, or political opinion."[114]

Unlike the 1965 Act's seventh preference, the new refugee definition lacked any reference to communist and Middle Eastern countries. (It also eliminated the 1965

[107] Cox & Rodríguez, *supra* note 87, at 493.

[108] Alex Stepick, *Haitian Boat People: A Study in the Conflicting Forces Shaping U.S. Immigration Policy*, 45 LAW & CONTEMP. PROBS. 163, 187–88 (1982).

[109] For a discussion of one explicit but little known racial classification that survived the 1965 Act, see Paul Spruhan, *The Canadian Indian Free Passage Right: The Last Stronghold of Explicit Race Restriction in United States Immigration Law*, 85 N.D. L. Rev. 301 (2009).

[110] *See* Malissia Lennox, Note, *Refugees, Racism, and Reparations: A Critique of the United States' Haitian Immigration Policy*, 45 STAN. L. REV. 687, 714–16 (1993); Andrew F. Brimmer, *The Haitian Exception*, WASH. POST, May 8, 1980, at A19 ("[O]ur policy has acquired a patina of racism that ought to be erased promptly.").

[111] *See* Cox & Rodríguez, *supra* note 87, at 508; Stepick, *supra* note 108, at 188.

[112] Kennedy, *supra* note 75, at 143; Moore, *supra* note 56, at 16 (noting that at the time of ratification, Congress and the administration "believed that the United States could comply with [the Protocol's] provisions without having to amend the Immigration and Nationality Act").

[113] H. Rep. No. 96–608, 96th Cong., at 1 (1979).

[114] Refugee Act of 1980, Pub. L. No. 96–212, 94 Stat. 102, 102.

Act's protection for victims of "catastrophic natural calamity"[115] – protection that had never actually been used.[116]) At least textually, then, the 1980 Act finally brought to refugee law the nondiscriminatory impulse that motivated the *rest* of the 1965 Act.

But definitions were one thing, practice another. Given that the president, after 1980, had the power to decide not just "how many overseas refugees to admit, [but] which ones,"[117] the discriminatory character of U.S. refugee policy was left largely up to him. The 1980 Act specified that the annual admissions quota was to be "allocated among refugees of special humanitarian concern to the United States,"[118] and the House Report accompanying the bill emphasized that "the plight of the refugees themselves, as opposed to national origins or political considerations, should be paramount in determining" who met that description.[119] And yet, "until the end of the Cold War, Presidents allocated almost the entire refugee quota to those who were fleeing communist countries."[120] Authorized admissions in 1981, for example, included 168,000 from Indochina, 37,500 from Eastern Europe and the Soviet Union, and 2,500 from Cuba, compared to 1,500 for the remainder of Latin America and the Caribbean and 3,000 for all of Africa.[121] Removing communism from the refugee definition had little effect on which refugees were actually welcomed.

This ideological focus has, if not dissipated, at least shifted dramatically since the end of the Cold War. After the most recent consultation with Congress, the Obama Administration authorized the admission of 70,000 refugees in fiscal year 2015: 33,000 from the Near East and South Asia; 13,000 from Africa; 13,000 from East Asia; 4,000 from Latin America and the Caribbean; 1,000 from Europe and Central Asia; and 2,000 more to be allocated as needed.[122] The region with the largest quota – the Near East and South Asia – includes refugees from Iraq, Afghanistan, and Syria. Among these, Iraqi refugees who worked with the U.S. government or armed forces have been identified as a group of special humanitarian concern. But so too have human rights activists in Cuba, ethnic minorities from Burma, Congolese in Rwanda, and – as a result of Congressional legislation (the so-called Lautenberg Amendment) – religious minorities in the former Soviet Union and Iran.[123] The

115 *Cf.* Act of October 3, 1965, Pub. L. No. 89–236, § 3(a)(7), 79 Stat. 911 (1965).

116 Janet L. Parker, *Victims of Natural Disasters in U.S. Refugee Law and Policy*, 3 MICH. Y.B. INT'L LEGAL STUD. 137, 140 (1982).

117 Legomsky, *supra* note 91, at 676.

118 Refugee Act of 1980, Pub. L. No. 96–212, 94 Stat. 102, 102, 103.

119 H. Rep. No. 96–608, 96th Cong., at 13 (1979).

120 STEPHEN H. LEGOMSKY & CHRISTINA M. RODRÍGUEZ, IMMIGRATION AND REFUGEE LAW AND POLICY 887 (5th ed. 2009).

121 126 CONG. REC. 31611, 31611–12 (Dec. 2, 1980).

122 PRESIDENTIAL MEMORANDUM – FY 2015 REFUGEE ADMISSIONS (2014), *available at* http://www.whitehouse.gov/the-press-office/2014/09/30/presidential-memorandum-fy-2015-refugee-admissions.

123 U.S. DEP'T OF STATE ET AL., PROPOSED REFUGEE ADMISSIONS FOR FISCAL YEAR 2015 at 9–11 (2014), *available at* http://www.state.gov/documents/organization/232029.pdf.

Lautenberg Amendment lowers the refugee standard applied to these groups, whose members only have to show a "credible basis for concern about the possibility of ... persecution," not a well-founded fear.[124]

As the latest refugee quotas show, political concerns and national origins distinctions remain part of U.S. immigration law even now, fifty years after the reforms of 1965. Geographic and, in some cases, country-specific distinctions are made explicitly within the annual refugee quotas that the president now sets, and Congress has legislated further distinctions among refugees based on their country of origin.

Of course, not all national origin discrimination is as invidious as the pre-1965 quotas undoubtedly were. If County X persecutes religious minorities but Country Y does not, admitting refugees from X but not Y hardly counts as discrimination at all. But what if religious minorities are protected in both X and Y, yet those from X have a lower burden in showing that they qualify as refugees? The Lautenberg Amendment allows for this. Alternatively, what if the United States, through its wars or foreign policy, may have played a role in bringing about the situation being fled in X, but not in Y? Such was the case in Vietnam and Cambodia in the 1970s, and it remains the case in Iraq now. To favor X's refugees in that instance would undoubtedly be to discriminate based on national origin, and to do so because of a historical connection between the United States and Country X. Still, the sense of moral indebtedness motivating the difference in treatment seems distinguishable from the kind of ethnically charged historical connections between the United States and certain foreign countries that gave rise to the pre-1965 quotas.

Related to this, however, is another kind of discrimination or distinction: that which occurs when refugees from X and Y both suffer persecution, but the United States has strong foreign policy reasons for calling attention to the human rights failures of X, or perhaps avoiding embarrassment for our ally, Y. Does the priority that would be given to X's refugees over Y's in such a situation count as discrimination based on *national origin*, or is the discrimination better described as ideological or political discrimination?

The point of these examples, in part, is that the wrongness of national origin discrimination – that which the 1965 Act is praised for ending, *except* in regard to refugees – is more complicated than it might first appear. The "harsh injustice of the national origins quota system"[125] surely stemmed from the racial and ethnic bias at its root. But when national origins are a proxy not for race, but for refugees' need,

[124] 8 U.S.C. § 1157 Note.

[125] Signing of the Immigration Bill, The President's Remarks at the Ceremony on Liberty Island, With His Offer of Asylum for Cuban Refugees. October 3, 1965, 1 WEEKLY COMP. PRES. DOCS. 364, 365 (Oct. 11, 1965).

or strategic value, or political affinity, or our own moral culpability it becomes far harder to say, as President Johnson did in 1965, that decisions to admit immigrants must never again be made "because of the land from which they sprung."[126]

Under the current system, disregarding a refugee's country of origin is hardly possible, since facts about that country are what make the person a refugee in the first place. The real question is which of those facts we want to consider when defining and prioritizing refugees: facts solely about the level or types of persecution in that country, or facts also about the country's historical or political connection to the United States. To treat countries interchangeably with regard to refugee admissions – to give Canada and Iraq the same number, for example – would be to avoid national origin discrimination only in the most absurdly formalist sense. Elsewhere in this volume, Kevin R. Johnson asks whether the same should be said for the rest of the post-1965 immigration system, which treats Mexico and Iceland alike, and thereby treats Mexicans and Icelanders far differently.[127] The shared insight is that discrimination happens just as much when we treat unequals equally as it does when we treat equals unequally. The difficulty is always in knowing what counts as equal, for that requires us to know what it is we are measuring.

Both before and after 1965, refugees have been measured both for their intrinsic need and their extrinsic value: refugees make humanitarian demands and serve foreign policy goals. The latter explains why national origins did not stop mattering in 1965, and have not stopped mattering to U.S. refugee policy ever since.

But refugees' humanitarian demands have never stopped mattering either, even if they have often been unevenly met. One of the lessons of 1965 is that Congress's desire to set firm limits on immigration does not preclude, and perhaps even requires, a willingness to let the executive branch circumvent those limits, especially when responding to humanitarian need. As it did in 1965, Congress can appear to narrow the humanitarian floodgates even while it allows the executive branch, with its parole authority, to nudge them back open when needed.[128] In the wake of the 1965 reforms, Congress may have complained about the executive branch's use of discretion, but, tellingly, that did not lead it to constrain the president's discretion much, if at all, when it again overhauled U.S. refugee law fifteen years later.

As Congress once again considers reform of the nation's immigration laws, amid claims, from both ends of the political spectrum, that the president has taken his discretionary powers too far, these are lessons worth remembering.

[126] *Id.*

[127] *See* Kevin R. Johnson, Chapter 3.

[128] Adam Cox and Cristina Rodríguez have shown a similar dynamic in the way Congress has ratcheted up the grounds of deportability while allowing the president the de facto authority to decide how many and which noncitizens are actually deported. Congress can show itself tough on immigration without suffering the costs of full enforcement. Cox & Rodríguez, *supra* note 87, at 510–30.

PART II

The 1965 Immigration Act and the Policy of Family Unification

5

The 1965 Immigration Act

Family Unification and Nondiscrimination Fifty Years Later

Rose Cuison Villazor

5.1 INTRODUCTION

Time has not been on the side of Rosalina Cuellar De Osorio. Seventeen years ago, on May 5, 1998, Rosalina's mother, a U.S. citizen, submitted a petition to the United States Customs and Immigration Enforcement (USCIS) to bring in Rosalina as a lawful permanent resident under the Immigration and Nationality Act's (INA) family-sponsored preference program.[1] In particular, this program allows U.S. citizens to sponsor their spouses, parents, children, adult sons and daughters, and siblings (and their families) to immigrate to the United States.[2] Because Rosalina was married, her mother petitioned her under the relevant category for Rosalina: third-preference family category,[3] which is reserved for married sons or daughters of U.S. citizens.[4] In addition, the petition included Rosalina's thirteen-year-old child, Melvin,[5] for under the INA's family-based program, the principal beneficiary's spouse (if still married) and child, defined as a person who is under twenty-one years old, may be included as derivative beneficiaries.[6]

1 Complaint for Declaratory, Mandamus and Injunctive Relief at 11, Zhang v. Napolitano, 663 F. Supp. 2d 913 (C.D. Cal. 2009) (No. EDCV 08-840 JVS(SHx)), 2008 WL 2723887.

2 *See* 8 U.S.C. § 1182(a)(3)(D)(iv) (2012).

3 Complaint for Declaratory, Mandamus and Injunctive Relief, *supra* note 1, at 11.

4 *See* 8 U.S.C. § 1153(a)(3).

5 Complaint for Declaratory, Mandamus and Injunctive Relief, *supra* note 1, at 11.

6 *See* Scialabba v. Cuellar de Osorio, 134 S. Ct. 2191, 2196–97 (2014) (noting, however, that in order for a beneficiary to actually obtain a visa, in addition to having their petition approved, there must also be a visa available).

Professor of Law, University of California at Davis King Hall School of Law. I am grateful to Gabriel "Jack" Chin, Bill Ong Hing, and Kevin Johnson and faculty at Brooklyn Law School, Brigham Young University School of Law, Loyola Law School (Chicago), SMU Law School and participants of the UC Davis School of Law Roundtable on the 1965 Immigration Act and the UCLA School of Law Whiteness as Property Symposium for their extremely helpful comments to earlier versions of this Article. I am also grateful to Noel Abcede ('14), Andrew Alfonso ('15), Channpreet Singh ('14), Steven Vong ('16) and Andrea Wu ('15) for excellent research and technical assistance.

It only took about two months for the petition to be approved.[7] After that, time began to work against Rosalina's favor. The petition's approval did not mean that Rosalina and Melvin would be able to immigrate to the United States immediately. Instead, they needed to wait until visas would be made available to them.[8] The availability of visas under the family-based preference program depends on a complicated formula comprised of, among other things, numerical caps on the number of visas available per year and limits on the number of immigrants from a particular country per year.[9] Critically, this template that demonstrates how the family-based preference program actually works in practice has led to a significant visa backlog and lengthy delays among family members before they can be reunited.[10] Thus, Rosalina and Melvin waited. And waited. They waited seven years.[11] Unfortunately, by the time visas became available – on November 11, 2005 – Melvin had already turned twenty-one years old and has thus "aged out" (i.e., no longer a "child" of a principal beneficiary).[12] Accordingly, Melvin became ineligible for a visa as a derivative beneficiary under Rosalina's mother's petition.[13] Faced with the choice of immigrating to the United States to reunite with her mother or staying in El Salvador to be with her son, Rosalina made the difficult decision of immigrating to the United States.[14] Thus, in August 2006, Rosalina left El Salvador and was admitted to the United States as a lawful permanent resident (LPR).[15] As an LPR or green-card holder, Rosalina would need to submit a separate petition to sponsor Melvin under the second-preference family category (unmarried adult son or daughter of a lawful permanent resident, or F2B category).[16] As of today, the current waiting time for a visa to be available under that category is six years.[17] Thus, Rosalina must wait several more years before she can be reunited with her son.

The Cuellar de Osorio family's story offers a useful launching-off point for exploring the contemporary family-based immigration law program and the law

7 Complaint for Declaratory, Mandamus and Injunctive Relief, *supra* note 1, at 11.

8 *Id.*

9 *See, e.g.*, *Scialabba*, 134 S. Ct. at 2197–99 (describing the mechanics per-country quotas in the United States' immigration regulation scheme).

10 *See* Section 5.4 *infra*.

11 Complaint for Declaratory, Mandamus and Injunctive Relief, *supra* note 1, at 11.

12 *Id.*; *see Scialabba*, 134 S. Ct. at 2196–97, 2202.

13 Complaint for Declaratory, Mandamus and Injunctive Relief, *supra* note 1, at 11; *see Scialabba*, 134 S. Ct. at 2202.

14 *Id.*

15 Complaint for Declaratory, Mandamus and Injunctive Relief, *supra* note 1, at 11–12.

16 *Cf.* 8 U.S.C. § 1153(a)(2)(B) (2012) (authorizing LPRs to submit a visa petition benefiting their unmarried adult sons or daughters).

17 *See* 9 U.S. Bureau of Consular Affairs, Dep't of State, Visa Bulletin, No. 74, *available at* http://travel.state.gov/content/visas/english/law-and-policy/bulletin/2015/visa-bulletin-for-november-2014.html.

on which such program is based – the Immigration and Nationality Act of 1965 (1965 Immigration Act).[18] Fifty years ago, Congress passed the 1965 Immigration Act and revolutionized immigration law[19] in at least two ways: by eliminating racially discriminatory immigration quotas that had been in place since the 1920s,[20] and by establishing family ties as the primary means of immigrating to the United States.[21] In so doing, Congress advanced two normative values and goals through immigration law: the promotion of a race-neutral policy in the immigration admissions process, and family unification. Data from the last five decades indicate that these normative goals have been achieved.[22] That is, without a doubt, millions of Americans and their immigrant families have been reunited and, notably, since 1965, the immigrant stream has been more racially diverse.[23] Such racial diversity represents a sea of change from a century-old formal policy of restricting immigrants on the basis of race.[24] For these reasons, the 1965 Immigration Act should rightly be hailed as an important civil rights achievement. Indeed, as Jack Chin has argued,[25] the 1965 Immigration Act was passed by essentially the same Congress that enacted the 1964 Civil Rights Act[26] and 1965 Voting Rights Act,[27] and should thus be considered as a path-breaking civil rights law as well.

Yet, as Rosalina and Melvin's story demonstrates, the achievements of the 1965 Immigration Act should be qualified. Despite the asserted goal of family reunification undergirding the 1965 Immigration Act, many Americans today continue to be separated from their families.[28] The lengthy delays and visa backlogs show that many families, especially those from China, Philippines, and India must wait between ten and twenty years before family reunification may be realized.[29] Additionally, the

[18] *See* Immigration and Nationality Act of 1965, Pub. L. No. 89–236, 79 Stat. 911 (codified as amended in scattered sections of 8 U.S.C.). It is also known as the Hart-Celler Act. *See* Gabriel J. Chin, *The Civil Rights Revolution Comes to Immigration Law: A New Look at the Immigration and Nationality Act of 1965*, 75 N.C.L. REV. 273, 297 (1996) (pointing out that the Immigration and Nationality Act of 1965 is also known as the Hart-Celler Act).

[19] *But see* President Lyndon B. Johnson, Remarks at the Signing of the Immigration Bill, Liberty Island, New York, 2 Pub. Papers 1037, 1038 (Oct. 3, 1965) (stating that "This is not a revolutionary bill. It will not reshape the structure of our daily lives" when he signed the Hart-Celler Act).

[20] *See id.* at 297 (explaining that the Hart-Celler Act was revolutionary by adopting race neutrality as a principle).

[21] *See* Kerry Abrams, *What Makes the Family Special?*, 80 U. CHI. L. REV. 7, 14 (2013) (stating that the Hart-Celler Act established our contemporary system of family-based law).

[22] *See* Section 5.3 *infra*.

[23] *See id.*

[24] *See id.*

[25] *See* Chin, *supra* note 18, at 317–18.

[26] Pub. L. No. 88–352, 78 Stat. 241 (codified as amended in scattered sections of 42 U.S.C.).

[27] Pub. L. No. 89–110, 79 Stat. 437 (codified as amended at 42 U.S.C. §§ 1971, 1973 to 1973bb-1 (2012)).

[28] *See* Section 5.4 *infra*.

[29] *Id.*

1965 Immigration Act privileges only certain family relationships – spousal, parent and child, and sibling – and rules out other family relationships such as aunt and nephew[30] or grandmother and grandchild.[31]

On the eve of the fiftieth anniversary of the 1965 Immigration Act, this chapter reflects on and evaluates both the law's normative goals and its impact on the racial makeup of the immigration population and American families today. In so doing, it makes three points. First, this chapter argues that the 1965 Immigration Act was an important civil rights law that utilized immigration law to promote family unification, which ultimately facilitated racial diversity. By establishing a norm of nondiscrimination in immigration law, the 1965 Immigration Act enabled the reunification of millions of U.S. citizens and lawful permanent residents with family members who would have faced barriers to immigration under the pre-1965, national-origins quotas-based system.[32] In so doing, the 1965 Immigration Act broadened the American family both literally and figuratively. The substantial number of immigrants from Asia, Africa, and Latin America led to more rapid demographic changes to the racial makeup of the United States than experienced in previous years.[33]

Second, this chapter maintains that any celebration of the 1965 Immigration Act should be done with caution. Despite the law's professed policy of family unification, millions of U.S. citizens and lawful permanent residents – the majority of whom are people of color – continue to experience years of separation from their families.

Third, it reconsiders the values undergirding the 1965 Immigration Act – promoting race neutrality and family unification – and argues that, as a normative matter, such values should continue to animate immigration law today. Using this normative position as a baseline, this chapter analyzes recent congressional proposals that seek to reform, among other areas, our family-based immigration system. Specifically, it examines two bills – one introduced in the U.S. House of Representatives and the other in the Senate – during the 113th Congress. Notably, both bills sought to limit family-based immigration law to the nuclear family. Such efforts, this chapter maintains, will have an adverse impact on Mexican Americans and Asian Americans and their families. Although neither bill became law, they are likely to serve as blueprints for proposed legislation in the future. Accordingly, understanding the consequence that a contraction of the family-based immigration law program would have on families and the immigrant stream is critical as Congress and policy makers continue to contemplate how to reform immigration law.

30 *See id.*

31 *See id.*

32 *See* Section 5.2 *infra.*

33 Bill Ong Hing, Deporting Our Souls 119 (2006) ("[o]ver time, Asian and Latin immigrants came to dominate most of the immigration to the United States").

Section 5.2 briefly discusses the history of the 1965 Immigration Act's family-based program and explains its current structure that privileges marital ties, the nuclear family, and parent-child relationships. Section 5.3 underscores the ways in which immigration law has facilitated reunification of families. Next, Section 5.4 complicates the "success" story of the 1965 Immigration Act by highlighting cases in which families have not been able to benefit fully from immigration law's policy of family unification. Section 5.5 considers two recent congressional bills that propose to limit family-based immigration system to the nuclear family only. Section 5.6 briefly concludes.

5.2 1965 IMMIGRATION ACT AND FAMILY-BASED IMMIGRATION PROGRAM

The creation of the system of family-based preferences in immigration law was, as Kerry Abrams noted, "not a carefully thought-out decision on Congress's part."[34] By contrast, Congress had, for years, sought to limit immigration to the United States on the basis of race, which had gendered and class consequences that impacted American families. It is against this racial history that the impact of the 1965 Immigration Act should be examined.

Brief History of Family Preferences in Immigration Law before the 1965 Act

Although the ability of noncitizens to immigrate to the United States based on familial relationship to a citizen dates as far back as the late nineteenth century,[35] it was not until the 1920s that Congress explicitly created a system that privileged family membership as a preferential basis for immigration.[36] Specifically, in 1921, Congress passed the Emergency Quota Act and expressly allowed U.S. citizens to

[34] *See* Abrams, *supra* note 21, at 10.

[35] *See, e.g.*, Act in Amendment to the Various Acts Relative to Immigration and the Importation of Aliens Under Contract or Agreement to Perform Labor, ch. 551, 26 Stat. 1084 (1891) (allowing "persons living in the United States [to send] for a relative" to immigrate to the United States); *see also* Abrams, *supra* note 34, at 10–11 (describing the incorporation of the concept of coverture into early immigration laws which allowed immigrant husbands to bring their wives into the United States); Janet M. Calvo, *Spouse-Based Immigration Laws: The Legacies of Coverture*, 28 SAN DIEGO L. REV. 593, 595–600 (2004) (same).

[36] To be sure, Congress had enacted other immigration laws before the 1900s that impacted the family. For instance, in 1891, it passed a law that made polygamists excludable from the United States. *See* Act in Amendment to the Various Acts Relative to Immigration and the Importation of Aliens Under Contract or Agreement to Perform Labor. ch. 551, § 1, 26 Stat. 1084, 1084 (1981). Moreover, in 1917, it prohibited noncitizens from the Asiatic Barred Zone, which covered the "entire area of Afghanistan to the Pacific, save for Japan," from immigrating to the United States. *See* MAE NGAI, IMPOSSIBLE SUBJECTS: ILLEGAL ALIENS AND THE MAKING OF MODERN AMERICA 37 (2005).

bring their family members to the United States.[37] Not all family members were treated equally, however. Although children of U.S. citizens who were younger than eighteen years of age were excluded from the quotas (that is, they could immigrate without numerical limitation), the other family members were subjected to the quota limits.[38] The gendered nature of the 1921 law was evident, for it defined family members to include "wives, parents, brothers, sisters, children, [and] fiancées."[39] Moreover, the 1921 Emergency Quota Act discriminated against Asians and Eastern and Southern Europeans by imposing national origins quotas that were based on the population of noncitizens in the United States in 1910.[40] By 1921, a series of other laws – the Page Act,[41] Chinese Exclusion Act,[42] and the Immigration Act of 1917 (which created the Asiatic Barred Zone)[43] – had virtually prohibited Chinese and other Asians from immigrating to the United States, and thus the Asian population in 1910 was significantly low.[44] Additionally, several barriers made it difficult for Eastern and Southern Europeans to enter the United States in the early 1900s, which led to their low population in 1910 as well. Moreover, many of the Asian and Southern and Eastern European countries were allotted minimal quotas. Consequently, for those

[37] *See* Emergency Quota Act, Pub. L. No. 67-5, § 2(d), 42 Stat. 5, 6 (1921) ("[I]n the enforcement of this Act preference shall be given so far as possible to the wives, parents, brothers, sisters, children under eighteen years of age, and fiancées [of United States citizens and legal residents].").

[38] *See id.* §§ 2(a), (d), 42 Stat. at 5, 6.

[39] *See id.*; Abrams, *supra* note 34, at 10–11.

[40] *See* Emergency Quota Act § 2(a), 42 Stat. at 5 (providing "[t]hat the number of aliens of any nationality who may be admitted under the immigration laws of the United States [annually] shall be limited to 3 per centum of the number or foreign-born persons of such nationality resident of the United States as determined by the United States census of 1910").

[41] *See* Page Act of 1875, ch. 141, 18 Stat. 477 (prohibiting the immigration of prostitutes, contract laborers and convicts from "China, Japan, or any Oriental country" from the United States, which had the intended effect of precluding Chinese from immigrating). For explorations of how the Page Act sought to exclude Chinese women, see Kerry Abrams, *Polygamy, Prostitution, and the Federalization of Immigration Law*, 105 COLUM. L. REV. 641, 692–702 (2005) (contending that the Page Act was enacted to prohibit Chinese women to enter the United States); Leti Volpp, *Divesting Citizenship: On Asian American History and the Loss of Citizenship through Marriage*, 53 UCLA L. REV. 405, 432–42 (2005) (same).

[42] *See* Act to Execute Certain Treaty Stipulations Relating to Chinese (Chinese Exclusion Act), ch. 126, 22 Stat. 58 (1882) (precluding Chinese from immigrating to the United States).

[43] Immigration Act of 1917, Pub. L. No. 64–301, § 3. 39 Stat. 874, 875–78 (creating the "Asiatic Barred Zone").

[44] *See* Campbell Gibson & Kay Jung, *Historical Census Statistics on Population Totals By Race, 1790 to 1990, and By Hispanic Origin, 1970 to 1990, For The United States, Regions, Divisions, and States* tbl. A-13 (U.S. Census Bureau, Working Paper No. 56, 2002), *available at* http://www.census.gov/population/www/documentation/twps0056/tabA-13.pdf. Note that Japanese were not excluded from entering the United States as a result of the Gentlemen's Agreement. Filipinos were also not barred from entering because the Philippines was a territory of the United States between 1898 and 1946 and Filipino nationals were considered subjects of the U.S. and not "aliens." *See* Toyota v. United States, 268 U.S. 402, 410–11 (1925).

noncitizens coming from countries that were allotted few quotas, the family-based preference system did very little to reunify them with their families.[45]

Congress would continue on its path of limiting immigration along racial and cultural lines until 1965. It passed the Immigration Act of 1924,[46] which modified the national origins system as well as the family-based immigration program established under the 1921 Act. Again, the family preference system that Congress created had racial distinctions by limiting the quotas allotted to Asian and Southern and Eastern European countries.[47] The 1924 Act also had gendered differences. For instance, wives of U.S. citizens, along with their children, were not subjected to quota limitations.[48] Husbands, parents, and children under the age of twenty-one of U.S. citizen women, however, were placed in numerically limited preference categories.[49] This meant that relatives whose immigration petitions were filed by female U.S. citizens had to wait much longer than those whose petitions were filed by male citizens.[50] Notably, the 1924 Act limited family-based immigration law to the nuclear family by cutting out preference categories for adult children and siblings of U.S. citizens that were previously part of the 1921 Act.[51]

More than twenty-five years later, Congress overhauled immigration law and enacted the Immigration and Nationality Act of 1952 (1952 INA).[52] It abolished racial restrictions to naturalization, which was previously only available to whites (beginning in 1790) and persons of African ancestry (1870) and, more recently, to Chinese, Filipinos, and Indians. The abolition of racial restrictions to citizenship had important implications to families. From 1924 until 1952, persons who were racially ineligible for citizenship were inadmissible to the United States. As I have written elsewhere, the combination of racial citizenship restrictions and inadmissibility provisions prevented thousands of Japanese women and American soldiers from residing together in the United States because Japanese were not eligible for naturalization and thus inadmissible.[53] Indeed, military leaders relied

[45] *See* Abrams, *supra* note 34, at 12.

[46] Pub. L. No. 68–139, 43 Stat. 153.

[47] *See id.* § 8, 43 Stat. 153, 155 (limiting the annual quota to two% of the number of foreign-born individuals of such nationality in the United States as of 1890 and providing for a minimum quota of one hundred individuals per nationality); *see also* Office of the Historian, U.S. Dep't of State, *The Immigration Act of 1924 (The Johnson-Reed Act)*, http://history.state.gov/milestones/1921–1936/immigration-act (last visited Sept. 17, 2014) (discussing the limited quotas available to Asians and Southern and Eastern Europeans).

[48] Immigration Act of 1924 § 4(a), 43 Stat. 153, 155.

[49] *See id.* § 6(a)(1), 43 Stat. 153, 155.

[50] *See* Abrams, *supra* note 34, at 12.

[51] *See id.* at 13.

[52] *See* Immigration and Nationality (McCarran-Walter) Act of 1952, Pub. L. No. 82–414, 66 Stat. 163 (codified as amended in scattered section of 8 U.S.C.).

[53] *See generally* Rose Cuison Villazor, *The Other Loving: Uncovering the Government's Racial Regulation of Marriage*, 86 N.Y.U. L. Rev. 1361 (2011).

on these citizenship restrictions to discourage and, in many cases, prevent American soldiers from marrying Japanese women.[54] Children of interracial couples also faced tremendous barriers to immigrating to the United States because of significant barriers to immigration for children born out of wedlock.[55] Thus, the elimination of racial restrictions to citizenship (ideally) made family unification for many mixed citizen/noncitizen status families a possibility.

The 1952 Act also promulgated a number of changes to the previous immigration laws. In particular, it allowed U.S. citizen women to have the same right to sponsor their family members as U.S. citizen men.[56] Additionally, children and spouses were once again considered non-quota immigrants.[57] Thirty percent of the visas were set aside for parents of citizens and 20 percent were allocated to spouses and children of lawful permanent residents. Moreover, the 1952 Act brought back categories for siblings and adult children,[58] and it also created preference categories for spouses and children of lawful permanent residents.[59]

It should be emphasized, however, that although Congress might appear to have expanded the family-based immigration program by creating preference categories for extended family members, it merely implemented symbolic changes. Siblings and adult children were placed at the bottom of the preference categories and were not guaranteed visa slots, but instead were entitled only to any unused visas.[60] Importantly, Congress maintained national origins quotas disadvantaging Asians and other disfavored groups.[61] This ensured that the family-preference system would continue to discriminate racially against many Asians and Asian Americans.[62]

54 *See id.* at 1403–16.

55 *See id.* at 1432–35.

56 *See* McCarran-Walter Act § 101(a)(27)(A), 66 Stat. 163, 169 (defining a "nonquota immigrant" as "the spouse of a citizen of the United States", thus abrogating the distinction between husbands and wives).

57 *See id.*

58 *See id.* § 203(a)(4), 66 Stat. 178–79.

59 *See id.* § 203(a)(3), 66 Stat. 178.

60 *See id.* § 203(a)(4), 182 Stat. 178–79 (providing that "[a]ny portion of the quota for each quota area for [a given] year not required for the issuance of visas to [all other preference classes]" shall be made available to siblings and adult children).

61 *See id.* at §201 (maintaining the quota system in place from the Immigration Act of 1924); *see also* Samuel W. Bettwy, *A Proposed Legislative Scheme to Solve the Mexican Immigration Problem*, 2 San Diego Int'l L.J. 93, 106 (2001)(acknowledging the continued bias of 1952 Act due to the continuation of the national origins quota system); Jonathon Zitney, *The State of Illegal Immigration in California and the Potential Effects of H.R. 4437: An Analysis of Human Rights Repercussions and Economic Consequences*, 34 W. St. U. L. Rev. 207, 209 (2007)(noting that the 1952 Act affirmed the national origins quota system).

62 *See* Enid Trucios-Gaynes, *The Legacy of Racially Restrictive Immigration Laws and Policies and the Construction of the American National Identity*, 76 Or. L. Rev. 369, 398–99 (1997) (stating that Congress's failure to do away with the national origins quota system indicates that Congress ignored the inherent racial bias that such a system placed on Asians).

The 1965 Family-Based Immigration System

The 1960s implemented radical legal and changes by passing major civil rights legislation, including the 1965 Immigration and Nationality Act.[63] In the 1965 Act, Congress explicitly prohibited discrimination on the basis of "race, sex, nationality, place of birth, or place of residence."[64] In place of the national origins quota system, the 1965 Act created a worldwide limit of 170,000 visas for the Eastern Hemisphere and 120,000 for the Western Hemisphere.[65] It allotted to each country in the Eastern Hemisphere up to 20,000 visas but did not impose an annual per-country cap on countries in the Western Hemisphere.[66]

Critically, the 1965 Act established family ties as the principal way of immigrating to the United States. Family members eligible to immigrate were classified as either "immediate relatives" or family-sponsored immigrants. It provided that "immediate relatives" – children, spouses, and parents of citizens[67] – would be exempted from numerical limitations.[68] That is, there would be unlimited visas for immediate relatives. Additionally, it set aside the majority of the 170,000 visas (75 percent) for relatives of U.S. citizens and lawful permanent residents, rather than based on employment or job skills.[69]

Importantly, the 1965 Immigration Act established a preference system that determines a noncitizen's eligibility for a visa based on his or her family relationship to a U.S. citizen or lawful permanent resident. The top of the hierarchy comprises of married sons and daughters of U.S. citizens. Up to 20 percent of the visas would be allocated to them first.[70] The next available visas (not to exceed 20 percent) would then be given to spouses and unmarried sons or daughters of lawful permanent residents.[71] Taking a break from family preferences, the next set of visas (not to exceed 10 percent) would then be made available to those members of the profession

63 Immigration and Nationality (Hart-Celler) Act, Pub. L. No. 89–236, 79 Stat. 911 (1965).

64 *Id.*, sec. 2, § 202(a), 79 Stat. 911, 911.

65 *See id.*, sec. 1, § 201(a)(ii), 79 Stat. 911, 911. Today, the cap is 480,000 visas per year. *See* 8 U.S.C. § 1151 (2012).

66 *See id.*, sec. 2, § 202(a), 79 Stat. 911, 911. Countries in the Western Hemisphere did not have numerical limits. In 1976, Congress passed an amendment to the Immigration and Nationality Act that imposed a 20,000 per-country quota on countries in the Western Hemisphere. *See* Immigration and Nationality Act Amendments of 1976, sec. 3, § 202(e), Pub. L. No. 94–571, 90 Stat. 2703, 2704.

67 8 U.S.C. § 1152.

68 *See* Hart-Celler Act, sec. 1, §201(a), 79 Stat. 911, 911.

69 *See id.*, sec. 3, §203(a), 79 Stat. 911, 912–15 (specifying the allotment of visas that are to go to family preference categories); Aubry Holland, *The Modern Family Unit: Toward A More Inclusive Vision of the Family in Immigration Law*, 96 CAL. L. REV. 1049, 1060–61 (2008) (stressing family unification as a primary focus of the Hart-Celler Act and describing the applicable familial categories).

70 *See* Hart-Celler Act, sec. 3, §203(a)(1).

71 *See id.*, §203(a)(2).

who "because of their exceptional ability in the sciences or arts will substantially benefit" the United States.[72] The Act then returns to privileging family members by setting aside the next set of visas (not to exceed 10 percent) to married sons or daughters of U.S. citizens.[73] Next, no more than 24 percent of visas would be made available to brothers and sisters of U.S. citizens.[74] Once again shifting away from family preferences and toward employment, the next set of visas (up to 10 percent) would be made available to immigrants "who are capable of performing specified skilled or unskilled labor" that are not temporary in nature.[75]

The blueprint for family-based immigration under the 1965 Immigration Act eventually led to the more complicated immigration system that we have today. Currently, there is a formula that determines admission to the United States as an immigrant, particularly for those family members who fall under the preference system. To begin, there is an annual worldwide level of 675,000 visas per year[76] and each country is limited to 7 percent of the worldwide level.[77] Of the worldwide level, 480,000 visas are allocated for immediate relatives and family-sponsored petitions.[78] The INA provides that the family-sponsored preference system may not fall below 226,000,[79] leaving 254,000 visas for immediate relatives.[80] As Table 5.1 shows, the allocation of 226,000 visas for family-sponsored immigrants is subdivided as follows: 23,400 (F1 or first preference); 114,200 (F2 or second preference, with 77 percent reserved for spouses and children of lawful permanent residents); 23,400 (F3 or third preference); and 65,000 (F4 or fourth preference).[81]

In sum, by privileging a noncitizen's ties to a U.S. citizen or lawful permanent resident, the system the 1965 Immigration Act established sought to promote the integrity of the family unencumbered by racial restrictions as prior immigration laws and policies have done. Through a combination of factors including a preference system, per-country limits, and caps per family category, the family-based

72 *See id.*, §203(a)(3).

73 *See id.*, §203(a)(4).

74 *See id.*, §203(a)(5).

75 *See id.*, §203(a)(6).

76 The 675,000 visa "cap" is the sum of family-sponsored visas (480,000), employment-based visas (140,000), and "diversity immigrant" visas (55,000). *See generally* 8 U.S.C. § 1151(a) (2012).

77 *See id.* § 1152(a)(2). There are two exceptions to the per-country ceiling. *See id.* § 1152 (a)(4). Seventy-five percent of the visas for spouses and children of lawful permanent residents are not subject to the per-country ceiling. *See id.* § 1152(a)(4)(A).

78 *Id.* § 1151(c)(1)(A)(i). Additionally, any unused employment-based visas from the prior year are added to the number set aside for immediate relatives and family-sponsored immigrants (480,000). *See id.* § 1151(c)(1)(A)(iii).

79 *See id.* § 1151(c)(1)(B)(ii).

80 In reality, family immigration often exceeds the 480,000 level because there are more than 254,000 immediate relatives that immigrate to the United States every year.

81 Note that any unused visas in each preference are then added to the next lower preferential group.

TABLE 5.1. *Family-preference system visa allocation*

Preference category	Familial relationship	Number of visas
F1	Unmarried children of U.S. Citizens	23,400
F2	Spouses and unmarried children of Permanent Resident Aliens	114,200
F3	Married children of U.S. Citizens	23,400
F4	Siblings of U.S. Citizens	65,000

immigration law program under the 1965 Immigration Act provided a workable framework for uniting U.S. citizens and lawful permanent residents with their families.

5.3 IMMIGRATION ACT OF 1965: THE PROMOTION OF FAMILY UNIFICATION AND RACIAL DIVERSITY

Without a doubt, the Immigration Act of 1965's creation of equal access to immigration has led to remarkable results in terms of reunifying family members. Such achievements in family unification correlated with the changing racial makeup of our country. That is, through family-based immigration law, the population of immigrants of color has increased such that by 2043, if not sooner, the United States will be a majority minority nation.[82]

Family Unification

The U.S. Department of Homeland Security's Office of Immigration Statistics ("OIS") has been publishing annual reports on immigration to the United States since 1996.[83] Such data from the OIS provides a valuable window through which we can evaluate how the 1965 Immigration Act has facilitated family unification between U.S. citizens and lawful permanent residents and their families.

As Table 5.2 shows, most immigration visas went to those who were sponsored under the family preferences program or because they were immediate relatives of U.S. citizens.[84] On average during this ten-year period, 65 percent of immigrants

[82] *See* Press Release, U.S. Census Bureau, U.S. Census Projections Show a Slower Growing, Older, More Diverse Nation a Half a Century from Now (Dec. 12, 2012), https://www.census.gov/newsroom/releases/archives/population/cb12-243.html.

[83] *See Archives: Yearbook of Immigration Statistics*, U.S. DEP'T OF HOMELAND SEC., http://www.dhs.gov/archives#1 (last modified Sept. 13, 2012).

[84] *See infra* Table 5.1. The remainder of noncitizens who immigrated to the United States did so through employment-based, diversity, refugee and asylum, and other programs. *See Archives: Yearbook of Immigration Statistics*, *supra* note 84.

TABLE 5.2. *Number of immigrant visas issued to immediate relatives and under the family-sponsored preferences program between 2003 and 2012*

	Total immigrants	Family sponsored	Immediate relatives	Combined	Percent out of total immigrants
2003	703,542	158,796	331,286	490,082	69%
2004	957,883	214,355	417,815	632,170	66%
2005	1,122,257	212,970	436,115	649,085	58%
2006	1,266,129	222,229	580,348	802,577	63%
2007	1,052,415	194,900	494,920	689,820	66%
2008	1,107,126	227,761	488,483	716,244	65%
2009	1,130,818	211,859	535,554	747,413	66%
2010	1,042,625	214,589	476,414	691,003	66%
2011	1,062,040	234,931	453,158	688,089	65%
2012	1,031,631	202,019	478,780	680,799	66%

Source: U.S. Department of Homeland Security, http://www.dhs.gov/archives#1.

who became lawful permanent residents acquired their status through family ties.[85] To be sure, the 1965 Immigration Act, as already discussed, was designed with family unification in mind.[86] Nevertheless, it is helpful to see actual numbers to gain a deeper appreciation of the impact the law has had in the United States.

Among all noncitizens who were petitioned by a family member, immediate relatives garnered the most visas.[87] Such numbers should not be surprising given that there are no numerical caps on immediate relatives[88] – as many as are eligible can come. Table 5.3 shows that between 2003 and 2012, an average of 44.9 percent of all immigrants entered the United States because they were spouses, children, or parents of U.S. citizens.[89] Among this group, spouses of U.S. citizens obtained the most visas, garnering an average of 57 percent of all visas allocated to immediate relatives.[90]

The foregoing numbers underscore the extent to which the 1965 Immigration Act has been able to effectively facilitate family unification. It should be noted, however, that the concept of family reunification comes in at least two different types. One type refers to those families who have been physically separated by national borders

85 *See infra* Table 5.1.
86 *See generally supra* Section 5.2.
87 *See supra* Table 5.2.
88 8 U.S.C. § 1151(b)(2)(A) (2012).
89 *See infra* Table 5.3.
90 *See id.*

TABLE 5.3. *Number of immediate relatives of U.S. citizens between 2003 and 2012*

	Total immigrants	Immediate relatives	Percent of immediate relatives out of total immigrants	Spouses	Percent out of total immediate relatives
2003	703,542	331,286	47%	183,796	55%
2004	957,883	417,815	44%	252,193	60%
2005	1,122,257	436,115	39%	259,144	59%
2006	1,266,129	580,348	46%	339,843	59%
2007	1,052,415	494,920	47%	274,358	55%
2008	1,107,126	488,483	44%	265,671	54%
2009	1,130,818	535,554	47%	317,129	59%
2010	1,042,625	476,414	46%	271,909	57%
2011	1,062,040	453,158	43%	258,320	57%
2012	1,031,631	478,780	46%	273,429	57%

Source: U.S. Department of Homeland Security, http://www.dhs.gov/archives#1.

and who are eventually reunited as a family in the United States.[91] Noncitizens who are reunited with their families under this type of family unification are referred to as new arrivals.[92] The second type gestures to those families who are *physically* together in the United States but who may or may not be legally authorized to remain together in the United States. That is, some noncitizen family members may be residing in the United States under a temporary status, which means that at the expiration of their visas they are required, in principle, to return to their home countries.[93] Other noncitizen family members may be living in the United States without authorized status.[94] Immigration law's family-based program allows U.S. citizens and lawful permanent residents to sponsor these nonimmigrants on

91 *Cf.* Randall Monger & James Yankay, *U.S. Legal Permanent Residents: 2012*, U.S. DEP'T OF HOMELAND SEC., OFFICE OF IMMIGRATION STATISTICS 2 (Mar. 8, 2013), http://www.dhs.gov/sites/default/files/publications/ois_lpr_fr_2012_2.pdf [hereinafter *2012 LPR Report*] (defining "new arrivals" as LPRs who become LPRs upon admission from a foreign nation into the United States at a port of entry).

92 *Cf. id.*

93 *Cf. Immigrant vs. Nonimmigrant Visas*, U.S. CUSTOMS & BORDER PROTECTION, https://help.cbp.gov/app/answers/detail/a_id/72/~/immigrant-visas-vs.-nonimmigrant-visas (last updated Sept. 4, 2014) (defining nonimmigrant visas as temporary for a limited period of time).

94 *See* Patricia Hatch, *U.S. Immigration Policy: Family Reunification*, LEAGUE OF WOMEN VOTERS (last visited Sept. 17, 2014), http://www.lwv.org/content/us-immigration-policy-family-reunification (noting a significant percentage of estimated unauthorized immigrants in the U.S. are family members of "anchor relatives").

temporary status, which would enable them to adjust their status to LPR status.[95] By acquiring LPR status, these previous temporary nonimmigrants are then considered to have reunified with their U.S. citizen or LPR family members.[96]

The distinction between new arrivals and those who adjusted their status is helpful in further understanding the impact of the 1965 Immigration Act on American families. As Table 5.4 demonstrates, a significant number of new arrivals (an approximate average of 35 percent) between 2003 and 2012 became LPRs because they fell in the categories of immediate relatives or family-sponsored preferences.[97] Moreover, new arrivals who are considered "immediate relatives" outnumbered those who fell in the "family-sponsored preferences" category.[98]

By comparison, as Table 5.5 illuminates, there were, on average, about 29.7 percent of noncitizens who adjusted their status to lawful permanent residents based on their connection to a U.S. citizen or an LPR.[99] Although the numbers are lower than those of new arrivals, they nevertheless underscore the ways in which immigration law has enabled families to remain together in the United States. For those noncitizens who were previously undocumented, the ability to come out of the shadows and adjust their status to LPR is incredibly important.[100]

As of this writing, the most recent annual statistical data from OIS is from the year 2013. Similar to the previous years, 2013 shows the ways in which the 1965 Immigration Act has helped reunite families. Specifically, in 2013, approximately 990,553 persons became legal permanent residents.[101] To be sure, this was the lowest number of total immigrants in a given year since 2004.[102] As Table 5.4 shows, during

[95] *See Green Card for a Family Member of a Permanent Resident*, U.S. CITIZENSHIP & IMMIGRATION SERVS., http://www.uscis.gov/green-card/green-card-through-family/green-card-family-member-us-citizen (last updated Aug. 29, 2013); *Green Card for a Family Member of a U.S. Citizen*, U.S. CITIZENSHIP & IMMIGRATION SERVS., http://www.uscis.gov/green-card/green-card-through-family/green-card-family-member-us-citizen (last updated Aug. 29, 2013); *Green Card for an Immediate Relative of a U.S. Citizen*, U.S. CITIZENSHIP & IMMIGRATION SERVS., http://www.uscis.gov/green-card/green-card-through-family/green-card-immediate-relative-us-citizen.

[96] *See Green Card for a Family Member of a Permanent Resident*, *supra* note 96 (describing steps to LPR status for family members and its purpose as "[t]o promote family unity"); *Green Card for a Family Member of a U.S. Citizen*, *supra* note 96 (same); *Green Card for an Immediate Relative of a U.S. Citizen*, *supra* note 96 (same).

[97] *See infra* Table 5.3.

[98] *See id.*

[99] *See infra* Table 5.5.

[100] *Cf.* Hatch, *supra* note 95 (discussing unauthorized immigrants who learn about bar to legal permanent residence choosing to remain undocumented rather than risk visa process for fear of separating from family again).

[101] *See* Randall Monger & James Yankay, *U.S. Lawful Permanent Residents: 2013*, U.S. DEP'T OF HOMELAND SEC., OFFICE OF IMMIGRATION STATISTICS 1 (May 29, 2014), http://www.dhs.gov/sites/default/files/publications/ois_lpr_fr_2013.pdf [hereinafter *2013 LPR Report*].

[102] *See supra* Table 5.5.

TABLE 5.4. *Population of new arrivals of family-sponsored immigrants and immediate relatives between 2003 and 2012*

	Total immigrants	New arrivals of family-sponsored	New arrivals of immediate relatives	New arrivals based on family membership/ percent out of total immigrants
2003	703,542	129,764	154,094	283,858 (40%)
2004	957,883	149,928	147,851	297,779 (31%)
2005	1,122,257	142,511	169,264	311,775 (28%)
2006	1,266,129	142,520	223,221	365,741 (29%)
2007	1,052,415	142,841	217,732	360,573 (34%)
2008	1,107,126	170,862	237,393	398,553 (36%)
2009	1,130,818	172,072	226,481	398,553 (35%)
2010	1,042,625	188,310	223,572	411,882 (40%)
2011	1,062,040	206,585	209,984	416,569 (39%)
2012	1,031,631	183,459	238,794	422,253 (41%)

Source: U.S. Citizenship and Immigration Services, http://www.uscis.gov/green-card/green-card-through-family/green-card-family-member-us-citizen.

that year, 957,883 noncitizens immigrated to the United States.[103] Since 2005, there have been well over 1 million noncitizens who immigrated to the United States as lawful permanent residents each year.[104]

Yet, despite the decrease in the overall number of LPRs, percentage wise, the total number of LPRs who immigrated to the United States based on family ties, consistent with prior years, was at 65 percent (or 649,763 people).[105] Of this group, the majority – 439,460 (or 44 percent of total LPRs) – was composed of immediate relatives.[106] The remainder of this group – 210,303 (or 21 percent of total LPRs) – was composed of family members of LPRs.[107] By comparison, the largest group of immigrants after the family-based immigration system – employment-based immigrants – was composed of 161,110 immigrants or about 16 percent of LPRs in 2013.[108]

103 *See id.*

104 *See id.*

105 *See* Monger & Yankay, *2013 LPR Report*, *supra* note 102, at 3 tbl.2. The total number of LPRs (990,553) may be divided into two general groups: persons who were new arrivals to the United States (459,751) and persons who were already present in the United States and adjusted their status (530,802). *See id.* at 2 tbl.1.

106 *See id.* at 3 tbl.2.

107 *See id.* The remainder of the LPRs obtained their status through the other legal channels, including employment, diversity, refugee and asylum. *See id.*

108 *See id.*

TABLE 5.5. *Total number of immigrants who adjusted their status based on ties to a U.S. citizen or lawful permanent resident family member*

	Total immigrants	Adjustment of status of family-sponsored	Adjustment of status of immediate relatives	Total adjustment of status based on family membership/percent out of total immigrants
2003	703,542	29,032	177,192	206,224 (29%)
2004	957,883	64,427	269,964	334,39 (35%)
2005	1,122,257	70,459	266,851	337,310 (30%)
2006	1,266,129	79,709	357,127	436,836 (35%)
2007	1,052,415	52,059	277,188	329,247 (31%)
2008	1,107,126	56,899	251,090	307,989 (28%)
2009	1,130,818	39,787	309,073	348,860 (31%)
2010	1,042,625	26,279	252,842	279,121 (27%)
2011	1,062,040	28,346	243,174	271,520 (26%)
2012	1,031,631	18,560	239,986	258,546 (25%)

Source: U.S. Citizenship and Immigration Services, http://www.uscis.gov/green-card/green-card-through-family/green-card-family-member-us-citizen.

Table 5.6 provides a further examination of the 2013 data. It demonstrates that, as in the past, spouses of U.S. citizens garnered the most visas (248,332) followed by parents of U.S. citizens (119,746) and children of U.S. citizens (71,382).[109] By comparison, the family preference immigrants' breakdown is as follows (in order of preferences): 24,358 (unmarried sons and daughters of U.S. citizens), 99,115 (spouses and children of LPRs), 21,294 (married sons and daughters of U.S. citizens) and 65,536 (siblings of U.S. citizens).[110]

In contrast to the significant numbers of immigrants who became new LPRs in 2013 based on their ties to a U.S. citizen or LPR, the number of people who became LPRs under either employment-based preferences, diversity programs, or refugee and asylum programs was not as high. As noted earlier, 161,110 immigrants (about 16 percent of total LPRs) acquired LPR status through the employment-based preference program.[111] Refugees and asylees were given 119,630 visas (12 percent), and immigrants under the diversity or "lottery" program received 45,618 visas (4 percent).[112]

[109] *See infra* Table 5.6; *see also* Monger & Yankay, 2013 *LPR Report*, *supra* note 102, at 3 tbl.2.

[110] *See infra* Table 5.6; *see also* Monger & Yankay, 2013 *LPR Report*, *supra* note 102, at 3 tbl.2.

[111] *See supra* note 109 and accompanying text.

[112] *See* Monger & Yankay, 2013 *LPR Report*, *supra* note 102, at 3 tbl.2.

TABLE 5.6. *Total number of visas received by immediate relatives and family-sponsored preference immigrants in 2013*

Immediate relatives	Total	Percent of total
Spouses of U.S. Citizens	248,332	57%
Parents of U.S. Citizens	119,746	27%
Children of U.S. Citizens	71,382	16%
Total Immediate Relatives	439,460	
Family Sponsored Preferences		
1st Pref: Unmarried Sons and Daughters of U.S. Citizens	24,358	12%
2nd Pref: Spouses and Children of LPRs	99,115	47%
3rd Pref: Married Sons and Daughters of U.S. Citizens	21,294	10%
4th Pref. Siblings of U.S. Citizens	65,536	31%
Total Family-Sponsored Preference	210,303	

Source: Randall Monger & James Yankay, U.S. Lawful Permanent Residents: 2013, U.S. DEP'T OF HOMELAND SEC., OFFICE OF IMMIGRATION STATISTICS 1 (May 29, 2014), http://www.dhs.gov/sites/default/files/publications/ois_lpr_fr_2013.pdf.

In brief, the foregoing data from the past ten years provides a meaningful way of understanding the impact of the 1965 Immigration Act. When set against the backdrop of the history of racially exclusionary immigration laws, which did not formally end until 1965, these numbers reflect the ways in which the law's goal of family unification has been achieved.

Racial Diversity

The 1965 Immigration Act's promotion of family unification cannot be fully appreciated without examining its role in increasing racial diversity in the United States. This is not to suggest that the Immigration Act of 1965 completely erased racial barriers to immigration. As scholars have argued, despite the 1965 Immigration Act's goal of race neutrality, it had racially discriminatory consequences.[113] Yet, as Jack Chin and other legal scholars and historians have also pointed out, the lifting of national origins quotas

[113] *See, e.g.*, Kevin R. Johnson, *The Beginning of the End: Anti-Latina/o Sentiment, the Immigration Act of 1965, and the Emergence of Modern Border Enforcement*, in LEGISLATING A NEW AMERICA: THE IMMIGRATION AND NATIONALITY ACT OF 1965 AND ITS CONTRIBUTIONS TO AMERICAN LAW AND SOCIETY __ (forthcoming 2015) (hereinafter LEGISLATING A NEW AMERICA); Bill Ong Hing, *African Immigration to the United States: Assigned to the Back of the Bus*, in LEGISLATING A NEW AMERICA ___.

facilitated the reunification of family members of U.S. citizens and lawful permanent residents who would have otherwise been separated from their families under the previous immigration law.[114]

Data from the OIS illustrate the ways in which the 1965 Immigration Act prompted a remarkable change in the racial demographics of immigrants between 1820 and 2012.[115] From 1820 until 1919, the majority of immigrants hailed from Europe.[116] As Table 5.7 shows, the total percentage of European immigrants ranged between 75 percent of all immigrants during the decade between 1820 to 1829 at its lowest to 96 percent during the last decade before the end of the nineteenth century.[117]

The same data shows that Asians had been immigrating to the United States since 1820 (three from China, nine from India, and nineteen from Turkey during the 1820–29 decade) and began coming in more significant numbers beginning the decade between 1850 and 1859.[118] During that decade, 36,080 Asian immigrants arrived, which included 35,933 Chinese.[119] That number shows a huge increase from the prior decade when only thirty-two Chinese immigrated to the United States.[120] Yet, it should be noted that the total number of Asian immigrants during the 1850–59 decade represented only 1 percent of the total number of immigrants during that decade, compared to 93 percent Europeans).[121] Indeed, subsequent decades indicate the same trend of limited immigration from Asia compared to Europe, as Table 5.8 illustrates.[122]

The low number of Asian immigrants to the United States during the foregoing period (1820–1919) was, of course, purposeful. As explained previously, Congress enacted several measures, including the Chinese Exclusion Act, during this period

[114] *See* Chin, *supra* note 18, at 317–18; *see, e.g.*, MARCELO M. SUÁREZ-OROZCO, CAROLA SUÁREZ-OROZCO & DESIRÉE QIN-HILLIARD, THE NEW IMMIGRANT AND THE AMERICAN FAMILY: INTERDISCIPLINARY PERSPECTIVES ON THE NEW IMMIGRATION 172 (2014) (stating Immigration Act of 1965 with its family reunification focus and abolishment of national origins quota system led to immigration of Chinese as family groups); Victor C. Romero, *On Elián and Aliens: A Political Solution to the Plenary Power Problem*, 4 N.Y.U. J. LEGIS. & PUB. POL'Y 343, 363 (2001) (noting large number of minority descent is due to lifting of national origins quota system); *cf.* Adam B. Cox & Eric A. Posner, *Delegation in Immigration Law*, 79 U. CHI. L. REV. 1285, 1316 (2012) (stating that family reunification is a core feature of immigration law in current times, whereas it only played a minor role when the national origins quota system was in place).

[115] *See 2012 Yearbook of Immigration Statistics*, U.S. DEP'T OF HOMELAND SEC., OFFICE OF IMMIGRATION STATISTICS 6–11 (Sept. 6, 2013), http://www.dhs.gov/sites/default/files/publications/ois_yb_2012.pdf [hereinafter *2012 Immigration Statistics*].

[116] *See id.* at 6–7.

[117] *See infra* Table 5.7; *see also 2012 Immigration Statistics*, *supra* note 116, at 6–7.

[118] *See 2012 Immigration Statistics*, *supra* note 116, at 6.

[119] *See id.*

[120] *See id.*

[121] *Compare id.* (listing 36,080 Asian immigrants out of a total of 2,814,554, or 1%, during the 1850–59 decade), *with id.* (listing 2,622,617 European immigrants out of a total of 2,814,554, or 93%, during the 1850–59 decade).

[122] *See infra* Table 5.8.

TABLE 5.7. *Total percentage of European immigrants from 1820 to 1919*

	Total immigrants per decade	Total immigrants from Europe	Percent of total immigrants from Europe
1820–1829	128,502	99,618	75%
1830–1839	538,381	422,853	78%
1840–1849	1,427,337	1,369,423	95%
1850–1959	2,814,554	2,622,617	93%
1860–1869	2,081,261	1,880,389	90%
1870–1879	2,742,137	2,252,050	82%
1880–1889	5,248,568	4,638,684	88%
1890–1899	3,694,294	3,576,411	96%
1900–1909	8,202,388	7,572,569	92%
1910–1919	6,347,380	4,985,411	78%

Source: U.S. DEP'T OF HOMELAND SEC., OFFICE OF IMMIGRATION STATISTICS 6–11 (Sept. 6, 2013), http://www.dhs.gov/sites/default/files/publications/ois_yb_2012.pdf.

to prevent Asians from immigrating to the United States.[123] Congress continued to pass laws during the subsequent decade (1920–29), particularly the National Origins Quota Act, which further reduced the number of Asian immigrants as well as southern and eastern Europeans.[124] The numbers during that decade shows the impact of such intentional discrimination.[125] Out of the 4,295,510 noncitizens who immigrated during that decade, 126,740 came from Asia (3 percent).[126] On the other hand, 2,560,340 came from Europe, which represented the lowest percentage of European immigrants (60 percent) since 1820.[127]

Immigration to the United States dropped significantly between 1930 and 1950.[128] Specifically, only 699,375 noncitizens immigrated during the 1930–39 decade and 856,608 immigrated during the 1940–49 decade.[129] During the 1930–39 decade, 64 percent immigrated from Europe and 3 percent from Asia, and during the

[123] *See supra* notes 36–46 and accompanying text.

[124] *See* Immigration Act of 1924, Pub. L. No. 68–139, 43 Stat. 153. The National Origins Quota Act was also known as the Immigration Act of 1924. *See* Tanya Kateri Hernandez, *The Construction of Race and Class Buffers in the Structure of Immigration Controls and Laws*, 76 OR. L. REV. 731, 738 n.38 (1997).

[125] *See* 2012 *Immigration Statistics*, *supra* note 116, at 8.

[126] *See id.* The National Origins Quotas was also designed to deter southern and eastern Europeans from immigrating to the United States, as these numbers demonstrate. *See* Chin, *supra* note 18, at 279, 327 n.258.

[127] *See* 2012 *Immigration Statistics*, *supra* note 116, at 6–8.

[128] *See id.* at 8.

[129] *See id.*

TABLE 5.8. *Total number of immigrants from Asia as compared to immigrants from Europe between 1860 and 1919*

	Total immigrants per decade	Total immigrants from Asia	Percent of total immigrants from Asia compared with Europe
1860–1869	2,081,261	54,408	3% vs. 90%
1870–1879	2,742,137	134,071	5% vs. 82%
1880–1889	5,248,568	71,152	1% vs. 88%
1890–1899	3,694,294	61,304	2% vs. 96%
1900–1909	8,202,388	300,441	4% vs. 92%
1910–1919	6,347,380	269,736	4% vs. 78%

Source: U.S. DEP'T OF HOMELAND SEC., OFFICE OF IMMIGRATION STATISTICS 6–11 (Sept. 6, 2013), http://www.dhs.gov/sites/default/files/publications/ois_yb_2012.pdf.

1940–49 decade, 55 percent of immigrants hailed from Europe and 4 percent came from Asia.[130]

Immigration in the following decade (1950–59) bounced back to well over 2 million.[131] Specifically, during that decade, 2,499,268 noncitizens immigrated to the United States.[132] The majority of majority of immigrants, as in the past, came from Europe (approximately 56 percent).[133] And, consistent with previous decades, the number of Asian immigrants was low – only 5 percent out of the total population of new immigrants.[134]

It was not until the decade beginning with 1960 that the United States experienced a sea change in immigration. Without a doubt, this change can be attributed to the elimination of the ongoing quota restrictions for Asian immigrants that the 1965 Immigration Act prompted. Indeed, during the 1960–69 decade, migration from Asia reached double digits in terms of percentage (11 percent of the total number of immigrants) for the first time.[135] The percentage of European immigrants dwindled

[130] *See id.* (recording 444,404 European immigrants out of 699,375 total, or 64%, during 1930–39; 19,292 Asian immigrants out of 699,375 total, or 3%, during 1930–39; 472,524 European immigrants out of 856,608 total, or 55%, during 1940–49; and 34,532 Asian immigrants out of 856,608 total, or 4%, during 1940–49).

[131] *See id.*

[132] *See id.*

[133] *See id.* (recording 1,404,973 European immigrants out of 2,499,268 total) or approximately 56%).

[134] *See id.* (recording 135,844 Asian immigrants out of 2,499,268 total, or 5%).

[135] *See* 2012 *Immigration Statistics*, *supra* note 116, at 8 (recording 358,563 Asian immigrants out of a total of 3,213,749, or 11%).

TABLE 5.9. *Comparison of immigrants from Europe and Asia between 1970 and 2009*

	Total immigrants	European immigrants	Asian immigrants
1970–79	4,248,203	826,327 (19%)	1,406,526 (33%)
1980–89	6,244,379	669,694 (10%)	2,391,356 (38%)
1990–99	9,775,398	1,349,919 (13%)	2,859,899 (29%)
2000–09	10,299,430	1,349,609 (13%)	3,470,835 (34%)

Source: U.S. DEP'T OF HOMELAND SEC., OFFICE OF IMMIGRATION STATISTICS 6–11 (Sept. 6, 2013), http://www.dhs.gov/sites/default/files/publications/ois_yb_2012.pdf.

to 35 percent.[136] The trend would continue in the decades leading up to the twenty-first century, as Table 5.9 indicates.[137]

Indeed, as the data from 2010, 2011, and 2012 indicate, the overall number of European immigrants continued to decrease while those from Asia increased to about 40 percent (see Table 5.10).

Most notable, perhaps, in the radical changes precipitated by the 1965 Immigration Act is the increase in immigrants from North America, particularly Mexico. To be sure, Mexicans, like immigrants from Asian countries, have been immigrating to the United States since well before 1965.[138] The OIS data shows, for example, that in the decade between 1820 and 1829, there were 3,835 Mexican nationals who became LPRs during that decade.[139] This represented 3 percent of the overall immigrants from Mexico during that decade, which constituted the *highest* percentage rate of immigration from Mexico for the next 100 years.[140] As Table 5.11 shows, for most of that period, less than 1 percent permanently immigrated from Mexico.[141] Between 1820 and 1920, Mexican immigration reached its lowest point during the 1890–99 decade (734 immigrants, which represents .0002 percent of the overall lawful permanent residents during that decade) and highest during the 1910–20 decade (185,334 or .03 percent during that decade).[142]

[136] *See id.* (recording 1,133,442 European immigrants out of 3,213,749 total, or 35%).

[137] *See infra* Table 5.9; *see also 2012 Immigration Statistics, supra* note 116, at 8, 10.

[138] *See 2012 Immigration Statistics, supra* note 116, at 6, 8.

[139] *See id.* at 6.

[140] *See id.* at 6, 8 (recording 3,835 Mexican immigrants out of 128,502 total, or 3%, during 1820–1829 and recording the number of Mexican immigrants for the next one hundred years).

[141] *See infra* Table 5.11.

[142] *See id.*

TABLE 5.10. *Comparison of immigrants from Europe and Asia between 2010 and 2013*

	Total immigrants	European immigrants	Asian immigrants
2010	1,042,625	95,429 (9%)	410,209 (39%)
2011	1,062,040	90,712 (8.5%)	438,580 (41%)
2012	1,031,631	86,956 (8%)	416,488 (40%)
2013	990,553	86,556 (8.7%)	400,548 (40.4%)

Source: U.S. DEP'T OF HOMELAND SEC., OFFICE OF IMMIGRATION STATISTICS 6–11 (Sept. 6, 2013), http://www.dhs.gov/sites/default/files/publications/ois_yb_2012.pdf.

During the following decades, the number of Mexican immigrants fluctuated tremendously. In the 1920–29 decade, the number of Mexican immigrants jumped to 498,945 – more than double the number from the previous decade.[143] This represented 12 percent of the total immigration from that decade (4,295,510) and was the highest percentage of Mexican immigrants since 1820.[144] However, the numbers dropped drastically to 32,709 (or 5 percent of 699,375 total immigrants) during the 1930–39 decade.[145] It increased slightly to 56,158 (or 7 percent of 856,608 total immigrants) during the 1940–49 decade and more than quadrupled to 273,847 (or 11 percent of the 2,499,268 total immigrants) during the 1950–59 decade.[146]

Notably, this 11 percent rate of overall immigration during the 1950–1959 decade constitutes the lowest in the latter half of the twentieth century. With the help of the 1965 Immigration Act, the population of lawful permanent residents from Mexico since then continued to rise, as Table 5.12 demonstrates.[147] It rose from 13 percent of overall immigration in the 1960s to as high as 28 percent in the 1990s.[148]

OIS has more specific data of noncitizens who became lawful permanent residents beginning in 2010.[149] The data evidences a dip in the population of new immigrants from North America, including Mexico. Specifically, as Table 5.13 indicates, between 2010 and 2012, the number of immigrants from the Americas remained at 40 percent, which is lower than the 43 percent average during the

143 *See 2012 Immigration Statistics*, *supra* note 116, at 8.
144 *See id.* at 6, 8.
145 *See id.* at 8.
146 *See id.* at 8.
147 *See infra* Table 5.12.
148 *See id.*
149 *See 2012 Immigration Statistics*, *supra* note 116, at 10–11.

TABLE 5.11. *Populatin of immigrants from Mexico out of total immigrant population between 1820 and 1919*

	Total immigrants per decade	Total immigrants from Mexico	Percent of total immigrants from Mexico
1820–29	128,502	3,835	3%
1830–39	538,381	7,187	1%
1840–49	1,427,337	3,069	.0021%
1850–59	2,814,554	3,446	.0012%
1860–69	2,081,261	1,957	.0009%
1870–79	2,742,137	5,133	.0018%
1880–89	5,248,568	2,405	.0004%
1890–99	3,694,294	734	.0002%
1900–09	8,202,388	31,188	.0038%
1910–19	6,347,380	185,334	.03%

Source: U.S. DEP'T OF HOMELAND SEC., OFFICE OF IMMIGRATION STATISTICS 6–11 (Sept. 6, 2013), http://www.dhs.gov/sites/default/files/publications/ois_yb_2012.pdf.

2000–09 decade.[150] Immigration from Mexico decreased to 13 percent in 2010 and 2011 but then increased to 14 percent in 2012.[151]

The most recent OIS data (2013) shows the continuing pace of immigration from Mexico. As Table 5.14 illuminates, out of the 900,553 immigrants, 135,028 (or 13.6 percent) came from Mexico.[152] Mexico dominated the field as the top country of origin in 2013.[153] The country that came closest to Mexico was China, which accounted for 7.2 percent of the total number of immigrants.[154] Indeed, Mexico had sent the most immigrants out of any other country since 1960.[155]

Demographers have long been noting that whites are to become a minority in the United States by the year 2040.[156] This should not come as a surprise given that the majority of immigrants in the last several years are people of color. For instance, in 2013, 40 percent of immigrants came from Asia (400,548 immigrants), followed by

[150] *See infra* Table 5.13; *see also 2012 Immigration Statistics*, *supra* note 116, at 10.

[151] *See infra* Table 5.13; *see also 2012 Immigration Statistics*, *supra* note 116, at 10.

[152] *See* Monger & Yankay, *2013 LPR Report*, *supra* note 102, at 4 tbl. 3; *infra* Table 5.14.

[153] *See* Monger & Yankay, *2013 LPR Report*, *supra* note 102, at 4 tbl. 3; *infra* Table 5.14.

[154] *See* Monger & Yankay, *2013 LPR Report*, *supra* note 102, at 4 tbl. 3; *infra* Table 5.14.

[155] *Compare 2012 Immigration Statistics*, *supra* note 116, at 8, 10 (listing number of Mexican immigrants from 1960 to 2012), *and* Monger & Yankay, *2013 LPR Report*, *supra* note 102, at 4 tbl. 3 (listing number of Mexican immigrants in 2013), *with 2012 Immigration Statistics*, *supra* note 116, at 8–11 (listing number of immigrants from other countries from 1960 to 2012), *and* Monger & Yankay, *2013 LPR Report*, *supra* note 102, at 4 tbl. 3 (listing number of immigrants from other countries in 2013).

[156] *See, e.g.*, *supra* note 83.

TABLE 5.12. *Population of immigrants from Mexico between 1960 and 2009*

	Total immigrants	Immigrants from America	Mexican immigrants
1960–69	3,213,749	1,674,185 (52%)	441,824 (13%)
1970–79	4,248,203	1,903,636 (44%)	621,218 (14%)
1980–89	6,244,379	2,694,504 (43%)	1,009,586 (16%)
1990–99	9,775,398	5,137,142 (52%)	2,757,418 (28%)
2000–09	10,299,430	4,441,529 (43%)	1,704,166 (17%)

TABLE 5.13. *Total immigrants from North America, including Mexico*

	Total immigrants	Immigrants from America	Mexican immigrants out of total immigrants
2010	1,042,625	426,981 (40%)	138,717 (13%)
2011	1,062,040	423,277 (40%)	142,823 (13%)
2012	1,031,631	409,664 (40%)	145,326 (14%)

31.9 percent from North America, which includes Mexico, Central America, and the Caribbean.[157] By contrast, Europe garnered 86,556 visas, or 8.7 percent of total LPRs.[158]

In sum, as the discussion in this section demonstrated, the combination of an immigration system that primarily privileged family ties and a norm of nondiscrimination essentially has led to a more diverse immigration stream in the last fifty years.[159] It is important to recognize and celebrate these achievements prompted by the 1965 Immigration Act. The United States would not be on a path to being a more racially diverse country without the assistance of the 1965 Immigration Act.

[157] *See* Monger & Yankay, *2013 LPR Report*, *supra* note 102, at 4 tbl. 3.

[158] *See id.*

[159] *See supra* Section 5.3.

TABLE 5.14. *Top sending countries to the United States in 2013*

Country	Total immigrants from that country	Percentage
Mexico	135,028	13.6%
China	71,798	7.2%
India	68,458	6.9%
Philippines	54,466	5.5%
Dominican Republic	41,311	4.2%

Source: Randall Monger & James Yankay, U.S. Lawful Permanent Residents: 2013, U.S. DEP'T OF HOMELAND SEC., OFFICE OF IMMIGRATION STATISTICS 1 (May 29, 2014), http://www.dhs.gov/sites/default/files/publications/ois_lpr_fr_2013.pdf.

5.4 ONGOING FAMILY SEPARATION

Although we ought to celebrate the 1965 Immigration Act for its achievements, as Section 5.3 highlighted, it is equally important to recognize its flaws. In particular, as this section discusses, the 1965 Immigration Act may also be described as a law that has facilitated the separation of families. The combination of caps on overall visas per year, limits on the number of visas available per family-sponsored preferences categories, and per-country limits has resulted in an extremely long visa backlog. In other words, the structure of immigration law itself has ironically delayed, if not obstructed, family unification.

Sponsoring Family Members

Sponsoring a noncitizen family member to immigrate to the United States requires two distinct steps. First, their visa application must be approved.[160] Second, there must be a visa available that would enable the noncitizen to immigrate to the United States.[161] A delay in the ability of the noncitizen may take place at either step in the process, but especially during the second stage.[162]

There are several factors governing the approval of a U.S. citizen or lawful permanent resident's petition to sponsor a non-citizen to immigrate to the United

[160] *See Green Card for a Family Member of a Permanent Resident*, *supra* note 96 (describing steps to LPR status for family members); *Green Card for a Family Member of a U.S. Citizen*, *supra* note 96 (same); *Green Card for an Immediate Relative of a U.S. Citizen*, *supra* note 96 (same).

[161] *See Green Card for a Family Member of a Permanent Resident*, *supra* note 96 (describing steps to LPR status for family members); *Green Card for a Family Member of a U.S. Citizen*, *supra* note 96 (same); *Green Card for an Immediate Relative of a U.S. Citizen*, *supra* note 96 (same).

[162] *See, e.g.*, Gene Demby, *For Asian-Americans, Immigration Backlogs Are a Major Hurdle*, NPR (Jan. 31, 2013, 12:50 PM), http://www.npr.org/blogs/itsallpolitics/2013/01/31/170744897/for-asian-americans-immigration-backlogs-are-becoming-a-major-hurdle.

States. These include evidence of family relationship, financial support for the noncitizen, and that the noncitizen is not inadmissible. Assuming that the petition is approved, the next requirement for immigrating is the availability of a visa. For immediate relatives, a visa is immediately available.[163] As explained in Section 5.3, there are no caps imposed on immediate relatives, and thus, when the petition is approved, it also means that the visa is available for the noncitizen to enter the United States as a new arrival or, if already in the United States, he or she may then adjust status to that of an LPR.[164]

By contrast, the process of immigrating to the United States for noncitizens who submitted petitions under the family-sponsored preferences program takes much longer. Like the immediate relative process, a visa application must first be approved. However, unlike immediate relatives, noncitizens do not have visas immediately available. As discussed earlier, there are limits on how many noncitizens may enter the United States in a given year.[165] For family-sponsored preferences, there is a minimum of 226,000 visas available, which are further subdivided among the various family preference categories. Additionally, there is a per-country cap of 7 percent imposed on almost all of the categories.

Finally, visa availability also depends on when the visa application was submitted before the "cut-off date" – the date when the demand for visas exceeded the available visas and the country is deemed oversubscribed. The cut-off date becomes the "priority date" for those who filed their applications before the visas ran out during a particular period and would thus be given priority over other applicants in the same family category.[166] The combination of all of these factors has led to a backlog in family-sponsored visa availability.[167] That is, although the immigration petitions may have been approved, there are no visas yet available for many of the family members – they must wait for visas to become available.

To be sure, as discussed earlier, a significant number of new immigrants have become LPRs each year as a result of the 1965 Immigration Act. Yet, these numbers obscure a critical reality for many U.S. citizens, LPRs, and their families today, namely the number of years it has taken for family unification to actually take place. Some have had to wait two years to be reunited. Others have had to wait almost twenty years. As explained in the next subsection, the delay is due to a backlog of available visas for the millions of eligible and approved visa applicants.

[163] *Green Card for an Immediate Relative of a U.S. Citizen*, *supra* note 96.
[164] *See supra* Section 5.3.
[165] *See supra* notes 77–82 and accompanying text.
[166] *See* 8 C.F.R. § 204.2 (2014).
[167] *Cf.* Demby, *supra* note 165.

Backlogs and Family Separation

The U.S. Department of State issues a monthly Visa Bulletin to inform the public on the current "cut-off dates" and to alert those who submitted under either family-based or employment-based preferences before the cut-off date that a visa is available.[168] The cut-off dates are different for each program. Indeed, the cut-off date is different per category. Notably, for some countries, especially Mexico and the Philippines, the cut-off dates are almost always earlier,[169] which means that noncitizens from these countries have a much longer wait.

These long waiting periods are evidenced in the most current visa bulletin as of this writing – December 2014. Specifically, it shows that for all countries but Mexico and the Philippines, those with the shortest waiting period are the spouses and children of lawful permanent residents. The cut-off date for them is May 1, 2012, which means that they have had to wait slightly longer than two years before their visas were available. Those with the longest waiting period are the siblings of U.S. citizens. Currently, the cut-off date is January 1, 2002, which means that, thus far, they have had to wait more than twelve years (see Table 5.15).

As Table 5.15 shows, immigrants from Mexico and the Philippines, which currently are the two most oversubscribed countries, have had a much longer wait. For instance, the cut-off date for married sons and daughters of U.S. citizens who are coming from Mexico is November 15, 1993, which translates into a wait of more than twenty-one years. This represents the longest waiting period for Mexican nationals. Those with the shortest waiting period are the spouses and children of LPRs from Mexico, which is currently set at January 1, 2013, which, as of this writing (December 2014), translates into approximately a two-year delay. Noncitizens from the Philippines similarly have much earlier cut-off dates than do others. Filipino siblings of U.S. citizens have the longest waiting period. The current cut-off date for this group is June 1, 1991, which represents an approximately twenty-three-year wait. Those with the shortest waiting period are the spouses and children of LPRs. Similar to countries other than Mexico, the cut-off date for them is March 22, 2013, or about eighteen months of waiting for the visas to become available. In sum, as these dates indicate, for a significant number of U.S. citizens, LPRs, and their families from Mexico and the Philippines, unification under immigration law could take from as little as two years to as long as twenty-three-plus years.

168 *See Visa Bulletin*, U.S. DEP'T OF STATE, http://travel.state.gov/content/visas/english/law-and-policy/bulletin.html (last visited Dec. 8, 2014).

169 *See infra* Table 5.15.

TABLE 5.15. *Department of State, Visa Bulletin, December 2014*

Family Sponsored	Worldwide	China	India	Mexico	Philippines
F1[a]	June 22, 2007	June 22, 2007	June 22, 2007	Aug. 15, 1994	Dec. 15, 2004
F2A[b]	March 22, 2013	March 22, 2013	March 22, 2013	Jan. 1, 2013	March 22, 2013
F2B[c]	Feb. 22, 2008	Feb. 22, 2008	Feb. 22, 2008	Oct. 1, 1994	Jan. 15, 2004
F3[d]	Dec. 15, 2003	Dec. 15, 2003	Dec. 15, 2003	Nov. 15, 2003	June 22, 1993
F4[e]	Feb. 22, 2002	Feb. 22, 2002	Feb. 22, 2002	March 1, 1997	June 1, 1991

[a] *See* 8 U.S.C. § 1153(a)(1) (2012).
[b] *See id.* § 1153(a)(2)(A).
[c] *See id.* § 1153(a)(2)(B).
[d] *See id.* § 1153(a)(3).
[e] *See id.* § 1153(a)(4).
Source: Bureau of Consular Affs., U.S. Dep't of State, Annual Report of Immigrant Visa Applicants in The Family-Sponsored and Employment-Based Preferences Registered at the National Visa Center as of November 1, 2014, available at http://travel.state.gov/content/dam/visas/Statistics/Immigrant-Statistics/WaitingListItem.pdf.

The National Visa Center issued its most current report detailing the total number of visa applicants currently waiting for their visas to be issued.[170] The numbers are staggering: as of November 1, 2014, there were a total of 4,331,750 visa applicants worldwide whose visa applications have been approved but have yet to receive a visa.[171] Of this group, more than 2 million – 2,455,964 visa applicants – are siblings of U.S. citizens.[172] Recall that there is an annual visa cap of 65,000 for this category, which demonstrates that the demand for such visas far exceeds the number of visas available. The countries with the largest number of applicants from this group are: Mexico (741,233),[173] India (244,813),[174] Vietnam (174,111), and the Philippines (159,538).[175] The next largest group of visa applicants is the third-preference group

[170] Bureau of Consular Affs., U.S. Dep't of State, Annual Report of Immigrant Visa Applicants in the Family-Sponsored and Employment-Based Preferences Registered at the National Visa Center as of November 1, 2014, *available at* http://travel.state.gov/content/dam/visas/Statistics/Immigrant-Statistics/WaitingListItem.pdf [hereinafter Annual Report].
[171] *See id.* at 2.
[172] *See id.* at 7.
[173] *See id.*
[174] *See id.*
[175] *See id.*

(married sons and daughters of U.S. citizens), consisting of 805,627 applicants.[176] This preference group is capped at 23,400.[177] Once again, Mexicans (189,794) and Filipinos (144,590) have the largest number of visa applicants.[178]

Unsurprisingly, when broken down by country, the countries with the highest number of visa applicants are Mexico (1,323,978), the Philippines (428,765), and India (323,089).[179] Recall that there is a per-country limit of 7 percent per year and, as indicated by the number of visa applicants in these countries, the demand for visas from these countries far outnumbers the number of visas available per year. Thus, new applicants go to the back of a decades-long line.

In brief, although Section 5.3 underscored the extent to which the 1965 Immigration Act facilitated both family unity and racial diversity, it is important to qualify the law's achievements by recognizing that, for many families, family unification did not take place immediately. The many years of separation, caused by the structure of the law itself, impose tremendous costs on many families.[180]

5.5 PROPOSED IMMIGRATION REFORMS

Twenty years ago, President Bill Clinton appointed U.S. Representative Barbara Jordan to chair a commission on immigration reform (Jordan Commission).[181] In 1995, the Jordan Commission submitted its report, which includes several recommendations on how to change immigration law.[182] One of its recommendations was the elimination of visa preferences for adult children and siblings of U.S. citizens.[183] Under the immigration law then and now, U.S. citizens may sponsor, without any numerical caps, their immediate relatives, including spouses, children (who are twenty-one years old or younger), and parents.[184] U.S. citizens may also sponsor their sons and daughters who are older than twenty-one years and they may also sponsor their siblings (who themselves may have their own spouses

[176] *See id.* at 6.

[177] 8 U.S.C. § 1153(a)(3) (2012).

[178] *See* ANNUAL REPORT, at 6.

[179] *See id.* at 3.

[180] Daniel Gonzalez, *Millions of Immigrants Waiting for Green Cards*, ARIZ. REPUBLIC, June 23, 2013, http://www.azcentral.com/news/politics/articles/20130614immigration-green-card-waiting-list.html.

[181] *Jordan Will Lead Study on Immigration*, Houston Chronicle, Dec. 15, 1993 (reporting on the presidential appointment of Barbara Jordan to lead a commission that would evaluate and recommend changes to immigration law).

[182] *See* U.S. COMM'N ON IMMIGRATION REFORM, *Executive Summary: Legal Immigration* xiii–xv (1995) (hereinafter JORDAN REPORT) (report by U.S. Commission that was chaired by U.S. Representative Barbara Jordan).

[183] *See id.* at xviii.

[184] *See* 8 U.S.C. § 1151(b)(2)(A)(i) (2012).

and children).[185] The Jordan Commission's proposal to eliminate the latter family categories was thus a purposeful desire to privilege the nuclear family. Doing so, according to the report, would help reduce the number of legal immigrants to the United States by one-third.[186]

Adopting the Jordan Commission's recommendations to limit family-based categories, Texas Republican Representative Lamar Smith introduced H.R. 1915, "Immigration in the National Interest Act." Ultimately, the recommendations were not adopted. Yet, since then, several other Congressional leaders have introduced bills that sought to restrict which family members of noncitizens may immigrate to the United States.[187]

Congressional Proposals

The 113th Congress discussed, without much action, the possibility of comprehensively reforming immigration law.[188] The various proposals considered, among other things, revamping immigration law's family-based program. One of these was H.R. 477, "Nuclear Family Priority Act," which was introduced in 2013 by Georgia Republican Representative Phil Gingrey.[189] Another one was S. 744, which was introduced by a bipartisan group and ultimately passed the Senate.[190] Notably, both bills sought to limit who counts as family for the purposes of immigration law. Importantly, these proposals would have had an adverse impact on Asian Americans and Mexican Americans. Although neither proposal became law, they are worth examining because they may form the basis of legislative recommendations in the future.

H.R. 477, "Nuclear Family Priority Act"

As its title suggests, H.R. 477 aimed to limit family-based immigration law by changing the definition of "immediate relatives" to mean the spouses and children or nuclear family members of U.S. citizens. By redefining "immediate relatives" in this way,

185 *See id.* § 1153(a).

186 *See* JORDAN REPORT, *supra* note 188.

187 *See* Hiroshi Motomura, *The Family and Immigration: A Roadmap for the Ruritarian Lawmaker*, 43 AM. J. COMP. L. 511, 513 (1995) (discussing that in 1995 the Commission on Immigration Reform recommended repealing the preference categories for unmarried sons and daughters, married sons and daughters, and siblings of citizens).

188 *See* David Nakamura & Ed O'Keefe, *Immigration Reform Effectively Dead Until After Obama Leaves Office, Both Sides Say*, WASH. POST, June 26, 2014, available at http://www.washingtonpost.com/politics/immigration-reform-deal-now-unlikely-until-after-obama-leaves-office-both-sides-say/2014/06/26/945d1210-fc96-11e3-b1f4-8e77c632c07b_story.html.

189 *See* H.R. 477, 113th Cong. (2013).

190 Border Security, Economic Opportunity, and Immigration Modernization Act, S. 744, 113th Cong. (as passed by Senate, June 27, 2013).

it purposefully eliminates parents from the category.[191] In so proposing, H.R. 477 intended to go beyond the Jordan Commission's recommendations, which would have allowed U.S. citizens to continue sponsoring their parents.[192] Instead, H.R. 477 created a new nonimmigrant status for parents of U.S. citizens.[193] The initial period of authorized admission for parents of U.S. citizens under this status would be five years, which can be extended as long as the U.S. citizen son or daughter resides in the United States.[194]

Additionally, H.R. 477 also sought to limit the family-preferences program to spouses and children of lawful permanent residents. That is, it intended to eliminate unmarried and married sons and daughters of U.S. citizens and lawful permanent residents and siblings of U.S. citizens, all of whom may be sponsored under the current law. In so recommending, H.R. 477 adopted the Jordan Commission's suggestions of removing these categories from the family-preferences program.[195] The bill's sponsor, Congressman Phil Gingrey, made the purpose of his bill known: "I introduced [H.R. 477] to reduce the number of family-sponsored immigrant entrants."[196]

Indeed, the bill sought to decrease the program not only by limiting it to certain members of the nuclear family but also by reducing the overall worldwide level of family preferences to 88,000 per year.[197] As discussed in Section 5.2, the worldwide allocation of visas for family members is currently set to 480,000.[198] The bill therefore aimed to decrease the present level by more than 80 percent.

H.R. 477 ultimately did not pass Congress. When Representative Gingrey introduced the bill on February 4, 2013, it had sixteen co-sponsors.[199] The bill was referred to the Subcommittee on Immigration and Border Security on February 28, 2013, and did not make it out of the committee. Still, H.R. 477's quest to limit immigration law's family-based and family-preferences program to only nuclear family members gives insight into how some members of Congress desire to narrow who counts as family for the purposes of immigration law.

[191] *See* H.R. 477 § 2.

[192] *See* Jordan Report, *supra* note 188.

[193] *See* H.R. 477 § 6.

[194] *See id.* § 6(b). The U.S. citizen son or daughter must also provide health insurance coverage to the parent during the parent's stay in the United States in order for the parent to be eligible for the nonimmigrant status. *See id.*

[195] *See* Jordan Report, *supra* note 188.

[196] Phil Gingrey, *Immigration*, Congressman Phil Gingrey, M.D., http://gingrey.house.gov/issues/issue/?IssueID=1594 (last visited Dec. 30, 2014).

[197] *Cf.* H.R. 477 § 4.

[198] *See* § 1151(c)(1)(A)(i).

[199] *See H.R. 477 – Nuclear Family Priority Act*, Congress.gov, http://beta.congress.gov/bill/113th-congress/house-bill/477 (last visited June 9, 2014).

S. 744, "Border Security, Economic Opportunity, and Immigration Modernization Act"

The Senate similarly has called for reforming family-based immigration law, although its approach is more nuanced. On June 27, 2013, the U.S. Senate passed the Border Security, Economic Opportunity, and Immigration Modernization Act (S. 744).[200] Proposed by a bipartisan group of senators,[201] S. 744 included a number of provisions that promote family reunification by, among other things, addressing the severe visa backlogs and ensuring that stepchildren and adopted children are treated like biological children. For instance, unlike the Jordan Commission and H.R. 477's approach, S. 744 sought to enlarge the group of family members considered "immediate relatives" by including in the group the spouse or minor child of LPRs.[202] Further, S. 744 aimed to equalize the treatment of stepchildren and biological children by allowing citizens and LPRs to petition for them up from the current age of eighteen years to twenty-one years.[203] Additionally, adopted children – whose adoptions were previously cut off at sixteen years old – may be adopted up until the age of eighteen years.[204]

S. 744 also attempted to provide a more accommodating approach to families. This is perhaps best reflected in the bill's proposal to return to immigration judges the ability to use their discretion to decline to remove a noncitizen if it would cause "substantial hardship" to the noncitizen or lawful permanent resident's spouse, child, or parent.[205] It further intended to confer to the Secretary of the Department of Homeland Security (DHS) discretion when deciding on whether to waive grounds for a noncitizen's inadmissibility.[206] Additionally, S. 744 would direct the Secretary of DHS to consider "family concerns" when making a determination about a noncitizen's repatriation or prosecution for violating immigration law.[207] Notably, S. 744 would give detained noncitizens the ability to have increased interactions with their minor children who will remain in the United States.[208] These proposals

[200] Border Security, Economic Opportunity, and Immigration Modernization Act, S. 744, 113th Cong. (as passed by Senate, June 27, 2013).

[201] *See, e.g.*, Rachel Weiner, *Immigration's Gang of 8: Who Are They?*, WASH. POST, Jan. 28, 2013, http://www.washingtonpost.com/blogs/the-fix/wp/2013/01/28/immigrations-gang-of-8-who-are-they/. In addition to Senator Schumer, the other members are Michael Bennet (D-CO), Richard Durbin (D-IL), Jeff Flake (R-AZ), Lindsey Graham (R-SC), John McCain (R-AZ), Robert Menendez (D-NJ), and Marco Rubio (R-FL). *Id.*

[202] *See* Border Security, Economic Opportunity, and Immigration Modernization Act, S. 744, 113th Cong. § 2305(a) (as passed by Senate, June 27, 2013).

[203] *See id.* § 2311.

[204] *See id.* § 2312.

[205] *See id.* § 2314(b).

[206] *See id.*

[207] *See id.* § 1115(b)(1).

[208] This subtitle of S. 744 is referred to as the Humane Enforcement and Legal Protections for Separated Children Act or the HELP Separated Children Act. *Id.* § 3801; *see generally id.* §§ 3802–07 (giving

illustrated the extent to which S. 744 aimed to provide greater rights to noncitizens with family members.

On the other hand, S. 744 sought to limit family-based immigration. First, S. 744 would have abolished the fourth preference, which is the category for siblings of U.S. citizens.[209] Specifically, S. 744 provided that eighteen months after the enactment of the Act, the fourth preference category would be eliminated.[210]

Second, S. 744 sought to remove married children older than thirty-one years of age from the program. Section 2307 of S. 744 provided:

> (B) the married sons or married daughters of citizens of the United States who are 31 years of age or younger at the time of filing a petition under section 204 shall be allocated visas in a number not to exceed 25 percent of the worldwide level authorized in section 201(c), plus the number of any visas not required for the class specified in subparagraph (A) current fiscal year.[211]

The language of the previous provision underscored Congress's intent to give preferences only to married sons or daughters of citizens who are *younger* than thirty-one years of age. In other words, any sons or daughters of citizens who are thirty-one years old would not be eligible to apply for admission under the family-based immigration system.

S. 744, as previously noted, received bipartisan support and passed the Senate. Yet, the failure of the House of Representatives to pass a bill ultimately meant that the 113th Congress was unable to submit a bill to the president that would have comprehensively reformed immigration law. Such an amendment would have included changing the family-based and family-preferences program in one way or another.

Consequences of Proposals to Reduce or Eliminate Certain Family Categories

Although efforts to pass comprehensive immigration reform were unsuccessful, many today are hopeful that Congress would eventually pass such a law. Discussions of such a bill would almost certainly include discussions of whether to change the current structure of the family-based and family-preferences program. Without doubt, any recommendation that reduces the overall number of visas reserved for family members or eliminates certain categories for family members, including parents, older children, and siblings, as H.R. 477 and S. 744 proposed, would have a

immigrants apprehended for immigration violations the right to regularly visit their minor children and arrange for their care).

[209] *See id.* § 2307(a)(1).

[210] *See id.* § 2307(a)(3).

[211] *See id.* § 2307.

considerably adverse impact on the number of immigrants – and their families – who enter the United States every year from Mexico, China, the Philippines, and India.

For starters, for many immigrants in these countries, the definition of family extends beyond the nuclear family.[212] Legislative efforts to narrow the meaning of the family would thus have a negative cultural impact on U.S. citizens and LPRs who wish to reunite with family members with whom they are close.[213]

Additionally, as explained earlier in the chapter, a significant number – indeed, a majority – of immigrants in the last several decades have hailed from Mexico, China, the Philippines, and India.[214] Millions of these immigrants were parents, unmarried and married sons and daughters, and siblings of U.S. citizens.[215] The elimination of these categories would therefore severely reduce the population of certain Asian groups and Mexican noncitizens from becoming LPRs of this country. Certainly, such reduced numbers may reinstate the pre-1965 Immigration Act's racial and ethnic annual immigration population.

Notably, these family members provide much needed support to their Asian American and Mexican American family members. Immigrant grandparents, for example, provide critical childcare for their grandchildren.[216] Indeed, thousands of grandparents who care for their grandchildren are undocumented and do not benefit from cancellation of removal from the United States under current immigration law.[217] Notably, Latino/a households have experienced an increase in reliance on grandparents as caregivers.[218] Thus, eliminating the ability of U.S. citizens to sponsor their parents would affect the stability of U.S. citizen and LPR families that rely on grandparents for caregiving. Similarly, Asian American families rely on extended family members, including parents, adult children, and siblings of U.S. citizens as well as adult children of LPRs, for childcare support. Such caregiving services enable family members to work outside the home.[219]

212 *See* Karen Narasaki, *Testimony on the Immigration Reform Act of 1995 Before the Subcommittee on Immigration, U.S. Senate Judiciary Committee*, 10 Geo. Immigr. L.J. 77, 83–84 (1996).

213 *See id.*

214 *See* Section 5.3.

215 *See id.*

216 Marcia Zug, *Deporting Grandma: Why Grandparent Deportation May Be the Next Big Immigration Crisis and How to Solve It*, 43 U.C. Davis L. Rev. 93, 205 (2009).

217 *See id.* at 213–14 (discussing cases in which undocumented grandparents did not qualify for cancellation of removal).

218 *See* Roy Grant, *The Special Needs of Children in Kinship Care*, 33 J. Gerontological Soc. Work 17, 18 (2000).

219 *See* Promoting Family Values and Immigration: Hearing on Role of Family-Based Immigration in the U.S. Immigration System Before the H. Judiciary Subcomm. on Immigration, 111th Cong. 7–10 (2007)(Testimony of Bill Ong Hing, Professor of Law and Asian American Studies, U.C. Davis); Asian American Justice Center, *Talking Points On H.R. 492: Nuclear Family Priority Act*, available at http://www.advancingequality.org/news-media/publications/talking-points-hr-692-nuclear-family-priority-act.

Indeed, as advocates have contended, these extended family members "are essential [not only] for the economic and overall well-being of U.S. citizen and legal permanent residents" but also the United States.[220] Many immigrants open their own businesses and are thus self-employed, and the success of their businesses depends on family members' ability to provide caregiving services.[221] These businesses in turn engage in activities that stimulate and support the U.S. economy. In brief, eliminating certain family categories from the family-based immigration law would have an adverse impact on Mexican Americans and Asian Americans as well as the U.S. economy.

5.6 CONCLUSION

The passage of the 1965 Immigration Act revolutionized immigration law and the makeup of the American family. It did so by erasing national origins quotas and promoting race neutrality as a principle for immigration law and policy. Additionally, it installed family ties as the dominant method for gaining lawful permanent immigration to the United States. Both changes to immigration law effected incredible family unification and racial diversity and helped to promote values of nondiscrimination and family unity. From this vantage point, the Immigration Act of 1965 should be celebrated as an important piece of legislation designed to achieve civil rights. To be sure, the modern family-based immigration program is far from perfect and requires rethinking in order to meaningfully achieve the policy goal of family unification. Proposals in Congress to change the current blueprint of immigration law could undermine the civil rights gains in the last fifty years.

[220] *See* Asian American Justice Center, *Talking Points On H.R. 492: Nuclear Family Priority Act*, at 2.

[221] *See* Jimy Sanders & Victor Nee, *Immigrant Self-Employment: The Family As Social Capital and the Value of Human Capital*, 61 American Sociological Review 231 (1996).

6

Workers without Families

The Unintended Consequences

Rhacel Salazar Parreñas and Cerissa Salazar Parreñas

6.1 INTRODUCTION

After twelve years in the United States, Sharon Seneriches,[1] a domestic worker for a wealthy family in New York City, finally returned to the Philippines and reunited with the family she left behind. Lacking proper documents, she had not been able to see her husband or children for more than a decade. Likewise, her children – without proper visa qualifications – could not visit their mother in New York City. The Seneriches family endured this long separation with the hope that eventually they would unify as a family in the United States. This sacrifice was made for the financial prospects available in the United States.

In 2001, after obtaining her green card, Sharon triumphantly returned to the Philippines. Sharon's new legal status allowed some of her dependents to obtain visas required to live permanently with her in the United States.[2] Thus, after a two-month visit to the Philippines, Sharon returned to the United States, accompanied by her twenty-year-old daughter JoAnn, nineteen-year-old son Mike, eighteen-year-old son Peter, and husband Frederico.

However, the migration of Sharon's family did not come with complete joy because one member of the family did not qualify to enter the United States. Her oldest daughter, Ellen, turned twenty-two years old by the time she was considered. No longer considered a "child" under the rubric of the immigration laws, Ellen belonged in a different visa preference category. Ellen qualified for a preference category that was lower than her younger siblings, one granted to unmarried adult

[1] In order to protect the identities of the interviewees, the authors used pseudonyms instead of actual names throughout the article. Moreover, the authors omitted the dates and locations of our interviews, but they are on file with the authors.

[2] *See generally* 8 U.S.C. § 1153 (2000).

Originally published in the *Asian American Law Journal*. Included here with permission.

children of permanent residents of the United States. In this category, she has to wait at least six more years[3] to receive a visa.[4]

Although left behind in the Philippines, Ellen still has the hope of eventually joining her family in the United States. However, in order to immigrate under the family-sponsored preference category, Ellen must put her life on hold. She cannot marry the man she has been dating for the last two years. If Ellen married her partner, her mother, who is a permanent resident, would no longer be able to petition for her entry. Alternatively, however, she could enter the United States legally as a skilled migrant.[5] With this in mind, Ellen has pursued a medical degree. However, she still has years of schooling and training to complete before she can even qualify to apply as a skilled migrant.[6] In the meantime, Ellen could also apply for a tourist visa.[7] This temporary measure would give her the possibility of joining her family for the holidays. Unfortunately, Ellen's recent application to obtain a tourist visa was denied at the U.S. embassy in Manila.[8]

Sadly, Ellen's story is not atypical. While conducting research in the Philippines, Professor Rhacel Parreñas met several young adult interviewees who could not petition for immediate visas to unify with their migrant parents in the United States.[9] We refer to these young adults as the "overlooked second generation."[10] Out of sixteen interviews

3 This is an estimate based on interviews conducted with community members in our field research site in the Philippines.

4 *Cf.* BUREAU OF CONSULAR AFFAIRS, U.S. DEP'T OF STATE, VOL. VIII. PUB. NO. 56, VISA BULLETIN (April 2003), *available at* http://travel.state.gov/visa_ bulletin.html (reflecting the longer waiting period for visas allocated to adult unmarried sons and daughters of permanent residents compared to children of permanent residents).

5 *See* § 1153(b)(2)(B)(ii); *see also* Susan Martin et al., *U.S. Immigration Policy: Admission of High Skilled Workers*, 16 GEO. IMMIGR. L.J. 619 (Spring 2002) (describing the contributions of skilled immigrant labor).

6 *See* § 1153(b)(2)(B)(ii).

7 *See* 8 U.S.C. § 1187(a) (2000); *id.* § 1101(a)(15)(B) (2002) (defining a tourist).

8 Consequently, Ellen must wait six more months before she can reapply for the same visa. In considering her application for a tourist visa, the consulate was concerned that Ellen would stay in the United States indefinitely since her entire family had already immigrated to the United States.

9 For eighteen noncontinuous months between 2000 and 2002, Professor Parreñas conducted fieldwork in the Western Visayas region of the Philippines for her gender-comparative study on the children of migrant workers. She interviewed sixty-nine children whose parents were working outside of the Philippines. In this sample, sixteen children had parents who were migrant workers in the United States. Thus far, only six of those children have qualified to enter the United States. Due to their adult status, the rest of the children did not qualify for immediate visas. The interviews are on file with the authors.

10 Our discussion of the overlooked second generation bears significance to the new direction in immigration studies as we begin to focus on the children left behind in the homeland by their migrant parents. Additionally, there is a growing interest on the lives of the foreign dependents, or the "immigrant second generation." Researchers believe that the immigrant second generation is significant because it helps illustrate the extent of the integration and acceptance of minorities in the U.S. population. *See generally* ETHNICITIES: CHILDREN OF IMMIGRANTS IN AMERICA (Ruben Rumbaut & Alejandro Portes eds., 2001); LEGACIES: THE STORY OF THE IMMIGRANT SECOND

conducted with children of U.S.-based parents, ten subjects fell in this category.[11] In addition, all the parents of these young adults have worked in the United States since their adolescence. On average, these families have been separated for 12.6 years.[12] As we will discuss in further detail, among these subjects were (1) Ellen Seneriches; (2) twenty-five-year-old Jeek Pereno, who has been repeatedly denied a tourist visa to the United States; (3) twenty-one-year-old Norbert Silvedirio, whose parents have worked in New York City for the last thirteen years; (4) twenty-three-year-old Gailanie Tejada, whose parents work as a teacher and a nursing aide at an elderly care facility in the Washington, DC area; and (5) Binky Botavara, who was fourteen years old when her mother left for the United States to work as caregiver for the elderly. After remarrying in the United States, Binky's mother filed for the immigrant visas for Binky and her siblings. Nonetheless, it was too late. As an adult child of a permanent resident, Binky no longer qualified for an immediate visa.[13] As a result, Binky chose to forgo marriage in order to qualify for the highest possible preference category.[14]

What legal entanglements prevent the overlooked second generation from uniting with their migrant families? The case of the overlooked second generation raises the question of the citizenship rights earned by labor migrants and the extension of any such rights to their children. As noted earlier, these young adults face formidable obstacles in joining their migrant parents in the United States. Further, as discussed later in the chapter, the prolonged separation strips away the benefits of childhood that traditional families often take for granted.

The overlooked second generation has fallen through the cracks because of the loopholes and inadequacies embedded in U.S. immigration policies. The predicament of the Seneriches family illustrates the unintended consequences of U.S. immigration laws that are deficient in its measures to reconcile migrant workers with their families. Moreover, our studies show that these deficiencies have a greater impact on countries providing a larger flow of migrant workers. More specifically, families from Mexico and the Philippines – two migrant-heavy countries – are more likely to confront unification difficulties than other migrant ethnic groups.[15] As we will discuss further, this greater

Generation (Alejandro Portes & Ruben Rumbaut eds., 2001); The New Second Generation (Alejandro Portes ed., 1996).

11 Professor Parreñas's study was not exclusive to sons and daughters of U.S.-based migrant workers. Parents of her interviewees also worked as merchant marines or migrant workers in parts of Asia, Europe, the Middle East, and North America. She gained access to these interviewees through a diverse sampling from schools, community organizations, and public spaces in her field research site. Nonetheless, ten of only sixteen interviewed sons and daughters of migrant workers in the United States were part of the overlooked second generation. The interviews are on file with the authors.

12 This calculation is derived from the ten young adults interviewed in the Philippines who are part of the overlooked second generation.

13 *See* 8 U.S.C. § 1151(b) (2000).

14 *See* Bureau of Consular Affairs, *supra* note 7 (noting priority dates for family-based visas).

15 *See* Sarah Vaughan, *Immigrant Visa Waiting List at 3.6 Million*, *in* Center For Immigr. Stud. Bull. No. 28 (1997), *available at* http://www.cis.org/articles/1997. In 1997, the two largest ethnic

likelihood is caused by the backlog generated by nationality limits imposed on immigrants from certain countries, affecting the admittance of relatives left behind.[16]

This chapter brings to light the plight of the overlooked second generation. It analyzes the limited citizenship rights of migrant parents whose labor has been maximized by the U.S. economy[17] while prospects for immediate family unification are ignored by U.S. immigration laws.[18] Furthermore, this essay discusses the hardships of migrant workers and how unintended consequences result in the limited integration of migrant workers and their families.

6.2 THE UNINTENDED CONSEQUENCES OF U.S. IMMIGRATION LAWS

The overlooked second generation represents a gaping hole in U.S. immigration laws. We argue that despite new laws, Asian migrant families (discussed later in the chapter) have been affected more than others by the government's lack of attention to the familial consequences of employing migrant workers.[19] Driven by economic incentives for low-cost labor, U.S. immigration laws serve as a valuable tool to satisfy labor shortages.[20] Nonetheless, given the unintended consequences discussed later, an issue arises as to how foreign families left in the homeland are accounted for by immigration laws. Specifically, how adequately do laws accommodate the foreign dependents of the migrant workers who are sought to satisfy the labor shortages in the United States?

To explain how the overlooked second generation emerged from the immigration policies, we begin by examining the visa preferences established by the 1965 amendments to the Immigration and Naturalization Act (the "1965 Immigration

groups waiting to unify with permanent resident family members in the United States were Mexicans and Filipinos, totaling approximately 1.6 million. A significant number of these individuals are unmarried adult children.

16 *See id.*

17 *See* Enid Trucios-Haynes, *Temporary Workers and Future Immigration Policy Conflicts: Protecting U.S. Workers and Satisfying The Demand for Global Human Capital*, 40 BRANDEIS L.J. 967, 990 (2002) (describing how the United States utilizes immigration laws to satisfy current labor shortages); *see also* KEVIN F. MCCARTHY ET AL., IMMIGRATION IN A CHANGING ECONOMY: CALIFORNIA'S EXPERIENCE–QUESTIONS AND ANSWERS 132 (1997).

18 *See* Carol Sanger, *Immigration Reform and Control of the Undocumented Family*, 2 GEO. IMMIGR. L.J. 295, 302–11 (1987) (discussing the effects of immigration laws on individual workers and their families).

19 The authors' usage of the term "Asians" refers to the Asian ethnic groups discussed in this essay.

20 *See, e.g.*, William R. Tamayo, *When the "Coloreds" Are Neither Black nor Citizens: The United States Civil Rights Movement and Global Migration*, 2 ASIAN L.J. 1, 6 (describing massive deportations of Mexican migrant agricultural workers when labor demands subside); Trucios-Haynes, *supra* note 20, at 990–98 (discussing how Filipina nurses are utilized to satisfy a nationwide shortage of registered nurses).

Act") and the implementation of these preferences. Then, we show how maximizing immigrant labor exponentially increases the population of the overlooked second generation. We show that this is the case even with the establishment of family-sponsored preference categories in the 1965 Immigration Act. Accordingly, we argue that as economic incentives drive immigration laws, labor shortages are resolved at the expense of turning a blind eye to the unintended consequences of prolonged family separation.

Immigrant labor generally benefits the U.S. economy. This has been the case throughout history. In the 1800s, Chinese immigrants alone were reported to have paid approximately $14 million in taxes, duties, and licenses.[21] Today, immigrants continue to influence the U.S. economy. According to the Urban Institute, "immigrants actually contribute a net surplus of $24.7 billion more than they contribute in taxes."[22] This is partially caused by their low use of welfare services.[23] For example, one in-home support services (IHSS) worker saves California taxpayers approximately $30,000 a year because of "[t]he difference between the cost of keeping a patient in a nursing home and the typical salary of $7,000 a year earned by an IHSS worker who works 30 hours a week."[24] Since immigrant workers currently make up 40 percent of the 170,000 IHSS workers in the United States, the inexpensive labor provided by immigrants saves California more than $2 billion per annum in welfare costs.[25] Considering such benefits, it comes as no surprise that U.S. immigration policies allow for the liberal entry of foreign workers.[26] Thus, as the demand for labor increases, so too does the flow of migrant workers to satisfy the shortages.

Nevertheless, declining immigrant visas become prevalent when labor demands are low. This ebb and flow is illustrated by the historical opening and closing of U.S. borders to Chinese immigrants beginning as early as the 1800s.[27] Initially, Chinese workers immigrated to California to work in the gold mines[28] and build the transcontinental railroads.[29] Throughout this time period, Chinese immigrants were depicted as perpetual foreigners who posed a threat to mainstream American

[21] *See* Bill Ong Hing, Making and Remaking Asian America through Immigration Policy, 1850–1990, at 20 (1993).

[22] Grace Chang, Disposable Domestics: Immigrant Women Workers in the Global Economy 32 (2000).

[23] *See id.* at 26–27.

[24] *Id.*

[25] *See id.* at 134.

[26] *See generally* David Reimers, Still the Golden Door: The Third World Comes to America (1985).

[27] *See* Keith Aoki, *No Right to Own?: The Early Twentieth-Century "Alien Land Laws" as a Prelude to Internment*, 40 B.C. L. Rev. 37, 40–45 (1998).

[28] *See id.* at 40–41.

[29] *See id.* at 41–42.

society.[30] While business owners benefited from Chinese labor, they eventually gave in to the massive labor union campaign against foreign workers.[31] As the economic downturn continued in the 1800s, the anti-Chinese movement eventually culminated into the Chinese Exclusion Act of 1882.[32] This illustrates how immigration laws are used pragmatically to address economic incentives.

The economic drive behind immigration laws still remains today, shadowed by the "anti-reproduction" and "pro-production" consequences[33] of existing policies. In recent years, the increase in the use of temporary visas (e.g., H1-B visas) for admitting workers but not their families attests to this pattern of limiting the integration of migrant families in the United States.[34] In the arena of globalization, migrant-intensive nations such as the United States incorporate immigrants under the guise of the "opposite turns of nationalism" – the simultaneous denationalization of economies and renationalization of politics.[35] According to political economist Saskia Sassen, nation-states maximize production in the global economy by opening borders and welcoming the flow of capital, information, and labor; simultaneously, they close borders when it comes to the permanent integration of immigrants.[36] Furthermore, integrating migrant workers while excluding their dependents preserves the wage requirement. The net result is a flexible army of cheap labor for the economy with benefits minimized for foreign workers.

As mentioned earlier in the chapter, to accommodate the production demands of the U.S. economy, temporary visas are granted in increasing numbers to prospective labor migrants willing to fill labor shortages in the United States.[37] In 1998, Congress passed legislation increasing the number of H-1B visas to as many as 142,500 in the following three years.[38] The H1-B visa grants temporary residency to people who can fill particular "specialty occupations," but ties these workers to a particular employer.[39] Essentially a form of bonded labor, H1-B visas circumvent the "free-worker" rights articulated in the Contract Labor Law of 1885,

30 *See id.* at 41.

31 *See id.* at 43.

32 *See id.*

33 The binary discourse of "pro-production" and "anti-reproduction" refers to the methods of the U.S. government in maximizing immigrant labor (pro-production) while creating obstacles to gaining permanent membership (anti-reproduction) in America.

34 *See generally* Mark Krikorian, *Captive Workers: A Disturbing Trend in Immigration Policy*, *in* CENTER FOR IMMIGRATION STUDIES BULLETIN NO. 3 (1998), *available at* http://www.cis.org/articles/1998 (discussing the use of temporary contract workers). *See also* Reimers, *supra* note 29, at 41–51.

35 SASKIA SASSEN, LOSING CONTROL?: SOVEREIGNTY IN AN AGE OF GLOBALIZATION 59–64 (1996).

36 *See id.* at 59.

37 Trucios-Haynes, *supra* note 20, at 990.

38 *See generally* Krikorian, *supra* note 37.

39 *See id.* (noting that high-tech computer programmers and physical therapists are two specialty occupations in demand).

which banned the importation of any form of contract labor to the United States.[40] Without the flexibility in switching employers, these workers cannot bargain for better wage rates or working conditions. Thus, H1-B visas maximize the production capabilities of the migrant workers. Moreover, there is little consideration given to the concerns or ambitions of the workers' families. Specifically, H1-B visas allow the children and spouses of the migrant workers to be considered for entry only under a family-sponsored preference category. This fact, coupled with the meager wages[41] earned by most H1-B visa holders, perpetuates the separation of migrant workers from their families.[42]

Despite the continued use of temporary visas to satisfy labor shortages, humanitarian incentives can be seen in the evolution of immigration laws. Over time, the United States refined its posture toward immigration policies with the 1965 Immigration Act, which completely removed the national-origins quota system created in the 1920s.[43] Instead of broad exclusionary practices, the government introduced a layered preference system giving priority to immediate relatives of U.S. citizens.[44] Immediate relatives were defined as (1) spouses, (2) unmarried minor children, and (3) parents of adult citizens.[45] Nonetheless, this system still limited the immigration of relatives left abroad by hierarchical categories based on relationships with the citizen or permanent resident and the limited number of visas granted each year.[46] The hierarchical preference categories include:

First preference: Adult unmarried sons and daughters of citizens.
Second preference: Spouses and unmarried children of lawful permanent resident aliens.
Third preference: Professionals who possess exceptional ability in the arts or sciences. In order to qualify, proof is required from the Department of Labor to show that the potential immigrant does not displace an available worker.
Fourth preference: Married children of citizens.
Fifth preference: Siblings of adult citizens.
Sixth preference: Workers who can satisfy U.S. labor shortages.

40 *See id.*
41 *See* Paul Ong, *Transforming Race Relations, in* The State of Asian Pacific America 179–80 (LEAP: Asian American Public Policy Institute & UCLA Asian American Studies Center ed., 2000); *see also* Office of Inspector General, U.S. Dep't of Labor, Report No. 06-96-002-03-321, The Dep't of Labor's Foreign Labor Certification Programs: The System Is Broken and Needs to Be Fixed (May 22, 1996) (showing a wide discrepancy between the wages declared by employers in visa applications and the actual wages earned by migrant employees).
42 *See generally* Rhacel Salazar Parreñas, Servants of Globalization: Women, Migration, and Domestic Work (2001).
43 *See* Hing, *supra* note 24, at 19–36.
44 *See id.* at 198.
45 *See id.*
46 *See id.*

Seventh preference: Displaced persons fleeing from a communist country, a Middle Eastern country, and persons uprooted by a national catastrophe.[47] While this preference structure is still in place, individual preferences have changed.[48] In 1980, the seventh preference was eliminated.[49] Moreover, the third and sixth preferences were incorporated into an employment-based scheme in 1990.

The establishment of family-sponsored and employment-based categories for immigrant entry further opened the U.S. borders. Nevertheless, the 1965 Immigration Act provided few obvious opportunities for prospective Asian immigrants. Because the majority of immigrants permitted under the 1965 Immigration Act were intended to be relatives of U.S. citizens and legally permanent migrants from Europe, lawmakers thought this law would lead to the growth of the majority European stock.[50] Thus, it is conceivable that the framers of the 1965 Immigration Act drafted family-sponsored provisions as a way of preserving the status quo of the ethnic makeup in the U.S. population at the time. Regardless, an unforeseen consequence of the 1965 Immigration Act was the rise in Asian immigration, as the framers underestimated the influx of Asian immigrants in response to the legislation. Many assumed that most immigrants would originate from Southern Europe, Greece, Italy, and Portugal.[51]

Stepping back, the 1965 Immigration Act seemingly implemented the humanitarian incentive of family unification. Of the available visas, 75 percent were granted to relatives of U.S. citizens and permanent residents according to the preference categories.[52] Significantly, these preference categories did not include the immediate relatives of U.S. citizens, who were not subject to any nationality limits. However, the beneficiaries of the preference categories were constrained by the annual limit of 20,000 immigrant visas granted for each country outside of the Western Hemisphere, regardless of the country's population.[53] Thus, India was allocated the same amount of visas as Madagascar was.[54] By imposing this nationality limit, lawmakers ensured the diversity of immigrants, but also accounted for the possibility of an overflow of any one particular nationality.

Coupled with the elimination of the national quotas act, the immigrant visas allocated under the 1965 Immigration Act suggested a turn towards migrant unification and a move away from a purely economic perspective. Yet, the

47 *See id.* at 198–99.

48 *See id.* at 199.

49 *See id.*

50 *See* George Borjas, Friends or Strangers: The Impact of Immigrants on the U.S. Economy 29–33 (1990).

51 *See* Hing, *supra* note 24, at 39–42, 79.

52 *See id.* at 40.

53 *See id.*

54 *See id.*

implementation of the nationality limit led to backlogs. More specifically, this limit created a severe backlog of potential migrants from more populous countries who were waiting to be united with their family members in the United States. According to the State Department, this backlog consists of almost four million individuals waiting to unify with their family members in the United States.[55]

Due to the nationality limit, the 1965 Immigration Act unintentionally delays the unification efforts of foreign dependents with their U.S.-based relatives, particularly with foreign families from migrant-heavy countries. Thus, the more migrants the United States allows from migrant-heavy countries, the greater the backlog imposed on the migrants' relatives. Consequently, the backlog for complete family unification is the longest for migrants from the largest migrant source countries of Mexico and the Philippines.[56] The arbitrary nationality limits inadvertently result in the "othering" of relatives abroad waiting to unite with their families.[57]

Alternatively, the 1965 Immigration Act created opportunities for the immigrant elite. The opening of borders on the basis of employment-based and family-sponsored preference categories transformed the face of Asian immigrant communities.[58] For instance, the Filipino community underwent a dramatic change.[59] Instead of merely a ready source of agricultural labor,[60] the Philippines also became a source for doctors, nurses, and other professionals after 1965.[61] As these professionals entered the United States and became naturalized, they took advantage of the family-based preference categories.[62] As a result, by 1989, approximately 8 percent of Filipino immigrants arrived through employment-based categories while 88 percent arrived via family-sponsored categories.[63]

Nonetheless, these figures are misleading. They suggest that migrants, even from migrant-heavy countries, such as the Philippines, have unrestricted access to family unification in the United States. Although many immigrants enter through family-sponsored categories, these numbers do not reflect the waiting periods and backlogs prolonging family separation.[64] Over time, high visa demands from anxious family members abroad develop into severe backlogs as applicants far exceed the number of available visas.[65]

55 *See* Vaughan, *supra* note 18.

56 *See id.*; *see also* Trucios-Haynes, *supra* note 20, at 990.

57 "Othering" refers to the process of alienating a racial group from the social landscape. *See generally* TRINH T. MINH-HA, WOMAN NATIVE OTHER: WRITING POSTCOLONIALITY AND FEMINISM (1987).

58 *See* HING, *supra* note 24, at 88–94.

59 *See id.*

60 *See id.* at 33.

61 *See id.* at 88.

62 *See id.*

63 *See id.* at 89.

64 *See id.* at 115.

65 *See id.*

The evolution of the immigration scheme has not resolved the unintended consequences of backlogs and family separations. Beginning in 1990, the immigration scheme underwent major revisions (the "1990 Immigration Act"). The visa limits per country remained in place.[66] However, family-sponsored and employment-based applicants were separated into two distinct categories.[67] For example, family-sponsored applicants fall under only four preference categories: (1) unmarried children of citizens; (2) spouses and unmarried children of permanent residents; (3) married children of citizens; and (4) siblings of citizens.[68]

Furthermore, the employment-based categories were substantially altered. There are now six different preference categories: (1) workers with extraordinary or outstanding ability; (2) members of a profession with an advanced degree; (3) skilled workers and professionals; (4) special immigrants; (5) employment creation via entrepreneurship; and (6) "K" special immigrants.[69]

Nevertheless, while the immigration scheme underwent change, prolonged family separation created by backlogs remained constant. In 1993, siblings of U.S. citizens from the Philippines waited an average of thirteen years.[70] In 2002, the waiting period for this preference category increased to twenty-one years.[71] For unmarried adult children such as Ellen Seneriches, the waiting period could last as long as nine years.[72] This lengthy waiting period reflects the existing inadequacies in current U.S. immigration laws.

Exacerbating the backlog is the narrow definition Congress affords "immediate family."[73] According to this definition, only spouses, minor unmarried children of citizens, and the parents of citizens are unrestricted by visa limitations.[74] Accordingly, not all family members are so lucky. For example, spouses and minor children of permanent residents are still subject to the visa preference system and, consequently, prolonged separations.[75] According to the State Department, this group constitutes approximately 45 percent of individuals on the waiting list.[76] Moreover, adult children of U.S. citizens and permanent residents have to wait years to receive approval.[77] As a result, migrant workers and their families are held

66 Immigration Act of 1990, Pub. L. No. 101–649, §§ 201(c) and (d), 202(a)(2), 104 Stat. 4978 (1990).

67 *See id.* § 203(a)-(b).

68 *See id.* § 203 (a)(1)-(4). The second preference group lengthens the waiting period for adult sons and daughters of permanent residents. *See id.* § 203 (a)(2)(A)-(B).

69 *See id.* § 203 (b)(1)-(6).

70 Bureau of Consular Affairs, *supra* note 7.

71 *Id.*

72 *Id.*

73 *See* Immigration Act of 1990, Pub. L. No. 101–649, § 201(b)(2)(A)(i), 104 Stat. 4978 (1990).

74 *See* Bureau of Consular Affairs, *supra* note 7.

75 *See* Hing, *supra* note 24, at 198.

76 *See* Vaughan, *supra* note 18.

77 *See* Bureau of Consular Affairs, *supra* note 7.

captive by administrative quagmires. Sharon Seneriches's family is one example of a split household affected by such unintended consequences.

As noted earlier, many minor children also fall through the cracks in qualifying for higher preference categories because the relevant age of the dependent child is determined at the moment of consideration of the petition rather than on the day of filing. Therefore, a child petitioned by her migrant mother at the age of seventeen would be ineligible for an immediate visa if the backlog extended the bureaucratic processing of visa applications past the year of minor eligibility. This loophole affected the ten interviewees in the Philippines.

Furthermore, the backlog caused by deficient U.S. immigration laws calls into question the adequacy of the laws in accounting for migrant workers' families. The operative effects of pro-production and anti-reproduction prolong the separation of families, particularly from migrant-heavy countries. Despite this separation, the U.S. economy continues to benefit from the labor of workers such as Sharon. In the 1980s, the nursing shortage was a crisis.[78] As a response to the demand for nurses, Congress enacted the Immigration Nursing Relief Act of 1989 ("IRNA"), granting permanent residency to foreign nurses working in the United States on temporary visas.[79] At the time, 75 percent of the foreign nurses originated from the Philippines.[80] However, while Congress passed IRNA, it neglected to address the prolonged waiting periods facing family members left behind in the Philippines.

In conclusion, the historical evolution of the immigration laws reveals that immigration policies have been heavily driven by economics and continue to ignore the unintended consequences illustrated by the overlooked second generation. It comes as no surprise that given the state of the current laws, the susceptibility of backlogs, and the neglect to address them, prolonged periods of separation continue to haunt migrant families.

6.3 CASE STUDIES: THE OVERLOOKED SECOND GENERATION

Every year, tens of thousands of Filipinos enter the Unites States as permanent residents. In 2001, the United States admitted 53,154 immigrants from the Philippines. The annual numbers have fluctuated between 30,000 and 65,000 in the last ten years.[81] However, as noted earlier in the chapter, migrants seldom immigrate

78 *See* Trucio-Haynes, *supra* note 20, at 990–98.

79 *See id.* at 991.

80 *See id.*

81 Bureau of Citizenship and Immigration Services, *Immigration and Naturalization Services Fiscal Year 2001 Statistical Year Book*, Table 3: Immigrants Admitted by Region and Country of Birth, Fiscal Years 1989–2001, *available at* http://www.immigration.gov/graphics/index.htm.

as a complete family unit. If they enter under employment-based categories, they often do so without all their family members. In addition, if they immigrate under family-sponsored categories, relatives are often still left behind. The case of the Seneriches family illustrates this point.

The fact that family members are often left behind in the origin country also raises questions about the quality of life for both ends of the migration spectrum. Looking at the "receiving end," numerous studies have shown the emotional difficulties of "transnational mothers" and the added pressures of raising children from a geographic distance.[82] Also, at the "sending end" of the spectrum, we found that growing up without parents poses distinct problems. The children of migrant workers suffer an incalculable loss when a parent disappears overseas; at the same time, they understand that the limited financial options for families in the Philippines initiate this loss. According to Jason Halili, an interviewee among the overlooked second generation: "[T]here are no opportunities for people unless you are filthy rich and your last name is Zobel. So people have no option but to go outside the country if they want to progress.... So it was the hardest route to take, but ... the best route to take." As scholars of Filipino family migration have argued, children struggle with variegated feelings of emotional insecurities including loneliness, unfamiliarity, the loss of quality time spent with the family, and abandonment.[83] Denied the care of their parents, they also feel that they are more likely to suffer from growing up without sufficient guidance and discipline.[84] Extended lengths of separation further aggravate these feelings.

For instance, Ellen Seneriches was only ten years old when her mother left for New York. She describes her loneliness over the physical distance of her mother as one that entailed the constant denial of wanting to "call her, speak to her, cry to her," and the dissatisfaction of having to rely on e-mails as their primary form of communication. Typically, children like Ellen often repress their longings to unite with their mothers. Knowing that their families have few financial options, they are left with no choice but to set aside their emotional shortcomings.

Although separated from her mother for as long as twelve years, Ellen has still managed to benefit from her frequent communication with her mother. In fact, Ellen and her mother exchange e-mails with each other at least two or three times a week. She even credits her mother for her success in school. Before attending medical school, Ellen graduated at the top of her class in both high school and

[82] *See* Pierrette Hondagneu-Sotelo & Ernestine Avila, *"I'm Here but I'm There" The Meanings of Latina Transnational Motherhood*, 11 GENDER & SOC'Y 548, 548–71 (1997). *See generally* PARREÑAS, *supra* note 45, at chs. 4 and 5.

[83] *See* PARREÑAS, *supra* note 45, at 116. *See generally* CECILIA GASTARDO-CONACO, IMPACT OF LABOR MIGRATION ON THE CHILDREN LEFT BEHIND (1996).

[84] *See* PARREÑAS, *supra* note 45, at 131–43.

college. According to Ellen, the key to her success has been the open communication she has maintained with her migrant mother. Moreover, Ellen always turns to her mother for advice about her problems. Significantly, she is more inclined to turn to her mother than seek the advice of her father at home.

Furthermore, children of migrant parents overseas often repress their feelings knowing that their mothers' care and attention have been diverted to other children. Such children are often forced to confront the jealousy of imagining their mothers caring for other children. However, this does not suggest that migrant mothers do not attempt to sustain ties with their children. On the contrary, migrant mothers often attempt to raise their children overseas and their children recognize and appreciate these efforts.[85]

Since the fortune of having a "super-mom" is not typical, it raises the questions of (1) whether children can withstand such geographical strains; (2) how they maintain solid ties with their distant parents; and (3) what circumstances lead some children to feel that such ties have been severed. Generally, frequent communication with migrant parents may ease much of the emotional insecurities arising from "transnational household" arrangements.[86] However, children who lack these ties have greater difficulty adjusting to the separation. Additionally, those who feel that their migrant parents have provided insufficient care are more likely to feel abandoned.

This includes Jeek Pereno. Jeek's life has been defined by sentiments of abandonment. Jeek was eight years old when his parents relocated to New York and left him, along with his three brothers, in the care of their aunt. Eight years later, Jeek's father passed away, and two of his brothers (the oldest and youngest) joined their mother in New York. Visa complications prevented Jeek and his other brother from following – their mother has not once returned to visit them in the Philippines. Jeek solemnly emphasized: "Never. It will cost too much, she said." At twenty-five, he is now a merchandiser for a large department store in the Philippines. His mother has somewhat provided for her children, with her meager wages first as a domestic worker and then as a nurse's aide, sending home $200 a month. However, Jeek is dissatisfied with his mother's financial support, as he wishes for more guidance, concern, and emotional care.

[85] Among a sample of sixty-nine children in the Philippines, we found that many migrant mothers communicated with their children on a regular basis to ensure a proper upbringing. For instance, some children reported that their mothers routinely called to check whether they had eaten breakfast, applied lotion in the morning, and finished their homework. *See also* ARLIE RUSSELL HOCHSCHILD, THE SECOND SHIFT (1989) (discussing the struggles of transnational mothers).

[86] "Transnational households" refer to households with members located in two or more countries. *See* PARREÑAS, *supra* note 45, at 80–85.

Years of separation breed unfamiliarity amongst family members, and Jeek does not have the emotional security of knowing that his mother has genuinely tried to improve their estrangement. For Jeek, perhaps a visit from his mother may provide this security after seventeen years of separation. Regardless, his mother's weekly phone calls do not suffice. Moreover, because he interprets his mother's absence as indifference, he does not feel comfortable communicating with her openly about his unmet needs.

Jeek feels that his mother has not only abandoned him, but failed to leave him with an adequate surrogate since his aunt already had a family and children of her own. Jeek recalls: "While I do know that my aunt loves me and she took care of us to the best of her ability, I am not convinced that it was enough … because we were not disciplined enough. She let us do whatever we wanted to do." He also feels that his education suffered from a lack of discipline. Now, he regrets that he did not concentrate more on his studies. Having only completed a two-year vocational program in electronics, he doubts his competency to pursue a college degree. Today, he feels inadequate, with the limited option of going from one low-paying job to another.

Unfortunately, even while extended kin may provide a sufficient amount of guidance and discipline, one cannot assume that surrogate parents do so willingly. For example, the uncle of Gailanie Tejada, Guillermo Tremaña, saw his surrogate responsibilities as an unwanted burden. He states:

> I never really chose to be anyone's guardian. Just that, you know, this responsibility had to fall on my lap because I was here most of the time. It was like, hey, you know, they are my nieces. I just feel responsible … but it wasn't really my responsibility because I was not their parent.… But being the brother of one of the parents, I felt it was my responsibility because they weren't there. And my mother was too old to deal with them.

In tears, Guillermo suggested that some guardians resent the unwanted responsibility. Moreover, this indifference leaves children susceptible to receiving inadequate care.

The case of Norbert Silvedirio is another example of the unintended consequences of U.S. immigration policies. Norbert is a twenty-one-year-old college drop-out whose mother and father have worked in New York City as domestic workers for more than thirteen years. Like Jeek, Norbert also feels that his schooling suffered from the lack of guidance caused by parental absence. Norbert's interview illustrates this void:

> I remember that I was in Grade 2 [when my parents left for the United States]. I was just left on my own. I was the one who looked after myself. [My older siblings] would just hand me my allowance and it was up to me to budget it … I would go to school everyday, but in high school, I would only go to class once in a while. I was

> always at the billiard hall. (Laughs) I think it would have been better if I grew up with them around. There was no one around to guide me. I just did what I wanted to do. I would go to school if I felt like it. My [older brother] would try to tell me to go to school, but I never really listened to him.

Without the option of following their parents to the United States, children like Norbert, Jeek, and Gailanie must rely on surrogate parents to provide guidance. However, as is the case with Guillermo, one cannot assume that extended kin are always willing to partake in such responsibilities. Alternatively, migrant parents do the best they can as transnational parents, as the monetary support they provide cannot, on its own, compensate for the emotional insecurities they have incurred on their children. Thus, migrant mothers, such as Sharon, must adjust to their roles as transnational mothers to ameliorate the insecurities of their children. These struggles underscore the added challenges for transnational families in their maintenance of strong intergenerational ties. Surely these challenges can be addressed by more adequate and sensitive immigration laws. In the meantime, life goes on for families separated by legislative loopholes.

6.4 CONCLUSION

Looking at the overlooked second generation, we see that loopholes impede the full integration of immigrants into U.S. society. Although immigration laws are premised on employment-based and family-sponsored preference categories, employment-based entry does not categorically result in the entry of the foreign dependents of the worker.[87] Ellen's case illustrates the unintended consequences caused by the government's neglect of backlogs and preoccupation with the growth of the local economy. Although liberals purport to support family unification, evidence shows that many families are still systematically denied reasonable access to any of the welfare benefits their working members have rightfully earned.[88]

As a solution, we propose some revisions in the implementation of the immigration laws concerning the dependents of legally permanent migrant workers. In doing so, we are not loosely advocating for an open-border policy, nor are we questioning the government's decision to restrict the number of immigrants they allow from each country. Instead, we ask for greater consideration of the citizenship rights earned by those who contribute to the economic growth of the United States and the extension of such rights to their relatives left abroad. For instance, immediate relatives of migrant workers, entering under H1-B visas, should be granted temporary working

87 *See* HING, *supra* note 24, at 115.

88 *Cf., e.g.*, Hope Lewis, *Universal Mother: Transnational Migration and the Human Rights of Black Women in the Americas*, 5 J. GENDER RACE & JUST. 197 (2001).

visas. This would reduce the number of migrant families geographically split apart and increase family incomes in order to afford them the financial ability to reside in America.

Furthermore, we also suggest that the government grant visas with priority given to dependent children of permanent migrant workers. The government must realize that backlogs may inadvertently move a dependent to a lower preference category over time. Given their immaturity, this adolescent pool of potential immigrants should be addressed with primary concern in order to unite them with their parents. This can be done without increasing the annual limits imposed by the law if the age determination of family-sponsored migrants is made when the petition is filed rather than when the petition is actually considered. Accordingly, families such as the Seneriches will not be penalized for originating from a migrant-heavy country.

Prior to the 1965 Immigration Act, many Asian immigrants in the United States left behind their spouses and children due to stringent immigration laws.[89] As a result, the number of split households increased exponentially.[90] In these households, relationships were unusually dichotomous, with one spouse laboring in the United States while the other managed domestic affairs in the homeland. After the family-sponsored preferences were established with the 1965 and 1990 Immigration Acts, many assumed that if any split households still existed, they remained by choice.[91] The dynamics of the overlooked second generation flies in the face of this assumption. Deceptively, the 1965 and 1990 Immigration Acts have increased the population of Asian immigrants in the United States, but not without the unintended consequences of workers without families.

89 *See* Hing, *supra* note 24, at 76–78 (discussing the predominant Asian male immigrant community and the ways immigration policies excluded workers' families from unification prior to 1965).

90 Evelyn Nakano Glenn, *Split Household, Small Producer, and Dual Wage Earner: An Analysis of Chinese-American Family Strategies*, 45 J. Marriage & Fam. 35, 35–46 (1983).

91 *See* Aihwa Ong, Flexible Citizenship: The Cultural Logics of Transnationality (1999) (discussing the transnational practices in the Chinese Diaspora).

7

Sexual Deviants Need Not Apply

LGBTQ Oppression in the 1965 Immigration Amendments

Atticus Lee

7.1 INTRODUCTION

> *"Upon consideration, it is ordered that your visa petition ... for classification of Anthony Corbett Sullivan as [your spouse] is ... denied for the following reasons:*
>
> *You have failed to establish that a bona fide marital relationship can exist between two faggots."*
>
> – letter addressed from the Immigration and Naturalization Service (INS), November 24, 1975.[1]

When the U.S. Supreme Court unveiled its long-awaited decision on the constitutionality of the Defense of Marriage Act (hereinafter DOMA), *Hollingsworth v. Perry*, and *US v. Windsor* in 2013, the legal landscape of LGBTQ[2] relationships in America forever shifted.[3] In this triumphant summer, the Supreme Court first declared unconstitutional DOMA's exclusion of LGBT marriages from federal recognition, and second, it upheld a California district court's ruling that a

[1] STEPHEN H. LEGOMSKY, IMMIGRATION AND REFUGEE LAW AND POLICY 139 (2d ed. 1997) (quoting Letter from INS to Anthony Sullivan, Nov. 24, 1975).

[2] A comment on terminology: the term "homosexual" gives offense to many in the lesbian, gay, bisexual, transgender, and queer (hereinafter "LGBTQ") community and is duly criticized for creating a false hetero-homo binary. However, using the contemporary "LGBTQ" or "queer" verbiage also misleadingly transfers modern sensibilities to an earlier, simpler, and more politically incorrect. After ruminating on this struggle of historical acuteness versus modern sensitivities, I have remained with "homosexual" as the terminology used by immigration officials in an attempt to stay authentic to the historical subject era.

[3] 1 U.S.C.A. § 7 (West); United States v. Windsor, 133 S. Ct. 2675, 186 L. Ed. 2d 808 (2013); Hollingsworth v. Perry, 133 S. Ct. 2652, 186 L. Ed. 2d 768 (2013).

Law Clerk to the Honorable Vanessa D. Gilmore, U.S. District Court for the Southern District of Texas; 2010 B.A., Stanford University; 2013 J.D., UC Davis School of Law. For criticism, guidance, and the immense privilege of participating in this project, I am indebted to Rose Cuison-Villazor, Gabriel "Jack" Chin, Sarah Song, and Kevin R. Johnson.

voter-approved ban on same-sex marriage was unconstitutional, thereby affirming the legality of same-sex marriage in California. In one fell swoop, same-sex couples regained the right to marry in California and the federal government began recognizing same-sex marriages for all federal purposes.

As a federal statute, DOMA governed the policies of immigration agencies and forcibly defined marriage as between one woman and one man. Thus, lawfully married same-sex couples were not considered married for U.S. immigration purposes and were denied the same immigration benefits that heterosexual couples received. Under DOMA, gay and lesbian U.S. citizens and permanent residents could not successfully petition for their spouses for naturalization, same-sex spouses could not accompany their Americans spouse under a family or employment-based visa, and LGBTQ noncitizens could not obtain a waiver from removal or relief based on their marriage to a U.S. citizen.

After DOMA's invalidation, binational same-sex couples gained the ability to sponsor foreign-born spouses for U.S. residency and to prevent the forcible separation of their families. Legally married same-sex spouses have begun to receive green cards following the Supreme Court decision, and are now able to sponsor the children of their same-sex spouse for permanent residency – finally furthering the American immigration tenet of family reunification.

Despite this recent progress in the recognition of LGBTQ civil rights, there remain unresolved immigration issues for LGBTQ persons. U.S. immigration law is burdened by a dark, discriminatory history against suspected homosexual immigrants. In particular, this chapter examines the status of homosexuals under the Immigration and Nationality Act (hereinafter INA), from the unspoken social morality condemnations of the 1875, 1917, and 1952 immigration acts, to the federal cases that highlighted Congress's homophobic intolerance during these years, to the Immigration and Nationality Act Amendments of 1965 itself and a political backlash that resulted in a wholesale ban on entry by HIV-positive persons, to the addition of "LGBT/HIV" as an asylum category, to the rise and fall of DOMA and its impact on the plight of LGBTQ people in the United States today.

The 1965 Act is largely credited with revolutionizing federal immigration policy in favor of unprecedented racial inclusion, family reunification, and skill-based contributions to the United States.[4] Prior to the 1965 Act, American immigration policies blatantly discriminated against Asian, African, and eastern and southern European persons.[5] However, what marked a new era of racial inclusivity also

[4] Immigration and Nationality Act Amendments of 1965, Pub. L. No. 89–236, 79 Stat. 911 (1965).

[5] Adam Francoeur, *The Enemy Within: Constructions of U.S. Immigration Law and Policy and the Homoterrorist Threat*, 3 STAN. J. CIV. RTS. & CIV. LIBERTIES 345, 352 (2007).

brought with it the sting of overt discrimination based on perceived sexuality and gender performance.

The otherwise liberal 1965 Act specifically defined homosexuals as "aliens afflicted with … sexual deviation" and prohibited them from receiving visas and gaining admission to the United States.[6] In this language, the INS cemented its long-standing unspoken policy of rejecting homosexual immigrants on the grounds that they were "mentally defective" or had a "constitutional psychopathic inferiority."[7] Ironically, as the budding LGBTQ movement slowly gained public understanding and social momentum in the 1960s,[8] federal immigration policies intentionally discriminated against homosexuals seeking admission to the United States.[9]

This prohibition against homosexuals in immigration remained on the lawbooks until the 1990 Immigration Act, which prohibited anyone who tested HIV-positive from entering the country.[10] This ban ironically resulted in the International Conference on AIDS to be moved from the United States to Italy, because the renowned researchers and public health specialists themselves were prohibited from entering the United States to attend the caucus.[11] Although this HIV prohibition is no longer in effect today, DOMA created additional exclusionary barriers for LGBTQ families and marriages until its repeal and invalidation in 2013.

7.2 BEFORE THE 1965 AMENDMENTS: IMMIGRATION ACT OF 1917 AND 1952 REFORMS

Systematic and institutional discrimination against homosexual immigrants to the United States began at the turn of the twentieth century with the Immigration Act of 1917. This Act, which passed with overwhelming support despite President Woodrow Wilson's veto, established many grounds for exclusion from the United States, such as

[6] Immigration and Nationality Act Amendments of 1965, Pub. L. No. 89–236, 79 Stat. 911 (1965).

[7] *Id.*

[8] For instance, Illinois became the first state to decriminalize homosexuality in 1962; the iconic homophilic Mattachine Society was founded in 1966; historic pro-gay Stonewall riots in New York City occurred three years later.

[9] *This Day in History: June 28 The Stonewall Riot*, HISTORY.COM, http://www.history.com/this-day-in-history/the-stonewall-riot (last visited Feb. 3, 2014); *Timeline: Milestones in the American Gay Rights Movement*, PBS AMERICAN EXPERIENCE, http://www.pbs.org/wgbh/americanexperience/features/timeline/stonewall/ (last visited Feb 3, 2014).

[10] Immigration Act of 1990, Pub. L. No.101–649, 104 Stat. 4978 (1990).

[11] Groups Vow Legal Action if U.S. Bars Homosexuals At Border, CHI. TRIB., June 10, 1990, *at* C22 (reporting controversy over whether INS would enforce the provision to exclude self-announced lesbians and gay men traveling to the United States to attend an international AIDS conference).

"mentally defective" persons or persons suffering from "constitutional psychopathic inferiority."[12]

Explicitly, the 1917 Act excluded:

> [a]ll idiots, imbeciles, feeble-minded persons, epileptics, insane persons; persons who have had one or more attacks of insanity at any time previously; persons of **constitutional psychopathic inferiority**; persons with chronic alcoholism; … persons afflicted with tuberculosis in any form or with a loathsome or dangerous contagious disease; persons not comprehended within any of the foregoing excluded classes who are found to be and are certified by the examining surgeon as being **mentally or physically defective**, such physical defect being of a nature which may affect the ability of such alien to earn a living.[13]

Prevailing pseudoscience at the time held that homosexuality was a psychological ailment, and thus the Immigration and Naturalization Service (hereinafter INS) held that homosexuality was evidence of "constitutional psychopathic inferiority" and grounds for exclusion.[14] Keeping in mind that homosexuality would not become listed as a "sociopathic personality disturbance" until Volume 1 of the Diagnostic and Statistical Manual of Mental Disorders (hereinafter DSM-1) in 1952, it is interesting that the 1917 Act never actually mentions homosexuality.[15] At a time in history when the moral depravity of homosexuality was not even publicly debatable, it is additionally strange that Congress chose to include homosexuality among the medical exclusions rather than the "moral exclusions," such as prostitution.

In the paranoid turbulence of the 1950s, the pervasive "Commie-pinko-fag" archetype was used by the federal government to link its two greatest enemies: homosexuals and communism. At a time when California was sending gay "offenders" to state prison and subjecting them to electroshock therapy and castration, and when the mere concept of civil rights for homosexuals was laughable, immigration laws echoed this social intolerance for anything outside of

[12] Act of February 5, 1917, 39 Stat. 874–89. *See also* Robert Foss, *The Demise of the Homosexual Exclusion: New Possibilities for Gay and Lesbian Immigration*, 29 HARV. C.R.-C.L. L. REV. 439, 446 (1994).

[13] Act of February 5, 1917, 39 Stat. 874–89 (emphasis added). *See also* Sarah Hinger, *Finding the Fundamental: Shaping Identity in Gender and Sexual Orientation Based Asylum Claims*, 19 COLUM. J. GENDER & L. 367, 408 (2010).

[14] Christopher S. Hargis, *Queer Reasoning: Immigration Policy, Baker v. State of Vermont, and the (Non) recognition of Same-Gender Relationships*, 10 LAW & SEXUALITY 211, 217–18 (2001).

[15] Act of February 5, 1917, 39 Stat. 874–89. In 1952, the APA listed homosexuality in the DSM as a sociopathic personality disturbance. *Homosexuality: A Psychoanalytic Study of Male Homosexuals*, a large-scale 1962 study of homosexuality, was used to justify inclusion of the disorder as a supposed pathological hidden fear of the opposite sex caused by traumatic parent-child relationships. This view was widely influential in the medical profession. Hargis, *supra* note 15, at 217.

the hyper-patriotic, defensively normal, and obsessively American mainstream.[16] This national anxiety and hysteria over the sudden suspicions of homosexuals among us in the McCarthy era led to heightened discrimination and diligent persecution of suspected homosexuals at home and at the border. Republican Senate leader Kenneth Wherry said, "You can't hardly separate homosexuals from subversives.... A man of low morality is a menace in the government, and they are all tied up together."[17]

Accordingly, the 1952 INA responded to this national paranoia and excluded "aliens afflicted with psychopathic personality, epilepsy, or a mental defect."[18] The bill's initial draft included the phrase "psychopathic personality" and excluded "aliens ... who are homosexuals or sex perverts."[19] However, this latter provision did not survive negotiations to Congress's ultimate enactment. According to legal scholars, the Public Health Services (PHS) had advised the Senate that the language of "psychopathic personality" and "mental defect" already included homosexuals and sex perverts, and thus including "homosexuals or sex perverts" would be redundant.[20]

The Act's legislative history explicitly relied on PHS's advisory opinion that this verbiage was broad enough to exclude "homosexuals and sex perverts."[21] Categorizing homosexuality as a mental defect reflected the pervasive social milieu, in no small part fueled by the DSM-1's listing of homosexuality as a "sociopathic personality disturbance," that homosexuality was a mental illness.[22] Nevertheless, many scholars and historians maintain that the homophobic exclusions were politically motivated by xenophobia against minority cultures – including sexual minorities. As historian William Eskridge, Jr. eloquently put, "[t]he homosexual as moral pollutant became

16 Foss, *supra* note 13, at 448; Francoeur, *supra* note 6, at 351–353; *see also* GABRIEL ROTELLO, SEXUAL ECOLOGY: AIDS AND THE DESTINY OF GAY MEN 53 (1997) (noting how one's identification as homosexual created a presumption of communist sentiment, and vice versa). The communist-homosexual association continues today, particularly in Catholic natural law and Thomist circles. *See* TPF COMMITTEE OF AMERICAN ISSUES, HIGHER LAW: WHY WE MUST RESIST SAME-SEX "MARRIAGE" AND THE HOMOSEXUAL MOVEMENT 16 (2004) ("[Harry Hay] made friends with movie director George Oppenheimer, who introduced him to the homosexual network in the movie capital. Communism was also making deep inroad into artistic circles.").

17 Immigration and Nationality Act of 1952, 8 U.S.C. §§ 1101–1537.

18 *Id.*; Francoeur, *supra* note 6.

19 Francoeur, *supra* note 6, at 354.

20 Report of the Public Health Service on the Medical Aspect of H.R. 2379, H.R. Rep. No. 1365, 82d Cong., 2d Sess., 46, 47 (1952).

21 *Id.*

22 AMERICAN PSYCHIATRIC ASSOCIATION, DIAGNOSTIC AND STATISTICAL MANUAL: MENTAL DISORDERS 38–39 (1952) (listing homosexuality as a type of "sociopathic personality disturbance"). For a general history of the characterization of homosexuality as a mental illness, *see* RICHARD BAYER, HOMOSEXUALITY AND AMERICAN PSYCHIATRY: THE POLITICS OF DIAGNOSIS (1981).

increasingly threatening as sexual deviants supposedly weakened the nation's moral fiber and sapped societal resources."[23]

Pat McCarran, U.S. Senator from Nevada and notorious anticommunist crusader, pushed through the 1952 INA, remarking that "our present laws are shot through with weaknesses and loopholes, and ... criminals, Communists, and subversives of all descriptions are even now gaining admission into this country like water through a sieve and we cannot under our present laws effectively exclude or deport them."[24]

Indeed, the 1952 amendment required all suspected homosexuals attempting to enter the country to undergo a medical examination by PHS.[25] If PHS diagnosed the individual seeking admission with a psychopathic, personality, or other condition, it issued a "Class A certificate," which "constituted the sole evidence for exclusion or deportation of the foreign national" under 8 U.S.C. 1182(a).[26] Of course, given that homosexuality is not a physically identifiable condition or objectively definable with reliable visual characteristics, PHS officials enjoyed arbitrary and subjective power over the fate of those at the border.[27] In fact, the 1952 Amendments were judicially used to exclude suspected homosexuals despite the fact that the act itself never mentions homosexuality.

The 1952 Act: Homosexuality as "Psychopathic Personality"

Following the 1952 textual replacement of "constitutional psychopathic inferiority" with "afflicted with psychopathic identity" in the INA, courts sought to flesh out the meaning of such a "psychopathic identity" as applied to actual humans. As the following three cases highlight, the DSM-1's inclusion of homosexuality as a mental illness directly facilitated the discriminatory exclusion experienced by homosexual immigrants prior to 1990. Courts frequently looked to the 1952 Act's legislative history in deciphering the term "psychopathic personality," and used the

[23] William Eskridge, Jr., *Law & the Construction of the Closet: American Regulation of Same-Sex Intimacy, 1880–1946*, 82 IOWA L. REV. 1007, 1047 (1997) (discussing the story of Nicholas P., who was deported in 1909 as a "public charge" after admitting to "unnatural intercourse with men" and to having been in the "habit of abusing himself, committing masturbation").

[24] Foss, *supra* note 13; Christopher A. Duenas, *Coming to America: The Immigration Obstacle Facing Binational Same-Sex Couples*, 73 S. CAL. L. REV. 811, 816–17 (2000)

[25] Immigration and Nationality Act of 1952, Pub. L. No. 414–477, § 212(a)(4), 66 Stat. 163, 182 (1952).

[26] Michael Rivers, *The Plight of Bi-National Same-Sex Couples in America*, 29 TOURO L. REV. 903, 908 (2013).

[27] Dennis A. Golden, *The Policy Considerations Surrounding the United States' Immigration Law As Applied to Bi-National Same-Sex Couples: Making the Case for the Uniting American Families Act*, KAN. J.L. & PUB. POL'Y, Spring 2009, at 301, 302; Shannon Minter, *Sodomy and Public Morality Offenses Under U.S. Immigration Law: Penalizing Lesbian and Gay Identity*, 26 CORNELL INT'L L.J. 771, 776–77 (1993).

prevailing medical and social perceptions of the time to identify, condemn, and expel suspected homosexual immigrants from the United States.

US v. Flores-Rodriguez: "A Sex Deviate so Afflicted" (Second Circuit, 1956)

The U.S. Court of Appeals for the Second Circuit was the first federal court to apply the "psychopathic personality" standard in the 1956 *United States v. Flores-Rodriguez*.[28] Roberto Flores-Rodriguez, a Cuban citizen, had been admitted to the U.S. as a twenty-nine-day visitor in 1949, but was arrested fifty-one days after entering the country by the New York Police Department (hereinafter NYPD) for disorderly conduct under New York Penal Law Section 722(8): frequent[ing] or [loiter]ing about any public place soliciting men for the purpose of committing a crime against nature or other lewdness.[29]

At trial, the witnessing NYPD officer testified that "Defendant did loiter for the purpose of inducing others to commit lewd and indecent acts, [and] from about 5 to 5:30 o'clock P.M. did move from one urinal to several others, did manipulate the exposed and naked parts of his person, to wit, his penis, to the view of others, and did motion with his head in the direction of deponent and several others in said toilet."[30] Flores-Rodriguez was tried and found guilty, and permitted to return to Cuba in lieu of serving his thirty-day sentence.[31] Two years later, Flores-Rodriguez applied (and was approved) for permanent residency to the United States at the American Consulate in Havana, Cuba. He did not disclose his prior conviction on his visa application.[32] When Flores-Rodriguez was arrested again in New York for violating the same disorderly conduct ordinance and sentenced to another thirty-day term, the authorities began investigating his immigration application.[33]

Upon discovering Flores-Rodriguez's past arrest and conviction for disorderly conduct, the government deemed him excludable under Section 212(a)(4) of the 1952 INA, which made him deportable under the INA.[34] Eventually Flores-Rodriguez was convicted of perjury for this failure to disclose, and a trial judge sentenced him to six months of imprisonment. The government asserted that Flores-Rodriguez was excludable under the INA as a person of "constitutional psychopathic inferiority," yet offered no evidence whatsoever or any data for purposes of judicial notice and that Congress intended to exclude homosexuals under the phrasing

28 237 F.2d 405 (2d Cir. 1956).

29 *Id.* at 407.

30 *Id.* at 407.

31 *Id.* at 407.

32 *Id.* at 407–08.

33 *Id.* at 407–08.

34 On January 14, 1955, the defendant stated that he was indeed a homosexual, that he had been practicing homosexuality all his life, and had engaged in such acts in the United States. Immigration and Nationality Act, § 212(a)(1–5, 7, 9), 8 U.S.C.A. § 1182(a)(1–5, 7, 9); Penal Law N.Y. § 722, subd. 8.

of "constitutional psychopathic inferiority."[35] Ultimately, the Second Circuit Court held that Flores-Rodriguez's homosexual loitering and solicitation was material to his admissibility, because Congress "designed to exclude homosexuals with exhibitionistic tendencies and other groups with lewd proclivities similarly repugnant to the mores of our society."[36]

Although the government failed to present any evidence of the link between homosexuality and the INA's exclusionary provisions, the Court nevertheless held that "a sex deviate so afflicted with such a defect of mentality as to publicly solicit an unnatural act is very likely to be brought into repeated conflict with our social customs, constituted authority, and social environment. He will find it extremely difficult to adapt himself, and to become a useful member of the American community."[37] Thus, the Court upheld the INS's deportation order, writing that "[i]t cannot be supposed that Congress did not intend to include such undesirables within the excluded classes of immigrants listed in subsections (a), (d) and (e) of Section 156 of Title 8 of U.S.C.A."[38]

Quiroz v. Neelly: Against the Advice of Medical Professionals (Fifth Circuit, 1961)

Following *Flores-Rodriguez*, the appellant in *Quiroz v. Neelly* also challenged homosexual exclusion from entry based on the verbiage of "psychopathic personality."[39] This case involved a Mexican woman who was deported from the United States in January 1960 under § 212(a)(4) of the 1951 INA.[40] Sara Harb Quiroz was a Mexico native and permanent resident of the United States; she was twenty years old and lived in El Paso where she worked as a domestic worker.[41] She was detained when trying to return to the United States after a brief trip to Juarez, Mexico, where her parents and her nine-year-old daughter resided.

Official documentation for Quiroz's detention and questioning no longer exists, but her attorney, Albert Armendariz, believed that Ms. Quiroz was stopped and detained "[b]ased on looks. Based on the way she dressed. The way she acted. The way she talked."[42] Armendariz asserted that Quiroz was detained at the border and

35 *United States v. Flores-Rodriguez*, 237 F.2d at 410.
36 *Id; see also* Immigration and Nationality Act, § 212(a), 8 U.S.C.A. § 1182(a).
37 *United States v. Flores-Rodriguez*, 237 F.2d at 412.
38 *Id.*
39 *Quiroz v. Neelly*, 291 F.2d 906, 907 (5th Cir. 1961).
40 *Id.* at 907.
41 *Id.* at 907.
42 Eithne Luibheid, *"Looking Like a Lesbian": The Organization of Sexual Monitoring at the United States-Mexican Border*, 8 J. HIST. OF SEXUALITY 3, 477–506 (1998). Interestingly, Quiroz's case is the only that has been discovered to involve a female Mexican immigrant deported on the basis of having a "psychopathic personality." Of the twelve published federal cases on the 1952 McCarren-Walter Act homosexual exclusions in the 1950s–60s, only two involved female immigrants.

ordered deported from the United States as being afflicted with homosexuality – a "psychopathic personality." Based on this subjective determination by the border patrol officer, who was not a medical doctor, Quiroz was deported under Section 212(a)(4) of the 1952 INA, and Quiroz challenged this order in the District Court of the Western District of Texas.[43] The Court affirmed the INS's deportation order, and Quiroz appealed to the Fifth Circuit Court of Appeals. Two medical doctors testified on Quiroz's behalf that homosexuals were not necessarily considered psychopathic personalities by the medical profession.[44]

In its review, the Fifth Circuit looked to legislative history to shed light on a standardized and applicable definition of "psychopathic personality." The court cited a report by the Senate Judiciary Committee, which cited the PHS advisory instructing that "the provisions for the exclusion of aliens afflicted with psychopathic personality … which appears in the instant bill is sufficiently broad to provide for the exclusion of homosexuals and sex perverts."[45] The Senate report also instructed that "[t]his change of nomenclature is not to be construed in any way as modifying the intent to exclude all aliens who are sexual deviates."[46]

Thus, the court upheld Quiroz's deportation because Congress intended to include homosexuals in the category of those having a "psychopathic personality."[47] The Fifth Circuit held that "[w]hatever the phrase 'psychopathic personality' may mean to the psychiatrist, to the Congress it was intended to include homosexuals and sex perverts."[48]

In a brave last-ditch effort, Quiroz married a man, Edward Escudero, less than two weeks before the date of her deportation and filed a motion to reopen her case.[49] Quiroz had vehemently denied the lesbian label throughout the proceedings (and argued that the birth of her daughter was evidence that she had had sexual relations with a man in the past), and presented her heterosexual marriage as evidence of her successful rehabilitation into becoming "a normal individual."[50] This claim fit neatly into the prevailing social assumption that one could be "cured" of homosexuality (for instance, by having a lesbian woman find the right man). However, the INS countered that Quiroz's marriage had no effect on her "psychopathic personality"

43 *Id.*

44 *Id.*

45 Laurie Martha Cochran, *The Changing Tide of Immigration Law: Equality for All?*, 26 GA. J. INT'L & COMP. L. 673, 677 (1997).

46 S.Rep. No. 1137, 82d Cong.2d Sess. (1952).

47 *Quiroz v. Neelly*, 291 F.2d 906, 907 (5th Cir. 1961).

48 *Quiroz v. Neelly*, 291 F.2d at 907 (holding that "We find it unnecessary 'to embark' as Judge Frank has said, 'on an amateur's voyage on the fog-enshrouded sea of psychiatry.") (citing *United States v. Flores-Rodriguez*, 237 F.2d 405, 412 (2d Cir. 1956)).

49 Because the circumstances of this marriage will probably never be known, this author resists hypothesizing on whether Quiroz was a lesbian. *See also* Luibheid, *supra* note 43.

50 *Quiroz v. Neelly*, 291 F.2d at 907.

because her deportation was determined by the existence of her condition upon entry in 1960, and not by "circumstances which may have arisen since that time."[51] The Board of Immigration Appeals agreed, and Quiroz was deported.

Fleuti v. Rosenberg: Void for Vagueness (Ninth Circuit, 1963)

Just two years later, the Court of Appeals for the Ninth Circuit ruled against the Quiroz court's application of the INA text to George Fleuti, a fifty-three-year-old Swiss national who was admitted to the United States and gained permanent resident status on October 9, 1952.[52] He remained in the United States continuously until a 1956 day trip to Ensenada, Mexico, "for a few hours."[53]

Three years later, the INS sought to deport Fleuti under 8 U.S.C.A. §1182(a)(4) based on the allegation that he was "afflicted with a psychopathic personality" when he reentered in 1956 after his three-hour international trip.[54] The government's formal charges did not state the medical condition that led to Fleuti's "psychopathic personality" diagnosis, but a PHS medical officer had certified that Fleuti had been "afflicted with the desire for sexual relations with members of [the same] sex for approximately the past twenty-two (22) years," "ha[d] indulged in the practice of sexual relations with members of [the same] sex at periodic intervals, averaging about once a month for the past twenty-two (22) years."[55]

During Fleuti's deportation hearings, Fleuti's psychiatrist testified that while Fleuti had in the past "demonstrated a greater than average capacity for interest in homosexual relations, [Fleuti] was not a sociopath, psychopath, or person of constitutional psychopathic inferiority."[56] The psychiatrist's letters defended that Fleuti "did not frequent homosexual hangouts, manifested no evident interest in youths and no irresponsible trends, and had his primary social contacts with respected members of the community."[57] Fleuti also testified that he had not engaged in homosexual relations prior to his 1956 entry, and that he had his homosexual inclination under control before he entered the country.[58] However, the District Court upheld the deportation.

[51] *Id.*

[52] 302 F.2d 652 (9th Cir. 1962), vacated on other grounds, 374 U.S. 449 (1963).

[53] *Id.* at 451.

[54] *Id.* at 452.

[55] Additionally, Fleuti provided a statement in 1959 that he had had no homosexual interests while in his teens; he was about twenty-four years old when he began having sexual relations with male friends; those relations occurred once a month or less; and in the roughly ten-month period immediately preceding his entry into this country, he had no homosexual relations. Fleuti, 302 F.2d at 654 n.3.

[56] *See* Golden, *supra* note 28.

[57] Peter N. Fowler & Leonard Graff, *Gay Aliens and Immigration: Resolving the Conflict Between Hill and Longstaff*, 10 U. DAYTON L. REV. 89, 628–29 (1985); and Samuel M. Silvers, *The Exclusion and Expulsion of Homosexual Aliens*, 15 COLUM. HUM. RTS. L. REV. 295, 306–08 (1984).

[58] *See* Golden, *supra* note 28.

Fleuti appealed his deportation, and the Ninth Circuit sided with Fleuti, enjoining enforcement of the INA's "psychopathic personality" provision, holding that the law was void for vagueness and violated constitutional due process guarantees.[59] The court wrote that the terminology of "psychopathic personality" and "mental defect" was too vague because these terms did not provide notice that homosexuality would fall under these exclusions. Thus, the law substantially prejudiced Fleuti because the statutory language was too vague to warn Fleuti that his behavior was forbidden and would subject him to deportation.

The U.S. Supreme Court granted certiorari to determine the constitutionality of the 1952 INA as applied to exclude homosexuals, but never reached that issue on the merits. Instead of reviewing the constitutionality of the statute, the Court decided the case in Fleuti's favor under the reentry doctrine. Because Fleuti's 1956 trip to Ensenada had been "innocent, casual, and brief" and had not meaningfully interrupted his permanent residency, the Court held that Fleuti did not in fact reenter the country and was thus not subject to the exclusion.[60] Thus, the Court vacated the Ninth Circuit's judgment and remanded the case for a judgment consistent with the Court's decision that Fleuti was not subject to deportation because he had never really left.[61]

7.3 THE 1965 IMMIGRATION AND NATIONALITY ACT AMENDMENTS

In response to the Supreme Court's decision in *Fleuti*, Congress immediately amended the 1965 INA to add the term "sexual deviation" to Section 212(a)(4).[62] In doing so, Congress explicitly affirmed its earlier intent to exclude homosexuals from entry to the United States.

In 1965, Congress passed revolutionary amendments to its 1952 Immigration Act. As other chapters detail, the 1965 INA abolished the quota system based on national origin and effectively eliminated national origin, race, or ethnic ancestry as bases for immigration to the United States.[63] From a racial standpoint, the effervescent effects of these reforms still reverberate today. These amendments dramatically transformed the racial, ethnic, and geographical makeup of the American melting pot. However, their effect for LGBTQ immigrants stands in sharp contrast and cruel irony in the face of this theme of family unification.

59 *Id.*
60 *Id.*
61 Duenas, *supra* note 25.
62 Immigration and Nationality Act Amendments of 1965, Pub. L. No. 89–236, 79 Stat. 911 (1965).
63 *Id.*

The 1965 amendments were proposed by Emanuel Celler, cosponsored by Philip Hart, and heavily supported by Senator Ted Kennedy. The Act operated on an overall theme of family unification and social togetherness – establishing a preference system for immediate relatives of U.S. citizens and permanent residents, as well as persons with special occupational abilities or training.[64] The new act maintained a numerical restriction, and placed a ceiling on Western Hemisphere immigration for the first time in U.S. history. Senator Ted Kennedy introduced and passionately pushed for the 1965 Hart-Celler Act. The House of Representatives voted 326 to 69 in favor of the act and the Senate passed the bill by a majority vote of 76 to 18.[65] President Lyndon B. Johnson signed the legislation into law on July 1, 1968. This new bill replaced the National Origins Quota System, which had favored European immigrants and bluntly and almost wholly excluded Asian ones. Under the feel-good banner of family reunification, the new legislation allowed U.S. citizens and permanent residents to sponsor their spouses, married and unmarried children, siblings and the spouses and children of siblings, as well as persons "of exceptional ability," laborers, and political refugees.

However, the racially liberal Immigration Reform Act of 1965 specifically addressed "aliens afflicted with … sexual deviation" and prohibited them from entering the United States.[66] Additionally, the statutory language explicitly required the INS to exclude and deport these afflicted aliens, and cemented the INS' long-standing policy of rejecting suspected homosexual immigrants on the grounds that they were "mentally defective" or had a "constitutional psychopathic inferiority."[67]

The 1965 Act had unexpectedly and transcendently demographic, cultural, and political consequences. Later scholars would remark that these reforms were "noble, revolutionary, and one of the most thoughtless of the many acts of the Great Society."[68] Unfortunately, for the homosexual in America, it unfolded into an era of fear, physical and legal insecurity, and forced retreat into the closet.

Boutilier v. INS (U.S. Supreme Court, 1967)

After the passage of the 1965 immigration reforms, the Supreme Court continued to exercise extreme deference to the will of Congress when it came to immigration.[69] In

64 *Id.*

65 Committee Report, H.R. Rep. No. 745, 89th Cong., 1st Sess. 16 (1965), and S. Rep. No. 748, 89th Cong., 1st Sess. 19 (1965)).

66 Immigration and Nationality Act Amendments of 1965, Pub. L. No. 89–236, 79 Stat. 911 (1965).

67 *Id.*

68 William McGowan, *The 1965 Immigration Reforms and the New York Times: Context, Coverage, and Long-Term Consequences*, Center for Immigration Studies, August 2008, http://cis.org/NYT_immigration_coverage.

69 Foss, *supra* note 13, at 455.

1967, the Supreme Court's decision in *Boutilier v. Immigration and Naturalization Service* affirmed Congress's plenary power over immigration and its power to exclude homosexuals from entering the United States.[70]

Clive Michael Boutilier was a twenty-one-year-old native of Nova Scotia, Canada, who was admitted in 1955 as a permanent resident. He joined his mother, stepfather, and three siblings who already resided in New York. He spent the next decade living and working in New York, and applied for citizenship in 1963. During the proceedings, Boutilier disclosed that he had been arrested for sodomy in 1959 with a seventeen-year-old male, but that the charges were dismissed. The INS immediately ordered his deportation as a person afflicted "with a psychopathic personality."[71] Boutilier appealed to the Special Inquiry Officer, and then to the Board of Immigration Appeals (hereinafter BIA), which dismissed his claim without opinion. Boutilier then appealed to the Court of Appeals for the Second Circuit, which also dismissed his claim. Ultimately, the Supreme Court granted certiorari and upheld Boutilier's deportation.

During these proceedings, Boutilier complied with various government requirements and submitted numerous affidavits detailing his sexual history – including answering invasive questions often based on offensive gender and sexual stereotypes. Based on his 1964 affidavit, in which he admitted to having homosexual tendencies, the PHS certified him as "afflicted with a class A condition, namely, psychopathic personality [as a] sexual deviate at the time of his admission."[72] During the hearings, both of Boutilier's psychiatrists conceded that he was gay, but that he did not have a "psychopathic personality."[73] Boutilier challenged the deportation on the grounds that the statute did not explicitly exclude homosexuals and that the law was void for vagueness.

Ultimately, a plurality of six justices upheld Boutilier's deportation, rejecting both defense arguments. The plurality held that the legislative history of the Act evidenced Congress's intent to exclude homosexuals from entry under the "psychopathic personality" category, and thus the statute was not void for vagueness.[74] The majority also held that Congress used the phrase "psychopathic personality" not in the clinical sense, but to exclude all "homosexuals and other sex perverts."[75] The Justices thus found that Boutilier's homosexuality "over a continuous and uninterrupted period prior to and at the time of [his] entry clearly [supported] the ultimate finding [of] deportation."[76] To add insult to injury, the Court's ruling published a harrowingly

[70] 387 U.S. 118, 122 (1967).
[71] *Id.*
[72] Duenas, *supra* note 25, at 819.
[73] *Id.*
[74] *Id.*
[75] *Boutilier v. Immigration and Naturalization Service*, 387 U.S. at 121.
[76] *Id.* at 123.

detailed and degradingly invasive description of Boutilier's sexual history, including his average annual number of homosexual and heterosexual partners and obsessively detailed descriptions of Boutilier's sexual acts and whether he was a "passive" or "active" participant in each of them.[77]

In its analysis, the Court examined the list of medical exclusions in INA Section 212(a)(4) – exclusions that required the government inspector to refer such immigrants to a PHS physician for medical examination.[78] One primary problem with this approach is that there existed no scientific or objective criteria to identify a homosexual, and this thus left the physician with only subjective belief based on speculation, personal feelings, and unfounded stereotypes. If a physician believed the immigrant to be homosexual, then he would issue a Class A certificate of that finding, which proffered conclusive evidence of excludability.[79] In affirming this policy under the 1965 act, the Court affirmed homosexuality as a pathological illness and a medically diagnosable defect of the mind.

Devastated by the Court's decision and the trauma of being forcibly separated from his entire family and life partner of eight years, Boutilier attempted suicide before his deportation.[80] His injuries left him in a month-long medically induced coma and resulted in permanent brain damage and lifelong disabilities. Boutilier died in Canada on April 12, 2003 from heart failure and other complications. Tragically, Boutilier's death was only weeks before Canada legalized same-sex marriage, and eleven weeks before the U.S. Supreme Court invalidated state sodomy laws in *Lawrence v. Texas*, thereby decriminalizing homosexuality in the United States.[81]

It is important to note here that Congress proudly touted the goal of family reunification in creating the 1965 amendments – the same family, Boutilier's family, that the Court tore apart in their non-medically based and arbitrary interpretation of "psychopathic personality." Boutilier's case is but one in a sea of broken lives that illustrate that neither Congress nor the Court was truly concerned with the effect of their actions on nontraditional or nonnuclear families. The plurality decided it was more important, and better, to tear apart a committed family of eight years than to allow a homosexual to enter the country.[82]

77 *See* Hargis, *supra* note 15.

78 *Boutilier v. Immigration and Naturalization Service*, 387 U.S. at n.6 (citing U.S. Public Health Service, Report on Medical Aspects of H.R. 2379, U.S.Code Cong. & Admin. News 1700 (1952).

79 *See* Hargis, *supra* note 15.

80 Mark Stein, *Forgetting and Remembering a Deported Alien*, History News Network, Nov. 3, 2003, http://hnn.us/articles/1769.html.

81 Francoeur, *supra* note 6.

82 In *Adams*, not even a marriage license and a religious wedding ceremony were strong enough evidence for the INS and the courts to conclude that two gay men could form a family. *See* Duenas, *supra* note 25.

7.4 1973: REMOVAL OF HOMOSEXUALITY AS A MENTAL DISORDER FROM THE DSM-II

Perhaps the single-most important twentieth-century event for the LGBTQ community was the removal of homosexuality as a mental disorder from the DSM-II. Beginning in 1973, the American Psychiatric Association (hereinafter APA) and other governing medical organizations have removed homosexuality from classification as a mental illness and sexual disorder – affirming that LGBTQ behaviors are fully within the range of natural human sexuality.[83] This declaration was due in large part to the clinical work of Dr. Evelyn Hooker, whose pioneering 1957 paper titled "The Adjustment of the Male Overt Homosexual" overthrew conventional thought and exposed the false correlation between homosexuality and mental illness.[84] Dr. Hooker's work showed there was no detectable difference between homosexual and heterosexual men in their mental adjustment, personality development, and social behavior.[85]

Relying on the APA's removal of homosexuality as a psychiatric disorder, the U.S. Surgeon General Julius Richmond in 1979 ordered the PHS to no longer issue class A certificates for medical exclusion based on suspected homosexuality.[86] Dr. Richmond instructed that the medical profession does not consider homosexuality to be a mental or medical disorder, and that homosexuality could not be determined through a physical examination. Thus began a legal conundrum for the INS: the 1965 Act required the INS to deport suspected homosexual immigrants after a medical examination and Class A certificate from the PHS, yet the PHS would no longer issue such certificates due to the overall lack of medical evidence. Moreover, the Department of Justice (hereinafter DOJ) maintained that it had a "legal obligation" to continue to exclude homosexuals from entering the United States as Congress had intended. The DOJ argued that the Surgeon General's discretion was trumped by congressional intent to prohibit homosexuals from entering the United States, and thus the INS must continue to exclude suspected homosexual immigrants. In response, the INS developed its own "Guidelines and Procedures for the Inspection of Aliens Who Are Suspected of Being Homosexual" and continued to exclude suspected homosexuals at the border.[87]

The removal of homosexuality from the DSM-II led to some early victories for homosexual immigrants. In 1971, *In re Labady* involved a twenty-four-year-old

[83] Silvers, *supra* note 58.
[84] *Id.*
[85] *Id.*
[86] 56 Interpreter Releases 387 (1989), quoted in Hill v. INS, 714 F.2d 1470, 1473 (9th Cir. 1983).
[87] Hill, 714 F.2d at 1473.

Cuban immigrant who first entered the United States at age fourteen.[88] Manuel Labady admitted his homosexuality to the authorities at the time of entry, but the border official did not certify Labady as a "sexual deviate" or as suffering from "psychopathic personality" under 8 U.S.C. §1182(a)(4). When Labady later applied for citizenship, the INS opposed his petition, claiming that Labady failed to timely establish that he "has been and still is a person of good moral character."

Like in *Boutilier*, the New York district court dwelled at length on the morbid details associated with Labady's homosexual encounters, focusing that on average Labady had engaged in homosexual activities about once a month, never with minors, privately behind locked hotel room doors, and never in a public park, school, theater, subway station, or other public place.[89] The Court also noted that Labady had never been arrested, did not drink or frequent bars, did not use narcotics, and was highly regarded at his place of employment.

Ultimately, Labady gained citizenship despite his admission of homosexuality, because the Court found that "petitioner validly entered the country without deceit."[90] Moreover, the Court held that *Boutilier* was not a controlling decision and that homosexuality per se did not preclude a finding of "good moral character." The Court wrote that "[p]rivate conduct which is not harmful to others, even though it may violate the personal moral code of most of us, does not violate public morality."[91]

Adams v. Howerton *(Ninth Circuit, 1982)*

Despite *In re Labady* and its astounding victory for LGBTQ immigration, appellate courts were not quite prepared to welcome homosexual immigrants of good moral character at the border with open arms. The opening line of this chapter, which quotes a letter written by the INS to the recipient "faggot[s]," presents the case of *Adams v. Howerton.*[92] Richard Adams, a U.S. citizen, and his life partner Anthony Sullivan, an Australian national, lived in Boulder, Colorado. When Sullivan's visitor

88 In re *Labady*, 326 F. Supp. 924, 926 (S.D.N.Y. 1971).

89 *Id.*

90 *Id.*

91 *Id.* More recently, in *Lesbian/Gay Freedom Day Committee, Inc. v. INS*, the court held that the homosexuality exclusion must be interpreted in light of modern medical knowledge. The court distinguished *Boutilier*, interpreting it narrowly to mean that a change in the medical classification of homosexuals would not affect their status as excludables, but that if it were determined that homosexuality is not a medical problem *at all*, then *Boutilier* would not apply. The court reasoned that "Congress could not have intended that an alien who has no medically recognized mental disorder or sexual deviation be excluded under Section 212(a)(4). *See* Golden, *supra* note 28; *Boutilier v. Immigration and Naturalization Service*, 387 U.S. at 121.

92 673 F.2d 1036 (9th Cir. 1982), cert. denied, 458 U.S. 1111 (1982) (refusing to admit the partner of a gay U.S. citizen, even though the court assumed the marriage between the two men was valid under state law).

visa expired, Adams married Sullivan in a religious ceremony in Boulder and the pair received a marriage license. Adams then sponsored Sullivan for permanent residency based on his status as an immediate relative (a spouse) of a U.S. citizen. The INS denied the petition, and the BIA affirmed. Adams and Sullivan challenged the denial based on constitutional and statutory grounds, but the California District Court awarded summary judgment for the INS. Their case eventually reached the Ninth Circuit Court of Appeals, which addressed two issues: (1) whether a "spouse" for immigration purposes must be an opposite-sex person, and (2) whether such a limitation is constitutional.[93]

On the first issue, the court concluded that Congress intended to restrict "spouse" under the INA to only members of heterosexual marriages.[94] This conclusion required a problematic and roundabout analytical leap, since the 1965 INA never defined "spouse." First, the court determined that an eligible spouse under the INA is one who is married to a U.S. citizen, and that a legitimate marriage is one that is valid under both state law and the INA. In these facts, a Colorado county official issued the Adams-Sullivan marriage certificate. However, because Colorado did not definitely permit or prohibit same-sex marriage at the time, the court could not determine whether the Adams-Sullivan marriage was legal under state law.[95] As for the legality of the marriage under the INA, the BIA previously determined that "the validity of a marriage [was] governed by the law of the place of celebration."[96] However, the court instead used the standard from the 1952 INA, and held that "[w]e think it unlikely that Congress intended to give homosexual spouses preferential admission treatment under section 201(b) of the Act when, in the very same amendments adding that section, it mandated their exclusion. Reading these provisions together, we can only conclude that Congress intended that only partners in heterosexual marriages be considered spouses under section 201(b)."[97] Thus, the court held that a "spouse" for immigration purposes must be an opposite-sex person.

Second, on the constitutional challenge, the court declined to apply the Equal Protection Clause in this case because "Congress has almost plenary power to admit or exclude aliens, and the decisions of Congress are subject only to limited judicial review."[98] The court also declined to apply strict scrutiny to Section 201, even though the case clearly implicated the fundamental right to marry as established

93 *Id.*; *see also* Sandra E. Lundy, *"I Do, But I Can't": Immigration Policy and Gay Domestic Relationships*, 5 YALE L. & POL'Y REV. 185 (1986).

94 *Adams v. Howerton*, 673 F.2d at 1040.

95 *Id.*

96 *Id.*

97 *Id.*

98 *Id.*at 1041.

in *Loving v. Virginia*.[99] The court instead used rational basis review to uphold exclusion of same-sex couples because they "never produce offspring, because they are not recognized in most, if in any, of the states, or because they violate traditional and often prevailing societal mores."[100] The Supreme Court declined certiorari. Thus, *Adams v. Howerton* demonstrated the federal courts' staunch unwillingness to reconsider Congress's previous intent in light of new medical knowledge and normalization of homosexuality.

Hill v. INS *(Ninth Circuit, 1983)*; In re Longstaff *(Fifth Circuit, 1983)*

After *Adams v. Howerton*, the battle between the U.S. Surgeon General (supported by the medical community and the PHS) and the U.S. Attorney General (supported by the DOJ) raged on. As a result of the Surgeon General's order to the PHS to stop issuing Category A certificates at the border, the INS faced the uneasy choice to either stop enforcing the medical exclusions or to come up with internal guidelines to continue the exclusions. The INS developed "Guidelines and Procedures for the Inspection of Aliens Who Are Suspected of Being Homosexual," under which border officials were not to question immigrants about their sexual orientation.[101] In these new guidelines, the medical exclusion for homosexuality under the 1965 Act would only trigger upon the entrant's voluntary written admission of homosexuality before an INS official. This in turn proved problematic because the INS was now enforcing a medical exclusion without any involvement of a physician or medical standards. Unsurprisingly, this controversy gave rise to two conflicting circuit opinions in the Fifth and Ninth Circuits.

In 1983, the Ninth Circuit's decision in *Hill v. Immigration and Naturalization Service* invalidated the INS guidelines for the exclusion of suspected homosexuals.[102]

[99] 388 U.S. 1 (1967).

[100] *See* Duenas, *supra* note 25; Rivers, *supra* note 27 (writing that "If the Adams court would have properly analyzed the Act, it would have realized that the exclusion of homosexuals was largely based on the belief that homosexuality was a mental disorder, which was manifested through sexually deviant behavior. In addition, the court would have been cognizant that Congress's intent was to exclude all aliens with mental disorders, not only homosexuals. Should the court have viewed the statute in light of the American Psychiatric Association's determination that homosexuality was not a clinical disorder, the court would have recognized that the congressional intentions of the 1965 Amendment were, in fact, moot.").

[101] In practice, firsthand reports by lesbians and gay men seeking to enter the country suggest that many INS inspectors continued both to interrogate entering aliens about their sexual orientation and to exclude persons appearing to be or suspected of being homosexual. *See* Hargis, *supra* note 15. Jorge L. Carro, *From Constitutional Pyschopathic Inferiority to AIDS: What Is in the Future for Homosexual Aliens?*, 7 YALE L. & POL'Y REV. 201, 212–13 (1989); Golden, *supra* note 28.

[102] 714 F.2d 1470, 1473 (9th Cir. 1983).

In 1980, Carl Hill, a British citizen, arrived at San Francisco International Airport with a tourist visa and disclosed to immigration authorities that he was gay. The INS handed him a form notifying him that he "appeared to be excludable under 28 U.S.C. §1182(a)(4)(1976)" and denied his entry.[103] The judge presiding over Hill's exclusion hearing ruled that Hill could not be excluded without medical certification. The INS appealed to the BIA, which reversed, and the INS once again appealed to the District Court for the Northern District of California. The court granted Hill a writ of habeas corpus and held that he could not be excluded without a medical certificate. When the INS was unable to obtain one (since the PHS no longer issued class A certificates for suspected homosexuality), Hill was released and admitted to the United States as a tourist. The INS then appealed to the Ninth Circuit.

In a unanimous decision, the Ninth Circuit invalidated the INS guidelines and reaffirmed the Section 212(a)(4) requirement that a medical exclusion can take place only after a medical doctor examines the immigrant and issues a Class A certificate.[104] The court cited the clear language of the 1965 Act that exclusion on the basis of "psychopathic personality" or "mental defect" must be based on medical certification. Thus, in a rising tide of medical acceptance of homosexuality as a healthy and normal part of human sexuality, the Surgeon General's recognition that homosexuality was not objectively diagnosable, and the PHS's refusal to issue certificates determining homosexuality, the 1954 homosexual exclusion was sinking fast.

However, the Fifth Circuit Court of Appeals reached the opposite result when presented with similar facts. The case of *In re Matter of Longstaff* involved a UK national who was admitted in 1965 for lawful permanent residence.[105] Fifteen years later, Longstaff owned and operated a clothing store and hair salon in Texas, and applied for naturalization. Longstaff admitted on his application that he was gay. The government denied his petition and ordered his deportation because "at the time of entry [he] was within one or more of the classes of aliens excludable by the law existing at the time of such entry."[106] The case eventually reached the Fifth Circuit Court of Appeals, which ruled in favor of the INS.

[103] *Id.* at 1473.

[104] Francoeur, *supra* note 6. The court, in disposing of *Lesbian/Gay Freedom Day Committee, Inc. v. INS* (consolidated with *Hill*), summed up the new policy in the Ninth Circuit: "Because the PHS refuses to issue medical certificates on the basis of homosexuality *per se* and because we today hold that the INS may not exclude homosexual aliens without such certificates, it is completely speculative that any aliens will be excluded in the future on the basis of their homosexuality *per se*."

[105] 716 F.2d 1439, 1447 (5th Cir. 1983).

[106] *Id.*

In stark contrast to *Hill*, the Fifth Circuit further held that Longstaff was excludable even without a medical certificate from a PHS physician, because a direct admission of homosexuality sufficed to exclude the immigrant under the 1965 Act. The court conceded that a Class A certificate was conclusive proof of the basis for exclusion, but maintained that the certificate was not absolutely indispensable. The court emphasized the plenary power of Congress to exclude aliens even for arbitrary or discriminatory reasons, because immigration issues were only subject to limited judicial review. The Fifth Circuit even cited *Boutilier* and recited that the verbiage of "psychopathic personality" is a legal rather than medical term, and that Congress's legislative intent to exclude homosexuals should govern regardless of medical status.[107]

As the two preceding cases demonstrate, the need for a Supreme Court resolution of the medical certificate requirement issue was quickly mounting. The Ninth Circuit sided with growing medical consensus that an immigration exclusion of homosexuals was based on faulty science and not in the interest of the country, while the Fifth Circuit held that Congressional intent in the INA trumped the existence of any medical opinion or certification.[108] In 1990, the need for a Supreme Court resolution evaporated as Congress passed the 1990 Immigration Act, which removed "sexual deviance" as grounds for exclusion.[109]

7.5 FREE AT LAST: THE 1990 IMMIGRATION AMENDMENTS

After witnessing the chaotically inconsistent application of Section 212(a)(4) by the circuit courts, Congress passed the Immigration Act of 1990 and finally ended the medical exclusions of suspected homosexuals.[110] The 1990 Act rewrote the INA's medical exclusions to eliminate all language involving sexual orientation or sexual deviance, and eliminated "psychopathic personality" and "mental defect" language that had been used for decades to exclude suspected homosexuals.[111] The 1990 Act also authorized the Department of Health and Human Services to come up with exclusion regulations and to ensure that national policy proceeded from sound medical truths and kept pace with new scientific advances. Thus, with the 1990 Act, the United States became the last industrialized nation in the world to lift its

107 *Id.*; Hargis, *supra* note 15.

108 Silvers, *supra* note 58.

109 Lyn G. Shoop, *Health Based Exclusion Grounds in United States Immigration Policy: Homosexuals, HIV Infection and the Medical Examination of Aliens*, 9 J. CONTEMP. HEALTH L. & POL'Y 521, 529–30 (1993).

110 Immigration Act of 1990, Pub. L. No.101–649, 104 Stat. 4978 (1990).

111 *Id.*

ban on homosexual immigrants and visitors. Tragically, the new law came after the United States had denied entry to international luminaries including Yves Montand, Gabriel Garcia Marquez, and Pierre Trudeau.[112]

Seven years after the Ninth Circuit's decision in *Hill*, President George H.W. Bush signed the 1990 Immigration Act as a result of strong support for immigration reforms in favor of family unification. In initially drafting the law, a Senate Commission found that family reunification serves the national interest "not only through the humaneness of the policy itself, but … psychologically and socially, the reunion of family members with their close relatives promotes the health and welfare of the United States."[113] During debates over the bill in 1985, Senator Alan Cranston stated that the 1965 INA was "unwise" and "harshly discriminatory" because it "attempt[ted] to use private sexual orientation as a criterion for judging who does and who does not qualify for admission to the United States."[114] Senator Cranston defended that the new law would "end a form of discrimination which has no valid scientific or medical basis and which violates traditional American respect for the privacy and dignity of an individual."[115]

Interestingly, when this Act repealed the homosexual exclusion, Congress remained silent on its intent to halt decades of discrimination against suspected homosexuals. Just as the homosexual exclusion was never explicitly stated in any of Congress's statutory text, their unceremonious repeal occurred without recognition or fanfare.[116] The new law took effect on June 1, 1991, and since that day, LGBTQ visitors, immigrants, and noncitizens have faced no legal barriers to entry on the basis of sexual orientation or gender performance.[117] However, many years would pass before LGBTQ individuals enjoyed equal treatment with respect to immigration laws, because violations of state morality and anti-sodomy laws could still result in deportation and exclusion.[118]

112 *Groups Vow Legal Action if U.S. Bars Homosexuals At Border*, CHI. TRIB., June 10, 1990, *at* C22 (reporting controversy over whether INS would enforce the provision to exclude self-announced lesbians and gay men traveling to the United States to attend an international AIDS conference).

113 Minter, *supra* note 28; James R. Edwards, Jr., *Homosexuals and Immigration: Development in the United States and Abroad*, CENTER FOR IMMIGRATION STUDIES, May 1999, http://www.cis.org/Immigration%2526Homosexuals-PolicyTowardHomosexuals.

114 Hargis, *supra* note 15.

115 Minter, *supra* note 28.

116 Foss, *supra* note 13.

117 *Id.*

118 Only since 2003, when the Supreme Court struck down laws restricting private, consensual sodomy as violations of the Fourteenth Amendment's Due Process Clause, have individual homosexuals had a reprieve from the United States' discriminatory immigration policies. *See* Lawrence v. Texas, 539 U.S. 558 (2003).

7.6 1996–2013: THE RISE AND FALL OF DOMA

Although the INS no longer openly discriminated against LGBTQ immigrants in written policy, the fight was far from over for binational same-sex couples. Even after the 1990 Act, U.S. citizens still could not sponsor same-sex partners as relatives under the law. Thus, many same-sex couples resorted to sham heterosexual marriages for immigration purposes.

In September 1996, Congress and the Clinton administration passed DOMA, which federally defined "marriage" as a legal union between opposite-sex adults.[119] Section 2 of DOMA allowed states to refuse to recognize same-sex marriages legally performed and officiated in other states.[120] In effect, states could also refuse to provide marital benefits or rights (such as hospital visitation rights) legally ordained in another state. Section 3 of DOMA defined marriage as one man and one woman. On the issue of immigration, DOMA also defined spouse as "a person of the opposite sex who is a husband or a wife."[121] Because immigration remains exclusively Congress's domain, any mention of "spouse" in immigration law would be governed by DOMA, and thus DOMA had devastating effects for binational same-sex couples. Whereas binational heterosexual couples could utilize the family-based paths for naturalization set up in the 1990 Act, same-sex couples had no way to petition their legal spouses for naturalization or permanent residence.[122]

DOMA was fiercely debated for its entire lifespan because it represented a huge shift in the powers of federalism. DOMA was the first instance in U.S. history where the federal government claimed the power to legally define marriage rather than deferring that determination to the individual states. With the exception of the Supreme Court invalidating antimiscegenation statutes in *Loving v. Virginia*, the federal government traditionally left it to the states to define marriage and domestic relations.[123] Indeed, DOMA was Congress's reaction to the Hawaii Supreme Court's decision that applied strict scrutiny analysis in its review of a statewide prohibition of gay marriage.[124] In *Baehr v. Lewin*, the Hawaii Supreme Court held that refusing to grant marriage licenses to same-sex couples was unconstitutional sex-based discrimination.[125]

119 1 U.S.C. § 7 (2006); 28 U.S.C. § 1738C (2006).

120 *Id.*

121 Francoeur, *supra* note 6.

122 *Id.* The impact of denying immigration benefits to binational same-sex couples is great. According to the 2000 U.S. Census, there are about 594,391 same-sex couples within the U.S. About 6% of those couples, or 35,820 couples, are binational same-sex couples. *Id.*, at n.27.

123 Hargis, *supra* note 15.

124 74 Haw. 530, 534 (1993).

125 *Id.*

In February 2011, U.S. Attorney General Eric Holder, Jr. announced in a letter to Congress that President Barack Obama determined that Section 3 of DOMA, "as applied to same-sex couples who are legally married under state law, violates the equal protection component of the Fifth Amendment."[126] This proclamation was the first death rattle and eventually led to DOMA's wholesale invalidation by the Supreme Court in 2013 in its determination of *Hollingsworth v. Perry* and *US v. Windsor*.[127] In reaction to the Attorney General's memorandum, House Speaker John Boehner and the House of Representatives Bipartisan Legal Advisory Group announced that it would be hiring a law firm to defend DOMA's constitutionality even if the DOJ refused. This conflict between the House's position and that of the executive branch left the fate of binational same-sex couples in limbo, until the invalidation of DOMA in the summer of 2013.[128]

After DOMA's invalidation, married LGBTQ people gained the ability to sponsor a noncitizen spouse for permanent residency to prevent the forcible separation of their families. Legally married same-sex spouses and their children are now able to receive green cards and be sponsored for permanent residency. Alas, the constitutionality of same-sex marriage has long been a hot-button issue in American politics and culture, but is certainly not the promised land of the LGBTQ community.[129] Moving forward, we must acknowledge that although this chapter details part of a long-arching journey to marriage and immigration equality, the convenient paradigm that true equality is fully achieved through homosexual inclusion in the institution of marriage is a myth.

[126] Letter from Eric Holder, Att'y Gen., to John A. Boehner, Speaker, U.S. House of Representatives (Feb. 23, 2011), available at http://www.justice.gov/opa/pr/2011/February/11-ag-223.html.

[127] United States v. Windsor, 133 S. Ct. 2675, 186 L. Ed. 2d 808 (2013); Hollingsworth v. Perry, 558 U.S. 183, 130 S. Ct. 705, 175 L. Ed. 2d 657 (2010).

[128] Rivers, *supra* note 27.

[129] A myriad of real, tangible, and socioeconomic injustices persist today to exclude LGBTQ persons from true equality – issues like poverty, homelessness, social stigma through harmful stereotypes, physical violence, disproportionate drug abuse and incarceration, and unique and terrible tribulations facing the transgender community.

PART III

The 1965 Immigration Act and Employment-Based Immigration

8

Coming to America

The Business of Trafficked Workers

Valerie Francisco and Robyn Magalit Rodriguez

8.1 INTRODUCTION

In November 2012, an explosion on an oil platform, not far from New Orleans, Louisiana, claimed the lives of three Filipino migrant workers: Avelino Tajonera, Ellroy Corporal, and Jerome Malagapo. These highly skilled migrant workers were recruited from the Philippines on temporary employment visas by Grand Isle Shipyards (GIS), Inc. and brought to the United States to work as welders, pipe fitters, and scaffolders on the Black Elk Energy–owned platform. The Gulf Coast's labor-intensive oil industry, following the massive British Petroleum oil spill in 2010, was in major need of workers.[1] Filipino migrant workers were among the groups recruited to fill that demand.

Hundreds of GIS Filipino migrant workers arrived in the Gulf Coast and found themselves working under severely exploitative conditions. However, they could not refuse the work because they had a contractual obligation to fulfill (they would later learn that the terms of their contracts were duplicitous) as well as massive debts incurred in the Philippines as a result of various migration-related expenses. These Filipino migrant workers were tethered to their contracts, debts, and dreams only to face abusive situations and, in some instances, the prospect of death.

Moreover, the GIS-recruited Filipino migrants were subject to a complex, transnational set of employment relations. While it was GIS (a U.S.-based staffing agency) that ensured migrants' employment and visas for entry into the United States, D&R Resources, a labor recruitment company based in Louisiana, facilitated their actual placement with Black Elk Energy.[2] After the workers filed suit against GIS and Black Elk, it was later revealed that D&R Resources was a shell company of GIS. The acquisition and recruitment of Filipino migrant workers by GIS was

[1] http://www.maptheimpact.org/state/louisiana/

[2] *See* Sabrina Canfield, *Filipinos Claim Enslavement in Louisiana*, COURTHOUSE NEWS SERV. (Nov. 14, 2011, 8:26 AM), http://www.courthousenews.com/2011/11/14/41400.htm.

a transnational effort that began with DNR Offshore and Crewing Services, yet another recruitment agency but in this case based in the Philippines.[3] Both DNR in the Philippines and D&R in the United States were owned by Danilo Dayao and Randolph Malagapo. They are both connected to GIS. In short, Filipino migrant workers had three different organizations (GIS, DNR Offshore and Crewing Services, and D&R Resources) facilitating and managing their migration to and employment in the United States.

Advocates with the National Alliance for Filipino Concerns conducted a series of fact-finding missions in New Orleans to hear from Filipino migrant workers firsthand. They learned that migrants were subject to abusive and oppressive working conditions. Workers were paid an emaciated wage of $5.50 per hour, despite the fact that GIS had promised them $16.25 for regular time and $24.37 for overtime when they were recruited in the Philippines. Moreover, the migrants' workdays ranged from ten to fourteen hours, sometimes for four months straight. The workers were not paid overtime or provided with breaks. In addition, GIS forced the migrants to pay $1,000 to $3,500 per month to live in a 10-foot by 10-foot room with four to six other workers. GIS also subjected them to curfews and surveillance in their living quarters on the GIS compound. GIS did not allow the workers to live off-site and cut them off from communication with the outside world. GIS even prohibited migrant workers from practicing their religious faith.[4]

Following the 2012 explosion, seventeen of Avelino Tajonera, Ellroy Corporal, and Jerome Malagapo's coworkers, also from the Philippines, initiated a class action lawsuit against GIS and the different Philippine and U.S.-based labor recruitment agencies involved in facilitating their migration to the United States to work for Black Elk, citing violations of the Fair Labor Standards Act of the United States. The lawsuit also claimed that the workers had been illegally trafficked from the Philippines. Among the issues contested was exactly which entity qualified as an employer. Different entities involved in the migration process filed motions to dismiss the workers' class action suit on the basis that there was no firm basis to establish that they were in fact employers.

What the GIS case reveals is the increasingly complex immigration process and employment relations that characterize more recent forms of migration from the Philippines to the United States. Indeed, the case sheds light on the changing dynamics of the U.S. guest worker program, the complexities of which have not garnered sufficient attention in the immigration scholarship.

[3] https://www.facebook.com/pages/DNR-Offshore-and-Crewing-Services-Inc/137172133140077?ref=stream

[4] This information was gleaned from email correspondence through the NAFCON listserv in 2012. Both authors are members of the listserv.

The Immigration Act of 1965, while perhaps notable for its elimination of race-based exclusions, which characterized pre-1965 immigration laws, as well as for its family reunification provisions, also contained provisions for the entry of temporary migrant workers. Perhaps the most utilized of these temporary employment visas is the H visa. Indeed, H visas have actually outnumbered employment-based immigrant visas since the Immigration Act of 1965, and subsequent amendments, were introduced. More people are entering the United States as temporary workers than as immigrant (long-term permanent resident) workers. In 2012, for example, the number of temporary employment H visas was almost double the number of immigrant visas. Asia is the region that sends the most H visas to the United States. In 2012, 175,003 Asians arrived in the United States as temporary workers.[5]

H-1 visas are set aside for professional workers while H-2 visas are for unskilled laborers. The most common of the H-1 visas is the H-1B, which is valid for a three-year period and renewable up to a six-year maximum. While a majority of H-1B visas go toward computer-related jobs, an increasing number are going to educators and health care workers. According to a report produced by the Department for Professional Employees, AFL-CIO, educators were the third-largest occupational group for H-1B visa recipients in 2009.[6] Indeed, an earlier report by the American Federation for Teachers found that between 2002 and 2007, the importation of educators through the H-1B visa program increased by 25 percent.[7] To qualify for the H-1B visa, a migrant must have the equivalent of a four-year college/university degree and relevant employment experience. Additionally, an H-1B applicant must have a job offer from an employer who also commits to file the H-1B visa on the migrants' behalf. Upon termination of employment, the visa is no longer valid; one cannot transfer one's H-1B visa to a new employer. Though less common than H-1 visas, H-2 visas for lesser-skilled workers are also offered. The H-2A is for agricultural workers and the H-2B is for nonagricultural workers. H-2B workers may stay in the United States for the duration of the approved petition and only up to a maximum of three years. Moreover, H-2B workers are authorized from only a specific number of countries.[8]

5 *See Characteristics of H1B Specialty Occupation Workers*, U.S. CITIZENSHIP & IMMIGRATION SERV. (June 26, 2013), http://www.uscis.gov/sites/default/files/USCIS/Resources/Reports%20and%20Studies/H-1B/h1b-fy-12-characteristics.pdf.

6 *See Gaming the System: Guest Worker Visa Programs and Professional and Technical Workers in the U.S.*, DEPARTMENT FOR PROFESSIONAL EMPLOYEES, AFL-CIO. (2009), http://dpeaflcio.org/pdf/DPE_Gaming_the_System_Report.pdf.

7 *See Importing Educators: Causes and Consequences of International Teacher Recruitment*, AMERICAN FEDERATION OF TEACHERS, 2009, https://www.aft.org/pdfs/international/importingeducators0609.pdf.

8 *See H-2B Temporary Non-Agricultural Workers*, U.S. CITIZENSHIP & IMMIGRATION SERV. (Jan. 17, 2014), http://www.uscis.gov/working-united-states/temporary-workers/h-2b-non-agricultural-workers/h-2b-temporary-non-agricultural-workers.

Notably, H-1 visa holders may be eligible to adjust their status to that of lawful permanent residents (green card).[9] Since 9/11, however, the ability of eligible temporary workers to convert their short-term visas to green cards has become increasingly more difficult. This puts them in a precarious situation; it is in this sense that they are, in effect, "probationary" Americans.[10] Temporary migrants may find themselves in legal limbo as they await the approval of their permanent residency (and indeed, may find themselves technically "out of status" or "illegal" for an indeterminate amount of time if their temporary visas expire before they receive green cards). Meanwhile, the pressures to maintain one's legality under conditions of stepped-up enforcement may make temporary migrants especially vulnerable to abuse by their employers who hold the power to keep them in legal status (even if only temporarily) and may even hold the key to long-term residency.

Legal status, whether it is temporary or long term, becomes a modality of labor control. The "carrot" that keeps migrants compliant in their places of employment is the promise of permanent residence in the United States for those who are eligible, or simply legal status for those who are not. Meanwhile, the "stick" is the prospect of losing the highly prized opportunity of work in the United States legally, albeit for a temporary period of time.[11]

Temporary migrant workers are increasingly being recruited and employed through a transnational network of labor recruitment and staffing firms. With labor market flexibilization occurring at a fast pace globally, demands for "flexible" (often defined as short-term, contractualized) workers have soared, and staffing firms have risen up to meet that demand. A crucial point made by Peck Theodore and Ward in their 2005 article, is that

> [s]taffing firms are not simply supplying services; in their role as private labour market intermediaries they are a major new institutional presence in liberalizing economies. They facilitate new kinds of intermediated employment practices and forms of labour contingency that otherwise would be logistically and socially infeasible (Peck and Theodore 1998); they shield employers from benefit liabilities and break apart the implicit contract of continuing employment (Vosko 2000); and in the process they help to shape new labour market practices and norms.[12]

The GIS case illustrates the ways that staffing firms play a role in shaping and mediating employment relations. As the Department of Professional Employees,

[9] *See* 8 U.S.C. § 1255 (2012).

[10] *See* Edward J.W. Park & John S.W. Park, *Probationary Americans: Contemporary Immigration Policies and the Shaping of Asian American Communities*, 2006).

[11] *See Gaming the System*.

[12] See Jamie Peck, et. al., Constructing Markets for Temporary Labour: Employment Liberalization and the Internationalization of the Staffing Industry, 5 GLOBAL NETWORKS 3, 4 (2005).

AFL-CIO states, "using a third party recruitment firm or 'body shop' as the employer of record decreases a domestic employer's risk of violating guest worker rights."[13]

Filipino migrants are an especially good case study for examining the U.S. guest worker program. Many Filipinos enter the United States through temporary employment H visas. Indeed, the Philippines was among the top five countries supplying temporary workers to the United States through the H-1B visa program as of the 2010 census and is one of the top ten recipients of nonimmigrant visas in the world.[14] A case study of Filipino migrant workers demonstrates that the U.S. guest worker program ultimately relies on multiple sets of actors transnationally.

As the GIS case illustrates, labor recruitment and staffing firms clearly play an important role in facilitating the migration process. They procure workers from the Philippines for U.S. employers, including getting them through U.S. immigration authorities. Yet what makes the migration industry proliferate in the Philippines and what ultimately enables Filipino workers to enter the United States as temporary workers is the Philippine state as a "labor broker."

According to Rodriguez, the Philippine state has a highly developed transnational bureaucratic apparatus through which it mobilizes and deploys workers overseas. Indeed, the migration industry depends on this apparatus for its very existence. The global labor markets to which private recruitment agencies send workers are countries with which various Philippine government agencies such as the Philippine Overseas Employment Administration and the International Labor Affairs Service engage in "labor diplomacy," both formal and informal agreements with labor-importing government's labor and immigration agencies that ensure the transfer of Filipino workers to fill specific employment needs.[15] As a "labor brokerage" state, the Philippines is crucial in producing flexible labor for the U.S. (and a global) labor market. However, labor brokerage is also highly profitable for the Philippine state. On one hand, the Philippines profits from its migrant citizens through more than $24 billion in annual remittance that fuels the national economy. On the other hand, it profits from fees secured from different migration industry actors as well as from mandatory pre-migration fees charged to migrants (and often collected by recruitment agencies) for seminars, forms, applications, and the like.[16]

[13] See Department of Professional Employees, AFL-CIO, 11 (2009).

[14] *See Nonimmigrant Visas Issued by Nationality – Fiscal Year 2012*, U.S. DEP'T OF STATE, http://travel.state.gov/content/dam/visas/Statistics/Graphs/FY2012/NIVIssuancesbyNationality.pdf (last visited July 22, 2014).

[15] *See* RODRIGUEZ, ROBYN MAGALIT, MIGRANTS FOR EXPORT: HOW THE PHILIPPINE STATE BROKERS LABOR TO THE WORLD (2010).

[16] *See id.*; *see also* Anna Romina Guevarra, MARKETING DREAMS, MANUFACTURING HEROES: THE TRANSNATIONAL LABOR BROKERING OF FILIPINO WORKERS (2009).

This chapter attempts to shed light on an often under-researched type of Asian migration since the passage of the 1965 Immigration Act. It illustrates the "illegal" aspects that characterize "legal" Asian migration through the U.S. guest worker program. We find that "legal" migration, as facilitated by the growing transnational migration industry and enabled by the Philippine labor brokerage state, becomes a thinly veneered form of labor trafficking. For example, in the GIS case, the Philippine-based recruiter DNR Offshore and Crewing Services drew up two different contracts with different wage rates when they recruited Filipino migrant workers in the Philippines.[17] One contract guaranteed a specific wage and the other guaranteed a substantially lower wage rate. The prospective migrants were practically coerced into signing both contracts if they hoped to leave the Philippines for highly coveted jobs in the United States. U.S. employment was contingent on workers signing both contracts. The contract with a higher wage was used to comply with the labor standards defined by the U.S government and was submitted to the U.S. embassy in Manila for H visa approval. The contract with the lower wage rate was filed in company records and was used as the legally binding document to which Filipino migrant workers were to conform upon their commencement of work in Louisiana. This situation is what migrant activists in the transnational alliance of Filipino migrant workers, Migrante International, call "contract substitution."[18] It is one mechanism, among many others, by which Filipino workers can be egregiously and illegally exploited even as they enter the United States legally.

We also find that many Filipino migrants, similar to the GIS workers, feel as if they have no option but to accept highly abusive working conditions because of the debts they have incurred to migrate. Indeed, there are numerous sets of agents that facilitate migration including the labor-sending state (the Philippines), the labor-receiving state (the United States), and labor recruiters (based in both the United States and the Philippines). Each set of agents generally requires workers to pay fees associated with documentary processing. Labor recruiters may "front" the money required for documentary processing and travel, or migrant workers may turn to lending companies for loans. Migrants are hence constrained by obligations (in some cases outright debt bondage), which shapes not only employment relations but impacts migrants' legal status. Not only do migrants endure difficult working conditions but they also may be forced to overstay the terms of their visas and become "illegal" in order to earn the wages necessary to pay off their debts.

In this chapter, we aim to look closely at the ways in which even legal migrants are dispossessed of labor rights and their legal statuses through contract substitution and

[17] *See* Mark Schleifstein, *Filipino Ex-employees Say Grand Isle Shipyard Pressed them into 'Involuntary Servitude'*, The Times Picayune, Nov. 19, 2012, http://www.nola.com/crime/index.ssf/2012/11/grand_isle_shipyard_charged_wi.html.

[18] *See* Migrante International, http://migranteinternational.org (last visited August 14, 2014).

debt bondage. We highlight migrant workers' stories garnered through qualitative research and campaigns advocating for migrant workers' rights. We highlight the new transnational complexities of U.S. immigration discussing the multiple actors that structure not only the immigration process but also the employment relations. To understand contemporary U.S. immigration by focusing solely on U.S. immigration policy is no longer sufficient for understanding global migration. We thereby contribute to new approaches in sociology and critical geography, which focus on sending states as well as collaborations between entrepreneurs, services, businesses, and sending states in shaping the social process of global migration.[19]

8.2 METHODS

For this chapter, we will be drawing from multiple sources of data. We will examine cases involving Filipino temporary workers as reported through the U.S. Department of Labor, migrant advocacy groups, and newspapers, both ethnic and mainstream. We pay close attention to cases of labor trafficking and migrant worker campaigns led by the National Alliance for Filipino Concerns (NAFCON). NAFCON is comprised of Filipino organizations across the United States including faith-based groups, youth and student organizations, community-based organizations, service providers, women's organizations, cultural groups, workers associations, health practitioners, academics, and human rights advocates.[20] NAFCON's mission is to advocate for the rights and welfare of Filipino migrants in the United States. They do so by responding to issues arising in migrant communities in the areas where member organizations are located like San Francisco/Bay Area, New York City, Los Angeles, and Chicago. As scholars and activists, we have been active in supporting recent NAFCON campaigns on labor trafficking. Indeed, we will draw from participatory research project endorsed by NAFCON called the Caregiver Research Project (i.e., CARE Project). Since 2011, both authors worked collaboratively with community organizers and migrant workers in the San Francisco/Bay Area to conduct participatory research with Filipino migrants working as caregivers and domestic workers. The research process was migrant-centered. The authors trained the Filipino migrants in research methods, but the migrants played a central role in the interview design, data collection, and analysis. From this project, the authors draw from the fifty interviews collected between December 2011 and November 2012.

[19] Ruben Hernandez-Leon, "The Migration Industry in the Mexico-U.S. Migratory System" *in* California Center for Population Research, University of California at Los Angeles (2005.), available in http://www.escholarship.org/uc/item/3hg44330; Thomas Gammeltoft-Hansen and Ninna Nyberg Srensen, *The Migration Industry and the Commercialization of International Migration* (2013).

[20] *See* NAT'L ALLIANCE FOR FILIPINO CONCERNS, http://nafconusa.org (last visited July 22, 2014).

8.3 THE ILLEGAL ASPECTS OF LEGAL MIGRATION

NAFCON has reported numerous cases of abuse, exploitation, and labor trafficking through H visas. One notable 2007 case was that of twenty-seven Filipino nurses working in a nursing home in New York. The nurses were brought to the United States on H-1B visas, and they experienced exploitative working as well as abusive living conditions.[21] The nurses resigned. They later found themselves targeted for prosecution by Thomas J. Spota, District Attorney of the Supreme Court, Suffolk County. The nurses were charged with conspiracy and endangering the welfare of a child and of a physically disabled person. The New York Supreme Court ultimately prohibited Spota with proceeding.[22] Indeed, the U.S. Department of Labor reported a similar case of exploitation where forty physical and occupational therapists hired through the H-1B visa program were owed back wages.[23]

The American Federation of Teachers documents a growing trend in the import of foreign teachers, including teachers from the Philippines, through the H-1B program.[24] These teachers are typically recruited to meet hard-to-fill jobs in urban centers as well as in rural areas. In 2010, the American Federation of Teachers, along with the Southern Poverty Law Center and the law firm of Covington & Burling LLP, brought a suit on behalf of Filipino teachers who had been recruited to fill positions in post-Katrina Louisiana. The petitioners accused the teachers' recruitment agency of illegally luring them to the United States and subjecting them to exploitative employment contracts. A federal court found in favor of the 350 teachers. It then ordered the teachers' recruitment firm and its owner to pay $4.5 million to the teachers.[25]

Another visa category through which migrants from the Philippines are able to secure employment in the United States is the H-2B. The H-2B brings in seasonal

[21] *See* Momo Chang, *Substandard Care*, National Nurse (October 2011), http://www.nationalnursesunited.org.

[22] In the Matter of Felix Vinluan et al., Petitioners, v. Robert W. Doyle, Justice of the Supreme Court, Suffolk County, et al., Respondents. 2008–02568 Supreme Court of New York, Appellate Division, Second Department 60 A.D.3d 237; 873 N.Y.S.2d 72; 2009 N.Y. App. Div. Lexis 199; 2009 NY Slip Op 219 January 13, 2009, Decided.

[23] Department of Labor. Wage and Hour Division. *US Labor Department Obtains More than $134,000 in Back Wages for 40 Therapists Employed by Orlando, Fla., Company under H-1B Visa Program Health Care Workers in 15 States Affected. Wage and Hour Division.* Department of Labor, 24 Oct. 2011. Web. 1 July 2012, http://www.dol.gov/whd.

[24] *See* Press Release, Recruiting Firm That Brought Filipino Teachers to Louisiana Ordered to Pay $4.5 Million in Damages for Exploitive Practices, Am. Fed'n of Teachers (Dec. 18, 2012), http://www.aft.org/newspubs/press/2012/121812.cfm.

[25] *See id.*; *Firm Must Pay $4.5 Million to Exploited Teachers in Precedent-Setting SPLC Case*, S. Poverty Law Ctr. (Dec. 18, 2012), http://www.splcenter.org/get-informed/news/firm-must-pay-45-million-to-exploited-teachers-in-precedent-setting-splc-case.

nonagricultural workers to the United States on a temporary basis. The H-1B is also a temporary employment visa, but it offers migrants the possibility of legal permanent residence if their employers petition on their behalf. The H-2B program does not. As with the H-1B visa, H-2B visa holders have also been subject to abuse as we find in our interviews with Filipino migrants through the CARE Project. Legal status, these cases reveal, does not protect one from what are practically "illegal" forms of exploitative employment.

We found that a participant in the CARE Project named Eric was recruited in the Philippines and came to the United States under an H-2B visa to work as a welder in Alabama. Eric recalled his migration to the United States:

INTERVIEWER: What was the reasons [sic] why you left the Philippines?

ERIC: It's, uh, a little bit difficult because, uh, the, I have the obligation to my family since I'm the eldest. You know, as what I told you, the difficulties, the hardship, coming to the U.S. can help me to earn good money. Before, I was only a factory worker at Unilever, Unilever Company. So I came to the U.S. to get better pay.

INTERVIEWER: Um, when, when did you come to the United States?

ERIC: Um, last, 2007. August 2007. I came first in the Alabama, the state, state of Alabama because our, our working place is in Alabama. That's where our agency delivered us.

INTERVIEWER: What did you do in Alabama?

ERIC: Welding, but because our visa expires in 15 days and the company asked us to pay $4,000 to renew our visa and we have not started our job, I could not pay. Even if they promised us in the Philippines for a renewal, they did not help us if we did not pay.

In this instance, Eric's story demonstrates the ability of migrants to avail of legal avenues to enter the United States with the intentions of working under a contract and viable visa. However, the costly fees of renewing his H-2B visa without the opportunity to work for a substantial amount of time and save money pushed him out of his prior documented status. The cohort of migrant welders with which Eric came to the United States with were under the impression that the company that employed them would assist in renewing their visas. When that assistance was not made available and further, the opportunity to work to pay fees was eclipsed, Eric's options to stay in the country narrowed. After arriving in the United States with the promise of earning better wages for his family, Eric did not want to shortchange his opportunity to pay debts, support his family, and earn dollars. Returning to the Philippines was to be his last option. Eric continued:

INTERVIEWER: So how did you stay in the U.S.?

ERIC: So in 2009, I came here in San Francisco, to do caregiving uh, but before I went to, Miami to look for work and I work in a hotel as a housekeeping. You know, every day we work, every day, with little pay like that.

Eric finds himself as an undocumented worker in different service industries in the United States because although he had been brought here through legal means, no one but Eric had wanted to be responsible for his legal status in the United States. Although his undocumented status had been a result of his recruitment agency misinforming him in the Philippines and the failure of his U.S.-based employer to provide ample time to renew his visa, this complex manipulation of legal avenues is invisible. Rather, Eric, as an undocumented worker is the overly visible representation of the migration industry.

NAFCON found that fifteen workers (the "Florida 15") were recruited to work as housekeepers for several Florida-based hotels under the H-2B program. The workers paid exorbitant fees to get employment in the United States and were paid much lower wages than their counterparts. Additionally, they were often paid late. They would later find themselves undocumented because the recruitment agency failed to renew the H-2B visa, which is only a one-year visa (though it is renewable for up to three years).[26] Indeed, according to a report on trafficking prosecutions in the state of Florida between 2007 and 2010 by Florida State University's Center for the Advancement of Human Rights, the second-highest source country for trafficking victims is the Philippines. Trafficking prosecutions, particularly labor trafficking, as reported by the Center, increasingly involve those who have entered the United States through the H-2B program to work in hospitality and tourism.[27]

Immigration and Customs Enforcement (ICE) has found cases where migrants from the Philippines have been trafficked into the United States through a variety of "legal" schemes, that is, labor recruiters and/or employers have managed to secure Filipino migrants with *non*-employment visas to gain entry into the United States with the intention of putting them to work. For instance, in 2012, three individuals were arrested on criminal charges for forcing migrants from the Philippines into conditions of virtual servitude. According to an ICE report, one of the defendants recruited migrants from the Philippines with promises of employment in the U.S. elder care facilities she owned. She then worked in partnership with another individual, an owner of a Taekwondo studio, to sponsor these migrants as "students" (i.e., on J visas) in order to secure visas for them. Once the migrants entered the United States, they were subjected to long hours of work but the wages they earned

[26] National Alliance for Filipino Concerns. *Florida 15, Sentosa 27 … Human Trafficking of Filipinos in the US Continues Under PNoy Administration–* NAFCON, http://nafconusa.org/. National Alliance for Filipino Concerns, 16 July 2011. Web. 16 July 2011.

[27] *See Florida Strategic Plan on Human Trafficking*, Fla. State Univ. Ctr. for the Advancement of Human Rights, http://www.cahr.fsu.edu/sub_category/Florida_StrategicPlanonHumanTrafficking.html (last visited July 22, 2014).

were used to pay off so-called "travel expenses."[28] According to a report by the Southern Poverty Law, "the J-1 Visa Exchange Visitor Program has been transformed into a source of cheap, exploitable labor for employers."[29]

In another case, a high-ranking Taiwanese official was actually deported from the United States for trafficking two domestic workers. Though she signed a contract with one of the workers and promised to pay her the US $1,240 per month for working forty hours a week, eight hours a day and promised her entry into the United States on B-1 (business) visas, she only paid the worker $450 a month and required her to work sixteen to eighteen hours per day as well as on weekends and holidays. In addition to ordering her deportation, a U.S. Federal Court ordered that she pay restitution to the workers.[30]

These cases highlight the role of the migration industry (from private labor recruiters to employers) in manipulating the United States' visa regimes to facilitate the migration of workers il/legally. We want to underscore, moreover, the role that the Philippine state plays as a "labor broker" in this process. Without the active role of the state in the export of workers, labor recruiters and overseas employers would not be able to function in the way that they do.

Jonny, another participant in the CARE Project who is currently undocumented and working as a caregiver, also shared with us the legal avenue in which he arrived to the United States. Jonny was granted a C-1B visa, a seaman transit visa, to be able to work on a ship whose company was based in the United States. Under his contract, Jonny worked on a cargo ship that took him all over the world, including the United States, and would bring him back to the Philippines at the end of his nine-month stint. He told us about this duties on the ship and the hardships of working under contract:

JONNY: *20 ako nung nagumpisa akong magtrabaho sa barco, tapos di na ako bumalik sa barco nung 25 ako nung nandito yung barco sa U.S. Limang taon sa barco.* I was 20 when I started working as a seaman on ships, I was 25 when I chose not to return to the ship when we were stopped in the U.S.

INTERVIEWER: What were your jobs on the ship?

JONNY: *Mga kritikal jobs, sa umpisa entry level job sa kitchen, mess boy, tagalinis ng kusina. Pag nakakuha ng maraming experience, punta ka sa deck. Doon yung talagang*

[28] *See Three Arrested for Bringing Filipino Aliens to the U.S. and Forcing*, U.S. IMMIGRATION AND CUSTOMS ENFORCEMENT. (April 4, 2008), http://www.ice.gov/news/releases/0804/080404losangeles.htm (last visited August 13, 2014).

[29] *SPLC Report: State Department Cultural Exchange Program Hijacked by U.S. Employers, Used for Cheap Labor*, S. POVERTY LAW CTR. (Feb. 11, 2014), http://www.splcenter.org/get-informed/news/splc-report-state-department-cultural-exchange-program-hijacked-by-us-employers-us.

[30] *See* Joseph Pimentel, *Taiwanese Official Deported After Abusing Filipinos*, INQUIRER.NET (Feb. 22, 2012, 6:44 PM), http://globalnation.inquirer.net/26485/taiwanese-official-deported-after-abusing-filipinos.

manual job, mahirap delikado pa kasi yung chemicals na dinadala naming, toxic. Puro chemical, hazardous na chemicals. After nun, navigation ng barco, how to drive the ship. Tapos navigate ka around the world, literally, mundo, ikot ka na. Lahat gagawiin mo.Pero overworked kami, beyond the contract, kasi pagdating sa barco hindi naman exacto sa contract mo ang gagawiin mo. Kagaya yung sa amin, konti lang yung crew para sa napakalaking ship, like ang laki ng ship yung crew naming 30 lang. So you have to exert effort din para compensate yung batch buddy mo.

Critical jobs, in the beginning entry level job in the kitchen as a mess boy, cleaning up the kitchen. When you gain experience, you are sent to the deck. That's the hard manual work, its hard because its hard work and dangerous because the chemicals we were handling were toxic. All the chemicals, hazardous chemicals. After that, ship navigation, how to drive the ship. Then you navigate around the world, literally the you circle the world. You do it all. But we were overworked, beyond the contract, because when we got to the ship, the work you do is not what is outlined in the contract. For example, in my case, we had such few crew members for such a huge ship like the ship was humungous and we had a 30-man crew. So you have to exert effort to compensate for the lack of crew members.

In this snippet, Jonny tells us about a life of hardship on a ship for nine months where the duties under contract were not what he encountered in his time on the ship. Jonny had experience doing all of the jobs he lists and attended to all of those tasks when needed since all of it were "critical jobs" for the ship to run. Work conditions were strenuous and Jonny continues to explain how this experience pushed him toward illegality:

> *Pagdating dito sa U.S. desidido akong pumirme dito at ayaw ko nang bumalik sa barco dahil sa hirap ng trabaho sa barco. Kahit na marami kaming ginagawa sa barco, di ka babayaran sa extra work mo. Hirap sa barco kumparado sa hirap dito sa U.S., iba. Barco is back breaking work. So ginamit ko ang aking legal na bisa para makapasok, at di na ako bumalik sa barco.*
>
> When I got to the US, I decided to not return to the ship because of the difficulty of working on the ship. Even if we did so much on the ship, you weren't paid for the extra work. The difficulty in working on a ship compared to the difficulty in working in the US, different. Working on a ship is back breaking work. So I used the legal visa to enter, and I didn't return to the ship.

Although Jonny is not covered under the H visa that we are chiefly discussing in this section, we want to highlight the legal avenues by which he came to the United States and the work conditions he endured as a seaman that pushed him toward illegality.

8.4 DEBT BONDAGE: AN ILLEGALIZING FORCE

If legal status does not protect migrants from highly exploitative living and working conditions, the transnational apparatus that structures Philippine migration often subjects migrants to incredibly onerous debts that ultimately render them undocumented. That is, in order to secure overseas employment, Filipino migrants depend on various migration industry actors (i.e., labor recruitment agencies that can be located in the Philippines, the United States, or both) as well as governments (i.e., the Philippines' and the United States' migration agencies). Both state and non-state actors charge migrants fees for their services. Often migrants do not have the funds to pay for these fees. They are then forced to borrow money from either private lenders or from labor recruitment agencies if these agencies have the capacity to front the funds that migrants' need. Of course, not only do migrants need funds to pay for service fees, they also need funds to travel. Most Filipino migrants' wages are garnished when they work abroad. This means that they have less to send back to their families. Those who do not pay risk having their families in the Philippines threatened by lenders' representatives. Moreover, the short-term contracts that migrants have often expire before they are able to repay their debts. Migrants, to avoid intimidation by lenders, willfully overstay their employment visas and become undocumented in order to continue to pay their debts.

In the NAFCON cases discussed earlier, the workers all found themselves saddled by oppressive debts. They are not alone. Reports from the Filipino media have covered several high-profile cases of debt peonage. For example, in Louisiana, Filipino teachers recruited in the state were forced to pay $16,000 placement fees before leaving the Philippines. In addition, they had to sign more thn 10% of their monthly salaries for two years to pay for agency-provided housing. Those unable to pay the initial $16,000 were referred to loan companies that charged them high interest rates. Anyone who complained about these debt repayment obligations were threatened with deportation.[31]

In Baltimore, the Prince George's County Public School (PGCPS) recruited 1,044 teachers from the Philippines on H-1B visas. PCGPS illegally required teachers to pay for the processing of their H-1B visas – the fees that are supposed to be borne by the employer. Instead, the PCPGS garnished teachers' wages to ensure that the visa processing fees were paid. The teachers ended up launching a campaign to challenge the school district on this and other issues. Although they were successful in getting the Department of Labor to intervene, the workers were ultimately rendered undocumented. The Department of Labor forced the school district to pay the teachers' back wages for the district's illegal deduction of migrants' salaries, and it barred the district from being able to hire through the H-1B program. But as their employment with the district was terminated, the teachers were left without

[31] Cynthia De Castro, *Victimized Pinoy Teachers Demand Justice at the White House*, Asian Journal, Aug. 10-12, 2011, *available at* http://www.ajdigitaledition.com/pdfs/PDF/2011_LA/2011_08_10/2011_LA_08_10_A%204.pdf.

visas and therefore without legal status. The onerousness of the debt the teachers had to bear is expressed by one of them, Ms. Gumanoy, who says:

> How in the world can I go back to the Philippines in 9 days? I have a car loan, doctors' appointments, financial obligations, etc. My family is with me here, we cannot just pack our bags and go home. This is our life at stake, we need to plan for it! Talk about injustice! They would not even give a 45-day notice like our apartment does.[32]

To better illustrate the impacts of debt peonage on migrants' everyday lives, we turn to interviews conducted as part of our participant action research with Migrante Northern California. Harry was brought to the United States on an H-2B visa as a first-class welder for employment in Alabama. Harry was first recruited from his hometown of Cebu with sixty-eight other workers. With a growing family of three children, he was forced to look for work overseas. Harry responded to a recruitment ad for welders in the United States. However, "*Sinabihan ng agency na kami magbabayad ng mga four hundred thousand pesos.* Our agency told us that we would have to pay four hundred thousand pesos. So it's about I would say, ten thousand U.S. dollars." Harry explains:

> *Binigyan ako nga* H-2B *visa, yung* H-2B *bisa ko is 15 days bago mag expired. Sinabi naming na walang kaming pang bayad sa three hundred fifty to four hundred thousand pesos yun ang range para sa pagbago ng bisa. So inofferan nalang nila ng offer na puntahan nyo itong lending company kasi may bisa na kayo, pakita nyo yung bisa sila na bahala sa pera nyo. So from lending yung pera hindi naman nahawakan, binigay na papuntang agency.*
>
> They gave me an H-2B visa, the H-2B visa is only 15 days before it expires. We said we didn't have the money to pay the range of 350,000 to 400,000 pesos for visa renewal. So the agency offered that we go to a lending company because we already had a visa but the lending would take care of the money. But the money from the lending company, we didn't get that money, it went straight to the agency.

Although anxious about the amount of money being charged by the recruitment agency, Harry also felt that it was a reasonable bargain for the opportunity to go to a coveted migrant destination, the United States. Harry's case illustrates how multiple state and non-state institutions are at work to produce a population of precarious workers before they even leave home. Yet, Harry ultimately saw his opportunity to earn in dollars as a promising opportunity to lift family members out of poverty.

Once he arrived in the United States, Harry was ready to work. He and his cohort of welders expected to work hard, but they ultimately found themselves in highly exploitative working conditions, "So *nagtrabaho kami ng 7 days a week, 12 to 14*

[32] See id.

hours. Yun yung trabaho namin. So we worked seven days a week, 12 to 14 hours. That's our workday." Despite working long hours, all of the wages Harry earned were used to repay his debt, which was accruing interest, to the Philippine-based lending company from which he borrowed funds to pay the recruitment agency, "*Walang mapupunta samin yung pera kasi, uh … pinagbabayad lang siya sa lending company.* None of our wages would end up with us because, uh … we are paying all of our wages to the lending company." Contrary to his expectation prior to leaving the Philippines for employment in the United States, Harry's ability to support his family was minimized by the need to pay his accruing debt within a specific timeline. Harry and the sixty-eight other migrant workers in his cohort were soon struck with the worst news about their employment:

> *After two months bigla nalang inninannounce nung company na wala na silang maibigay na project so yon. May utang pa kami pero wala pa kaming trabaho pag dating dito sa U.S.* After two months, they surprisingly announce that the company did not have any projects to provide to the workers. We still had debts but we had no work when here in the U.S.

The cohort of migrant workers with whom Harry came to the United States soon realized that their agency's promise of employment and legalization was a sham.

> *Nakita yung status na talagang human trafficking. Parang ghost company lang ginawa. Binigyan muna kami ng … parang ginawa sabing totoo na may trabaho binigyan namin muna ng dalawang bwan na trabaho tapos wala na, bigla nalang nawala. So nag watakwatak kami tapos ah …*
>
> We saw immediately that our status was human trafficking. It was a ghost company that was made to bring migrant workers, the company created a job contract that would give us work for two months and then it was gone, it was all of the sudden gone. After that all of the workers dispersed after we couldn't find work with company.

The case of Harry and sixty-eight of his colleagues begins in the culture of migration in the Philippines. Prospective migrants not only desire employment overseas; they are particularly motivated by fantasies of stable work in America. After migrants are able to secure employment in the United States, debt peonage keeps them working under any set of conditions. The interests of the migration industry become very clear, Harry says:

> *Parang nakita ko ano lang, yung habol nila sa pera yung pera talaga. Oo, utang from the lending kasi malaki yon pero ginamit nila yung U.S., ginamit nila yung pangalan ng America.*
>
> From what I saw, what they [the agency] were after is money. Yes, the debts from the lending [company] were huge but they used the US, they used the name of "America".

Debt is a heavy burden for migrant workers to bear. In Harry's case, when the job he was recruited for disappeared without the possibility of renewal or placement, he was not able to continue to pay his debts. The lending company, however, used strong-arm tactics transnationally to ensure that Harry would find some way, even if it meant becoming undocumented, to pay the debts back:

> *Bumigat noon yung problema kasi, tapos may trip na sa pamilya ko. Yung asawa ko tinatawagan na ng lending companies, mga lawyers sinasabi makukulong asawa ko pag hindi ako magbayad. Hindi na nakakatulog, yung pormisyo na yung labas. At apektado na yung pamilya ko.*
>
> The problem became heavier because there were threats to my family. The lending company was calling, the lawyers said that my wife could be jailed if I didn't pay my debt. I wasn't able to sleep because of the situation because it affected my family.

Threats made to his family because of the debt he incurred for leaving them forced Harry to ultimately stay in the United States, with or without documentation, to pay back what he owed to the lending company to ensure his family's safety. As Harry's story illuminates, the transnational regulation of migrant workers through debt peonage is a key reason why many immigrants choose to let their legal status expire. Harry's migration started with the desire that working abroad would help stabilize his family. The migration industry created an avenue through which he could satisfy those desires. Harry believed that he would be able to pay back the debt incurred to be able to migrate. However, his story illustrates how the precariousness of his employment and his debt bondage worked toward his illegalization in America. The corporation he worked for relied on these conditions to retain him as a highly exploited, low-wage worker.

In another example, a migrant worker named Angelito described his inescapable tie to his debt in his migration to the United States:

> *Do you believe may utang na ang alam ko lang noong pumunta ako rito is more than a million pesos? And it never stop. Kaya hanggang ngayon, hanggang ngayon, kaya I don't want to go back.*
>
> Do you believe that my debts when I came to the U.S. is more than one million pesos? And it never stopped growing. That's why until now, until now, I don't want to go back.

Angelito accrued debts up to a million pesos in his years as a migrant worker, which is equivalent to almost $23,000 in today's currency. He was first recruited to a job in Saudi Arabia working in a factory and then to Papua New Guinea as an electrical worker and was able to gain a multiple-entry visitor's visa to the United States. As a worker in Saudi Arabia and Papua New Guinea, Angelito lamented that his work in those places bankrupted him instead of stabilizing his financial status:

> *I didn't know that the agency that I applied for is not legalized in Saudi Arabia and they're asking money to deduct in our salary in which it is not in our contract. Ayoko ko yung ganun. Na idideduct maliit na yung sahod na tinanggap ko tapos babawasan mo pa.*
>
> I didn't know that the agency that I applied for is not legal in Saudi Arabia and they're asking to deduct money from our salary which is not in our contract. I didn't like that. That they would deduct from our already measly wage.

When Angelito's short-term contracts did not prove to be a viable way of supporting his family's livelihood or an avenue to receive steady income to pay back his debts, Angelito turned to his visitor's visa to gain legal entry to the United States. This migration was mostly influenced by the need to pay his debts coupled with the promise of the American dollar. In what Anju Paul calls stepwise migration,[33] Angelito follows a trend where Philippine migrants ultimately "collect" temporary contracts and visas and engage in stepwise migration wherein they migrate to multiple destinations for short periods of time until they are able to get to their final destination goal, most often countries in the West. Moreover, this stepwise migration is motivated by debt accrued from past contracts. And once in the United States, Angelito felt he had no other option but to remain in the country undocumented because of the insurmountable debts he had in the Philippines.

8.5 CONCLUSION

Debates about immigration, particularly undocumented immigration, have been raging across the United States for more than a decade. Indeed, state and municipal governments have attempted to introduce policies to discourage the settlement of immigrants in different communities in the absence of major, comprehensive immigration reform at the federal level.

Currently, the Obama administration's proposal for immigration reform calls for more border security, enhanced mechanisms by which employers can verify the immigration status of prospective employees as well as a pathway to citizenship for the undocumented, especially long-time residents of the United States. Some public commentators suggest that the United States expand the current guest worker program to allow low-wage, unskilled migrants to enter the United States legally, albeit without the possibility of permanent residence or citizenship. Indeed, President George W. Bush initially proposed expanding the guest worker program in earlier debates on immigration reform in the months prior to the 9/11. The events of

[33] Anju Mary Paul, *Stepwise International Migration: A Multistage Migration Pattern for the Aspiring Migrant*, 116 American Journal of Sociology 1842–86 (2011).

9/11, of course, dashed those initiatives, but they have resurfaced in subsequent years and are a topic of discussion in the current debate.

Although the guest worker program – that is, the provision of temporary employment visas – has been a key aspect of (im)migration to the United States since the passage of the 1965 Immigration Act, the experiences of workers who come to the United States through the H visa and the mechanisms by which they get here have been rarely explored in the scholarship.

Filipinos are among the top five groups who come to the United States on H visas and are therefore an important population for study. We find that Filipinos' entry into the United States on H visas is due to a growing transnational migration industry. The transnational migration process can be the source of "dispossession" for migrant workers who are both illegally exploited for their labor and even illegalized as a consequence of debt bondage. It is important, however, to situate the transnational migration of Filipinos within the context of labor brokerage on the part of the Philippine state. The Philippine state is responsible for the flourishing of the migration industry in the Philippines. Even if comprehensive immigration reform were to be introduced in the United States, including the expansion of the guest worker program, undocumented migration, especially from the Philippines may not be fully addressed. The Philippine state is among the top labor-sending countries in the world. Along with private recruitment agencies, the Philippine labor brokerage state plays a critical role in mobilizing, facilitating, and regulating migration from the Philippines. Hence, Filipino migrants find themselves living and working in nearly 200 countries around the world as both short-term contractual and immigrant workers. We argue that the Philippines' labor brokerage state plays a critical role in producing undocumented migration.

The systematic and aggressive institutionalization of labor export in the Philippines continues to export migrants on a large scale globally. Many migrants leaving the Philippines secure their departure through temporary contracts in precarious forms of employment. These short contracts are profitable, as stepwise migration and circular migration ensures remittances that have been incorporated into the fabric of the Philippine national economy. Aneesh states that contractual labor is crafted through transnational labor regulation.[34] This research demonstrates that companies in recruitment, placement, and consultation profit from garnishing one-third to two-thirds of migrant workers' wages per month. We have confirmed in our research that recruitment agencies and consultancy firms, here in the United States and in the Philippines, pocket a great deal of profit from the recruitment and placement of migrant workers. The role of these agencies and firms creates

34 A. Aneesh, Rethinking Migration: High-skilled Labor Flows from India to the United States, CENTER FOR COMPARATIVE IMMIGRATION STUDIES (2000).

a complex employment relation with migrant workers as agencies "technically" employ workers. Therefore, migrant workers are legally bound to the recruitment agency that facilitates their employment in the United States. Debt peonage becomes a key condition for migrant workers that are then pushed into "illegality" in the United States.

We argue that the U.S. guest worker program is part of a neoliberal regime of transnational regulation of migrant labor. For Filipino workers, this regime includes the Philippine state's labor brokerage acting in concert with a growing migration industry consisting of recruitment agencies, lending companies, and employers in low-wage industries in the United States. The role of sending states in the production of "illegal" forms of legal migration as well as facilitating the illegalization of migrants must be interrogated as the profits from the labor of migrant workers are not only collected in receiving states and economies but in sending as well; migrant workers' blood and sweat are becoming more and more profitable for both receiving and sending states.

9

The Impact of 1965 Immigration and Nationality Act on the Evolution of Temporary Guest Worker Programs, or How the 1965 Act Punted on Creating a Rightful Place for Mexican Worker Migration

Leticia M. Saucedo

9.1 INTRODUCTION

As much as the Immigration and Nationality Act of 1965 (1965 Act) did to end the discriminatory national origins provisions embedded in immigration law, it did far less to stabilize the status of countless temporary workers in the United States, including those under the former Bracero Program. The vast majority of these workers were of Mexican descent. While Congress and the federal agencies overseeing contract labor programs historically dealt with foreign workers outside the immigration system, Congress's failure to incorporate provisions for the stabilization of Braceros into the 1965 Act created a huge undocumented, exploitable worker population for U.S. employers. In the meantime, the image of the Mexican as temporary or transient went unchallenged in the political debates leading up to the 1965 Act. The failure of the 1965 Congress to bring these temporary workers into the legal permanent migration stream followed a historical trajectory of treating Mexicans as transient workers. The result was the transformation, beginning in 1965, of the Mexican worker from legal and temporary to permanent and undocumented.

This essay explores the development of temporary labor regulation involving Mexicans and the politics behind Congress's failure to include former Braceros into the 1965 Act's provisions. It also discusses the effects of the failure on future discussions of temporary labor programs and employment-based immigration regulation in the United States, including current talks surrounding comprehensive immigration reform.

Several scholars have written about the sometimes schizophrenic goals of temporary worker and contract labor programs to (1) provide a steady labor supply to some of the most needy industries (mostly agricultural), (2) protect jobs for available U.S. workers, and (3) regulate immigration flows into the United States.[1] Through these programs, the interests of labor and the interests of employers who need the temporary labor are mediated by federal agencies, namely the Department of Labor and the Department of Homeland Security, or its legacy agency, the Immigration and Naturalization Service.[2] In ongoing negotiations over the need and the number of immigrants required to fill positions, the related goals of adequate employment law enforcement and preservation of living-wage standards for the available jobs have become secondary to the twin goals of preserving jobs for Americans and immigration enforcement. The image of the Mexican always as a temporary worker, moreover, has affected the nature of the discourse around Mexican migration in particular. The stakeholders in the negotiations over the future of immigration policy, in addition to the agencies, have traditionally been seen as labor and employer groups. The missing players have been the migrants themselves, always considered transient or temporary and without a real stake in the consequences.

Legal historian Mae Ngai notes that historically the agencies regulating work and immigration have constructed the Mexican migrant as both temporary, always potentially illegal, and without a rightful place in the legal system of immigration.[3] An example during the period of the Bracero era (1948–64) makes her point. Deportation policy during the 1940s and 1950s revolved around a suspension of deportation system that allowed those who entered the United States without inspection to seek admission through Canada. By law, the system was not available to Mexicans, Caribbeans, or Canadians who could not secure admission to Canada. Under this system, almost 58,000 cases were heard and approved between 1935 and 1959, mostly of European refugees.[4] At the same time, the Bracero Program was in full swing and allowed temporary entry of about 200,000 Mexicans a year, on average, between 1948 and 1964.[5] While European immigrants had their status adjusted to permanent residence, however, Braceros were required to leave the country and reapply for admission at the end of every contract period. This unequal pattern of permanent European migration and temporary Mexican migration was not unique to the era, and the 1965 Act did nothing to change it.

1 *See, e.g.*, George C. Kiser, *Mexican American Labor Before World War II*, 2 JOURNAL OF MEXICAN AMERICAN HISTORY 122 (1972).

2 *See* KITTY CALAVITA, INSIDE THE STATE: THE BRACERO PROGRAM, IMMIGRATION AND THE I.N.S., 181 (2d. ed. 2010).

3 Mae Ngai, *The Strange Career of the Illegal Alien: Immigration Restriction and Deportation Policy in the United States*, 1921–1965, 21 LAW & HIST. REV. 69, 71 (2003); see also, MAE NGAI, IMPOSSIBLE SUBJECTS (2004)[hereinafter SUBJECTS].

4 Ngai, *The Strange Career*, *supra* note 3 at 104.

5 SUBJECTS, *supra* note 3 at 139.

9.2 THE HISTORICAL TRAJECTORY OF TEMPORARY MEXICAN LABOR

Early Concessions to Agriculture and the Labor Contractor

Since the enactment of restrictive requirements and national origins quotas into the immigration system in the 1920s, agricultural employers have sought exemptions and variances to ensure a steady supply of seasonal foreign agricultural labor. In 1917, Congress passed a restrictive immigration law that gave the Attorney General (AG) the power to impose literacy requirements, to expand the categories of inadmissible aliens, and to bar categorically from admission anyone from the Asia-Pacific Zone. Pursuant to the law, the Immigration Bureau, housed at the time in the Department of Labor, implemented a head tax and a literacy requirement for entry into the United States.[6] A provision of the 1917 law also allowed the Attorney General to provide a system for temporary labor during the transition period required to implement the law. The AG allowed temporary workers into the country under this provision through inadmissibility waivers.[7] It was through these exceptions to general immigration policy, therefore, that Mexican workers were able to enter the country for contract labor.

Agricultural growers took advantage of the waivers, negotiating time extensions for their Mexican laborers for several years. Approximately 80,000 Mexicans entered under the waiver program, working in agricultural fields or in railway work. This program ended under pressure from the American Federation of Labor in 1918, although the agricultural segment was continued and extended until 1921 under "certain particularly meritorious cases."[8]

Many attribute to this period the beginning of the federal government's experimentation with guest worker programs. One scholar described these early efforts as the "'Bracero' program of World War I."[9] Another report noted, "Over the objection of labor advocates, Congress created the first guest worker program, allowing Mexican nonimmigrant admissions between 1917 and 1920, and then exempted Mexicans and other Western Hemisphere migrants from per-country immigration limits imposed on the rest of the world in 1921."[10] Pursuant to the 1917

[6] Immigration Act of 1917, Sec. 3, 39 Stat. 875.

[7] Immigration Act of 1917, Ch. 29, § 2, Pub. L. 301, 39 Stat. 874, 875, 877–78 (Feb. 5, 1917).

[8] Education and Public Welfare Division, Cong. Research Serv., Temporary Worker Programs: Background and Issues 6 (1980) [hereinafter CRS Worker].

[9] Kiser, *supra* note 1 at 126.

[10] Cong. Research Serv., R42560, Mexican Migration to the United States: Policy and Trends 6 (2012); see also Kiser, *supra* note 1 at 132–33, for a description of efforts to place a quota on Western hemisphere immigration.

Act, the Secretary of Labor issued a directive allowing the admission of temporary agricultural workers on May 23, 1917. The directive called for detailed procedures that are in essence the precursors to the Bracero Program as well as the labor certification system we have today.[11]

A 1980 Congressional Research Service Report on temporary immigrant labor explicitly describes the compromises in the 1917 act as the prototype for future guest worker programs that occurred well into the middle of the twentieth century:

> The H-2 provision evolved from a combination of the 4th and 9th provisos to section 3 of the Immigration Act of 1917. Section 3 set forth a list of inadmissible aliens including contract laborers. The fourth proviso authorized the Attorney General to grant waivers of the exclusion clause regarding skilled contract laborers upon a finding that "labor of like kind unemployed can not be found in this country." The ninth proviso allowed for a waiver of excludability for inadmissible aliens, including contract laborers, for temporary entry, and was the principal authority for the admission of agricultural worker (sic) during the periods before and after the enactment of special legislation for that purpose during World War II. Administrative procedures developed jointly in 1948 by the Commissioner of the Immigration and Naturalization Service and the Director of the U.S. Employment Service required that before such waiver could be issued, the need for the workers had to be investigated by INS and certified by the U.S. Employment Service; and it had to be shown that their admission would not displace or otherwise detrimentally affect labor in this country.[12]

The 1917 proviso allowing the Attorney General to extend waivers to resolve labor shortages formed the foundation for the future Bracero and H-2 programs.[13] The Attorney General invoked it in 1942 just before the implementation of the initial Bracero Program.[14] It was used again to implement the H-2 program in 1952.[15] Importantly, the H-2 program amounted to "a recasting of the waiver of inadmissibility of temporary contract workers in positive rather than negative terms."[16]

Social scientist George C. Kiser noted about this period that even after this temporary World War I program ended, employers continued to hire undocumented workers informally. He noted:

[11] *See* CRS Worker, *supra* note 7 at 10.

[12] CRS Worker, *supra* note 7 at 63. According the CRS report, the ninth proviso states: "Provided further, that the Commissioner General of Immigration with approval of the Secretary of Labor shall issue rules and prescribed conditions, including exaction of such bonds as may be necessary, to control and regulate the admission and return of otherwise inadmissible aliens applying for temporary admission." *Id.*

[13] George C. Kiser, *supra* note 1 at 127.

[14] CRS Worker, *supra* note 7 at 8.

[15] *Id.*

[16] *Id.*

> Even when the formal policy turned against the employers, their interests were still informally accommodated. The government continued to maintain an informal Mexican labor program by simply refusing to apply the immigration laws vigorously and systematically. Far from reducing the number of Mexican workers, the end of the emergency program marked the beginning of a decade which brought Mexican workers to the United States in vastly increased and unprecedented numbers.[17]

It was clear given its history that the H-2 program – and the Bracero Program that existed alongside it – was developed outside of the confines of regular migration in immigration law. Its initial casting as a waiver of inadmissibility placed the temporary worker program in a realm of its own, with its contours formed by negotiations involving the Attorney General, the Department of Labor, and, at times, the Department of Agriculture, organized labor, and even foreign governments.

The Bracero Program

Having successfully navigated the restrictions in the 1920s, employers sought to establish a more permanent source of seasonal labor. They lobbied heavily for the implementation of contract labor agreements with other countries, including Mexico and the British West Indies. The labor shortage caused by World War II created an opening for the establishment of a labor agreement between Mexico and the United States through which the Mexican government would supply its citizens as labor to U.S. employers. The Mexican contract labor agreement, also known as the Bracero Program, was by far the largest, involving more than 4 million Mexican laborers over a twenty-two-year period.[18] During this period, the stakeholders again considered temporary worker programs outside the strictures of immigration law. They sought to replicate the program that had been developed out of the 1917 proviso as the exception to immigration law's restrictions. By this time, however, the history of the temporary programs demonstrated the need for increased worker protections. The Bracero Program initially included those protections. Historians note, however, that the initial protections were highly contested throughout the duration of the programs. As historian Otey Scruggs notes,

> [W]hen the two governments exchanged notes on a Mexican farm labor agreement on August 4, 1942, it was on a document that contained guarantees against exploitation and provided for joint United States-Mexican enforcement. The subsequent history of the farm labor program can be viewed largely in terms of the conflicting efforts of southwestern farmers to turn the clock back to 1917 on the one

[17] Kiser, *supra* note 1 at 136.

[18] *See*, Philip Martin, Manolo Abella, and Christiane Kuptsch, Managing Labor Migration in the Twenty-First Century, 87 (2006) (chart describing Bracero admissions from 1942 to 1964).

> hand and those of the Mexican government to secure for the workers more and stronger protective guarantees on the other.[19]

As the Mexican government pushed for broader protections, organized labor in the United States pressed for the program's elimination. Labor supporters lobbied for the same broad protections for U.S. workers that were afforded to Braceros under the program's contracts.[20] They were not strong enough politically to ensure passage of such proposals at the time. The 1951 amendments to the Bracero agreement did, however, include a provision similar to today's labor certification requirements for certain workers. Sec. 503 of P.L. 78 implementing the program stated:

> No workers recruited under this title shall be available for employment in any areas unless the Secretary of Labor has determined and certified that (1) sufficient domestic workers who are able, willing and qualified are not available at the time and place needed to perform the work for which such workers are to be employed, (2) the employment of such workers will not adversely affect the wage and working conditions of domestic agricultural workers similarly employed, and (3) reasonable efforts have been made to attract domestic workers for such employment at wages and standard hours of work comparable to those offered foreign workers.[21]

This provision provided some leverage to the Department of Labor. It provided the agency a mechanism by which it could recruit U.S. workers for jobs before certifying that no workers were available in general. It also gave the DOL exclusive authority over certification.[22]

In response to complaints that the Bracero Program was stimulating undocumented immigration, several proposals suggested its elimination. The public debate centered on the social costs of illegal immigration and Bracero labor.[23] Importantly, during this period, advocates and detractors called for a more rigorous form of immigration regulation that included the workplace. As early as 1946, some stakeholders, including the Mexican government, suggested employer sanctions for knowingly hiring undocumented labor outside of the parameters of the Bracero agreement.[24] While this trial balloon was floated at the time of debates over the 1952 and 1965 Acts, it was not until Congress considered the 1986 Immigration Reform and Control Act that it was implemented.[25]

[19] CRS Worker, *supra* note 7 at 13–14.

[20] *Id.* at 32–36.

[21] *Id.* at 33.

[22] *Id.* at 62.

[23] Juan Ramón Garcia, Operation Wetback: The Mass Deportation of Undocumented Workers in 1954, 159 (1980).

[24] CRS Worker, *supra* note 7 at 39–40.

[25] Immigration Reform and Control Act, Pub. L. No. 99–603, 100 Stat. 3359 (codified as amended at 8 U.S.C. §§ 1150-24 (Supp. 1987))(signed into law Nov. 6, 1986).

Debates over Mexican Labor Leading Up to the 1952 Act: Guest Worker Provisions Specifically Exclude Braceros

Congress formally debated guest worker programs as part of immigration law in the early 1950s. Part of the debate at the time was whether authority over a guest worker program should rest the Department of Labor or the Immigration and Naturalization Service (INS). This debate reflected the tug-of-war between the DOL and INS over the use of the immigration system enforcement mechanisms to regularize Mexican workers for employers.[26] The debate was consistently framed on the assumption that Mexicans would enter the United States and return to Mexico after the work was completed. This assumption reflects the view of Mexicans and Mexican labor as transient.

The Judiciary Committee in 1950 issued a report recommending that the immigration agency maintain oversight of a temporary guest worker program:

> [P]rovisions should be made in permanent legislation which would permit the admission of temporary agricultural labor in a nonimmigrant classification when like labor supply cannot be found in this country. The determination of the necessity for the importation of such labor in any particular instance should be made by the Commissioner of Immigration and Naturalization upon application by the interested employer before the importation and after a full investigation of the facts and consultation with appropriate agencies.[27]

The recommendation gave DOL advisory rather than final authority over the admission of temporary workers. This was in contrast to the provisions of the Bracero Program, which gave the DOL full authority for implementing, monitoring, and enforcing the provisions of the agreement.[28]

The Judiciary Committee's recommendation became the H-2 provision of the Immigration and Nationality Act of 1952 with the very important omission of the Mexican agricultural labor program. Although there was much lobbying for folding the Bracero Program into the developing guest worker provisions, Congress ultimately declined. Beginning in 1951, the Mexican Bracero Program was authorized by separate legislation, Public Law 78. Thus, even when Congress merged contract labor and immigration law, it did so in a piecemeal way. Nonetheless, the 1952 Act set the precedent in its H-2 provision that employers hoped would be expanded in the 1965 Act into a full-scale guest worker program. Because the DOL and the INS had similar authority for two different sets of workers, the debate over control of contract labor flows grew after passage of the 1952 Act.

26 *See* SUBJECTS, *supra* note 3 at 152–55.
27 S. Rep. 1515, 31st Cong., 2d sess., 578 (1950).
28 CRS WORKER, *supra* note 7 at 64.

During this period, the calls for curbing undocumented immigration were growing. President Truman advocated for stiff penalties against employers who knowingly hired undocumented workers, as well as increased immigration authority to inspect workplaces without warrants. Employer sanctions were hotly debated and ultimately defeated by a large margin.[29] After much debate, the 1952 Act included a compromise: the criminalization of the willful importation, transportation, or harboring of illegal aliens. Such a crime was considered a felony punishable by a $2,000 fine or imprisonment of up to five years, or both. The provision was initially introduced as a penalty on employers. The compromise was initially designed to reach employers actively engaged in recruiting and bringing workers into the country. After much lobbying, however, employment of undocumented workers was specifically exempted from the harboring definition.[30]

After the 1952 Act was enacted, proposals continued to emerge in Congress to curtail the undocumented immigration that migrated alongside Bracero labor. Hearings during the period focused on getting rid of illegal immigration from Mexico.[31] Around the same time, the immigration agency began a massive deportation campaign known as Operation Wetback.[32] Proposals for employer sanctions also arose, with the purpose of encouraging employers to use the Bracero Program for their labor needs.[33]

The 1952 Act and the actions the immigration agency took in its wake set the stage for future discussion over the control of temporary labor flows, employer sanctions, and the effectiveness of labor certification and the H-2 program. All of these issues served as background to the professed reason for the 1965 Act, namely the elimination of the national origins quota system embedded in the Act.

9.3 DEBATES OVER MEXICAN LABOR DURING THE 1965 ACT

The End of the Bracero Program and the Discussion over Temporary Work

In 1964, the federal government officially ended its Bracero agreement with Mexico. By the time it was terminated, the Bracero Program had issued 4.6 million temporary visas.[34] The meaning of the Bracero Program's cancellation was widely disputed heading into the debates surrounding the 1965 Amendments to the Immigration

[29] *Id.* at 40.
[30] *Id.* at 39–40.
[31] GARCIA, *supra* note 21 at 161.
[32] *Id.* at 183.
[33] *Id.* at 161.
[34] CONG. RESEARCH SERV., MEXICAN MIGRATION, *supra* note 9 at 7.

and Nationality Act. Federal agencies, employers, labor unions, and the Mexican government all had different views about whether the Bracero Program would or should be folded into the existing but small H-2 guest worker program already in the Act.

In December 1964, Secretary of Labor Willard Wirtz implemented DOL regulations effectively excluding Braceros from the H-2 program.[35] The regulations were aimed at providing a smooth transition between the termination of the Bracero Program and the use by agricultural growers of U.S. workers.[36] The purpose of the regulation was to ensure that "foreign workers will not be admitted where unemployed domestic workers are available, and in no event, will be admitted under circumstances adversely affecting domestic wage levels."[37] The regulations also prohibited certification to any employer "who is found to have had in his employ after the effective date of these regulations, any foreign worker when such employer knows or has reasonable grounds to believe or suspect or by reasonable inquiry could have ascertained that such foreign worker is not lawfully within the United States."[38] This administrative form of employer sanction was eventually toughened and made part of the 1986 Immigration Reform and Control Act.

Growers responded with loud and persistent calls to Congress to clarify the standing of Mexican migrants and former Braceros and their ability to take advantage of the existing H-2 program to import Braceros. In response to a proposed amendment that would prohibit the importation of contract labor in the agricultural industry, the National Council of Farmers Cooperatives asserted its understanding that Congress never meant to end the importation of foreign temporary workers. The NCFC letter to the Judiciary Committee in 1965 noted that "our basis for this opinion is supported by actions which would refute the interpretation that it was the intent of Congress to terminate the use of all foreign workers in agriculture."[39] The letter noted that the Secretary of Labor, responsible for certifying the need for foreign workers, was still certifying a need three weeks before the Bracero Program ended. The NCFC deduced from the federal agency's actions that "this act scarcely 3 weeks before the termination of Public Law 78 [the Bracero Program] would not have been logically undertaken if it had been the express intent of Congress to terminate the use of all foreign workers in agriculture."[40] The NCFC urged Congress at the time to resist any attempts to end foreign labor contracting for agricultural work.

[35] CRS WORKER, *supra* note 7 at 64–67.

[36] 29 Fed. Reg. 19,101–19,102 (Dec. 19, 1964).

[37] *Id.*

[38] 29 Fed. Reg. 19,102 (Dec. 19, 1964).

[39] 1 OSCAR M. TRELLES, II & JAMES F. BAILEY, III, IMMIGRATION AND NATIONALITY ACTS: LEGISLATIVE HISTORY AND RELATED DOCUMENTS 1, 871 (1979).

[40] *Id.*

The Secretary of Labor, on the other hand, testified in hearings on S. 500, the 1965 Amendments to the INA, that the bill as written – that is, without reference to the Bracero Program – provided adequate protections for U.S. workers and at the same time provided the type of skilled immigrants that the country needed. In other words, there was no need for Congress to incorporate the Bracero Program into the then-current program. The Department's main concern at the time was protecting U.S. workers, and the Department wanted to ensure that all employers, including agricultural employers, used the certification system in place for H-2 workers. In response to questions about the use of the H-2 program as an alternative, Wirtz stated that the INA temporary worker provision would not allow for the importation of workers "if there are people in this country qualified to do the work."[41] Wirtz indicated that the DOL did not envision using the H2 program to replace the Bracero Program.[42] At the same time, he left open the possibility that growers could use the H-2 program if they followed its certification procedures. The following exchange between the Secretary of Labor and the 1965 Act's sponsor illustrates the lack of transparency in the DOL's position:

> Senator Hart: On that Bracero thing, is it your opinion or what is your opinion with respect to the adequacy of the now only existing law, 414 [INA sec. 214, the nonimmigrant temporary worker provision], in terms of permitting you to enable growers in this country to make decent harvesting plans? Specifically, can you make a determination far enough in advance of the harvest season that domestics are not available, and therefore admissions are permitted under 414?
>
> Secretary Wirtz: Yes, I can, Senator. I would want to urge that the first question is whether growers will take the affirmative action which in my judgment is necessary to discharge their responsibility in this situation, but assuming that first step, my answer to your second step is that the procedures could be used if that determination still showed that there was no available U.S. work force.[43]

Although Wirtz conceded that the H-2 program could theoretically accommodate or replace the now defunct Bracero Program, his statement reflected the DOL's long-time struggle to get employers to abide by the program's certification requirements. The DOL had, in fact, been pushing for its demise for years before its termination in 1964 precisely because it could not enforce its provisions effectively.[44]

The governors of states that benefited from Bracero labor, including Governor Pat Brown of California, lobbied hard for an extension of the program or, alternatively,

[41] *Id.* at 109.

[42] *Id.* at 110.

[43] *Id.* at 111.

[44] Cong. Research Serv., Mexican Migration, *supra* note 9 at 7, fn. 18.

for the inclusion of former Braceros in the existing H-2 temporary labor program.[45] Brown sought a phase-out period for Braceros, on behalf of California growers who claimed they would suffer greatly without the Bracero labor pool.[46] The governor sought an administrative DOL program for the use of Mexican workers under the H-2 provisions for a transitional period of five years.[47]

The Mexican government also opposed ending the Bracero Program, arguing that the program should be phased out rather than ended abruptly.[48] The government also argued that it was undocumented workers, and not Braceros, who depressed wages for U.S. workers, and that ending the program would only increase the undocumented worker population.[49]

Sensing that the DOL would not expand the current H-2 program, proponents of an expanded program sought a labor program through the Department of Agriculture instead of either the DOL or the INS.[50] They argued to Congress that the Agriculture Department would have a better idea than the DOL of the needs of the industry and of harvests' tight timelines. They debated the idea in the context of the Food and Agriculture Act of 1965, a multiyear commodity program for growers of wheat, grains, and cotton. There was even an amendment to the Food and Agriculture Act of 1965 to legislatively transfer the advisory certification responsibility for importation of farm workers from the DOL to the Department of Agriculture. It was the belief of these senators that the DOL was violating "the express congressional intent that Mexican workers be admitted under Public Law 414 after the expiration of Public Law 78."[51] The amendment failed.[52]

In sum, the several parties involved in the development of the 1965 Amendments to the INA were aware of the Bracero Program's expiration. It was unclear whether the majority of Congress understood that the Bracero Program would not be replaced by the then-current H-2 guest worker program, except that the Secretary of Labor gave indications that Braceros might be included if they met the DOL requirements of no loss of jobs to American workers or adverse effects on the prevailing wage. The issue was highly contested in hearings, testimony, and debate. Ultimately, however, the DOL's interpretation and implementation of the H-2 program was a narrow one, and the temporary Mexican labor pool was never fully absorbed into the H-2 program.

45 Gilbert Gonzalez, Guest Workers or Colonized Labor?: Mexican Labor Migration to the United States, 146 (2006).

46 *Id.*

47 *Id.*

48 *Id.* at 147.

49 Gonzalez, *supra* note 42 at 147. In fact, without an alternative program created in the 1965 Amendments, the undocumented Mexican worker population grew.

50 *See* 111 Cong. Rec. S-23504 (1965).

51 CRS Worker, *supra* note 7 at 67.

52 *Id.*

The 1965 Act

> Every American can be proud today because we have finally eliminated the cruel and unjust national origins system from the immigration policy of the United States. We have righted a longstanding wrong. So today, any man, anywhere in the world can hope to begin a new life of freedom and a life of greater opportunity in the United States. No longer will his color or his religion or his nationality be a barrier to him.[53]

The 1965 Act abolished the long-held tradition of national origins quotas embedded in immigration law. The law is seen as a triumph of liberalism over the conservative restrictionist views that excluded generations of Asians and others from a rightful place in the migration stream. That the law was passed in the same era as other civil rights laws is no coincidence.[54] On the one hand, it was considered as much a civil rights triumph as the Voting Rights Act of 1965 and the Civil Rights Act of 1964.[55] Just as the termination of the Bracero Program at the end of 1964 was hailed as a humanitarian and progressive move,[56] so was Congress's attempt to diversify the stream of permanent immigrants to the United States. Senator Edward Kennedy proclaimed when the Act passed that it "stands with legislation in other fields – civil rights, poverty, education and health – to reaffirm in the 1960's our nation's continuing pursuit of justice, equality, and freedom."[57] Moreover, the 1965 Congress came to a general agreement that "matters corollary to the basic issue of eliminating the national-origins quota system should be left for deliberation at a future time."[58]

On the other hand, critics of the proposed legislation fought hard for some form of restriction that would curb increased immigration from third-world countries, Mexico in particular. Ultimately, Congress – at the same time that it abolished the national origins quotas – set quotas for the Western hemisphere, which includes Mexico, at 120,000 per year.[59] Notably, the United States had not imposed a quota before on this hemisphere. This was part of the price paid for eliminating the national

[53] President Lyndon B. Johnson, Remarks to the Committee on Italian Migration on the Occasion of the Termination of the National Origins Quota System (July 1, 1968) (transcript available at http://www.presidency.ucsb.edu/ws/?pid=28974).

[54] Gabriel J. Chin, *The Civil Rights Revolution Comes to Immigration Law: A New Look at the Immigration and Nationality Act of 1965*, 75 N.C. L. Rev. 273, 276 (1996).

[55] *Id.* at 276.

[56] Willard Wirtz letter reprinted in Appendix H of Secretary of Labor, Year in Transition: Seasonal Farm Labor (1965).

[57] Edward M. Kennedy, *The Immigration Act of 1965*, Annals Am. Acad. Pol. & Soc. Sci. 137, 138 (1966).

[58] *Id.* at 148.

[59] In 1976, Congress further restricted the quotas, setting country quotas in the Western hemisphere.

origins quotas.[60] The measure was undertaken at the same time that the national origins restrictions were lifted without much debate over the possible repercussions of such a move. As historian Timothy Henderson notes of the provision, "Oddly, the debate surrounding the immigration reform of 1965 omitted discussion of the Western Hemisphere generally, and of the undocumented Mexican immigrants specifically, as if those were entirely separate matters, unrelated to mainstream immigration."[61] The move confirmed the belief of even the liberal reformers of the time that there was no place for permanent migration from Mexico. An AFL-CIO lobbyist at the time of the passage of the 1965 Act noted that while immigration was legitimately foreseen from Europe and Asia, Mexican immigration "swarms in at the back door and through the windows."[62] The law also limited the number of immigrant visas available for unskilled manual work, a decision that mostly affected Mexican workers.[63] Mexican immigration had taken the place of Asian immigration as undesirable and unmentioned in the 1965 Act.

The Act was not generous to temporary workers, in part because of the heavy pressure from organized labor and others to end foreign contract labor programs. The hostility to temporary workers translated to a hostility toward Mexicans, who were historically viewed as temporary and transient residents. During the hearings on the 1965 Act the AFL-CIO urged that any amendments to the Act allow only for permanent and not temporary immigration for work.[64] The House Report on the 1965 amendments also clarified that there was no path to permanent status in the proposed preference categories that were to replace national origins quotas. The House Report on the 1965 amendments addressed the issue of foreign agricultural workers as follows:

> [T]he committee has given much thought to the practice of importing foreign labor to work in agricultural endeavors. Inasmuch as the Agricultural Act of 1949, as amended, has not been extended, it is the firm position of the committee that the provision of the INA, pertaining to temporary admission of laborers, shall not be abused.... The bill makes specific provision that skilled or unskilled labor of a temporary or seasonal nature is not entitled to any preference under the selective system."[65]

[60] David M. Reimers, *An Unintended Reform: The 1965 Immigration Act and Third World Immigration to the United States*, J. AM. ETHNIC HIS. 9, 18–19 (1983).

[61] TIMOTHY J. HENDERSON, BEYOND BORDERS: A HISTORY OF MEXICAN MIGRATION TO THE UNITED STATES, 100 (2011).

[62] AFL-CIO lobbyist Hyman Bookbinder, quoted in DANIEL TICHENOR, DIVIDING LINES: THE POLITICS OF IMMIGRATION CONTROL IN AMERICA, 247 (2002).

[63] *See* INA § 203(b)(3); *See also* CRS REPORT, MEXICAN MIGRATION, *supra* note 9.

[64] CRS WORKER, *supra* note 7 at 68.

[65] *Id.*

The Senate report on the 1965 amendments was also silent on the subject of temporary agricultural labor, noting that "[t]he bill specifically provides that skilled or unskilled labor of a temporary or seasonal nature is not to be entitled to any preference under the selection system for the allocation of immigrant visas."[66]

Most important, in a concession to organized labor, the Act included a provision requiring that before a worker could seek entry, the Department of Labor had to certify that there were not enough American workers to perform the jobs for which employers requested temporary help and that employment of such workers would not affect wages of American workers.[67] In the 1952 version of the Act, petitioners seeking entry to perform skilled or unskilled labor could not enter *if* the Secretary of Labor certified that there were sufficient able and qualified U.S. workers to fill the job category or that the petitioner would adversely affect the wages and working conditions of the U.S. work force.[68] Few certifications – fewer than sixty – were issued under the 1952 version of the statute, which placed the DOL in a secondary, advisory role.[69] The 1965 version of the provision reversed the procedure and placed the burden on the employer seeking temporary work to obtain a certification.[70] Importantly, the provision now gave the DOL greater leverage and control over the flow of work-based migration into the United States because the agency was now directly involved in individual decisions regarding entry.[71] This provision mirrored the authority that the DOL had under the Bracero Program. The provision applied to the professional and skilled and unskilled categories of permanent immigration as well as to non-preference categories and –importantly – to all Western hemisphere applicants.[72] Ultimately, Secretary Wirtz applied the labor certification provision to limit the use of the H-2 program and to ensure it did not simply replace the Bracero Program as a vehicle for temporary labor. A DOL report issued in 1965 on the transitional use of Braceros noted an 83 percent reduction in the use of foreign labor from 1964 to 1965.[73]

To ensure, moreover, that the temporary Mexican labor program was not simply replaced with a path to permanent residence, the 1965 Congress imposed caps on the immigrant visas available to the Western hemisphere countries. The move was made in the name of fairness. Congressmen denounced the inequity of the caps on the rest of the world while the Western hemisphere remained relatively free of such

66 CRS Worker, *supra* note 7 at 69.

67 *See* INA § 212(a)(5); *See also* Henderson, *supra* note 58 at 101.

68 McCarran-Walter Act, Sec. 212(a)(14).

69 Reimers, *supra* note 57 at 17–18.

70 INA § 212(a)(5).

71 Reimers, *supra* note 57 at 17–18. Under the 1952 Act, the DOL's role had been advisory.

72 Immigration Act of 1965, Pub.L. 89–236, 79 Stat. 911.

73 Secretary of Labor, Year in Transition: Seasonal Farm Labor (1965).

regulation. The 1965 Congress ignored, however, the level of regulation occurring both through temporary work programs and through inadmissibility provisions aimed at controlling Mexican immigration. Once the temporary programs were eliminated and caps places on immigration, the rise of undocumented immigration was inevitable. Sociologist Douglas Massey notes that while the numbers of legal immigrants remained fairly constant between 1965 and 1985, the number of temporary workers decreased and the numbers of illegal entrants increased at roughly the same levels. According to Massey's calculations, the temporary worker population went from about 450,000 in 1955 to almost zero by 1968, while the undocumented population went from about 50,000 to about 450,000 in the same period.[74]

9.4 THE CONSEQUENCES OF NOT INCORPORATING BRACEROS INTO 1965 ACT

As a result of the termination of the Bracero Program and the failure of the INA of 1965 to incorporate former Braceros into a viable guest worker program, the undocumented Mexican population, which was already considered a problem in the 1950s and 1960s, increased after the law went into effect.[75] Employers shut out of the H-2 labor market simply resorted to undocumented Mexican labor. The failure of the 1965 Act to create a place for Braceros soon transformed into a failure of the government to control illegal immigration and growing public alarm about the problem.[76] In 1968, when the law went into effect, 151,000 Mexicans were deported. When the law was further amended in 1976 to reduce Mexican quotas to 20,000 per year, 781,000 Mexicans were deported.[77] By the end of the 1970s, the INS was apprehending nearly one million undocumented persons along the U.S.-Mexico border. The number was almost eight times the number of undocumented immigrants from the rest of the countries combined.[78]

The CRS 1980 Report on Temporary Workers acknowledged the problem as one of undocumented immigration created in the wake of the 1965 reforms:

> On August 4, 1977, President Jimmy Carter announced his program for the control of undocumented aliens.... In apparent recognition of the likelihood that an effective curtailment of the flow of undocumented aliens would increase pressures for the legal importation of temporary foreign workers, President Carter also

[74] Douglas A. Massey and Karen A. Pren, *Unintended Consequences of US Immigration Policy: Explaining the Post-1965 Surge from Latin America*, 38 POPULATION AND DEVELOPMENT REVIEW 4 (2012).

[75] HENDERSON, *supra* note 58 at 99; Reimers, *supra* note 57 at 23.

[76] *Id.*

[77] HENDERSON, *supra* note 58 at 102.

[78] *Id.*

> announced that he is requesting a comprehensive review of the temporary foreign worker (H-2) program.... [T]he possibility of the elimination of undocumented aliens as a fairly dependable source of labor was a matter of serious concern to some employers during this period, particularly in the area of agriculture.

Congress was placed on notice that the failure of the 1965 Act to incorporate Braceros into the existing H-2 program was contributing to undocumented population growth. A Congressional Research Service report on temporary worker programs placed the problem in the hands of the DOL and its restrictive interpretation of the H-2 provisions in the statute:

> A relatively small number of Mexicans has been admitted under the H-2 provision; this is despite the fact that, unlike Public Law 78, the H-2 provision has no geographic restrictions. The limited number of Mexican H-2's has been partly the result of administrative determinations by the U.S. Labor Department, either that domestic workers have been available in the areas and occupations for which Mexican workers have been requested, or that employers have failed to meet the requirements of the regulations governing the importation of H-2s. Thus, the decision to admit onion pickers into Presidio, Texas in June 1977, reportedly at the urging of President Carter, was contrary to the recommendation of the Department of Labor.[79]

In the meantime, the undocumented population continued to grow as employers found labor in the undocumented market. The failure to incorporate Braceros into a legal path to citizenship was framed as a growing undocumented population problem throughout the 1970s and 1980s. Legal scholar Kitty Calavita notes that the problem was one of short-term solutions creating the next generation of problems:

> In 1986, twenty years after the last Braceros left the field, apprehensions of illegal immigrants reached over 1.5 million. With the Bracero solution to illegal immigration dismantled, not only did employers return to using illegal labor, but the flow was redoubled. The contract labor system had strengthened the historical dependence of western growers on Mexican labor. And so the dialectical sequence of contradictions and conflicts plays on, as the solution of one period prepares the way for the conflicts of the next.[80]

Continued Pressure for an Expanded Guest Worker Program to Replace the Bracero Program

Growers continued their pressure on the federal government to replace the Bracero Program with something similar. The H-2 program as implemented by the DOL was

[79] CRS Worker *supra* note 7 at 62.

[80] Kitty Calavita, *supra* note 2 at 181.

too restrictive for them. It was easy to choose undocumented labor as an alternative. One senator noted,

> I think any association will tell you that in the past on the west coast illegal aliens have been used extensively. You do not like that. I do not like that. Growers do not prefer it. They have been unable to get any other satisfactory source of help. So long as illegals were available and so long as INS was not seriously enforcing the laws, it was a practical solution to a problem that exists. That is a problem that cannot be allowed to continue.[81]

He went on to warn that any tightening of restrictions on illegal entry would have to be balanced out with an expansion of the current guestworker program:

> The day of the illegal alien in this country is going to dwindle very rapidly, I think, and should. You take that factor away and you are going to have, if the growers are believed, a substantial shortage. They think they are going to have a substantial shortage and they are especially worried about trying to produce 7,000 workers in a small valley on a short-term basis.[82]

Growers opposed to the DOL's restrictive application of the H-2 program did not end their lobbying for an expanded temporary worker program after 1965. They also sought an end to the DOL's role in labor certification. In 1977, for example, the Senate Select Committee on Small Business held hearings on the "feasibility of an expanded legal temporary worker program as an alternative to illegal entrants, particularly in the context of the Labor Department's less than enthusiastic attitude toward the foreign worker program."[83]

The lobbying during this period was now done in the context of a growing call for employer sanctions in the immigration statute. In the 1970s, Perry Ellsworth of the National Council of Agricultural Employers noted, "if Congress passes legislation prohibiting the employment of undocumented aliens, Congress must enact legislation that will set forth inflexible rules which the Department of Labor must follow in arriving at a decision regarding the certification of small growers for the use of temporary foreign agriculture workers."[84]

Leading up to the Congressional activity of 1986, the DOL tried to restrict the H-2 program even more. In consultation with a firm that culled through hearing testimony, it decided not to restrict the program, in part because the firm found that growers perceived a relationship between undocumented and temporary work:

Many agricultural employers, particularly those in the western states, apparently are looking toward the alien certification process as a future alternative to present

[81] CRS Worker, *supra* note 7 at 73.
[82] *Id.*
[83] *Id.* at 72.
[84] *Id.*

use of illegals in the event that employers are made legally responsible for hiring illegals, or as they put it, if the supply of illegals is cut off. Pointing to the decline of the seasonal agricultural labor force, they are concerned that any tightening up of the alien certification process may pose future problems."[85]

The 1986 Act

By 1986, the consequences of failing to create a legal path to immigration to the United States from Mexico were evident, although their implications were highly contested. On the one hand, immigration advocates joined with employers and others to push for a path to permanent residence and citizenship. On the other, restrictionists called for increased border enforcement and employer sanctions to curb illegal immigration flows. The result was again a compromise.

In the Immigration Reform and Control Act of 1986, Congress finally made agricultural workers available to agricultural growers through the H-2A program. It created a path to permanent status for workers who were initially temporary agricultural workers.[86] It also created a separate path for legalization for those who had been in undocumented status in the United States before the Act's effective date. The IRCA finally implemented the employer sanctions provisions that had been debated since the 1950s.[87] The provision was touted as an effective tool for closing down illegal immigration by including employers in the immigration enforcement scheme.[88] The provision was weakened at the last minute, however, by an amendment that created a safe harbor for employers that requested documentation from workers regardless of their validity.[89] The practical effect of the employer sanctions provision has been to drive undocumented workers deeper into the shadows and to place the onus on the workers for violations of the provision. In fact, one of the ways that employers have eluded enforcement has been through extensive subcontracting of workers.[90]

9.5 THE CURRENT SITUATION AND THE LABOR-EMPLOYER COMPROMISES FOR THE FUTURE

Eventually, under pressure from employers, the DOL relaxed its certification requirements, allowing more Mexican temporary labor to enter under the temporary H-2 program. Mexico is now one of fifty-eight countries eligible as a sending

85 CRS WORKER, *supra* note 7 at 75.

86 The Special Agricultural Worker provision is found at INA §210; 8 U.S.C. §1160.

87 INA § 274A; *See* CALAVITA, *supra* note 2 at 182.

88 CALAVITA, *supra* note 2 at 182.

89 *Id.* at 183.

90 *Id.*

country for H-2 visas. Today, Mexicans comprise the majority of H-2 visa holders. Mexicans accounted for almost 83% of the H2A and 2B visas issued in 2010.[91] The undocumented population, meanwhile, has reached an estimated 11 million. Today's employers have conflated undocumented immigrants with Latinos and express preferences for these workers in low-wage workplaces. The undocumented and temporary labor population Congress failed to find a place for in the 1965 Act, or in the 1986 Act is now entrenched and more vulnerable than ever. The same narratives that existed in 1917, moreover, perpetuate themselves today: Latinos are hard workers and will do the jobs that native-born workers will not do.

Even the proposals for comprehensive immigration reform today rely on the narrative that there are some jobs Americans will not do and that require temporary labor. Even the so-called W visa in the Senate's 2013 failed comprehensive immigration reform plan created an expanded nonimmigrant temporary worker category based on the same assumptions as the old guest worker programs (i.e., Americans will not perform these jobs). This time, the employers won some of their battles of the 1965 era. The U.S. Department of Agriculture (USDA) would now be involved in the regulation of this guest worker contract labor. The USDA would have to establish a process to certify employers as "designated agricultural employers." The USDA, in consultation with the DOL,[92] would make determinations about the number of workers needed every year based on a number of factors, including (as the growers of the 1965 era strongly advocated) a demonstrated shortage of workers, the number of nonimmigrant workers sought the previous year, and the number who worked in agriculture the previous year.[93] There are already estimates that the program would reach suggested caps of 337,000 by its third year of operation.[94] This is close to the numbers of Braceros brought into the U.S. around the peak of the program.[95] Most importantly during and after the initial period of adjusting the caps, the USDA would remain a major player in establishing annual caps. The USDA would also have the authority to establish procedures for adjusting annual allocation levels in cases of emergency labor shortages.[96]

The W visa for nonagricultural workers would be available under criteria established by DHS (as employers strongly advocated during the 1950s). Employers would register with DHS to become "registered" employers for "registered"

[91] Cong. Research Serv., Mexican Migration, *supra* note 9.

[92] Note that the DOL is once again relegated to a consultative role.

[93] Border Security, Economic Opportunity, and Immigration Modernization Act, S. 744, sec. 2232, 113th Cong. (2013).

[94] Economic Policy Institute, Future Flows and Worker Rights in S. 744, 32 (2013).

[95] Year in Transition, *supra* note 53 at Appendix H.

[96] Border Security, Economic Opportunity, and Immigration Modernization Act, S. 744, sec. 4703, 113th Cong. (2013).

positions.[97] Rather than seeking certification from the DOL, the employer would attest to a shortage of workers in the registered position, that a required wage level would be met, that the working conditions of W visa holders would not adversely affect the working conditions of other workers employed in similar positions, and that no qualified U.S. worker is ready, willing, and available for the position. Note that this requirement (which is already available for high-skilled immigrant work visas) shifts the balance of power that weighed in favor of the DOL upon implementation of the 1965 Act. In fact, it shifts the power decidedly in favor of the DHS, which under the proposed law would have the authority (although not exclusive) to investigate and bring claims related to the terms and conditions of a W visa holder's employment or related to the nonhiring of a U.S. worker.[98]

The W visa program would be available only for the most undesirable jobs and only on a temporary basis. Although the plan allows for a path to citizenship after a three-year period, the plan continues to try to protect certain jobs for American workers. The program would be capped, for example, for workers in the construction industry,[99] even though in some parts of the country immigrants now perform most of these jobs.

9.6 CONCLUSION

From the assumptions about the transiency and labor skills of temporary workers to the debates over which federal agency has the best capacity to regulate labor flows, the discussion continues to center on the place of Mexican workers outside of a more permanent and regular immigration system. The history of debates over undocumented migration after 1965, moreover, demonstrates that the issues have yet to be resolved. In fact, they are amazingly similar in their content and character.

The failure of the 1965 Congress to adequately resolve the struggles between employers, the DOL, and the (at that time) INS over control of temporary labor flows resulted in a decades-long discussion about undocumented immigration. In part because the 1965 Congress failed to clarify the place of former Braceros in the migrant stream, the discussions over illegal immigration devolved into a conflation of illegal immigrant and Mexican.[100] It is unsurprising, given the history of temporary worker programs, that the 1965 Congress was unable to clarify the position of Mexican workers. Ultimately, important parties have been left out of negotiations surrounding the creation of contract labor agreements and temporary

97 *Id.* at sec. 4703.

98 *Id.*

99 Border Security, Economic Opportunity, and Immigration Modernization Act, S. 744, sec. 4703, 113th Cong. (2013).

100 The conflation had started with earlier characterizations of Mexicans as "wetbacks," and continued after the 1965 Act. *See* SUBJECTS, *supra* note 3 at 149.

worker programs in the United States. If the goal of such programs includes enhanced worker protections, sincere commitments to the temporary nature of the programs from participants, a predictable, documented labor supply, and a fair employer-employee relationship that adheres to current labor and employment standards, the content of the discussions must change. That can only happen if the workers themselves are given a place at the table. This observation holds true as much today as it did for the discussions surrounding the 1965 Act.

PART IV

Political and Economic Issues

10

The 1965 Immigration Act

The Demographic and Political Transformation of Mexicans and Mexican Americans in U.S. Border Communities

Jeannette Money and Kristina Victor

10.1 INTRODUCTION

The Mexican and Mexican American community in the United States has grown extraordinarily rapidly since the passage of the Immigration and Nationality Act Amendments of 1965. The Integrated Public Use Microdata Series (IPUMS) allows us to track the changes in the Mexican and Mexican American population in the United States encompassing the years 1960 through 2010.[1] Table 10.1 shows the Mexican and Mexican American (MMA) population in the United States over the last five decades has increased from 4 million in 1960 to more than 32 million in 2010 – an eightfold increase. Yet their influence on border security issues, central to the lives of many in this community, has not kept pace. In this chapter we examine the influence of the 1965 Act on the demographic and political transformations of the Mexican and Mexican American community and explore their growing influence on U.S. border security along the U.S.-Mexican border.

The 1965 Act is often perceived as the rectification of an antiquated immigration system based on racially discriminatory quotas. Yet it also carried some significant burdens for at least one immigration flow into the United States: Mexicans. By placing a cap on Western Hemisphere migration for the first time, it limited legal migration that had previously been virtually unlimited, at least in principle. Legal Mexican migration was further restricted when the 20,000 per-country quota was imposed on Western Hemisphere migration in 1976. Migrant networks were

[1] The IPUMS-USA datasets use samples drawn from the federal censuses in conjunction with data from the American Community Surveys. The IMPUMS-USA dataset is a 1% sample of the U.S. Census; for person-level analyses, the data are weighted with the variable "PERWT" that gives the population represented by each individual in the sample. The Mexican/Mexican American designation is self-identified.

TABLE 10.1. *Mexican and Mexican American population in the United States*

Census year	Total U.S. population	Total MMAs living in the U.S.	Percent of U.S. population
1960	179,292,732	4,024,429	2.2%
1970	203,392,031	10,252,700	5.0%
1980	226,862,400	8,771,800	3.8%
1990	248,107,628	13,374,999	5.3%
2000	281,420,906	20,867,722	7.4%
2010	309,349,689	32,915,983	10.6%

Source: IPUMS.

already well developed through the Bracero Program, so the restrictions quickly generated a larger, more permanent, and more undocumented population. In this essay we document the demographic impact of the 1965 law in terms of increased permanence and increased illegality.

Political empowerment of the Mexican and Mexican American community was gradually enhanced through four channels: second-generation access to citizenship through birth on U.S. soil; legalization via the Immigration Reform and Control Act of 1986; increased naturalization when the Mexican government recognized a form of dual nationality in 1998; and finally, through geographic concentration. In the second half of this chapter we explore the political power of the Mexican and Mexican American community to shape border security policy along the U.S.-Mexican border, illustrating the delayed but growing influence of the largest group of immigrants in the United States.

The essay begins with an overview of Mexican immigration patterns to the United States prior to the passage of the 1965 Immigration Act. The Act is then analyzed in terms of its specific impact on Mexican immigration. The Section 10.4 delineates the four channels through which the Mexican and Mexican American community gradually enhanced its political power. Section 10.5 presents our dependent variable, border security, and draws on the literature addressing the role of immigrants in U.S. foreign policy to generate hypotheses about the influence of the Mexican and Mexican American community on border security issues. Sections 10.6 and 10.7 present qualitative and quantitative analyses of the impact of the Mexican and Mexican American community on border security policy along the U.S. Mexican border. In the Conclusions section we point to the need for additional research on the role of immigrants in the U.S. political system.

10.2 PATTERNS OF MEXICAN IMMIGRATION PRIOR TO THE 1965 ACT

We first acknowledge the 1848 Treaty of Guadalupe Hidalgo, which ceded about 55 percent of Mexican territory to the United States. The nationals living in that territory were given the choice of relocating to within the new boundaries of the Mexican state or becoming U.S. citizens with full rights. Of the approximately 100,000 individuals affected, 90 percent chose to become U.S. citizens. These individuals are the original Mexican Americans in the United States.[2]

Subsequent Mexican immigration to the United States was limited until the regime of Porfirio Diaz initiated policies that led to tighter economic ties with the United States and the beginnings of economic growth that dislocated agrarian populations. Economic growth in the American Southwest was the pull, compounded by labor demand generated by World War I; subsequent restrictive U.S. immigration policy limited the influx of immigrants from elsewhere, generating a strong demand for Mexican labor.[3] The U.S. border agency recorded almost half a million Mexican entries during the 1920s. We point out that although Western Hemisphere migrants, and hence Mexicans, were not subject to quotas, undocumented migration has always been fairly common.[4] The land border between the United States and Mexico facilitated illegal entry. By avoiding ports of entry into the United States, migrants were able to avoid head taxes, visa fees, and, after 1917 legislation, literacy tests and other potential grounds for exclusion. However, migration remained limited in scope and circular in nature. Most estimates suggest that nearly three in every four immigrants returned to Mexico in the 1920s.[5]

The Great Depression elicited both voluntary repatriation of Mexicans, encouraged by the Mexican government, and deportations by the U.S. government. Controversy exists on the levels of deportation and the number of U.S. citizens who were deported, but the largest portion of repatriation was voluntary and reproduced

2 TIMOTHY J. HENDERSON, BEYOND BORDERS: A HISTORY OF MEXICAN MIGRATION TO THE UNITED STATES (Wiley-Blackwell 2011).

3 *Id.*

4 Immigration legislation was also routinely waived for Mexicans, making legal what would have been undocumented entry. For an overview of various ad hoc regulations that privileged Mexican migrants, see Gary P. Freeman & Frank D. Bean, *Mexico and U.S. Worldwide Immigration Policy*, *in* AT THE CROSSROADS: MEXICO AND U.S. IMMIGRATION POLICY, Frank D. Bean et al., eds., Rowman & Littlefield 1997 and ARTHUR F. CORWIN, ED., IMMIGRANTS – AND IMMIGRANTS: PERSPECTIVES ON MEXICAN LABOR MIGRATION TO THE UNITED STATES (Greenwood Press 1978).

5 Brian Gratton & Emily Merchant, *Immigration, Repatriation, and Deportation: the Mexican-Origin Population in the United States, 1920–1950*, 47 (4) INT'L MIGRATION REV. 944–975 (2013). *See* Freeman & Bean *supra* note 4.

the circular migration experienced during the 1920s.[6] Poor economic conditions in the United States during the 1930s drew fewer migrants, and census data confirm that the Mexican and Mexican American population in 1940 was less than that population a decade earlier, a pattern similar to all other immigrant groups.[7]

Labor shortages during World War II resulted in an agreement between the United States and Mexico that reconstructed and expanded the circular migration patterns that had previously existed. The "Agreement Respecting the Temporary Migration of Mexican Agricultural Workers" incorporated Mexican demands for protection of Mexican migrant workers and fulfilled the demands of U.S. employers, in particular agricultural interests, with a legal temporary supply of workers. A maximum of 62,000 Mexicans was authorized annually during the war; after the war ended, the program was renewed annually until 1964. Maximum annual admissions reached almost 450,000 at the peak of the program in the late 1950s. This program generated a legal process for admissions but, given the demand in agriculture, also elicited an undocumented flow that is estimated to be equal to the legal flow.[8] This illegality was dealt with in part by mechanisms that "dried out" the "wetbacks." Undocumented workers were sometimes taken back to the border, stepped over, and were then readmitted as legal Bracero workers. However, these flows remained predominantly cyclical rather than permanent.

Table 10.2 provides an overview of the Mexican population resident in the United States prior to the 1965 Immigration Act. The settled Mexican population grew relative to the circular flow and generated a growing portion of the population that was Mexican American. By 1960, 86 percent of the population was U.S.-born, although that was a small proportion of the U.S. population as a whole.

10.3 THE 1965 IMMIGRATION ACT AND ITS IMPACT ON MEXICAN IMMIGRATION

Before describing the impact of the 1965 Immigration Act on Mexican migration, it should be noted that the Bracero Program came to an end in 1964. Its legacy was a densely knit migration network of Mexicans who had a continuous but cyclical attachment to U.S. labor markets.[9] Given that a substantial portion of the circular flow was undocumented, it is unsurprising that this flow would continue, even though the program was discontinued.

6 *See* Gratton & Merchant, *supra* note 5.

7 *Id.*

8 *See id.*; HENDERSON, *supra* note 2.

9 Douglas S. Massey & Zai Liang, *The Long-term Consequences of a Temporary Worker Program: The US Bracero Experience*, 8 POPULATION RESEARCH & POL'Y REV. 199–226 (1989).

TABLE 10.2. *Mexican origin persons in the United States by generation, 1900–1960*

Census year	Born in Mexico	Second generation	Subsequent generations	Total of Mexican origin	Percent foreign born	Percent of U.S. population
1900	99,286	116,324	171,299	386,909	26	0.5
1910	237,196	160,874	211,485	609,555	39	0.7
1920	499,547	249,755	235,553	984,855	51	0.9
1930	649,207	614,988	427,561	1,691,746	38	1.3
1940	387,600	685,200	518,900	1,591,700	24	1.2
1950	456,390	914,430	906,840	2,277,660	20	1.5
1960	582,603	–	–	4,024,429	14	2.2

Source: Reproduced from Gratton & Merchant, *supra* note 5; originally from IPUMS.

The impact of the 1965 Immigration Act was twofold. First, at the end of the Bracero Program, the Act prevented migrants who circulated to the United States from entering legally under different auspices. Second, by preventing the circular movement of migrants, it created incentives for the circular migration to become permanent.

The Act is most noted for its dismantling of the National Origins Quota System and the creation of a first-come, first-served policy toward immigration, based on family and employment preferences, with an annual overall Eastern Hemisphere quota of 170,000 and a maximum quota of 20,000 per country. The entry of close family members of U.S. citizens (spouse, unmarried minor children, and parents) was not subject to numerical restriction. However, the Act also introduced a 120,000 annual quota on Western Hemispheric migration for the first time, although the 20,000 per-country quota along with the preference system was not imposed on Western Hemisphere migration until 1976. The alternative to the Bracero Program was to enter legally under the 120,000 annual quota. Given that the circular flow of migrants from Mexico during the prior period ranged from 450,000 to upward of 900,000,[10] this annual quota prevented the vast majority of previously circular migrants from entering the United States under legal auspices. Once implemented on July 1, 1968, a backlog of requests for legal entry quickly developed.[11]

[10] *See* Gratton & Merchant, *supra* note 5. "Operation Wetback"in 1954 deported some 1.3 million Mexicans, so this probably is a conservative estimate of the prior annual flows.

[11] *See* Freeman & Bean, *supra* note 4.

The inability to circulate freely increases the costs of migrating and leads migrants to develop more permanent migration patterns.[12] The replacement of circular migration with permanent migration is a pattern typical of guest worker programs, particularly when they are phased out. Germany is a case in point where the end of its guest worker program in 1973 led to the decrease of male migrant workers but to an increase in the overall migrant population with a dramatic drop in labor force participations rates from 70 percent to 40 percent almost overnight.[13] The same is true with the Mexican migrants. However, unlike the German case that permitted family reunification for legal guest workers, Mexicans were very likely to be undocumented. However, their undocumented status did not prevent but enlarged family reunification.

The ultimate consequence of the 1965 Immigration Act on the Mexican immigrant population was to increase its undocumented status and to increase its permanence. The 1976 revisions to the Immigration and Nationality Act only aggravated the problem of illegality by moving from an annual quota of 120,000, which could be used by any Western Hemisphere migrant and therefore allowed Mexicans a disproportionate share, to imposing a per-country quota of 20,000 on Mexico and all other nations in the Western Hemisphere. Mexicans already took more than half of the annual allotment, three times more than the new quota.[14] And the lack of documentation of the Mexican community prevented its political enfranchisement.

Table 10.3 illustrates that legal resident alien entries expanded rapidly after the turn of the twentieth century and peaked at about 46,000 per year during the 1920s. Legal entries plummeted during the Great Depression and recovered only slowly in the 1940s. The 1950s, when annual circular migration through the Bracero Program and the accompanying undocumented entries achieved levels of 450,000 to 900,000 annually, total legal entry averaged 30,000 per year, less than one-tenth of the annual circular flow. It was not until the late 1960s, after the passage of the Western Hemisphere quotas, that the demand for legal entry began to expand and reached the levels of the 1920s. Legal entries expanded to accommodate need for permanent legal residence, but the 1965 Act did not provide sufficient visas to meet demand. Undocumented entry and residence continued unabated and began to be reflected in documented entry after the passage of the 1986 Immigration Reform and Control Act that offered amnesty

[12] *See* Massey & Liang, *supra* note 9; Douglas S. Massey, Jorge Durand & Nolan J. Malone, Beyond Smoke and Mirrors: Mexican Immigration in an Era of Economic Integration (Russell Sage Foundation 2002); Florian K. Kaufmann, Mexican Labor Migrants and U.S. Immigration Policies from Sojourner to Emigrant? (LFB Scholarly Publishing 2011).

[13] Jeannette Money, *Immigrants as Fellow Citizens?*, *in* Migrants and Minorities: The European Response (Adam Luedtke, ed. Cambridge Scholars Publishing 2011).

[14] *See* Freeman & Bean, *supra* note 4.

TABLE 10.3. *Decennial legal entries from Mexico*

Year	Legal entries	Year	Legal entries	Year	Legal entries
1821–30	4,817	1881–90	1,913	1941–50	60,589
1831–40	6,599	1891–1900	971	1951–60	299,811
1841–50	3,271	1901–10	49,642	1961–70	453,937
1851–60	2,078	1911–20	219,004	1971–80	640,294
1861–70	5,162	1921–30	459,387	1981–90	1,655,843
1871–80	5,162	1931–40	22,319		

Source: DHS Yearbooks.

to more than 3 million undocumented aliens, more than half of whom were Mexican (see Table 10.3).

This overview documents the impact of the 1965 Immigration Act on the Mexican and Mexican American community in the United States. The circular movement prevalent through the mid-1960s was halted, leading to a growing permanent Mexican and Mexican American population but one that was dominated by undocumented flows. This severely limited the ability of the Mexican and Mexican American community to participate in local, state, and national policy making where their interests were affected. In the next section we delineate the four determinants that slowly enhanced the political power of the Mexican community in the United States.

10.4 ENFRANCHISEMENT OF THE MEXICAN AND MEXICAN AMERICAN COMMUNITY

Given the large undocumented Mexican population, it is not surprising that their political influence was limited. These immigrants confronted many barriers in their daily lives in terms of low wages, poor working conditions, lack of access to health, education, and other provisions of the welfare state, and widespread discrimination. However, existing and new legal provisions ultimately provided access of the Mexican population to political voice.

Jus Soli Provisions. The 14th Amendment to the U.S. Constitution confirmed the *jus soli* nature of U.S. citizenship. Therefore, all children born to Mexicans (or anyone else) on U.S. territory became citizens at birth. Second-generation Mexicans were Mexican Americans. But their political participation awaited their growth to majority. Thus, the earliest beneficiaries of the post-1965 Mexican immigrants came of age only in 1983.

Table 10.4 documents the rise of the U.S.-born Mexican American population. The table comes from census data and divides the Mexican and Mexican American

TABLE 10.4. *Mexican and Mexican American demographics*

Census year	Total MMAs in US	U.S. citizens	Born in Mexico, total	Born in Mexico, naturalized	Not U.S. citizens
1960	4,024,429		582,603	–	14.4%
1970	10,252,700	3,957,300	1,685,000	326,200	58.2%
1980	8,771,800	6,459,760	2,242,100	568,900	19.1%
1990	13,374,999	8,779,290	4,409,033	991,330	25.6%
2000	20,867,722	12,048,622	9,325,452	1,916,322	32.3%
2010	32,915,983	20,969,793	11,964,241	2,696,328	27.3%

Source: IPUMS, 1% sample of U.S. census data.

community into those born in the United States and those born in Mexico (foreign and naturalized).[15] The MMA population rose by 250 percent from 1960 to 1970, following the passage of the 1965 Immigration Act, but the citizen population rose by only 15 percent. Thereafter, the citizen population of U.S.-born rose rapidly, by 63 percent from 1970 to 1980, 35 percent from 1980 to 1990, 37 percent from 1990 to 2000, and 74 percent from 2000 to 2010.

Immigration Reform and Control Act (IRCA). The passage of this Act in 1986 provided amnesty to undocumented immigrants who could demonstrate their continuous residence in the United States since January 1, 1982. It also created a category of Special Agricultural Workers (SAW) and provided legal residency status for some of those individuals. As a result of this amnesty program, 3.1 million immigrants, more than half of whom were Mexicans, were granted legal residence status that provided a gateway to citizenship. However, again, the effects on enfranchisement of the Mexican community were delayed for a minimum of five years, the required minimum legal residence for application for naturalization. Moreover, Mexican immigrants faced an external barrier to naturalization imposed by Mexican laws that did not recognize dual nationality and therefore penalized Mexicans who naturalized.

Table 10.5 provides evidence of the legalization of the Mexican immigrant community based on the IRCA amnesties. The bulk of the IRCA entries are recorded in 1989, 1990, and 1991, when almost one million Mexicans were granted permanent legal residence status based on continuous residence in the United States since January 1, 1982.

[15] In the 1970 census, 57.9% of this population refused to disclose their legal status. This may understate the U.S. citizen population.

TABLE 10.5. *Legal permanent resident entries of Mexicans subsequent to IRCA amnesties*

1986	66,533	1992	214,128
1987	72,351	1993	126,642
1988	95,170	1994	111,415
1989	405,660	1995	90,045
1990	680,186	1996	163,749
1991	947,923		

Source: DHS Yearbooks.

Dual Nationality and Naturalization. Naturalization is the central mechanism for obtaining political voice in the immigrant's host country. However, the laws of the host state are only one component of the equation. The laws of the home state can either penalize or facilitate the attainment of citizenship in the host country. The literature on home country policies toward their emigrants is relatively small but it suggests that there are at least four possible positions the home country can take.[16] In the first case, the emigrant is an enemy of the state, seeking to overthrow the government in power. These individuals are often labeled as exiles and/or refugees. A milder but still negative position would be to view immigrants as deserters of the nation, seeking their fortunes elsewhere rather than contributing to the development of their home country. States could also take a neutral position on emigrants, ignoring their departure as being irrelevant to the home country's goals and trajectory. Finally, states could take a positive view of immigrants as a valued community with whom the state would like to retain ties. The immigrant community could be seen as a potential resource for development purposes as well as a potential actor in the host state to extract favorable policies from the host state toward the home state.

Empirically, in the case of Mexico,[17] Mohar argues that the Mexican state has followed a trajectory from immigrants as deserters to immigrants as resources.[18] Mexico began to organize immigrant communities in the United States in 1990 with the creation of the Program for Mexican Communities Living Abroad (PCME). But a more important reform was the 1998 modification of nationality law to allow naturalized citizens of another country to retain (or regain) their Mexican

[16] David FitzGerald, A Nation of Emigrants: How Mexico Manages its Migration (University of California Press 2009); Gustavo Mohar, *Relations with the Mexican Diaspora*, *in* Latinos and U.S. Foreign Policy. Representing the "Homeland"? (Rodolfo O. DelaGarza & Harry P. Pachon, eds., Rowman & Littlefield, 2000).

[17] *See* Mohar, *supra* note 16.

[18] *Also see* FitzGerald, *supra* note 16.

TABLE 10.6. *Citizenship acquisition by Mexicans*

Year	Mexican naturalizations	Total naturalizations	Percent	Year	Mexican naturalizations	Total naturalization	Percent
1991	22,066	308,058	7.1%	2002	76,310	572,646	13.3%
1992	12,880	240,252	5.3%	2003	55,946	462,435	12.0%
1993	23,630	314,681	7.5%	2004	63,840	537,151	11.9%
1994	46,186	434,107	10.6%	2005	77,089	604,280	12.7%
1995	79,614	488,088	16.3%	2006	83,979	702,589	11.9%
1996	217,418	1,044,689	20.8%	2007	122,258	660,477	18.5%
1997	134,494	598,225	22.4%	2008	321,815	1,046,539	22.0%
1998	109,065	563,060	23.5%	2009	111,630	743,715	15.0%
1999	207,072	837,418	24.7%	2010	67,062	619,193	10.8%
2000	189,051	886,026	21.3%	2011	94,783	694,193	13.6%
2001	102,736	606,259	16.9%	2012	102,181	757,434	13.5%

Source: DHS Yearbooks.

nationality.[19] This allows Mexicans to avoid prior penalties associated with the loss of Mexican citizenship. It allows dual nationals to legally work in Mexico, to establish Mexican businesses, and to buy property in the "forbidden zone," that is, within 100 kilometers of the border or 50 kilometers of the coast – properties that cannot be owned by foreigners. Therefore, we would anticipate that naturalization and the accompanying political power of Mexicans resident in the United States to rise after this reform.

Table 10.6 presents the record of Mexican naturalizations. The absolute number of naturalizations and their proportion of total naturalizations rose beginning in 1994, exactly five years after the initial granting of permanent residence status based on IRCA amnesties. The absolute number peaked at more than 200,000 in 1996, as the INS cleaned out a backlog of citizenship applications and the Mexican applications as a proportion of total applications peaked in 1999 at almost 25 percent of all naturalizations. The impact of the Mexican nationality law reform of 1998 does not appear to create much of a spike in U.S. naturalizations, but the level subsequent to the reform – ranging from 10.8 percent to 24 percent – is significantly higher than the rate of naturalizations pre-IRCA.

Geographic Concentration. Although the MMA population is large and growing, it is still a small minority of the U.S. population if evenly dispersed across the

[19] Mexico, Secretary of Foreign Relations, *The Law of Nationality*, www.mexicanlaws.com/SRE/nationality.htm, accessed Jan. 21, 2014.

TABLE 10.7. *Distribution of Mexican immigrants by state of residence*

State	1910	1920	1940	1950	1960	1970	1980	1990
Arizona	11.6%	14.1%	7.2%	6.7%	6.3%	4.5%	3.3%	3.4%
California	16.9%	21.6%	35.6%	34.0%	41.9%	52.7%	57.0%	57.8%
Illinois	0.3%	0.8%	2.5%	2.6%	4.8%	6.2%	7.7%	5.2%
New Mexico	4.5%	3.2%	4.2%	2.1%	1.8%	0.8%	0.8%	1.9%
Texas	55.2%	49.9%	39.5	44.5%	35.9%	26.5%	22.6%	22.1%
Other states	11.2%	10.5%	11.1%	10.2%	9.4%	9.4%	8.5%	10.3%

Source: Jorge Durand, Douglas S. Massey & Fernando Charvet, *The Changing Geography of Mexican Immigration to the United States: 1910-1996*, 81 (1) Soc. Sci. Q. 1–15 (2000).

United States. But the Mexican and Mexican American population has increased at different rates across the United States. Over the last five decades the list of the states with the largest numbers, and the greatest percentage, of Mexican and Mexican Americans has consistently included the southwest border states where, until 1990, 90 percent of the MMA population was concentrated: California, Texas, Arizona, and New Mexico (Table 10.7).

Tracing the Enfranchisement of the Mexican Population. The impact of the 1965 Immigration Act and the subsequent channels of enfranchisement are summarized in Table 10.8. We have argued that the act created a more permanent undocumented population. Since 1965 that population has grown through natural increase and new legal migration flows generated in large part by the family reunification provisions for U.S. citizens (outside quota controls) and the family preference system for legal resident aliens. These flows are supplemented by the legalization of the previously undocumented flows through IRCA amnesty provisions.

The MMA community's political enfranchisement followed slowly as the children of Mexicans born in the United States came of age and through higher rates of naturalization following the IRCA amnesty and Mexican nationality law reform.

The last column in Table 10.8 provides an indication of the "political participation gap." In 2010, the MMA community represented 10.6 percent of the U.S. population but only 7.5 percent were citizens (with 26.5 percent under the age of twenty-five, so they either cannot participate or have low levels of political participation). So it is not surprising that this community has less political weight than its size would suggest. Nonetheless, its geographic concentration allows it to speak with a louder voice in those states in which it is concentrated – the border states with Mexico. It is to that political participation we now turn.

TABLE 10.8. *Political participation gap*

Year	Decennial legal permanent residence entries	Total MMAs	Citizen	Naturalized	Percent citizen of U.S. population	Percent of U.S. population	Political participation gap
1960	453,937	4,024,429	3,441,826[a]		1.9%	2.2%	0.3%
1970	640,294	10,252,700	3,957,300	326,200	2.1%	5.0%	2.9%
1980	1,655,843	8,771,800	6,459,760	568,900	3.0%	3.8%	0.8%
1990	1,009,586	13,374,999	8,779,290	991,330	3.9%	5.3%	1.4%
2000	2,757,418	20,867,722	12,048,622	1,916,322	4.9%	7.4%	2.5%
2010	1,704,166	32,915,983	20,969,793	2,696,328	7.5%	10.6%	3.1%

[a] We only know the number of MMAs born in Mexico; this figure assumes that none of that population of 582,603 born in Mexico was naturalized.
Sources: Decennial legal permanent residence entries from DHS Yearbooks. MMAs from IPUMS.

10.5 BORDER SECURITY POLICIES

There is no doubt that the MMA community has become a significant actor in U.S. politics, especially in the recent past. However, we choose to focus on their influence on U.S. foreign policy because of the controversy this influence generates in the American political scene.[20] There is a long tradition of concern expressed by well-known academics and policy analysts about immigrants' influence on their host country's foreign policy and the potential diversion of the "national interest" as a result.[21] Nathan Glazer and Daniel P. Moynihan argue that "[t]he immigration process is the single most important determinant of American foreign policy. This process regulates the ethnic composition of the American electorate. Foreign policy responds to that ethnic composition. It responds to other things as well, but probably *first of all* to the primal fact of ethnicity."[22] Samuel Huntington adds a note of alarm: "Diasporas can influence the actions and policies of their host country and co-opt its resources and influence to serve the interests of their homeland."[23] Although this level of concern appears uniquely American, extreme right or populist parties in many European countries are stoking the fears of the native populations about immigrant activities of all sorts, including their influence on foreign policy.

Given this rhetoric, it is surprising that the MMA community influence on U.S. foreign policy has been judged as virtually nil.[24] In *Latinos and U.S. Foreign*

[20] There is a rich literature on immigrant and ethnic groups' impact on U.S. foreign policy. *See* MOHAMMAD E. AHARI, ED., ETHNIC GROUPS AND U.S. FOREIGN POLICY (Greenwood Press 1987); THOMAS AMBROSIO, ED., ETHNIC IDENTITY GROUPS AND U.S. FOREIGN POLICY (Praeger 2002); STEPHEN M. SAIDEMAN, THE TIES THAT DIVIDE: ETHNIC POLITICS, FOREIGN POLICY AND INTERNATIONAL CONFLICT (Columbia University Press 2001); Scott McConnell, *Not So Huddled Masses: Multiculturalism and Foreign Policy*, WORLD AFF. J., http://www.worldaffairsjournal.org/article/not-so-huddled-masses-multiculturalism-and-foreign-policy, accessed Sep. 5, 2013; Will H. Moore, *Ethnic Minorities and Foreign Policy* 22(2) SAIS Rev. 77–91 (2002); Stephen M. Saideman, *The Power of the Small: The Impact of Ethnic Minorities on Foreign Policy*, 22(2) SAIS REV. 95–105 (2002); Yossi Shain, *Multicultural Foreign Policy*, 110 FOR. POL'Y 69–87 (1995); Steven Vertovec, *The Political Importance of Diasporas*, MIGRATION INFO.SOURCE, www.migrationinformation.org/Feature/display.cfm?ID=313, accessed Jan. 18, 2009; Kenneth D. Wald, *Homeland Interests, Hostland Politics: Politicized Ethnic Identity among Middle Eastern Heritage Groups in the United States*, 42(2) INT'L MIGRATION REV. 273–301 (2008); Paul Y. Watanabe, *Asian American Activism and U.S. Foreign Policy*, *in* ACROSS THE PACIFIC: ASIAN AMERICANS AND GLOBALIZATION (Evelyn Hu-DeHard, ed. Temple University Press 1999).

[21] NATHAN GLAZER & DANIEL PATRICK MOYNIHAN, ETHNICITY: THEORY AND EXPERIENCE (Harvard University Press 1975); Alan Dowty & Gil Loescher, *Refugee Flows as Grounds for International Action*, 21 (1) INT'L SEC'TY 43–71 (1996); Samuel Huntington, *The Erosion of American National Interests*, 76(5) FOR.AFF'S 28–49 (1997); John J. Mearsheimer & Stephen M. Walt, *The Israel Lobby and U.S. Foreign Policy*, 28 (6) LONDON REV. BOOKS, available at www.lrb.co.uk (2006).

[22] *See* GLAZER & MOYNIHAN, *supra* note 22 at 23.

[23] *See* Huntington, *supra* note 22 at 39.

[24] The literature on Mexican and Mexican American influence on U.S. foreign policy is much more limited. In addition to the edited volume cited below, see Michael Jones-Correa, *New Directions for Latinos as an Ethnic Lobby in U.S. Foreign Policy*, 9 HARV. J. HISP. POL'Y (1995–1996).

Policy, two distinguished scholars and their colleagues provide original research on the role of these groups on U.S. foreign policy. Rodolfo de la Garza and Harry Pachon examine Latino elites, Latino diplomats for the U.S. State Department, and the Latino population at large. They conclude that "Latino attitudes toward foreign policy and international relations are like those of most Americans. That is, international issues are not their top priority."[25] Although Latinos are systematically involved in Latin America around "cultural, economic, and social issues," they are "disengaged ... from foreign policy issues."[26] They suggest that "Latinos' mobilization reflects their domestic rather than foreign policy concerns"[27] and that "Latinos do not engage in the regular foreign policy process."[28] Although the authors talk about Latinos as a group, they also provide statistics on Latino subgroups, including Mexican Americans. This lack of influence can be easily explained in terms of the political and demographic changes describe in the previous section. However, given the expanded political voice in the last decade, this is an interesting arena in which to trace their growing influence.

To better capture conditions under which the MMA community may affect U.S. foreign policy, we focus on border security. At least on the surface, border security represents an issue on which public opinion in the MMA community differs dramatically from public opinion at large in the United States, as well as an issue on which MMA preferences are fairly homogeneous. Recent CNN/ORC polls put support for "more federal law enforcement officials ... along the border with Mexico" at 88 percent (2010) and 74 percent (2006).[29] However, a Reuel Group 2010 poll of Mexican Americans living in border communities reveals that this community believes that the border area is safe and favors fewer deployments on the border. Moreover, the MMA community remains highly concentrated along the southern border between the United States and Mexico. If the MMA community does have influence over U.S. foreign policy, it is more likely to see that influence where its preferences are distinctive and homogeneous, and where geographic concentration allows them to play a central role in politics.

U.S. Border Security Policy. As it turns out, there are multiple border security policies that lack overall coordination.[30] Here we trace the evolution of border security policy in the United States, beginning in the early 1990s, to provide an

[25] Rodolfo O. De la Garza & Harry P. Pachon, eds. Latinos and U.S. Foreign Policy: Representing the "Homeland"? 45 (Rowman & Littlefield, 2000).

[26] *Id.* at 14.

[27] *Id.* at 47.

[28] *Id.* at 14.

[29] CNN Poll: *Support for Border Crackdown Grows*, available at http://politicalticker.blogs.cnn.com/2010/05.26,cnn-poll-support-for-border-crackdown-grows/, accessed Feb. 20, 2014 (2010).

[30] Rey Koslowski, The Evolution of Border Controls as a Mechanism to Prevent Illegal Immigration (Migration Policy Institute 2011).

overview of this dimension of U.S. foreign policy, in order to select specific dependent variables that we can analyze over time and space. Most researchers would describe the increasing "securitization" or "militarization" of the southwest U.S. border over the past two decades. This process began in the early 1990s with the implementation of Operation Blockade in El Paso in 1993 and Operation Gatekeeper in San Diego in 1994. The Border Patrol, initially operating within the Immigration and Naturalization Service (INS) structure, developed two National Strategies in 1994 and 2004. The Border Patrol was incorporated into the Customs and Border Protection Unit in the Department of Homeland Security (DHS) subsequent to the terrorist attacks on September 11, 2001. The DHS implemented the Secure Border Initiative in 2005, and the U.S. Congress passed the Secure Fence Act in 2006. Additional policies include the Southwest Border Security Initiative, promulgated in 2009 and complimented by the Merida Initiative, providing more than $2 billion in aid to Mexico to facilitate border security.[31]

Although these are the major initiatives and active border enforcement units, many other agencies have responsibilities and deployments on the southwestern U.S. border. These include the Department of Defense and the National Guard, the Department of Justice, including the Drug Enforcement Administration and the Federal Bureau of Investigation, the Coast Guard, and Immigration and Customs Enforcement. These deployments are, in some cases, supplemented by state and local law enforcement agencies. In particular, the 287(g) program was included in the immigration reform legislation (IIRIRA) in 1996 and allows state and local law enforcement agencies to partner with the INS/DHS to enforce federal immigration policy.[32] The Secure Communities Program also exists to deport criminal aliens; Secure Communities is based on a Congressional mandate for the FBI to share its database with DHS; a 2008 law established procedures for the Immigration and Customs Enforcement division of DHS to employ arrest information from local and state jurisdictions, through the FBI database, to determine if criminal aliens are deportable.[33]

From this complex and overlapping deployment of border security we have taken as possible dependent variables – that is, policy that the MMA community might affect – to include the following: number of Border Patrol agents deployed (by county or by "border sector"); the size of the Border Patrol budget (by county or by

[31] *Id.*

[32] The 287(g) program has recently been "discontinued" by the Obama administration; no new state and local communities can sign on, but existing agreements are honored. *Delegation of Immigration Authority Section 287(g) Immigration and Nationality Act* (2014), www.ice.gov/287g/, accessed Feb. 20, 2014.

[33] *Secure Communities* (2014), www.ice.gov/secure_communities/, accessed Feb. 20, 2014.

"border sector"); adherence to the 287(g) border enforcement program; and early adherence to the Secure Communities program.

10.6 THEORIES OF POLITICAL INFLUENCE ON U.S. FOREIGN POLICY

We can draw on the diaspora research to generate several hypotheses to guide our research on the Mexican and Mexican American community. Rubenzer's synthetic evaluation of the various explanations of influence suggests that only two factors are systematically related to influence over foreign policy: organizational strength and level of political activity.[34] Building on Rubenzer, we argue that two factors contribute to the influence of immigrant groups over foreign policy choices. The first is the immigrant group's political power, based on organizational and material capabilities, or what Rubenzer has labeled "organizational strength." The second is the cohesion and distinctiveness of diasporic preferences on foreign policy, or what Rubenzer labels "level of political activity."

Organizational Strength. Once we examine this issue closely, we argue that the organizational strength of the diasporic community depends on two factors: the personal attributes of the immigrants that affect their political participation, and their ability to participate in the political process. The migrant's ability to participate in the political process is a function of the host country's institutions that facilitate or minimize immigrant political participation and the home country's laws that can penalize or promote the political integration of its population living abroad. In a comparative setting, these factors differ cross-nationally. In the U.S. context, these variables change over time.

First, immigrants and their offspring may or may not have the characteristics associated with higher levels of political participation across Western democratic societies. We argue that the higher the levels of education, wealth, and status the immigrant community has, the more likely they are to affect foreign policy outcomes.[35] Education includes the ability to speak the host country's language. These variables change over time in the MMA community in the United States and across the first and second generations of immigrants.

Second, the political context in which immigrants live also matters. Immigrants and their offspring have varying levels of ability to participate in the political process. Although political organization does not require citizenship, it is a central attribute that allows immigrants to maneuver various levers of political power.

[34] Trevor Rubenzer, *Ethnic Minority Interest Group Attributes and U.S. Foreign Policy Influence: A Qualitative Comparative Analysis*, 4 (2) For. Pol'y Analysis 169–85 (2008).

[35] Yossi Shain, *Ethnic Diasporas and U.S. Foreign Policy*, 109 (4) Pol. Sci. Q. 811–41 (1994–95).

Shain, for example, argues that citizenship is the central attribute that affects diasporic influence on the host country's foreign policy.[36] The larger the proportion of immigrants that become citizens, the larger their ability to participate in the political process through voting and the larger their impact on policy choices.

Preferences and Level of Political Activity. Regardless of the level of political power in the immigrant community, the level of political activity is driven by the preferences of the immigrant community and their variance from the host country's policy position. The lack of Latino political influence on foreign policy observed by de la Garza and Pachon is attributed in large part to the lack of salience of foreign policy for the Latino and Mexican American communities. This lack of salience is often observed but is not uniform across immigrant communities. The Cuban and Cuban American population is well known for its interest in American foreign policy toward Cuba.[37] Homogeneity of preferences is also crucial to the influence of the immigrant community; if two, or multiple, positions are adopted by an immigrant community, the host state is better able to deflect the demands of the groups or to co-opt the part of the immigrant community that is congruent with its interests into its foreign policy choices.

Size and Geographic Concentration. Mexican immigrants constitute the largest single immigrant group in the United States, more than five times larger than the second-largest group. Nonetheless, this represents less than 4 percent of the U.S. population. Even when counting the second generation of Mexican Americans born in the United States, this still only represents 10.6 percent of the total U.S. population. Although size alone is not the only factor that determines influence in the U.S. political system, if immigrants are geographically concentrated, their weight might provide them an important swing position in the electorate, with a plurality, or even a majority of the vote. So the location and size of the diasporic community is important in predicting the level of influence over foreign policy.

Hypotheses. These theoretical frames lead to specific expectations or hypotheses about the conditions under which diasporas, including the Mexican and Mexican American community, can influence U.S. foreign policy.

H1: The greater the salience of the issue to the diasporic community, the greater the political organization.

H1A: When issues are politically salient and preferences are more homogeneous, there will be an increase in political influence.

36 *Id.*

37 Nedim Ögelman, Jeannette Money & Philip Martin, *Immigrant Cohesion and Political Access in Influencing Foreign Policy*, 22(2) SAIS REV. 145–65, (2002); Patrick J. Haney & Walt Vanderbush, *The Role of Ethnic Interest Groups in U.S. Foreign Policy: The Case of the Cuban American National Foundation*, 43(2) INT'L STUDIES Q. 431–61 (1999).

H1B: When issues are politically salient and the citizen proportion of the diasporic community is increasing, the political influence will also increase.

H1C: When issues are politically salient and when socioeconomic status of the diasporic community is increasing, the political influence will also increase.

H1D: When conditions H1 through H1C are met, an increase in the geographic concentration will lead to an increase in the political influence of the diasporic community.

10.7 A QUANTITATIVE EXAMINATION OF THE POLITICAL INFLUENCE OF MEXICANS AND MEXICAN AMERICANS ON BORDER SECURITY

We have selected a mixed-methods research design to evaluate each of our hypotheses. This research design utilizes the county as the unit of analysis, with an emphasis on the border counties. There are twenty-four border counties, in four states, forming the U.S. side of the U.S.-Mexican border. Since the county unit is a basic unit in the U.S. Census, we are able to trace the Mexican and Mexican American population, including the size of the population, the citizenship status of the population, and the usual socioeconomic indicators associated with political participation.

Previous research has examined the political influence of Mexican and Mexican Americans at the *national level* and found little evidence of their political influence. It is entirely plausible that a more appropriate unit of analysis could be the state or the city level. Cities or metropolitan areas are natural units of organization and community. However, the county unit often overlaps with the city unit along many measures, such as population trends, racial and ethnic demographics, income, language ability, migration, and geography. Additionally, the county unit of analysis facilitates the collection of certain information about socioeconomic status variables and political outcomes. In many cases the city and county will be relatively indistinguishable, so it may be possible to blend the city and county. The city or metropolitan level of analysis is important if we think about how individuals organize and attempt to effect change based on preferences, since it is not clear that individuals think in terms of their county.

The overlapping city/county units examined in this research design are distinctive in four ways: (1) population distribution, (2) representation, (3) geographic proximity, and (3) ongoing immigration. The percentage of MMA's is very high in the border communities we examine; in McAllen the MMA population is nearly 80 percent of the population. It may be that at a certain threshold of the population it no longer matters that the population is poor, undereducated, and Spanish-speaking since they constitute the majority. Furthermore, in these communities there are Latinos at all levels of government and in many governmental functions (school board, city, mayor, judges, county), so it is possible that once there is widespread descriptive representation in local government, the population is more likely to express preferences to their representatives and also hold them accountable for acting on these preferences. Furthermore, in the border communities there are political issues that are geographically proximate to the MMA population. These political issues are not issues that exist at a more abstract level, or issues specific to Washington, DC; these are political issues proximate to where MMAs live and work. Lastly, the individuals living in these communities are likely to have at least some friends or family members who are first generation/new immigrants. This may make certain political issues more salient, regardless of preferences.

Using the state-level unit of analysis may be tempting, since moving from the city/county unit to the state unit would allow us to gather far more information about aggregate preferences using public opinion data. But the trade-off is that we lose much of the variation produced among border communities in the state. A large state like Texas or California may have different preferences along the border versus inland communities. At the state level it may be difficult to make sense of null findings. Utilizing the city/county unit takes more time to develop case studies, but in the end they may yield more information about how and why Mexicans and Mexican Americans influence politics at the local level.

We are interested in the conditions under which Mexicans and Mexican Americans are able to overcome the typical barriers to political participation. There are three important barriers to consider: first, there is a set of typical socio-economic status (SES) variables, such as income, age, language ability, and educational attainment, that would seem to indicate certain communities may not be able to effectively organize or effect change based on their preferences; second, the MMAs must hold distinct and salient preferences; and third, MMAs must have the capacity to act on those preferences, to influence politics and policy.

To test the hypotheses, we operationalize and carefully measure each of the concepts as described in the four hypotheses. One of the most important concepts to define and measure is the political salience and preferences of the Mexican and Mexican American community. We focus our efforts on the salience and preferences of MMAs on a single issue: border security. By selecting border communities, we are able to isolate an issue that is politically salient to the border and on which preferences are homogeneous. This political issue is geographically proximate and has an impact on the daily life of MMAs in border counties. The populations residing in the border communities have not been systematically surveyed on the issue of border security. Of the few surveys that have been fielded there is an overwhelming preference, among MMAs, for a reduction in the number of Border

TABLE 10.9. *Border patrol sectors and border counties*

Border sector	Counties	Border sector	Counties
Big Bend	Brewster, Culberson, Hudspeth, Jeff Davis, Presidio, Terrell	Rio Grande Valley	Cameron, Hidalgo, Starr
Del Rio	Kinney, Maverick, Terrell, Val Verde	San Diego	San Diego
El Centro	Imperial	Tucson	Cochise, Pima, Santa Cruz
El Paso	Dona Ana, El Paso, Luna	Yuma	Imperial, Yuma
Laredo	Webb, Zapata		

Patrol staff, a reduction in the presence of Border Patrol staff in the community, and an overwhelming belief that the border communities are far safer than political rhetoric in the state capitals or in Washington, DC would seem to indicate.

In our quantitative analysis, salience is constant, so that we can evaluate the impact of the other independent variables: citizen proportion, socioeconomic status, and geographic concentration. In the qualitative analysis, we compare a border county with a non-border county and allow the salience of the issue and homogeneity of the preferences to vary.

Measures of Dependent Variables. In order to measure the political influence of MMAs on border security issues we use several operationalizations to approximate the broader concept. The first method of approximating "political influence" is to look at changes in border policy, including: changes in the number of border patrol staff, changes in the spending for border security, changes in the policy at the local level, and non-adoption of border security policies.

As mentioned in the previous section, to test our hypotheses we examine several dependent variables. The first dependent variable is the number of Border Patrol agents deployed by county by "border sector" in a given year. As noted in Table 10.9, there are nine border sectors; the number of Border Patrol officers per border sector is reported, by year, by the DHS and the INS. Two counties are split between two border sectors; in this case we average the number of Border Patrols between the two sectors.

The second dependent variable is the size of the Border Patrol budget per border sector per year, as measured in U.S. dollars. This information is reported by the DHS, and by the INS prior to the formation of the DHS. The third dependent variable is participation in the 287(g) border enforcement program. This dependent variable is a dichotomous measure, in terms of adherence (0,1), and it is also measured in terms of the date of participation so that we are able to distinguish early adopters from late adopters. The fourth dependent variable is the early adherence to the Secure Communities program. This variable will also be measured in terms of the date of adherence. The last dependent variable we examine is the number of Latino elected officials in each county. This variable is standardized by the total population in the county and the number of MMA's in the county.

Measures of Independent Variables. This analysis includes several independent variables that may have an effect on collective action either at the level of the individual or community. We examine the effect of several socioeconomic status (SES) variables that are hypothesized to affect political participation. Each of the measures is taken from the American Communities Surveys and the U.S. Census data for the relevant years. The first SES variable is educational attainment, measured by the percentage of MMAs living in the county who receive a ninth grade education or less. The lower levels of education are correlated with low levels of voter registration and turnout. The second SES variable is the percentage of unemployment, by year, at the county level. The third SES variable is the median home price, by year, at the county level. The last SES variable is the percentage of families living in poverty, by year, at the county level. We would expect high levels of unemployment, low median home prices, and higher levels of poverty to be correlated with lower levels of influence on policy.

We also examine several demographic variables, including the percentage of the population who is MMA, the percent foreign-born, the percent Spanish dominant, and the percent naturalized. Again, we use the IPUMS dataset, the American Communities Surveys, and the U.S. Census for the relevant years. The percentage of the population who is MMA includes all generations of MMA individuals regardless of legal status. The percentage of foreign-born includes all MMA individuals reporting foreign birth, regardless of their legal status. The percent of naturalized MMA individuals includes all foreign-born MMAs who have gone through the process of becoming a naturalized U.S. citizen. The percent Spanish dominant is the percentage of MMA individuals reporting that they primarily speak Spanish in their homes and that their English is "not very good".

Preliminary Analyses. In the preliminary analysis, for each of the border counties, we have collected data on three of the dependent variables for the year 2010. The completed dataset will also include observations from 1986, the year of the passage of IRCA, 1996 ten years post-IRCA and two years post-proposition 187 in California, and 2010. The final analysis will have time series comparison between the border counties. We will compare change over time as well as differences across county units. The completed dataset will also have two additional independent variables measuring the level of crime reported in border counties and the number of official ports of entry in each county. The completed dataset will also have an additional dependent variable; the variable will measure the number of policies per county

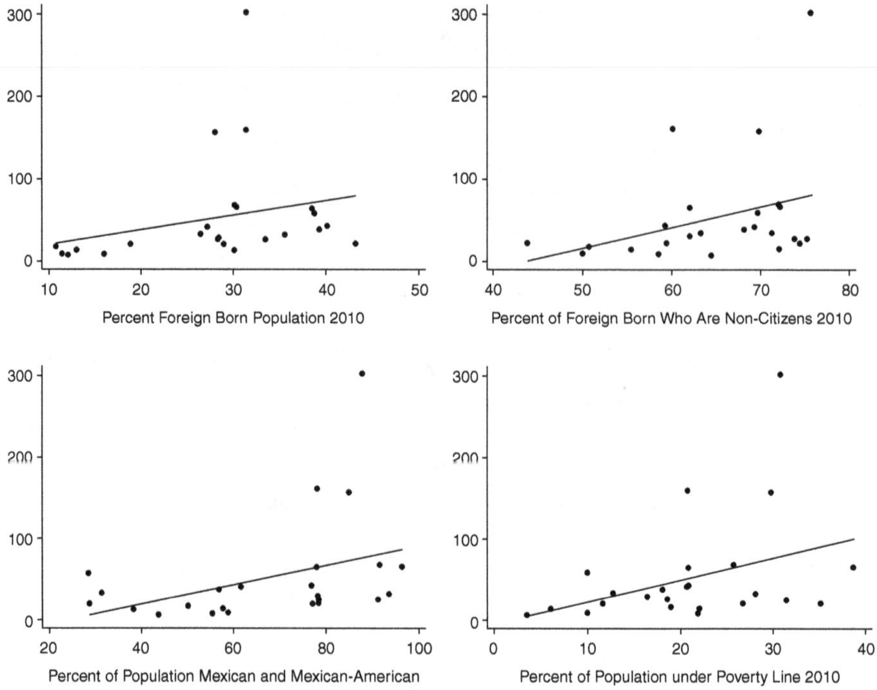

FIGURE 10.1. Total Latino representation (y-axis) by county as a function of various MMA political competence variables, 2010 (x-axis).

aimed at strengthening border security, or the number of policies aimed at providing sanctuary to immigrant populations.

Preliminary Results. Figure 10.1 shows the number of Latino political representatives as a function of county demographics. The only graph that is consistent with our hypotheses is Graph 3, which demonstrates a positive relationship between the proportion of the county that is Mexican and Mexican American and Latino representation. The percent foreign-born who are noncitizens and the percent of the population that lives in poverty are both highly correlated with the Mexican and Mexican American population and show a similar positive relationship, despite the supposed infirmities these demographic variables are supposed to confer. These graphs, although preliminary, suggest that the politics in majority-minority districts may function differently than in other political settings, at least for descriptive representation.

Figure 10.2 shows the relationship between selected independent variables and the dependent variable measuring the number of Border Patrol staff in each border sector. Here, too, the relationships are nonexistent or work in the opposite of the hypothesized direction. As the proportion of MMAs with less than ninth grade

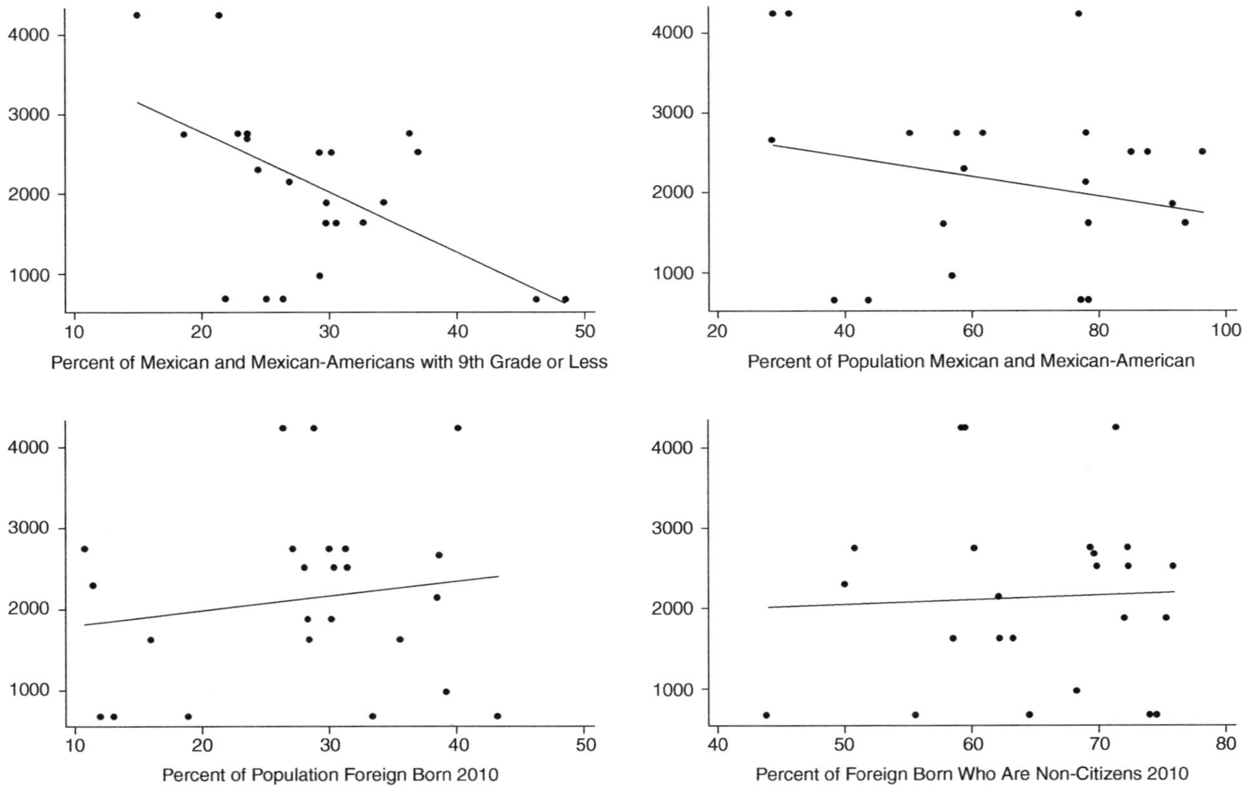

FIGURE 10.2. Number of Border Patrol staff (y-axis) as a function of various MMA political competence variables, 2010 (x-axis).

education increases, the number of Border Patrol agents declines, suggesting that lack of education is not a barrier to affecting policy decisions. There appears to be little relationship between the other three political competence variables: the proportion of the population that is Mexican and Mexican American, the percent of foreign born who are noncitizens, and the percent of the population that is foreign born.

We hope that by constructing a time series data set and controlling for other variables, such as the crime rate and the level of cross-border activity, we can better understand the influence of the Mexican and Mexican American community on border security policies. At present, the bivariate analyses are not very revealing.

10.8 QUALITATIVE ANALYSIS OF THE POLITICAL INFLUENCE OF MEXICANS AND MEXICAN AMERICANS ON BORDER SECURITY

In this section we contrast a border community with a non-border community and present evidence to suggest that the border community has characteristics central to political success and that these characteristics allowed the MMA community to influence border security, whereas the non-border county, lacking these characteristics, was much less successful.

Measuring impact or influence may be the most difficult part of this research agenda. As mentioned previously, research has focused on how Latinos have influenced foreign policy at the national level. We argue that impact or influence can be measured in many more ways than simply looking at direct policy shifts at the national level. When measuring influence and impact we may also want to include:

1. Did MMAs participate in collective action and did elected officials react to the effort?
2. Did the organizational effort(s) lead to new laws or new policies?
3. Did the organizational effort(s) lead to the repeal of old laws or policies?
4. Did the organizational effort(s) lead to a rejection of proposed legislation?
5. Did the organizational effort(s) lead to purposeful inaction by local officials or law enforcement officers?
6. Did the organizational effort(s) lead to rejection of increases in funding or staffing for the enforcement of old laws and policies?
7. Did the organizational effort(s) lead to election of certain individuals over other individuals (when those individuals' border preferences were known)?

A Border Community in Texas. Hidalgo County, located along the U.S. border with Mexico north of the Rio Grande and west of the Gulf of Mexico, is an official U.S.-Mexico border-crossing area. Built in 1926, the McAllen-Hidalgo-Reynosa

International Bridge is a very busy and important port of entry. As a result, Hidalgo County is often named as an area in need of increased border security.

County Preferences. There have been sustained efforts in the U.S. Congress, by senators and members of the House of Representatives, to introduce legislation aimed at security at the U.S.-Mexico border. The proposed legislation is often at odds with the preferences of local politicians and populations living in border communities. While many local individuals in McAllen *are* concerned about the number of migrants crossing and, at times dying, in their county, they are also concerned about the security-centric approach.[38] Residents and elected officials in McAllen frequently counter the claims of lawlessness in their border communities by citing the decline in crime over the last several years. Additionally, local officials have voiced concerns that border patrol and securing have taken precedence over equally important issues such as increasing the efficiency of trade and legal crossings.

The growth of the maquiladora industry along the Mexican border along with the signing of NAFTA corresponded with a population boom in McAllen during the 1990s and 2000s. In the period post-NAFTA the border cargo and border traffic have increased by more than 345 percent and 36.4 percent, respectively.[39] Additionally, McAllen is the host of the country's first inland Foreign-Trade Zone (FTZ) and the U.S. Border Patrol. Due to its strategic location and economic activity, individuals residing in McAllen may have developed common preferences about border security and border policy. A poll conducted by the Reuel Group in July 2010 examined preferences on border security. The poll showed that the majority of residents in McAllen do have similar preferences regarding security and the border.[40] Residents reported they feel safe living in their community (visiting parks, walking and driving in town) and that their communities are no more dangerous than other U.S. communities. If residents hold a widespread belief that border communities are safe, we might assume residents of those communities will resist efforts to increase the securitization of the border.

County Political Characteristics. According to U.S. Census data, Hidalgo County is one of the fastest-growing counties in the country. The county has grown from approximately 180,000 in 1960 to just under 800,000 in 2010. The largest city in the county is McAllen with approximately 130,000 people in the city proper and nearly 800,000 in the larger metropolitan area. The U.S. Census reports that in 2000 the total population of McAllen was 66.9 percent Mexican and Mexican American, and by 2010 Mexican and Mexican Americans had grown to 78.8 percent of the total

[38] Alexa Ura, *Border reps slam Texas Sen. Ted Cruz for his border security claims*, El Paso Times, Sept. 16, 2013.

[39] The McAllen Chamber of Commerce 2011.

[40] The poll was conducted in July of 2010 by the Reuel Group; there were 1,222 respondents to an automated telephone poll. The poll was conducted in Arizona, Texas, New Mexico, and California.

population. More importantly, the Mexican and Mexican American community is a long-standing one. Less than 30 percent of the population is foreign-born, although most of these are not naturalized citizens (IPUMS). So the demographic concentration of the MMA community offsets the disability of a foreign population. This should be a county where the MMA community is able to effectively participate in the political process.

County Outcomes. Given the high numbers of Mexicans and Mexican Americans it is perhaps unsurprising that McAllen is the home to many Latino elected officials. The elected officials hold a range of offices: school board members, city council members, state representatives, and state senators. So descriptive representation is strong. And the community is organized effectively to address border security concerns. In 2011, McAllen law enforcement officials and community leaders participated in the Reform Immigration for Texas Alliance (RITA) law enforcement summit. The summit brought together community leaders and immigration policy aides for the members of the state legislature. Additionally, the law enforcement leaders from McAllen participated in a media press conference to explain their opposition to the Texas statewide proposal to ban sanctuary cities in Texas.[41] The official statement released by the law enforcement executives reflects the policy preferences of the several constituencies in McAllen. The statement notes that "mandating local police to enforce the federal immigration code alienates a significant and growing sector of our society, especially in the Latino community."[42] The official statement of law enforcement executives also explains how restrictive border control policies lead to distrust in the community and negative economic impacts. The participation of McAllen law enforcement officials reflects a community with stable preferences between leaders, agencies, and residents. It also reflects a desire of residents to participate in changing existing and proposed border policies at the state and federal level. As a result, at the local level, activism was able to prevent proposed statewide legislation aimed at banning so-called sanctuary cities.

A *Non-Border Community in Texas.* The second county we examine in Texas is Harris County, a non-border county and the largest county in Texas. The 2010 U.S. Census reports the population of Harris County as just over 4 million, up from approximately 1.2 million in 1960. The largest city in Harris County is Houston with approximately 2.1 million individuals in the city proper.

County Preferences. The community organizations and politically active leaders in Houston, a non-border city, have focused on policies affecting immigrants in general, more than border issues specifically. Harris County is more economically diverse than Hidalgo, and as a result it is not dependent on cross-border traffic.

41 The effort to ban sanctuary cities, none of which were legally recognized sanctuary cities, was seen as an effort to restrict immigration and immigrant movements in the state.

42 *Texas Can Do Better*, <reformimmigrationfortexas.org/actnow/sign-on/>, accessed June 7, 2015.

In Houston, the main argument against the securitization of the border and the apprehension of immigrants as criminals seems to focus on the unfunded mandates handed down to cities by the federal government and the state government. The Mexican and Mexican American community in Houston is not centrally affected by border security and therefore is not strongly focused on border security issues.

County Political Characteristics. Harris County has a large population of Mexicans and Mexican Americans, 28.8 percent, who report speaking Spanish at home, but the MMA community is not majoritarian, as Houston is a melting pot of many immigrant groups. Harris County also has high levels of childhood poverty and lower levels of educational attainment for Mexicans and Mexican Americans. These characteristics suggest that the Mexican and Mexican American community will be much less effective in affecting border security policies.

County Outcomes. As a result of its large population size, Harris County has several congressional districts, and the city of Houston is represented in four of the congressional districts. Harris County also has twenty-four state legislative seats and seven state senate seats. The city of Houston has many Latino elected officials. Similar to McAllen, the elected officials hold a range of offices: council members, district court judges, mayor pro-tem, and state representatives. The large number of Latino elected officials across all levels of government could indicate increased access and increased capacity to participate in the political process for Mexican and Mexican American individuals in Houston.

The city of Houston is host to many community organizations focused on reforming border security and associated immigration policies. For many years Houston was described as a de facto sanctuary city for immigrants.[43] Candidate Rick Perry targeted Houston's informal sanctuary city policies in his 2010 race for governor in Texas. The anti-immigrant sentiment in the 2010 campaign for governor, and the victory of several Tea Party candidates resulted in the formation of the "Texas Can Do Better Campaign." Community activists and residents of Houston participated in the campaign, in addition to other related collective action movements, such as the Reform Immigration for Texas Alliance (RITA) discussed earlier in the chapter. The RITA organization was formed by civil rights leaders, law enforcement agencies, unions, and businesses. The RITA campaign brought together community leaders with the Speaker of the House, the lieutenant governor, and other state senators.[44] Community members from Houston participated in the RITA demonstrations in Austin in January 2011. Additionally, in 2011, law enforcement officials from Houston participated in the "Texas Residents United for a Stronger Texas" (T.R.U.S.T.) law enforcement summit. Law enforcement officers testified that the restrictive

[43] "Texas can do better: Lessons from Reform Immigration for Texas Alliance's successful campaign to stop the Arizona-style anti-immigration agenda in Texas," August 2011.

[44] "Texas can do better," August 2011.

immigration legislation banning sanctuary cities was unnecessarily restrictive and burdensome on enforcement agencies. The local community-based organizations and law enforcement officials joined together to release a "Statement of Principles" on state-based immigration policies. In many ways, these results indicate similar activities to those in Hidalgo. However, the size of these organizations is smaller and therefore less effective.

Although individuals and communities in Houston have been active participants in the immigration policy debates over the last decade, they have been much less effective than the community groups and leaders in Hidalgo. The Border Network for Human Rights identifies Houston as a city that is still underorganized and has not yet met its full potential.

10.9 CONCLUSIONS

The 1965 Immigration Act has affected the Mexican migrant population in very different ways than other immigrant groups, based on prior patterns of circular migration from a neighboring state. We have presented evidence to suggest that the Western Hemisphere restrictions that were part of the Act, along with the application of the 20,000 per-country quota limitation and preference system in 1976, generated pressures for more permanent migration and, with limited legal entry, generated a largely undocumented migrant population. This disenfranchised the Mexican community. Political empowerment was gradually enhanced through four channels: second-generation access to citizenship through birth on U.S. soil; legalization via the Immigration Reform and Control Act of 1986; increased naturalization subsequent to IRCA and subsequent to the Mexican government nationality reform in 1998; and through geographic concentration. We have provided a measure of the "political participation gap" that helps illuminate how political participation has grown but still lags behind the demographic weight of the Mexican and Mexican American community.

The quantitative dataset is insufficiently developed to confirm our hypotheses about the determinants of Mexican and Mexican American influence on U.S. border security, and by implication on politics in general, but the qualitative evidence suggests that the proportion of citizens within a political unit (here, the county) that are the Mexican and Mexican American can help explain the degree of influence over border security policy in locations where immigrants are concentrated. Clearly, further research is warranted that explores the political dynamics in majority minority communities, but many of the demographic characteristics that explain U.S. political participation in general are useful in understanding Mexican and Mexican American political influence. Finally, the exact mechanisms that channel influence should be explored, as there are multiple possible mechanisms that might translate the demographic weight of the community into political outcomes.

Appendix A

Tracing the Rise of the Mexican and Mexican American Community in the United States

This study utilizes the Integrated Public Use Microdata Series (IPUMS-USA) to track the changes in the Mexican and Mexican American population in the United States encompassing the years 1960 through 2010.[45] The IPUMS-USA datasets use samples drawn from the federal censuses in conjunction with data from the American Community Surveys. Over the last five decades the Mexican and Mexican American population in the United States has increased from more than 4 million in 1960 to more than 32 million in 2010. Additionally, the Mexican and Mexican American population has also increased as a percentage of the overall population from 2.2 percent to 10.6 percent in 2010 [see Table 10A.1].

In 1960, 14.5 percent of the Mexican and Mexican American population in the United States was foreign born. Unfortunately, the 1960 census data provided by IPUMS-USA does not allow us to make distinctions between Mexican Americans born in the United States, or foreign-born naturalized, or foreign-born noncitizens [see Table 10A.2].

In 1970, the census following the 1965 Immigration Act showed the total Mexican and Mexican American population increasing from slightly more than 4 million to more than 10 million people. Additionally, the percent of foreign-born also increased from 14.5 percent to 16.4 percent. Of the foreign-born population 21.2 percent were either naturalized citizens or legal citizens because of being born abroad to U.S. parents. The remaining 78.8 percent of foreign-born population reported they were either not U.S. citizens, or they chose to not disclose their legal status. Furthermore, of the total Mexican and Mexican American population residing in the United States in 1970, 57.9 percent either refused to disclose their legal status or they disclosed they were not citizens.

[45] The IMPUMS-USA dataset is a 1% sample of the U.S. census; for person-level analyses the data is weighted with the variable "PERWT"; the variable gives the population represented by each individual in the sample.

TABLE 10A.1. *Mexican and Mexican American population in the United States*

Census year	Total U.S. population	Total MMA's living in U.S.	% of U.S. population
1960	179,292,732	4,024,429	2.2%
1970	203,392,031	10,252,700	5.0%
1980	226,862,400	8,771,800	3.8%
1990	248,107,628	13,374,999	5.3%
2000	281,421,906	20,867,722	7.4%
2010	309,349,689	32,915,983	10.6%

Source: IPUMS, 1% sample U.S. Census data.

TABLE 10A.2. *Mexican and Mexican American demographics*

Census year	Total MMA's in U.S.	U.S. citizens	Born in Mexico, living in U.S	Born in Mexico, naturalized citizens	Not U.S. citizens	Born abroad to U.S. parents
1960	4,024,429	–	582,603	–	–	–
1970	10,252,700	3,957,300	1,685,000	326,200	503,900	36,600
1980	8,771,800	6,459,760	2,242,100	568,900	1,678,700	64,440
1990	13,374,999	8,779,290	4,409,033	991,330	3,432,722	171,323
2000	20,867,722	12,048,622	9,325,452	1,916,322	6,747,195	155,583
2010	32,915,983	20,969,793	11,964,241	2,696,328	9,011,262	238,600

Source: IMPUMS-USA, 1% sample of U.S. census data.

In 1980, the census shows the total Mexican and Mexican American population decreasing from approximately 10 million to fewer than 9 million people. The percentage of foreign-born individuals increased from 16.4 percent in 1970 to 25.6 percent in 1980. Of the foreign-born population 28 percent were either naturalized citizens or legal citizens because of being born abroad to U.S. parents and approximately 72 percent report they are not U.S. citizens. In 1980, there is a large increase in the number of individuals identified as foreign-born non-citizens. A portion of this change is undoubtedly due to new immigration from Mexico, but a portion of the change might also be due to better reporting and classification of individuals during the census.

In 1990, the census shows the total Mexican and Mexican American population increases from fewer than 9 million to 13 million over ten years. During this period

Mexicans and Mexican Americans comprise 5.3 percent of the total population. Of the total population of Mexicans and Mexican Americans 65.6 percent are native-born citizens. The percentage of foreign-born individuals increased from 25.6 percent in 1980 to 33 percent in 1990. Of the foreign-born population 26.4 percent are naturalized citizens or legal citizens and approximately 77.8 percent report they are not U.S. citizens. Similar to the 1980s, the 1990s have larger numbers of foreign-born individuals who are not U.S. citizens.

In the 2000s the census data show the total Mexican and Mexican American population increasing from 13 million to slightly more than 20 million. During this period Mexicans and Mexican Americans comprise 7.4 percent of the total U.S. population. Of the total population of Mexicans and Mexican Americans 57.7 percent are native-born citizens. Similar to the previous decade, the percentage of foreign-born individuals increases from 33 percent in 1990 to 44.7 percent in 2000. Of the foreign-born population 22.2 percent are naturalized citizens, a decrease from the previous decade. Additionally, of the foreign-born population, 72.3 percent report they are not U.S. citizens. The trends of the 1980s and 1990s continue into the 2000s as large numbers of individuals report being foreign-born and not holding citizenship.

In 2010 the census data shows the total Mexican and Mexican American population increased from approximately 20 million in 2000 to 32 million in 2010. Mexicans and Mexican Americans comprise 10.6 percent of the total U.S. population in 2010. Of the total population of Mexicans and Mexican Americans 63.7 percent are native-born citizens. The percentage of foreign-born individuals decreased from 44.7 percent in 2000 to 36.3 percent in 2010. Similar to the figures from the 2000 census, the percentage of the foreign-born who are naturalized citizens is 22.5 percent; of the foreign-born population 75.3 percent report they are not U.S. citizens.

The IPUMS-USA data provides additional information about the age of the Mexican and Mexican American population and the proportion of the population who were second-generation Mexican Americans in 1960 and 1970. The percentage of Mexican and Mexican American population under the age of twenty-five may be relevant to our study, since younger individuals typically do not participate in politics (voting, for example) at the same rates that older individuals participate. In 1960 approximately 20 percent of the Mexican and Mexican American population was under the age of twenty-five. In 1970 the percent had increased slightly to 22 percent, in 1980 and 1990 the percent dropped slightly to 20 percent, in 2000 the percent again increased slightly to 22 perent, and in 2010 the percent of the population under the age of twenty-five increased to 26.5 percent.

The IMPUMS-USA data provides information for 1960 and 1970 on second-generation Mexican Americans. In 1960, of the Mexican and Mexican American population, approximately 1.1 million reported they had a mother or father born in Mexico. By 1970, 2.3 million Mexicans and Mexican Americans reported having a mother or father who was born in Mexico.

The Mexican and Mexican American population has increased at different rates across the United States. Over the last five decades the list of the states with the largest numbers, and the greatest percentage, of Mexicans and Mexican Americans has consistently included the four border states: California, Texas, Arizona, and New Mexico. This paper examines the effect of Mexicans and Mexican Americans residing in border communities on U.S. foreign policy, specifically border security.

Appendix B

TABLE 10B.1. *Distribution of MMA population and foreign-born population by county*

Foreign born	MMA under 50%	MMA over 50%
Less than 20%	Brewster, Jeff Davis	Culberston, Hidalgo, Terrell, Cameron, Donan Anna
20–30%	Cochise, Pima	Kinney, Val Verde, Webb, Zapata, El Paso, Imperial, Hidalgo, TX, Hudspeth, Luna
30–50%	San Diego	Maverick, Presidio, Santa Cruz, Staff Webb, Yuma

Source: IPUMS, 1% sample U.S. Census data.

TABLE 10B.2. *Distribution of MMA population and foreign-born non-citizen population by county*

Foreign born non-citizens	MMA under 50%	MMA over 50%
40–60%	Cochise, Brewster	Culberson, Hidalgo, Kinney, Santa Cruz, Terrell
60–70%	Jeff Davis, San Diego	Cameron, Donan Ana, Imperial, El Paso, Maverick, Val Verde, Yuma
70–80%	Pima	Hidalgo, TX, Hudspeth, Luna, Presidio, Starr, Webb, Zapata

Source: IPUMS, 1% sample U.S. Census data.

11

Economic Performance of Immigrants Following the Immigration and Nationality Act of 1965

Giovanni Peri

11.1 INTRODUCTION

The Immigration and Nationality Act Amendments of 1965 still stands as the last major legislative overhaul of the Immigration system in the United States. Fifty years have passed, and the United States today is a very different country from an economic and demographic point of view than it was in the 1960s. Average economic growth over fifty years has made the average U.S. resident much wealthier in 2015 than they were in 1965. However, the gains in earnings for American workers have not been distributed equally. College education has become the necessary condition for economic success. Job growth and wage growth have benefited those who are college-educated, while the economic performance of workers with only a high school degree or less has stagnated, and since 1980, their income in real terms has decreased. Moreover, the young labor force of the 1960s, when Baby Boomers had just reached working age, has turned into an aging and shrinking group, with most of those Baby Boomers about to retire or already retired as of 2015.

The immigration system set in place in 1965 has, in some respect, served well the U.S. economy and society. It has allowed, one way or another, a substantial inflow of two types of economic immigrants: low-skilled menial workers and high-skilled scientists and engineers (as we will document later in the chapter). The net demand for both types of workers has been high. It has allowed foreign-born to become a very substantial percentage of the U.S. population (14 percent in 2010, up from a mere 4 percent in 1970). It has provided a way to economic success to many people born in Asia and Latin America who moved to the United States. In a global shift of migration flows, Europe (previously favored by laws and suppliers of virtually all U.S. immigrants in the early decades of the twentieth century) has relinguished its position to Asia and Latin America as the source region of most immigrants. Many of those immigrants have been extremely successful economically in the United States, and their children, who are U.S. citizens, show promising signs of economic success.

However, fifty years of immigration history and a long list of amendments, extensions, correction, and changes to the system have also made clear that some features of this system do not serve well a changing economy and society such as the modern United States. The heavily family-based system of admission of permanent immigrants set up by the Immigration and Nationality Act has forced employment-based immigration to take the back seat. A long list of disconnected and cumbersome temporary visa programs have been introduced as partial remedy to allow workers, in high demand by U.S. firms, laboratories, and universities, to enter the country. The draconian limitations to the inflow of low-skilled workers and the long processing time for family unification applications have created bottlenecks and have contributed to generate a very large number of undocumented immigrants, who participate to the economy of the country but not fully to its society. While overall immigrants are economically successful in the United States, there are groups that struggle significantly, especially those undocumented. These are well-known problems, and the need for a comprehensive reform is clear, although the road to get there can be politically challenging. In the concluding section I provide some suggestions for it.

In this chapter I review some of the aggregate economic and demographic trends relative to U.S. immigrants from 1960 to 2010, using U.S. Census and other administrative data. In particular, the question I try to address is: What type of immigrants have entered the United States since the 1965 reform? And how have they performed from an economic point of view relative to natives? With this goal in mind I analyze the characteristics of immigrants and how they have changed over time, how successful they have been economically compared to natives, and how they improved their living conditions relative to those in their countries of origin. In particular I focus on the interesting differences between two of the largest groups of immigrants: Mexicans and Asians, who constituted two of the largest and fastest-growing groups in the past fifty years. Mexicans, on the one hand, are chosen as they have represented the vast majority of Latin American immigrants, and from an economic perspective, they typify the immigrants from Central America. On the other hand we collectively consider the group of Asian immigrants including people from different countries (the largest groups are Chinese, Indians, and Filipinos) as they also share economic and job market characteristics. In particular, as we will see, there are several characteristics in terms of selection, education, and type of occupations that are shared by immigrants from Asia and that contrast with immigrants from Mexico. Hence considering these as two groups, with roughly similar size, while somewhat simplistic, makes sense and is useful in economic terms.

I emphasize how the opening of immigration options in 1965, interacting with the preexisting communities of Mexicans and Asians in the United States, have combined to produce two very different groups of immigrants, from an economic point of view. While both groups have been attracted in large part by jobs and by the perspectives of economic success, the type of jobs, the selection of skills, the mode of entry, and the economic outcomes of these two groups of immigrants, Mexicans and "Asians," could not be more different. Paradoxically, the group of Mexican immigrants has entered the United States in large part through family ties (and sponsors), which was the preferred channel of legal entry in the 1965 Nationality Act, while the group of Asian has used the "employment sponsor" option in much larger share. However, the group of Mexicans is also the group that has the largest incidence of undocumented entry, and this is because their occupational specialization precluded them from being in the standard categories of economic immigrants, restricted essentially to highly educated individuals. While most of Mexican immigrants came to work, very few of them had an appropriate permit related to their job.

The trends presented in this chapter show that within the same immigration system, groups of immigrants differ substantially in terms of their selection, their economic success, and their mode of entry, even coming from countries at similar levels of development (in Asia and Latin America). We then emphasize the important role of education for economic success (of immigrants and natives alike), and we point out the failure of the immigration system in managing labor-related immigration for less educated persons. While labor demand from U.S. firms may not be the only relevant criterion to admit immigrants, job-driven immigration is a key component of a successful immigration system. There is a very large literature emphasizing that labor immigrants are more productive and have an easier time integrating, adjusting to the receiving country, and contributing to its society.[1] With other economists, I have suggested in the past that an efficient immigration system should manage labor flows of immigrants, more and less skilled, as efficiently as possible and to promote growth, employment, and success of the economy. A reform of the current system should make progress in this direction.[2]

The rest of the chapter is organized as follows. Section 11.2 shows the evolution of the immigrant population in the United States and begins to draw comparisons between the group of Mexican (i.e., born in Mexico) and Asian (i.e., born in a country of Asia) immigrants. Section 11.3 illustrates the importance of skills (education) to predict economic performance of native-born and immigrants alike. Section 11.4 shows how native-born and immigrant populations have become

[1] See Jennifer Hunt & Marjolaine Gauthier-Loiselle, *How Much Does Immigration Boost Innovation?*, 2 American Economic Journal: Macroeconomics 31–56(2010).

[2] See Giovanni Peri, Rationalizing U.S. Immigration Policy: Reforms for Simplicity, Fairness, and Economic Growth, Discussion Paper, The Hamilton Project, Washington D.C. (May 2012); Pia Orrenius *et al.*, *Overhauling the Temporary work Visa System*, in *New Sources of revenue and Efficiency*, The Hamilton Project, Washington D.C. (February 2013).

progressively more college-educated, with the exception of Mexicans. We emphasize how Mexican immigrants have filled a niche in the labor market focused on menial type of jobs, quite different from other immigrants. In Section 11.5, we emphasize how skill-selected was the group of Asian immigrants, a feature that has become even stronger over time possibly because of the type of network of Asian in the United States that has selected highly educated professionals. Mexicans, instead, have become more concentrated in low-skilled jobs. Selection of migrants from the population in the country of origin, rather than country of origin characteristics, explains large part of the economic differences across these groups of immigrants. Section 11.6 shows how the "mode of entry" of immigrants reflects these differences and how it penalizes Mexicans, whose main motivation to immigration is labor related but not in those jobs that could ensure a legal immigration permit. Section 11.7 suggests some ideas for reforming the immigration system moving it beyond the 1965 Immigration and Nationality Act.

11.2 AGGREGATE EVOLUTIONS: MEXICAN AND ASIAN IMMIGRANTS

In 1960, only 5 percent of the U.S. population was born abroad, and almost two-thirds of them were born in Europe. The Nationality Act Amendments of 1965, by removing the country quotas and introducing a system based on family and employment sponsors, opened the doors to immigration from the rest of the world. By 2010, according to the U.S. Census, 17.1 percent of the population of the United States was foreign-born and more than half of it was born either in Mexico or in a country of Asia. Mexico was the individual country supplying the largest number of immigrants to the United States since 1965 and the overwhelming majority of this immigrant group consists of Latin Americans. While in 1960 only one in fifty U.S. immigrants was born in Mexico,[3] in 2010 almost one in four was. Mexico shares a long border with the United States and its income per capita as of 2010 was about one-third of the U.S. income per person, so it is clear that U.S. jobs are attractive for potential Mexican migrants.

Another group of source countries whose immigration to the United States surged since 1965 are grouped in Asia. China, India, and the Philippines are the countries providing the largest share to this group, but in these statistics we include all immigrants born in a country of Asia. Asian-born immigrants, as a group, increased from one-tenth to almost one-third of the whole U.S. foreign-born population between 1960 and 2010. Their countries of origin were, in general, significantly poorer than

[3] *See* U.S. Census 1960.

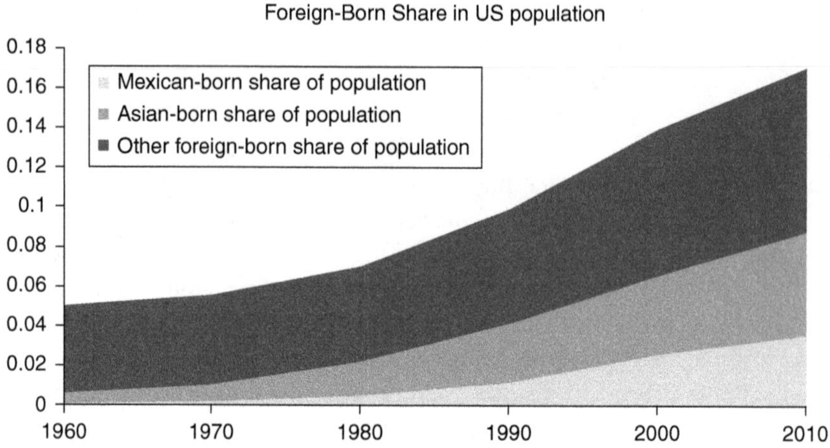

FIGURE 11.1. Foreign-born share in US population.
Note: All people born in any country of Asia are included among Asian-born, in this and in all figures below. People born in Mexico are included among Mexican-born.
Source: Author's Calculations Based on Data from the U.S. Bureau of Census, 1960–2010.

Mexico, especially in 1965 when income per capita in China, India, and the Philippines was less than one-tenth of the U.S. income per capita (while Mexico's was about one-fourth of it), and also the average level of schooling in their countries of origin was much lower than it was in Mexico. Figure 11.1 shows the time evolution of total foreign-born in the United States, and of the Mexican and Asian born within it. These two groups accounted for more than two-thirds of the growth in share of foreign-born between 1960 and 2010, and their size and time evolution are similar.

While immigration from Europe and Canada continued after 1965, and in general mobility across rich countries increased in the recent decades, the new phenomenon, representative of the South-North migration, that has accelerated so drastically in the 2000s, is well represented by Mexican and Asian migrants. Their inflow started in the 1970s, but in the fashion typical of network processes, in which presence of migrants facilitates the entry of new immigrants, it accelerated in the 1980s and 1990s. Recently, as pointed out by Timothy Hatton and Jeffrey Williamson, the aging of the population and the growth in income per capita in those regions of origin has slowed down the growth in immigration rates of these groups, as is already visible from the trend in the 2000s.[4]

[4] Timohty Hatton & Jeffrey Williamson, *Are Third World Emigration Forces Abating?* University of Essex Working Paper (December 2010).

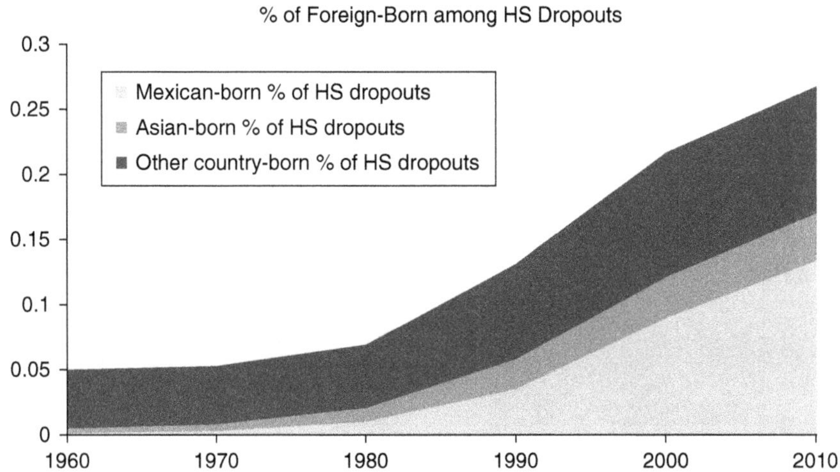

FIGURE 11.2. Percentage of foreign-born among high school dropouts.
Source: Author's Calculations Based on Data from the U.S. Bureau of Census 1960–2010.

Migrants from these two areas could expect to increase their income by a factor between three and ten when moving to the United States, and as I argue, both groups largely came attracted by jobs. However, their composition in terms of education and skills and their performance in the United States in terms of wages, relative to native-born, has been quite different. These differences do not have much to do with characteristics of their countries of origin; rather, they stem from the different selection, generated by the initial type of networks that fueled immigration, by the type of jobs where these groups were concentrated, and possibly by the immigration options available to them. The same immigration policies produced a large increase in the numbers of immigrants from both groups, but they also resulted in different trajectories in the education and skills characteristics of those immigrants.

We can begin to visualize the different characteristics between Mexican and Asian immigrants looking at immigration by schooling group. If we group individuals by their level of schooling, the two groups that received the largest inflow were the groups at the top and at the bottom of the distribution. Among people with no high school degree almost 27 percent were foreign-born in 2010, while among college-educated almost 20 percent were foreign-born, vis-à-vis an average of 14 percent of foreign-born in other education groups. Figures 11.2 and 11.3 show the time evolution of the share of foreign-born among high school dropouts and college-educated, respectively. We also distinguish within these groups those from Mexico and from Asia. We notice an almost symmetric behavior

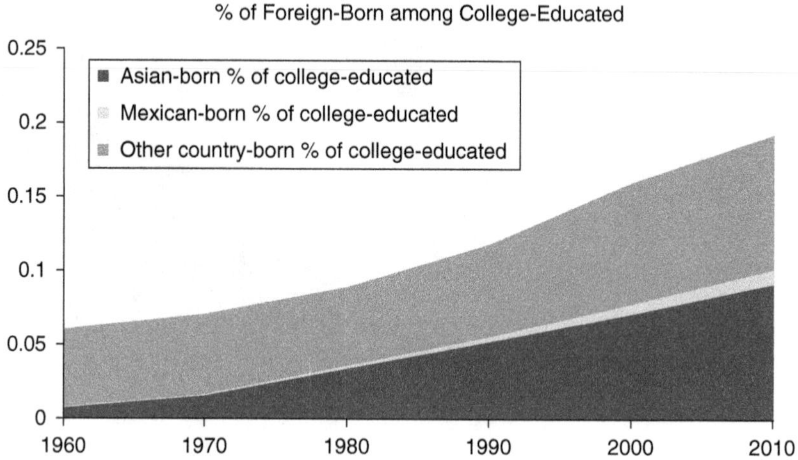

FIGURE 11.3. Percentage of foreign-born among college-educated.
Source: Author's Calculations Based on Data from the U.S. Bureau of Census 1960–2010.

of the two groups (Mexican and Asian) in the two educational partitions. Looking at Figure 11.2 we see that Mexicans accounted for about half of the foreign-born in the high school dropout group as of 2010. Even more strikingly, about 60 percent of the overall growth of the foreign-born share in that group, between 1960 and 2010, was contributed by Mexican nationals. To the contrary, Asians collectively accounted for only 10 percent of the total in 2010 and less than 15 percent of the growth of foreign-born dropouts between 1960 and 2010.

The opposite is true about each of the two groups' contribution when we analyze the growth of foreign-born among college-educated U.S. residents. While the overall share of foreign-born among college-educated more than tripled between 1960 and 2010, Asian-born accounted for almost half of the foreign-born in this group as of 2010, and for 65 percent of the 1960–2010 growth. Mexicans instead were a mere 5 percent of the total in 2010 and they accounted for less than 10 percent of the 1960–2010 growth. These differences in schooling of immigrants from the two groups have deep roots, as we will see, as well as important implications. As education is the most important dimension in determining economic success, wages and income of these two groups of immigrants will be very different as well. We can also say that the bimodal distribution of immigrants in the United States, concentrated at the low and at the high end of the schooling distribution, which has been a feature of the post-1965 immigration, corresponds also to two geographically distinct immigration flows. Mexicans are responsible for the high inflow at the low end and Asians for the high inflow at the high end.

11.3 THE IMPORTANCE OF SKILLS AND SCHOOLING

Let us emphasize that the evidence is consistent with the idea that both more and less educated immigrants have come to the United States mainly to work. While in Europe some researchers have found some evidence in support of immigration driven by "welfare" magnets, namely generous assistance for the less wealthy attracting immigrants[5] in the United States there is no evidence of such phenomenon.[6] Moreover, looking at the employment/population ratio of foreign-born and natives, we see that those are very close. In fact, immigrant employment/population ratio for male individuals between eighteen and sixty-five was 77.5 percent versus 77.2 percent for natives in 2010. If anything, less-educated immigrants worked in higher proportions than less-educated natives. That ratio was larger for college-educated, but in that case, natives (94.8 percent) had larger employment/population ratio than did immigrants (88 percent).

Employment per se, however, has not been sufficient to ensure good economic performance. The considered period, in particular, has experienced a massive shift in demand of productive skills from those linked to primary/secondary education and menial skills to those provided by tertiary education and cognitive abilities. Technological changes in production (mechanization, computerization, and information technologies) have changed the skills needed by workers.[7] At the same time improvements in schooling opportunities, especially during the 1980s and 1990s, have allowed a much larger part of the population to achieve a college education[8] and to benefit from this increase in demand for complex skills. The types of skills that a worker needs in order to be successful in the labor market and earn higher wages evolved from 1965 to 2010. Did immigrants change their skills as much as natives did? Did they respond to the increased premium to high education by becoming more educated? Did this allow them to earn the same wages as natives? The answer to each of these questions is a resounding yes, with one exception: the Mexican immigrants. Let us illustrate.

5 Assaf Razin & Jackline Wahba, *Migration Policy and the Generosity of the Welfare State in Europe*, CESifo DICE Report, 9 Ifo Institute for Economic Research at the University of Munich 28–31(2012).

6 Neeraj Kaushal, *New Immigrants' Location Choices: Magnets Without Welfare*, 23 Journal of Labor Economics 59–80 (January 2005).

7 David H. Autor et al., *Trends in U.S. Wage Inequality: Revising the Revisionists*, 90 Review of Economics and Statistics 30–23 (May 2008); Daron Acemoglu *Technical Change, Inequality and the Labor Market*, 40 Journal of Economic Literature 7–72 (March 2002); David Autor *et al.*, *The Skill Content of Recent Technological Change: An Empirical Exploration*, 4 The Quarterly Journal of Economics 1279–1333 (Nov. 2003).

8 Claudi Goldin & Lawrence F. Katz, The Race between Technology and Education (Harvard University Press 2008).

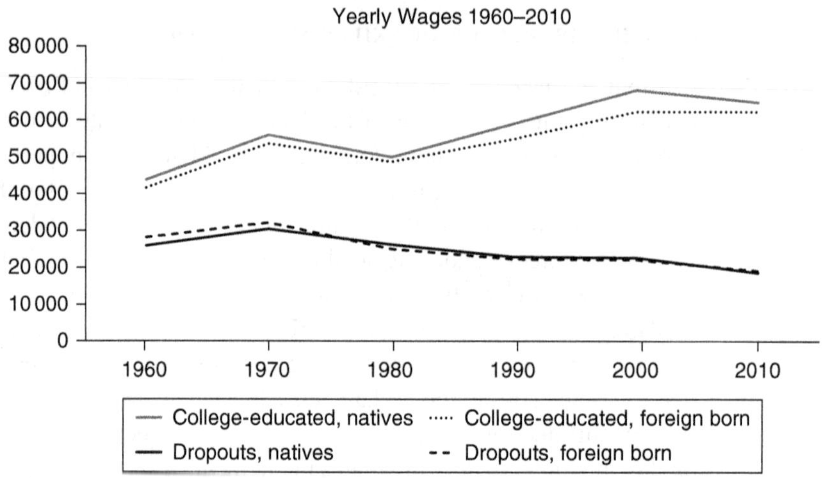

FIGURE 11.4. Yearly wages 1960–2010.
Source: Author's Calculations Based on Data from the U.S. Bureau of Census 1960–2010.

Figure 11.4 shows the evolution of yearly wages expressed in constant 2000 U.S. dollars over the 1960–2010 period for four groups: high school dropouts and college graduates, each of them divided into U.S. natives and foreign-born.[9] The gray lines show yearly wages for college-educated (native and foreign-born) and the black lines show yearly wages for high school dropouts (native and foreign-born). Two facts are striking. First, within educated groups, native and immigrants had similar wages. This implies that the foreign-born had productivity and careers comparable to those of the natives with the same education level. Second, while wages for college-educated grew significantly over time (although the effects of the oil crisis in the 1970s and of the great recession in the 2000s are visible), the wage of high school dropout stagnated and declined. In relative terms, while high school dropouts were earning more than half of the salary of college-educated individuals in 1960, as of 2010, their annual earnings, on average, were less than one-third of that of college-educated.

Immigrants were subject to the same economic and demand forces as natives were, driven in large part by technological growth and relative skill supply.[10] Hence, their level of schooling mattered significantly for their economic success in the United States. In this respect, the post-1965 immigration policies did not put immigrants at

[9] The averages are annual wage earnings obtained from our calculations on males, ages eighteen to sixty-five, who worked at least one week per year and earned non-zero salary.

[10] *See* Goldin & Katz, *supra* note 8.

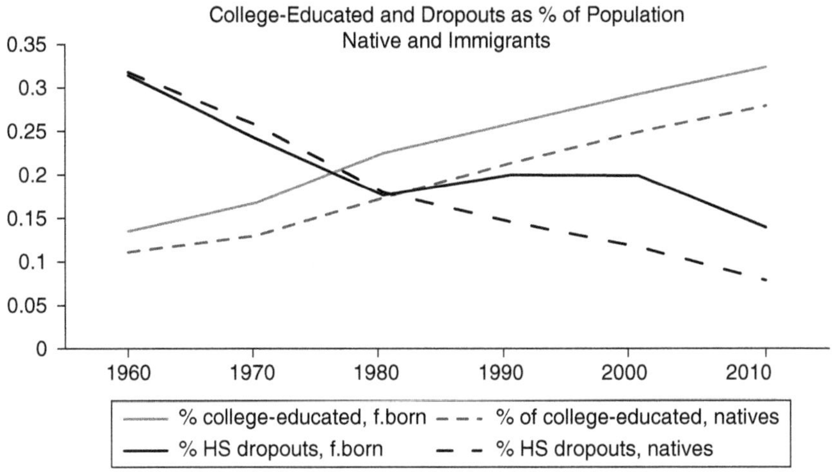

FIGURE 11.5. College-educated and high school dropouts as percentage of population, native and immigrants.
Source: Author's Calculations Based on Data from the U.S. Bureau of Census 1960–2010.

a disadvantage relative to natives, but the market forces affecting the wages of natives also operated on immigrants.

Given this very strong positive premium on college education, did the immigrant population respond accordingly? Namely, did the inflow of immigrants become more college-intensive and less dropout-intensive? And was this shift similar to what happened to the native population? The answer, shown in Figure 11.5, is that by and large, the flow of immigrants became more and more concentrated among college-educated and less in high school dropouts, mirroring what was happening to the native population. The gray lines in Figure 11.5 show the percentage of college-educated in the native (dashed line) and immigrant (solid line) populations. While college-educated always represented a higher share of the immigrant (than native) population, those percentages were similar, and they show a similar time trend. They go from around 12 percent in 1960 to 30 percent in 2010. In an opposite trend, high school dropouts in the same time period decrease from about 30 percent to less than 10 percent for natives. However, in the 1980s and 1990s, corresponding to the period of the largest Mexican immigration, the share of high school dropouts among immigrants did not decrease (while it continued to decrease among natives), so that still 15 percent of immigrants did not have a diploma in 2010. During the 1980s and 1990s, less-educated Mexicans filled a large portion of the menial jobs in manufacturing, agriculture, and services that a shrinking group of native dropouts was leaving. While those jobs ensured employment, their wages were stagnating, and, as we will see, this affected the income of the Mexican group.

So while the selection of Asian immigrants was becoming more and more skewed toward highly educated ones during the 1965–2010 period, Mexican immigrants remained heavily represented among high school dropouts (we will show this more in detail later). They continue to fill those jobs not requiring college education, but they were employed and they kept coming to the United States, attracted by the larger salaries relative to those they could earn in Mexico. The type of immigrants attracted determined their wages, and it explains crucially the mode of entry and the immigrant status of Mexicans in the United States, given that the immigration laws did not allow obtaining permanent employment permits for the jobs they were filling.

11.4 ECONOMIC PERFORMANCE OF IMMIGRANTS AND NATIVES: EARNINGS

The significantly different educational composition of Mexicans explains their significantly different performance in earnings. As shown in Figure 11.5, college graduates, be they immigrants or natives, have enjoyed sustained growth of their earnings between 1960 and 2010. To the contrary, high school dropouts have experienced wage decline. Hence, the way in which the average earnings of a population have increased over this period is either because individuals had a college degree or because the composition of the group shifted away from low schooling and to college degree. Both of these phenomena were taking place for the native population. Figure 11.6 shows that these tendencies were even stronger for the group of Asian immigrants. Asian immigrants were underrepresented among high school dropouts in 1960, but what is more remarkable is that they were overrepresented among the college-educated. Their share of college-educated also grew substantially. By 2010, 50 percent of Asian-born in the United States had a college education (the lighter line in Figure 11.6) and only 5 percent of them did not have a high school degree (the darker line).

To the contrary, Mexican immigrants did not increase their share of college-educated, nor did the share of high school dropouts decrease for this group. These are the fundamental tendencies that explain the behavior of average wage for each of these two groups.

Figure 11.7 shows the average wage of Asian-born and Mexican-born, together with that of natives and other immigrants between 1960 and 2010. Wages are expressed in constant 2000 U.S. dollars. While the average yearly earnings of Asian-born increased substantially, to the point that this group overtook the natives in terms of average wages, the earnings of Mexicans, on average, have been declining. The

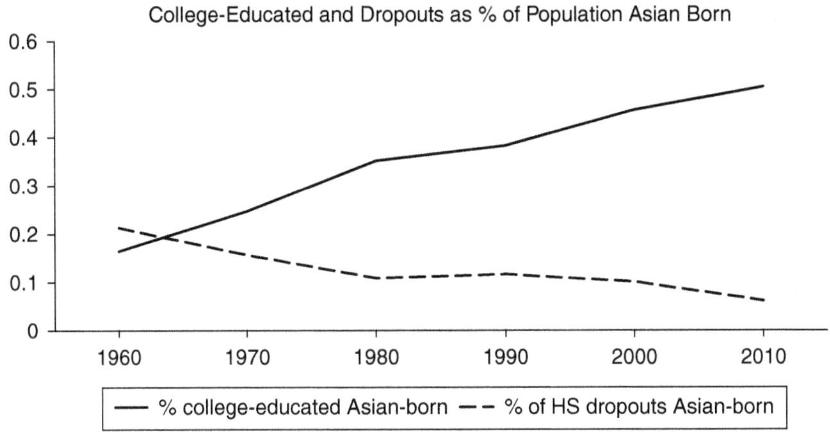

FIGURE 11.6. College-educated and high school dropouts as percentage of population, Asian born.
Source: Author's Calculations Based on Data from the U.S. Bureau of Census 1960–2010.

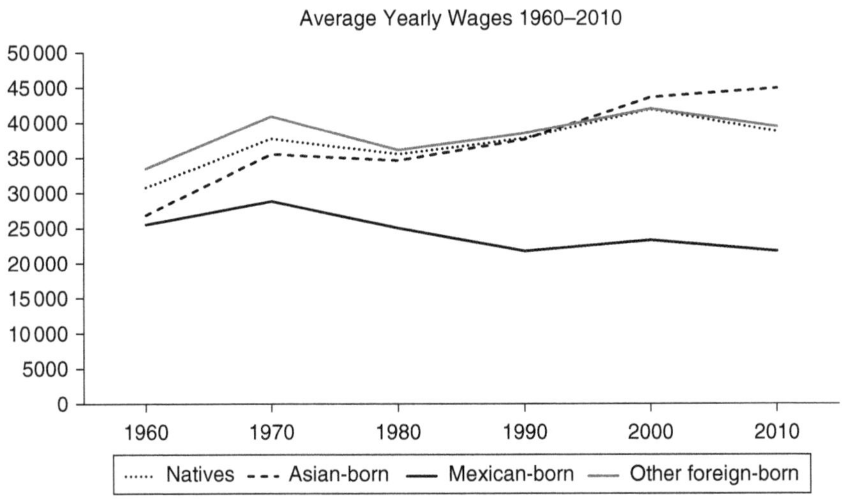

FIGURE 11.7. Average yearly wages, 1960–2010.
Source: Author's Calculations Based on Data from the U.S. Bureau of Census 1960–2010.

"polarization" of these two groups of immigrants in the earning scale has been remarkable and has mirrored the polarization in their educational distribution combined with the significant relative decline in the wages of jobs accessible to people with no high school diploma.

While it is true that many more Mexicans are undocumented, compared to any other immigrant group, and some people argue that there can be discrimination against them, those factors do not seem to contribute much to the explanation of the Mexican underperformance in terms of wages. Once their schooling level is accounted for, because of their much larger share of high school dropouts and because of the poor performance of this group in the labor market, we can explain the whole disadvantage of Mexicans in terms of wages. In fact, from the Census data for 2010 we can calculate that, considering only high school dropouts, the average yearly wages of Mexican-born were $18,019 per year (2000 constant dollars), while natives with no high school degree received $18,592. Once we account for the low level of education, Mexicans received essentially the same earnings as the native-born did.

11.5 SELECTION OF IMMIGRANTS

The striking differences in educational level and income between Mexicans and Asian-born prompts the questions of whether one can explain those by looking at differences in their countries of origins. As we have already mentioned, both groups had a small presence in 1960 relative to the dominant immigrant group of Europeans, and both groups grew in number and as a share, becoming much larger than the European group. Both groups were coming from countries at intermediate-to-low levels of income relative to the United States, and in fact Mexico was (and still is as of 2015) richer than most Asian countries of origin when measured in terms of income per capita. It certainly had higher income per person than India, China, and the Philippines throughout the whole 1960–2010 period. These two groups were also subject to the same "immigration rules" as the post-1965 legislation was not making any difference among countries of origin in terms of ease of access to the United States.

Considering the selection of immigrants among the population of their country of origin within a typical economic model,[11] one would predict that countries with more unequal income distribution would generate immigrants that are more negatively selected along the educational dimension. Namely, as highly skilled workers have a higher relative wage return at home, in more unequal countries they would have fewer incentives to migrate. If we consider as determinant of migration incentives, in the Jeffrey Grogger and Gordon Hanson tradition,[12] the absolute wage

[11] A. D. Roy Some Thoughts on the Distribution of Earnings, Oxford Economic Papers, 235–246 (1951); George Borjas, *Self-Selection and the Earnings of Immigrants*, 77 American Economic Review 531–53 (September 1987).

[12] Jeffrey Grogger & Gordon H. Hanson, *Income maximization and the selection and sorting of international migrants*, 95 Journal of Development Economics, *Elsevier* 42–57 (May 2011).

differentials between origin and destination, then the lower average income per person in Asia (especially India and China), relative to Mexico, implies a larger relative benefit for highly educated to migrate from those countries vis-á-vis highly educated from Mexico. Hence larger wage gains can be a first reason for stronger positive skill selection from Asia than from Mexico.

Are the low education of Mexican immigrants to the United States and their low wage and income partly explained by the skill supply in Mexico? Did Mexico simply produce such a small number of college-educated and Asia such a large number of them that migrants to the United States mirror the schooling features of people in those countries? Or is it that the pre-1965 selection of immigrants, combined with wage differentials, has generated job-specific networks that have reproduced and perpetuated the selection of immigrants?

It is well known that the geographical location of immigrants is rather persistent, so that metropolitan areas that had a large immigrant population at the beginning of the twentieth century still have a large immigrant share now.[13] This is usually attributed to the strength of immigration networks. Could those networks also be characterized by schooling levels or by specific occupations, so that certain groups come to fill some labor market niches, and this persists over time? If this is the case, immigrants can be very different from the average worker in the country of origin: specific networks only select workers similar to the existing type, because they can find the best job opportunities within the network. This seems to be exactly what happened with the Asian and Mexican networks.

To illustrate this point, Figure 11.8 shows the share of population with no high school degree (as dashed and dotted lines) and with college degree (in shades from black to gray) for four different groups. The solid lines represented these shares in the population of China, India, and the Philippines, the countries of origin of most U.S. Asian-born immigrants.[14] The dashed lines represent the percentages among the Asia-born U.S. immigrants (obtained from the U.S. Census). What is absolutely striking is the extent of selection of Asian immigrants, relative to their country of origin, already in 1960, which then was simply maintained throughout the fifty years. In 1960, only 20 percent of Asian-born in the United States had no high school education. In China, India, and the Philippines, the corresponding figures were 98 percent, 99 percent, and 87 percent, respectively.

[13] David Card, *Is the New Immigration Really so Bad?*, 115 ECONOMIC JOURNAL, ROYAL ECONOMIC SOCIETY F300–F323 (November 2005); David Card, *Immigrant Inflows, Native Outflows, and the Local Labor Market Impacts of Higher Immigration*, 19 JOURNAL OF LABOR ECONOMICS 22–64. January 2001.

[14] These data are from the Barro-Lee dataset, available at http://www.barrolee.com/data/dataexp.htm

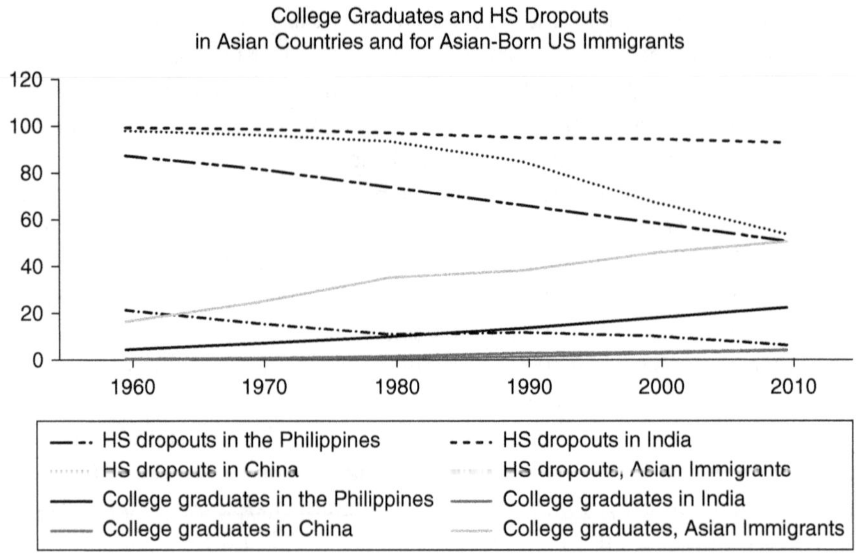

FIGURE 11.8. Percentage of college-educated and high school dropouts in Asian countries and for Asian-born US immigrants.
Source: Author's Calculations Based on Data from the U.S. Bureau of Census, 1960–2010.

Conversely, while about 18 percent of the Asian-born residing in the United States had a college degree, less than 1 percent of the population in India and China did. The Asian "diaspora" in the United States was already a select group in 1965, more likely to be professionals and highly educated. Historical accidents, the very large wage incentives for highly educated to migrate, and the very few opportunities for non-college-educated before 1965 contributed to create this "elite" type of migration from Asia pre-1965. They likely took jobs requiring more education and skills, and the newcomers were selected in a similar group and were admitted, as we will show, in large part with skilled work permits. When the Immigration and Nationality Act Amendment of 1965 opened the possibility for more immigrants from Asia, the existing professional network reproduced in the new flow the characteristics of the existing immigrants.

Very different was the situation of Mexicans. The population of Mexican-born in the United States as of 1965, far from being selected among the education elites, was in fact even less educated than the population of Mexicans in Mexico. A large part of the immigration had been linked to agricultural jobs (post–Bracero Program), and hence was filled with individuals originating from rural Mexico. Moreover, as of 1965, the incentives of more educated/wealthy Mexicans to migrate to the United States were probably lower as they were relatively highly

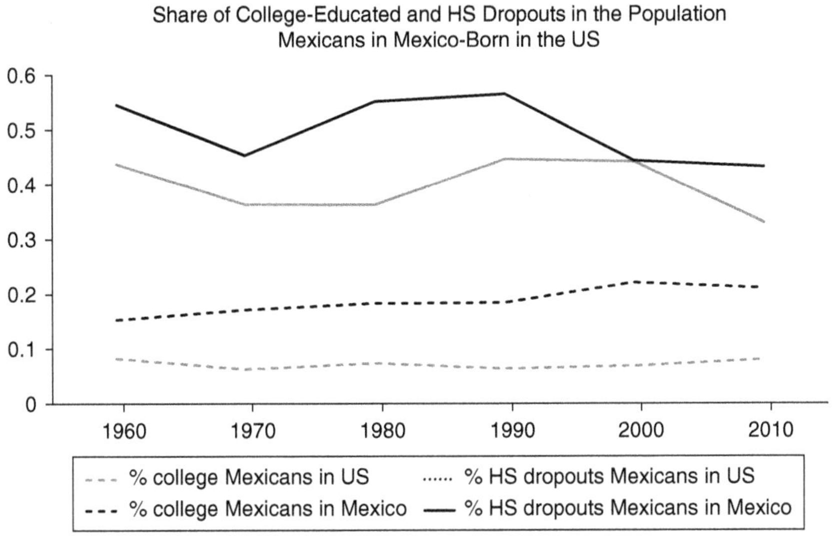

FIGURE 11.9. Percentage of college-educated and high school dropouts in Mexico and for Mexican-born US immigrants.
Source: Author's Calculations Based on Data from the U.S. Bureau of Census, 1960–2010.

paid in Mexico.[15] The percentage of college-educated among Mexican-born in the United States was 8 percent vis-à-vis 15.3 percent of college-educated in Mexico. On the other hand, the percentage of high school dropouts was similar between Mexicans in the United States (43 percent) and residents of Mexico (53 percent). As the number of Mexican immigrants grew, their composition remained unchanged. Still in 2010, Mexican-born in the United States show a share of college-educated close to only 8 percent. The role of the job-related network in reproducing this composition, combined with the rather unequal distribution of income in Mexico, must have been very strong. In fact, the Mexican resident population reached a share of college-educated of 21 percent in 2010, but none of the educational gains in Mexico have been passed on to the Mexican-born immigrants to the United States (Figure 11.9). This is probably because the type of jobs and occupations filled by that group of immigrants, and for which the network provides information, were and still are concentrated in menial sectors in manufacturing, agriculture, and services.

[15] Geoge Borjas, *Self-Selection and the Earnings of Immigrants*, 77 AMERICAN ECONOMIC REVIEW 531–53 (September (1987).

Previous studies have analyzed the selection of immigrants[16] and have emphasized the role of country-of-origin characteristics as well as immigration laws in determining the type of immigrants a country receives. The United States is an interesting case, as the immigration system set in place in 1965 is not explicitly favoring high-skilled immigrants, although the employment-related permanent permits have a skilled component to it. In fact, it has generated two types of immigration flows, both very prominent: one of highly educated people (from Asia) and one of much less-educated ones (from Mexico). The persistence of these flows, together with the link to the jobs performed by these immigrants, suggests that immigration laws are not enough to understand the selection and economic performance of immigrants. The role of job network, selection from countries of origin, and the evolution of labor conditions must also be understood. This is where the 1965 Immigration and Nationality Act was the weakest.

11.6 DIFFERENT MODE OF ENTRY: HAS THE IMMIGRATION SYSTEM WORKED FOR THE LESS EDUCATED?

The evolution of schooling and wages of foreign-born overall has followed the same economic forces that have affected the evolution of the U.S. economy and of its residents. However, the immigration system of the United States has been mainly based on family sponsoring and family reunification. If we look at the data on permanent legal residents to the United States (Yearbook of Immigration Statistics, Office of Homeland Security), more than 75 percent of all permanent immigrants are admitted under family sponsorship or immediate family reunification. In many cases economic immigrants find it easier to obtain their permanent residence through family sponsor (spouse, siblings, or parents). Only a minority of people among the permanent residents obtain the permits for working reasons. The constraint imposed by the family-based system is clear: it reduces the options of immigrants who do not have access to highly skilled types of jobs or to family members in the United States, even if they have a job in the United States and an employer ready to hire them. If this is correct, we should observe a clear difference in the way in which the Mexican-born and the Asian-born are admitted to the United States. For the Asian-born, the option of obtaining a permit via employment sponsor, albeit limited, should be available to many. College-educated individuals are the group that should benefit from it. As a consequence, a significant part of the inflow of immigrants should have been

[16] Jeffrey Grogger & Gordon H. Hanson, *Income Maximization and the Selection and Sorting of International Migrants*, 95 JOURNAL OF DEVELOPMENT ECONOMICS, *Elsevier* 42–57 (May 2011).

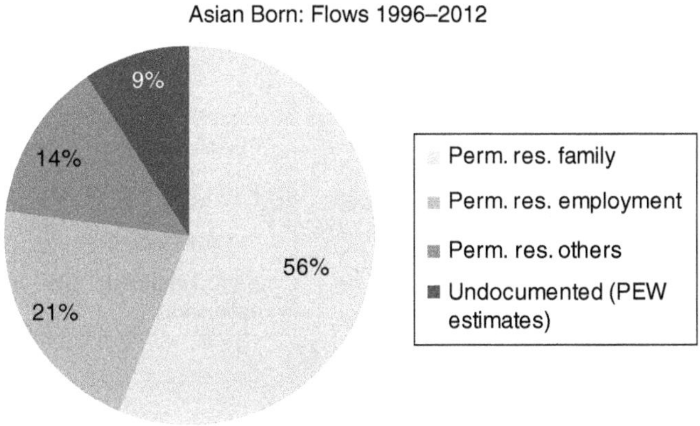

FIGURE 11.10. Asian born: flows 1996–2012.
Source: Author's Calculations Based on Data from the U.S. Bureau of Census 1960–2010.

through employment sponsor, although the majority will still likely to be through family sponsor. For Mexicans, to the contrary, employment in menial jobs does not really afford the possibility of a permanent legal permit. Hence we should observe a much larger share of the total entries as family reunification, and this will also create incentives for undocumented immigration.

In Figures 11.10 and 11.11 we show the data on total cumulated entry in the United States either as legal resident or as undocumented for Mexican and Asian immigrants. The data combine information from the yearbook of Immigration Statistics and from the PEW Hispanic publications that reports estimates on the stock of undocumented immigrants and a partial breakdown into countries of origin. We consider the 1996–2012 period and we cumulate the yearly permanent residence permits, dividing them among those obtained via family sponsor, those obtained via employment sponsor, and those obtained from other sources. Furthermore, we calculate the net inflow of undocumented immigrants (from Mexico and Asia) obtained as difference in the estimated stock (PEW Hispanic center) in 2012 and in 1998. The pie chart represents how the total number of net new entries for the 1998–2012 period is distributed across the four different types of entry, three legal (via family, employer, or others) and one undocumented.

For the Asian-born immigrants, family reunification is the largest way of entry (56 percent), but then employment sponsors accounted for 21 percent of the inflow. If we think that a large part of the family entries are immediate relatives of workers, we can think that labor-sponsored entry was a very important channel for Asians. Much smaller are undocumented entry and entry for other causes (asylum,

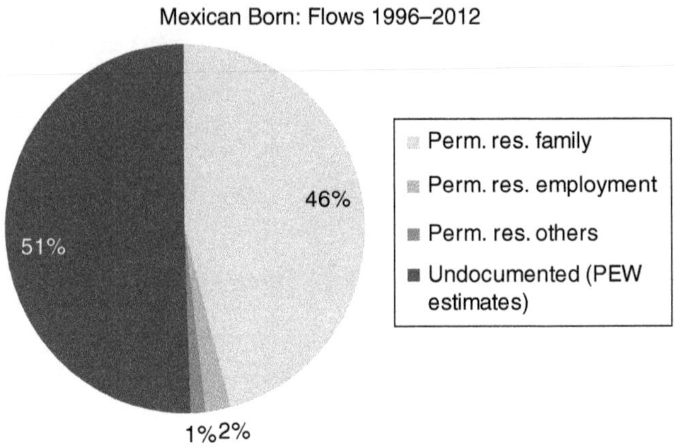

FIGURE 11.11. Mexican born: flows 1996–2012.
Source: Author's Calculations Based on Data from the U.S. Bureau of Census, 1960–2010.

lottery). When considering the corresponding chart for the Mexican immigrants to the United States, however, we see that employment sponsor only provides a negligible 2 percent of the entries. This pushes the whole immigrant population to find entry either as undocumented or through family unification.

As we know from the previous analysis, most of the Mexicans in the United States as of 2010 were working, but as they had low levels of education and hence access mostly to unskilled types of jobs, the current immigration system does not provide them with any legal channel of entry through their jobs. It is also worth emphasizing that even temporary entry for working reasons (not included in these statistics) and allowed through a large variety of visas is strongly biased in favor of college-educated. The larger visa programs, counting more than 100,000 entries per year, are the H1B and the L, which only allow entry to "specialty occupations" typically requiring college education. Only the H1A and H2A visa allow seasonal and agricultural workers, but their caps are low and their requirements very cumbersome. Ultimately the availability of legal entry permits for non-college-educated would not change their economic opportunities much, which are driven mainly by schooling and human capital. However, legal presence in the United States would make these immigrants more mobile and more willing to invest in training, and would improve the options and opportunities for the second generation. In the last section I analyze the features that would improve the current immigration system, still based on the 1965 Immigration and Nationality Act.

11.7 COMPONENTS OF AN IMMIGRATION REFORM: AN ECONOMIST'S VIEW

For its very important role in opening the doors to more immigrants, the 1965 Immigration and Nationality Act has been a fundamental step in the social and economic policy of the United States. Its focus on family reunification and its rigid quotas, however, have become a significant limitation on its benefits. Immigration can be managed much more effectively to be an engine of growth and economic productivity.

One of the most visible signs of malfunctioning of the current system has been the accumulation of millions of undocumented immigrants. A large part of the current debate is focused on them. However, they are only one part of the puzzle. Certainly finding a reasonable path to legal status for this group would bring economic benefits. Most of the undocumented are already working. Probably with legal status they will be able to obtain somewhat higher wages, 5–10% higher, most studies say, and consume and spend more. The fees and back taxes paid to achieve legal status also will be a welcome source of revenue for the government. The really significant payoff, however, will be when the newly legal immigrants are more willing to invest in training and to move between employers as they participate fully in the economy and feel more certain about their future. The younger among them will be more likely to pursue an education. These investments will increase their human capital, wages, productivity, and taxpaying ability, with positive effects on the economy.

Yet the problem of undocumented immigrants is likely to come back unless we find better ways to legally accommodate new immigrants. In particular, as we saw in the case of Mexican-born, the existence of demand for menial workers without a legal channel to allow them in the country has produced abuses of the system. While less-educated menial jobs attracting non-college-educated immigrants will continue to pay significantly less than other jobs do, they will still be attractive to motivated, hardworking immigrants as they constitute a three- to fourfold increase of their income relative to what they can earn in their countries of origin. Managing inflows of less-educated immigrants that respond to the economic demand would be an important role of immigration reforms. Significant economic gains are achievable if we reorganize the immigration system following three fundamental principles.

The first is simplification. There are many different kinds of temporary visas, each with specific provisions, numeric limits, requirements, and fees, that have accumulated over time since 1965. The disconnect between temporary visas and permanent residence permits implies that people who have worked for years and are well integrated in the United States have no guarantee of obtaining permanent residence. A more rational approach would have the government set overall targets and simple rules for temporary and permanent working permits, deciding the balance between permits in "skilled" and "unskilled" jobs. But the government should not micromanage permits, rules, and limits in specific occupations. Employers should compete to hire immigrants, and they are best suited at selecting the individuals who will be the most productive in the jobs that are needed.

The second important principle is that the number of temporary work visas should respond to the demand for labor. Currently the limited number of permits is set with no consideration for economic conditions. Their number is rarely revised. Recognizing, as we did in this chapter, that most immigrants come for economic reasons implies that the number and skills of admitted immigrants should also mirror labor markets and their changes. In periods of high demand, the economic incentives to bypass the limits and hire undocumented workers are large. Work visas and permanent residence permits that are responsive to labor demand would make enforcement of the immigration laws easier.

The third principle governing immigration reform should also emphasize that scientists, engineers, and innovators are the main drivers of productivity and economic growth. More scientists and more innovation in the United States mean more labs, universities, and companies doing research and creating jobs for Americans. There is abundant research showing that foreign scientists and engineers contribute substantially to science, innovation, and productivity growth in the United States, with benefits spreading well beyond the lab and research facility where they work.[17] Fifty years after the Immigration and Nationality Act, the time has come to introduce immigration policies more suited to our economy and society in the twenty-first century.

[17] William Kerr & William F. Lincoln, *The Supply Side of Innovation: H-1B Visa Reforms and U.S. Ethnic Invention*, 28 Journal of Labor Economics 473–508 (2010); Jennifer Hunt & Marjolaine Gauthier-Loiselle, *How Much Does Immigration Boost Innovation?* 2 American Economic Journal: Macroeconomics 31–56 (2010); Giovanni Peri *et al.*, *Foreign STEM Workers and Native Wages and Employment in U.S. Cities*, NBER Working Papers 20093, National Bureau of Economic Research (2014).

Index

Note: An *f* following a page number indicates a figure; a *t* following a page number indicates a table.

For EU product safety concerns, contact us at Calle de José Abascal, 56–1°,
28003 Madrid, Spain or eugpsr@cambridge.org.

www.ingramcontent.com/pod-product-compliance
Lightning Source LLC
Chambersburg PA
CBHW060334210525
27036CB00003B/223
* 9 7 8 1 1 0 7 0 8 4 1 1 7 *